PSYCHOLOGY
and
LANGUAGE

AN INTRODUCTION TO PSYCHOLINGUISTICS

Under the General Editorship of

Jerome Kagan

Harvard University

PSYCHOLOGY
and
LANGUAGE

AN INTRODUCTION TO PSYCHOLINGUISTICS

HERBERT H. CLARK
Stanford University

EVE V. CLARK
Stanford University

HARCOURT BRACE JOVANOVICH, INC.

NEW YORK   CHICAGO   SAN FRANCISCO   ATLANTA

ISBN: 0–15–572815–6

Library of Congress Catalog Card Number: 76–62594

Printed in the United States of America

Cover: *Landscape of a Thought* by Benedict Umy.

Copyrights and Acknowledgments appear on page vi,
which constitutes a continuation of the copyright page.

To our parents

Helen, Cushman, Nancy, and Desmond

Copyrights and Acknowledgments

The authors wish to thank the following for permission to reproduce material in this book:

Picture Credits

Preface

Over the last two decades psycholinguistics has become an especially lively and influential field of study, one that promises to yield fresh insights into the nature of the human mind. It has grown with help from linguistics and cognitive psychology and with encouragement from areas of study as far apart as anthropology and neurology. But this diversity of influences has led to a problem: The aims and organizing principles that give psycholinguistics integrity—that make it worthy of study in its own right—have never been spelled out clearly enough.

In *Psychology and Language* we have tried to do just that. We have put together an introduction to psycholinguistics that attempts to be both comprehensive and balanced, reflecting the best theories and evidence available in the field today. We have designed this book primarily for undergraduate and graduate students in psychology, linguistics, and related fields—anthropology, communication, education, rhetoric, speech and hearing sciences, and the like —but it can profitably be read by anyone with an interest in psycholinguistics, for it does not require technical knowledge of either psychology or linguistics.

One of the principles that gives the field coherence is that psycholinguistics is fundamentally the study of three mental processes—the study of listening, speaking, and of the acquisition of these two skills by children. We have therefore organized the text around these processes. Part 1 is introductory. In Part 2 we take up listening, tracing it from the initial perception of speech sounds to the interpretation of and memory for what was said. In Part 3 we discuss speaking, beginning with the gross planning of monologues and dialogues and working through to the pronunciation of individual speech sounds. In Part 4 we deal with acquisition, following the development of language in children from birth to adolescence. In Part 5 we take up meaning—its role in listening, speaking, and acquisition—and the relation of language to thought.

Another principle that gives the field coherence is that the primary use of language is for communication. Curiously, this fact has played practically no role in previous treatments of the field. Listening, speaking, and acquisition have usually been considered for the way they reflect language structure—syntax, morphology, and phonology—with little regard for the way they reflect people's aims in communicating with one another. In *Psychology and Language* we have tried to correct this imbalance. For example, we have discussed not only the language structures children acquire but also their function—how children use them to communicate with other people. And, as the title of the book suggests, we have drawn freely on psychology and linguistics for insights into the role of communication in language use.

Readers may have more interest in some areas of psycholinguistics than in others. Those who wish to focus on speaking and listening but not on acquisition could pass over Part 4 and Chapter 13 in Part 5. Those interested in acquisition and listening but not in speaking could omit Part 3. Those who wish to concentrate on acquisition alone could read Chapter 1, the first part of Chapter 5, and Chapters 8, 9, 10, and 13. Readers interested in the three basic mental processes but not in speech sounds could leave out Chapters 5 and 10 and perhaps the second half of Chapter 7. And those not interested in word meaning could omit Chapters 11, 12, and 13.

In writing this book we have been helped by many people. We are grateful to our colleagues in the Departments of Psychology and Linguistics at Stanford University, who encouraged us in many ways, and to the undergraduate and graduate students in our courses who commented on early drafts. We are particularly indebted to the many psychologists and linguists whose constructive reviews of parts of the early drafts have led to major improvements in the book: Dwight L. Bolinger, Professor Emeritus, Harvard University; Brian Butterworth, Cambridge University; Jack Catlin, late of Cornell University; Philip S. Dale, University of Washington; Lila R. Gleitman, University of Pennsylvania; David W. Green, University College London; James A. Hampton, University College London; Lise Menn, Research Laboratory of Electronics, Massachusetts Institute of Technology; David B. Pisoni, Indiana University; Jacqueline S. Sachs, University of Connecticut; Neilson V. Smith, University College London; Eric Wanner, Rockefeller University; and Deirdre Wilson, University College London. We would like to single out Charles E. Clifton, Jr., University of Massachusetts; Dan I. Slobin, University of California, Berkeley; and Edward E. Smith, Stanford University, who reviewed and left their mark on virtually every part of the manuscript. We are also grateful to William Dyckes, Judith Greissman, and Abigail Winograd at Harcourt Brace Jovanovich for their skill and care in guiding the book from manuscript to print. And, finally, we thank Ann Edmonds and Joyce Lockwood for typing the manuscript and for handling it and us with such patience.

This book has also benefited from financial support for which we are grateful. Much of the final manuscript was written with the aid of a John Simon Guggenheim Fellowship for Herbert H. Clark, a Mellon Fellowship for Eve V. Clark, and the hospitality of the Departments of Psychology and Linguistics at University College London. Our own research has been supported by grants from the National Institute of Mental Health and the National Science Foundation.

HERBERT H. CLARK
EVE V. CLARK

Contents

Chapter 3   Utilization of Sentences   87

Chapter 4   Memory for Prose   133

Chapter 5   Perception of Speech   175

③

PRODUCTION

4

ACQUISITION

5

MEANING AND THOUGHT

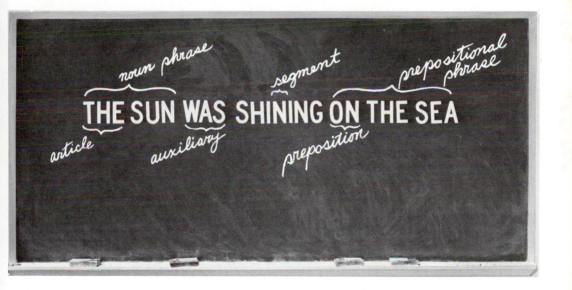

part 1

LANGUAGE

1

The Nature of Language

The essence of language is human activity—activity on the part of one individual to make himself understood, and activity on the part of that other to understand what was in in the mind of the first. These two individuals, the producer and the recipient of language, or as we may more conveniently call them, the speaker and the hearer, should never be lost sight of if we want to understand the nature of language.

Otto Jespersen

1

The Nature of Language

Language stands at the center of human affairs, from the most prosaic to the most profound. It is used for haggling with store clerks, telling off umpires, and gossiping with friends as well as for negotiating contracts, discussing ethics, and explaining religious beliefs. It is the medium through which the manners, morals, and mythology of a society are passed on to the next generation. Indeed, it is a basic ingredient in virtually every social situation. The thread that runs through all these activities is communication, people trying to put their ideas over to others. As the main vehicle of human communication, language is indispensable.

THE PSYCHOLOGY OF LANGUAGE

Communication with language is carried out through two basic human activities: speaking and listening. These are of particular importance to psychologists, for they are mental activities that hold clues to the very nature of the human mind. In speaking, people put ideas into words, talking about perceptions, feelings, and intentions they want other people to grasp. In listening, they turn words into ideas, trying to reconstruct the perceptions, feelings, and intentions they were meant to grasp. Speaking and listening, then, ought to reveal something fundamental about the mind and how it deals with perceptions, feelings, and intentions. Speaking and listening, however, are more than that. They are the tools people use in more global activities. People talk in order to convey facts, ask for favors, and make promises, and others listen in order to receive this information. These actions in turn are the pieces out of which casual conversations, negotiations, and other social exchanges are formed. So speaking and listening ought to tell us a great deal about social and cultural activities too.

Although speaking and listening are so commonplace they are normally taken for granted, they are actually very complex activities. We get an occasional glimpse of this complexity when, for example, someone mishears **I'm all covered in chalk dust** as **I'm all covered in chocolate**. Why did the listener come up with **chocolate** and not some other word? And when someone takes an impatient **Why don't you leave?** as an invitation for a long explanation, we wonder how that person could have missed the intended interpretation. Or when a nervous groom says **With this wing I thee red**, we wonder how the **w** and **r** got interchanged. Why these and not some other sounds? When someone wrecks a conversation by talking out of turn, we wonder why that person didn't wait for the previous speaker to finish. And when a three-year-old says **I falled it**, we wonder how the child came up with **falled**, a word that adults don't use. It is examples like these that begin to reveal speaking and listening for the complicated skills they are.

The psychology of language, the subject of this book, is fundamentally concerned with these two skills and their acquisition. That is, it is concerned with three broad questions:

(1) By what mental processes do people listen to, comprehend, and remember what they hear? (*Comprehension*)

(2) By what mental processes do people come to say what they say? (*Production*)

(3) What course do children follow in learning to comprehend and produce their first language, and why? (*Acquisition*)

These questions lead to others: How does language influence thought? How does thought influence language? How does language fit into other human activities? Why does language have the structure it does? Do animals have language? And so on. But these further questions are intimately tied to the three fundamental questions and must be taken up with respect to them, so that is how we will proceed.

The Study of Language

Where should the study of speaking and listening begin? For over two thousand years, philosophers, orators, and linguists have answered: "With the study of language, its structure and function." They have argued that language has the structure it has because humans are subject to certain general laws of thought. Thus, if one could only discover the true structure and function of language, one could discover these universal laws of thought. For traditional scholars, speaking and listening were an integral part of language, so by studying language, they were also finding out how people speak and understand. In one form or another, this view has been held up to the present day, although the study of language structure—the discipline of linguistics—has recently been separated from the study of speaking and listening—the psychology of language. But as traditional scholars thought, if we are to understand speaking and listening, we must understand the relation between language structure and the processes of speaking and listening.

Grammar

In speaking or comprehending a language, people implicitly conform to a system that relates sounds to meanings. This has traditionally been called the *grammar* of the language. In speaking or understanding French, for example, people adhere to the conventions of the French language about which combinations of words convey which meanings. **Chien** means "dog," and **C'est un chien** means "That is a dog." These conventions are said to be described by the grammar of French. This view of a grammar is a far cry from the dull prescriptive rules most people are taught about what is and what is not "good grammar." The grammar of French is intended to be a complete description of the language as it is actually spoken.

What does a grammar look like? Recently, especially under the influence of Zellig Harris and Noam Chomsky, many linguists have argued that a grammar is a system of rules (see Bach, 1974; Akmajian and Heny, 1975). The rules for English, for example, have the capability of "generating" all the legitimate sentences of English and no illegitimate ones. They can generate **The sun is shining**, but not **Sun the shining is**. One rule in English states that for **the** and **sun** to form a "noun phrase," they must be ordered **the sun** and not **sun the**, while another rule states that for **is** and **shining** to form a "verb phrase," they must be ordered **is shining** and not **shining is**. There are grammatical rules to deal with three major aspects of language:

Phonology: the sounds and their structure.

Syntax: the way words combine to form sentences.

Semantics: the meaning of words and sentences.

Taken together, the rules form a complex system that is supposed to capture all aspects of language structure. This, of course, is only an ideal, for so far only partial grammars have been worked out for English and some other languages.

What makes the grammar important for the psychology of language is the possibility that it will help in the study of speaking and listening. Grammatical rules, in effect, summarize regularities in the behavior of people speaking a language. Consider this approximate rule for the structure of English noun phrases:

A noun phrase can consist of an article followed by a noun.

As this rule states, people say **the gazelle**, **an aardvark**, and **a toad**, but not **gazelle the**, **aardvark an**, and **toad a**. This rule summarizes a regularity in people's production of noun phrases, and the ideal grammar of English would summarize all such regularities. But if grammatical rules summarize facts about behavior, they should surely help in the study of that behavior—in the study of speaking and listening. From the traditional point of view, grammatical rules should also take us a long way toward understanding the fundamental laws of thought and the nature of the human intellect. Noam Chomsky (1965, 1968) has tried to make much of this explicit in his discussion of competence and performance.

Competence and Performance

Most people know how to add a column of numbers, but when they actually do an addition, they require time and sometimes make mistakes. Put another way, people have a "capacity" for addition, but in "applying" that capacity on any occasion, they require time to think and sometimes make errors in their computations. Likewise, nearly all people have a "capacity" for a particular language. But in "applying" this capacity in speaking or listening, they too require time to think and sometimes make mistakes. In speaking, they sometimes hesitate, repeat themselves, stutter, or make slips of the tongue. In listening, they sometimes misunderstand. Considerations like these led Chomsky to distinguish between *linguistic competence*—one's capacity to use a language—and *linguistic performance*—the actual application of this competence in speaking or listening.

Chomsky went on to propose an important hypothesis: the competence of a person who knows a language ideally well is described by the grammar of that language. As Chomsky put it (1968, p. 23):

> The person who has acquired knowledge of a language has internalized a system of rules that relate sound to meaning in a particular way. The linguist constructing a grammar of a language is in effect proposing a hypothesis concerning this internalized system.

People's competence in English, Russian, or Eskimo, then, is described by implicit rules—ones people are not aware of—that form the grammars of those languages. In English, for example, people's competence in the use of noun phrases such as **the gazelle**, **an aardvark**, and **a toad** is described in part by the rule, "A noun phrase can consist of an article followed by a noun."

But what about linguistic performance? What about speaking and listening? Chomsky has often argued that the grammar a person has learned, one's competence in a language, is something one "puts to use in producing and understanding speech" (Chomsky, 1970, p. 184). At first reading Chomsky appears to be saying that the rules themselves are "put to use" in speaking and listening—for example, that the rule "A noun phrase can consist of an article followed by a noun" is put to use when people produce or understand **the gazelle, an aardvark,** or **a toad**. In fact, Chomsky meant his argument to be taken only abstractly, almost metaphorically. There is no direct relation, he has argued, between the rules of grammar and the way people proceed to produce or under-

> Grammar, n. A system of pitfalls
> thoughtfully prepared for the feet of
> the self-made man, along the path by
> which he advances to distinction.
>   Ambrose Bierce, The Devil's Dictionary

stand speech. The relation is only indirect, and it is up to the psychologists of language to discover what it is. On the other hand, he has followed traditional scholars in arguing that the grammar of each language reflects something fundamental about the human intellect. That is one reason why it is so challenging—and important—to discover the grammar of each language.

At this point in the argument, then, the place of a grammar in the study of speaking and listening has once again become cloudy (see Watt, 1974a,b). It is essential to put it all into perspective.

Structure, Function, and Process

Language is fundamentally an instrument of communication. People talk as a way of conveying ideas to others—of getting them to grasp new facts, answer questions, register promises, and so forth. A language has not only a structure —what linguists try to capture with their rules—but also a function to which that structure is put.

Building a Bicycle

Function is intimately tied to structure. Take the sentence **Who knows George?** The function it can serve—that of asking someone for the name of a person who knows George—depends on its structure—the fact that it is an interrogative construction with the words **who, knows,** and **George** in that order. And its structure is designed in part for that particular function. Language is much like any other instrument humans have invented. The function of a bicycle, for example, is to transport one person plus baggage for moderate distances at moderate speeds. This function could not be served if the bicycle did not have the structure it did. Its frame, two wheels, handlebars, pedals, and chain have had their form imposed on them in part by the function the bicycle was meant to serve. Although the precise materials and measurements may not be critical, the overall structure is. In sentences, structure has to be studied in relation to function, and function in relation to structure.

But, leaving comprehension aside for the moment, how does a speaker produce a sentence? In the bicycle analogy the question would be, How does someone build a bicycle? First, the builder must have the right workshop, tools, and materials. Then he might proceed like this:

    (1) Make frame from steel tubing.
    (2) Paint frame.
    (3) Make two wheels from hoops, spokes, and rubber.
    (4) Make handlebars from chrome-plated steel tubing.
    (5) Attach handlebars to frame.
    (6) Attach wheels to frame.
    (7) Make chain from steel links and rivets.
    (8) Make pedals from steel and rubber.
    (9) Attach pedals to frame.
(10) Sling chain from pedals to rear wheel.

Building a bicycle, then, is a process with a series of steps, or physical operations, carried out in a particular order, the product of which is a completed bicycle. Likewise, building a sentence can be thought of as a process with a series of steps, or *mental operations*, carried out in a particular order, the product of which is a completed sentence.

What Structure and Function Say About Process

In the bicycle analogy, one can distinguish three facets of the problem:

Structure: A designer's blueprint of the bicycle.

Function: A description of how the bicycle is used to transport a person and baggage for moderate distances at moderate speeds.

Process: A description of the materials, tools, and procedure used in building the bicycle.

It is easy to see that the structure and function of a bicycle do not specify the process by which it is constructed. The goal of the builder, of course, is a finished bicycle that conforms to the blueprint and fulfills the functions meant for it. But this goal can be reached by many different procedures, with many different tools and materials, and in many different amounts of time—from days to months. The blueprint and functional description have nothing directly to say about the process. They do, however, give hints about it. The two wheels, because they are alike, are probably built at the same time and in the same way. The pedals and rear wheel have to be attached to the frame before the chain can be slung. The frame is probably painted before anything is attached to it. The list of hints could go on. The lesson, however, is simple. It is highly profitable to know the product before studying the process by which it is arrived at.

    The lessons are the same for the sentence as for the bicycle. Once again one can distinguish three facets:

Structure: The grammar of the language.

Function: A description of how sentences communicate what they are meant to communicate.

Process: A description of the mental tools, materials, and procedures people use in producing or comprehending them.

Again it is easy to see that the structure and function of a sentence do not specify the process by which it was produced or understood, but they probably do give hints about it. So it is profitable to know something about structure and function in language before digging into comprehension and production in earnest.

Complexity and Creativity in Language

Automobiles require a much more complicated procedure in their manufacture than do bicycles. The reason for this is that automobiles are structurally much more complex than bicycles, as one can conclude from their blueprints alone. For centuries the same argument has been made for speaking and listening as compared with other forms of human communication. The system of nautical

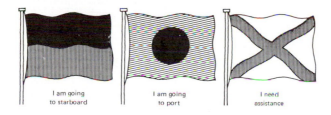

I am going to starboard	I am going to port	I need assistance

flags for signaling from boats, for example, can be summarized in a short handbook with a few easy rules. It has a simple blueprint. No one, however, has yet been able to summarize the structure of a language in a handbook of any length. Its blueprint is extremely complex. Speaking and listening, therefore, must be infinitely more complicated skills than the use of nautical flags or other such signaling systems.

What makes these skills even more complicated is that they are creative. As scholars have noted for a long time, speaking and listening are fundamentally different from signaling systems like the nautical flags, for in speaking and listening people are able to use a virtually unlimited variety of sentences they have never used before. Most of what people say and hear is not mere repetition of something they have said or heard before. It is novel—something that has been created on the spot. Yet all this creativity happens within the confines of language, within the blueprint for its structure. The novel sentences that are produced and understood still fit within the conventions of the language being spoken.

When scholars noticed this complexity and creativity in language, what puzzled them was how people were ever able to learn or use such a complicated system. No matter how unintelligent people are, they seem able to speak and listen with at least some effectiveness. How do they manage that? And how is it that children are able to master these two skills so rapidly and with so little apparent effort? The structure of language has been searched for clues to this puzzle—one reason why language has been studied for centuries with such intense interest. But clues should also be found in speaking and listening—one more reason for studying language processes in addition to structure and function. The puzzle has even more general significance, for its solution ought to provide insights into complexity and creativity in human thought itself.

THE STRUCTURE OF LANGUAGE

Speech has the appearance of being a succession of ideas expressed bit by bit in words, phrases, and clauses. But just how are the ideas expressed? This is an important question for the psychology of language, for the goal is to discover how speakers turn ideas into words and how listeners turn words into ideas. This quest has been aided by a remarkable conclusion linguists have reached in their analysis of language structure: sentences can be divided into parts that reveal the elementary ideas being expressed and their conceptual relations to each other. It is essential, then, to begin with some understanding of this insight.

We will start, therefore, with the sentence. By many it is considered the basic unit of language, for of all linguistic units it can best stand on its own and in everyday speech has the most coherent function. The focus in this discussion will be on the order and arrangement of words within the sentence. Next we will consider the structure of words themselves and the ways in which they are used in sentences. Finally we will deal with the sounds that are strung together to make up words.

In linguistics, much labor has gone into devising large rule systems to represent the structure of a variety of languages. Obviously we cannot describe the details of these systems in a single chapter and must therefore leave them to texts in linguistics. Yet we will give an informal description of language structure and illustrate it with English examples. This description should give a basic idea of what these rule systems might be like. We will consider other general properties of the world's languages in Chapter 14.

Sentences and Their Structure

Most complex sentences are built out of smaller sentences, or *clauses*. Sentence 1, for example, is built out of the clauses in 2:

1. George's friend, who lives in Valley Forge, likes winter because he likes snow and because he hates summer tourists.

2. a. George's friend lives in Valley Forge.
    b. George's friend likes winter.
    c. He likes snow.
    d. He hates summer tourists.

Sentence 2a corresponds to the *relative clause* in 1, sentence 2b to the *main clause*, 2c to the first *adverbial clause*, and 2d to the second. What is not so obvious is that most simple sentences, despite their unified appearance, consist of smaller sentences too. Sentence 3, for example, can be thought of as having been built out of the sentences in 4:

3. The fresh young troops defeated Napoleon's army.

4. a. The troops were fresh.
   b. The troops were young.
   c. The army belonged to Napoleon.
   d. The troops defeated the army.

The main point in 3 is expressed in 4d. What 4a, 4b, and 4c do is qualify elements in 4d to make it clear what troops and what army are being talked about. Sentences 4a and 4b specify that the troops were young and fresh, and 4c specifies that the army belonged to Napoleon. Thus, 3 seems to be all the simple sentences of 4 packed into a single clause.

Propositions as Units of Meaning

This is an important insight. Sentence 3 can be said to express four different things, while each sentence in 4 expresses one of them. But what are these things? They are clearly not sentences or even clauses, for 3 is not made up of the "sentences" or "clauses" in 4. Rather, they are units of meaning called *propositions*. This is the reason for saying that each sentence in 4 *expresses* a proposition instead of saying that each one *is* a proposition. When the propositions expressed in 4 are put together in just the right way, they constitute the meaning of 3. As a next step, one can think very loosely of each proposition as corresponding to a unitary idea. Thus in 3 there are four ideas—about the freshness of the troops, the youth of the troops, the possession of the army by Napoleon, and the defeat of his army by the troops.

What makes this analysis so important is that it shows that meaning units have a relatively simple form. Propositions come in only a few different types. The main ones are illustrated in 5:

	Sentence	*Verbal unit*	*Nouns*
5. a.	Max walks.	walks	Max
b.	Max is handsome.	is handsome	Max
c.	Max eats fruit.	eats	Max, fruit
d.	Max is in London.	is in	Max, London
e.	Max gives Rex to Molly.	gives	Max, Rex, Molly

As these examples suggest, each proposition consists of a *verbal unit* plus one or more nouns. The propositions expressed by 5a and 5b have a verbal unit plus one noun; those expressed by 5c and 5d have a verbal unit plus two nouns; and the one expressed by 5e has a verbal unit plus three nouns. Although the verbal unit is often expressed by a single verb (**walks**, **eats**, and **gives**), it can also be expressed by **be** + adjective (**is handsome**) or by **be** + preposition (**is in**). The important point is that each proposition describes an elementary state or action —spelled out in the verbal unit—and one or more entities involved in that state or action—spelled out in the nouns. Thus, **Max eats fruit** describes the action of eating and specifies that the entities involved in this action are Max and fruit. (Propositions will be considered in greater detail in Chapter 2.)

Surface Structures and Underlying Representations

Every sentence, then, has two levels of structure. Its *surface structure* is its linear arrangement of clauses, phrases, words, and sounds. Its *underlying representation* is its meaning, which consists of propositions that are interrelated in a particular way. Loosely speaking, the surface structure says how the sentence is to be spoken, and the underlying representation says how it is to be understood.

FIGURE 1–1
A HIERARCHICAL TREE

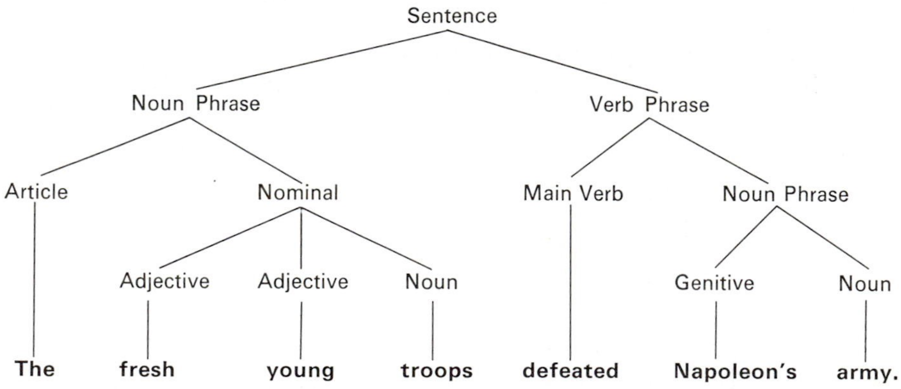

These two levels of structure can be illustrated for 3, **The fresh young troops defeated Napoleon's army**. Its surface structure is often represented in the form of a hierarchical tree, as in Figure 1–1, which shows how each large phrase consists of one or more smaller phrases. The sentence as a whole consists of a noun phrase (**the fresh young troops**) and a verb phrase (**defeated Napoleon's army**). The noun phrase in turn consists of an article (**the**) and a nominal (**fresh young troops**), which itself divides into two adjectives and a noun. The verb phrase divides further into a main verb (**defeated**) and a noun phrase (**Napoleon's army**), which consists of a genitive and a noun. All the words consist in turn of sounds. Its underlying representation, in contrast, consists of the four proposi-

tions expressed in 4 in a particular arrangement. The main proposition is in 4d
and the other three restrict its parts.

The four meaning units in 4 can be combined in different ways to yield
surface structures and underlying representations that differ from those of 3.
Consider these:

6. a. The young troops that defeated Napoleon's army were fresh.
   b. The fresh troops that defeated Napoleon's army were young.
   c. The army that the fresh young troops defeated belonged to Napoleon.
   d. The troops that were fresh and young defeated the army that belonged
      to Napoleon.

Although these sentences all express the four propositions in 4, they do so in
different ways. The main idea in 6a is that the troops were fresh. The remaining
propositions in 6a serve to restrict or qualify parts of this idea. In contrast, the
main idea in 6b is that the troops were young, in 6c that the army belonged to
Napoleon, and in 6d that the troops defeated the army. The sentences in 6 have
different underlying representations—different meanings—because the underlying representation of a sentence consists of propositions *in a particular arrangement*. Yet because the sentences in 6 are all built from the same propositions,
they are *paraphrases* of each other. They all refer to the same objective situation.
Dividing sentences into propositions shows how paraphrases like these are
related to one another.

It is easy to see how all of these notions—surface structure, underlying
representation, proposition, and paraphrase—might play a role in speaking and
listening. Speaking is the process of turning meaning into sounds—of building
surface structures for particular underlying representations—and listening is
more or less the reverse. Speakers and listeners must be able to relate the elements
of surface structure (sounds, words, phrases, and clauses) to the units of underlying representations (propositions). If propositions really do correspond to
the basic ideas people try to express in language, they should play a role in
speaking and listening. And if paraphrases (like those in 6) are related to each
other by the propositions they express in common, this too should have consequences for speaking and listening. Indeed, when people try to remember a
sentence, they often confuse it with its paraphrases—reporting they heard 6b
for example, when they actually heard 6a.

Combining Propositions

Speech would be very odd if people had to speak in sentences that expressed
only one proposition each. Every sentence would be short and unrelated to its
neighbors, and it would take a long time to say anything. Languages therefore
have systematic ways of relating propositions to each other while economizing
on speaking and listening time. On the one hand, they have ways of combining
propositions to form complex surface structures. The propositions expressed in
Max eats apples and **Susan eats oranges** can be combined to form **Max eats**

apples and Susan eats oranges. On the other hand, languages have methods for condensing complicated surface structures into neater, more concise ones, without any alterations in meaning, for example, **Max eats apples and Susan oranges**. These two devices will be taken up in turn.

Propositions combine in three different ways, technically called coordination, relativization, and complementation. Their functions are fundamentally different. Roughly speaking, coordination *links* ideas, relativization *qualifies* ideas, and complementation *fills in* ideas. These three functions seem to exhaust the basic ways people have for thinking of one idea in relation to another.

Coordination

Coordination links two propositions by **and**, **but**, **or**, or some other coordinate conjunction, as illustrated in 7 and 8:

>   7. The troops are young, and the army belongs to Napoleon.

>   8. Max likes fruit, but Max gave the apple to Molly.

The two propositions are placed on a par with each other, and this makes coordination quite unlike the next two ways of combining propositions.

Relativization

In *relativization*, one proposition is attached to a part of another proposition in order to restrict or qualify that part. The most obvious examples are found in relative clauses. Consider the propositions expressed in 9:

>   9. a. The troops defeated the army.
>   b. The army belonged to Napoleon.

The proposition expressed by 9b can be turned into the relative clause **that belonged to Napoleon** and attached to **the army** in 9a to give 10:

>   10. The troops defeated the army that belonged to Napoleon.

This relative clause serves to restrict or qualify **army**. It wasn't just any army that the troops defeated, but the army that belonged to Napoleon. Or take the propositions expressed in 11:

>   11. a. The troops were fresh.
>   b. The troops were young.

The proposition in 11b can be made into the relative clause **that were young** and attached to **the troops** in 11a in order to restrict or qualify it, as in 12:

>   12. The troops that were young were fresh.

Not all relativization takes the form of relative clauses. Without any change in meaning, for example, 10 and 12 can be condensed into 13a and 13b:

13. a. The troops defeated Napoleon's army.
    b. The young troops were fresh.

By this time all that is left of the relativized propositions are the single words **Napoleon's** in 13a and **young** in 13b. In fact, most modifiers are types of relativization. These include adjectives inside noun phrases (like **young** in **the young troops**), possessives (like **Napoleon's** in **Napoleon's army**), most adverbs (like **happily** in **happily married**), most prepositional phrases (like **behind the barn** in **the tub behind the barn**), and many other types of constructions. Restriction and qualification are very useful functions and so relativization is an important way of combining propositions.

Complementation

In *complementation*, the final way of combining propositions, one proposition is used to fill in an empty part of another. Imagine beginning with 14:

14. Something was nice.

Something, here, is an "empty" noun. We want to know what it was that was nice. One way to specify this is to insert another proposition, called the *complement*, in place of the empty **something**. Imagine, for example, that the complement was the proposition expressed by **Wellington won the battle**. That would give 15:

15. [Wellington won the battle] was nice.

But 15 cannot be left like that. **Wellington won the battle** must be explicitly marked to show that it is a complement and not some other kind of clause. For this English has three main devices, as shown in 16:

16. a. That Wellington won the battle was nice.
    b. For Wellington to win the battle was nice.
    c. Wellington's winning of the battle was nice.

What has been introduced in 16a is the word **that**, in 16b the words **for** and **to**, and in 16c the possessive **-'s**, **-ing**, and **of**. Complements like these don't have to remain in their original places. For example, the complementation in 16a and 16b could have been expressed instead with the surface structures in 17a and 17b:

17. a. It was nice that Wellington won the battle.
    b. It was nice for Wellington to win the battle.

There are other forms complementation can take as well

Recursion

What makes coordination, relativization, and complementation so powerful is that they can apply again and again to form very complex sentences. For example, relativization and complementation are both used in sentences like **Wellington thought that Napoleon sent an army that was young**. This sentence in turn can be used as the complement of another sentence, **Everyone suspected that Wellington thought that Napoleon sent an army that was young**, and so on. The process is *recursive*, and in theory could go on indefinitely, a limit that children seem to be testing when they recite **This is the cow with the crumpled horn that tossed the dog that worried the cat that killed the rat that ate the malt that lay in the house that Jack built**.

This is what makes coordination, relativization, and complementation of interest psychologically. With these devices propositions can be combined in a variety of ways. But in speaking, *by what process* are they combined, and in listening, *by what process* are they pulled apart? How do children come to learn that propositions can be put together, and what do they find easy, and what hard? At this point one can only marvel at the complex and creative ways in which the processes of listening, speaking, and acquisition handle combinations of propositions.

Condensing Sentences

Surface structures can often be condensed into very compact forms. This has already been illustrated for relativization, where **the troops that were young** was condensed into **the young troops**, and **the army that belonged to Napoleon** was condensed into **Napoleon's army**. But there are other types of condensation as well. The two most important are *ellipsis* (the omission of words) and *pronominalization* (the use of pronouns). The function of ellipsis is to leave out repetitious and unnecessary words, and the function of pronominalization is to replace complicated expressions by simple ones. Both make sentences more compact without altering their meaning.

Ellipsis

With ellipsis, certain words can be omitted from surface structure when they repeat content given elsewhere in the sentence—usually earlier. In the following pairs of sentences, the first sentence has no obvious omissions, whereas the second contains ellipsis with the omission of the words in italics:

18. a. Napoleon conquered Italy, *Napoleon conquered* Prussia, and *Napoleon conquered* Austria.
    b. Napoleon conquered Italy, Prussia, and Austria.

19. a. Napoleon fought for France, and Wellington *fought* for England.
    b. Napoleon fought for France, and Wellington for England.

20. a. The general who said he could take Moscow didn't *take Moscow*.
    b. The general who said he could take Moscow didn't.

In the elliptical versions the missing words can safely be left out because they are predictable from the rest of the sentence. This kind of ellipsis could therefore be called *sentential ellipsis.*

Another form of ellipsis is *contextual ellipsis,* where one can tell what has been left unsaid only from context. Consider these two examples:

21. *King George:* Where did you defeat Napoleon?
    Wellington: At Waterloo.

22. *Father to child searching for lost toy:* Over here, honey.

In 21, Wellington's answer on its own does not indicate what he has omitted— that he has given an elliptical version of **I defeated Napoleon at Waterloo.** The missing elements can be determined only from context, namely the King's question, and even then **you** must be changed to **I.** But 22, an elliptical version of **The toy you are looking for is over here, honey,** demonstrates that even verbal context isn't necessary. The missing elements here are determined by the father's and child's concurrent activities. Contextual ellipsis like this is common in informal speech.

Pronominalization

Whereas ellipsis achieves condensation by leaving out certain predictable words entirely, *pronominalization* does it by using simple expressions (like pronouns) to stand for complicated ones (like full noun phrases). The condensation this achieves is illustrated in the following pairs of sentences:

23. a. After the very wily young English general won the battle, *the very wily young English general* became the talk of the town.
    b. After the very wily young English general won the battle, he became the talk of the town.

24. a. Jefferson wanted the capital of the United States to be in Virginia, and his friends *wanted the capital of the United States to be in Virginia* too.
    b. Jefferson wanted the capital of the United States to be in Virginia and his friends did so too.

In 23b, the pronoun **he** takes the place of **the very wily young English general,** or at least refers to the same person as the longer noun phrase, and it thereby makes the sentence more compact. In 24b, the expression **do so** is a "pro-verb." Like its cousin the pronoun, it takes the place of a long verb phrase and thereby condenses the sentence.

Just as ellipsis is either sentential or contextual, so is pronominalization. The examples in 23 and 24 involve sentential pronominalization, for **he** in 23 and **do so** in 24 refer back to something expressed in the same sentence. But pronouns and pro-verbs can also refer to objects and events known to the speaker and listener only in that context. Here are two examples:

25. *King George:* What happened to Napoleon at Waterloo?
    Wellington: I defeated *him.*

26. *Airline flight attendant to passenger watching the woman in the next seat putting on her safety belt:* Would *you* please *do that* too?

The commonest examples of contextual pronominalization are **I** and **you**. Their referents can only be determined from the context: **I** refers to the speaker, and **you** to the person being addressed. In 25, the referent of **him** can be determined from the previous question, but in 26, the referent of **do that** can only be determined from what is happening around the speaker and listener.

Ellipsis and pronominalization, then, offer a distinct challenge to the investigators of the psychology of language. In comprehension, how do listeners "fill in" the information missing from elliptical sentences? How do they "find" the objects to which pronouns refer? In production, how do speakers decide when to use ellipsis and pronominalization? How do they know that their listeners can "fill in" the ellipses and "find" the objects to which the pronouns refer? And in acquisition, how do children acquire these two skills? The answers to these questions are not obvious, yet are clearly central to a complete account of speaking, listening, and their acquisition.

Ambiguous Sentences

With all the ways of combining propositions and condensing surface structures, many sentences turn out to be ambiguous. Some surface structures correspond to two or more underlying representations. Consider 27:

27. Visiting relatives can be tiring.

This sentence has two interpretations, or two *readings.* One is that relatives who visit can be tiring, and the other is that going to visit relatives can be tiring. The two readings can be accounted for by noting that the surface structure in 27 corresponds to not one but two underlying representations, as shown roughly in 28:

28. a. [One visits relatives] can be tiring.
    b. Relatives [relatives are visiting one] can be tiring.

In 28a, **One visits relatives** serves as a complement replacing the "empty" noun in **Something can be tiring**. In 28b, on the other hand, **relatives are visiting one** is attached as a relative clause to **relatives** in **Relatives can be tiring**. These two underlying representations could have surfaced, with very little ellipsis, as 29a and 29b:

29. a. One's visiting of relatives can be tiring.
    b. Relatives who are visiting one can be tiring.

Yet with the omission of **one's**, **who are**, and **one**, and with some rearrangement of words, they actually emerge with the same surface structure, namely 27, and hence 27 is ambiguous. Ambiguity like this is common.

So just because two sentences have similar surface structures, they don't necessarily have similar underlying representations. One often quoted example from English is the pair of sentences in 30:

30. a. John is eager to please.
    b. John is easy to please.

On the surface, these two sentences look the same; they differ only in the words **eager** and **easy**, both of which are adjectives. Yet their underlying representations are quite distinct, as shown in these less elliptical versions:

31. a. John is eager for John to please someone.
    b. For someone to please John is easy.

Their complements are the reverse of one another: 31a contains **John pleases someone**, whereas 31b contains **someone pleases John**.

Examples like these show how indirect the correspondence is between surface structures and underlying representations. But if this is so, how do listeners and speakers cope? For ambiguous sentences listeners must be able to comprehend the several readings and decide which one was meant. And speakers must be able to produce such sentences with the confidence that their listeners will be able to decide correctly. Speakers and listeners must also be able to handle sentences with virtually identical surface structures.

Grammatical Relations

In English almost every complete sentence has a subject and a predicate. In **Wellington beat Napoleon at Waterloo**, **Wellington** is the subject, and the rest is the predicate. Traditionally, subject and predicate have been tied to the notion that every sentence is composed of what is being talked about—the subject— and what is being said about it—the predicate. Wellington is what is being talked about, and that he beat Napoleon at Waterloo is what is being said about him. In addition, the predicate often contains a direct object and sometimes an an indirect object. In **King George sent Wellington his congratulations**, **his congratulations** is the direct object and **Wellington** is the indirect object. All these notions—subject, predicate, direct object, and indirect object—are called *gramatical relations*, and they are properties of the surface structure of a sentence.

The subject can take a variety of forms, as illustrated in 32:

32. a. *He* is reciting poetry to Ophelia.
    b. Him *I* have known for a long time.
    c. *What Carnell wanted to do* was meet the great Mr. Fields.
    d. Is *he* reciting poetry to Ophelia?
    e. Where is *the kite society* going to meet, Mr. Franklin?

Because each italicized word or phrase is the subject, it determines whether the verb is singular or plural. In 32a, **he** is singular, and so **is** must be singular too. Change **he** to the plural **they**, and **is** must be changed to the plural **are**. Not all verbs are different in the singular and plural, but whenever they are, with few exceptions they must agree with the subject. Besides that, the subject in English is always in the nominative case, and the direct and indirect objects in the objective case. This shows up only in the *nominative pronouns* (**I, he, she, we, they**) versus the *objective* ones (**me, him, her, us, them**). In some languages this distinction may show up in nouns as well as in pronouns, and they may be explicitly tagged as direct or indirect objects too.

In the typical English declarative sentence, the subject comes just before the verb it governs, and in the typical English question, it comes just after. This holds for all the examples in 32. Although there are exceptions such as **Rarely does Ben fly kites any more**, **In the garden stood four goats**, and **Who has been sitting in my chair?**, even these exceptions are predictable. That is, English has rules that say where the subject in a sentence can go. This turns out to be of considerable practical importance in comprehension, for in many English sentences there is no way of identifying the subject except through word order. We know that **Wellington** is the subject of **Wellington beat Napoleon** only because it precedes the verb.

Summary of Sentence Structure

Every sentence, then, has two different levels of structure—one to specify how it is to be spoken and the other to specify what it means. Its surface structure consists of sounds, words, phrases, and clauses. Some of these units can be classified in terms of their grammatical relations as subjects, predicates, direct objects, indirect objects, and so on. The surface structure can be condensed through various kinds of ellipsis and pronominalization. At the same time, every sentence has an underlying representation that consists of propositions combined with each other by coordination, relativization, or complementation.

Words and Their Structure

Words, the basic building blocks in the surface structure of sentences, have a structure all their own. This structure is something speakers and listeners must take account of. First of all, people must grasp the function each word has in phrases, clauses, and sentences. **In**, for example, is a preposition, used as part of a prepositional phrase to express a verbal unit. **Dog**, however, is a noun, used as part of a noun phrase that denotes a role in some proposition. People must also grasp the internal structure of words. For example, to pick out a single dog, speakers must use **dog**, but to pick out more than one dog, they must use **dog + s**, or **dogs**. For their part, listeners must be able to break **dogs** down and see that it means more than one dog. Speakers and listeners must even be able to create and understand novel words—for example, **duckhouse** as a house for ducks. For children, mastering the functions, internal structure, and creative possibilities for words cannot be easy—these have to be learned along with the rest of language.

Novel words like duckhouse *often have several conceivable meanings.*

Content and Function Words

In our treatment of sentence structure, some words were accorded a certain amount of respect, while others were pushed around, added, deleted, and changed almost at will. This division in privilege corresponds roughly to a traditional distinction between *content words*, sometimes called contentives, and *function words*, sometimes called functors. Content words are those that carry the principal meaning of a sentence. They name the objects, events, and characteristics that lie at the heart of the message the sentence is meant to convey. They include nouns, main verbs, adjectives, and most adverbs. Function words, in contrast, are those needed by the surface structure to glue the content words together, to indicate what goes with what and how. They include articles, pronouns, conjunctions, auxiliary verbs, and prepositions. A fairly complete listing of the different types of content and function words is shown in Table 1–1.

What distinguishes content and function words, however, is that content words belong to "open classes" of words, and function words belong to "closed classes." The open classes of nouns, verbs, adjectives, and adverbs are constantly

TABLE 1–1

THE MAJOR WORD CLASSES IN ENGLISH

CONTENT WORDS

Nouns: dog, apple, matriarchy, elation, etc.

Verbs: go, receive, believe, trip, etc.

Adjectives: happy, naughty, pusillanimous, etc.

Adverbs: sadly, understandably, aptly, etc.

FUNCTION WORDS

Pronouns: I, you, she, . . . there.

Determiners: a, an, the, this, . . . some.

Quantifiers: much, a few, more, . . . three.

Prepositions: in, on, beside, to, . . . of.

Intensifiers: very, too, a little, . . . quite.

Coordinate conjunctions: and, but, or, nor, also, so, yet.

Adverbial conjunctions: although, if, because, . . . before.

Conjunctive adverbs: besides, nevertheless, . . . hence.

Relative pronouns: who, which, whose, . . . that.

Auxiliary verbs: can, may, have, . . . must.

Linking verb: be.

Based on Bolinger (1975).

acquiring new members, many of which find their way into people's everyday vocabularies. The closed classes of function words, however, each have a fixed roster, and once this roster has been learned—by about age twelve—few new members are ever added. New function words are added to a language only very rarely. Altogether the function words number just a few hundred and take up a very minor part of the dictionary. Yet as syntactic glue, they are by far the most frequent words we use. **The** is the commonest word in written English, and the other function words crowd in close behind. The division between open and closed classes makes good sense. As people discover new ideas to talk about and want to express them in new propositions, they have to invent new content words, which carry the weight of these propositions. But because the way in which propositions are put together remains relatively fixed, the roster of function words remains fixed too.

Morphemes and Inflections

Words themselves consist of one or more *morphemes*, the smallest carriers of meaning. Take the single morpheme **man**. Add the morpheme **gentle** and it becomes **gentleman**; add the morpheme **-ly** and it becomes **gentlemanly**; and add the morpheme **un-** and it becomes **ungentlemanly**. The final product **ungentle-manly** consists of four morphemes. Indeed, most complex words consist of some combination of stems, prefixes, and suffixes, each of which is a morpheme. Here are several more examples:

> blackboard: black + board
> inactivity: in + act + ive + ity
> bloodiness: blood + y + ness
> steelworker: steel + work + er
> disabled: dis + able + ed
> antidisestablishmentarianism: anti + dis + establish + ment + ary + an + ism

By the addition of prefixes and suffixes, content words often change classes. The noun **blood** can be made into the adjective **bloody**, the adjective **active** into the verb **activate**, the verb **relate** into the noun **relation**, and so on. In the psychology of language the question is whether speakers and listeners make use of the internal structure of words, and if so how. Do speakers build **activate** from **active** plus **-ate** every time they say the word? Do listeners break down **activate** into **active** plus **-ate** in order to understand it?

Inflections are an especially important type of morpheme. These are morphemes—in English generally suffixes—that do not change the class of the word they are affixed to and can generally be added to every word within the class. Here are the major English inflections:

Plural nouns: boys = boy + s

Singular verbs: works = work + s

Past tense verbs: worked = work + ed

Progressive verbs: working = work + ing

Comparative adjectives: bigger = big + er

Superlative adjectives: biggest = big + est

Possessive nouns: Mary's = Mary + 's

For the most part inflections follow general rules. For example, the plural of a noun consists of the noun plus the suffix **-s**. But there are many exceptions—for example, the plural of **man** is **men**, the past tense of **go** is **went**, and the comparative of **bad** is **worse**. For children the rules are easy enough to learn, but the exceptions aren't. Most children go through a stage where they say things like **mans, goed**, and **badder**. But are children producing these by "rules"? If so, how do they learn the rules? How do inflections figure in speaking and listening generally?

Sounds and Their Structure

Words themselves consist of a succession of sounds called *phonetic segments*. The English word **pat**, for example, consists of three phonetic segments: a consonant sound **p**, followed by a vowel sound written as **a**, followed by another consonant sound **t**. Each language builds up its words from a fairly small inventory of phonetic segments, although languages vary widely in the particular inventory they make use of. In English there are approximately forty different phonetic segments to choose from—the exact number depends on the dialect spoken and the phonetic segments technically counted as "different"—and these combine to form all the words in the language.

Phonetic segments have their own properties. One property is defined by where in the mouth the segment is pronounced. For example, **p**, **b**, **m**, and **w** are all pronounced with both of the lips, and so they are called "bilabial consonants." Another property is defined by the manner in which they are pronounced. The sounds **p**, **b**, **t**, **d**, **k**, and **g** are all pronounced with a complete closure of some part of the mouth followed by the release of that closure. For this reason they are called "stop consonants." One can speak of each segment as having a collection of such properties. For example, **p** is a consonant, a stop, a bilabial, and several other things.

The properties of phonetic segments in turn determine which segments can follow which in the formation of syllables and words. In English, for example, a word cannot normally begin with two stop consonants in a row, as in **tpop**, **kpog**, or **bdopper**. It isn't just that English doesn't have such words, but that speakers and listeners reject these as even possible English words. All languages have constraints like these, but never the same ones. In Russian and Czech, for example, it is not unusual for a word to begin with two stop consonants. The phonetic regularities that go into sound combinations constitute an important part of the structure of every language.

What possible interest, the skeptic might ask, could phonetic structure ever have for the psychology of language? Phonetic structure is concerned with the physical process of pronunciation—the movement of the muscles in and around the mouth—not with the processes of comprehension and production. In fact, however, phonetic structure is vital to explanations of how people produce, understand, and acquire language. It is needed to explain why people mishear **deaf in Venice** for **Death in Venice**, why they mis-say **Fillmore's face grammar** for **Fillmore's case grammar**, and why children begin by saying **mouse** instead of **mouth**. It is also needed to explain how we "know" that **blurg** is a possible English word and **tpop** isn't, and that the **c** in **elasticity** is pronounced with an **s** sound and not with the **k** sound it has in **elastic**. More generally, the sound structure of a language is very complex, and it is essential to explain how people are able to hear and produce these sounds so deftly. A detailed examination of phonetic structure, however, will be postponed until Chapter 5.

THE FUNCTION OF LANGUAGE

In language, function goes hand in hand with structure, for the structure of each sentence specifies the uses to which it can be put. **Napoleon was exiled to Elba**, for example, has the structure of a declarative sentence with **Napoleon** as subject and **was exiled to Elba** as predicate. Because of its structure it can be used to tell someone that Napoleon was exiled to Elba. It cannot be used to tell someone that Benjamin Franklin invented bifocals, to thank the President for a pleasant evening, or to ask the waiter to bring another cup of coffee. Like the bicycle, this sentence has a structure specially engineered for a particular function, that of telling someone that Napoleon was exiled to Elba. For this reason, function is as important to the study of language as structure.

The fundamental function of language is communication. In this activity there are three main elements:

(1) a speaker

(2) a listener

(3) a signaling system (for example, the English language)

Furthermore, the signaling system must be one that speakers and listeners are both able to use. Communication begins with speakers. They decide, for example, to impart some information in a particular way. They then select a signal—a particular English sentence—that they believe is appropriate and utter it. The listeners receive the signal—the uttered sentence—and take it in for immediate use or for storage in memory. With that, one stage of communication is complete.

As this description shows, the function of language is intimately bound up with the speakers' and listeners' mental activities during communication, in particular with the speakers' intentions, the ideas speakers want to convey, and the listeners' current knowledge. First, speakers intend to have some effect on their listeners, and must get them to recognize these intentions. The sentences used must therefore reflect these intentions. Second, speakers want to convey certain ideas, and to do this the sentences must also reflect the listeners' ways of thinking about objects, states, events, and facts. And third, speakers must have some conception of what is on their listeners' minds at the moment and of where they want the communication to lead. The sentences used must reflect these conceptions as well. These three aspects of language function have been studied under the labels of speech acts, propositional content, and thematic structure.

Speech Acts

Each sentence, taken as a whole, is designed to serve a specific function. It may be meant to inform listeners, warn them, order them to do something, question them about a fact, or thank them for a gift or act of kindness. The function it serves is critical to communication. Speakers expect listeners to recognize the functions of the sentences they speak and to act accordingly. Whenever they ask a question, for example, they expect their listeners to realize that it is a request for information. If the listeners fail to appreciate this intention, they are judged as having "misunderstood," even though they may have taken in everything else about the utterance. But just how is this function of sentences to be characterized? And how does each sentence convey its particular function?

Performative Utterances

These questions have been answered in part by Austin (1962) and Searle (1969) in their theory of speech acts. According to them, every time speakers utter a sentence, they are attempting to accomplish something with the words. Speakers are performing a *speech act* (Austin called it an illocutionary act). What is meant by speech act can be shown by such examples as:

33. *Judge to prisoner:* I hereby sentence you to five years in jail.

34. *Minister to couple:* I pronounce you husband and wife.

35. *One football fan to another:* I bet you $15 the Dolphins will lose.

36. *Debtor to lender:* I promise to pay you $50 on July 1st.

In each instance the speaker performs a speech act in the very utterance of the words. The judge's words, for example, constitute the formal act of sentencing. Properly speaking, the prisoner would not have been sentenced and obliged to go to jail without the judge's words. The minister's pronouncement, likewise, constitutes the act of marrying the couple; without it the ceremony would have been incomplete. Analogously, the football fan makes a bet by saying "I bet you," and the debtor makes a promise by saying "I promise you." Before uttering these sentences the football fan and the debtor had not yet performed the acts of betting and promising; by the end of their utterances they had.

Sentences like these have structural properties in common. Each of these examples contains a "performative" verb (**sentence**, **pronounce**, **bet**, **promise**) that indicates the speech act the speaker meant the utterance to perform—the function it was meant to fulfill. Other verbs that can be used performatively include **appoint**, **order**, **bequeath**, **warn**, **urge**, **announce**, **nominate**, **guarantee**, **apologize**, **thank**, **congratulate**, **dare**, **request**, **affirm**, and **state**.

The performative verbs have a special place in these sentences, fitting into a sentence frame like this:

37. I [verb] to you [sentence complement].

That is, each performative sentence consists of the subject **I**, a performative verb in the present tense, the indirect object **you**, and a complement inserted in place of an empty direct object. The debtor's sentence, for example, has roughly this form:

38. I [promise] to you [I will pay you $50 on July 1st].

With ellipsis, the sentence becomes simply **I promise to pay you $50 on July 1st**. This sentence frame makes good sense. In every utterance the speaker (**I**) must

Drawing by Ross; © 1974 The New Yorker Magazine, Inc.

"I hereby pronounce you authorized personnel."

indicate which speech act is being performed in relation to the addressee (**you**), and this is specified by the verb. Since the speaker indicates the speech act while actually performing it, the verb must be in the present tense. It can normally be modified by **hereby** to emphasize that fact. The speaker must also indicate the particular consequences or conditions of the speech act, and this is done in the complement, the "embedded" sentence in brackets. In the debtor's utterance, for example, it isn't that she promised to burn $100 on July 2nd or to stand on her head on New Year's Eve, but rather to pay the lender $50 on July 1st.

Declaratives, Interrogatives, and Imperatives

Among the many speech acts one can perform, three of the commonest are assertions, questions, and commands, as illustrated here:

> 39. a. I tell you that it's raining out.
>   b. I ask you to tell me who invented the Franklin stove.
>   c. I order you to stand still.

Like other performative sentences, these three fit the sentence frame in 37. Each has a performative verb in the present tense, **I** as subject, **you** as indirect object, and a complement sentence as direct object. But in English, as in most other languages, assertions, questions, and commands don't normally require the full performative constructions in 39, but only the shortened constructions in 40:

40. a. It's raining out.
    b. Who invented the Franklin stove?
    c. Stand still.

Telling is normally done with declaratives, questioning with interrogatives, and ordering with imperatives.

The reason English has these shortened constructions is not hard to guess. Telling, asking, and ordering are so common that it would be a waste of time and effort to have to use the full performative sentences. How tedious it would be if every assertion had to be introduced by the words **I tell you that**. To avoid excess verbiage English has an efficient arrangement for "marking" or specifying speech acts. Every utterance is assumed to be an assertion—by far the commonest of the speech acts—unless it is "marked" (tagged or labeled) otherwise. It is a request for information when marked by the use of the interrogative form, or a command to do something when marked by the use of the imperative form. An utterance is taken to be some other speech act when it is introduced by the appropriate performative verb, as in **I warn you that it's raining out**. This is an efficient system, for in general, the commoner the speech act, the simpler it is to produce and take in.

Direct and Indirect Speech Acts

What has been said so far, however, is not quite right. Although in English the standard way to command someone to do something is to use the imperative form, that isn't the only way. It can also be done indirectly with declarative constructions, interrogative constructions, and other special devices, as illustrated here:

Direct command: Open the door.

Indirect commands: Can you open the door?
Would you mind opening the door?
The door should be open.
Why not open the door?
Haven't you forgotten to do something?
I would prefer the door open.
You will open the door right this minute or else.
It's hot in here.

Under the right circumstances each of these constructions could be used to get someone to open the door, although they differ in their politeness, directness, and so forth. Most other speech acts have alternative forms of expression too. There is a distinction, then, between direct and indirect speech acts. *Direct speech acts* are those expressed by the constructions specifically designed for those acts. *Indirect speech acts* are those expressed by other constructions.

It isn't easy to characterize the indirect correspondence between speech acts and sentence types. **It's hot in here** could be used in different situations to assert that it is hot in the room, request someone to open the window, request someone to close the window, warn someone not to enter the room, and so on. But how do listeners decide which way the utterance is to be taken? And how do speakers select this sentence, confident that listeners will arrive at the right interpretation? Besides relying on an appropriate intonation pattern, speakers obviously depend heavily on the immediate situation to tell listeners which interpretation to select, and listeners obviously make use of this information. It is not obvious, however, how all this is done. That remains an intriguing question in the psychology of language.

Propositional Content

Sentences can be used to inform people of something, ask them about something, warn them about something, or request them to do something. Each of these **somethings**—each of these empty nouns—must have content to convey the ideas the listeners are to be informed of, asked about, warned about, or requested to fulfill. So a very important function of sentences is to specify the ideas around which a speech act is built. These ideas are conveyed by the *propositional content*, sometimes called the ideational content, of a sentence. Of course, if listeners are ever to grasp these ideas, this content must fit people's requirements for what is a "proper idea." Thus, the study of propositional content is important because of its potential for revealing the fundamental nature of human ideas—at least those ideas that can be communicated.

The propositional content of a sentence is nothing more than the combination of propositions it expresses. **The young troops defeated the army**, as we observed earlier, expresses two propositions—the ones expressed separately in **The troops were young** and **The troops defeated the army**. Combined as they are, these propositions convey what it is the speaker wants to inform the listener of.

The Functions of Propositions

Propositions, as wholes, have one of three basic functions: they denote states or events; they denote facts about states or events; or they qualify parts of other propositions (Vendler, 1967). Take the proposition expressed by **The troops defeated the army**. It can be used to denote an event, as when it is the complement replacing the empty noun in **Something took a long time**:

The troops' defeating of the army took a long time.

Here, **the troops' defeating of the army** specifies an event. It can also be used to denote the fact of an event, as when it is the complement replacing the empty noun in **Something surprised the king**:

That the troops defeated the army surprised the king.

Here it is the *fact* that the troops defeated the army that surprised the king, not the event itself. Finally, it can be used to qualify part of another proposition, as when it appears as a relative clause modifying **the troops** in **The troops were delighted**:

The troops that defeated the army were delighted.

Spoken sentences, however, consist of words, phrases, and clauses—the constituents of surface structure—and not of propositions. What, then, is the connection between these constituents and the underlying propositions? The simplest answer is that each constituent directs the listener to some aspect of the underlying propositions and their functions. Precisely how they do this is an important question for the study of speaking and listening.

The connection between constituents and underlying propositions might be illustrated in the following way. Because it is an assertion, a sentence like **Van Gogh painted a chair** functions as if it were the complement of **I tell you that**—as in **I tell you that Van Gogh painted a chair**. But complements of this sort denote facts about events, and this sentence denotes the fact of Van Gogh's having painted a chair. Each constituent of the sentence picks out one or other aspect of this event. The verb **painted** denotes the nature of the event, and the noun phrases **Van Gogh** and **a chair** denote the two participants. All sentences, no matter how complex they may appear, express a state or event or a fact about a state or event. The main verb normally denotes the state or event, and the other constituents normally denote participants in that state or event.

Sources of Complexity

Sentences become complex for several reasons. First, to enable listeners to pick out the participants in a state or event accurately, speakers are often forced to expand on the noun phrases that denote the participants:

the army
the first army that defeated Napoleon
the very first army that historians found had defeated Napoleon soundly

With more and more such qualifications, listeners can determine more precisely which army a speaker is thinking of. Second, in some events, one or more of the participants are themselves events or facts. The **something** in **John thinks something**, for example, has to be a fact, not just an object. It must therefore be replaced by a complement, as in **John thinks that Van Gogh painted a chair**. The use of such complements makes sentences more complex too. Third, it is possible to slip one whole sentence inside another. For example, the declarative sentence **The king, who feared Napoleon, praised the army** actually makes two assertions, **The king praised the army** and **The king feared Napoleon**. It is as if the speaker, in the middle of asserting **The king praised the army**, also wanted to assert **The king feared Napoleon**, and so he slipped it in as a "non-restrictive" relative clause. Languages have many such parenthetical devices, most of which make sentences more complex.

In short, the propositional structure of a sentence is used to denote the objects, states, events, and facts that make up the core ideas behind a sentence. Because the propositions themselves are not present in surface structure, it falls on the words, phrases, and clauses to make clear what propositions are being expressed. Since speech itself is linear, with words following one another in succession as they are uttered, the expression of these propositions has to be forced into a single line, and this is what makes sentences complex. For speakers the problem is how to express propositions in strings of words, and for listeners, it is how to reconstruct the underlying propositions. These two problems are not easily solved.

Thematic Structure

To be effective in conversations, speakers also have to pay close attention to their listeners. They have to keep track of what their listeners do and don't know, refer to things they do know, and tell them things they don't. Speakers must also keep track of where they are leading their listeners, and steer the conversation in the right direction. Speaking is a cooperative enterprise. Speakers talk to satisfy their listeners' reasons for listening, which are normally to learn what information is being conveyed, what actions are being requested, what promises are being made, and so on. The speakers' judgments about the listeners' current mental states are reflected in what is called *thematic structure* (Halliday, 1970, 1973).

At first it seems as if these judgments must be impossible. How could Dickens, writing *Oliver Twist* more than a century ago, possibly know what is on people's minds as they read it now? The solution is quite simple. He introduces everything readers need to know as he goes along—at least everything that is not part of "common knowledge." He can then assume that they know everything in the novel up to the current sentence. He can also assume that they don't otherwise know the story he is telling. With these two assumptions he can accurately gauge what readers do and don't know at each point in the novel. In everyday conversations this task is even easier. Speakers know not only what has been said, but also what is available to their listeners to see, hear, or feel.

In English as in all languages, thematic structure has three main functions. The first is to convey given information and new information, the second subject and predicate, and the third frame and insert.

Given and New Information

Speakers must tailor their sentences to fit what they think their listeners know. Take 41, for example:

41. It was your BROTHER who stole the money.

To use this, the speaker would expect the listener to know that someone had stolen some money, but not that that someone was his brother. The speaker's purpose in saying 41 would be to tell the listener, not that some money had been stolen, but that the thief was his brother. Sentence 41 is therefore said to have two parts:

Given information: Someone stole the money.
New information: That someone was your brother.

These two parts are signaled in the structure of the sentence. It is up to the speaker to use the sentence in the right circumstances. The sentence **It was the MONEY that your brother stole**, with different given and new information, is appropriate to different circumstances, even though it too expresses the idea that the listener's brother stole the money. It should be used when the listener knows his brother stole something, but doesn't know that what he stole was the money.

Sentences signal given and new information by stress or accent on particular words (e.g., Halliday, 1967). In 41, as the capital letters indicate, **brother** is spoken with the greatest emphasis and highest pitch. It is said to carry the *focal stress* of the sentence. The word with focal stress, or a phrase containing it, always conveys the new information. The rest of the sentence conveys the given information. The focal stress (indicated by capital letters) signals the new information in these sentences too:

42. a. Your BROTHER is the one who stole the money.
    b. Your BROTHER stole the money.
    c. The money was stolen by your BROTHER.

In most ordinary sentences, however, focal stress falls on the final content word. Take 43:

43. Mr. Fields juggled the BOXES.

This sentence, unlike the other examples, can be divided into given and new information in three possible ways:

44. a. *Given information:* Mr. Fields juggled something.
       New information: That something was the boxes.

    b. *Given information:* Mr. Fields did something.
       New information: That something was to juggle the boxes.

c. *Given information:* Something happened.
New information: That something was that Mr. Fields juggled the boxes.

These three ways correspond to the three phrases of which **boxes** is a part:

45. a. the boxes (*a noun phrase*)
    b. juggled the boxes (*a verb phrase*)
    c. Mr. Fields juggled the boxes (*the whole sentence*)

Here, then, the focal stress signals the new information, but leaves open the three possibilities.

The three ways of dividing up 43 also correspond to the three questions for which 43 is an appropriate answer:

46. a. *What did Mr. Fields juggle?* Mr. Fields juggled the BOXES.
    b. *What did Mr. Fields do?* Mr. Fields juggled the BOXES.
    c. *What happened?* Mr. Fields juggled the BOXES.

The question in 46a, for example, takes it as known that Mr. Fields juggled something and asks what it was. For the answer to be appropriate, it must take what is known as given information and provide the answer as new information. Determining which questions are appropriate is often a good way of discovering the given and new information of a sentence. Note that the following questions are *not* appropriate for 43 with its particular stress pattern:

47. a. *Who juggled the boxes?* Mr. Fields juggled the BOXES.
    b. *What did Mr. Fields do with the boxes?* Mr. Fields juggled the BOXES.

From these it is clear that the new information of 43 cannot be that the juggler was Mr. Fields or that the action done was juggling. It must be one of the three possibilities in 44.

Subject and Predicate

When people talk, they also tailor their sentences to suit themselves. They have something they want to talk about, and something they want to say about it. These functions are conveyed, respectively, by the subject and the predicate, the two grammatical categories discussed earlier. These functions can be illustrated in 48 and 49:

48. The police investigated the robbery.

49. The robbery was investigated by the police.

When speakers use 48, they are talking about the police and what they did. When they use 49, they are talking about the robbery and what happened to it. It is as if in 48 a speaker had said, "I have a fact I want you to remember about the police: they investigated the robbery." And in 49, "I have a fact I want you to remember about the robbery: it was investigated by the police." It is easy to imagine that listeners would comply and store this fact one way given 48 and another way given 49. Subject and predicate are therefore important for carrying out the purposes of a conversation. They allow the participants to keep track of what each other is talking about at all times.

In most sentences the subject is given information and the predicate new information. In **Mr. Fields juggled the BOXES**, for example, the subject (**Mr. Fields**) is usually given information, and the predicate (**juggled the boxes**) usually contains the new information. This makes good sense. Normally, listeners know what speakers are talking about (the subject) but not what they are saying about it (the predicate). It is then appropriate to make the subject given information and the predicate new information. However, this need not be the case. Take 50:

50. The OWNERS investigated the robbery.

In using this sentence, the speaker indicates that although for the listener it is new information that the owners did it, for the speaker, the owners are what he is talking about, the subject of the sentence. In English and perhaps most other languages, then, the functions served by given and new and by subject and predicate are signaled separately. In English, given and new are signaled by stress, and subject and predicate by position and other relations within the sentence.

Frame and Insert

When speakers place a particular phrase at the beginning of a sentence, they are deliberately trying to orient their listeners toward a particular area of knowledge—to give them a point of departure for the sentence. Speakers then use the rest of the sentence progressively to narrow down what they are trying to say. For this reason, the first phrase can be called a *frame*, and the remainder of the sentence an *insert* for that frame. These two notions are illustrated in the following sentences, with the frame in italics:

51. a. *On the film set* Mr. Fields was delightful.
    b. *Hardly ever* did Mr. Fields crack a smile.
    c. *Down his gullet* went the last nip of gin.
    d. *Mr. Fields* was a good juggler.

The point of departure for 51a is being on the film set. It is the frame within which the fact that Mr. Fields was delightful is to be inserted. Similarly, the point of departure for 51b is the rarity of an event, for 51c the swallowing of things, and for 51d Mr. Fields himself.

In the simplest sentences, the frame coincides with the subject and is part of the given information. In **Mr. Fields juggled the BOXES, Mr. Fields** is not only the subject and part of the given information, but also the frame. The point of departure that speakers plan for an utterance (the frame) is normally the same as what they are talking about (the subject), and that in turn is usually information known to their listeners (the given information). Yet the frame can be separated from both the subject and the given information, as in this sentence:

52. MR. FIELDS she met.

While the frame is **Mr. Fields**, the subject is **she**, and the given information is that she met someone. Given and new information, subject and predicate, and frame and insert, therefore, are three separate pairs of functions, although normally given information, subject, and frame coincide.

A final note of warning. The notions of frame and insert have been very difficult for linguists to characterize and so have been surrounded by controversy and confusing terminology (see Chafe, 1976). For example, they have been labeled topic and comment by some investigators, while topic and comment have been used by others to label given and new information. They have been labeled theme and rheme by Halliday (1967, 1973), but elsewhere theme has been used for other notions. We have selected frame and insert to keep these notions separate at least from given and new information and subject and predicate. As Chafe has argued, so much confusion has arisen over frame and insert probably because they play a relatively minor role in English compared to such languages as Chinese (see Li and Thompson, 1975). Indeed, frame and insert will receive little attention in our discussions of comprehension, production, and acquisition.

Discourse

The concern so far has been with the sentence and its parts. Yet hardly any of our day-to-day use of language stops after one sentence. People engage in conversations, stories, gossip, and jokes that consist of a succession of sentences in a highly organized social activity. It is common knowledge that stories, jokes, and essays have structure, but so do even the most trivial conversations. Indeed, speech acts and thematic structure make no sense except within the larger framework of discourse. The nature of the discourse determines which speech acts are appropriate, and what should be given information, subject, and frame in each utterance. To neglect discourse would be to miss some of the most important aspects of language. It will therefore be taken up in relation to comprehension, production, and acquisition at various points throughout the book.

PROCESSES IN THE USE OF LANGUAGE

The point has already been made that the structure and function of a language do not by themselves reveal the processes involved in language use. Imagine that Professor Smith had uttered **Washington chopped down his father's cherry tree.**

Structurally, the sentence has a subject, predicate, direct object, nouns, verbs, and underlying propositions. Functionally, it is a speech act asserting the fact of George's cutting down a particular tree, with Washington as subject, frame, and part of the given information. Yet none of this says what mental activity Smith went through in uttering the sentence. How did she plan it? How did she select the words—all at once, from first to last, from content words to function words, or some other way? How did she retrieve the right words from memory and produce them in an order that conforms to English syntax? Nor does any of this say what mental activity her listeners went through in comprehending it. How did they identify her words? How did they work out what the words were meant to refer to? How did they decide she was asserting a fact and not asking for information or making a demand?

Sources of Evidence

For insight into these questions, one must study the activities of speaking and listening themselves. But how does one study an "activity," especially a "mental activity"? That all depends on what such an activity is assumed to be. Most investigators have taken it for granted that speaking and listening consist of a collection of mental operations, just as building a bicycle consists of a collection of physical operations. These operations feed on certain basic mental resources, just as building a bicycle requires tools and raw materials. Furthermore, these operations take effort and tax people's capacity to perform them in a limited amount of time. From these assumptions it was natural for investigators to turn to two types of information as clues to the nature of speaking and listening: the responses that are actually made under various circumstances and the length of time these responses take.

Actual responses, especially mistakes, are an important resource in the study of speaking and listening. Consider the person who said **Yew Nork** instead of **New York.** This example allows one to infer that at some point before the words were spoken, both **New** and **York** were in the speaker's "working" memory—otherwise their parts could not have been interchanged. And it also allows one to infer that at that point the two words consisted of separable sound segments; otherwise the **n** and **y** could not have been cut loose and exchanged. A systematic investigation of speech errors can lead to inferences about how words are planned just before they are spoken. Other types of responses reveal other aspects of speaking and listening.

Response times, or "response latencies," are another important resource. Take the speaker who says **I met a** (pause) **machiavellian old man yesterday.** Why did he take so much time between **a** and **machiavellian?** One could infer that deciding on this word and retrieving it from memory required complicated mental operations and therefore took a relatively long time. A systematic investigation of speech pauses can give clues as to how speakers plan their speech, decide on each word, and retrieve it from memory. More generally, response times provide a sensitive measure of the time and effort mental operations require. With the proliferation of sophisticated tape recorders and accurate chronometers, response times have become more and more available in the study of speaking and listening.

Methods in the Study of Language

The psychology of language is built on theories. These theories—sometimes precise but more often loose and programmatic—are attempts to explain the mental processes behind speaking, listening, and acquisition by a systematic account of the phenomena in these three areas. But theories are only as good as the evidence behind them, and so great effort has gone into the search for evidence—both pro and con—that bears on the validity of each theory. There are two methods that have been used in this search: experiments and naturalistic observations.

Experiments are designed to test theories by the use of controlled observation. Briefly, an experiment consists of five phases:

(1) *Theory:* Investigators begin with a theory to be tested.

(2) *Prediction:* From the theory they derive a prediction of the form: If X occurs, then Y should occur.

(3) *Manipulation:* In the experiment proper they then set up the conditions needed for X to occur.

(4) *Observation:* They observe whether Y occurs.

(5) *Conclusion:*
   (a) If Y occurred, the prediction is upheld, and they conclude they have support for the theory.
   (b) If Y didn't occur, the prediction is contradicted, and they conclude they have evidence against the theory—that the theory is partially or wholly incorrect.
   (c) If the observations are equivocal, they conclude nothing.

In this procedure, investigators must take care that the predictions follow from the theory (Phase 2), that the manipulation is truly appropriate (Phase 3), and that they can unequivocally decide whether Y did or didn't occur (Phase 4).

Naturalistic observations, which are also used for testing theories, lack the Phase 3 manipulation of experiments. In observational studies investigators simply observe ongoing behavior without any intervention. Observational studies are important for several reasons. For one thing, they are often essential for studying behavior that occurs naturally and is not open to manipulation. Slips of the tongue, for instance, are difficult to induce, and so one often has no choice but to observe and record them as they occur naturally. For another, investigators sometimes judge that an experimental manipulation might contaminate or even destroy the phenomenon they are studying. For example, telephone conversations in the laboratory will surely be different from everyday telephone conversations. If investigators are interested in the everyday kind, they must observe them under everyday conditions.

Naturalistic observations and experiments often go hand-in-hand. Naturalistic observations are used to explore a phenomenon, and experiments are then brought in to clean up the details. Imagine that a psychologist named Jugend is interested in the two-year-old's understanding of questions. His first step might be to observe natural conversations between parents and children in the home as they go through their daily routines. From a tape-recording and accompanying notes, he can then tally up those questions put by the mother or father that the child did and didn't answer appropriately. With luck, the parents will have asked a variety of questions, and Jugend can decide which ones the children have and haven't answered appropriately. In this study, Jugend did not set out to test any particular hypothesis. He merely wanted to see which questions two-year-olds could understand.

Jugend's next step might be to build a theory about the comprehension of questions by two-year-olds and test it in an experiment. The theory might predict that certain types of question should be easier under one circumstance than under another. He might then get mothers and fathers to ask their two-year-olds a fixed set of questions under these two circumstances. He would observe how they answered and draw his conclusions depending on whether the answers went with the prediction, went against it, or were equivocal. The same theory, however, could have been tested with naturalist observations. Jugend could simply have looked through his tape-recordings of natural conversations for the right questions asked under the right circumstances. The trouble is, he may never find them, or if he does, they may be interrupted by a barking dog or an inquisitive older sister. Experiments make controlled observation possible.

Naturalistic observations and experiments, however, are not as different as they might first appear. In observational studies, the investigator always applies some controls. Jugend might try to find a time of day when two-year-olds are alone with their mothers and are playing with a selected set of toys. The best observational studies have just such natural controls in natural settings. In experiments too, the investigator tries to be as naturalistic as possible. If Jugend had sat a two-year-old in a chair and had a stranger ask her the questions, it wouldn't be surprising if he got odd results. In this way, experiments must always be evaluated for their adequacy as tests of a theory. Considerations of naturalness and control will often be just as important as the logic of the test itself.

Linguistics is an empirical science too. The grammar of a language is a theory about its structure, and so the rules of grammar must be tested for their validity. For this, linguists combine naturalistic observations with experiments too. Imagine that a linguist named Langue is studying the structure of Eskimo. She begins by observing Eskimo spoken under relatively uncontrolled conditions. Then she looks for regularities in these observations and devises rules to account for them. In effect, these rules constitute a theory about the structure of Eskimo, and the next step is to test the theory. She does so by devising new sentences that should be good Eskimo if the rules are correct and then presenting them to an Eskimo speaker for judgment. If they are good Eskimo, she has support for the rules. If they are not, she must try again. When linguists work on their own languages, the task is much easier, and naturalistic observations and experiment often merge into a continuous procedure. Each rule they devise is tested immediately, so they spend their time devising systems of rules that are as complete as possible.

The theories that methods like these test require extensive work in their own right. There are three main criteria for judging a theory:

(1) *Correctness:* Does the theory accord with the facts?

(2) *Completeness:* Does it cover all relevant aspects of the facts?

(3) *Compatibility:* Is the theory consistent with others that have been shown to hold in adjacent areas?

Thus the adequacy of theories must be judged as well as the adequacy of experiments designed to test them.

Four Topics in This Book

This book takes up theories and evidence for four broad topics: comprehension, production, acquisition, and meaning and thought. These topics are covered in Parts 2, 3, 4, and 5, respectively. Any one of them would be formidable if it could not be broken down into smaller parts. But just as building a bicycle divides into roughly successive stages of activity—collecting the materials, building the parts, and assembling them—so do comprehension, production, and acquisition. Thus it is possible without too much distortion to look at each of these processes stage by stage. The final topic can be divided into the study of meaning, its role in comprehension, production, and acquisition, and its implications for the nature of human thought.

SUMMARY

For over two thousand years language has intrigued scholars, not only because it is an intricate and powerful tool for human communication, but also because it seems to reflect the very nature of human thought. Traditionally, philosophers and linguists have paid most attention to the structure and function of language. In the psychology of language, however, we are concerned with three processes: comprehension, production, and acquisition.

Structurally, the basic unit of language is the sentence. It has roughly two levels: a surface structure consisting of sounds, words, phrases, and clauses— surface constituents of various sizes—arranged so that they form a linear succession of units; and an underlying representation consisting of propositions combined with each other by coordination, relativization, or complementation. These propositions, woven together in complex patterns, bear an indirect, but specifiable, relation to the constituents in surface structure. In effect, the surface structure says how the sentence is to be pronounced, and the underlying representation indicates what ideas it was meant to convey.

Functionally, the sentence has three relatively separate aspects: speech acts, propositional content, and thematic structure. Speakers utter sentences in order to perform speech acts—to ask questions, assert facts, promise favors, make bets, and the like. The speech act that a sentence is meant to express is reflected directly or indirectly in its structure. In performing speech acts, speakers also convey propositional content—to indicate the objects, states or events, and facts their speech acts are about. The sentences they use express propositions, and these denote objects, states or events, and facts in particular ways. Finally, speakers are careful to use their sentences in cooperation with their listener. In each sentence they indicate given and new information (what they judge their listener does and doesn't know), subject and predicate (what they are talking about and what they are saying about it), and frame and insert (the framework of their ideas and its contents). In short, different aspects of a sentence fulfill different functions.

The mental processes by which people speak and understand, however, are not revealed directly in the structure and function of language. They are beyond structure and function and need to be studied on their own, and by their own methods. That is the focus of this book. We will take up the processes of comprehension, production, and acquisition in turn, with meaning and the relation between language and thought left to the end.

Further Reading

For more complete introductions to language and linguistics, there are many excellent texts, among them Bolinger (1975), Fromkin and Rodman (1974), Langacker (1973), and Sampson (1975). For syntax Cattell (1969) and Langendoen (1970) are introductory, while Akmajian and Heny (1975) and Bach (1974) are more thorough. For word formation V. Adams (1973) and Matthews (1974) provide excellent introductions. Noam Chomsky's influence—especially with his discussions of competence and performance, grammar, and the human intellect—have come mainly from five sources, spanning two decades: *Syntactic Structures* (1957), *Aspects of the Theory of Syntax* (1965), *Cartesian Linguistics* (1966), *Language and Mind* (1968), and *Reflections on Language* (1975). Of these the most readable is *Language and Mind*. For balance on Chomsky's views, one might consult the critical essays edited by Harman (1974). Less has been written about function in language. Yet Austin's *How to Do Things with Words* (1962) and Searle's *Speech Acts* (1969) introduce speech acts very clearly; Vendler (1967) and Fillmore (1968) have excellent discussions of the use of propositions; and Halliday's *Explorations in the Function of Language* (1973) describes his views on thematic structure. For a good sampling of essays in these and other areas one might read *New Horizons in Linguistics*, edited by Lyons (1970). As for methods, B. Anderson (1971) gives a brief introduction to psychological experiments, G. Olson and H. Clark (1976) survey methods for studying language processes, and Langacker (1974a) has an extensive discussion of linguistic methods.

COMPREHENSION

Take a sentence of a dozen words, and take twelve men and tell to each one word. Then stand the men in a row or jam them in a bunch, and let each think of his word as intently as he will; nowhere will there be a consciousness of the whole sentence.

William James

2

Comprehension of Sentences

Day after day people listen to thousands of sentences about many topics from a variety of sources and manage to understand them. To do this, they have to make an intricate series of decisions that require detailed knowledge and delicate judgments of all sorts. As a rule, they have no difficulty in understanding what they hear, and tend to think of comprehension—if they think about it at all—as a relatively simple matter. Yet every so often they make mistakes that make the complex nature of comprehension apparent. As when a driver turns left after misunderstanding a sign that says: " No Left Turn Except Commercial Vehicles." Or when the American people misunderstood President Calvin Coolidge as implying that he might be available for a second term when he announced, " I do not choose to run." Or when a neighbor fails to detect the sarcasm of " What a beautiful job the painters did on your house." But what are the processes people go through in comprehending a sentence? How do they come to the right—or wrong—interpretation? What sorts of knowledge and delicate judgments does the process demand?

WHAT IS COMPREHENSION ?

Comprehension has two common senses. In its narrow sense it denotes the mental processes by which listeners take in the sounds uttered by a speaker and use them to construct an interpretation of what they think the speaker intended to convey. More simply, it is the building of meanings from sounds. With a little thought it is possible to make some good preliminary guesses about what comprehension in this narrow sense must be like.

Imagine listeners trying to comprehend this sentence:

1. The old man lit his awful cigar.

They must begin with what they hear, the temporal sequence of words: **the** first, **old** second, **man** third, and so on. To understand this sequence, they probably have to identify these words and see that they fall into natural groups. **The**, **old**, and **man** go together to form a unit—a phrase—that denotes one entity; **his**, **awful**, and **cigar** go together to form a phrase that denotes another entity; and **lit** ties the two phrases together into a larger unit—a sentence—that denotes an event. But these words and phrases, and their classification, correspond roughly to the surface structure of 1 (see Chapter 1). Thus it is a crude but plausible guess that the sound end of the comprehension process starts by identifying the surface structure of a sentence—its words, their temporal order, and their grouping.

At the meaning end of the process, listeners have to build an interpretation for 1. What is this interpretation like? One approach is to ask what 1 conveys, which is not just one indivisible lump of information but rather all the separate pieces of information expressed in 2:

2. a. A man has been mentioned.
   b. He is old.
   c. A cigar has been mentioned.
   d. It belongs to him.
   e. It is awful.
   f. He lit it.

The main idea in 1 is expressed by **He lit it** (2f). The other ideas (2a through 2e) are there only to specify more exactly what "he" and "it" are. "He" is a man, and he is old; "it" is a cigar, it is awful, and it belongs to "him." This description, of course, is roughly the underlying representation of 1 (see Chapter 1). The sentences in 2 express the propositions underlying 1; 2f expresses the main one, and 2a through 2e express propositions that are combined with 2f by relativization as "modifiers" of the nouns in 2f. Thus it is again a crude but plausible first guess that the meaning end of the comprehension process builds an interpretation that resembles the underlying representation of a sentence—a set of propositions plus their interrelations.

Comprehension in its broader sense, however, rarely ends here, for listeners normally put the interpretations they have built to work. On hearing an assertion, they normally extract the new information it conveys and store that information in memory. On hearing a question, they normally search for the information asked for and compose an answer. On hearing an order or request, they normally decide what they are supposed to do and do it. In brief, under most circumstances listeners figure out what they were meant to do with a sentence and do it. For this, they must have at their disposal additional mental processes that make use of the interpretation they have constructed so far.

The Two Processes

This preliminary tour through comprehension in both of its senses suggests that it divides naturally into two somewhat distinct areas of study. The first will be called the *construction process*. It is concerned with the way listeners construct an interpretation of a sentence from the speakers' words. They seem to begin by identifying surface structure and end up with an interpretation that resembles an underlying representation. The second area of study will be called the *utilization process*. It is concerned with how listeners utilize this interpretation for further purposes—for registering new information, answering questions, following orders, registering promises, and the like. The construction process will be taken up in this chapter, and the utilization process in Chapter 3.

It would be a mistake, however, to think of the construction and utilization processes as truly separate. People listen because they want to cooperate with speakers—to register the information they are offering, answer their questions, and carry out their requests. Their goal is to discover how they are expected to utilize speakers' sentences. This goal should motivate and guide comprehension from beginning to end—from identifying words through building interpretations to utilizing those interpretations. For example, when people build interpretations, they try to build ones that when utilized will make sense in this particular context. How they do this will become clearer in this and the next chapter.

THE CONSTRUCTION PROCESS

When listeners interpret a sentence, their immediate goal is to build an underlying representation for the sentence. Yet when they hear **The old man lit his awful cigar**, they aren't presented with its underlying representation directly. They must build up the six propositions expressed in 2 and their interrelations bit by bit from the words as they hear them. How do they do that? It is instructive first to look more closely at underlying representations and their relation to surface structure.

Underlying Representations

In Chapter 1, propositions were shown to consist of a verbal unit plus one or more nouns. In the basic types shown in Table 2–1, each proposition is expressed as a verbal unit (**walks**, **is handsome**, **is a bachelor**, **hit**, **is in**, and **gave**) plus one or more nouns (**John**, **Bill**, **Paris**, **Fido**, and **Mary**). (The reason for treating **bachelor** in 3 as part of the verbal unit will become clear later.) To be more precise, each of these propositions is a *predication* about one or more entities. The proposition in 1 predicates the activity of walking of John; 2 predicates the state of handsomeness of John; 3 predicates the state of bachelorhood of John; 4 predicates the activity of hitting between John and Bill; and so on. Viewed this way, propositions are important for what they predicate of

TABLE 2–1

PROPOSITIONAL FUNCTIONS

Examples of Six Simple Sentences and Their Corresponding Propositional Functions

SIMPLE SENTENCES	SENTENCES WITH VARIABLES	PROPOSITIONAL FUNCTIONS
1. John walks.	x walks	Walk(x)
2. John is handsome.	x is handsome	Handsome(x)
3. John is a bachelor.	x is a bachelor	Bachelor(x)
4. John hit Bill.	x hit y	Hit(x,y)
5. John is in Paris.	x is in y	In(x,y)
6. John gave Fido to Mary.	x gave y to z	Give(x,y,z)

entities: walking, handsomeness, bachelorhood, and the like. The proper nouns **John**, **Bill**, **Paris**, **Fido**, and **Mary** can just as well be replaced by variables such as **x**, **y**, and **z**, as shown in the middle column in Table 2–1. From there it is a short step to denote what is predicated as logicians might, as *propositional functions*, which are shown in the right-hand column in Table 2–1.

Propositions

Propositional functions have an important notational advantage. When **x is handsome** is written as **Handsome(x)**, it is clear that being handsome is a function with one argument, **x**. For those familiar with algebra, **Handsome(x)** is analogous to **f(x)**, which is also a function with one argument. Imagine, for example, that $f(x) = x^2 + 4$. Given any value of **x**, say **6**, one can uniquely determine the value of **f(x)**, here **40**. As for **Handsome(x)**, given any value of **x**, say **John**, one can uniquely determine the value of **Handsome(x)**—it is either true or false. Of the six propositional functions in Table 2–1, **Walk(x)**, **Handsome(x)**, and **Bachelor(x)** are all one-place functions; **Hit(x,y)** and **In(x,y)** are both two-place functions; and **Give(x,y,z)** is a three-place function. In English some functions are expressed as verbs, namely **Walk(x)**, **Hit(x,y)**, and **Give(x,y,z)**; some as adjectives, **Handsome(x)**; some as prepositions, **In(x,y)**; and some as nouns, **Bachelor(x)**.

Once the arguments of a propositional function have been filled in, the result is a proposition. **Walk(John)**, for example, is a proposition that specifies all the information, except tense, that goes into the sentence **John walks**. Propositions are very different from sentences. Whereas the sentence **John walks** is something one can pronounce, the proposition **Walk(John)** is not. **Walk(John)** represents the meaning of **John walks** and nothing more. To put it another way, whereas there is temporal significance in the fact that **John** comes first and **walks** second in the sentence **John walks**, there is no temporal significance to the order of **Walk** and **John** in the proposition **Walk(John)**. The order of the arguments in **Give(John, Fido, Mary)** specifies only how they function in the action of giving. The first argument, **John**, is the agent; the second, **Fido**, is the object;

and the third, **Mary**, is the indirect object. In spoken sentences they may even occur in the reverse temporal order, as in **Mary was given Fido by John**. Although it will sometimes be easier to speak loosely of the "proposition" **John walks** without using the more cumbersome notation **Walk(John)**, propositions should not be endowed with temporal properties.

Constructing Interpretations

In the construction process, listeners must take a linear string of words and from it construct a hierarchical arrangement of propositions. They would be helped tremendously in building the propositions if they could work out the surface structure of each sentence first. This will be demonstrated for **The old man lit his awful cigar**.

With the new notation, the propositions for this sentence are the following:

3. $\text{Known}(E_{57})$ $\text{Known}(E_8)$
      $\text{Man}(E_{57})$ $\text{Cigar}(E_8)$
      $\text{Old}(E_{57})$ $\text{Awful}(E_8)$
                                                  $\text{Belong}(E_8, E_{57})$

                        $\text{Light}(E_{57}, E_8)$

In these propositions, the symbols E_{57} and E_8 stand for two specific entities—hence the E's—that listeners have to keep track of; the arbitrary choice of **57** and **8** emphasizes that these numbers have no meaning in themselves. What this list shows is that E_{57} is an entity that is known to the listeners, is a man, and is old, and E_8 is an entity that is known, is a cigar, is awful, and belongs to E_{57}. $\text{Light}(E_{57}, E_8)$ specifies that E_{57}, so characterized, lit E_8, so characterized.

Constituents

The surface structure of a sentence, on the other hand, divides up into phrases and subphrases called *constituents*. They are implicit in the function and order of the words. The breakdown of 1 into constituents looks something like this:

4.

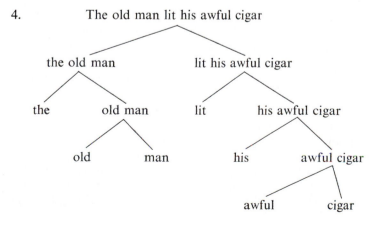

The whole sentence divides into two *immediate constituents*, **the old man** and **lit his awful cigar**; these in turn each divide into two immediate constituents; and so on. At the bottom are the ultimate constituents **the, old, man, lit, his, awful,** and **cigar**.

As a rough guide, a constituent is a group of words that can be replaced by a single word without a change in function and without doing violence to the rest of the sentence. The replacement need not have the same meaning. **The old man** is a constituent because it can be replaced by **Amos, George,** or **he** without altering the structure of the rest of the sentence. Similarly, **old man** is replaceable by **oldster, lit his awful cigar** by **smoked, his awful cigar** by **it,** and **awful cigar** by **stogie**. On the other hand, **the old** is not a constituent since it is not replaceable by a word with the same function. **Man lit, lit his awful, old man lit his,** and other groups of words are not constituents for the same reason. In a more exact definition of constituent, the criterion of replaceability must be used along with other criteria, such as the ability of a group of words to move as a unit. In particular, these other criteria are needed to classify **the old man** as a noun phrase, **old man** as a modified noun, **lit his awful cigar** as a verb phrase, and so on.

Constructing Underlying Propositions

What is remarkable about this analysis is that most underlying propositions can be constructed from single constituents. Ignoring the ultimate constituents—the single words—there are the following rough correspondences:

Constituent	Underlying propositions
old man	$Man(E_{57})$, $Old(E_{57})$
the old man	$Known(E_{57})$
awful cigar	$Cigar(E_8)$, $Awful(E_8)$
his awful cigar	$Known(E_8)$, $Belong(E_8, X)$
the old man lit his awful cigar	$Light(E_{57}, E_8)$

Because **old man** is a constituent, there must be an entity E_{57} that is both a man and old. It is a man that is old, not a cigar or something else. With **the old man**, this old man, E_{57}, must be known to the listeners. Similarly, from **awful cigar** alone, there must be some entity, E_8, that is both a cigar and awful. **His awful cigar** adds two more propositions, but the second, **Belong(E_8, X)** has an argument that cannot be filled from the constituent alone. In fact, **his** could refer, not to the old man, but to someone not even mentioned. With the complete sentence, one can add the proposition **Light(E_{57}, E_8)**. The first argument must be E_{57}, the old man, and the second E_8, the awful cigar.

So constituents are potentially very useful. Once listeners have identified a constituent, they can decide on its underlying propositions with little or no reference to the rest of the sentence. In 1, once they have taken in **the old man**, they can build three of the eight propositional functions—**Man(x), Old(x),** and

Known(x)—and "bind" them to the same entity E_{57}. It would be surprising if listeners didn't do this. Indeed, we normally have the intuition that we understand a sentence as we hear it—that we understand **the old man** before we come to **lit his awful cigar**. The hypothesis, then, is obvious. As listeners go along, they parse a sentence into its constituents and for each one build up the appropriate propositions.

If listeners are to have enough time to build propositions from each constituent, however, they must retain in memory its phonological representation —its verbatim content. Constituents larger than single words are generally complete at the ends of noun phrases, clauses, and sentences. So once listeners have built the underlying propositions of a constituent after these points, they could safely purge their memory of its verbatim content. No longer useful, that content will probably only interfere with the next batch of words put into memory. It is a reasonable hypothesis, then, that listeners' verbatim memory for a constituent should fade rapidly after it has been processed.

Preliminary Outline

These preliminary remarks suggest that listeners construct the underlying representation for a sentence in roughly four steps:

(1) They take in the raw speech and retain a phonological representation of it in "working memory."

(2) They immediately attempt to organize the phonological representation into constituents, identifying their content and function.

(3) As they identify each constituent, they use it to construct underlying propositions, building continually onto a hierarchical representation of propositions.

(4) Once they have identified the propositions for a constituent, they retain them in working memory and at some point purge memory of the phonological representation. In doing this, they forget the exact wording and retain the meaning.

These four steps are probably not applied one after the other but are all in action at the same time. Listeners may well identify constituents (Step 2) while taking in new speech (Step 1), identify propositions (Step 3) while organizing constituents (Step 2), and purge memory (Step 4) simultaneously with many other activities.

Although preliminary, this outline will help make sense of facts that have been discovered about the role of surface structure in comprehension. The first task ahead is to examine the evidence for this outline, correcting and refining it where possible. The next task is to look at specific theories meant to describe how listeners build underlying representations from surface constituents. The final task is to see how listeners resolve the ambiguities that appear in almost every sentence.

SURFACE CONSTITUENTS

In the four steps of the construction process, constituents play a central role. But is there any evidence for this assumption? Studies from various viewpoints suggest that listeners (a) feel constituents to be conceptually unified wholes, (b) use them in the organization of speech, (c) store them in working memory as units, and (d) purge them from memory when a sentence has ended.

The Conceptual Unity of Constituents

Constituents have a clear conceptual reality. The definition alone attests to this. For a group of words to be replaceable by a single word with an equivalent function, it must have a conceptual coherence, for it has a single unified function. Consider **The likable general collapsed**. By definition, **the likable** is not a constituent: it has no unified function and would not be *judged* as particularly unified. Yet **likable general** is a constituent—it is replaceable, for example, by **officer**—and seems to possess a conceptual unity. Even if there were no other evidence, then, the very definition of constituent establishes its holistic nature.

Both Levelt (1970a, b; 1974) and E. Martin (1970), however, went beyond this and asked people to give judgments of constituent structure. They then compared their subjective constituents with linguistically defined constituents. Experimentally, the problem was how to get people to reveal their intuitions about constituents. Levelt presented people with sentences such as **The boy has lost a dollar** followed by a triad of words from the sentence thus:

a   boy

has

People were to judge which two words of this triad were most closely connected in the given sentence (say, **boy** and **has**) and which two were least closely connected (say, **boy** and **a**). Levelt then applied a so-called hierarchical clustering technique (S. Johnson, 1967) to a collection of such judgments and identified the constituents implicit in them. For his part, Martin asked people "to arrange the words of each sentence into natural groups." A person might, for example, arrange the above sentence into three groups: **the boy**, **has lost**, and **a dollar**. Following the same hierarchical clustering procedure, Martin was able to derive the constituents implicit in these subjective arrangements.

The subjective constituents generally coincided with the "objective," or linguistically defined constituents. For Levelt's sentence **The boy has lost a dollar**, for example, both the objective and subjective constituents were as follows:

((The boy)((has lost)(a dollar)))

In this notation, each constituent larger than a single word is enclosed in a pair of parentheses. So **has lost** is one constituent, **a dollar** another, **has lost a dollar** a third, and so on. The subjective and objective structures coincide completely, as they do in the following sentence tested by Martin:

((Children (who (attend regularly)))((appreciate lessons) greatly))

Although the agreement was not always this good, the discrepancies there were probably arose from difficulties inherent in the technique itself (Levelt, 1974). In any event, people clearly appreciate the conceptual unity of constituents.

Constituents as Aids in Perception

Listeners, it is argued, may immediately try to isolate the constituents in the speech they hear. They should be greatly aided, then, if the speech is already broken down into constituents. To pick an obvious device, pauses between each major constituent should help considerably. Indeed, language has the convention that if speakers want to pause for thought or take a breath, they are *supposed* to do it between, not within, constituents. Speakers who are not fluent, however, do not follow this dictum. They often hesitate in the middle of a constituent to find a word or change their phrasing (see Chapter 7). These mid-constituent hesitations almost certainly make the listener's job harder. It is significant that the constituent is the natural unit of perfectly fluent or "ideal" speech.

Few psychologists have studied whether isolating constituents by pauses helps listeners or not. Graf and Torrey (1966), however, isolated constituents for readers and found that it helped. They presented people with a prose passage in a machine that exposed the print line by line, with each line visible for only a fixed period of time. Immediately afterwards, these people were given a short multiple-choice test to see how well they had understood the passage. Some were shown the passage divided in one way, and some in another. Form A of the passage had been segmented so that the end of each line coincided with a major constituent boundary. Form B had been segmented so that the end of each line coincided with the middle of a major constituent. In all other respects, Forms A and B were alike. The first sentence of Forms A and B looked like this:

Form A	*Form B*
During World War II, even fantastic schemes received consideration if they gave promise of shortening the conflict.	During World War II, even fantastic schemes received consideration if they gave promise of shortening the conflict.

If isolating constituents helps the reader, Form A should be easier to read and understand than Form B. This is just what Graf and Torrey found. The comprehension test yielded better scores for Form A than for Form B (see also Wood, 1974).

Constituents in Working Memory

Once listeners have isolated constituents, they should hold them verbatim as constituents in working memory until they have no more need for them—until they have used them to construct the underlying propositions. There is relatively good evidence that a sentence is divided into constituents in working memory (but see Kempen, 1976). Ammon (1968) used a "probe-latency technique" to show this. People would listen to a tape-recording of a sentence such as 5:

> 5.   The *polite actor* thanked the *old woman who* carried the black umbrella.
>   1   2   3   4   5

Immediately after, they would hear a "probe word," e.g., **polite**, and be asked to give the next word in the sentence (here, **actor**) as quickly as they could. Ammon looked at five different probes, the italicized words labeled 1 through 5. If the sentence is divided into constituents in working memory, people should be quick in giving the next word if the probe and its response are from the same constituent.

Ammon confirmed this prediction on several types of sentences. Sentence 5 divides into constituents this way:

> 5′. ((The (polite actor))(thanked ((the(old woman))(who(carried(the (black umbrella)))))))

Ammon found that the fastest probe-response pairs were **polite-actor** and **old-woman**. In each pair, the response belongs to the same constituent as its probe: there is no major constituent boundary between the probe and its response. The slowest probe-response pairs were **actor-thanked** and **woman-who**. Both have three major constituent boundaries between the probe and its response. The probe-response pair **who-carried** was intermediate. It has only one major constituent boundary between the probe and response. Other types of sentences showed much the same pattern (see also Suci, Ammon, and Gamlin, 1967).

Listeners must eventually purge their working memory of the verbatim contents of constituents. Several experiments by Jarvella (1970, 1971) suggest that listeners typically begin purging memory only *after* a sentence boundary has passed. In Jarvella's study, people listened to a long prose passage that was interrupted every so often for them to "write down as much of the end of the passage just immediately preceding the interruption" as they could remember word for word. The passages were designed so that the two sentences just preceding each interruption were of one of two types:

6. The tone of the document was threatening. *Having failed to disprove the charges*, Taylor was later fired by the President.

7. The document had also blamed him for *having failed to disprove the charges*. Taylor was later fired by the President.

The three major clauses in 6 and 7 can be called A, B, and C: A is the first clause; B is the clause in italics; and C is the final clause. In Sequence 6, the clauses are grouped as constituents A(BC), whereas in Sequence 7, they are grouped (AB)C. Yet the wording of Clauses B and C is identical in the two sequences. If people purge memory once they are through with a sentence, they should have purged Clause B by the time they were interrupted in Sequence 7, but not by the time they were interrupted in Sequence 6. Thus they should recall Clause B well in Sequence 6, but poorly in Sequence 7, even though it is the identical clause in the same position.

These predictions were borne out remarkably well. For Sequence 6, people recalled complete clauses 12 percent, 54 percent, and 86 percent of the time for Clauses A, B, and C. For Sequence 7, they did so 20 percent, 21 percent, and 84 percent of the time. So people always did well on Clause C and poorly on Clause A. This was hardly surprising. But on the critical Clause B, they did much better when it belonged to the same sentence as C than when it did not, 54 percent to 21 percent. Verbatim memory, therefore, fades very quickly once a sentence has been processed completely (see also Chapter 4).

Constituents in the Construction of Propositions

When sentences are divided into constituents by pauses or printed lines, listeners appear to understand more easily because these breaks help them do what they eventually do anyway: isolate and identify each constituent. How early in the listening process, however, do constituents normally become relevant? Fodor, Bever, and Garrett have argued in an extensive series of studies that constituents play a role in the "perception" of speech. Their hypothesis was simply this: "The unit of speech perception corresponds to the constituent [Fodor and Bever, 1965, p. 415]."

Fodor and Bever (1965) were the first to test this hypothesis. They argued that in perception genuine units tend to preserve their integrity by resisting interruption from other sources. So if the constituent is a basic unit in speech perception, it should resist interruption by a click from an extraneous auditory source. Imagine that a listener, while attending to speech in one ear, incidentally hears a click in the other. If the click falls at a constituent boundary, it doesn't interrupt the constituent either before or after it and should be heard as occurring at that boundary. But if it comes in the middle of a constituent, it should be perceived as falling nearer one of the constituent boundaries than it actually does, since the constituent tends to resist interruption.

In Fodor and Bever's experiment, people listened to a tape-recorded sentence in one ear, heard a click in the other, and afterwards wrote down the sentence and marked the location of the click with a slash. The type of sentence they used is illustrated here (with its constituents enclosed in parentheses):

((That (he (was happy)))(was (evident (from ((the way) (he smiled))))))
   1 2 3   4 5   6 7 8 9

The extraneous click was placed at one of the nine positions indicated with numbers. A click placed at position 5 does not interrupt a constituent—it falls at a boundary with four parentheses—so it should be perceived as occurring where it objectively occurred. A click in the last syllable of **happy**, however, does interrupt a constituent and should be perceived as occurring at or nearer the closest main constituent boundary, namely 5. The same goes for a click in **was**. In general, clicks at all nine positions should "migrate" toward 5, and this is just what Fodor and Bever found. Clicks at 5 were "misheard" less often than clicks at other positions, while the other clicks were misheard as having occurred closer to 5. These findings appear to support the hypothesis that the constituent is the unit of speech perception.

In other experiments, Garrett, Bever, and Fodor tried to rule out alternative explanations for the click displacements. In one study (1966), for example, they compared pairs of sentences like 8 and 9 (in which only the two immediate constituents of the full sentence are enclosed by parentheses):

8. (As a result of their invention's *influence*) (*the* ∗ *company was given an award*).

9. (The chairman whose methods still *influence the* ∗ *company*) (*was given an award*).

The italicized parts of 8 and 9 were made identical acoustically by splicing the same tape recording onto the end of two different sentence beginnings. Yet because of the sentence beginnings, the italicized portions differed in their constituent structure. As predicted, a click centered on **the company** (shown by the asterisk ∗) tended to be displaced left toward the major constituent boundary in 8, but right toward the major constituent boundary in 9. So acoustic differences are not needed for clicks to be displaced.

Alternative Explanations of Click Displacements

Yet how do constituents influence click displacements? Fodor and Bever's hypothesis that the perception of constituents resists interruption has come under heavy fire. In their experimental procedure, a person: (1) listens to the speech with the superimposed click, by hypothesis isolating and identifying the constituents in working memory; (2) encodes the click's position with respect to these units; and (3) recalls the sentence, writes it down, and marks where the click occurred. The critics have noted that click displacements could have occurred during any one of these three stages, the perceptual stage (1)—as Fodor and Bever proposed—the encoding stage (2), or the response stage (3).

One set of critics (Ladefoged, 1967; Reber, 1973; Reber and Anderson, 1970) have argued that click displacements arise during the response stage. In Fodor and Bever's procedure, much time elapses between hearing the sentence and click and marking the click in the written sentence. During this time, people may forget exactly where the click occurred and be forced to guess a little. Intuitively aware of constituents, they are biased to put clicks they are not sure about at or near constituent boundaries. To show this, Ladefoged (1967) and Reber and Anderson (1970) had people listen for clicks in sentences that sometimes had no objective clicks at all. People were told that the experiment was on subliminal perception, so the clicks would not always be audible. The nonexistent clicks tended to be placed at or near major constituent boundaries, just as genuine clicks were. Also, Green (1973) compared people who marked the click's position immediately after hearing a sentence with people who marked it only after recalling the sentence. Immediate marking led to many fewer misplacements than delayed marking, although both led to misplacements toward constituent boundaries. Thus, although response bias may not account for all click displacements (see Bever, 1973; Fodor, Bever, and Garrett, 1974), it probably accounts for many. This weakens the evidence for the original hypothesis.

Click displacements could also plausibly occur during the encoding stage. To "locate" a click, listeners have to become conscious of other units with respect to which they can locate the click—units like phonetic segments, syllables, words, phrases, and clauses. But as McNeill and Lindig (1973) have shown, if people listen for the whole sentence, as they must in order to recall it, they will find it easier to become conscious of constituents the larger they are. If so, they will find it easier to locate clicks around large constituents than around small units like phonetic segments and syllables, and they will more likely locate clicks nearer the boundaries of large constituents.

The literature on click displacements, in brief, fits what was concluded earlier. Listeners try to isolate and identify constituents in working memory, for they are useful in building propositions. But whether or not click displacements occur at the initial perceptual stage is still an open question.

Real-Time Processing

Listeners have a limited capacity for processing what they hear in the time available. Their ability to deal with speech breaks down if it is too fast, in a language they know imperfectly, or in competition with another conversation. Their limited capacity shows up even in normal speech, for sentences are quite uneven in the demands they make. Imagine how listeners build up a semantic representation for **The old man lit his awful cigar**. They take in and isolate the first constituent, **the old man**, but while trying to construct propositions from it, they have to take in the remainder, **lit his awful cigar**. If for some reason they find it difficult to construct propositions from **the old man**, their ability to take in **lit his awful cigar** will suffer. They may delay isolating the constituents from **lit his awful cigar** until they are finished with **the old man**.

There is ample evidence that a difficulty in processing at one point in a sentence slows down processing immediately after that point. Foss and his associates have demonstrated this with a simple technique. People were asked to listen to a sentence, knowing they would be responsible for what it meant afterwards, and simultaneously listen for the sound **b** in one of the words. They were to press a button as quickly as possible when they heard the **b**. If processing was difficult immediately before the **b**, they should have taken longer to detect the **b** than otherwise.

In one study, Foss and Lynch (1969) compared sentences with "right-branching" relative clauses as in 10 to sentences with "self-embedded" relative clauses as in 11:

10. The store sold the whisky that intoxicated the rioter that broke the window.

11. The rioter that the whisky that the store sold intoxicated broke the window.

In both sentences people pressed the button on hearing **broke**, since it was the first word to contain a **b**. But they took 0.2 seconds longer on the average for 11 than for 10. As Foss and Lynch argued, self-embedded sentences place much greater demands on listeners' processing capacity than right-branching sentences, and that slows up the extraneous task of monitoring for a **b**. In another study, Foss (1969) compared sentences such as 12 and 13:

12. The *traveling* bassoon player found himself without funds in a strange town.

13. The *itinerant* bassoon player found himself without funds in a strange town.

Since **itinerant** is a rarer word than **traveling**, it should be more difficult to process, delaying the detection of the **b** in **bassoon** in Sentence 13. This is exactly what happened.

The delay in detecting a **b** or any other extraneous signal should increase with the amount of processing the sentence requires. Using a technique like Foss's, Green (1977) had people listen to sentences and simultaneously listen for an extraneous click, pressing a button when they heard it. Some people (the "memorizers") had merely to recall the sentence afterwards; others (the "comprehenders") had to compose a continuation for it, a task that presumably required much deeper comprehension. The clicks were responded to much faster by the memorizers than by the comprehenders. And whereas the memorizers heard clicks as quickly in the middle as at the end of the sentence, the comprehenders were slower to spot clicks at the end, where comprehension is presumably most taxing. Thus, the listener's limited capacity for processing speech is real enough (see also Aaronson, 1974a, b). Not only is this capacity taxed more in some parts of a sentence than others, but it is also more taxed the more "deeply" the listener tries to comprehend the sentence (see Chapter 4).

So far, then, there is good evidence for the preliminary four-step outline of the construction process. The main idea is that listeners try to isolate and identify surface constituents and build propositions for each. According to the evidence, listeners think of constituents as conceptually coherent units. They isolate them soon after taking in speech and hold them in working memory as units. They eliminate them from memory soon after they have passed a sentence boundary. All of these processes take time and may interfere with other mental activity. It is clear that constituents play a major role in the comprehension of sentences. But from the evidence so far it is not clear that the four steps always occur in that order—that listeners always begin with sounds, isolate constituents, and *then* build propositions for them. Actually, there is evidence to the contrary. But to examine this evidence it is necessary to take up more specific proposals about the nature of the construction process.

SYNTACTIC APPROACHES TO THE CONSTRUCTION PROCESS

If listeners isolate and identify constituents, how do they do it? Nothing in the speech sounds themselves unambiguously marks where one constituent ends and another begins. And nothing there labels a constituent, even once isolated, as a noun phrase, prepositional phrase, auxiliary verb, or something else. The constituents and their implicit classifications are something listeners *infer* about the speech they hear. Given **The old man lit his awful cigar**, they infer that **the old man** is a constituent, is a noun phrase, and refers to an entity they are expected to know. On what basis do they draw these inferences? There have been two broad approaches to this question: the syntactic and the semantic.

In the syntactic approach, listeners are assumed to use the surface features of a sentence in coming to its interpretation. They identify sounds, words, and larger constituents and from them build and connect propositions in an interpretation for the whole sentence. In the semantic approach, on the other hand, listeners are assumed to work from the interpretation a sentence must be conveying. They work on the assumption that the sentence refers to entities, events, states, and facts; that it was meant to get them to do something; that its subject, predicate, given information, and new information are appropriate to context; and so on. They then actively search for sounds, words, and constituents that satisfy these assumptions and expectations.

Listeners probably use some mixture of these two approaches. So the question is not just how they use syntactic and semantic information, but also how much they use of each. The older and more thoroughly investigated of these two approaches is the syntactic, so it will be taken up first. Yet in recent years the semantic approach has gained considerable favor, even though its details have not yet been worked out as fully. One reason for its appeal is its emphasis on the goal-directed nature of comprehension—listeners comprehend in order to discover how they are meant to use a sentence.

Building Up Constituents

The major proposal in the syntactic approach, as developed by Bever (1970), Fodor and Garrett (1967), Kimball (1973), Watt (1970b) and others, is this. Listeners have at their command a battery of mental strategies by which they segment sentences into constituents, classify the constituents, and construct semantic representations from them. These strategies rely on the fact that sentences contain elements listeners can use as clues to proper segmentation. Whenever they hear **the**, for example, they know they have the first word in a constituent, specifically a noun phrase, and they can expect to find a noun soon after, as in **the old man**. These strategies seek out the best clues and try the most likely segmentations first. So if the first strategy applied does not work, another is tried, and so on. When strategies become inapplicable because the surface clues they rely on are absent, listeners must try other strategies, and this may make comprehension more difficult.

As listeners identify constituents, they must not only locate them, but also implicitly classify them—as noun phrases, verb phrases, determiners, and the like. They must do this before they can build underlying propositions. Imagine the process listeners might implicitly go through on taking in the first word of **The man left**. They identify the word as **the**, classify it as a determiner (Det), and note that it is the first word in a noun phrase (NP). They further note that this NP must be the first constituent of a clause or sentence (to be labeled S). They can therefore set up three labeled constituents, each one inside the next, like this:

$$[[[the]_{Det} \cdots]_{NP} \cdots]_S$$

Here each constituent is enclosed in "labeled brackets" instead of the simple unlabeled parentheses used so far. The right-hand bracket around a constituent has a subscript that labels the constituent. So $[\ldots]_{Det}$ is a determiner, $[\ldots]_{NP}$ is a noun phrase, and $[\ldots]_S$ is a sentence or clause. When listeners encounter the next word **man**, they identify it as a noun, note it will complete the noun phrase, and leave the structure like this:

$$[[[the]_{Det}[man]_N]_{NP} \cdots]_S$$

The next word is **left**, which they identify as a verb, and they find nothing more. So they finish out the structure this way:

$$[[[the]_{Det}[man]_N]_{NP}[[left]_V]_{VP}]_S$$

By this point, listeners have isolated and labeled each constituent according to its function—determiner, noun, verb, noun phrase, verb phrase, and sentence. They then use this labeled bracketing for constructing the underlying representation.

TABLE 2–2
VARIETIES OF STRATEGY 1

Strategy 1a: Determiners and quantifiers
Whenever you find a determiner (**a, an, the**) or quantifier (**some, all, many, two, six,** etc.), begin a new noun phrase (NP).

Strategy 1b: Prepositions
Whenever you find a preposition (**to, at, in,** etc.), begin a new prepositional phrase (PP).

Strategy 1c: Pronouns
Whenever you find a definite pronoun (**I, you, he, she, it, we, they**), begin a new noun phrase (NP).

Strategy 1d: Auxiliaries
Whenever you find an auxiliary verb with tense (**is, are, was, were, have, can, could,** etc.), begin a new verb phrase (VP).

Strategy 1e: Relative pronouns
Whenever you find a relative pronoun (**that, which, who, whom**), begin a new clause (S).

Strategy 1f: Complements
Whenever you find a complementizer (**for–to, that,** etc.), begin a new clause (S).

Strategy 1g: Subordinating conjunctions
Whenever you find a subordinating conjunction (**because, when, since, if,** etc.), begin a new clause (S).

Strategy 1h: Coordinating conjunctions
Whenever you find a coordinating conjunction (**and, or, but, nor**), begin a new constituent similar to the one you just completed.

Use of Function Words

Function words—determiners, prepositions, conjunctions, pronouns, quantifiers, and the like—may play a crucial role in the strategies for segmenting speech into constituents. Kimball (1973) has proposed the following strategy:

> *Strategy 1:* Whenever you find a function word, begin a new constituent larger than one word.

This strategy reflects the observation that function words are very reliable clues to constituent structure because in English each one signals the beginning of a major constituent. Most function words also signal the type of constituent they are part of. **A, an,** and **the** begin noun phrases, not prepositional phrases, verb phrases, or necessarily sentences. The prepositions **to, at, in, on,** etc., mark the beginning of prepositional phrases, not noun phrases, verb phrases, or necessarily sentences. Viewed this way, Strategy 1 is a collection of specialized strategies for identifying and labeling constituents. These specialized strategies are listed in Table 2–2. Each indicates how a different type of function word signals an appropriate constituent.

These strategies, however, cannot always be applied unequivocally, for some words belong to more than one class of function words. **That**, for example, may be a determiner (**that boy**), a definite pronoun (**that is the one**), a relative pronoun (**the man that she loves**), or a complementizer (**I know that she left**). Listeners encountering **that** cannot know which. So Kimball proposed that listeners can look ahead one word—that is, wait for the next word—before deciding on the class a function word belongs to. The word after **that**, along with the preceding context, is often enough to fix it as a determiner, pronoun, relative pronoun, or complementizer.

Function words usually signal not only the beginning of a new constituent, but also the end of the previous one. In **The man was leaving**, **was** signals the beginning of a verb phrase and the end of the earlier noun phrase thus:

$$[[[\text{the}]_{\text{Det}}[\text{man}]_\text{N}]_{\text{NP}}[[\text{was}]_{\text{Aux}}\cdots]_{\text{VP}}]_\text{S}$$

Sometimes function words signal the presence of other larger constituents as well. In **the man in the parlor**, the preposition **in** tells the listener to close off **the man** as a noun phrase and begin a prepositional phrase, like this:

$$[\text{the man}]_{\text{NP}}[[\text{in}]_{\text{Prep}}\cdots]_{\text{PP}}$$

But it also signals the formation of a larger noun phrase encompassing both major constituents formed so far, like this:

$$[[\text{the man}]_{\text{NP}}[[\text{in}]_{\text{Prep}}\cdots]_{\text{PP}}]_{\text{NP}}$$

In rare cases, a function word does not mark the end of the previous constituent. The verb phrase **is leaving** in the sentence **Is he leaving?**, for example, has just this problem, since **is leaving** is a so-called *discontinuous constituent*. According to Strategy 1d, **is** marks the beginning of a verb phrase. But **he** should not lead listeners to close off the verb phrase, in this instance because **is** comes at the beginning of a sentence. Listeners must wait until after the interrupting noun phrase is completed and check the next word.

Evidence for Strategy 1

What evidence is there for Strategy 1? In an early study, Fodor and Garrett (1967) noted that some function words in English are optional. Compare 14 and 15:

14. The pen which the author used was new.

15. The pen the author used was new.

These two sentences have roughly the same meaning; it is just that the relative pronoun **which** has been deleted in 15. Fodor and Garrett argued that this deletion should impair comprehension. When listeners come to **which** in Sentence

14, they know by Strategy 1e that they are beginning a clause. Yet when they get to the second **the** in Sentence 15, they know that they are beginning a new noun phrase, but not that they are beginning a new clause. They learn about the clause in 15 only later, and this should delay its identification and the construction of its interpretation. The prediction is clear. Sentence 15 should be more difficult to take in than Sentence 14.

To test this prediction, Fodor and Garrett (1967) read people more complicated "self-embedded" sentences, like those in 16 and 17, and required them to paraphrase the sentences in their own words immediately afterwards:

16. The pen which the author whom the editor liked used was new.

17. The pen the author the editor liked used was new.

Sentences with the relative pronoun, like 16, were paraphrased more quickly and accurately than those without, like 17.

Following up Fodor and Garrett, Hakes and Foss (1970; Hakes, 1972) noted that listeners should have the most difficulty comprehending a sentence right after the point at which the relative pronouns were deleted. To demonstrate this momentary difficulty, Hakes and Foss used the monitoring task, described earlier, in which people listen to a sentence for meaning while simultaneously monitoring for a specific sound. They might, for example, have to listen for a **g** in the following two sentences:

18. The zebra which the lion that the gorilla chased killed was running.

19. The zebra the lion the gorilla chased killed was running.

The **g** in **gorilla** should be detected faster in 18 than in 19, since 18 provides the helpful surface clues just before, and 19 does not. Hakes and Foss confirmed this prediction. But they did not always find more accurate paraphrases to 18 than to 19, as Fodor and Garrett had. Perhaps, they suggested, the lack of a relative pronoun impairs comprehension only temporarily. If the sentence is not too complex, listeners eventually compute the right interpretation whether the relative pronoun is there or not.

Anticipating Content Words

Function words should also help listeners classify neighboring content words. On encountering a content word—according to the syntactic approach—listeners must identify its function and place it within the appropriate constituents. Yet most content words cannot be identified unambiguously. **Man**, for example, can be either a noun (**the man**) or a verb (**to man a ship**), and to decide which, listeners must rely on other information. One possible strategy, the complement of Strategy 1, goes as follows:

Strategy 2: After identifying the beginning of a constituent, look for content words appropriate to that type of constituent.

TABLE 2–3
VARIETIES OF STRATEGY 2

Strategy 2a: Noun phrases
After identifying a determiner or quantifier, look for a noun, which closes out the noun phrase (as in **the dirty old man**).

Strategy 2b: Prepositional phrases
After identifying a preposition, look for a noun phrase, which closes out the prepositional phrase (as in **through the broken window**).

Strategy 2c: Pronouns
After identifying a definite pronoun, close out the noun phrase (as in **he**).

Strategy 2d: Auxiliaries
After identifying a tensed auxiliary verb, look for a main verb, which closes out the verb (as in **would have been going**).

Strategy 2e: Relative pronouns
After identifying a relative pronoun, look for a sentence with one noun phrase missing (as in **the man that I saw**).

Strategy 2f: Complements
After identifying a complementizer, look for a sentence (as in **Mary knew that I left**).

Strategy 2g: Subordinate conjunctions
After identifying a subordinate conjunction, look for a sentence (as in **although he was drunk**).

Strategy 2h: Coordinate conjunctions
After identifying a coordinate conjunction, look for content words of the same kind identified in the previous constituent (as in **Mary and Bill**).

For example, since **the** marks the beginning of a noun phrase, it should lead listeners to expect a noun that "heads" the noun phrase, e.g., **man** in **the old man**. Like Strategy 1, Strategy 2 consists of a series of specialized strategies, labeled 2a through 2h in Table 2–3.

Strategy 2 works together with Strategy 1. By Strategy 1a, for example, encountering a **the** leads listeners to begin a new noun phrase. By Strategy 2a, it also leads them to look for a noun to head that noun phrase. Together, Strategies 1a and 2a lead listeners to set up the structure:

$$[[\text{the}]_{\text{Det}} \ldots [\ldots]_{\text{N}}]_{\text{NP}}$$

Although the space between the determiner and anticipated noun need not be filled, the slot set up by $[\ldots]_{\text{N}}$ must be, except in rare cases. So when listeners encounter **the man**, they can tentatively assume **man** is a noun: there is a noun slot $[\ldots]_{\text{N}}$ after the word **the** that must be filled, and **man** fits. Similarly, by Strategy 2d listeners would identify **man** in **will man** to be a main verb, since the auxiliary verb **will** sets up the structure

$$[[\text{will}]_{\text{Aux}} \ldots [\ldots]_{\text{MV}}]_{\text{V}}$$

thereby forcing them to fill the main verb slot [...]$_{MV}$ before going on. Strategy 2 often even allows us to identify the function of nonsense words, as in Lewis Carroll's famous verse "Jabberwocky": **Twas brillig, and the slithy toves did gyre and gimble in the wabe; all mimsy were the borogoves, and the mome raths outgrabe.**

Use of Affixes

As these lines suggest, listeners may also be helped by suffixes and prefixes. Most such affixes can be added to only one or two kinds of content words, so they can be used to pick out what kind of content word a word is. For example, **-ing** and **-ed** mark a word as a verb; **-ly** usually marks a word as an adverb; and **-y**, **-ic**, **-al**, and **-ive** usually mark words as adjectives. Suffixes that mark concrete and abstract nouns include **-tion (description)**, **-ity (activity)**, **-ness (rudeness)**, and **-er (believer)**. The suffix **-s** marks nouns as plural (**the bears sleep**) and verbs as singular (**the bear sleeps**). Hence one might propose the following general strategy:

> *Strategy 3:* Use affixes to help decide whether a content word is a noun, verb, adjective, or adverb.

By Strategy 3 along with other information, one can be certain that Lewis Carroll's **slithy** and **mimsy** are adjectives; that **toves, borogoves**, and **raths** are nouns; and that **outgrabe** is a verb. More typically, listeners can use suffixes to rule out structural ambiguities. Compare:

20. Maggie knows the boys cook.

21. Maggie knows the boys cooked.

In the spoken version of 20, **cook** could be either a noun (**Maggie knows the boy's cook**) or a verb (**Maggie knows that the boys cook**). In 21, because of the suffix **-ed** on **cook**, there is only one possibility: **cook** must be a verb. These clues often make the difference between an ambiguous and an unambiguous parsing of a sentence.

Use of Verbs

Content words themselves limit what can occur around them. Among content words, verbs restrict their environments the most. Within simple sentences, for example, the verb often specifies whether there should be one, two, or three noun phrases with it, as in the following sentences:

22. The man slept.

23. The man hit the ball.

24. The man put the dog into the house.

Slept in 22 requires only one noun phrase—its subject—though it may have more. **Hit** in 23 requires at least a subject and an object, two noun phrases. **Put** in 24 requires a subject, an object, and a location, three noun phrases. When listeners encounter **put**, for example, they know they must find an object and location and will identify upcoming content words as an object and location. Listeners could use such information to good advantage with a strategy like this:

Strategy 4: After encountering a verb, look for the number and kind of arguments appropriate to that verb.

Fodor, Garrett, and Bever (1968) noted that verbs also limit the syntactic form of the objects, or complements, they can occur with. **Hit**, for example, requires a noun phrase that is *not* a complement:

25. John hit [the doctor]$_{NP}$

On the other hand, **believed** allows in addition several types of complements:

26. John believed [the doctor]$_{NP}$
27. John believed [that the doctor had left]$_S$
28. John believed [the doctor to have left]$_S$

On encountering **hit**, listeners can restrict their search to noun phrases that are not complements, but on encountering **believed**, they cannot. They should find sentences with **believe** more difficult to parse than those with **hit**. In an experiment requiring people to give paraphrases, Fodor and his associates found evidence that sentences like 26 were more difficult than ones like 25. In similar experiments, however, Hakes (1971) found little or no evidence for this difficulty. At present, the support for Strategy 4 is equivocal.

By the syntactic approach, Strategies 1 through 4 seem not only sensible, but even necessary if listeners are to make full use of syntactic information. Yet the direct evidence for their use is sparse. It consists, really, of one main finding. When optional relative pronouns (**who, which, that**) or complementizers (**that**) are deleted, comprehension is temporarily impaired. Yet informal examples like 29 and 30 bring even this finding into question:

29. The fellow who I told you that I managed to see yesterday said that he thought that he'd buy the car that he discovered that the dealer who I referred him to had just acquired.
30. The fellow I told you I managed to see yesterday said he thought he'd buy the car he discovered the dealer I referred him to had just acquired.

Of the two sentences, 30, the one with deletions, seems less ponderous and probably easier to understand than 29, the one without deletions. Writing experts like Flesch (1972) even advise authors to delete **who, which**, and **that** wherever possible to make prose easier to understand. Thus, although these optional words may be helpful if ambiguities arise, they may actually hinder comprehension otherwise. So far, the evidence for the syntactic approach is problematic.

Memory Capacity

Some sentences seem intrinsically difficult to understand:

31. I gave the dream I had cherished all my life about living in Ullapool during herring season up.

32. The squid the blowfish the shark ate ate tasted awful.

33. The man offered a hundred dollars for the bottle of 1962 vintage Mouton Rothschild is my uncle.

In 31, the discontinuous constituent **gave up** is interrupted by too much speech. In 32, there are too many confusing self-embedded relative clauses. And in 33, by the time the listener reaches **is** it is too difficult to infer that **who was** had been deleted from between **the man** and **offered.** What these three sentences have in common is that they tax the listener's memory. To account for this, Kimball (1973), following up suggestions by Bever (1970) and Watt (1970b), proposed that listeners are subject to special constraints on memory.

Listeners try to minimize memory load, according to Kimball, by relying on the following strategy:

Strategy 5: Try to attach each new word to the constituent that came just before.

When this strategy works, listeners are saved from searching memory any further back than the last constituent. Strategy 5, of course, affects only how listeners deal with discontinuous constituents: it makes the two halves of the constituent difficult to put together, especially when they are separated by too much speech (as in 31 above).

To see how Strategy 5 works, consider:

34. *The dog that was rabid* came from New York.

35. *The dog* came from New York *that was rabid.*

36. *The dog* bit the fox *that was rabid.*

Imagine that it is always the dog that was intended to be rabid. In 34, the relative clause **that was rabid** is directly preceded by **the dog**, so Strategy 5 immediately gives the intended interpretation. In 35, listeners first try to attach **that was rabid** to **New York**, reject that on semantic grounds, and then attach it to **the dog**. Even though they come to the right interpretation, it takes more tries, fitting our intuition that 35 is more awkward than 34. In 36, however, listeners try to put **that was rabid** with **the fox**, find it makes sense, and never arrive at the intended meaning with **that was rabid** attached to **the dog**. Strategy 5 correctly predicts that 36 will be misinterpreted to mean that it is the fox that was rabid. It also helps explain the wit in the following slogans urging people to read the classified ads of a London evening paper on their way home in the London underground trains:

Stunt man finds job sitting in front of underground train.

Zoo-keeper finds Jaguar queueing for underground ticket.

Young couple finds house at lost property office.

Two Principles of Memory Capacity

Kimball also proposed a "principle of fixed structure" and a "principle of two sentences." According to the first, once listeners have parsed speech into constituents one way, it is very costly in processing capacity to go back in memory and reparse the constituents another way. This principle explains why 37 and 38 are so hard:

37. The horse raced past the barn fell.

38. The dealer offered two dollars for the painting refused to sell.

In 37, listeners are led by Strategy 7 (to be discussed later) to identify **[The horse raced past the barn]$_S$** as a clause. But because **fell** is left over, they have to go back in memory and reparse the sentence as **[The horse [that was raced past the barn] fell]**. In 38, listeners get into the same trouble and have to reparse it as **[The dealer [who was offered two dollars for the painting] refused to sell]**. Revising speech into a new constituent structure takes considerable thought and effort, when it is possible at all.

According to Kimball's principle of two sentences, it is very costly in memory capacity to parse more than two constituents labeled S at a time. Compare:

39. John's departure bothered Mary.

40. That John departed bothered Mary.

41. That that John departed bothered Mary surprised Max.

Of these, 39 seems easy, 40 slightly difficult, and 41 very difficult. When the bracketings labeled with an S are put in. it is easy to see why:

39′. [John's departure bothered Mary]$_S$

40′. [[that John departed]$_S$ bothered Mary]$_S$

41′. [[that [that John departed]$_S$ bothered Mary]$_S$ surprised Max]$_S$

In 39′ there is no point at which listeners are keeping track of more than one constituent labeled S—of more than one clause. In 40′, they must keep track of two constituents labeled S from the very first word. In 41′, on reaching the second **that**, they must keep track of three such constituents. Kimball's principle predicts that 41 ought to be very difficult, and it is. It isn't that the content itself is so difficult, because 42, with only one S, seems much easier than 41:

42. [John's departing's bothering Mary surprised Max]$_S$

Yet 42 seems harder than 40, a judgment that does not follow neatly from the principle of two sentences. The issue, then, is more complex than this principle alone suggests.

Kimball used the principle of two sentences to explain why the notorious doubly self-embedded sentence is so difficult (see G. Miller and Isard, 1963; Blumenthal, 1966; Stolz, 1967; Schlesinger, 1968; Freedle and Craun, 1970). Consider 43 and its labeled bracketing in 43′:

43. The boy that the girl that the man saw met slept.

43′. [The boy [that the girl [that the man saw]$_S$ met]$_S$ slept]$_S$.

By the second **that**, listeners are keeping track of three constituents labeled S. Earlier, Bever (1970) had argued that sentences like 43 are hard because they contain constituents that serve two functions at once. In 43, **the girl** is both the subject of **met (the girl met the boy)** and the object of **saw (the man saw the girl)**. Yet for many instances of double function, comprehension is relatively simple. In **John's aunt's dog's tail is brown**, the dog is both the possessor of the tail and the object possessed by the aunt, but the sentence seems perfectly comprehensible, at least in comparison to 43. At present, Kimball's principle of two sentences appears to account for the difficulty of 43 better, for it accounts for other facts too.

Clauses

Although Strategy 1 can be used to isolate and classify a constituent as a clause, there are probably additional strategies for identifying just how that clause functions in the current sentence. Halliday (1970) has observed that in English we know fairly accurately what function a clause fulfills from its first constituent alone. The strategy corresponding to Halliday's observation might go like this:

> *Strategy 6:* Use the first word (or major constituent) of a clause to identify the function of that clause in the current sentence.

Strategy 6 breaks down into the specialized strategies listed in Table 2–4.

The strategies in Table 2–4 divide clauses first into main clauses and "non-main" clauses. Non-main clauses are easy to identify (by Strategies 6a through 6c) since they all begin with a function word specifically marking them as adverbial clauses (**because Mary met John**), relative clauses (**that Mary met**), or complements (**for Mary to meet John**). Main clauses, in effect, are what is left over. They begin not with function words specially designed to subordinate, relativize, or complementize, but with constituents that indirectly tell listeners what function the sentence conventionally serves as a speech act. An initial WH- word, for example, normally signals that the sentence functions as a WH-question. This fact is captured by Strategy 6d. Strategies 6e through 6h are similar. It is probably not accidental in English that if a sentence functions as something other than a question, statement, command, or exclamation, the performative clause that signals the intended speech act (**I** + performative verb + **you** + **that**) also comes first in the sentence, as in **I promise you I won't leave**, **I bet you George won't come**, and **I sentence you to six years in jail**. In brief, syntactically oriented listeners can find much valuable information about the function of clauses in their initial constituent, and they may well have use of something like Strategy 6.

Bever (1970) proposed a slightly different strategy to cover some of the same ground as Strategy 6:

> *Strategy 7:* Assume the first clause to be a main clause unless it is marked at or prior to the main verb as something other than a main clause.

TABLE 2–4
VARIETIES OF STRATEGY 6

Strategy 6a: Adverbial clauses
Whenever a clause begins with a subordinate conjunction (**because, if, before, since**, etc.), it is an adverbial clause subordinate to a main clause.

Strategy 6b: Relative clauses
Whenever a clause begins with a relative pronoun (**who, which, that**, etc.), it is a relative clause modifying a noun.

Strategy 6c: Complements
Whenever a clause begins with a complementizer (**for . . . to, that**), it is a complement, i.e., a sentence functioning as a noun phrase.

Strategy 6d: WH- questions
Whenever a clause begins with a WH- word (**why, who, what, how, where**, etc.), it is a WH- question.

Strategy 6e: Yes/No questions
Whenever a clause begins with an auxiliary verb with tense (**is, has, was, did, can, will**, etc.), it is a yes/no question.

Strategy 6f: Imperatives
Whenever a clause begins with a main verb in its infinitive form (**go, wash, leave, be**, etc.), it is an imperative.

Strategy 6g: Exclamations
Whenever a clause begins like a WH- question but does not have its subject and verb inverted, it is an exclamation.

Strategy 6h: Assertions
Whenever a clause is not classifiable by any of the above strategies, it is an assertion.

This strategy distinguishes main from non-main clauses by noting whether there is a special warning flag on a clause saying it is not a main clause. So Strategy 7 subsumes Strategies 6a, 6b, and 6c, which note when subordinate conjunctions, relative pronouns, and complementizers mark clauses as non-main clauses. But it also catches clauses marked as subordinate in the verb alone, as in the first clauses of 44 and 45:

44. The burglar *having* stolen everything, the family was destitute.

45. *Taking* a shower, Molly sang one bad piece after another.

In 44 and 45, the first clause has a " non-finite verb "—one not marked for present or past tense—and this marks the clauses as subordinate. So Strategy 7 adds one valuable new procedure for identifying subordinate clauses to the procedures contained in Strategy 6.

Historical Evidence

In arguing for Strategy 7, Bever and Langendoen (1971) appealed to the history of relative clauses in English. Consider:

46. The doctor talked to the woman (that) John had married.

47. The woman (that) John had married left the room.

48. The doctor talked to the woman (that) was John's wife.

49. The woman (that) was John's wife left the room.

In Modern English, **that** can be deleted from 46 and 47, but not from 48 or 49, where it is the subject of the relative clause. In earlier forms of English, the facts were different. For several centuries one could omit **that** in sentences equivalent to 48, producing **The doctor talked to the woman was John's wife**, but at no time in the history of English could one omit **that** in sentences equivalent to 49, producing **The woman was John's wife left the room**.

These facts make sense, according to Bever and Langendoen, only if English listeners always had Strategy 7. By this strategy, listeners assign the first verb with tense to the main clause unless they find contrary indications prior to the verb. So in 48, tenth-century listeners would classify **The doctor talked to the woman** as the main clause, and this is correct. But in 49, they would classify **The woman was John's wife** as the main clause too, and this is not correct. To avoid such confusing misparsings, English has never allowed **that** to be deleted when it was the subject of a relative clause preceding the verb of the main clause. With such sentences disallowed, listeners can always apply Strategy 7 and will never mistakenly interpret 48 to mean "The doctor that talked to the woman was John's wife." Even in Modern English, there are rare cases of **that**-deletion in sentences like 48 (as Kipling's **It was haste killed the yellow snake** or Wilde's **There are lots of vulgar people live in Grosvenor Square**), and because of Strategy 7 there is no confusion about their interpretation. In the spirit of Strategy 7, English speakers also generally prefer to use sentences with the main clause before the subordinate (as in 50) over those with the subordinate clause before the main clause (as in 51) (see H. Clark and E. Clark, 1968):

50. John talked to the doctor after he had his accident.

51. After he had his accident, John talked to the doctor.

Building Underlying Propositions

In the syntactic approach, once listeners have isolated and labeled constituents, they are still not through. They must use these labeled constituents to construct an interpretation for the sentence—a hierarchy of underlying propositions. Investigators stressing the syntactic approach have said little about how listeners might do this (though see Woods, 1970, 1973; R. Kaplan, 1972, 1973). Yet listeners would probably have specialized strategies for dealing with each type of constituent—noun phrases, verb phrases, clauses, and the like. By applying these strategies in the right order, they could build a hierarchy of underlying propositions appropriate to the sentence.

Noun phrases provide one example. Consider the constituent structure of **the old man**:

$$[[\text{the}]_{\text{Det}}[[\text{old}]_{\text{Adj}}[\text{man}]_{\text{Noun}}]_{\text{Modified-noun}}]_{\text{NP}}$$

From the ultimate constituents **old** and **man**, listeners can build **Old(x)** and **Man(x)**; from the more inclusive constituent **old man**, they can give them the same argument **Old(E_{39}) & Man(E_{39})**; and from the full constituent **the old man**, they can add **Known(E_{39})**. When the relative clause **who yelled** is added, the noun phrase looks like this:

$$[[\text{the old man}]_{NP}[[\text{who}]_{Pronoun}[\text{yelled}]_{Verb}]_S]_{NP}$$

From the constituent **who yelled** alone, listeners can build **Yell(x)**. To find a value for **x**, they have to consider the complete constituent **the old man who yelled**, inserting the argument E_{39} for **the old man** in place of **x**. The interpretation of the full noun phrase, then, contains these propositions: **Man(E_{39}) & Old(E_{39}) & Yell(E_{39}) & Known(E_{39})**.

Although not all noun phrases work like this, certain features are common to most. The head noun classifies the entity being referred to; associated adjectives and relative clauses characterize it further; and determiners and quantifiers (like **the, many, much, six**) specify such information as the knowability, number, and amount of the entity. Interpreting noun phrases is a complicated matter. The many strategies involved must work together in an intricate way (for two specific examples, see Winograd, 1972, 1973; Woods, 1970, 1973). Other constituents undoubtedly require even more complex collections of strategies.

Evaluation of the Syntactic Approach

The syntactic approach has its good and its bad points. Its strongest appeal is that it accounts for certain difficulties that arise from syntactic sources—from self-embedding, missing relative pronouns, discontinuous constituents, and the like. It also takes full advantage of surface clues in identifying constituents and building propositions.

The syntactic approach, of course, has not been worked out very far. Ultimately, it must provide strategies that take care of every detail described in the grammar of a language (like English). Strategies 1 through 7 are first attempts to handle some details for English, but the range is actually small. Strategies 1a and 2a, for example, handle very little of what is known about noun phrases. They handle those that begin with a determiner (**the, a, an, few, much, two**, etc.) and end with a noun. Woods (1970) and Winograd (1972) have proposed strategies to handle more details about noun phrases, but only a few. It will be a truly Herculean feat to specify strategies to cover all details.

Problems

Yet as the sole account of the construction process, the syntactic approach has problems in principle. In this approach, listeners are assumed to make heavy use of function words (see Strategies 1, 2, and 6) and prefixes and suffixes (Strategies 3 and 7). But to be used, these must be identifiable from their sounds alone. In actual speech, these are just the words and elements that are most difficult to identify (Pollack and Pickett, 1964; Woods and Makhoul, 1973). People speak so quickly and sloppily that their words, especially their function words, are often unintelligible out of context (see Chapter 5). More than that, actual speech is so full of incomplete words, repeats, stutters, and outright errors (see Chapter 7) that these strategies should often be stymied from the very start. It is difficult to see how by working from syntactic information alone listeners could ever fill in all the unintelligible words and get around the other mistakes speakers make.

But the most serious criticism is that the pure syntactic approach doesn't take advantage of semantic and pragmatic information until very late in the process. The semantic approach, on the other hand, does.

SEMANTIC APPROACHES
TO THE CONSTRUCTION PROCESS

Listeners usually know a lot about what a speaker is going to say. They can make shrewd guesses from what has just been said and from the situation being described. They can also be confident that the speaker will make sense, be relevant, provide given and new information appropriately, and in general be cooperative. Listeners almost certainly use this sort of information to select among alternative parses of a sentence, to anticipate words and phrases, and sometimes even to circumvent syntactic analyses altogether. Just how is not yet very clear. The main progress in the semantic approach has come from workers in artificial intelligence, who have attempted to program computers to "understand" natural language (see Schank, 1972; Winograd, 1972; Woods and Makhoul, 1973). This work is based on several general principles, and others have proposed tentative strategies that fit in with these principles.

The Reality and Cooperative Principles

The basic premise behind the semantic approach is that the listener's goal is to determine how each sentence was meant to be utilized. In practice listeners achieve this by following two working principles—the *reality principle* and the *cooperative principle*. The reality principle is concerned with the substance of a sentence, the ideas being talked about, and the cooperative principle is concerned with the way these ideas are expressed.

According to the reality principle, listeners interpret sentences in the belief that the speaker is referring to a situation or set of ideas they can make sense of. On this basis, listeners can build up an internal model of that situation piece by piece. The model might be of a country scene, a murder mystery plot, a series of actions to be performed, or a mathematical problem. Because of concrete facts they know about country scenes, mystery plots, actions, and mathematics in general, they can set limits on the situation the speaker is likely to have been referring to. They can parse and interpret the current sentence in such a way that it adds the next logical piece onto the model they are building. The reality principle is potentially very powerful. It could help listeners rule out ambiguities, fill in misheard words, and avoid other incorrect interpretations.

Listeners use the cooperative principle to interpret sentences in the belief that the speaker is trying to tell the truth, tell them all they need to know and no more, say things that are relevant, and use sentences clearly and unambiguously. The consequences of the cooperative principle are potentially far reaching too, for these assumptions help listeners come to the interpretation the speaker intended. Although the main consequences of the cooperative principle will be taken up in Chapter 3, it plays an implicit role in the strategies to be discussed here.

Making Sense of Sentences

The first strategy to be considered (suggested by Bever, 1970, among others) goes as follows:

> *Strategy 8:* Using content words alone, build propositions that make sense and parse the sentence into constituents accordingly.

Here listeners assume, in line with the cooperative principle, that speakers intend their sentences to make sense. For example, if listeners had heard the words **flower, girl, picked,** and **red** without any other syntactic information, they could guess that two propositions were involved: **the girl picked the flower** and **the flower was red**. They could make the same guess on hearing **The flower the girl picked was red** and then attempt to confirm the guess by finding constituents to match. By making the guess, they could constrain their search to a small set of possible constituents. They might sometimes get away without reference to any further syntactic information at all.

Stolz (1967) tested for Strategy 8 by asking people to paraphrase doubly self-embedded sentences of two kinds:

52. The vase that the maid that the agency hired dropped broke on the floor.

53. The dog that the cat that the girl fought scolded approached the colt.

Sentences of type 52 were highly constrained semantically. **Vase, maid, agency, hired, dropped,** and **broke on the floor** can easily be sorted into three sensible propositions: **the vase broke on the floor; the maid dropped the vase;** and **the agency hired the maid.** Not so with sentences of type 53. Dogs, cats, and girls can all fight, scold, and approach colts, so the words cannot be sorted into propositions. As expected, people correctly paraphrased sentences of type 52 more often than sentences of type 53 (see also Schlesinger, 1968). These sentences, however, may be so difficult that they are treated more as jigsaw puzzles than as sentences.

Strategy 8 has been demonstrated more directly with simpler sentences. Strohner and Nelson (1974) found that children aged two and three interpreted the sentences:

54. The cat chased the mouse.

55. The mouse was chased by the cat.

56. The mouse chased the cat.

57. The cat was chased by the mouse.

all in the same way—as "the cat chased the mouse." They were always correct on 54 and 55 and always wrong on 56 and 57. These children apparently assumed very strongly that what they were told ought to make sense—cats chase mice and not vice versa. They gave that assumption precedence over any syntactic information. By age four or five, children interpreted all four sentences correctly, taking account of the syntactic information. Yet as Herriot (1969) found, even when interpreted correctly, sentences analogous to 56 and 57 take longer to interpret than sentences analogous to 54 and 55. Listeners apparently take longer when the propositions make less sense (but see Forster and Olbrei, 1973).

A demonstration by Fillenbaum (1971, 1974a, b) brings home the reality principle and Strategy 8 the most clearly of all. In one study people were given sentences to paraphrase in their own words. Among them were "perverse" sentences like:

58. John dressed and had a bath.

59. John finished and wrote the article on the weekend.

60. Don't print that or I won't sue you.

They are perverse in that one normally dresses *before* bathing, writes an article *before* finishing it, and sues someone for *printing*, not for failing to print, something. But in their paraphrases, over 60 percent of the people "normalized" the perverse sentences, as in this incorrect paraphrase of 60:

60'. If you print that, I'll sue you.

Fillenbaum went a step further, asking people to look carefully at their paraphrases and say if there was any "shred of difference" between the original sentences and their rewordings. Nevertheless, people replied that there was no difference between the original and their incorrect paraphrase 53 percent of the time. It is as if the reality principle—"what is described in discourse will be sensible," as Fillenbaum put it—blinded them to the syntactic information that made the sentences perverse. They often justified their incorrect paraphrases the other 47 percent of the time by saying that they knew what the original sentences were trying to say and so they said it correctly. The reality principle is a powerful force in comprehension, even in artificial experiments like Fillenbaum's (see also Gleitman and Gleitman, 1970).

Anticipating Constituents

Listeners probably have specialized strategies for searching for constituents, especially for anticipating ones to come. Fodor (1971), Schank (1972), Winograd (1972), and others, for example, have suggested that listeners center their attention on verbs and look for noun phrases that fit their semantic requirements. **Put**, for example, requires three noun phrases—an agent to do the placing, an object to be placed, and a location to receive the object. **John put the book on the table** expresses the three-place proposition **Put(John, book, table)**. Listeners can put this information to good advantage once they have identified the verb:

John put ...

Here listeners can look for the two remaining arguments of **Put(John,x,y)** by searching for two noun phrases, one interpretable as an object and the other as a location. They can bypass conceivable but unintended analyses of the remaining part of the sentence.

More generally, the verb-centered strategy might be expressed this way:

Strategy 9: Look for constituents that fit the semantic requirements of the propositional function that underlies each verb, adjective, adverb, preposition, and noun.

Just as verbs require certain noun phrases, adjectives require certain nouns; adverbs require certain verbs, adjectives, or adverbs; prepositions require certain noun phrases; and some nouns require certain other noun phrases. Here are examples of each:

Put requires three noun phrases: an agent, an object, and a location

Tall requires one noun: an object with height

Quickly requires one verb: an action of movement

In requires two noun phrases: an object and a container

Son sometimes requires one noun phrase: a person old enough to be the son's parent (as in *George's son*)

The assumption is that listeners can quickly identify these words, determine their propositional functions, and narrow in on constituents that fit the missing arguments. Although there is little *direct* evidence for Strategy 9, it is highly plausible because of its potential helpfulness. Yet it has at least one drawback. It suggests that sentences ought to be easiest to comprehend when the verb is first. Yet in many languages, like Japanese and Turkish, the verb normally comes at the end of the sentence. If Strategy 9 were essential, these languages should be more difficult for native speakers to understand than they are.

Tying Sentences to Context

Listeners are especially anxious to make sense of a sentence in the circumstances they are in at the time. From the cooperative principle they assume that the speaker has made his utterance relevant to the ongoing discourse—for example, that the speaker has used definite noun phrases like **the general** to refer to entities they know. They can therefore use this strategy:

Strategy 10: Look for definite noun phrases that refer to entities you know and replace the interpretation of each noun phrase by a reference to that entity directly.

For illustration, imagine that someone had said 61 followed immediately by 62:

61. Claire and Kent climbed Mt. McKinley last summer.

62. She photographed the peak, and he surveyed it.

Listeners, having heard 61, expect the next sentence to be relevant and perhaps refer to Claire, Kent, Mt. McKinley, last summer, the climb itself, or even the speaker. So on hearing 62, they search for noun phrases that refer to these entities and find **she**, **the peak**, **he**, and **it**. If Claire, Kent, and Mt. McKinley had been assigned the indices E_9, E_{82}, and E_{17}, then the listener can replace **she, he, the peak**, and **it** by their corresponding indices and build the propositions:

62'. Photograph(E_9, E_{17}) & Survey(E_{82}, E_{17})

This strategy enables listeners to restrict their search to a small number of noun phrases; Claire, Kent, the speaker, and the listener, for example, would almost certainly be referred to by the noun phrases **she**, **he**, **I**, and **you**.

Any restriction like this should make it easier to perceive the individual words (see Chapter 5). Moreover, Strategy 10 ties the sentence in with the on-going discourse.

One place Strategy 10 may take on special importance is in selecting between alternative interpretations of a single sentence (Winograd, 1972). Consider:

63. John put the block in the box on the shelf.

This could mean either that the block in the box was put on the shelf, or that the block was put in the box on the shelf. By Strategy 10, listeners can decide which interpretation was intended. If in that situation there is a block in the box and no box on the shelf, the first interpretation must have been intended; if there is no block in the box and the box is on the shelf, the second interpretation must have been intended.

As Springston (1975) has demonstrated, listeners look for noun phrases that refer to recently mentioned entities first. Consider 64 and 65:

64. John said that Bill hit him.

65. John said that Mary hit him.

On reaching **him** in 64, listeners are open to noun phrases referring to either John or Bill. Since **him** could refer to either, they must note that **him** cannot refer to Bill for syntactic reasons—**him** would have to be **himself**—and then settle on John. On reaching **him** in 65, on the other hand, listeners are open to references to either John or Mary, and **him**, because of its gender, can only refer to John. As expected, in Springston's study people managed to pick out the correct referent for **him** faster in 65 than in 64, even though it refers to John in both sentences. In a series of similar comparisons, Springston demonstrated that listeners are faster at identifying a referent the more recently it has been mentioned and the more ways alternative candidates (like Bill and Mary in 64 and 65) can be eliminated on syntactic, semantic, or pragmatic grounds.

By Strategy 10, listeners actively anticipate references to known entities, yet many facts in its support can as easily be accounted for by Strategy 11:

> *Strategy 11:* On finding a definite noun phrase, search memory for the entity it was meant to refer to and replace the interpretation of the noun phrase by a reference to the entity directly.

With Strategy 11 applied to 61 and 62, listeners would come upon **she**, realize it has to refer to a female person, search working memory for such an entity, find Claire, or E_9, and replace **she** by E_9. Instead of anticipating **she**, as Strategy 10 does, Strategy 11 identifies **she** first and then works backward. Such a strategy would account for Springston's findings. The listener would identify **him** in 64 and 65 first, and by working backward, manage to settle on John as its referent more quickly in 65 than in 64. Strategies 10 and 11 may both be used. Strategy 11 is a special case of a " given-new strategy " discussed more completely as part of the utilization process in Chapter 3.

Use of Word Order

The order of words and clauses within sentences has considerable consistency, both in English and in many other languages, and listeners could make good use of that consistency. As Bever (1970) has noted, for example, most English sentences have the order agent-action-object, as in **John struck Bill**, and so listeners could make use of Strategy 12:

> *Strategy 12:* Look for the first noun-verb-noun sequence to be an agent, action, and object, unless the sequence is marked otherwise.

This strategy, he argued, accounts for why young children often misinterpret passive sentences like **The cow was kissed by the horse** as an agent-action-object sequence meaning " the cow kissed the horse " (Fraser, Bellugi, and Brown, 1963).

Along similar lines H. Clark and E. Clark (1968) and E. Clark (1971) have noted that events are normally described in the order in which they occur. **The boy jumped the fence and patted the dog**, for example, indicates that the boy jumped the fence before and not after he patted the dog. Thus listeners may use Strategy 13:

> *Strategy 13:* Look for the first of two clauses to describe the first of two events, and the second clause the second event, unless they are marked otherwise.

E. Clark (1971) found that very young children rely heavily on Strategy 13, ignoring the caveat " unless they are marked otherwise." For example, they often misinterpret sentences like **The boy jumped the fence after he patted the dog** to mean that the boy jumped the fence and *then* patted the dog. Unlike Strategy 12, Strategy 13 appears to be applicable in all languages.

Halliday (1967) among others has observed that given information tends to come before new information, as in **The man caught a beaver**, in which **the man** conveys given information and **caught a beaver** new information. When new information comes before given information, special syntactic devices are often needed, as in **It was a beaver that the man caught**. This suggests Strategy 14:

> *Strategy 14:* Look for given information to precede new information, unless the sentence is marked otherwise.

Like Strategy 13, Strategy 14 appears to apply to all languages.

Evaluation of the Semantic Approach

Like the syntactic approach, the semantic approach has its good and bad points. Its advantages are obvious. Whereas the syntactic approach exploits mostly function words and the classification of content words as nouns, verbs, and the like, the semantic approach exploits the real meat of a sentence—the content words and their meaning. Listeners know that sentences make sense and refer to their surroundings, and the semantic approach exploits these facts as much as possible. It accounts for the many sentences that are difficult to understand merely because they make little sense internally or make little sense in context.

Yet a "pure" semantic approach won't work any more than a "pure" syntactic approach. Listeners might sort the content words of **The flower the girl picked was red** into its two main propositions **the girl picked the flower** and **the flower was red**, but that isn't enough. They must also find constituents that reflect these propositions, the noun phrase **the flower the girl picked** for the first proposition and the whole sentence for the second. Without the second step they could not know that the sentence asserts that the flower was red, not that the girl picked the flower. Strategies 8 through 14 in this section serve only as guides in the search for constituents, which then have to be "confirmed" or "checked" by strategies very much like Strategies 1 through 7. Precisely how they guide listeners has not yet been spelled out in any detail.

There are major issues yet to be resolved in the semantic approach. Are syntactic strategies tried before semantic strategies, semantic before syntactic, or do they work simultaneously? How much do listeners anticipate what is to come and how much do they wait, collecting phonological information in working memory, and then attempt an analysis? In general, how do all these strategies fit into a *system* of comprehension? The essence of the semantic approach is captured in the reality and cooperative principles: listeners assume that the sentence a speaker uses was meant to be utilized for some purpose. Some of these issues, then, cannot be resolved without knowing more about how sentences are utilized, a process taken up in the next chapter. Indeed, it may be impossible to draw a line between many of the strategies used in the construction process and those used in the utilization process.

AMBIGUITY

Ambiguity ought to be the bane of comprehension because many—probably most—sentences have more than one interpretation, or reading. Although people ought to have great trouble selecting the intended reading, in practice they are rarely aware of more than one reading, which they select immediately. Consider, for example:

66. The farmer put the straw on a pile beside his threshing machine.

At first glance 66 is unambiguous. Yet on closer examination it is seen that **straw** could mean either "grain stalk" or "drinking tube." Since the rest of the sentence makes "grain stalk" much more plausible than "drinking tube," people normally accept the "grain stalk" reading and fail to notice the ambiguity. This illustrates the paradox of ambiguity: although most sentences are technically speaking ambiguous, practically speaking they are unambiguous. This paradox needs explaining.

"Usual guff about a bearded stranger."

The Garden Path Theory

Many investigators have proposed the Garden Path, or One Meaning, Theory of ambiguity. As listeners proceed through a sentence they compute only one reading for each ambiguous construction. In 66, they compute only one meaning for **straw**—namely "grain stalk." Only if this reading later becomes implausible or contradictory do they go back and compute a second, third, or fourth interpretation. The Garden Path Theory has two points in its favor. First, it solves the paradox. It claims that the reason people do not see a sentence as ambiguous is that they never compute more than one reading. Second, it explains why people are startled when they are " led down the garden path ":

67. I was afraid of Ali's powerful punch, especially since it had already laid out many tougher men who had bragged they could handle that much alcohol.

In 67 **punch** is first interpreted as a blow, and only after a reference to alcohol is it reinterpreted as a drink. The Garden Path Theory handles these " garden path " sentences with ease.

The defect in the Garden Path Theory is that it cannot account for the early findings by MacKay (1966). In his study people were presented with a sentence fragment typed on an index card and asked to provide a sensible completion as quickly as possible. Some were presented ambiguous fragments, as illustrated here (with the ambiguity in italics):

68. After taking the *right* turn at the intersection, I

69. Although Hannibal sent troops *over* a week ago,

70. Knowing that *visiting relatives* could be bothersome, I

Others were presented unambiguous fragments that corresponded to them:

68'. After taking the left turn at the intersection, I

69'. Although Hannibal sent troops almost a week ago,

70'. Knowing that some relatives could be bothersome, I

People were timed from the moment they began reading the fragment to the moment they began their completion.

MacKay found that people took longer to begin completing ambiguous than unambiguous fragments. The fragments with more than one ambiguity took longer than those with just one. And, oddly enough, people were more likely on ambiguous fragments to stutter, repeat themselves, become ungrammatical, and even titter. Yet even these people were not aware of the ambiguities.

These findings led MacKay and others (MacKay, 1970a) to suggest two alternatives to the Garden Path Theory. The Many Meanings Theory claims that listeners compute two or more readings for each ambiguous construction and then immediately pick one on the basis of context. For 66 they would compute the " grain stalk " and the " drinking tube " readings for **straw** and pick the first. By the No Meaning Theory, on the other hand, listeners compute no meaning for an ambiguous construction at first, but let the context " give weight " to one reading until it pops out. In 66 the facts about farming give weight to the " grain stalk " reading for **straw** and so it becomes conscious. At first this theory seems to contradict itself, for how could listeners know a construction was ambiguous until they had computed at least two readings? In MacKay's version, however, each reading tries to suppress the others in a struggle to become conscious. The reading furnished with the most weight from surrounding context is the one that eventually wins. The state of having no meaning is relatively brief. In neither theory are listeners conscious of the ambiguity or of selecting a reading.

The Mixed Theory

Work on ambiguity since MacKay's suggests a combination of the Many Meanings and Garden Path Theories that most popularly goes like this (see Garrett, 1970; Lackner and Garrett, 1972; Bever, Garrett, and Hurtig, 1973):

(1) When listeners encounter an ambiguous construction, they compute multiple readings.

(2) Using the context, listeners then attempt to select the most plausible reading.

(3) If the ambiguity has not been resolved by the end of the clause, they select one reading and stick to it.

(4) If later context contradicts the selected reading, they try to retrieve the surface structure of the prior clause and compute a new compatible reading.

By this mixed theory, listeners are influenced by ambiguities as they go along—each one consumes extra time. But once a clause is closed, they choose the reading they intend to stick with. Recall that listeners tend to purge working memory of the verbatim context of a just completed clause, especially if it is in the previous sentence. By the mixed theory, they do this just after they have resolved all the ambiguities in the clause and no longer need the verbatim content.

The mixed theory has received mostly positive support. Foss and his associates (Foss, 1970; Foss and Jenkins, 1973) examined the momentary processing difficulties people have just after encountering an ambiguous word. They used a monitoring task where people listen to a sentence for meaning while simultaneously monitoring for, say, a **b**. Ambiguous sentences like 71 were compared with unambiguous ones like 72:

71. The merchant put his straw beside the machine.

72. The merchant put his hay beside the machine.

People took longer to detect the **b** in **beside** in 71 than in 72, suggesting that the ambiguous word **straw** in 71 required more mental processing than the unambiguous word **hay** in 72. Yet some slowing down occurred even in sentences like 73:

73. The farmer put his straw beside the machine.

The initial word **farmer** in 73 should enable listeners to resolve the ambiguity in **straw** very quickly toward "grain stalk," but apparently even this easy resolution adds some processing difficulty. Thus, consistent with the mixed theory, it takes extra mental processing to resolve ambiguities.

In the mixed theory, listeners compute more than one reading for each ambiguity and resolve it immediately—if there is enough information. This has been demonstrated by Lackner and Garrett (1972) and MacKay (1973a) with a remarkable technique. In their studies people heard in one ear a sentence they were to attend to and later paraphrase, and in the other ear a sentence they were to ignore. As earlier research had shown, listeners are not "conscious" of the message beamed to the unattended ear, although they are affected by it—they have to analyze it a little simply to reject it as the wrong conversation (see Chapter 5). In Lackner and Garrett's study, the attended sentence was sometimes ambiguous, like 74, while the simultaneous unattended sentence was one that could potentially resolve the ambiguity, like 75 or 76:

74. The spy put out the torch as our signal to attack.

75. The spy extinguished the torch in the window.

76. The spy displayed the torch in the window.

Note that 75, if properly heard, ought to bias listeners toward the "extinguish" reading of **put out** in 74, whereas 76 ought to bias them toward the "display" reading.

The findings agreed with the mixed theory. People most often paraphrased 74 with an "extinguish" reading when 75 had come to the unattended ear, and with a "display" reading when 76 had come to the unattended ear. For the interpretation of **put out** to be pushed around like this, listeners must have had both readings available at first and selected the "extinguish" or "display" reading only afterwards. The unattended message had to be analyzed just enough —without becoming conscious—to sway the choice in one direction or the other. The critical part of the unattended message (for example, **extinguished** in 75) affected the choice of reading even when it preceded or followed the ambiguous word (**put out** in 74) by small intervals. This phenomenon, incidentally, is consistent with the semantic approach to the construction process.

In the mixed theory clause boundaries are critical. When listeners cross one, they should fix on one reading and behave from then on as if the clause were unambiguous. To demonstrate this point, Bever, Garrett, and Hurtig (1973) repeated MacKay's (1966) sentence completion study with a twist. Some sentence fragments they presented were incomplete clauses, as in 77, while others were complete clauses plus a word or two, as in 78:

77. Although flying airplanes can

78. Although flying airplanes can be dangerous, he

Both fragments, of course, are ambiguous, since **flying airplanes** can mean either " someone's flying of airplanes " or " airplanes that fly." These fragments were compared to unambiguous fragments, as in 77' and 78':

77'. Although some airplanes can

78'. Although some airplanes can be dangerous, he

According to the mixed theory, fragment 77 has two readings available at the time people try to complete it, since they have not yet crossed a clause boundary. Completing 77 ought to be much harder, therefore, than completing 77'. Fragment 78, on the other hand, should have only one reading when people complete it, since they will already have crossed a clause boundary (after **dangerous**). So completing 78 should be only slightly harder than completing 78'. These predictions were confirmed.

Criteria for Theories of Ambiguity

For any theory of ambiguity to be correct, it must conform to the strategies considered earlier, for they were explicitly designed to resolve potential ambiguities. Strategy 3, for example, selects between the " person " and " operate " readings of **man** in **the man** and **will man** by use of the function words **the** and **will**. It resolves the ambiguity so quickly and locally that **man** is hardly seen to be ambiguous. For **The horse raced past the barn fell**, Strategy 7 chooses " the horse did race " over " the horse that was raced." It resolves the ambiguity so quickly and locally that listeners are led briskly down the garden path. For **Being pregnant, the hospital wouldn't accept the woman's offer of a blood donation**, Strategy 8 from the very beginning would put **being pregnant** with **the woman** instead of **the hospital.**

Fortunately, most aspects of the mixed theory of ambiguity are natural consequences of Strategies 1 through 14. Ambiguities should take time to resolve, for the strategies that resolve them take time to apply. Most ambiguities should be resolved as one goes along, for most strategies make use of local information, like the function words in **the man** and **will man**. Most ambiguities should be settled by the end of the clause, for most strategies deal with constituents no larger than the clause. And ambiguities should be resolved with virtually any kind of information one can get one's hands on, for the strategies proposed make use of a broad range of information. The correspondences between the mixed theory and the comprehension strategies, however, are still only approximate. In the end, the correct theory of ambiguity will be the one that corresponds exactly to the system of strategies that listeners are assumed to apply in the process of comprehension.

SUMMARY

What is comprehension? In its narrowest definition it is the process by which listeners come to an interpretation for a stream of speech, and this is called the construction process. In its broader definition it also includes the process by which listeners use those interpretations for their intended purpose—called the utilization process. This chapter focused on the construction process.

In the construction process, listeners take in the raw speech, isolate and identify the constituents of surface structure, and build propositions appropriate to each. As they build each proposition, they add it to the interpretation they have formed of the sentence so far, and the propositions taken together constitute the finished interpretation. In this process listeners normally hold the constituents verbatim in working memory until they have passed a sentence boundary, and then they eliminate them and retain only the finished interpretation. The major question is how listeners do all this. How do they isolate constituents, identify them, and build propositions, and in what order?

It is assumed that listeners have a number of strategies by which they infer what the constituents are and what they are meant to convey. Two major types of strategies were taken up: the syntactic and the semantic. In the syntactic approach, the strategies use function words, suffixes, prefixes, and grammatical categories of content words as clues to the identity of constituents, and other strategies build propositions from these constituents. In the semantic approach, the strategies take advantage of the fact that sentences refer to real objects, states, and events, and fit the ongoing discourse. Generally, these strategies begin with propositions that make sense in context and then check for surface constituents that express these propositions. Listeners probably rely on some flexible combination of these strategies. Whatever the strategies look like, their purpose is to resolve potential ambiguities as listeners go along. These ambiguities are normally resolved without awareness, but each resolution takes time. Sometimes, however, the strategies listeners use lead them down the garden path, as in **The pitcher pitched the ball pitched the ball**, and listeners have to retrace their steps and reparse the sentence if they are to arrive at the correct interpretation.

Further Reading

Fodor et al. (1974), especially Chapters 5 and 6, and Levelt (1974) both consider many of the issues taken up in this chapter, but from different points of view. Bever (1970) and Kimball (1973) provide good introductions to strategies in comprehension, especially syntactic strategies. Winograd (1972), Schank (1972), and Woods (1975) describe computer systems for comprehending natural language, providing another view, mostly from the semantic approach, of comprehension strategies.

I remember once when I had been talking on this subject that somebody afterwards said: "You know, I haven't the least idea what he
means, unless it could be that he simply means what he says." Well,
that is what I should like to mean.

J. L. Austin

3

Utilization of Sentences

People talk for a purpose—to assert beliefs, request help, promise actions, express congratulations, or ask for information. Listeners would be remiss if they
did not register this purpose and act accordingly—recording the beliefs, providing
the help, recording the promises, acknowledging the congratulations, and providing the information. The construction process described in Chapter 2, however, does not extend this far. In that process listeners figure out what a sentence
was meant to express, but they do not register how the sentence was meant to
carry forward the purposes of the speaker. Although the listeners have inferred
the underlying propositions, they have not yet used them in the way the speaker
intended. This is the goal of the utilization process. Of course, this is a rough
division; the line between the construction and utilization processes is not a
sharp one. Formally, it is not easy to say when listeners are building a representation and when they are using it. And psychologically, it is often not possible to
infer the propositions underlying a sentence without simultaneously registering
the speaker's purpose. Nevertheless, in this chapter the focus will be on utilization—the listeners' mental processes in utilizing a sentence as the speaker
intended.

WHY PEOPLE LISTEN

Speakers convey their purposes in three separable parts of their utterances—
the speech act, the propositional content, and the thematic content (Chapter 1).
For example, Kathy, in saying **Does George own a car?** to Jeff, is probably performing the speech act of requesting information. She wants Jeff to say whether
the proposition **George owns a car** is true or false. But she is also indicating by

the thematic content that she takes Jeff's knowledge of George for granted and that she wants to know specifically whether owning a car is something that can be said of George. Jeff, if he is to utilize the sentence properly, must register these three bits of information, search memory for the right information, and provide an answer of yes, no, or maybe. Since these three parts of an utterance are critical to the utilization process, it is instructive to examine them in more detail.

Speech Acts

Speech acts are limited in their variety. There are only some things people can do by uttering a sentence, and this is reflected in the limited purposes that can be imparted by their utterances. **George owns a car** usually has the force of an assertion, while **Does George own a car?** has the force of a request for information, and **I warn you that George owns a car** the force of a warning. Each utterance is said to have a different kind of *illocutionary force*. Yet according to Searle (1975a), every speech act falls into one of only five very general categories:

(1) *Representatives*. The speaker, in uttering a representative, conveys his belief that some proposition is true. The representative *par excellence* is the assertion. When someone asserts **George owns a car**, he conveys his belief that the proposition **George owns a car** is true. When someone suggests, hypothesizes, swears, flatly states, or hints that George owns a car, he is also uttering a representative but at the same time conveying the strength of his belief in the truth of the proposition.

(2) *Directives*. By uttering a directive, the speaker attempts to get the listener to do something. By ordering, commanding, requesting, begging, or pleading, the speaker is trying to get the listener to carry out some action. By asking a yes/no question like **Does George own a car?** or a WH- question like **What does George own?**, he is trying to get the listener to provide information. Requests and questions are the two main types of directives.

(3) *Commissives*. By uttering a commissive, the speaker is committing himself to some future course of action. A prime example is the promise, but the category also includes vows, pledges, contracts, guarantees, and other types of commitments.

(4) *Expressives*. If the speaker wishes to express his "psychological state" about something, he utters an expressive. When he apologizes, thanks, congratulates, welcomes, or deplores, he is expressing how good or bad he feels about some event and is therefore uttering an expressive.

(5) *Declarations*. When the speaker utters a declaration his very words bring about a new state of affairs. When he says **You're fired, I resign, I hereby sentence you to five years in prison**, or **I christen this ship the H.M.S.** *Pinafore*, he is declaring, and thereby causing your job to be terminated, his job to be terminated, you to spend five years in prison, or this ship to be named H.M.S. *Pinafore*. Most declarations are specialized for use within a particular cultural system, such as employment, the church, law, or government.

Each of these categories requires something different of the listeners. Representatives require them to take note of the speaker's beliefs. Directives require them to determine some course of action and carry it out. Commissives, expressives, and declarations all require them to take note of new information: namely, the speaker's intended course of action, his feelings about some fact, or the change in formal status of some object. Of the five categories, the first two are the most important. They are the most common and the best studied of the speech acts. For these reasons we will focus on these two categories—especially assertions (a representative), yes/no questions, WH- questions, and requests (all directives).

Propositional and Thematic Content

When the speaker makes an assertion, what beliefs is he attempting to convey? And when he utters a directive, what action does he want carried out? The answers are found in the propositional and thematic content of his utterances.

When Robert asserts **It was Julia who discovered the virus**, he is not only conveying his belief in the statement **Julia discovered the virus**, but also how he thinks the proposition fits into the ongoing discourse. He takes it as given that someone discovered the virus. He expects listeners to know, or to be able to figure out, that someone discovered the virus. What he is really asserting is the new information that that someone was Julia. If listeners are to register his beliefs properly, they must take note of this given-new distinction. Robert also distinguishes between subject and predicate, between Julia—what he is talking about—and her discovery of the virus—what he is saying about the subject. Listeners must keep track of this information too, for that moves the conversation or discourse along.

Requests and questions have propositional and thematic content too. In asking **Was it Julia who discovered the virus?**, the speaker expects the listeners to know the given information that someone discovered the virus. He is requesting them to say whether or not that someone was Julia, the new information. Questions like **Who discovered the virus?** and requests like **Feed the dog** have similar thematic content. Once again listeners must deal not only with the propositions underlying **Julia discovered the virus**, but also with the thematic content associated with them.

What listeners do with this content depends on the speech act. For the assertion **It was Julia who discovered the virus**, they must search memory for the fact they are expected to know—that someone discovered the virus—and add to their memory the missing name. For the question **Was it Julia who discovered the virus?**, they must search memory for the same fact, decide whether the discoverer was Julia, and answer yes or no. For both speech acts, they have to search memory, compare one proposition with another, and carry out other mental operations. The fundamental question in the utilization process is just how this is done.

The Utilization Process

It is possible, therefore, to characterize very roughly how listeners utilize sentences:

(1) On hearing an utterance, listeners identify the speech act, propositional content, and thematic content.

(2) They next search memory for information that matches the given information.

(3) Finally, depending on the speech act, they deal with the new information:
   a. If the utterance is an assertion, they add the new information to memory.
   b. If the utterance is a yes/no question, they compare the new information with what is in memory and, depending on the match, answer yes or no.
   c. If the utterance is a WH- question, they retrieve the wanted information from memory and compose an answer conveying that information.
   d. If the utterance is a request, they carry out the action necessary to make the new information true.

But is this outline correct? For that we must consult the evidence and must test, correct, and elaborate this first guess. The first parts of this chapter will take up the utilization of four speech acts in turn: assertions, yes/no questions, WH-questions, and requests.

What has been discussed so far could be called the *direct* utilization of sentences. Listeners directly interpret declarative sentences as assertions, yes/no interrogatives as questions, WH- interrogatives as questions, and so on. Yet many speech acts are conveyed only indirectly. In the right circumstances, the statement **It's hot in here** will be construed as a request to open the window, the interrogative **Did you know Julia discovered the virus?** as an assertion that Julia discovered the virus, the statement **George owns a car** as a warning to be careful of George and his car, and so on. To handle these utterances, listeners must go beyond the outline just described, and infer what the speaker meant them to understand. The indirect utilization of utterances will be taken up in the last part of this chapter.

The utilization processes to be taken up rely on three major principles. The first two are the reality and cooperative principles, discussed in the previous chapter, which lead listeners to assume that the speaker is referring to things and ideas in the real world and is trying to coordinate speech with his listeners. (The cooperative principle is especially important in indirect utilization and will be explored more completely later.) The third principle, the *congruence principle*, governs the listeners' search for information in memory. Imagine a grocer searching a shelf for Oxford marmalade. He must check each package to see whether its label matches the words "Oxford marmalade." If it does, he accepts the package as what he is looking for; if it does not, he rejects the package and moves on. That is, he searches for a label "congruent" with a target label, and when there is a mismatch, he takes extra time in rejecting the label. Like the grocer, listeners search memory for a target proposition and seize on a proposition only if it matches the target. When there is a mismatch, they must reject the information and move on, and that takes extra time and effort. The search for matching or "congruent" information in memory plays a central role in the utilization process.

RECORDING ASSERTIONS

When a speaker utters an assertion, he is trying to convey his belief that some proposition is true. If listeners are to utilize this utterance appropriately, they should take note of this belief and incorporate it into memory. They should "record" the assertion. How might they do that? According to the preliminary outline, listeners must register the fact that the speaker's utterance was an assertion, determine its propositional and thematic content, and add the new belief to memory. To do this they must make important assumptions about the roles that propositional and thematic content play in assertions.

The Function of Assertions

Imagine Ann trying to tell Ed she has just seen John hit Bill. She could do so in many different ways, for example:

John hit BILL.

Bill was hit by JOHN.

It was JOHN who hit Bill.

It was BILL John hit.

What John did was HIT BILL.

Although each sentence expresses the proposition **John hit Bill**, the one Ann used would depend on what she assumed Ed already knew. If she said **It was JOHN who hit Bill**, it would mean that she assumed he already knew somebody hit Bill and that she wanted to supply him with the name of the person who did it, John. However, if she said **It was BILL John hit**, it would mean she assumed he already knew John hit someone and that she wanted to supply him with the name of the victim, Bill.

The Given-New Contract

What Ann is trying to do is comply with what H. Clark and Haviland (1977) called the *given-new contract*. Each of these assertions has structural devices for distinguishing between given information and new information (see Chapter 1). **It was JOHN who hit Bill**, for example, has its given and new information as follows (where X denotes "someone" or "something"):

> Given: X hit Bill.
> New: X = John.

Now Ann and Ed—indeed all speakers and listeners—have an implicit agreement, or contract, about how to cooperate with each other in the use of given and new information. The agreement is roughly this:

> *Given-New Contract:* The speaker agrees (a) to use given information to refer to information she thinks the listener can uniquely identify from what he already knows and (b) to use new information to refer to information she believes to be true but is not already known to the listener.

Put more simply, given information should be identifiable and new information unknown. So Ann would tell Ed **It was JOHN who hit Bill** when she thought Ed could uniquely identify the event of someone hitting Bill and when she wanted to convey her belief that that someone was John, which she judged that Ed didn't already know. For his part, Ed would work on the assumption that Ann was trying to follow the agreement. Thus the agreement has important consequences for the listener too.

Because of the given-new contract, listeners can be confident that the given information conveys information they can identify uniquely. They understand that it is information the speaker believes they both agree on and that the speaker is asserting his beliefs about. Hornby (1972) demonstrated that listeners normally consider the given information to be "what the sentence is about." Hornby prepared the five sentences listed in Table 3–1. He told people that he would show them some pictures, and: "You will hear something said about one of the pictures, but there will be something wrong with what is said. I would like you to tell me which picture the sentence is about, even though it is not exactly correct." He showed people pairs of pictures like the following:

A.

B.

He then read them a sentence, such as **It is the BOY who is petting the cat** (Sentence 1 in Table 3–1). The assumption was that if they thought that the sentence

TABLE 3–1
GIVEN AND NEW INFORMATION
Five types of sentences and their given and new information

SENTENCE	GIVEN AND NEW INFORMATION
1. It is the BOY who is petting the cat.	Given: X is petting the cat
	New: X = the boy
2. It is the CAT which the boy is petting.	Given: the boy is petting X
	New: X = the cat
3. The one who is petting the cat is the BOY.	Given: X is petting the cat
	New: X = the boy
4. What the boy is petting is the CAT.	Given: the boy is petting X
	New: X = the cat
5. The BOY is petting the cat.	Given: X is petting the cat
	New: X = the boy

was about the boy or the boy petting something, they would point to Picture A, since these appear in A but not in B. But if they thought that it was about the cat or the petting of the cat, they would point to Picture B.

For each sentence in Table 3–1, people overwhelmingly selected the picture depicting the given information. For 1, they selected the picture depicting someone petting a cat (Picture B). Note that in 3 and 4 the given information comes before the new information, while in 1, 2, and 5 it comes after. Yet in both types the given information was selected as " what the sentence is about." And in 5, **the boy** was not selected despite its role as the subject. Because it receives " contrastive stress," listeners take it to be new information and not what the sentence is about. Listeners, then, are clearly aware of given and new information and of the given-new contract.

Active and Passive Sentences

Simple active and passive sentences have long interested linguists and psychologists because of their clear difference in function. Consider 6 and 7:

6. The boy is petting the CAT.

7. The cat is being petted by the BOY.

Although both express the proposition **the boy pets the cat**, 6 seems to be " about" the boy and 7 " about" the cat. Indeed, 6 and 7 were included in Hornby's study and yielded just this finding. In other studies people have been shown to reflect this property in a variety of other judgments too (H. Clark, 1965; H. Clark and Begun, 1968; Johnson-Laird, 1968a, b; Tannenbaum and Williams, 1968).

Active and passive sentences, however, are particularly versatile. As explained in Chapter 1, when Sentence 6 is spoken with only normal stress on the last word, it has one of three given-new divisions:

Given information	New information
6′. a. X is happening	X = the boy pets the cat
b. the boy is doing X	X = pet the cat
c. the boy is petting X	X = the cat

Similarly, when 7 is spoken with normal stress on the last word, it has one of these three divisions:

7′. a. X is happening	X = the boy pets the cat
b. X is happening to the cat	X = the boy pets
c. X is petting the cat	X = the boy

Because of its possible given-new divisions, 6 is an appropriate answer to the questions **What is happening?, What is the boy doing?,** and **What is the boy petting?,** and 7 is an appropriate answer to **What is happening?, What is happening to the cat?,** and **Who is petting the cat?** This versatility makes 6 and 7 functionally more adaptable than 1 through 5: 6 and 7 can fit more situations. Hornby's subjects, in their judgments of "what the sentence is about," reflected this versatility. They agreed with each other less on the given information in 6 and 7 than on the given information in 1 through 5. In addition, the passive 7 was found to be less versatile than the active 6 (Anisfeld and Klenbort, 1973; Hornby, 1974).

The article **the** is a special device to mark information in a noun phrase as given information, as in:

8. I met the general.

When a speaker says 8, he expects listeners to be able to identify the particular general he is referring to—often because that general has just been mentioned. In Chapter 2, this complicated notion was denoted by the simple proposition **Known(x)**. It is not the same with the article **a**, however, as in:

9. I met a general.

When a speaker says 9, he expects listeners to set up a new entity, call it E_{74}, and predicate it to be a general, **General(E_{74})**. Listeners are specifically "instructed" not to look for a general they already know. Thus, **the general** conveys given information, and **a general** normally conveys new information. If so, what about 10?

10. It was the GENERAL that I met.

In this case **the general** is said to "convey" new information. Technically speaking, however, **the general** itself is not new information. What is new is the general's *identification* as the person the speaker met. If the speaker was confident that the general in question could be identified by **Eisenhower**, or **Ike**, or **Mamie's husband**, he could have used one of them instead with exactly the same result, as in 10':

10'. It was IKE that I met.

Nevertheless, in this book we will often speak loosely of **the general** as "conveying" new information.

Integrating Information into Memory

When Ann tells Ed **It was JOHN who hit Bill**, Ed must do more than identify the speech act, propositional content, and thematic content. He must integrate Ann's message into memory. According to H. Clark and Haviland (1974, 1977; H. Clark, 1977; Haviland and H. Clark, 1974), he accomplishes this feat by what they called the *given-new strategy*. This strategy works very much as if Ed were a postal clerk putting a letter into a pigeonhole. The sentence is a letter consisting of an address and a message. If Ann is adhering to the given-new contract, the given information **X hit Bill** is the address of the memory pigeonhole where the message should go, and the new information **X = John** is the message itself. What Ed must do is identify the address and the message, find the memory pigeonhole that corresponds to the address, namely **X hit Bill**, and insert the message **X = John** into that pigeonhole. This way he will have delivered the message just as the sender, Ann, had intended. He will have inserted the belief **X = John** with what he already knew of Ann's earlier beliefs.

The given-new strategy is presented more formally in Table 3–2 and is illustrated for the following pair of sentences.

11. Someone hit Bill. It was JOHN who hit Bill.

In this illustration, Ed has just comprehended and stored away the first sentence, and he is now applying the given-new strategy to the second. Initially his memory is filled with a number of propositions, labeled p_1 through p_n, one of which represents the just preceding sentence **E_8 hit Bill**, "some particular entity E_8 hit Bill." Ed now attacks the present sentence **It was JOHN who hit Bill** in three steps. At Step 1, he divides the sentence into given and new information. At Step 2, he searches his memory for information that matches the given information **X hit Bill**. In this instance he manages to find the matching proposition **E_8 hit Bill**, which is the antecedent. At Step 3, because **E_8** corresponds to **X**, he replaces the **X** in **X = John** by **E_8** and adds the resulting **E_8 = John** to memory. By these three steps, Ed adds to memory not just an unanchored "somebody who hit Bill is John" but rather the properly anchored "the somebody mentioned before who hit Bill, namely E_8, is John." He has revised his memory

TABLE 3–2

THE GIVEN-NEW STRATEGY

The given-new strategy as applied to the sentence

It was JOHN who hit Bill.

A. *Prior contents of memory:*
   $p_1, \ldots, E_8$ **hit Bill,** $\ldots, p_n$.

B. *Apply strategy to* **It was JOHN who hit Bill:**
   Step 1: Divide current sentence into given and new information.
   Given: X hit Bill.
   New: X = John

   Step 2: Search memory for unique antecedent that matches the given information.
   Antecedent: E_8 hit Bill

   Step 3: Integrate new information into memory by replacing **X** by the appropriate index in the antecedent.
   Add: E_8 = John

C. *Resulting contents of memory:*
   $p_1, \ldots, E_8$ **hit Bill,** E_8 **= John,** $\ldots, p_n$.

---

precisely as intended, inserting the new information in the pigeonhole where it belongs.

For the given-new strategy to work smoothly, given information must refer to information the listener has readily available in memory, typically facts that have just been mentioned. If the necessary facts have not been mentioned or have been mentioned too long ago, then integration by the given-new strategy ought to become more difficult. To demonstrate this, Carpenter and Just (1977) presented people with a series of sentences to read one at a time and measured how long they took to read and understand each one. The sentences formed a brief story, and people were to say when a sentence contradicted something that had gone before. Prior to any contradictory sentence, two of the sentences might have been these:

12. The ballerina captivated a musician during her performance.

13. The one who the ballerina captivated was the trombonist.

The given information in 13, **the ballerina captivated X**, is mentioned explicitly in 12, and so 13 ought to be integrated quickly. But imagine 14 in place of 13:

14. The one who captivated the trombonist was the ballerina.

In this case the given information **X captivated the trombonist** is not mentioned in 12, and so 14 ought to be integrated much more slowly. Indeed, it was. Moreover, the more sentences that intervened between 12 and 13, the longer subjects took to read and integrate 13. Listeners apparently expect given information to refer to facts just mentioned or to facts "on stage" at the moment in the discourse (Chafe, 1974).

Implicatures

Fundamentally, the given-new strategy is a method for deciding what the speaker is referring to. Take the sequence in 15:

15. Patience walked into a room. The room was enormous.

On reaching **the room** in the second sentence, listeners must decide what room the speaker was referring to. They must find an antecedent for the given information that there is a room they can identify. In 15 it is natural to infer that **the room** picks out the same room referred to by **a room** in the first sentence. The given-new strategy works so smoothly that we hardly notice the inference that is being drawn. In 16, however, the inference is not so simple:

16. Patience walked into a room. The chandeliers burned brightly.

On reaching **the chandeliers**, listeners must decide what chandeliers. Since there is no mention of any chandeliers, there is no antecedent for **the chandeliers**, and Step 2 of the given-new strategy reaches an impasse. How do listeners proceed from here?

By a proposal of H. Clark and Haviland's (1974, 1977), listeners get over such impasses by building bridging assumptions. Whenever they cannot identify an antecedent directly, they suppose they are expected to do so indirectly—at least if the speaker is being cooperative. In 16, they note that if they assumed that the room had chandeliers, they would have a direct antecedent for **the chandeliers**. Since this is an assumption the speaker could expect them to grasp, they add this bridging assumption, or *implicature*, to memory as part of what the speaker meant to convey. Thus, they add to memory not only the information in 16, but also the implicature in 16':

16'. The room referred to by *a room* had chandeliers in it.

Most assertions are accompanied by implicatures of this sort. Speakers cannot be bothered to spell out each tiny bit of information they refer to, and so they leave the most obvious pieces for listeners to supply as bridging assumptions. More examples of two-sentence sequences and their implicatures are shown in Table 3–3.

The formation of bridging assumptions, however, takes time. Haviland and H. Clark (1974) had people read pairs of sentences, one after the other, as in 17 and 18:

17. Mary got some beer out of the car.   The beer was warm.

18. Mary got some picnic supplies out of the car.   The beer was warm.

TABLE 3–3
IMPLICATURES
Sequences of two sentences and the implicatures induced by the second sentence

---

1. **Sequence:** Bill had a black eye. It was JOHN who hit him.
   Implicature: Bill had a black eye because someone hit him.

2. **Sequence:** John had been murdered. The knife lay NEARBY.
   Implicature: John had been murdered with a knife.

3. **Sequence:** Judy is an editor. BILL is very smart TOO.
   Implicature: Editors are very smart.

4. **Sequence:** Jake called Jess a conservative. Then SHE insulted HIM.
   Implicature: Calling someone a conservative is an insult.

In 17, the beer referred to by **the beer** is explicitly mentioned in the first sentence. In 18, however, it must be inferred to be among the picnic supplies. The listener has to draw the implicature in 18′:

18′. The picnic supplies include some beer.

Building this bridging assumption ought to take time, and it did. People took more time to read and comprehend **The beer was warm** in sequence 18 than in sequence 17.

Denials

Denials are a special kind of assertion. They are like an affirmative supposition and its cancellation all rolled into one. To see this, consider first a supposition plus cancellation, as when Ann tells Ed, " Remember yesterday when I told you that it was John who hit Bill. Well, I was wrong." In her second sentence Ann has asserted that the statement **It was JOHN who hit Bill** is not true. But what precisely has she canceled? Did John do something, but not hit Bill? Did John hit someone, but not Bill? Did something happen, but not the hitting of Bill by John? Probably none of these. Ann almost certainly meant that although someone hit Bill, it wasn't John, but someone else. She meant to imply that the given information **X hit Bill** was true and assert that the new information **X = John** was not. She presupposed the given information and canceled the new. For comparison, consider a denial, as when Ann tells Ed " It wasn't John who hit Bill." Denials are assertions with a negative attached to their main verb. This denial has the very same interpretation as Ann's supposition plus cancellation: Although someone hit Bill, it wasn't John, but someone else. In other words, the denial in 19 is interpreted as if it were 20:

19. It wasn't JOHN who hit Bill.

20. You may think it was JOHN who hit Bill, but that is false.

From THE NEW WORLD (Harper & Row). © 1961 Saul Steinberg. Originally in The New Yorker.

Denials almost always leave the given information of the corresponding affirmative intact and negate only the new information. This can be illustrated for the denials of Sentences 1 through 5 in Table 3–1:

1'. It isn't the BOY who is petting the cat—it's the GIRL.

2'. It isn't the CAT which the boy is petting—it's the DOG.

3'. The one who is petting the cat isn't the BOY—it's the GIRL.

4'. What the boy is petting isn't the CAT—it's the DOG.

5'. The BOY isn't petting the cat—the GIRL is.

Switch the continuation of 1' to **it's the DOG he is petting** and the sentence becomes nonsense. The same idea applies to the rest (see Klenbort and Anisfeld, 1974; Hupet and le Bouedec, 1975).

The Use of Denials

If denials are truly suppositions plus cancellations rolled into one, as in 19 and 20, then they have a very special purpose. They should be used only when speakers want to deny beliefs they have some reason to think their listeners might hold. To see this (see Givón, 1975), imagine Margaret meeting George and asking him, "What's happening?" George might say, "Oh, my wife is pregnant," and Margaret would carry on normally. But if he had said, "Oh, my wife isn't pregnant," Margaret is likely to balk and exclaim "Wait a minute

—is she *supposed* to be pregnant?" She balks because she expects George's denial to cancel something he thought she might believe, and he had no reason to think she might believe his wife *was* pregnant.

Because denials have this function, they sometimes reveal more about speakers than they are meant to reveal. Take the little boy who snitches a cookie. When his mother asks him what he is eating, he might blurt out, "I'm not eating a cookie," thereby revealing his suspicion that his mother knew exactly what he was eating all along. A cleverer child would have hidden his suspicions and lied with an affirmative sentence. Or take the example of Richard M. Nixon, who shortly before resigning as President of the United States said at a press conference, "I am not a crook." Instead of saying "I am an honest man," he denied that he was a crook, suggesting that he supposed his audience might think that he *was* a crook. Until that time Nixon had managed to appear cool in the face of growing criticism of his activities in the Watergate affair. Here, finally, was an unwitting public admission that he was in political trouble.

Denials are probably integrated into memory in the same way as any other assertion except that they often require bridging assumptions. When Ed is confronted with **It wasn't JOHN who hit Bill**, he goes through three steps in the given-new strategy. At Step 1, he divides the sentence into given information (**X hit Bill**) and new information ($X \neq$ **John**). At Step 2, he searches memory for information matching the given information, finds let us say E_{19} **hit Bill**, and calls this the antecedent. However, he also expects to find $E_{19} =$ **John**, the supposition being canceled. At Step 3, he then adds the new information, namely $E_{19} \neq$ **John**. In propositions, he inserts **Be(E_{19}, John)** into the proposition **False(x)** to form **False(Be(E_{19}, John))**. When there is no direct antecedent to attach the information to, as in 21, then the listener is forced to add the bridging assumption in 21':

21. My wife is in the hospital. She isn't pregnant.

21'. The speaker must think I might believe that his wife is in the hospital because she is pregnant.

Beyond this, however, little is known about the process of recording denials.

ANSWERING YES / NO QUESTIONS

When listeners are confronted with a yes/no question, their goal is normally to answer it. They realize that it is a speech act requesting them to provide information about the truth or falsity of one or more propositions. If Ann asks Ed, "Was it JOHN who hit Bill?" he realizes she wants him to affirm or deny that it was John who hit Bill. If Ed is cooperative, he searches memory for who it was that hit Bill. If he finds it was John he replies "Yes," and if he finds it was someone else he replies "No."

As this example suggests, there is an intimate connection between yes/no questions, affirmations, and denials, as in 22, 23, and 24:

22. Was it JOHN who hit Bill?

23. It was JOHN who hit Bill.

24. It wasn't JOHN who hit Bill.

The speaker of 22 assumes the listener already knows that someone hit Bill. What he is requesting is whether that someone is John. Thus, 22 has given and new information as in 22′, where the question mark goes only with the new information:

22′. Given: X hit Bill.
    New: X = John?

The answers to 22, **yes** and **no**, are really shorthand expressions for the affirmation in 23 and denial in 24, which have roughly the given and new information in 23′ and 24′:

23′. Given: X hit Bill.
    New: X = John.

24′. Given: X hit Bill.
    New: X ≠ John.

The parallels here are striking. The three sentences have the same given information, but vary in their new information. Where the question in 22 requests confirmation of **X = John**, the **yes** answer in 23 asserts **X = John**, and the **no** answer in 24 asserts **X ≠ John**.

The given-new strategy ought therefore to be useful for yes/no questions too, but with a slight change in procedure. For 22, listeners should assume they can identify the antecedent for the given information **X hit Bill**. But they should take the new information **X = John** not as unknown information, but as information being queried. Instead of adding **X = John** to memory, as they would for the assertion in 23, they should compare **X = John** with what is already in memory and compose an answer equivalent to 23, **yes**, or to 24, **no**.

Although there has been little experimental work on yes/no questions, there has been a lot on how people judge whether a sentence is true or false—the process of *sentence verification*. In a typical verification experiment people might read **The boy is hitting the girl**, look at a picture of a girl kicking a boy, and say "false" as quickly as possible while being timed. In this task the goal is not to integrate the information into memory (the usual goal for assertions), but rather to provide the experimenter with information about the truth or falsity of the sentence. Formally, then, verifying assertions is virtually identical to answering yes/no questions. Judging **The boy is hitting the girl** to be true or false is like answering the question **Is the boy hitting the girl?** with "yes" or "no." Because of this relationship, sentence verification gives us insights into the process of answering yes/no questions.

Verifying Assertions

People judging a sentence to be true or false often have the impression of going through a series of steps. When told **It's raining out**, they interpret the sentence, look out the window to characterize the weather for themselves, compare their interpretation of **It's raining out** with their characterization of the weather, and respond "true" or "false." H. Clark and Chase (1972, 1974; Chase and H. Clark, 1971, 1972) have formalized this intuition in a model with four stages (see also Trabasso, Rollins and Shaughnessey, 1971; Carpenter and Just, 1975). Each stage is expressed as a command to carry out certain mental operations:

Stage 1: Represent the interpretation of the sentence.

Stage 2: Represent the relevant external evidence.

Stage 3: Compare the representations from Stages 1 and 2.

Stage 4: Respond with the answer computed at Stage 3.

Listeners begin at Stage 1, and by Stage 4 they are able to respond "true" or "false." These four stages will be called the *verification model.*

The operation of the verification model can be illustrated with a task used by Clark and Chase. On each trial, people were shown a card that displayed a sentence on the left and a simple picture on the right, as shown here:

The sentence contained either **above** or **below**, and **star** and **plus** in either order; the picture depicted either a plus above a star, as shown here, or a star above a plus. People were required to read the sentence first, look at the picture second, and then indicate as quickly as possible whether the sentence was true or false of the picture. They gave their answer by pressing a "true" button or a "false" button in front of them. They were timed from the moment the card first appeared to the moment they pressed one of the buttons, an interval called the response or verification latency. For simplicity, the stars and pluses will be replaced by A's and B's such that the picture is always an A above a B.

In the verification model, each stage has one or more mental operations, shown in Table 3–4 for the sentence **B is above A**. At Stage 1, people represent **B is above A** in its propositional form **Above(B,A)**. At Stage 2, they represent the picture, an A above a B. If they are ever to compare it with the sentence,

TABLE 3–4

THE VERIFICATION MODEL

Mental operations and their results in the verification model. The sentence illustrated is **B is above A**, and the picture is of an A above a B.

MENTAL OPERATION	RESULT
Stage 1: Represent the sentence.	Above(B,A)
Stage 2: Represent the picture.	Above(A,B)
Stage 3: Compare the two representations.	
Rule 0: Set Truth Index at true.	Truth Index = True
Rule 1: If 1 does not match 2, change Truth Index to its opposite.	Truth Index = False
Stage 4: Respond with final value of the Truth Index.	Press "false" button

they must represent it in a format compatible with the sentence—as a proposition. Hence the command " Represent the picture " here results in the proposition **Above(A,B)**. At Stage 3, people compare the two representations just formed. Their goal is to compute a " truth index," an index that will eventually carry the correct answer. The comparison process consists of two rules. First, people start with the truth index set at *true*. This is shown as Rule 0, with the result on the right. Second, they compare the two representations. If the two match in every respect, the truth index is left alone. If the two do not match, as in this illustration, the truth index is changed to its opposite, *false*. At Stage 4, people take note of the final value of the truth index, *false*, and press the corresponding " false " button. With that the process is complete.

One prediction of the verification model is that for simple sentences true ought to be faster than false. When the sentence is true of the picture, Rule 1 will not be used. Although the two representations are compared, they match and do not require a change in the truth index. When the sentence is false, however, the two representations do not match and Rule 1 will be required to change the truth index from *true* to *false*. This process ought to consume time. This prediction ultimately relies on the congruence principle, described earlier, which states that it is easier to decide that two representations match than to decide that they mismatch. This prediction has been confirmed in studies by H. Clark and Chase, Trabasso et al. (1971), and many others.

The verification model bears a distinct resemblance to the given-new strategy discussed earlier (Table 3–2). Yet in comparison, the verification model is still lacking in certain ways. For example, how do listeners know what to represent at Stage 2? Even when they are shown a picture with an A above a B, why do they code A's and B's spatial relations rather than other pictorial features—like their size, their place on the display, or their color? And how do listeners compare the representations at Stage 3? Do they check the propositional function **Above(x,y)** first and *x* and *y* later, or the other way around? With more complex sentences and pictures these questions become critical. It should come as no surprise that given and new information play a key role in their answers.

The Role of Thematic Structure in Verification

If verifying sentences is like answering yes/no questions, given and new information *should* play a key role. Imagine listeners asked to decide whether 25 is true or false of a picture:

25. It is the BOY who is petting the cat.

They should assume that the given information **X is petting the cat** is true, a fact they can find in memory. They should also see that their task is to check whether the new information **X = the boy** is true or false. As a result they should selectively code the pictorial information relevant to the truth of **X = the boy**.

Hornby (1974) has demonstrated that listeners do just that. He read people a sentence like 25 and then showed them a picture they were to judge true or false. But the picture was shown for only $\frac{1}{20}$ of a second, and so they often chose the wrong pictorial features to attend to and made mistakes. But which features did they attend to? Sentence 25, for example, was false for two pictures:

A.   B.

If they assume **X is petting the cat** is true and concentrate on checking the truth of **X = the boy**, as the given-new strategy prescribes, they will search the picture for the agent of the action, code whether or not it is a boy, and say "true" if it is and "false" if it isn't. This search strategy will pay off for Picture A but not for Picture B. For the latter they will miss the fact that there is a dog instead of a cat, and say "true" when it is "false." This is what happened not only for sentences like 25, but also for ones like 26 through 28:

26. It is the CAT which the boy is petting.

27. The one who is petting the cat is the BOY.

28. What the boy is petting is the CAT.

When the picture contradicted the new information, errors occurred only 39 percent of the time. When it contradicted the given information instead, errors occurred 72 percent of the time (see also Carpenter and Just, 1977; Loftus and Zanni, 1975).

Active and Passive Sentences

Given and new information may also govern the way listeners verify active and passive sentences. In a series of trials, Gough (1965, 1966) and Slobin (1966a) read people an active or passive sentence, showed them a compatible or incompatible picture the moment the sentence ended, and timed them from the appearance of the picture to their judgment of " true " or " false." In line with the verification model, true sentences were judged faster than false sentences. But in addition, actives were judged faster than passives. Why?

In one experiment Gough tested the possibility that passives take longer only because they are physically longer. He compared full actives like **The boy hit the girl** with the shorter so-called " truncated " passives like **The girl was hit**. Even so, the passives took longer than the actives. In another experiment he tested the possibility that passives take longer to encode initially. He introduced a three-second interval between the end of the spoken sentence and the appearance of the picture and start of the timer. This interval should be long enough for people to interpret the passives—and actives—fully before they view the picture. Yet even with this interval, passives took longer to judge than actives.

What may make passives so difficult is that they lead listeners to code the picture in a way that takes extra time, although this conclusion is still tentative and not fully confirmed. Consider an active sentence Gough used and the given and new information most often ascribed to it in other experiments (Hornby, 1974; Klenbort and Anisfeld, 1974):

29. The boy is hitting the girl.
    Given: The boy is doing X.
    New: X = hit the girl.

If Hornby's study is any guide, people normally assume the given information is true and attempt to verify the new information. For a picture of a girl kicking a boy—which will make the sentence false—here is how the verification model might look:

Stage 1. Represent the given and new information of 29.

Stage 2. Search picture for the agent of the action, A, and code what it is doing: **Kick(A, the boy)**.

Stage 3. Compare the new information in 29 with the representation of the picture.
    Rule 0. Set truth index at *true*.
    Rule 1. Since **Hit(A, the girl)**, does not match **Kick(A, the boy)**, change the truth index to *false*.

Stage 4. Respond " false."

The new information in 29 leads people to search the picture for and code what the agent is doing, namely kicking the boy, and that is what enables them to say "false."

For comparison, consider the corresponding passive in Gough's study:

> 30. The girl is being hit by the boy.
> Given: X is happening to the girl.
> New: X = the boy hits.

For 30, instead of searching for the agent and coding what it did, people would search for the object of the action and code what happened to it. For the picture of a girl kicking a boy, the subject would find the object 0 and code **Kick(the girl, 0)**. But as D. Olson (1972) has shown, it takes longer to search pictures for objects than for agents. Thus, it should take longer to code the appropriate pictorial information for 30 than for 29, and this would explain why passives take longer.

Under the right circumstances, passives can actually be easier than actives. D. Olson and Filby (1972) showed people a picture of, say, a boy hitting a girl and told them to attend to either the agent (the boy) or the object (the girl) in the action. What this did, presumably, was induce them to code the pictures "around" the agent or object, with the agent or object as given information. They were then shown an active sentence like 29 or a passive sentence like 30 to judge as true or false as quickly as possible. When the agent had been coded as given information, the active was faster, but when the object had been coded as given information, the passive was faster. Thus, actives and passives fit different circumstances, and, when used appropriately, may be equally easy to understand.

Picture Codes

The coding of the picture, therefore, plays a critical role in the process by which a sentence is verified against it. This is especially clear when the picture is shown before the sentence to be judged. Then listeners have to represent the picture without knowing which features will be useful for judging the new information true or false. How they represent the picture in these instances is strongly influenced by the nature of the picture itself. Take the pictures in 31 and 32:

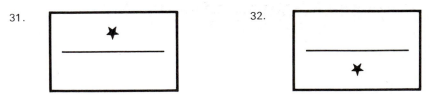

Because the lines make such strong perceptual references, the "star" is seen in relation to the line, and not vice versa. Picture 31 would normally be represented as **Above(star, line)** and 32 as **Below(star, line)**. H. Clark and Chase (1974) had people view one of these two pictures and then read and judge one of the following sentences:

Sentence	Propositional content
33. The star is above the line.	Above(star, line)
34. The line is below the star.	Below(line, star)
35. The star is below the line.	Below(star, line)
36. The line is above the star.	Above(line, star)

If Picture 31 is represented as **Above(star, line)**, Sentence 33 should be judged faster than 34, because 33 matches and 34 does not. And if Picture 32 is represented as **Below(star, line)**, Sentence 35 should be judged faster than 36, because 35 matches and 36 does not. These predictions were confirmed. But when pictures do not have strong references, like this one,

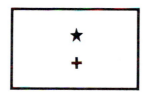

they should normally be represented as **Above(A,B)**. For these, sentences with **above** were verified faster than ones with **below**. The perceptual characteristics that influence how people represent pictures, however, are as yet not very well understood (H. Clark, Carpenter, and Just, 1973).

In verifying assertions, then, just as in recording them, given and new information have a directive function. Listeners normally assume the given information to be true and search for facts relevant to the truth of the new information. When possible they use the new information to select which features of a picture to represent and which not to represent. In the verification model in Table 3–4, then, the representation of the picture at Stage 2 depends critically on the representation of the sentence at Stage 1. This is even more evident in the verification of denials.

Verifying Denials

It is often particularly difficult to judge the truth or falsity of denials. Although **San Francisco is north of Los Angeles** seems easy enough, **It isn't to be denied that San Francisco isn't south of Los Angeles**, which comes to the same thing, strikes us as much more difficult. Because of this complexity, denials have been among the most intensively studied sentences in comprehension. The pioneering work was carried out by Wason (1959, 1961, 1965, 1972; Wason and Jones, 1963; Wason and Johnson-Laird, 1972). In one study he had people judge the truth or falsity of sentences like **57 is not an even number** and **24 is an odd number** and among other things found that denials took about half a second longer to judge than affirmatives. Since then denials have been investigated with strikingly similar findings by many others (see H. Clark, 1974a).

Denials ought to be verified in accordance with their function. Remember that denials are equivalent to suppositions plus their cancellations—as, for example, 37 is equivalent to 38:

37. It wasn't JOHN who hit Bill.

38. You may believe it was JOHN who hit Bill, but that is false.

If Ann says 37 to Ed, he ought to verify it by checking the supposition first, having retrieved from memory the person who did hit Bill. After all, Ann has claimed that he may believe that that person is John. If he believes that it *was* John, then her supposition is true. But since she canceled it, the denial itself must be "false." On the other hand, if he finds that it was Ian who hit Bill, then her supposition doesn't fit the facts and must therefore be false. But since Ann canceled this supposition, her denial must be true anyway.

Roughly speaking, this is what listeners appear to do in verifying denials. They first check the truth of the supposition. When it matches the facts, they are fast, and when it doesn't, they are slow. Listeners then note that the speaker has canceled the supposition, and it takes additional time to realize that if the supposition is true, the denial must be false, or if the supposition is false, the denial must be true. This process leads to two major predictions. First, denials should take longer to judge than affirmatives because taking account of the cancellation takes time. Second, false denials should be easier to judge than true denials because the suppositions in false denials match the facts, while in true denials they do not. These predictions have generally been borne out.

The Amended Verification Model

These ideas have been formalized as part of the verification model by H. Clark and Chase (1972). In their study people sometimes judged sentences like **Star isn't above plus**—schematically **A isn't above B**. This sentence can be represented as a supposition plus its cancellation, as **Above(A,B)** inserted in place of **x** in **False(x)**, "*x* is false." In other words, the denial **A isn't above B**, would be represented as **False(Above(A,B))**. Thus, in the Clark and Chase study there were four kinds of sentences, shown here for the picture of an A above a B:

Sentence Type	Sentence	Underlying propositions
True Affirmative	A is above B	Above(A,B)
False Affirmative	B is above A	Above(B,A)
True Negative	B isn't above A	False(Above(B,A))
False Negative	A isn't above B	False(Above(A,B))

TABLE 3–5

THE AMENDED VERIFICATION MODEL

Mental operations and their results in the amended verification model. The sentence illustrated is the true negative **B isn't above A**, and the picture is of an A above a B.

MENTAL OPERATION	RESULTS
Stage 1: Represent the sentence.	False(Above(B,A))
Stage 2: Represent the picture.	Above(A,B)
Stage 3: Compare the two representations.	
Rule 0: Set Truth Index at true.	Truth Index $=$ true
Rule 1: If embedd*ed* propositions do not match, change Truth Index to its opposite.	Truth Index $=$ false
Rule 2: If embedd*ing* propositions do not match, change Truth Index to its opposite.	Truth Index $=$ true
Stage 4: Respond with final value of the Truth Index.	Press "true" button

The verification model given earlier has to be amended to handle denials, which have two propositions to check instead of one. What has been added in the revised model, shown in Table 3–5, is Rule 2, the sole purpose of which is to handle the **False(x)** in denials. Table 3–5 illustrates how the model applies to **B isn't above A,** which is true of a picture of an A above a B. Stage 1 represents the sentence as **False(Above(B,A))**. Stage 2 represents the picture as **Above(A,B)**. At Stage 3 there are now two comparisons to be made. After Rule 0 has set the truth index at *true*, Rule 1 compares the "embedd*ed*" proposition of the sentence—the supposition **Above(B,A)**—with the picture **Above(A,B)**. Because they don't match, Rule 1 changes the truth index from *true* to *false*. Rule 2 compares the "embedd*ing*" proposition of the sentence—the canceling proposition **False(x)**—with the absence of one in the picture, finds a mismatch, and changes the truth index back to *true*. Stage 4 produces the response "true" corresponding to the final value of the truth index, *true*. These four stages "compute" the correct answer for this true negative sentence, and they also do so for the other three types of sentences.

How long should each sentence take? True affirmatives should obviously be the fastest, since they require the fewest mental operations. The other sentences require one or more additional mental operations:

a. Extra time to represent **False(x)** at Stage 1.

b. Extra time to carry out Rule 1.

c. Extra time to carry out Rule 2.

False affirmatives require *b*; false negatives require *a* and *c*; and true negatives, the hardest of all, require *a*, *b*, and *c*. In one of Clark and Chase's experiments, *a* and *c* together were estimated at about 0.7 seconds, and *b* at about 0.2 seconds.

TABLE 3–6

LATENCY COMPONENTS

Latency components for true and false affirmative and negative sentences in seconds.

SENTENCE TYPE	BASE TIME FOR TRUE AFFIRMATIVE	EXTRA TIME FOR RULE 1: b	EXTRA TIME FOR STAGE 1 AND RULE 2: a + c	TOTAL LATENCY
True Affirmative	1.8			= 1.8
False Affirmative	1.8	+ 0.2		= 2.0
True Negative	1.8	+ 0.2	+ 0.7	= 2.7
False Negative	1.8		+ 0.7	= 2.5

Based on H. Clark and Chase (1972).

If the verification model is right, the times for the four sentence types should be as shown in Table 3–6. False affirmatives, true negatives, and false negatives should take longer than true affirmatives by the increments of time required for their extra mental operations. People's actual latencies fit these predictions almost exactly.

Many people have the intuition that they change their answers very much as the verification model in Table 3–6 suggests. They start by assuming the sentence to be true, change their answer once on false affirmatives and false negatives, and change their answer a second time on true negatives. Take **The dot isn't blue**, said of a red dot. People work as if they first set aside the negative and judge the positive supposition **The dot is blue**. Since it is false, they change their answer to false. But because they had put aside the negative, they must change their answer back to true again. Changing their answer twice takes a great deal of time, and this is why true negatives take so long to verify.

Further Evidence About Denials

By following eye movements as people verified sentences, Just and Carpenter (1976a) were able to demonstrate more directly that the suppositions of denials are checked first. People were shown displays like this:

+

$ isn't north $

$

The sentence contained **is** or **isn't**, and **north, east, south,** or **west**; the plus was in the north, east, south, or west position. People first read the sentence—**isn't**

north meant " The plus isn't north "—and then judged it true or false as quickly as possible. Their eye movements during each trial suggest how they made these judgments. Initially, they spent nearly 0.1 seconds longer reading negative than affirmative sentences. But after that they focused virtually the whole time on the position named in the sentence—north, east, south, or west. For affirmative sentences, then, they checked the new information, and for denials, the new information of the supposition. For **isn't north**, with the supposition **the plus is north**, people checked the north position, not the east, south, or west positions. And the time they spent gazing north closely reflected the number of mental operations required to come to the right answer. Thus, the verification model makes good sense of eye movements too (see also Carpenter and Just, 1972).

The position of the negative in a sentence can make a great difference to the way it is judged (H. Clark, 1974a). For example, Carpenter and Just (1975) compared " predicate negatives," as in 39, with genuine denials, as in 40:

39. It's true that the dots aren't red.

40. It isn't true that the dots are red.

These two sentences are equivalent in truth value, for whenever 39 is true so is 40, and vice versa. Yet they differ subtly in their suppositions. In 39, the speaker affirms a belief that is negative—**the dots aren't red**—while in 40, he denies a belief that is positive—**the dots are red**. When people judged affirmatives, predicate negatives, and denials against pictures for truth or falsity, they were fastest on affirmatives, next fastest on predicate negatives, and slowest on denials

Because denials make certain assumptions about listener beliefs, they should be particularly appropriate when these assumptions are fulfilled. **My wife isn't pregnant** will be appropriate only when the listener might believe that the speaker's wife is pregnant. Wason (1965) argued that denials should be particularly useful for describing an exception to a rule. For example, **Senator Smith isn't a man**, which describes an exception to one's expectations, seems more plausible than **Senator Smith isn't a woman**, which describes a fact as *not* being an exception. Wason confirmed this conjecture by having people view a row of circles all of which were the same color except one. They then judged an affirmative or negative sentence true or false, where the sentence described either a majority circle or the exception. Denials were judged more quickly when they described the exception, although even these took longer to judge than affirmatives.

An Evaluation of Sentence Verification

What can be concluded from this work on sentence verification? Generally the findings are these:

(1) *Mental operations.* Listeners verify sentences in a series of mental operations by which they represent the sentence, represent the relevant external information, compare the two representations, and respond true or false.

(2) *Given and new information.* Listeners generally take the given information as true and identifiable, and they concentrate on trying to verify the new information.

(3) *External evidence.* When possible, listeners try to represent evidence relevant to the truth of the new information. For external evidence they may consult their general knowledge (as for **29 isn't an odd number**), pictures (as for **Star isn't above plus**), or previous sentences (see Greene, 1970a, b).

(4) *Congruence principle.* In comparisons of two representations, it takes less time to find a match than a mismatch.

(5) *Negation.* The extra proposition **False(x)** in denials has at least three repercussions on the verification process. First, it makes denials take extra time to represent initially. Second, it takes up extra memory capacity and slows down the search for relevant external evidence (Howard, 1975; D. Meyer, 1973; Sherman, 1976). And, third, it requires an additional comparison operation—namely, Rule 2—for computing the truth or falsity of the sentence.

The work on verification should nevertheless be read with caution, for in some studies people adopted strategies that probably bear little relation to what they do "naturally." To take one example, after repeated trials in Wason's study, some people reported converting denials into affirmatives before judging them to be true or false. They converted **29 is not an even number** into **29 is an odd number** and then verified the latter. This strategy leads to entirely different verification latencies (see Carpenter and Just, 1975; H. Clark and Chase, 1972; Trabasso et al., 1971). But is this strategy natural? Presumably not. Most everyday denials, like **Robert's car isn't blue**, cannot be converted into affirmatives without loss of information. They have to be handled as denials, and to be optimal, other denials should be handled the same way. To take another example, after many trials, people in Glucksberg, Trabasso, and Wald's study (1973) devised a strategy that ignored the distinction between given and new information. In this particular experiment such a strategy was optimal and decreased latencies, whereas normally it is optimal to pay close attention to given and new information. So this strategy is probably unnatural too. Listeners may turn to such strategies when they have exhausted their normal strategies without success. Even in these two special strategies, however, listeners were shown to represent the sentence, proceed through a series of mental operations, and work by the congruence principle. The special strategies alter only the representations used and the steps taken.

Yes/no questions, to return full circle, exhibit a curious phenomenon that the study of sentence verification can never illuminate—the subtle contrast between **Is Irene there?** and **Isn't Irene there?** In both questions, the listener is requested to say whether **Irene is there** is true or false. Yet for **Is Irene there?** the questioner is noncommittal about the answer, whereas for **Isn't Irene there?** he indicates that while he hopes Irene is there, he expects a no answer (Fillenbaum, 1968). Even more complicated expectations are set up in the contrast between **Do you want some soup?** and **Do you want any soup?** (R. Lakoff, 1969). Since these contrasts do not appear in the corresponding assertions, sentence verification cannot reveal how people go about answering these questions.

TABLE 3–7

GIVEN-NEW STRATEGY FOR ANSWERING WH- QUESTIONS

The question illustrated is **Who sold the book to Mary?**; the listener knows **John sold the book to Mary**.

Step 1: Divide the question into given and new information.
Given: X sold the book to Mary.
New: X = ?

Step 2: Search memory for a unique antecedent that matches the given information.
Antecedent: John sold the book to Mary.

Step 3: Retrieve the wanted (new) information from memory, insert it in place of the question mark, and produce the resulting assertion in simplified form.
New: X = John
Produce: *"John* sold it to her" or *"John* did" or "John."

ANSWERING WH- QUESTIONS

The WH- question **Who stole my Dusenberg?** is a request, not for the truth or falsity of some proposition, but for a specific piece of information. The questioner wants the listener to supply a replacement for the **X** in **X stole my Dusenberg** so that the proposition will be true. The listener's aim then is normally to represent the question, search memory for the requested information, and supply it in a well-formed answer. The aim is the same for all the varieties of WH-questions, as in **What did you steal?, How did you take it?, Why did you take it?, When did you last see it?**, and **Where is it now?**

Like assertions and yes/no questions, WH- questions are utilized largely on the basis of their given and new information. In WH- questions the given information is what results when the WH- word is replaced by **X**, sometimes with certain other adjustments. The new information is really the wanted information that is indicated by the WH- word in itself. This is illustrated in 41:

41. Who sold the book to Mary?
Given: X sold the book to Mary.
New: X = ?

Here again we can turn to the analogy of the postal clerk. The question **Who sold the book to Mary?** is like a request from a customer for a certain message. The postal clerk must search for the pigeonhole labeled **X sold the book to Mary**, take from it the message already there—the name to replace the question mark in **X = ?**—and hand the message over to the customer requesting it. What is critical is that the clerk is guided by the address—the given information—and he must find a pigeonhole that exactly matches that address before he can retrieve the wanted message, the new information.

More formally, answering WH- questions can be broken down into three steps parallel to those in the given-new strategy. These steps are illustrated in Table 3–7 for listeners who know the proposition **John sold the book to Mary** and are asked **Who sold the book to Mary?** At Step 1 they represent the given and new information in the question. At Step 2 they search memory for information matching **X sold the book to Mary** and find the proposition **John sold the book to Mary**, which is then labeled the antecedent. At Step 3, they retrieve what **X** is, namely **John**, and form an answer. The answer is always an assertion formed by replacing the new information in the question **X = ?** by the information just retrieved. The assertion is usually produced in highly simplified form, as in **JOHN sold it to her**, **John did**, **It was John**, or just **John**. The question and answer have the same given information, but where the question has a WH-word, the answer has a piece of new information.

Simple Questions and Answers

So long as listeners have the right information—a proposition in memory that matches the given information—Step 2 is straightforward and answering questions is uncomplicated. In reality this is rare. More often listeners have the relevant information, but have to deduce the answer. Imagine that listeners had in memory, not the proposition **John sold the book to Mary**, but the proposition **Mary bought the book from John**, which is represented as **Buy(Mary, book, John)**. When asked **Who sold the book to Mary?** they will search memory for an antecedent of the form **Sell(X, book, Mary)**, and not be able to find one. Somehow they must realize that the proposition **A sold B to C** entails the proposition **C bought B from A**, and vice versa, and by a series of mental operations, change **Buy(Mary, book, John)** to **Sell(John, book, Mary)**. With that they have an antecedent for **Sell(X, book, Mary)**, and they can proceed to Step 3, retrieve the wanted information, and compose an answer, **John**. These extra mental operations, however, ought to take time, and the question should therefore take longer to answer. The general idea is, then, that whenever the given information of the question doesn't match the information in memory exactly, the process of answering the question should take longer.

This general idea has been demonstrated in a variety of experiments. One such study is K. Smith and McMahon's (1970). On each trial people were presented with a statement like **Bill is leading Bob** and were timed as they answered either **Who is ahead?** or **Who is behind?** The four types of statements and two types of questions that were used are shown in skeleton form in Table 3–8. Smith and McMahon also used **precede** and **trail**, which behaved just like **lead** and **follow**. How should these statements and questions be represented? **Who is ahead?** and **Who is behind?** should be represented as **Ahead(X,Y)** and **Behind(X,Y)**, respectively. Similarly, **A is leading B** ought to be represented as **Lead(A,B)** and **B is following A** as **Follow(B,A)**. But **Lead(A,B)** itself implicitly contains the locative notion **Ahead(A,B)**, and **Follow(B,A)** the locative notion **Behind(B,A)**. If the questions are ever to match the information in these statements, this is the information that must be available.

With these representations, it is easy to see which statement-question sequences should be fast, and which should be slow. **Ahead(X,Y)**, the representation for **Who is ahead?**, matches the representations for 1 and 3, but not 2 and

TABLE 3–8

UNDERLYING CODES

Four statements and two questions used by Smith and McMahon (1970) and the assumed codes corresponding to each. The body of the table shows the answers to each question. The asterisks mark answers for which a readjustment is required to form a match between statement and question.

STATEMENTS	UNDERLYING CODES	WHO IS AHEAD? AHEAD(X,Y)	WHO IS BEHIND? BEHIND(X,Y)
1. A is leading B.	Ahead(A,B)	A	B*
2. B is following A.	Behind(B,A)	A*	B
3. B is led by A.	Ahead(A,B)	A	B*
4. A is followed by B.	Behind(B,A)	A*	B

4. For 2 and 4, people have to realize that **Ahead(A,B)** entails **Behind(B,A)**, and vice versa, and translate from one representation into the other. This should take time, and it did for the people in Smith and McMahon's study. Analogously, **Who is behind?** should be answered quickly for 2 and 4, but not for 1 and 3, and this prediction was borne out too.

The match between question and stored information, therefore, is critical in answering simple questions. This has also been demonstrated for questions about temporal order, comparisons, locations, and actions, as illustrated by these statement-question sequences (see H. Clark, 1974a; H. Clark and Haviland, 1977):

42. The new lady in town was carefully watching the organ grinder and his new monkey. Who was being watched? (Wright, 1969, 1972)

43. Before Max drank the beer, Sally left the party. What happened second? (K. Smith and McMahon, 1970)

44. If John isn't as bad as Pete, then who is best? (H. Clark, 1969)

45. If Mary isn't as high (on the stairway) as John, then where is John? (H. Clark, 1972)

46. It is John who Jim is following. Where is Jim? (Carpenter and Just, 1977)

47. The car hit the truck. What was hit? (D. Olson and Filby, 1972)

In each study the answer was quicker when the question matched the stored information in all the appropriate ways. Yet there is little indication of how people adjust the stored information when it doesn't match the question—they just do. The details of the mental operations required by these simple questions must wait on further research.

Complicated Questions and Answers

Questions in everyday life are rarely as simple as those just illustrated. Many questions, for example, require highly specialized knowledge about the world, as do **What is the capital of Scotland?**, **What are the prime numbers between 20 and 30?**, **How does a car work?**, and **When did Freud write** *The Interpretation of Dreams?* For these one must consult one's knowledge of geography, mathematics, mechanics, and psychology. Many other questions require information about specific events or episodes—for example, **Who came to the party?**, **Why did you leave Muskogee?**, **When did I say that?**, and **Where does Max live?** Before the theory of answering questions is complete, it must specify how knowledge about general facts and specific events is stored in memory and how listeners search, find, and retrieve just the right facts. Here we come to a dead standstill, for little is known about the storage of general or specific facts. Still less is known about the schemes by which listeners retrieve these facts. Indeed, there is no clear line between these complicated questions and the simple ones we looked at earlier. Virtually all questions require knowledge and search schemes of some kind. What the studies on simple questions have done is minimize these factors to bring out the match between question and stored information.

Some questions are complicated because their answers are difficult to compute in the first place, and others because their answers, once computed, are difficult to express. **What is the square root of 113?**, for example, is difficult because its answer requires a long and tedious set of calculations. Once computed, the answer is easy to express. The same goes for the classical " algebra word problems " (Paige and Simon, 1966):

> A stream flows at a rate of two miles per hour. A launch can go at the rate of eight miles per hour in still water. How far down the stream does the launch go and return if the downstream trip takes half as much time as the upstream trip?

Both examples show how close the utilization of sentences is to what is normally called *problem solving*. The question directs people to the problem they have to solve, and from there on, finding the answer is no different from any other type of problem solving. Even the simple questions examined earlier give people simple problems to solve.

Formulating Answers

For other questions listeners must think hard about how their answers ought to be expressed. Take Ann asking Ed **Where is the British Museum?** His answer should depend on where the two of them are standing. If they are in America, he might answer **In London**. If they are in Piccadilly Circus in London, he might answer **In Bloomsbury**. If they are a few blocks away, he might answer **Just down Great Russell Street on the left**. If they are in the London subway system, he might answer **Near the Tottenham Court Road station**. Or take Ann asking

Ed **How does a car work?** If Ann is an adult, Ed will answer one thing, and if she is a four-year-old, he will answer something quite different. In both examples Ed must assess Ann's frame of reference and formulate the answer accordingly. How he does this belongs to the process of planning sentences, a topic taken up in Chapter 6.

Answers may also take hard planning because the listener has to hedge (R. Lakoff, 1973). If David is asked **Where is Madeleine?**, he might reply **Well, she was in the dining room a few minutes ago**. He has implied that Madeleine is *probably* in the dining room, and the reason he thinks so is that she was there a few minutes ago. Unlike the direct answer **In the dining room**, this answer provides the wanted information along with a hedge and a reason for the hedge. Indirect answers are common. People often have only partial answers to questions, and indirect answers enable them to be as helpful as possible.

FOLLOWING INSTRUCTIONS

When listeners are instructed, requested, commanded, ordered, invited, begged, or advised to do something, they are being directed to carry out a series of actions. In English the construction specially designed for many of these directives is the imperative. Imagine that Nancy says to Jeffrey **Wash the dog**. He will have successfully utilized her directive if he figures out what he is being asked to do, plans how to do it, and does it. Most studies of directives have been concerned with instructions, and our discussion here will be confined to them. The utilization question, then, is how people follow instructions.

Drawing by C. Barsotti; © 1974 The New Yorker Magazine, Inc.

Instructions vary enormously in the detail with which they specify the actions to be carried out. Some spell them out step by step, as in the typical recipe:

Simmer and chop about $\frac{1}{2}$ pound of white raisins or put through a blender. Mix 3 cups sugar with enough tepid water to make $4\frac{1}{2}$ quarts in all. . . .

This might be called a *means-oriented instruction*. Others specify only the end product desired, as in the summary request:

Make some choke-cherry wine.

This might be called a *goal-oriented instruction*. The goal-oriented instruction will be easy if the listener has a ready procedure for attaining the goal, but may be very difficult if he does not. Ultimately, every instruction requires a series of actions, and the problem listeners have to solve is what actions will do the job most efficiently. The way they plan their actions depends critically on the instruction.

Following Simple Instructions

The goal-oriented instruction confronts listeners with a problem to solve—how to attain the goal. Imagine a little girl sitting at a table holding a red block, and in front of her a ladder-like structure with a blue block on its middle shelf. For simplicity let us call the red block A and the blue block **B**. The situation is pictured at the top of Figure 3–1. She is then instructed **Make it so that A is above B.** How will she proceed? Roughly speaking, she must go through these steps:

(1) *Decide on the goal.* The goal is to make it so that the proposition **A is above B** is true.

(2) *Code the present situation.* A is movable, and B is fixed in the ladder.

(3) *Plan the actions.* The actions to be planned must change the present situation into the situation described by the goal **A is above B.** This itself requires three steps:
   a. Find something that can be changed. (Since A is movable it can be changed.)
   b. Determine how to make a change so that the present situation is more like the goal. (The child implicitly asks **Where should A go?**, and this is answered by the proposition **A is above B**. She should plan to change A to be above B.)
   c. Check that the planned action achieves the goal. If it does not, return to step 3a and begin again. (Putting A above B will indeed achieve the goal.)

(4) *Carry out the actions planned.* The child picks up A and puts it above B.

Although Steps 1, 2, and 4 are obviously intrinsic to the following of instructions, it is Step 3, the *planning stage*, where the child solves the central problem and most of her difficulties arise. This has been neatly demonstrated in the work of Huttenlocher and her colleagues on goal-oriented instructions. They investigated three situations like the one just described, sometimes with children and sometimes with adults, but always with two blocks and one or more ladders. These are depicted in Figure 3–1. The instructions varied in several ways, but their essential properties can be illustrated by these two sentences:

48. Make it so that A is above B.

49. Make it so that B is above A.

FIGURE 3–1
GOAL-ORIENTED INSTRUCTIONS
Three situations used by Huttenlocher and colleagues.

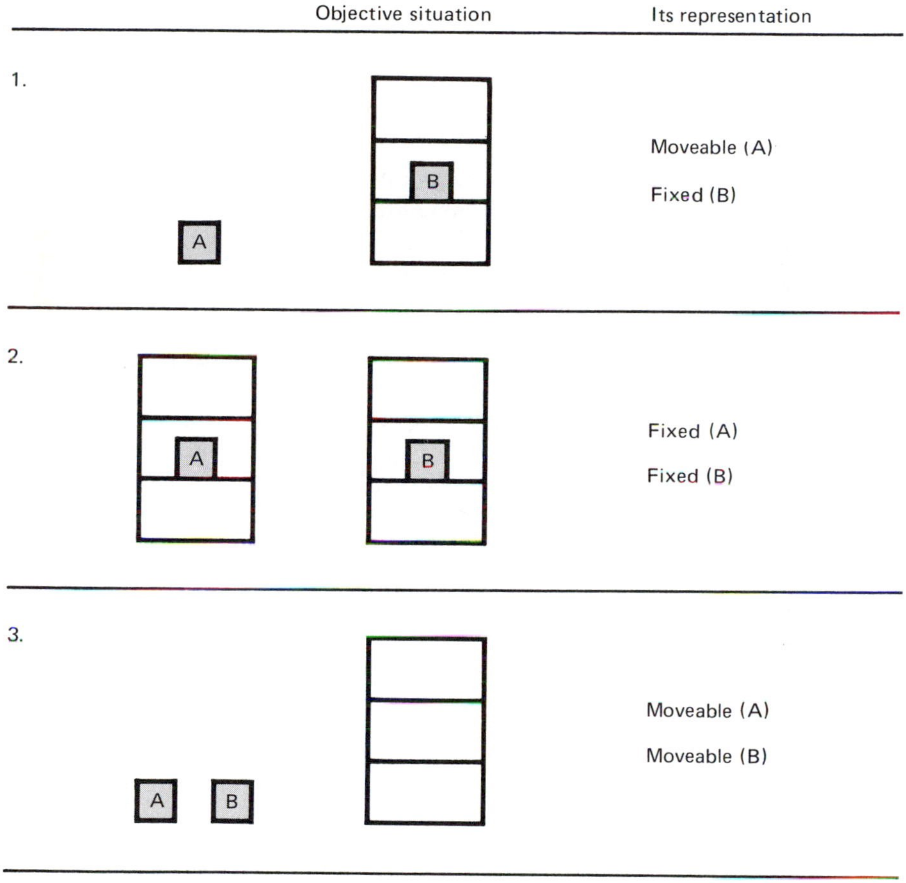

Objective situation	Its representation

How, then, does the child follow these two instructions, and which is harder?

In the first situation (Huttenlocher and Strauss, 1968), A is movable and B fixed, and the planning stage for instruction 48 would proceed as just described:

(a) Which block should be moved? Since A is movable, move A.

(b) Where should A go? Since the goal is **A is above B**, A should be changed so that it is above **B**.

(c) Is the goal attained? Yes.

The critical step here is *b*. **Where should A go?**, with its given information **A is in X direction from B**, matches the information in memory given by the goal **A is**

above B. The question is easy to answer. For instruction 49, however, the question doesn't match the information given by the goal **B is above A**, and so 49 should take longer and lead to more errors. Indeed, 49 led to many more errors among schoolchildren than 48. Instructions like 49 also took adults longer to follow than ones like 48 (H. Clark, 1972; Harris, 1975).

In the second situation (Huttenlocher and Weiner, 1971), blocks A and B are each in the center shelf of a ladder. It is plausible to suppose people plan their actions for instruction 48 by these steps:

(a) What should be changed? Since A and B are both in place, consult the goal **A is above B**. Since this characterizes A as the object located with respect to B, move A.

(b) Where should A go? Since the goal is **A is above B**, A should be changed so that it is above B.

(c) Is the goal attained? Yes.

For instruction 49, where the goal is **B is above A**, the planning would be identical except that people would move B. In fact, A was moved for instruction 48 and B for instruction 49, just as this process suggests (see also Seymour, 1974).

In the third situation (Huttenlocher and Weiner, 1971), people are faced with one ladder and two potentially movable blocks. Here they must move both blocks, but which will they move first? For instruction 48 it is plausible that they proceed this way:

(a) What should be changed? Since A and B are both movable, consult the goal **A is above B**. Since this characterizes A as located with respect to something, move A.

(b) Where should A go? Since A is to go into the ladder and no other block is there yet, A simply goes on one shelf of the ladder.

(c) Is the goal attained? No. Therefore plan further actions.

(a′) What else should be changed? Since B is movable and A is now fixed, move B.

(b′) Where should B go? Since the goal is **A is above B**, which entails **B is below A**, B should be changed so that it is below A.

(c′) Is the goal attained? Yes.

So given 48, children should move A into the ladder first and B second, and, given 49, they should move B first and A second—which is just what Huttenlocher and Weiner found. Yet note that the third situation is more difficult than the second. At step b′, **Where should B go?** should be difficult to answer because it doesn't match the goal **A is above B**. In the second situation there is no such difficulty at step b. And indeed, the third situation elicited more errors than the second.

Following goal-oriented instructions, therefore, is largely a matter of solving problems. Listeners, in effect, ask themselves, "How can I change the present situation into the goal described in the instruction?" The route they take will depend on their perception of the present situation and on the description of the goal. In the Huttenlocher experiments, instructions 48 and 49 led to different actions for each situation, and the three situations led to different actions for each instruction. It is easy to see how the problem to be solved will become harder for more complex situations and more distant goals. In general, the more difficult the problems themselves are to solve—as in **Make some choke-cherry wine**, **Build a house**, or **Figure out your income tax**—the less central a role the instruction itself plays in the process.

With instructions, we have come to the last of three directives: yes/no questions, WH- questions, and instructions. They have two things in common: they direct listeners to act, and in deciding on their action, listeners have a problem to solve. They differ, however, in the act requested and the problem to be solved. Generally, the three directives are progressively less restrictive in the acts requested. For yes/no questions, listeners are restricted to one of two replies—**yes** or **no**. For WH- questions, they are restricted to a reply replacing the WH- word in the question. For instructions, they are hardly restricted at all, so long as they accomplish the goal. On the other hand, the three directives generally require progressively more problem solving. The problems are simplest for yes/no questions, more complex for WH- questions, and typically most complex for instructions. In any event, problem solving plays a vital role in the utilization process. Its role takes on added importance in indirect utilization.

INDIRECT UTILIZATION OF UTTERANCES

Utterances would be relatively easy to utilize if they always carried a clear indication of their illocutionary force. But they do not. Apologies often masquerade as assertions, assertions as questions, questions as requests, requests as predictions, and so on. Under the right circumstances, any one of these sentences can be used as a request to open the window:

Open the window. (*literally a request*)

Would you mind opening the window? (*literally a question*)

I would appreciate it if you opened the window. (*literally an assertion*)

It's hot in here. (*literally an assertion*)

Didn't you forget to do something? (*literally a question*)

What do you think this room is, an oven? (*literally a question*)

Yet not just any sentence can serve this purpose. If so, communication would be chaotic. Listeners would never know what speech act was being performed. Indirect meaning of this sort must, therefore, have bounds—bounds that speakers adhere to in composing utterances and bounds that listeners use in interpreting and utilizing them. Perhaps the most insightful analysis of these bounds has come from H. P. Grice (1967) in his discussion of what he called the cooperative principle.

The Cooperative Principle

In order to communicate accurately and efficiently speakers and listeners try to cooperate with one another. They cooperate, for example, on the simple mechanics of speech. Speakers talk in audible voices, use languages they believe their listeners know, and adhere to the phonology, syntax, and semantics of those languages. Just as important, however, are the conventions speakers and listeners observe in what is said and how it is expressed. Put concisely, speakers try to be informative, truthful, relevant, and clear, and listeners interpret what they say on the assumption that they are trying to live up to these ideals. As Grice put it, speakers and listeners adhere to the *cooperative principle*.

Four Maxims

In observing the cooperative principle, according to Grice, speakers normally try to satisfy four maxims. These maxims are expressed as precepts to speakers as to how they should contribute to a conversation. They are, in summary:

(1) *Maxim of Quantity*. Make your contribution as informative as is required, but not more informative than is required.

(2) *Maxim of Quality*. Try to make your contribution one that is true. That is, do not say anything you believe to be false or lack adequate evidence for.

(3) *Maxim of Relation*. Make your contribution relevant to the aims of the ongoing conversation.

(4) *Maxim of Manner*. Be clear. Try to avoid obscurity, ambiguity, wordiness, and disorderliness in your use of language.

It is easy to see how communication can break down when speakers do not adhere to these maxims. Take a violation of the maxim of quantity:

Steven: Wilfred is meeting a woman for dinner tonight.

Susan: Does his wife know about it?

Steven: Of course she does. The woman he is meeting is his wife.

> [The rules of literary art] require
> that the author shall
> —Say what he is proposing to say, not
> merely come near it.
> —Use the right word, not its second
> cousin.
> —Eschew surplusage.
> —Not omit necessary details.
> —Avoid slovenliness of form.
> —Use good grammar.
> —Employ a simple and straightforward
> style.
>
> Mark Twain, "Fenimore Cooper's
> Literary Offenses"

When Steven described the woman as **a woman** instead of **his wife**, he was not being as informative as he could have been, and Susan took him to mean that the woman was *not* Wilfred's wife. By violating the maxim of quantity, Steven misled Susan. Or take the maxim of quality. Information could hardly be exchanged accurately if listeners could not tell which statements were true and which were not. As for the maxim of relation, communication would also break down if listeners could not tell which utterances were relevant and which were not. Conversations would only progress toward their goals very slowly without the maxim of relation. And the maxim of manner is just as important. Ambiguous, obscure, disorderly, and wordy sentences can have just as deleterious effects on communication as the violation of any other maxim.

Implicatures

These maxims are more than a code of conversational etiquette. They are critical to the very meaning of what the speaker said. Consider this exchange (from Grice, 1967):

Barbara: I am out of gas.

Peter: There is a gas station around the corner.

On the surface Peter has merely asserted the presence of a gas station nearby. But by implication he has conveyed something more. He expects Barbara to realize he has adhered to the maxim of relation and so his contribution is relevant to what she had just said. And if she takes it to be relevant, she will see that he means that the station is probably open and sells gas. This is an instance of what Grice called *conversational implicature*. Although Peter hasn't said directly that the gas station is open and sells gas, he has " implicated " it. If Barbara is to utilize Peter's utterance as he intended her to, she must construct this implicature as part of what he meant to convey.

Grice noted that speakers can also bring about conversational implicatures by flouting one of the maxims—by blatantly violating a maxim while still holding to the cooperative principle. Take sarcasm, as when Barbara tells Peter **That was certainly a terrific play we saw tonight** while knowing that he knows she thinks it was a terrible play. In saying this Barbara is flouting the maxim of quality—she is obviously not being truthful. But she expects Peter to see that, and that she is still adhering to the cooperative principle, so by implication she means her comment to be taken as sarcasm, as meaning the opposite of what she said. Understatement, irony, and metaphor work in much the same way. Or take Marion's reply when asked how well she liked the man she had dinner with the night before: **He had neatly polished shoes**. In so saying, Marion is flouting the maxim of quantity—she is not being as informative as is required. By picking out an irrelevant attribute to remark on, she implicates that his important attributes didn't please her. Or take Malcolm's circumlocution in **Miss Gainsborough produced a series of sounds that corresponded closely with the score of "Home Sweet Home."** By avoiding the simple **Miss Gainsborough sang "Home Sweet Home,"** Malcolm has flouted the maxim of manner and has implicated that Miss Gainsborough's singing wasn't very good.

Listeners, then, must always ask themselves implicitly " Why did the speaker say what he said?" Knowing that the speaker is adhering to the cooperative principle, with its maxims of quantity, quality, relation, and manner, they can usually see why quite accurately. Yet nothing has been said so far about *how* they see. What is the process by which listeners construct the implicatures they were meant to see? One area where this question has been studied is in the comprehension and utilization of indirect speech acts, especially indirect requests.

Indirect Speech Acts

The cooperative principle plays an especially important role in indirect speech acts. When a duke says to his servant **It's hot in here, Charles**, the servant realizes that the duke has asserted that it is hot in the room. But the servant reasons further: " Why did the duke assert that here, now, under these circumstances? Being hot is uncomfortable, and since my job is to attend to his comforts, he must be asking me to make it less hot in the room by opening the window." The duke's direct speech act is an assertion. That is its literal meaning. Yet by uttering this assertion he has also performed an indirect speech act, a request to open the window. That is its indirect meaning. In Grice's terms, the duke has implicated, by the maxim of relation, that he is requesting the servant to open the window, and the servant has understood it as such. The duke could have accomplished the same thing by asking **Does the window need to stay closed?** As a question, it would elicit the answer **No**, but it would also be taken as a request to open the window. In such cases listeners utilize *both* the direct *and* the indirect meanings, even though their ultimate interest is in the indirect meaning (Searle, 1975b).

The Use of Felicity Conditions

How are indirect speech acts conveyed? The problem has been studied most extensively for indirect requests, and for them there are four general methods by which A can indirectly request B to perform some action (see Gordon and Lakoff, 1971; Searle, 1975b):

(1) *Ability.* Assert to B that he is able to do that action, or ask B whether or not he is able to do that action, as in **You can leave me the car keys** and **Can you reach the salt?**

(2) *Desire.* Assert to B that you want him to perform the action, as in **I want you to hand me the car keys** and **I would appreciate it if you passed me the salt.**

(3) *Future action.* Assert to B that he will do that action, or ask B whether or not he will do that action, as in **You will leave me the keys to the car** and **Would you pass the salt?**

(4) *Reasons.* Assert to B that there are good reasons for doing the act, or ask B whether or not there are good reasons for doing the act, as in **You should hand me the keys to the car** and **Why don't you pass me the salt?**

These four methods of making indirect requests are closely tied with what it means to make a sincere request in the first place. For A to request B to close the window, for example, A must:

(1) believe that B has the ability to close the window,

(2) have the desire that B should close the window,

(3) believe that B will close the window if requested,

(4) have good reasons for B to close the window.

As the numbering shows, each of these conditions on the proper use of requests —Austin (1962) and Searle (1969, 1975b) called them "felicity conditions"— corresponds to one of the methods for making indirect requests. This is an extraordinary correspondence. It suggests, in effect, that speakers make indirect requests by making use of the social conventions that cover proper use of requests, and listeners interpret them by use of the same conventions. In the same way, speakers and listeners make use of social conventions about promises, questions, assertions, and warnings when they utter and interpret indirect promises, questions, assertions, and warnings (Heringer, 1972; Searle, 1975b). This process works because speakers and listeners expect each other to be co-operative and adhere to these social conventions about the sincere use of speech acts.

Computing Indirect Meaning

Just how listeners compute indirect meaning is far from clear, but as a first approximation the process has these four major steps (H. Clark and Lucy, 1975; Gordon and Lakoff, 1971; Searle, 1975b):

> *Step 1:* Compute the direct meaning of the utterance.
>
> *Step 2:* Decide if this meaning is what was intended. Are there sufficient and plausible reasons for the speaker to have intended to convey this meaning, or this meaning alone, in this context?
>
> *Step 3:* If not, compute the indirect meaning by way of the cooperative principle and the conventions on speech acts.
>
> *Step 4:* Utilize the utterance on the basis of its indirect meaning.

For the duke's utterance **It's hot in here, Charles**, the servant would compute the direct meaning at Step 1, decide it was not the sole meaning intended at Step 2, conclude it must be a request to open the window at Step 3, and utilize the utterance on the basis of its indirect meaning at Step 4, opening the window.

In an attempt to test for aspects of this process, H. Clark and Lucy (1975) had people deal with various pairs of positive and negative indirect requests, as illustrated here:

> 50. a. Can you open the door?
>   b. Must you open the door?
>
> 51. a. Why not open the door?
>   b. Why open the door?
>
> 52. a. I would love to see the door opened.
>   b. I would hate to see the door opened.

In the right circumstances, 50a, 51a, and 52a will be taken as requests to open the door, and 50b, 51b, and 52b will be taken as requests *not* to open the door. Request 50a gets its interpretation from the method called Ability; 50b, 51a, and 51b from the method called Reasons; and 52a and 52b from the method called Desire. Many other pairs of positive and negative requests were included as well. The interest was in two points. First, if listeners utilize these sentences on the basis of their indirect meaning (Step 4), then the positive requests should behave like other affirmative sentences, and the negative requests like other negative sentences, regardless of their direct meanings. Second, if listeners compute the direct meaning (Step 1) in getting to the indirect meaning (Step 3), the difficulty of computing the direct meaning should make a difference too.

On each trial people were presented with a request, like **Can you open the door?**, together with a picture, like one of an open door. They were timed as they decided whether or not the request was satisfied by the situation depicted. In effect, this task was equivalent to a sentence verification task, and that enabled Clark and Lucy to use the logic of the verification model as it applies to affirmative and negative sentences. The indirect requests yielded verification times very much as predicted. Each negative request took longer than its affirmative counterpart. In other critical respects too, the negative requests behaved like negative sentences and the affirmative requests like affirmative sentences. What is striking here is that the surface features of the requests were often in conflict with their indirect meaning. Although **Can you open the door?** and **Must you open the door?** are both superficially positive questions, **Can you?** behaved like a positive sentence and **Must you?** behaved like a negative. Among other things, **Must you?** took about 0.3 seconds longer to judge than **Can you?** More dramatically, although **Why not open the door?** is superficially negative and **Why open the door?** superficially positive, **Why not?** behaved like a positive sentence and **Why?** like a negative. **Why?** took about 0.3 seconds longer to judge than **Why not?** What counted, then, was not whether the direct meaning was positive or negative, but whether the indirect meaning was.

Yet there was also evidence that people computed the direct meaning first. Consider these two pairs of indirect requests:

53. a. I'll be very happy if you open the door.
    b. I'll be very sad if you open the door.

54. a. I'll be very sad unless you open the door.
    b. I'll be very happy unless you open the door.

Although the corresponding requests in 53 and 54 are identical in their indirect meanings—they mean either "open the door" or "don't open the door"—they differ in their direct meanings. The two assertions in 53 make the happiness of the speaker dependent on the door being opened, whereas those in 54 make it dependent on the door *not* being opened. That is, the pair in 54 is more complex in direct meaning than the pair in 53—**unless** is implicitly the negative of **if** (see Chapter 12). If people compute the direct meaning (Step 1) before they come to the indirect meaning (Step 3), they should take longer on 54 than on 53. This prediction was confirmed. On the average, 54 took about one second longer than 53.

Do listeners sometimes get at the indirect meaning without first computing the direct meaning? Imagine this conversation:

Barbara: What did you ask me to do?

Peter: Could you open the door?

By Peter's reply, Barbara is ready for a request, not a question, and so she might try to compute a request meaning directly. She could do so on the basis of very little of his reply—maybe only the words **open the door.** Very young children do just that. Before they understand how indirect requests work, they respond to such requests as **Can you open the door?**, **Must you open the door?**, and **Should you open the door?** by opening the door (Shatz, 1974). Note that they are led to the *incorrect* action on the latter two requests. If adults use this method, they must usually go on to compute the direct meaning. Otherwise, how could Barbara know she should answer Yes to Peter's direct question before acting on his indirect request? Also, listeners are keenly aware of politeness distinctions among indirect requests. Between equals, **Open the door, I want you to open the door**, and **You will open the door** are normally impolite, while **Could you open the door?**, **Would you mind opening the door?**, and **Won't you open the door?** are polite. To notice these gradations, listeners must normally compute the direct meaning, noting the method the speaker had used to convey the request (R. Lakoff, 1973). The issue, however, is complex and needs more investigation.

Other Kinds of Indirect Meaning

The cooperative principle appears to be critical to the utilization of sentences in other ways too. One is in the finding of referents by the given-new strategy, as discussed earlier. Reconsider these two pairs of sentences:

17. Mary got some beer out of the car. The beer was warm.

18. Mary got some picnic supplies out of the car. The beer was warm.

To find the referent for **the beer** in 17 and 18, listeners have to assume that the speaker has been cooperative—that he has used **the beer** to refer to some beer they can identify uniquely. For 18 they are therefore forced to add the bridging assumption in 18′:

18′. The picnic supplies include some beer.

We called 18′ an implicature, and indeed it has all the hallmarks of other Gricean implicatures (H. Clark and Haviland, 1977; H. Clark, 1977). Thus, the given-new contract—the agreement about how to use given and new information—can be thought of as one part of the cooperative principle.

There are many other agreements like the given-new contract. One governs the use of **and** in conjunctions (Fillenbaum, 1974b, R. Lakoff, 1971):

The common topic contract. Conjoin two ideas with **and** or **or** only if they belong to a common topic.

To see its importance, compare 55 and 56:

55. He will eat an orange and she will drink tea.

56. He will eat an orange and the horse lost the race.

Whereas one can find a common topic for the ideas conjoined in 55—consuming food—one cannot find one for 56. And while 55 is plausible enough, 56 is very strange indeed—despite the fact that it is *logically* possible. Another agreement is this (H. Clark and E. Clark, 1968; E. Clark, 1971, 1973c; Grice, 1967; Schmerling, 1975; Wilson, 1975):

The order of mention contract. Mention two events in the order in which they occurred.

This explains why the order of sentences in narratives is taken to convey the order of the events being described, unless there is some indication to the contrary.

These two contracts, along with other parts of the cooperative principle, may explain why the word **and** is interpreted differently in these four sentences:

57. John is handsome and Bill is tall.

58. John got up and left.

59. John fell down and broke his arm.

60. Fall down and you'll break your arm.

The simplest interpretation of **and** is in 57, where it is equivalent to the logician's **&**. **And**, however, means "and subsequently" in 58, "and consequently" in 59, and "and if that happens, consequently" in 60. These three interpretations are indirect. In 58, **and** is interpreted as **&**, but by the order of mention contract the two actions—getting up and leaving—are assumed to have occurred in that order. In 59, **and** is again interpreted as "and subsequently," but by the common topic contract, the falling down is assumed not only to have preceded the arm-breaking, but also, as part of the same episode, to have caused the arm-breaking. In 60, the same logic applies, but the two events are hypothetical and in the future. A similar explanation accounts for the different interpretations of **or** in these sentences:

61. John will arrive by train or by plane.

62. John will wear a brown jacket or hat.

63. Be careful or you'll break your arm.

Little is known about the process by which listeners utilize the ordered events in 58, 59, and 60 or the ordered alternatives in 63. There is evidence, however, that the ordered alternatives in 63 take more time to represent and utilize than the ordered events in 60. Consider 64 and 65, and their paraphrases in 64' and 65':

64. Flip the switch and the light will go on.

65. Flip the switch or the light will go on.

64'. Flip the switch, and if you do, the light will go on.

65'. Flip the switch, and if you don't, the light will go on.

As their paraphrases show, 64 is like a simple conditional, whereas 65 is like a negative conditional. For this reason Springston and H. Clark (1973) argued that 65 ought to take longer to interpret and utilize than 64. They timed people as they solved a variety of problems like this:

66. If the sign says " Don't flip the switch or the fan goes on " and the fan did go on, then did you flip the switch?

People were faster on **and** than on **or**. And the time they took fit the idea that ordered alternatives, as in 65, have a negative element somewhere in their indirect interpretation, whereas simple ordered events, as in 64, do not (see also Fillenbaum, 1974b).

Word Choice

Very generally, listeners draw inferences from the speaker's choice of one word over another. In reporting the death of King Henry VIII's second wife Ann Boleyn, for example, a historian could say one of four things:

67. Ann Boleyn died in 1536.

68. Ann Boleyn was killed in 1536.

69. Ann Boleyn was executed in 1536.

70. Ann Boleyn was beheaded in 1536.

If the historian had said 67, readers would assume that, so far as was known, she had died a natural death. They infer this from the maxim of quantity—that the historian will provide as much information as is required. If he knew she had been killed, executed, or beheaded, he would have been more specific, using Sentences 68, 69, or 70. In a demonstration of this phenomenon, Kintsch (1972) asked people to say what they could infer from various types of sentences. For **Ivan was killed**, they inferred that he had intentionally been killed by someone. If Ivan had been killed by accident, the speaker would have been more specific. For **Ivan was shot**, they inferred that the instrument used was a gun. If he had been shot by some other means, the speaker would have specified the means. Neither inference, of course, is strictly legitimate. Yet most listeners would draw much the same inferences because they assume the speaker is being cooperative.

The few examples considered here have barely scratched the surface of indirect meaning. They suggest that listeners go beyond virtually every word they hear in search of what is really meant. A large proportion of what people understand of an utterance probably comes not from what it says directly, but from what is inferred from it indirectly, via the cooperative principle and the implicatures it induces. It is clear, however, that very little is known about the process by which people make these inferences. There is an extraordinary amount left to be learned.

SUMMARY

When people listen to someone speak, their job is normally to try to see what he meant them to do with his utterance and then do it. He has performed a speech act, and he means his listeners to identify it and react accordingly. This is the utilization process, and it was discussed in this chapter for four major types of speech acts: assertions, yes/no questions, WH- questions, and instructions. The assertion **It's raining out** expresses the speaker's belief that it is raining out, and listeners are meant to record the belief. The yes/no question **Is it raining out?** directs listeners to tell the speaker whether the proposition **It is raining out** is true or false. Cooperative listeners will provide a yes or no answer. The WH- question **Who killed Cock Robin?** directs listeners to provide the speaker with an X such that the proposition **X killed Cock Robin** is true, and cooperative listeners will produce a description of this X. And the instruction **Go home** directs listeners to do something to accomplish the goal of going home, and they will have complied once they have planned the action and carried it out. Other speech acts require still other reactions.

Given and new information play an especially important role in the utilization of utterances. For the assertion **It was JOHN who hit Bill**, for example, listeners generally take the given information **X hit Bill** as identifiable, search memory for its antecedent, and attach the new information **X = John** to that antecedent. For the yes/no question **Was it JOHN who hit Bill?**, they compare the new information **X = John** against their knowledge of who hit Bill for a match or mismatch. And for the WH- question **Who hit Bill?** they retrieve information from memory to complete the new information **X = ?**, where X is the someone who hit Bill. Given and new information determine what listeners take as known and unknown, how they search memory, and what they attend to in pictures.

Inference and problem solving are central to the utilization process—from beginning to end. For a start, listeners have to infer what speech act is being performed. Is the speaker asserting something, asking a question, making a request, or what? Although the answer can often be inferred directly from the direct meaning of the utterance, it sometimes has to be inferred indirectly using the cooperative principle. From there on, listeners have other problems to solve. What does the given information refer to? Do I know the answer the questioner wants? How should I express the answer? How can I accomplish the goal being requested? What implicatures should I add to the direct meaning of the utterance? Solving all these problems is no easy matter. It takes all the knowledge, skill, and attention listeners can apply, and even then they sometimes fail. It is in the utilization of utterances that language makes full contact with our full cognitive abilities.

Further Reading

This chapter relies heavily on two notions: speech acts, and given and new information. Fortunately, there are excellent discussions of both. Austin (1962) and Searle (1969, 1975a) describe speech acts with great clarity. Chafe (1970), Halliday (1970), Jackendoff (1972), and Kuno (1972, 1975) each take up the linguistic distinction between given and new information (Jackendoff uses the terms "presupposition" and "focus"). There are several further sources for more detailed discussions of the utilization process itself. H. Clark & Haviland (1977) and Carpenter and Just (1977) both review the role of given and new information in recording assertions. H. Clark (1974a) takes up more of the details about sentence verification, with special emphasis on the role of negation. Wason and Johnson-Laird (1972) present a provocative discussion of the role of negatives, comparatives, and other constructions in reasoning. As for answering questions and following instructions, Winograd (1972) and Woods (1968, 1975) have excellent discussions of the utilization of language by computers. Finally, there are good discussions of indirect speech acts available by both linguists and philosophers. The book edited by Cole and Morgan (1975) includes Grice's seminal essay on the cooperative principle, Searle's and Gordon and Lakoff's discussions of indirect requests, and other pertinent papers. Sadock (1974) presents another view of indirect speech acts.

Recollect, v.   To recall with additions something
not previously known.

Ambrose Bierce, *The Devil's Dictionary*

Memory for Prose

Memory plays an integral part in listening from the moment the first sound
hits our ears to our recollection, years later, of what was said. In the construction
process it is the halfway house where sounds and words are stored, and it is the
final storehouse for the propositions that are built from them. In the utilization
process it is the place where new information is stored, asked-for information is
sought, and planned actions are placed. It is also the archive for the facts and
and general knowledge that are used in inferring indirect meanings. This chapter
focuses on one aspect of this capacity: memory for passages once heard or read.
This is a natural continuation of the construction and utilization processes discussed in Chapters 2 and 3.

WHAT AFFECTS MEMORY?

Memory for prose depends on many factors:

(1) *Type of language*. Was the passage an ordinary conversation, a formal
lecture, a play, a poem, or a list of unrelated sentences in a psychology
experiment?

(2) *Input*. Did we hear it passively, try to memorize it word for word, listen
for the gist only, or listen for nothing but grammatical errors?

(3) *Retention interval*. Did we hear it a moment ago or a year ago?

(4) *Output*. Are we trying to recall it verbatim, or only trying to decide for a
test sentence whether or not it was what we had originally heard?

All of these factors affect the content and accuracy of what we remember.

To say "I remember x" is to make one of three claims. For example, the statement "I remember that Ken told Julia 'Come here'" is a claim that Ken uttered the exact words **Come here**. However, "I remember that Ken told Julia to come here" is a claim, not about Ken's exact words, but about the intended interpretation or "gist" of his message. Again, "I remember Lincoln's *Gettysburg Address*" is a claim about one's ability to repeat the speech word for word. It is not a claim about an event that took place at the time something came into memory, but about an enduring piece of general knowledge. These distinctions between verbatim and gist memory, and between episodic and general memory, are each important to the remembering process.

But what is most important about this characterization is that remembering is *making claims about* past events, not merely "retrieving" representations of the events themselves. While remembering does require that information be retrieved from memory, like notes fetched from a pigeonhole, these notes are used only as a starting point for the claims. The notes will usually be incomplete, garbled, and even contrary to common sense. But since people can safely assume that the original passage did not contain these flaws, they will not want to claim that it did. They will make corrections to insure that their claim sounds sensible. For reasons like this, remembering is often said to be a reconstructive process. People remember passages by piecing together what information they can retrieve, adding outside information and making corrections wherever necessary to get them to make sense.

In its barest outlines, remembering has three stages: input, storage, and output. The pigeonhole analogy will serve nicely here. On hearing a passage, listeners jot down notes about its contents on pieces of paper. This is the input. Next, they place these notes in a pigeonhole in memory until they need them. This is storage. During this time some of the notes can become lost or smudged. At the time of recall, they fetch the notes from their pigeonhole and from this fragmentary information reconstruct what they thought was in the original message. This is the output. It is instructive to examine these three stages more closely before turning to memory more generally.

Input

Normally, in conversation, people take in speech, build interpretations, purge memory of the exact wording, and go on to use their interpretations for their intended purposes. People generally listen for meaning. They do not store the verbatim wording or even the direct meaning of the speech, which is used only for drawing further inferences. Instead, they normally store the inferences themselves, the situation modeled, or whatever else the interpretations have been used for. It should come as no surprise, then, that people cannot usually recall speech word for word. They were listening not for what was said but for what was meant.

In "unusual" situations, however, verbatim memory can become important.

An actor may have to memorize *Hamlet*, a student Keats's "Ode on a Grecian Urn," and a churchgoer the Lord's Prayer. When they do this, they apply a rather special skill, one that requires repetition and much hard work. The same people would be utterly unable to listen to a conversation and reproduce it word for word an hour later. So memorization, though clearly a topic of memory, is unrepresentative of the "normal" course of input and may require very different processes.

The input situations that have actually been studied run the gamut from the "normal" to the "unusual"—from listening for meaning to outright memorization. Most fall nearer the "unusual" end of the continuum. For example, when people are asked to read ten unrelated sentences and then recall them, they do not read for meaning alone. They try to memorize, to pay close attention to the surface details, for they want to be able to recall the sentences word for word. So what do these experiments tell us about the "normal" situations? Recent experiments suggest that "normal" situations are quite different. The input situation is one of the most critical determinants of what people remember.

Storage

Psychologists have traditionally distinguished between short-term memory and long-term memory (but see Craik and Lockhart, 1972). *Short-term memory* is a place where exact wording is stored for brief periods of time. Words can be maintained there only through active rehearsal—as when we repeat telephone numbers to ourselves—and are otherwise lost very rapidly. Short-term memory has a limited capacity. It can hold only about seven or so unrelated words at a time. *Long-term memory*, on the other hand, is the place where more permanent information is stored. It deals generally in meaning rather than sounds, and for all practical purposes it has unlimited capacity. The information in long-term memory is often divided theoretically into episodic information (facts about everyday events that can be dated) and general knowledge (facts and generalizations that cannot be dated) (Tulving, 1972). Although this chapter will continually refer to general knowledge, it is primarily concerned with memory for episodic information.

In the traditional framework, short-term memory corresponds roughly to what has been called the working memory in the construction process. You will recall that working memory is where the phonological content and isolated constituents of a sentence are placed. Just like short-term memory, it stores surface features, can handle only a limited capacity, and loses its contents very rapidly. But working memory is also the place where the interpretation of a sentence is first stored. Unfortunately, very little is known about the storage of interpretations in short-term memory, so it is hard to see whether it corresponds to working memory in this way or not (but see Craik and Lockhart, 1972; Shulman, 1970, 1972). Working memory, then, may differ slightly from traditional views of short-term memory.

Long-term memory for episodes is most often claimed to be in the form of a network of propositions, perhaps accompanied by visual, auditory, and other kinds of imagery (see Chase and H. Clark, 1972; Kintsch, 1972, 1974; Rumelhart, Lindsay, and Norman, 1972). This view has been implicit so far in the construction and utilization processes. The interpretations of a sentence consist of propositions, and in the utilization process, they were added to memory, retrieved from memory, and compared against other propositions in memory. The role of imagery in memory for prose is much less clear and will be touched on only peripherally.

In the memorization of prose, however, long-term memory must also be able to store verbatim forms accompanied perhaps by such auxiliary information as "the first word was **four-score**," "the sentence was in the active voice," and "there were many multisyllabic words." The verbatim content may not even be accompanied by meaning in the usual sense. Some Hausa-speaking Nigerians, for example, memorize the whole Koran without knowing a word of classical Arabic, the language of the Koran. So long-term memory must have the capacity to store verbatim forms alone.

Output

The two methods for tapping memory are recognition and recall. In a recognition test, people are shown a sentence and asked if it was one they had seen or heard before. They may be shown two or more sentences and asked to point to the one they had seen or heard before. In a recall test, on the other hand, people have to produce or write down a sentence or passage they had been given previously. Sometimes they are prompted with a word or phrase—like the subject of a sentence—and asked to recall the corresponding sentence. Recognition is usually more accurate than recall.

In both recognition and recall, people utilize three kinds of outside information. They may refer to their language to decide what are possible, sensible constructions, and what are not. They may use world knowledge to decide what are plausible realistic situations or events, and what are not. (This is the reality principle.) And finally, they may refer to conventions about discourse to decide how stories are constructed, how paragraphs are organized, and how conversations proceed. Such information makes it possible to rule out sentences that could not have occurred and settle on ones that could. Linguistic knowledge, world knowledge, and conventions of discourse have striking consequences for the recognition and recall of prose.

The rest of this chapter takes up the input, storage, and output processes pertinent to memory for prose. It begins with verbatim recall, works through memory for more and more abstract features of the language input, and concludes with memory for paragraphs, stories, and other kinds of discourse. This progression follows the characteristics of the input—what people were listening for, and what kind of passage they were listening to. Memory adheres to the dictum: You can't get out what you haven't put in.

SHORT-TERM MEMORY

Psychologists have traditionally studied short-term memory by asking people to recall digits, letters, or unrelated words. People are presented a series of from six to twelve random digits, one per second, and are immediately required to repeat them back in their correct order. Most people can do this up to about eight digits, after which they make mistakes, and so are said to have a memory span of eight digits. For letters the memory span is about seven items, and for unrelated words, about six. This makes short-term memory seem like a tape recorder with a limited length of tape. It records exactly what it hears and can repeat it back exactly, as long as it hasn't gone past the limit of the tape available.

But this comparison is not really valid. First, memory span is limited not by the number of digits, letters, or words it can hold, but by the number of "chunks" it can hold, where a chunk is a meaningfully coded unit. For example, when words make up larger constituents, as they do in sentences, memory spans in terms of *words* increase dramatically—up to twenty to twenty-five words depending on the sentence. This suggests that constituents and their interpretations play a central role even in immediate verbatim recall. Second, short-term memory does not simply store the order of the words as they arrive at the ear. In recalling unrelated words or digits, people often interchange pairs of items in the sequence, and the same happens in recalling sentences. Third, short-term memory doesn't record exactly what it hears.

Fallibility of Short-Term Memory

Intuitively, six-word sentences ought to be exceedingly easy to repeat. If the memory span is about seven chunks of material, six-word sentences with perhaps only three major constituents should fall well within the span. Yet some six-word sentences are consistently repeated incorrectly, and the reasons why are instructive. This has been shown in an elicitation technique called the "compliance test" in which people were read a sentence and asked to write it down immediately after performing a simple modification (Greenbaum, 1969; Greenbaum and Quirk, 1970; and Quirk and Svartvik, 1966). For example, given the sentence **He badly needed the money**, they might have to change **he** to **they** and write down **They badly needed the money**. Although they were strongly urged to make only the one alteration, and despite the simplicity of the task, they made a surprising number of additional changes, apparently without awareness. Words were left out, moved around, and sometimes changed altogether. At the same time, the sentences they wrote down were almost always normal English sentences.

What these people did was write down sentences that conformed to the normal use of words in English. Here, for example, are three sentences compared by Greenbaum (1970):

1. He badly needed the money.
2. He badly wounded the elephant.
3. He badly treated the servant.

For 1, people had to change **he** to **they**, and for 2 and 3, they had to change the verbs from past to present tense. (Elsewhere these two changes were shown to be about equal in difficulty.) There were 100 percent correct responses on 1, 77 percent on 2, and only 34 percent on 3. The three sentences appear to have the same structure, so why the difference in errors? Greenbaum argued that **badly**, when it means "much" as in 1, conventionally goes just before the verb it modifies. But when it means "a bad wound" as in 2, or "in a bad manner" as in 3, it conventionally goes at the end of the clause. Since 2 and 3 violate this ordering preference, **badly** is often unwittingly placed at the end of the clause where it belongs. Greenbaum, Quirk, and Svartvik examined many other preference rules and demonstrated that people tended to err consistently there too.

Where in the memory process do these changes arise? There are at least two plausible answers. Assume that short-term memory is very bad about preserving word order. Then, to get the word order right, people must rely on the constituents they have isolated and the interpretation they have built. These usually enable them to reconstruct a unique word order, the right one. But where there are options, as in **He badly treated the servant**, they are often led to reconstruct the wrong word order in conformity with the preference rules. Alternatively, assume that short-term memory is accurate in preserving word order, but people don't believe what they find there. They say to themselves, "**Badly** before **treated** sounds wrong; my memory must be in error; **badly** must have been at the end." And so they "correct" the sentence in their reconstruction. Of these two explanations, the first is favored by the work on digits and unrelated words.

Short-term memory records even less information about the hesitations, repeats, and stutters so common to spontaneous speech. J. G. Martin and Strange (1968; J. G. Martin, 1971) had people listen to speech that was replete with hesitations and had them repeat it back verbatim. Some people were specially urged to include all pauses. As expected, no one was able to reproduce the hesitations accurately. The people with special instructions inserted more hesitations into their reproductions all right, but at the wrong places. At the same time, the more closely people listened for hesitations, the worse they became in their verbatim recall of the sentence. It appears that people normally filter out these "errors" and store only the words they think were intended. So having to attend to and encode speech errors takes away from people's processing and storage capacity for normal content and leads them to more errors in recall. Short-term memory is apparently not equipped to store the irrelevancies of speech.

Short-Term versus Long-Term Memory

All the same, short-term memory tends to preserve verbatim content, whereas long-term memory tends to preserve meaning. In a striking demonstration of this distinction by Sachs (1967) people were asked to listen to tape-recorded passages taken from factual articles. At odd intervals the passage was interrupted by a bell and they were shown a test sentence to judge as "identical" to, or "changed" from, one they had heard before. The test sentence came either zero, forty, or eighty syllables after the original. For the original sentence **A wealthy manufacturer, Matthew Boulton, sought out the young inventor**, there were four types of test sentences:

4. A wealthy manufacturer, Matthew Boulton, sought out the young inventor. (*identical*)

5. A wealthy manufacturer, Matthew Boulton, sought the young inventor out. (*formal change*)

6. The young inventor was sought out by a wealthy manufacturer, Matthew Boulton. (*passive/active change*)

7. The young inventor sought out a wealthy manufacturer, Matthew Boulton. (*semantic change*)

Sentence 4 should be judged "identical," and 5, 6, and 7 "changed." Note, however, that 5 and 6 preserve the meaning of the original approximately, whereas 7 does not.

The percentages of test sentences judged correctly are shown in Figure 4–1. Test sentences 4, 5, and 6, which preserved the meaning of the original sentence, looked almost exactly alike and are plotted as a single line marked "same meaning." Test sentence 7 is plotted separately and marked "different meaning." These curves show that immediately after hearing a sentence (at zero syllables), people are quite accurate on all test sentences. They still have enough verbatim content to detect the subtle change in wording of test sentence 5. But after forty syllables (about twelve and one half seconds), they have lost most verbatim content and fail to detect even the gross change of wording in test sentence 6. The "same meaning" test sentences are not much above chance level (50 percent) after forty or eighty syllables. Yet, as time passes, people remain quite accurate in detecting gross changes in meaning. The "different meaning" curve for test sentence 7 remains relatively high at both forty- and eighty-syllable intervals. In short, verbatim wording is lost very rapidly, but meaning is retained over much longer periods.

Sachs's findings fit very comfortably with the construction process described in Chapter 2. In that process, listeners build an interpretation from verbatim wording, but then get rid of this wording soon after crossing a sentence boundary, leaving only the interpretation. Accordingly, they are good at verbatim recognition immediately after hearing a sentence and poor thereafter. Yet they remain accurate in detecting gross changes in meaning (see also Flores d'Arcais, 1974a).

The contrast between short-term and long-term memory has been demonstrated in retrieval time as well. J. Anderson (1974) read people a story, then showed them a "test sentence" to be judged true or false of an event in the story. These events were sometimes expressed in the active voice (**The painter**

FIGURE 4–1
SACHS'S EXPERIMENT

Percentage of correct judgments of "same" or "changed"
when the test sentence had the same meaning as the original
sentence, and when the test sentence had a different
meaning from the original sentence (at three intervals).

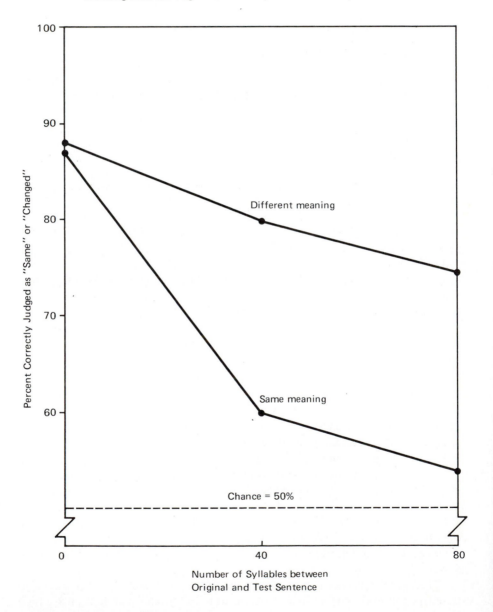

Adapted from J. S. Sachs (1967).

visited the missionary), sometimes in the passive (**The painter was chased by the missionary**), and the test sentences were sometimes active and sometimes passive. When an event was tested right after it had been mentioned in the story and was still in short-term memory, there was a strong influence of verbatim content. The test sentences were judged true much faster when they were in the same voice as the original sentence. But when an event was tested two minutes after it had occurred in the story, the influence of such verbatim content was almost nil. Garrod and Trabasso (1973) demonstrated much the same phenomenon but found that the first sentence in short paragraphs also appeared to be retained verbatim, even after some interval of time.

Yet even after a two-minute interval, people in Anderson's study were able to recall some information verbatim. The explanation Anderson favored was that people retain at least *some* verbatim wording over longer intervals—especially when they know they are going to be tested. An alternative explanation is that people retain thematic information, like what is subject or given information (see Perfetti and Goldman, 1974). In Anderson's experiment, when the test and original sentences had the same subject, they were judged slightly faster. The same explanation could be applied to the first sentence in Garrod and Trabasso's short paragraphs.

All this evidence suggests that both verbatim wording and semantic interpretations are retained in short-term memory, but "normally" only semantic interpretations in long-term memory. Yet in no sense does short-term memory retain all the surface features of an utterance. Hesitations, stutters, and other irrelevant features are normally filtered out and cannot be reproduced with any accuracy after a short time. Word order is not represented accurately either, and subtle changes can creep in during immediate recall. Generally, short-term memory is merely a halfway station in the course of comprehension. The more time listeners have had to work on an utterance, the less they have of its form and the more they have of its substance.

MEMORIZATION

At some time or another everyone has committed to memory a poem, a passage from Shakespeare, or the lyrics of a song, and it wasn't easy. The passage had to be repeated again and again with special attention paid to its exact wording. With great dedication people have been able to memorize very long passages indeed—*The Hunting of the Snark*, the New Testament, or the *Iliad* and the *Odyssey*. The principles behind memorization are mostly obvious. Passages will be easier to memorize if they are meaningful, grammatical, short, in the learner's own language, and complete with rhyme and meter to anchor the surface structure. But what does the work on memorization say about the storage of exact wording in long-term memory? The answer to this question is much less obvious.

In memorization the goal is to be able to reproduce a passage word for word. Since the surface features are normally jettisoned soon after a sentence is understood, memorization requires that these features be specially represented and placed in memory. But which features? Presumably, they include specific words—synonyms will not do—and the constituent structure, with all that it entails. Yet they do not include repeats, stutters, hesitations, and other such irrelevancies. These are normally not deemed worthy of memorization, for they are not part of the sentence, but part of the speaker's attempt to utter the sentence. What is not so obvious, however, is that people also make heavy use of interpretations in memorizing a sentence. In recall they use what is retrieved about the interpretation to help reconstruct what the surface structure must have been.

The importance of meaning in memorization was demonstrated neatly by Marks and Miller (1964; see also N. Johnson, 1968) in an experiment in which people were asked to memorize one of three types of sentences: "grammatical" sentences like 8, "anomalous" sentences like 9, and "ungrammatical strings" like 10.

8. Accidents kill motorists on the highways.

9. Trains steal elephants around the highways.

10. Between gadgets highways passengers the steal.

Sentence 8 should be easiest, since it contains constituent structure and makes sense; 9 should be harder, since it has constituent structure but does not make sense; and 10 should be hardest, since it neither has constituent structure nor makes sense. This is what Marks and Miller found. Since both 8 and 9 have constituent structure, people must be relying on the interpretation of 8 to help them recall it better than 9.

But what units of surface structure are represented? As studies of mistakes in recall reveal, the units are constituents of various sizes. In a study by N. Johnson (1965; 1966a, b; 1968), people memorized sentences like:

11. ((The (tall boy))(saved (the (dying woman))))

12. (((The house)(across (the street)))(burned down))

In the course of memorization, they were less able to proceed to the next word when it belonged to a new constituent. **The tall boy** was recalled as a unit; **tall boy saved** was not. The more constituent boundaries people had to cross, the less likely it was they could go on.

This finding alone has two interpretations. People could have stored the words and each more-inclusive constituent. Or they could have stored both constituents and their interpretation. The findings of Marks and Miller add weight to the second explanation. **The tall boy** is easy to recall as a unit not just because it forms a constituent, but because the constituent has a coherent interpretation. **Motorists on the highways** is easier to memorize than **elephants around the high-**

ways. It seems likely that most memorization reflects two kinds of stored information: surface constituents and underlying propositions. Memorization without meaning is rare and very difficult.

MEMORY FOR UNRELATED SENTENCES

In many investigations, people are put through a grueling and frustrating experience. They are shown a series of unrelated sentences one at a time and are later asked to recall them. This is just one step away from memorization but without all its advantages. They know they will have to recall each sentence, and for that they will need the exact wording. But they have only one chance to study each sentence, and the sentences do not form a coherent passage. It shouldn't be surprising that the recall of unrelated sentences bears some resemblance to memorization, even though recall typically allows one viewing and memorization many. In both, people are intent on storing both the exact wording and the underlying propositions.

Of course the task was designed not to please people, but to induce errors that would reveal the nature of what is stored in memory. To this end the task has been relatively successful. It has shown that:

(1) the proposition is a basic unit in long-term memory,

(2) reconstructions from memory are subject to strong biases, and

(3) the instructions at input are critical to what is remembered.

The most fundamental issue is probably the first: the proposition is a basic unit in memory for sentences.

The Proposition in Memory

In 1962 George Miller brought what were at the time new and innovative linguistic principles to bear on the question of what people remember of a sentence. His proposal, as applied to 13, went something like this:

13. Was the boy hit by the girl?

To understand 13, people "de-transform" it into a simple active affirmative declarative, or "kernel," sentence (**The girl hit the boy**) plus some "footnotes" specifying the linguistic transformations needed to reconstitute the original. For 13 the kernel sentence would have to be "transformed" to a passive to give **The boy was hit by the girl** and then into a question to give **Was the boy hit by the girl?** so 13 would be represented as 14:

14. The girl hit the boy $+ T_{Passive} + T_{Question}$

T$_{Passive}$ indicates the passive transformation, and T$_{Question}$ the question transformation. This is what is stored in memory. In recall, people retrieve these three elements (the kernel and two footnotes) and put them together to reconstruct the original sentence in 13.

The most direct consequences of Miller's proposal were for comprehension. It implies that the more transformations to be undone in comprehending a sentence, the longer comprehension should take and the more difficult it should be. This proposal was later called the *theory of derivational complexity*. Despite initial support (for example, G. Miller and McKean, 1964), the theory soon ran into deep trouble. The problem was that it mispredicted a host of examples about which sentences should be easy or hard to comprehend (see Fodor and Garrett, 1967; Watt, 1970b). It predicted, for example, that **That that that David wanted to go amazed Hazel is obvious** should be easier to understand than **It is obvious that Hazel was amazed that David wanted to go**. The theory was eventually replaced by the collection of proposals discussed in Chapters 2 and 3.

Yet there was a grain of truth in Miller's proposal. It assumed that sentences are ultimately represented as kernel sentences plus information about how they fit together. Altered a little and put into our terminology, it assumed that sentences are represented as propositions plus their interrelations. This, of course, is what has been assumed to be the end product of the construction process, as discussed in Chapter 2. In particular, Miller argued that for a sentence like 13, people were likely to retain the kernel sentence (**The girl hit the boy**) and forget the rest (the two footnotes). This has been demonstrated in restricted circumstances both for recall (Mehler, 1963) and for recognition (Clifton and Odom, 1966).

Propositions and Constituents

If propositions are basic units in memory, they should be remembered and forgotten as units. Consider 15 and its propositions in 16:

15. The thief who owns the car despises bankers.

16. a. The thief owns the car.
    b. The thief despises bankers.

People should sometimes remember 16a and not 16b, or vice versa, recalling **The thief owns the car**, or **The thief despises bankers**, without being able to recall 15 itself. One consequence of this view is that surface constituents should be recalled as units, since most constituents specify a single proposition plus its arguments. In a study by H. Clark (1966) people were required to recall unrelated sentences of this form:

17. ((The (old man))(closed (the door)))

When they recalled **man**, for example, they were more likely to recall **old**, another immediate constituent of **old man**, than **closed** or **door**, immediate constituents of **closed the door**. The proposition **Old(man)** that underlies the constituent **old man** may be what makes this possible.

But there is a problem in interpreting this evidence. Do people remember the surface constituents themselves, or the propositions that underlie them? The evidence fits either interpretation. Wanner (1974), following up work by Blumenthal (1967), suggested a way around this problem. First, one must use two types of sentences with the same surface constituency, but with different underlying representations. Any difference in memory between the two sentence types can then be attributed to their different underlying representations. Second, one might use prompts for recall. People can be given one word from a sentence and be required to recall the remainder. If propositions are units of memory, people should be able to recall all those words that belong to propositions the prompt word is also part of, but not necessarily any words from other propositions.

Memory Prompts

This reasoning can be applied to several experiments by Blumenthal (1967; Blumenthal and Boakes, 1967). In one study, people had to recall sentences of two types:

18. (John (is (eager (to please))))

19. (John (is (easy (to please))))

As the parentheses show, the constituents of 18 and 19 are alike. Superficially, the two sentences differ only in the adjective **eager** versus **easy**. But 18 and 19 have different underlying representations, as shown in 18′ and 19′:

18′. a. John is eager for something.
    b. John pleases someone.

19′. a. Something is easy.
    b. Someone pleases John.

In 18′ the complement inserted in place of the empty noun **something** is **John pleases someone**, while in 19′ it is **Someone pleases John**. While 19 can be paraphrased as **It is easy to please John**, 18 does not have the corresponding paraphrase **It is eager to please John.**

In recall, people were given a single word from 18 or 19 as a prompt. How effective should **John** be as a prompt? In 18, it is part of both proposition 18′a and proposition 18′b. In 19, on the other hand, it is part of only one of the two propositions: 19′b. So in 18, prompting with **John** should lead to the recall of both propositions, while in 19 it should lead to the recall of just the one, which is only part of the sentence. **John** should be a more effective prompt for 18 than for 19. That is what Blumenthal and Boakes found. Also, **please** was as effective a prompt for 18 as for 19, as it should be. **Please** gets at only one of the two propositions in either sentence.

The same logic has been applied in other studies too (see Blumenthal, 1966; Levelt and Bonarius, 1973; Wanner, 1974), but these have been plagued with problems. The main one is methodological. Note that in 18 **John** is the agent of the proposition **John pleases someone**, while in 19, it is the object of the proposition **Someone pleases John**. **John** may be a better prompt in 18 because it is an agent—an active, salient role—while in 19 it is not. The prompting effectiveness of agents and objects cannot be distinguished from the prompting effectiveness of a word from one versus two propositions. It is also difficult to find sentences like 18 and 19 that are equal in "semantic coherence" (Levelt, 1974). For example, in a comparison of **Children are anxious to play** (type 18) with **Rome is fun to visit** (type 19), **children** may be a better prompt than **Rome** because of the stronger semantic link between **children** and **playing** than between **Rome** and **visiting**. When Levelt and Bonarius (1973) repeated Blumenthal and Boakes's study in Dutch and Finnish with these factors carefully controlled, they failed to find the predicted result. Other predicted findings have failed to materialize too.

Propositions in Recall and Memory Search

Perhaps the most thorough attempt to show that propositions are units of memory has been made by J. Anderson and Bower (1973). They carried out a long series of studies, using a variety of techniques, and provided much evidence for the propositional nature of memory. Only a taste of that evidence can be presented here.

In one study Anderson and Bower demonstrated that when a proposition is repeated in new sentences on successive lists to be recalled, it aids in that recall. People were first given a list of sixteen sentences to recall, and on it was a sentence like this:

20. The hippie who touched the debutante was tall.

They were then given a second list to recall, and on it was one of two sentences:

21. The *hippie* who kissed the prostitute was *tall*.

22. The captain who kissed the *debutante* was *tall*.

Both 21 and 22 repeat a pair of words from 20 on the first list: **hippie** and **tall**, and **debutante** and **tall**. These two words constitute a single proposition in 21—**The hippie was tall**—but not in 22. Which kind of repetition should help more, the repetition of two words constituting a proposition (as in 21), or the repetition of two words not constituting a proposition (as in 22)? The answer, obviously, is the first. If propositions are units of memory, people hearing 21 have only one new proposition to learn (**The hippie kissed the prostitute**), while people hearing 22 have two (both **The captain was tall** and **The captain kissed the debutante**). As expected, Anderson and Bower found that the recall of 21 was helped by the repetition, while the recall of 22 was not.

A second technique Anderson and Bower used was to provide people with selected prompts for recall, as Blumenthal and Wanner had done, and then to look at what parts of the sentence they were able to recall. In one study people were shown many sentences all of this form:

23. The hippie who kissed the prostitute touched the debutante who liked the captain.

Later, they were given prompts in the form of a sentence frame:

24. The ____ who kissed the ____ ____ the ____ who liked the ____.

They were to fill in the blanks.

What should happen here? Sentence 23 expresses the following three propositions:

25. a. The hippie kissed the prostitute.
    b. The hippie touched the debutante.
    c. The debutante liked the captain.

The verb **kissed** should therefore prompt proposition 25a, enabling people to recall both **hippie** and **prostitute**. In some instances, however, they will recall **hippie** and not **prostitute**, or **prostitute** and not **hippie**. As Anderson and Bower argued, those people recalling **hippie** but not **prostitute** should recall **touched** quite often, since **hippie** is part of proposition 25b too and enables them to get at **touched**. But those people recalling **prostitute** but not **hippie** have no element from proposition 25b and so they should recall **touched** much less often. Anderson and Bower confirmed this and several other similar predictions. Note that the evidence here goes against a theory that predicts simply that recall of one word in a sentence leads to recall of the next. If this theory were right, people should have recalled **touched** more often when they had first recalled **prostitute** (the previous word) than when they had recalled **hippie** (five words before). This did not happen. So here again, propositions seem to be basic units in memory.

Another technique of Anderson and Bower's showed the role of propositions in memory search. They used lists of sentences with elements repeated one, two, or three times, as in this short list:

A hippie is in the park.
A policeman is in the park.
A sailor is in the park.
A sailor is in the store.
A judge is in the church.

After studying longer lists of this kind, people were shown test sentences and asked to say, as quickly as possible, whether the sentence was or was not on the list.

The rationale was that people will attach all those propositions about one kind of person, or about one location, to a single "node" in memory. When tested, they first find the person and location mentioned (say, **hippie** and **park**) and then search all the propositions containing those two elements until they find the test sentence. The more propositions they have to search, on the average, the longer they should take. For example, people should be fastest in saying "yes" to **A judge is in the church**, since both its elements appear just once in the list; they should be slower on **A sailor is in the store**, since **sailor** appears twice; they should be slowest on **A sailor is in the park**, since **sailor** appears twice and **park** appears three times. Anderson and Bower confirmed these predictions. From evidence like this, they argued that such sentences are stored in memory as propositional units, for those units are what people search through in judging whether or not a sentence was on the list.

All in all, the hypothesis that propositions are units in memory has good though not conclusive support. The problem is that it is a difficult proposal to test unambiguously. So many other factors can reduce the influence of propositions that it can almost disappear. One of these factors is people's biases in reconstructing sentences.

Biases in Reconstructing Sentences from Memory

In remembering, people retrieve bits and pieces from memory in order to reconstruct sentences they can honestly claim to have heard or read before. Although they rely on propositions for some of these pieces, they may use quite incidental pieces of information too. Bregman and Strasberg (1968), after testing people's recognition for a list of unrelated sentences, questioned them on how they selected the test sentences they did. Most reported using *adjunct information*, information not actually part of the meaning of the sentence. Some remembered that a particular sentence was controversial, or contrary to fact; others remembered some vivid action they associated with the sentence; and still others remembered details about specific words ("the word **boy** came first" or "the sentence had **by** in it, so it must have been a passive"). The important point is that people are often quite aware they are reconstructing sentences from partial and often adjunct information.

Bias Toward Normality

Because people work from incomplete information, they are highly susceptible to biases in their reconstructions. Principal among these is the *bias toward normality*. Imagine that Ann has just studied many unrelated sentences, some active and some passive. In trying to recall one of them, she remembers that it was about a pirate finding a treasure. But was it active or passive? Since she cannot remember, she reasons as follows (though, of course, not explicitly). Actives are the normal sentence. Passives are used mainly when the object of the verb is the thing of interest, or when the agent is new information. Both of these circumstances are out of the ordinary. If the sentence about the pirate finding the treasure had been passive, she would have remembered that it had been "marked" for one of those special purposes. Since she doesn't, it must have been active, that is, **The pirate found the treasure**. Like other people, she implicitly knows which of two constructions is normal and which is "marked" for special use. At recall, she selects the normal construction unless she retrieves information that specifically indicates it should be a non-normal construction.

E. Turner and Rommetveit (1968) demonstrated how strong the bias toward normality can be. School children were asked to study active and passive sentences each paired with a picture. Later, they were shown a series of pictures and asked to recall the sentence appropriate to each. The sentences used were of two types:

26. The cat chases the dog.

27. The dog is chased by the cat.

In the study period, each sentence was paired with one of three types of pictures:

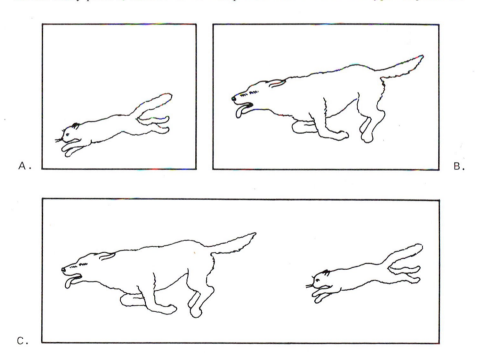

At the time of recall, the children were probed for a particular sentence (say, 26 or 27) with any one of the three pictures, not necessarily the one it was paired with at the time of study. As it turned out, it mattered very little which picture had been paired with which sentence at the time of study, but it mattered a great deal which had been paired with which at the time of recall.

The children were biased toward treating the picture they were probed with as what the sentence was about—as the subject of the sentence. When probed with Picture A, they produced actives (like 26) 54 percent of the time and passives (like 27) only 11 percent of the time, although the two percentages ought to have been equal. When probed with Picture B, on the other hand, they produced actives 12 percent of the time and passives 50 percent of the time. For both pictures the overwhelming choice was a sentence in which the subject referred to the thing in the picture. When probed with Picture C, the children produced actives 74 percent of the time and passives 23 percent of the time. So when the picture didn't create a bias of its own, they responded in conformity with the well-attested bias toward actives: the bias toward normality.

There are similar biases with other constructions. In another study (H. Clark and E. Clark, 1968) people were required to recall sentences with main and subordinate clauses. Included among the sentences were four types:

28. He caught the rabbit before he jumped the stream.

29. Before he jumped the stream he caught the rabbit.

30. He jumped the stream after he caught the rabbit.

31. After he caught the rabbit he jumped the stream.

In recall, people were biased toward two assumptions:

(1) the main clause should come before the subordinate clause (as in 28 and 30), and
(2) the two events should be mentioned in chronological order (as in 28 and 31).

The first bias reflects the strong preference in English sentences for the subject to come first. In 29 and 31 it doesn't. The second bias reflects the "order of mention contract" mentioned in Chapter 3. Unless marked otherwise, two clauses normally describe events in the order in which they occurred. From the two biases together, 28 should be produced most often, and 29 least often, and that is what happened. There are also biases toward comparative (**bigger than**) over equative (**as big as**) constructions (H. Clark and Card, 1969), and toward affirmative over negative sentences (Cornish and Wason, 1970).

Instructions

What and how much people remember of a sentence depends on how they dealt with the sentence in the first place. People cannot possibly recall the meaning of a sentence if they didn't put that meaning into memory during the time of study. The only information retrievable from memory is information placed there at the time of study, and that is greatly affected by the instructions. If people are told to ignore meaning, they can hardly be expected to recall it later. It should come as no surprise that instructions play a critical role in determining what is remembered.

The two major hypotheses as to what instructions do are about *depth of processing* and *focus of processing*. The first, stated earliest by Bobrow and Bower (1969), is that the more deeply people comprehend a sentence, the more of it they will be able to recall. The second, investigated principally by Tieman (1972), is that the aspect of a sentence people focus on in study will be remembered better than other aspects of the sentence. These two hypotheses complement each other. By focusing on different aspects of a sentence—for example, its surface structure or its meaning—people will recall the sentence differently. But recall is best when people know the meaning of a sentence, so the more attention that is focused on meaning, the better their recall.

Depth of Processing

Depth of processing was examined by Bobrow and Bower (1969) in two related studies. In the first, people were shown a series of sentences of the form **The cow chased the rubber ball**. After reading each sentence aloud, they were asked one of two kinds of questions. One group was asked whether a specific word, say **ball**, was misspelled or not; the other was asked which meaning **ball** had in that sentence, "round object" or "dance." Later, without warning, they were told this was a memory experiment; they were given the first noun of each sentence (e.g., **cow**) and were required to recall the second (**ball**). The people who had looked for misspellings, which required rather shallow processing, recalled the second noun only 18 percent of the time. The people who had answered questions about word meanings, which required rather deep processing, recalled 49 percent of the words, almost three times as many. In a second study, people were shown a sentence and required either to repeat the sentence aloud several times, a task that required rather shallow comprehension, or to provide a sentence that could sensibly follow the study sentence in a story, a task that required rather deep comprehension. Again, without warning, these people were later given the first noun and asked to recall the second. The repetition people recalled the second word only 22 percent of the time; the continuation people recalled it 43 percent of the time, about twice as often. Greater depth of processing clearly led to better recall.

The depth of comprehension hypothesis was examined by Mistler-Lachman (1974) in tasks that all required processing for meaning. People were given a series of sentences and asked to do one of three things:

(1) decide whether each sentence was meaningful or anomalous,
(2) decide whether each sentence followed from a previous sentence, or
(3) make up a sentence that could follow the sentence in a story.

Mistler-Lachman argued that these three tasks require increasing depth of comprehension and should therefore lead to increasing amounts of recall. As expected, people recalled 19 percent of the words in the sentences in the first condition, 26 percent in the second, and 29 percent in the third.

Focus of Processing

The focus of processing hypothesis has been tested by Tieman (1972) in several studies. In each, people were read a long list of comparative sentences like 32:

    32. The butcher is smarter than the baker.

Later they were given a recognition test with four choices (in random order) and asked to check the correct alternative:

    33. a. The butcher is smarter than the baker. (*completely correct*)
        b. The butcher is dumber than the baker. (*noun-order preserving*)
        c. The baker is smarter than the butcher. (*adjective preserving*)
        d. The baker is dumber than the butcher. (*meaning only preserving*)

If they had remembered 32 exactly, they should of course check alternative *a*. But if they made an error, they would check *b*, *c*, or *d*, depending on what aspect of the sentence they had remembered. If they had remembered the meaning but not the exact wording, they should check *d*, since it alone preserves the ordering of the butcher and baker in intelligence—the "meaning" of the sentence. But if they had remembered some part of the exact wording but not the meaning, they should check *b* or *c*, for *b* preserves the order of the two nouns **butcher** and **baker**, while *c* preserves the adjective **smarter**. They should not check *d*, since it preserves none of the exact wording of 32. In short, this test could determine which information people remembered better: exact wording or meaning.

   The focus of processing was varied by the instructions Tieman gave. Some people were told to remember the sentences by forming a visual image of the relations in each—to get the meaning right and not worry about the exact wording. Others were told instead that they would be tested on the exact wording, so they should not be fooled by sentences that meant the same thing but were worded differently. As expected, alternative *d* was checked more often by people with the imagery instruction than by those with the verbatim-focused instruction. Alternative *d* comprised 50 percent of the errors of the meaning-focused group, but 30 percent for the verbatim-focused group. On the other hand, alternatives *b* and *c* together were given more often by people with the verbatim-focused instruction than by people with the meaning-focused instruction, 70 percent to 50 percent. So people remember the surface features of a sentence when they focus on its exact wording, but its "meaning" when they focus on its meaning. In addition, the meaning-focused group chose the correct alternative *a* more often than the verbatim-focused group. This suggests a greater depth of comprehension under the meaning-focus instruction.

" *Normal* " *Study*

But if conscious strategies at study time are so critical, what do people normally do—when there is no memory test looming in the future? In an inspired study of this problem, Wanner (1974) concealed a memory experiment within a very normal situation. He gave people taking part in an experiment the following sentence as part of their instructions:

> When you score your results, do nothing to your correct answer but mark carefully those answers which are wrong.

At the end of the instructions he gave them a surprise test on this sentence, which they had listened to closely but had not expected to be tested on. The test looked like this:

When you score your results, do nothing to $\begin{Bmatrix} \text{correct your} \\ \text{your correct} \end{Bmatrix}$ answer but $\begin{Bmatrix} \text{mark carefully} \\ \text{carefully mark} \end{Bmatrix}$ those answers which are wrong.

People were to circle the pair of words they thought they had heard.

The two different pairs of words led to quite different results, as Wanner had expected. **Correct your** and **your correct** give the sentence entirely different meanings, whereas **mark carefully** and **carefully mark** are stylistic variants and almost identical in meaning. People were correct 100 percent of the time on **your correct** but only 50 percent of the time on **mark carefully** (where 50 percent is chance level). Other people who were warned they might be asked to remember the instructions did about the same on **your correct** (93 percent), but reliably better than the unwarned group on **mark carefully** (73 percent). A warning like this apparently invites people to focus more attention on such superficial features as word order, and that leads to the better recognition of **mark carefully**. From Wanner's study, one might conclude that memory in "normal" situations is for meaning.

MEMORY FOR SUBSTANCE

Is memory in normal situations really memory for "meaning"? Not exactly. It is really memory for the products of comprehension, and they aren't necessarily the same as the meaning of a sentence. Take Wanner's experiment. In it people "studied" the instructions (including the critical sentence) for no other reason than to know what to do in the experiment. What they intended to remember was not the meaning of the instruction itself, but rather some product of their comprehension of it. For example, in accordance with the utilization of instructions like this, they might have represented and stored the series of actions they were expecting to carry out. In Chapter 3, we examined many products of the utilization process—what normally goes on after one has taken in the direct meaning of a sentence. It is these products people should store in memory, having discarded the immediate product of the construction process— the direct meaning of the sentence. This type of memory will be called *memory for substance*.

Considerations like these might lead one to criticize the work just reviewed on memory for unrelated sentences. These studies, the argument would go, do not simulate normal comprehension and cannot tell us much about memory for substance. Because the sentences are unrelated, people cannot organize them, fit them into a larger context, provide referents for the nouns, or rely on external information in their comprehension, all strategies they would normally use. This criticism is correct, but overstated. Studies of memory in normal situations, because of their inherent imprecision, could probably not have shown that propositions are basic units in memory, that the reconstruction of sentences is subject to strong syntactic biases, and that the kind and amount of information remembered depends critically on the study strategies people use. Indeed, the studies of unrelated sentences tell us what to look for in "normal" situations— for propositions, reconstruction biases, and even different "study" strategies. Memory for substance simply pushes us to take a more global view of memory, for there are many new external factors influencing people's comprehension of the sentences to be remembered.

If memory for substance is memory for the products of comprehension, what are they? The listeners' main goal in comprehension, it will be recalled, is to integrate the new information from assertions with what they already know, to find answers for questions, to develop plans for instructions, and so on. In each instance, they go beyond the direct interpretation of a sentence. For example, they identify the real-world entities that definite noun phrases (e.g., **the dog**) refer to. And they compute the indirect meaning of an utterance whose intended meaning does not coincide with its direct meaning. A number of studies suggest that it is these products that people normally store in memory.

Implications

One thing people commonly do in comprehension is draw the obvious implications. On hearing **The policeman was shot**, people infer from their knowledge of the world that the instrument used was probably a gun, not a bow. On hearing **The fragile glass was dropped on the floor**, they infer that it probably broke. People seem to draw these inferences easily and automatically, and in memory tasks especially, they draw them as a strategy for giving them more information from which they can reconstruct the sentence later on. The immediate implications of a sentence should turn up as objects of memory. This has been demonstrated many times over.

Among the first to demonstrate it was Fillenbaum (1966). He read people a long list of unrelated sentences of the type **The sailor is alive**, **The window is not closed**, and **The postman is dishonest** and later gave them a multiple-choice recognition test for each sentence. Take the sentence:

34. The window is not closed.

For 34 the multiple-choice test consisted of these alternatives (in random order):

35. a. The window is not closed. (*completely correct*)
    b. The window is closed. (*preserves the main proposition*)
    c. The window is not open. (*preserves the negative only*)
    d. The window is open. (*preserves the substance, or "gist"*)

Many people, of course, picked the correct alternative *a*, but of those who did not, the interest lay in which of *b*, *c*, and *d* they picked. Alternative *b* preserves the proposition **Closed(window)** of the original; *c* preserves the negative proposition **False(x)**; and *d* preserves neither. Yet because of the meaning of **open**, **closed**, and **not**, *d* is an obvious implication of 34. People selected *d* far more often than *b* and apparently more often than *c*. They selected the alternative that expressed a product of their comprehension of 34, not one that merely preserved one of its two propositions.

Among the adjectives Fillenbaum used were **open** and **closed**, and **tall** and **short**. **Open** and **closed** are said to be contradictory antonyms because from **The door is not open** one can infer **The door is closed**, and vice versa. **Tall** and **short**, on the other hand, are said to be contrary antonyms because from **The man is not tall** one cannot legitimately infer **The man is short**. The man could be neither tall nor short. What this suggests is that people should readily draw the inference from **not closed** to **open**, two contradictory adjectives, but not from **not tall** to **short**, two contrary adjectives. This was confirmed in Fillenbaum's data. Just and Carpenter (1976b) showed in addition that the inference from **The window is not closed** to **The window is open** has to be made at the time the sentence is studied. If it isn't, people take much longer at testing time to judge **The window is open** to be true (see also Fillenbaum, 1973; Frederiksen, 1975).

World Knowledge

Most implications are based wholly or partially on world knowledge in conformity with the reality principle (Chapter 2). M. Johnson, Bransford, and Solomon (1973), for example, had people study sentences like 36:

36. John was trying to fix the bird house. He was *pounding/looking for* the nail when his father came out to watch him and to help him do the work.

When 36 contains **pounding**, we easily infer that the instrument used was a hammer, but when it contains **looking for**, we do not draw this inference. For a recognition test, these people were shown single sentences and asked to judge whether or not they had occurred before. Among them was this sentence, which had not occurred before:

> 36'. John was using the hammer to fix the bird house when his father came out to watch him and to help him do the work.

Yet 36' is a probable inference of 36 with the verb **pounding**, though not with **looking for**. In fact, people claimed (incorrectly) to have seen 36' fully five times as often when 36 contained **pounding** as when it contained **looking for**. People easily mistake the inference for the original sentence.

Many other studies have demonstrated the intrusion of implications into memory. Bransford, Barclay, and Franks (1972) had people study sentences like 37 and tested them on sentences like 37':

> 37. Three turtles rested *beside/on* a floating log and a fish swam beneath them.
>
> 37'. Three turtles rested *beside/on* a floating log and a fish swam beneath it.

When the preposition is **on**, 37 easily implies 37' based on our knowledge of turtles, floating logs, and fish. But when it is **beside**, the implication does not go through. Note that this major difference in inference hangs on a minor difference in wording: the replacement of **on** by **beside**. As expected, errors in recognition favored 37' only when the preposition was **on**.

Referents

During comprehension listeners normally try to integrate new information with what they already know, and for this, we assume, they use the given-new strategy discussed in Chapter 3. Whenever they encounter a definite noun phrase, like **the reporter that Bill met,** they have to determine its referent before they can integrate the new information into memory. Take 38:

> 38. The reporter that Bill met left.

On hearing this, listeners search memory for an entity that fits two descriptions: **x is a reporter** and **Bill met x**. Imagine they are successful and find an entity to be designated E_{42}. What they do then, in effect, is "replace" **the reporter that Bill met** by E_{42} to form the proposition E_{42} **left**, which they add as new information to memory. Listeners may already know a lot of other things about E_{42}—for example, that he is a bachelor, lives in Apartment 3G, and works for the CIA. These facts are as much a part of their knowledge of E_{42} as are the facts that he is a reporter and that Bill met him. So in a recognition test they should readily claim that they had originally seen any one of these sentences:

38'. a. *The bachelor Bill met* left.
    b. *The reporter who lives in Apartment 3G* left.
    c. *The bachelor who works for the CIA* left.

Since the italicized noun phrases all pick out the same E_{42}, they are equivalent and difficult to tell from **the reporter that Bill met**. Memory errors like this should be common.

Such errors of reference have been demonstrated by J. Anderson and Bower (1973). People were read a long list of sentences that included at different places sentences like 39 and 40:

39. George Washington had good health.

40. The first president of the United States was a bad husband.

Later, in a recognition test, they were given this multiple-choice item:

41. a. George Washington had good health.
    b. The first president of the United States had good health.
    c. The first president of the United States had bad health.
    d. George Washington had bad health.

The correct alternative of course is *a*, but *b* is also "correct" for those people who treated **George Washington** and **the first president of the United States** as referring to the same entity. In fact, when people did make errors (about 40 percent of the time), 58 percent of the errors were selections of alternative *b*, and the rest were split between alternatives *c* and *d*.

The referent of a noun phrase, however, must be identified during the initial comprehension if these errors are to arise easily. In a study by J. Anderson and Hastie (1974), people were required to learn a series of related facts and later judge test sentences for their truth or falsity. One group of people, for example, learned 42 followed by many facts like 43 and 44:

42. James Bartlett is the lawyer.

43. James Bartlett rescued the kitten.

44. The lawyer caused the accident.

Because of 42 they knew that **James Bartlett** and **the lawyer** referred to the same entity, say E_3, and so they could store in memory these four facts:

42'. a. E_3 is named James Bartlett.
    b. E_3 is a lawyer.

43.′ E_3 rescued the kitten.

44′. E_3 caused the accident.

They were later asked to verify these two sentences (among others):

45. James Bartlett rescued the kitten. (*a sentence they had heard*)

46. The lawyer rescued the kitten. (*a new sentence*)

They were as fast at verifying 46 as 45 even though they had not heard 46 before. Because of 42′, they found it as easy to get to E_3 in 43′ from **James Bartlett** in 45 as from **the lawyer** in 46. It is remarkable that a novel sentence like 46 could be judged as quickly as an original sentence like 45.

But in this study, another group of people learned facts like those in 43 and 44 first and only at the end learned the crucial fact that would tie them together —namely 42, that James Bartlett was the lawyer. Presumably, people in this group had to store 43 and 44 with separate entities, like this:

43″. a. E_3 rescued the kitten.
    b. E_3 is named James Bartlett.

44″. a. E_{17} caused the accident.
    b. E_{17} is a lawyer.

Finally, with the presentation of 42 they could enter this proposition into memory:

42″. $E_3 = E_{17}$

They too were later asked to verify 45 and 46, repeated here:

45. James Bartlett rescued the kitten. (*a sentence they had heard*)

46. The lawyer rescued the kitten. (*a new sentence*)

They could judge 45 directly, of course, because all the relevant facts are stored directly in 43″. Since James Bartlett is E_3, and E_3 rescued the kitten, 45 is true. For 46, on the other hand, they had to draw an inference via 42″. The lawyer is E_{17}, and since E_{17} is E_3, and E_3 rescued the kitten, 46 is true. This roundabout route should take time, and in fact, people in this group took considerably longer to verify 46 than 45. So listeners appear to replace each definite noun phrase (like **James Bartlett** or **the lawyer**) by a "pointer" to its referent only at the time they comprehend it. Retrieving information about a referent later will be delayed if the "pointer" is indirect, as in this study (see also Frederiksen, 1975).

Referents in Discourse

Definite noun phrases are especially important in cementing discourse together. In stories, an entity may be introduced in one sentence as **an engineer** and referred to in the next as **the engineer** or **she**. By noting that the definite noun phrase refers to an entity mentioned before, listeners can piece the story together, putting the right facts with the right people. Unless they do, they won't have understood the story as it was intended. But these links should also make the story easy to recall. Once they have retrieved one fact about the engineer, for example, they can get at the other facts about her too and use these to reconstruct a coherent story.

This reconstructive process has been demonstrated by P. de Villiers (1974). In his study one group of people were read a series of sentences that began like this:

47. The store contained a row of wooden cages. The man bought a dog. The child wanted the animal. The father drove to his house. Etc.

Later they were asked to recall as many sentences as they could. Although they hadn't been told that the sentences formed a story, most assumed that they did and proceeded to infer that **the father** and **the man** referred to the same entity, that **a dog** and **the animal** referred to the same entity, and so on. Another group of people were read the same list of sentences, but with **the** replaced everywhere by **a**:

48. A store contained a row of wooden cages. A man bought a dog. A child wanted an animal. A father drove to his house. Etc.

The people in this group did not take the sentences as forming a story, nor did they tie the sentences together with common referents. As a result, the first group recalled far more sentences than the second. On the other hand, the first group often made the mistake of recalling, for example, **The child wanted the animal** as **The child wanted the dog**. As before, they tended to confuse two noun phrases that referred to the same entity. The first group may also have recalled more than the second simply because there were fewer different entities for them to remember.

Storing all the facts about a single referent together in memory can lead to even more dramatic confusions. In a study by Sulin and Dooling (1974), one group of people were read this brief story:

Carol Harris's need for professional help. Carol Harris was a problem child from birth. She was wild, stubborn, and violent. By the time Carol turned eight, she was still unmanageable. Her parents were very concerned about her mental health. There was no good institution for her problem in her state. Her parents finally decided to take some action. They hired a private teacher for Carol.

Comprehended in the normal way, **she** in the second sentence should be taken as referring to **Carol Harris**, and the facts that she was wild, stubborn, and violent should be stored with the other facts about her. Another group of people, however, were read the identical story but with **Carol Harris** replaced everywhere by **Helen Keller**. It was natural to expect these people to store these facts with the other facts they already knew about Helen Keller—for example, that she was deaf, dumb, and blind and that she had discovered "language" from her teacher. Five minutes or a week later, both groups were asked among other things whether **She was deaf, dumb, and blind** had occurred in the story. Very few people in the first group claimed that it had occurred, but many in the second did, especially a week later (see also Pompi and Lachman, 1967; Perfetti and Goldman, 1974).

So people try to attach all the facts they know about a single entity to a single "point" in memory. This is economical and allows them to see all the facts about that entity at a glance. But it also leads to confusion in memory. To recall the Helen Keller story, people have to distinguish the facts they learned from the story from those they knew before. When all of the facts have been stored together, this is difficult to do.

Indirect Meaning

In normal comprehension, listeners try to build the interpretation they think they were meant to build, and that may take them beyond the direct meaning of a sentence to its indirect meaning (Chapter 3). **Must you open the door?**, for example, will in certain contexts be construed not just as a question to be answered "yes" or "no" but as a polite request not to open the door. Because listeners probably store this indirect interpretation, they should often confuse **Must you open the door?** with other requests with the same interpretation, for example **Please don't open the door**.

This has been demonstrated by Jarvella and Collas (1974). In their study people were asked to take the part of an actor reading a script aloud. The script included, for example, 49:

49. The food is on the table.

But the script was cleverly written so that in context 49 would be interpreted as an invitation, roughly "Please take the food that is on the table." Afterwards they were given a second script and asked to judge for certain sentences in the script itself whether they were the "same as" or "different from" what they had read in the first script. The second script, for example, included one of four sentences related to 49:

Sentence	*Interpretation*	*"Same" judgments*
50. The food is on the table.	*Invitation*	89%
51. The food is on the table.	*Assertion*	77%
52. Please take the food on the table.	*Invitation*	69%
53. The food is on the chair.	*Invitation*	7%

The second script was written to give 50, 52, and 53 the interpretations of an invitation and 51 the interpretation of a simple assertion.

Indirect meaning had a distinct influence on people's memory for 49. Although both 50 and 51 are identical to 49 in their direct meaning, only 50 is identical in its indirect meaning. As the percentages to the right of these sentences show, people were reliably more willing to say "same" to 50 than 51. And although both 52 and 53 are invitations, only 52 is identical to 49 in its indirect meaning. People were far more willing to say "same" to 52 than 53. These findings suggest that people store both the direct and indirect meaning. The direct meaning isn't enough, for otherwise 50 and 51 should have had the same percentages. The indirect meaning isn't enough either, for otherwise 50 and 52 should have had the same percentages. This isn't surprising. **The food is on the table**, used as an invitation, does two things: it asserts that the food is on the table and it invites the listener to take it. Both parts are relevant and both *should* be stored.

Creating Global Representations

In comprehending prose passages, people not only draw implications as each sentence comes along, but also create new representations, unrelated to any single sentence, to capture the global situation being described. Take the following scene:

> The two of them glanced nervously at each other as they approached the man standing there expectantly. He talked to them for about ten minutes, but spoke loudly enough that everyone else in the room could hear too. Eventually he handed over two objects he had been given, one to each of them. After he had said a few more words, the ordeal was over. With her veil lifted, the two of them kissed, turned around, and rushed from the room arm in arm, with everyone else falling in behind.

Eventually this is recognized as a wedding scene even though no sentence by itself implies this. Only with the cumulative evidence does the global situation become clear. Then it is inferred that the man is a judge, minister, or the like, the couple are a man and woman, the objects handed to them are rings, and so on. The global representation is based on all the information taken together embellished by knowledge of the world according to the reality principle. People should be liable to confuse what was in the global representation with what was in the original passage. Memory errors ought to be legion, and indeed they are.

Linear Arrays

Memory for global representations has been carefully examined for linear arrays by Barclay (1973), Potts (1972; 1973; 1974; Scholz and Potts, 1974), and Trabasso and Riley (1975). What happens, they asked, when a linear array is described with one set of sentences and quizzed with another? Take this linear array used by Barclay:

lion   bear   moose   giraffe   cow

Here, the lion is left of the bear, the bear left of the moose, and so on. Call these five elements A B C D E. When all possible pairs of these elements are combined with the relations **is to the left of** and **is to the right of**, there are forty possible sentences, half of them true of the array and half of them false. Barclay selected eleven of the twenty true sentences to specify the array (even though four is quite enough), told some people to memorize the eleven sentences, and told others to use them to figure out the linear array being described. Later, everyone was given a recognition test.

This study provided striking evidence for the existence of global representations of linear arrays. On the recognition test were three kinds of sentences:

(1) true sentences that had been studied (11 possible sentences),
(2) true sentences that had not been studied (9 possible sentences),
(3) false sentences that had not been studied (20 possible sentences).

The array builders—the people told to build the linear arrays—were as willing to claim they had seen the true sentences they had *not* studied (the second kind) as they were the true sentences they *had* studied (the first kind). At the same time they were very confident they had not seen any of the twenty false sentences. The memorizers, on the other hand, could generally distinguish the eleven sentences they had memorized from all the rest. If the array builders had formed only a global representation, this is what we should expect. They should be able to distinguish true from false, but shouldn't be able to distinguish among the true sentences. The memorizers may build global representations too, but they should use their word-for-word memory for the sentences to help them distinguish between the two kinds of true sentences.

What about the time needed to retrieve information about a linear array from memory? In a study by Potts (1972) people were read a brief story that described animals differing in intelligence. Schematically, the array had four elements, A B C D. In the story the array was specified by these three sentences:

54. A is smarter than B.

55. B is smarter than C.

56. C is smarter than D.

Later, these people were shown test sentences and asked to decide as quickly as possible whether each was true or false of the array. The test sentences included 54 through 56, but also 57 through 59, sentences they had not seen before:

57. A is smarter than C.

58. B is smarter than D.

59. A is smarter than D.

The simplest theory would predict that decisions on 54 through 56 should be faster than those on 57 through 59. After all, 54 through 56 had been stored in memory, and 57 through 59 would require inferences from 54 through 56. Sentence 57 requires an inference based on 54 and 55; 58 requires one based on 55 and 56; and 59 requires one based on 54, 55, and 56.

This simple theory, however, collapses with Potts's findings. Not only were 57 through 59 no slower than 54 through 56, they were even faster. In fact, the fastest sentence was 59, which theoretically should be slowest because it requires more inferences than any other sentence. With the idea of a global representation, however, all this makes sense. In such a representation, two elements can be judged faster the farther apart they are. In addition, the two ends, A and D, have special status as "end anchors," enabling statements containing them to be judged even more quickly than other statements. This characterization of the linear array in memory has been corroborated, extended, and refined in an intensive series of studies by Potts and others (Barclay, 1973; Holyoak, 1977; Moyer and Bayer, 1976; Potts, 1972, 1973, 1974; Scholz and Potts, 1974). Although there are disagreements about the representation, one thing is clear. Most of its properties have little to do with the specific sentences originally used to describe it. It is truly a global representation.

Misfits in Global Representations

For any fact to be remembered easily, it must fit within the global representation being built. In a study by Bransford and Johnson (1973), people were read the following short passage after being told that its title was *Watching a Peace March from the Fortieth Floor*:

> The view was breathtaking. From the window one could see the crowd below. Everything looked extremely small from such a distance, but the colorful costumes could still be seen. Everyone seemed to be moving in one direction in an orderly fashion and there seemed to be little children as well as adults. The landing was gentle and luckily the atmosphere was such that no special suits had to be worn. At first there was a great deal of activity. Later, when the speeches started, the crowd quieted down. The man with the television camera took many shots of the setting and the crowd. Everyone was very friendly and seemed to be glad when the music started.

Immediately afterwards, people were able to recall the passage well, except for the sentence about the landing. Because it did not fit within the global representation being built, it was badly represented initially and therefore badly recalled. A second group of people heard the same passage, but were told it was titled *A Space Trip to an Inhabited Planet*. They recalled the sentence about the landing

very much better. It was easy to incorporate into the global representation initially and was therefore easy to retrieve later.

What is put into the global representation, then, is critical to what can be
retrieved from it. E. Loftus (1975) has demonstrated this for the important legal
problem of eyewitness reports. In one of her experiments people were shown a
short film of a car accident and later asked ten questions about it. The first was
either 60 or 61, and the last was always 62:

60. How fast was Car A going when it ran the stop sign?

61. How fast was Car A going when it turned right?

62. Did you see a stop sign for Car A?

In reality there was no stop sign in the film, so 60 is based on a false assumption.
To answer 60, one needs to assume there was a stop sign; but to answer 61,
one does not. Loftus argued that people answering 60 should therefore alter
their representation of the accident, adding a stop sign, whereas people answering 61 should not. As expected, 53 percent of those asked Question 60 said "yes"
to 62, whereas only 35 percent of those asked Question 61 did. From other
experiments Loftus argued that people in this first group were not just remembering the earlier sentence, but were basing their incorrect answers on an altered
representation. Because of such questions people would add buildings and
people, make cars go faster or slower, and add actions not originally there. All
of these alterations made their later recall of these facts inaccurate. Together
with the earlier studies, Loftus's work suggests that the global representation
people create is relatively divorced from the source of their information.

How is Substance Represented?

One of the most critical questions in memory has been skirted in this discussion:
What is the nature of a global representation? This question is related in turn to
an even more general one: How is knowledge represented in memory? These
questions are among the toughest in the study of memory and have no clear
answers.

Propositional and Non-Propositional Memory

The proposals that have been made fall into two categories.

(1) *Propositions*. Theorists like J. Anderson and Bower (1973), Kintsch
(1972), and Rumelhart, Lindsay, and Norman (1972) have argued that most facts
are represented in memory as a complex network of propositions. In the strong
form of this position, all facts are propositional. In weaker forms, some are and
some aren't. But even if information is represented in forms other than propositions, one might argue that it must be transformed into propositions before it
can take part in the utilization process or in memory retrieval for the reconstruc-

tion of sentences. This is implicitly the position we have taken in discussing comprehension, although other positions are clearly possible too.

(2) *Modality-specific memory*. Theorists like Shepard (Shepard and Chipman, 1971; Shepard, Kilpatric, and Cunningham, 1975), Kosslyn (1975) and Paivio (1971), on the other hand, have argued that there are types of memory representations that are specific to one of the sense modalities—vision, hearing, touch, and so on—and these have certain "continuous" properties. Visual imagery, for example, is a type of memory representation that is tied to the visual system and is treated in a continuous fashion. People seem able to move, rotate, and reshape mental images smoothly and without discrete jumps (L. Cooper and Shepard, 1973; Shepard and Metzler, 1971) and to scan them as if they had continuous spatial extent (Kosslyn, 1975). Mental images don't seem to be discrete, disjointed objects. That distinguishes them from propositions with their discrete predicates and arguments. There is considerable evidence that such modality-specific information is used immediately after an event has been experienced (Brooks, 1968), but less evidence that it remains available in long-term memory.

The issue of propositional versus non-propositional memory is complicated by the fact that the two positions are in principle difficult to distinguish (see Pylyshyn, 1973). Just what is a proposition? How does it differ from a modality-specific representation of a fact? The answers to these questions hinge on the nature of propositions—on the nature of meaning—and that won't be taken up until Chapters 11, 12, and 13. Even there, the issue will not be fully resolved.

The most that investigators have done is examine particular global representations to lay bare as many of their properties as possible. This has been tried for linear arrays, as described earlier, and also for short paragraphs.

Structure in Paragraphs

Kintsch and Keenan (1973; Kintsch, 1976) began with the hypothesis that at least some paragraphs are represented as a hierarchy of propositions. What people recall of a paragraph, therefore, should vary with the number of propositions in that paragraph and with the "position" of each proposition within it. Two of the shortest "paragraphs" they used were these:

63. Romulus, the legendary founder of Rome, took the women of the Sabines by force.

64. Cleopatra's downfall lay in her foolish trust in the fickle political figures of the Roman world.

By Kintsch and Keenan's count, 63 has four propositions and 64 has eight. (The propositions of 63 will be given later.) Yet the two sentences are about the same length in words. The paragraphs they used contained from two to twenty-two propositions and varied from seven to fifty-eight words in length. People were required to read each paragraph silently, press a button when they had finished, and immediately recall as much of the paragraph as they could.

Kintsch and Keenan predicted that the more propositions that have to be stored in memory, the longer a sentence should take to read and understand, and this was confirmed. For paragraphs of about fifteen words, reading time increased from ten seconds for four-proposition paragraphs to about fifteen seconds for eight-proposition paragraphs. When the paragraphs were short, reading time increased about 1.5 seconds per additional proposition. When they were long, it increased about 4.5 seconds per additional proposition. Apparently, the more complex the global representation already built, the more time it takes to integrate a new proposition into it.

In recall, people were much more likely to reproduce propositions the "higher" they were in the presumed hierarchy of propositions. Take the four propositions that according to Kintsch and Keenan underlie 63:

> 65. a. Take(Romulus, women, by force)
>   b. Found(Romulus, Rome)
>   c. Legendary(Romulus)
>   d. Sabine(women)

These propositions form a hierarchy in that 65a is the main proposition, and the other three modify its parts in various forms of relativization (see Chapter 1). Proposition 65a is the highest in the hierarchy, and the three others are one level lower. Other paragraphs had a similar hierarchy, some running four levels deep (instead of two, as in 65). The highest-level proposition was recalled most often in these paragraphs, and the lower levels were recalled progressively less often. What this suggests is that these paragraphs each had a global representation that was a hierarchy of propositions. The more propositions it had, the longer it took to build. Once it was built, the higher in the hierarchy a proposition was located, the easier it was to retrieve. The suggestion, in effect, is that paragraphs are organized around the main facts (the highest propositions), and the incidental facts (the lower propositions) are more difficult to retrieve.

MEMORY FOR STORIES

Stories stand as one of the ultimate challenges to theories of memory for prose. They are natural units of discourse, genuinely interesting and meaningful, and yet complicated enough that people can't remember them in any detail. Every influence on memory discussed in this chapter so far affects story memory with strengthened force. As people listen to stories, they bring in outside knowledge, draw inferences, keep track of referents, and build global representations. Their attempts at recalling stories show this dramatically. But stories have an additional structure all their own. A person describing a building, a football game, or the history of a country isn't thought to be telling a story. Stories have a special kind of beginning, middle, and end. Five- and six-year-old children already know what can and cannot pass as a proper story. This structure adds yet another dimension that influences memory for stories.

Among the first to study memory for stories extensively was F. Bartlett (1932). He had people read a story through twice and then either immediately or after some delay attempt to recall it. Not surprisingly, people made a great many errors in their reproductions. They added some details, left out others, and altered still others. Bartlett talked about the three processes of sharpening, leveling, and rationalization, about how people sharpen some details, level out others, and give rationalizations for what had happened within the story (see also Allport and Postman, 1947).

Folk Tales and Schemata

These processes can be illustrated with a folk tale Bartlett used from the Kwa-kiutl Indians of British Columbia called "The War of the Ghosts." It tells of a young man who was drawn into a war party of ghosts. The last three paragraphs of the story go like this:

> So the canoes went back to Egulac, and the young man went ashore to his house, and made a fire. And he told everybody and said: "Behold I accompanied the ghosts, and we went to fight. Many of our fellows were killed, and many of those who attacked us were killed. They said I was hit, and I did not feel sick."
>
> He told it all, and then he became quiet. When the sun rose he fell down. Something black came out of his mouth. His face became contorted. The people jumped up and cried.
>
> He was dead.

To Bartlett's British readers, this was a very strange story indeed, and they tended to mold their reproductions after their own customs and beliefs. Here, for example, is the corresponding part of one person's attempt to reproduce the story immediately:

> In the evening he returned to his hut, and told his friends that he had been in a battle. A great many had been slain, and he had been wounded by an arrow; he had not felt any pain, he said. They told him that he must have been fighting in a battle of ghosts. Then he remembered that it had been queer and he became very excited.
>
> In the morning, however, he became ill, and his friends gathered round; he fell down and his face became very pale. Then he writhed and shrieked and his friends were filled with terror. At last he became calm. Something hard and black came out of his mouth, and he lay contorted and dead.

The story has obviously undergone significant changes. Certain details have been sharpened. The young man was shot with *an arrow*; he *writhed* and *shrieked* as he lay dying; his face was *pale*; and something *hard* and black came out of his mouth. Many details have been rationalized as well. In explanation of the odd death to come, the young man remembered that the battle had been queer; in explanation of his death, he became not just calm, but ill; and in explanation of his friends' cries, they were filled with terror. Finally, certain details have been omitted altogether. The person reproducing this story was strongly influenced by his own frame of reference.

Bartlett attempted to explain these influences by appealing to the notion of *schema*, a kind of mental framework based on cultural experience into which new facts are fitted. For example, we may have one schema for cause and effect —that certain causes lead to certain effects and others don't—whereas people in other cultures may have a slightly different one. For us certain events are important and basic; for others the same events may be trivial or incidental. Unfortunately, the notion of schema is so loose that it can accommodate almost any influence on the recall of stories. Yet the phenomenon Bartlett investigated is very real and in need of explanation. Since his work, others have refined the idea of structure in discourse and have shown the critical role it plays in recall.

Structure in Stories

Every type of prose passage—descriptions, explanations, jokes, paragraphs, and stories—has a structure within which each sentence plays a role. A paragraph, for example, can have one of several different structures (see Irmscher, 1972). Some paragraphs proceed from the general to the specific, or from the particular to the general; others alternate topics in order to compare and contrast; and still others lay out details in a chronological order, a spatial order, or an order that builds to a climax. People "know" that paragraphs have structure, for they object to ones that do not conform to these possibilities. The same goes for other units of discourse. Stories have a particularly clear structure, as Colby (1973), G. Lakoff (1972a), and Propp (1968) have demonstrated for Russian, Eskimo, and other folk tales. It is instructive to look at the structure Rumelhart (1975, 1977) has formalized on the basis of this and his own work on fairy tales. (See also Mandler and Johnson, 1977; Thorndyke, 1977.)

The Story Hierarchy

The structure of stories, according to Rumelhart, is hierarchical. At the highest level, each story consists of a *setting* followed by an *episode*. In formal notation:

story = setting + episode

The setting and episode, in turn, break down into further parts. The setting is denoted like this:

setting = state + state + · · · + state

It is a *series* of states (time, place, and characters) that sets the scene for the episode. The episode that follows consists of an *event* and its *reactions*:

episode = event + reaction
   event = episode, or
        = change-of-state, or
        = action, or
        = event + event
reaction = internal response + overt response

Note that these equations are *recursive*. An episode can itself contain an episode, and an event can contain an event. This way a story can be expanded out indefinitely, as happened in Homer's *Odyssey*, in which the overall episode, the voyage, consisted of a series of smaller episodes, and as happened in *The Arabian Nights*, in which Scheherezade spun out one story within another to fill a thousand and one nights.

Along with these equations, there are certain relations. An episode, for example, does not merely follow a setting—it is "allowed" or "enabled" by the setting. Likewise, a reaction is "initiated" by an event, and an overt response (for example, crying) is "motivated" by an internal response (sadness). Not only do stories have identifiable parts, but these parts are welded together by gross relations such as allowing, initiating, and motivating.

This hierarchical structure can be illustrated with a simple story analyzed by Rumelhart. Its units are numbered for reference:

(1) Margie was holding tightly to the string of her beautiful new balloon.
(2) Suddenly, a gust of wind caught it
(3) and carried it into a tree.
(4) It hit a branch
(5) and burst.
(6) [sadness]
(7) Margie cried and cried.

These seven units belong to the hierarchy in Figure 4–2.

Although this is an exceedingly simple story, complex stories fit the same sort of hierarchical structure. Since each episode, by Rumelhart's equations, can itself contain another episode, a story can become as deep and complex as one wants to make it. Yet getting in and out of events and episodes is a highly structured business. By Rumelhart's scheme, each episode must be resolved eventually, and the story ends with a resolution of the hierarchically highest episode.

Summarizing Stories

Not all parts of a story are equally critical to its structure. As Rumelhart noted, when people summarize stories, they have highly regular ways of condensing,

FIGURE 4-2
HIERARCHY OF RUMELHART'S STORY

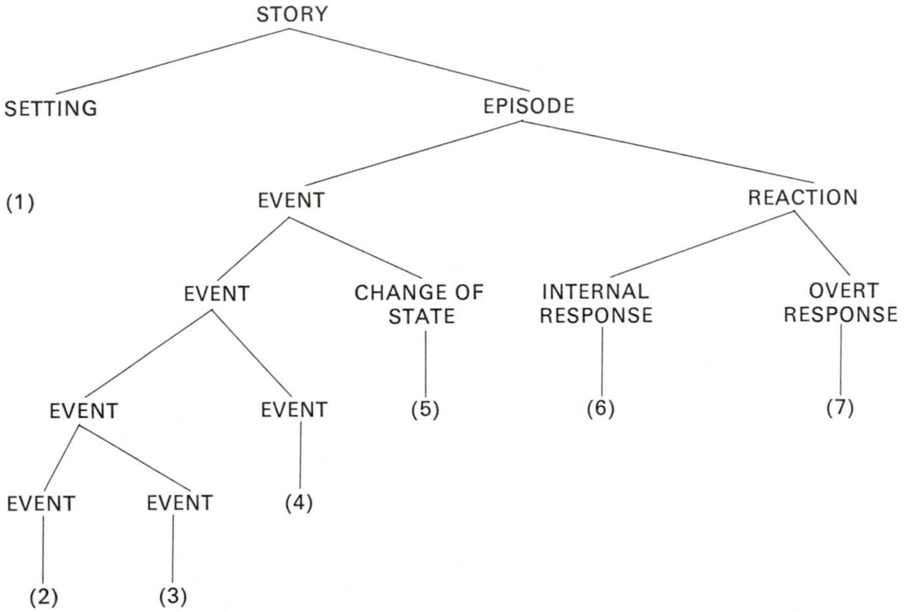

```
                        STORY
                  _____|_____
                 |                 |
            SETTING             EPISODE
                            _____|_____
               |           |               |
              (1)        EVENT          REACTION
                      _____|_____       ____|____
                     |           |     |         |
                   EVENT    CHANGE OF  INTERNAL  OVERT
                            STATE      RESPONSE  RESPONSE
                 ____|____     |          |         |
                |         |   (5)        (6)       (7)
              EVENT     EVENT
            ____|____     |
           |         |   (4)
         EVENT     EVENT
           |         |
          (2)       (3)
```

coalescing, and omitting various parts of the story. The general rule is this. Stories are goal-oriented, and therefore goals tend to be preserved. Causes are omitted or absorbed into their effects: **The prince chopped off the head of the dragon with a sword and the dragon died** might be shortened to **The prince killed the dragon with his sword**, or simply **The prince killed the dragon**. Events are omitted or absorbed into reactions to these events; **The prince killed the dragon and that pleased the king** might be shortened to **The prince pleased the king**. Internal responses are omitted or absorbed into the resulting overt responses: **The princess was pleased and so she agreed to marry the prince** might be abbreviated to **The princess agreed to marry the prince**. In short, goals are important, and stories can be shortened by reducing or omitting causes, initiators, and enabling events.

Recall of Stories

This structure ought to be critical in both the initial comprehension of a story and its recall. According to Rumelhart, people build up a hierarchy as they listen to stories, identifying each unit (normally each sentence) as some part of this hierarchy—a setting, event, action, change-of-state, internal response, overt response, and so on. By the end they have constructed a global representation for the story. When asked to recall the story, they retrieve this hierarchy and its parts and try to reconstruct the story. In doing so, they fill in whatever pieces of setting, action, events, internal responses, and the like they need to add to make the story complete. Thus, Bartlett's subject filled out "The War of the Ghosts" in a way consistent with the structure as he had originally understood it.

Stories should be recalled according to their hierarchical structure. The higher a sentence is in the hierarchy, the more likely it should be recalled. Thorndyke (1977) confirmed this by identifying the level of sentences in the hierarchical graphs of several stories. In the graph for Margie and her balloon, for example, (1) would be highest, (5), (6), and (7) the next level down, (4) the third level down, and (2) and (3) the lowest. For Thorndyke's stories, people were far more likely to recall a sentence the higher it was in such a graph. The highest-level sentences were recalled 95 percent of the time, and the lowest-level ones only 50 percent. When the same sentences were presented to other people in random order, the story hierarchy no longer mattered. Sentences that would have been at different levels in the story were recalled about equally often. In the random condition, recall was also much lower (see also B. Meyer, 1975). The hierarchy, then, has two effects. It influences which parts of a story will be recalled, and it enables people to recall more of it.

The story hierarchy, however, appears to be remembered separately from other aspects of a story. In another study by Thorndyke (1977), people were presented two stories and asked to recall both. Their recall depended on the relationship of the two stories to each other. Sometimes the two had the same hierarchy but a different content (that is, different characters and actions), sometimes a different hierarchy and a different content, and sometimes a different hierarchy with the same content. The group that read the first of these pairs of stories was helped by the fact that they had only one hierarchy to learn, and they recalled more than the second group. The third group, however, was hindered by the fact that they had the same content to learn for both hierarchies. Thus, the common hierarchy, or framework, helped recall, whereas the common characters and actions only confused. It is as if the story hierarchy is understood independently of the characters and actions that are part of it.

When a story hierarchy is complex, the story is also more difficult to recall. Among the stories Thorndyke (1977) used, some had clear, neatly defined hierarchies, while others had more complex ones. The less complex the hierarchy, the more comprehensible a story was judged to be and the better it was recalled. In one comparison, two stories had the same sentences, but in one story the order didn't quite fit the simplest hierarchical structure. Of the two, the better structured story was the better recalled.

In our examination of comprehension in its broadest sense, the story marks the end of a journey from the smallest units to the largest. At the beginning were constituents, like **the man**, which had a structure that was critical to the construction process. Next came larger units, principally the sentence, which had a structure—including speech acts, propositional content, and thematic content—that played a critical role in the utilization process. At the end was an even larger chunk of discourse, the story. Its structure affected not only the utilization of each sentence but also the understanding of the whole discourse. But because stories are so large, they cannot be studied in the same immediate and direct way that words, constituents, and sentences have been studied. Their influence on comprehension can only be inferred indirectly from studies of memory. Yet with the story, the lessons have remained the same. The structure of the whole affects the understanding of each part. People listen for what they were meant to understand, and that affects what they do with language from the smallest units to the largest.

SUMMARY

Memory for prose is a complicated product of how the prose is studied, how its content is represented in memory, and how retained information is used in reconstructing the original prose.

Normally, people "study" speech by listening to it for its meaning and by discarding its word for word content very quickly. They try to identify referents, draw inferences, get at indirect meanings, and in general build global representations of the situation being described. When they later try to remember this speech, they fail miserably on its verbatim content. They confuse different names for the same referent, sentences with their implications, and pieces of a global representation with one another. Yet when they have to, people can "study" speech word for word and later recall it verbatim. Memorization, however, usually requires repetition and special concentration on the surface features of the speech to be remembered.

The storage of information can take several forms. Over the short term, speech can be represented verbatim in the form of constituents. Speech errors, hesitations, and stutters, however, are generally not represented. The propositions built from a sentence are also available over the short term. Over the long term, information is often represented as a network of propositions. Yet in "normal" situations, information is incorporated into global representations that are relatively independent of the sentences from which they were built. The same global representation may result from radically different initial descriptions. These global representations may or may not consist of a network of propositions.

Remembering is a reconstructive process. To recall or recognize a sentence, people retrieve bits and pieces of what is stored in memory and use them to reconstruct what they could plausibly claim to be the original sentence. To do this they fill in missing details based on their knowledge of situations, beliefs, and customs. They are also heavily swayed in their choice of constructions by a bias towards normality. When the discourse has a structure of its own, as stories do, they try to reconstruct a passage that fulfills the prerequisites for that type of discourse.

Further Reading

For an introduction to memory in general, see such sources as Herriot (1974), Klatzky (1975), G. Loftus and Loftus (1976), and Norman (1976). Within the specialized area of memory for prose, J. Anderson and Bower (1973), Fillenbaum (1973), and Wanner (1974) provide rather detailed discussions, especially of the role played by syntax. Bransford and Johnson (1973) and Bransford and McCarrell (1974) review their own work on memory for global representations. The form of global representations has also been a concern to investigators in artificial intelligence; see Minsky (1975) and Schank and Abelson (1975), among others. Bartlett's (1932) *Remembering* and Allport and Postman's (1947) studies on the spreading of rumors are still good reading. For some more recent approaches to stories, one can consult G. Bower (1977), van Dijk and Kintsch (1977), Kintsch and van Dijk (1975), and several of the papers in Just and Carpenter (1977).

Take care of the sense and the
sounds will take care of themselves.

Lewis Carroll

5

Perception of Speech

Although comprehension takes in interpretation, utilization, and memory of language, it begins with the raw speech sounds themselves. Speakers move their lips, tongue, and vocal cords and emit a stream of sounds that arrive at the listeners' ears. Listeners are somehow able to analyze the sounds and identify the sentences that have been uttered. Because this end of the comprehension process draws heavily on the perceptual system, it is called *speech perception*. To some this term may suggest that the process of identifying sound sequences as words, phrases, and sentences involves nothing more than auditory perception—the analysis of sounds by the ears—and can be divorced from the interpretive processes discussed in the previous chapters. This is not correct. Meaning and the ultimate use of a sentence play an important role even in the "simple" process of identifying speech sounds.

THE PROBLEMS OF IDENTIFYING SOUNDS

How is a sentence like **Bill is a writer** identified from its sounds? Imagine that the speech stream was like a printed sentence with its sequence of letters separated by spaces. In speech the units corresponding to letters would be *phonetic segments*, and the spaces between letters would be silences. In this view the stretch of sounds up to the first silence would be taken in and identified from its unique acoustic properties as the phonetic segment **b**. The next stretch would be taken in and identified as an **i** and so on through the sentence. At word boundaries there would be longer silences, and at sentence boundaries even longer ones. This way it would be easy to identify phonetic segments, words, and finally sentences.

Lack of Discreteness and Invariance

At first glance this model of speech perception seems attractive and plausible. Unfortunately, it fails at almost every turn—largely because the speech stream is quite unlike printed language. There are three major problems.

(1) *Speech is continuous and not chopped up into discrete stretches of sound.* Although there may appear to be silences between words and sentences, and boundaries between phonetic segments, there are not. Speech is a continuously varying signal, like a warbling siren, with few genuine breaks or discontinuities. Most silences and boundaries people hear are illusory and arise from the way they perceive the speech stream.

(2) *Phonetic segments do not have invariant properties.* The **b**'s in **bill**, **ball**, **bull**, **able**, and **rob** are printed in exactly the same way: the letter **b** is invariant from word to word. Not so with the pronunciation of these **b**'s. Although they are judged to be the same sound, each has distinct acoustic properties. As if this lack of invariance weren't enough, different accents and voice qualities add even more variation to the acoustic signal, and so do different modes of speaking—whispering, talking with food in the mouth, and talking with the mouth wired shut. Despite dramatic variations in the pronunciation of **b**, it is still identified as a single sound.

(3) *Phonetic segments do not stand in a one-to-one relation to stretches of the speech stream.* Take **writer** and **rider**. Since they are heard to differ in the **t** and the **d**, they ought to differ in the corresponding stretch of sound in the speech stream. But no. In American English pronunciation, they differ only in the length of the vowel corresponding to the **i**. In the phonetic notation that will be used in this book, they have this pronunciation:

> writer: [rayDer]
> rider: [ray:Der]

The **t** and **d** are both pronounced with a "flap **d**," symbolized by the **D**. But **writer** has a short vowel and **rider** a long vowel (indicated by the colon). What is perceived as **t** or **d** here corresponds only indirectly to differences in the speech stream itself.

Speed and Intelligibility

The comparison of speech to printing presents still other problems. Even if the speech stream could be cut up into phonetic segments, these segments would race by so quickly that they could not be identified one by one. To identify a word like **pass**, people have to identify not only the three phonetic segments **p**, **a**, and **s**, but also their order, so as to distinguish **pass** from **sap**, or **asp**, or **apse**. Warren, Obusek, Farmer, and Warren (1969) found that when people were given sequences of sounds consisting of a hiss, a vowel, a buzz, and a tone, they could not determine the order of the four elements unless they occurred no faster than about 1.5 elements per second. Yet speech normally runs along at about twelve segments per second and is still quite intelligible at rates up to fifty segments per second (Foulke and Sticht, 1969). Clearly, phonetic segments are not identified sequentially in this way.

Another problem lies in the quality of the speech stream itself. Imagine trying to proceed letter by letter through a printed page when half the words have been blanked out. The page would be very difficult to read. Yet most naturally occurring speech is like a half-printed page, for the pronunciation is so sloppy that more than half the words are unintelligible when taken out of the speech and presented alone. As sloppy as speech is, however, it is perceived as perfectly intelligible and not at all like a printed page with half its words missing. Or imagine trying to read a printed page with two or three passages typed one over the other. That should prove extraordinarily confusing too. Yet at cocktail parties people often listen to one conversation when there are other equally loud competing conversations all around them. They are able to pick out the right conversation and stick with it perfectly. Both the sloppiness of speech and the cocktail party phenomenon suggest that the later stages in comprehension—the construction and utilization processes—are deeply involved in the perception of speech. Without meaning there is little to make sloppy speech intelligible or a cocktail party conversation coherent.

Speech perception, then, poses some challenging puzzles. People identify words and sentences from the speech stream even though phonetic segments have no clear-cut boundaries, have many different pronunciations, and correspond only indirectly to parts of the speech stream itself. People hear speech as intelligible even though it is sloppy, and they can pick out the right speech stream from a number of competing ones. This chapter will try to offer answers to these and other puzzles by examining speech perception from two complementary directions, bottom up and top down. The first task is to see how the acoustic properties of the speech stream might be used in identifying phonetic segments, syllables, and words. This is working from the bottom (the acoustic level) up. The second task is to see how syntactic and semantic constraints might help the listener identify and "hear" the words in the speech stream. This is working from the top (syntax and semantics) down.

PHONETICS AND PHONOLOGY

Before speech perception can be examined intelligently, one must be aware of what linguists know about the systematic nature of speech sounds. They have approached the problem from two complementary points of view, phonetics and phonology. *Phonetics* is concerned with the raw speech sounds and how they are produced. Phoneticians have studied the acoustic properties of speech sounds and how the tongue, lips, larynx, and mouth cavity behave in their production. *Phonology*, on the other hand, is concerned with speech sounds as a system of language. Phonologists have attempted to give an abstract representation of the sound system that will explain how sounds are added, changed, and omitted in the formation of words and sentences. They have been interested, for example, in how the final **k** sound in **electric** is changed to an **s** sound in the formation of **electricity**.

Speech sounds, then, can be represented at two levels. The phonetic level specifies all the features that are needed in the pronunciation of the sounds. The more abstract phonological level, on the other hand, represents only certain "nonredundant" features. Consider the **p** sound in **pill** and **spill**. Phonetically, at the level of pronunciation, these two sounds are different. The first **p** is accompanied by a slight puff of air, an "aspiration," whereas the second **p** is not. The two **p** sounds, then, are distinct phonetic segments and are normally written in a special phonetic alphabet with square brackets around them. So [pʰ] is the aspirated **p** sound and [p°] is the unaspirated **p** sound. At the more abstract phonological level, however, these two **p** sounds are said to be manifestations of the same underlying phonological segment, or phoneme. This phonological segment is also written in a special alphabet within square brackets, as in [p] although it is often placed within two slashes, as in /p/. So [pʰ] and [p°] are said to be two phonetic segments, or allophones, derived from the same phonological segment, or phoneme, [p].

But how does one distinguish phonetic from phonological segments? The essential idea is that phonetic segments point to any systematic difference in pronunciation, and phonological segments point only to those that make a difference to meaning. Consider these two phonetic sequences:

$$\left.\begin{array}{l} [pʰɪl] \\ [p°ɪl] \end{array}\right\} \text{No difference in meaning.}$$

Both of these would be identified as **pill**. Although **pill** would normally be pronounced the first way, it would still be recognizable as **pill** if pronounced the second way. Indeed, French speakers learning English often make the mistake of pronouncing **pill** the second way because unlike English French doesn't ever aspirate **p**. Since [pʰ] and [p°] do not signal a difference in meaning, they must be two manifestations of the same phonological segment [p]. But consider these two phonetic sequences:

$$\left.\begin{array}{l} [pʰɪl] \\ [kʰɪl] \end{array}\right\} \text{Difference in meaning.}$$

This difference in pronunciation signals a difference in meaning: **pill** versus **kill**. Not only are [pʰ] and [kʰ] different phonetic segments, but they are also manifestations of two different phonological segments, namely [p] and [k]. Any systematic difference in pronunciation is captured in the phonetic segments, but only those that change meaning in the phonological segments.

Phonetic differences that change meaning are often called "distinctive," and what is distinctive in one language may not be distinctive in another. In English, for example, it doesn't matter to meaning whether a **p** sound is aspirated or unaspirated, [pʰ] or [p°]. In Thai, it does. The phonetic sequence [p°aa]

TABLE 5–1
PHONETIC SYMBOLS

The major consonants, vowels, and diphthongs of English and their phonetic symbols.

CONSONANTS				VOWELS		DIPHTHONGS	
p	pill	θ	thigh	i	beet	ay	bite
b	bill	ð	thy	ɪ	bit	æw	about
m	mill	š	shallow	e	bait	ɔy	boy
t	till	ž	measure	ɛ	bet		
d	dill	č	chip	æ	bat		
n	nil	ǰ	gyp	u	boot		
k	kill	l	lip	ʊ	put		
g	gill	r	rip	ʌ	but		
ŋ	sing	y	yet	o	boat		
f	fill	w	wet	ɔ	bought		
v	vat	ʍ	whet	a	pot		
s	sip	h	hat	ə	sofa		
z	zip			i	marry		

means "forest," whereas [pʰaa] means "split." And in English, the phonetic segments [l] and [r] are distinctive phonologically, whereas in Japanese, they are not. This explains why [l]s become [r]s in words the Japanese adopt from English, as for example when **high class** is turned into **hi-kurasu, love hotel** into **rabu hoteru,** and **Lockheed scandal** into **rokkeedo sukandaru** (Whynant, 1976).

Articulatory Phonetics

Over the years phoneticians have developed a system and vocabulary for talking about the articulatory gestures people use in the pronunciation of phonetic segments. The segments have been described in terms of the shape of the mouth, place of the tongue, shape of the lips, and so on. This system can be illustrated with the phonetic segments in English. In this extended illustration we will generally ignore articulatory differences on the level of those between [pʰ] and [p°], which would bog us down in too much detail, and concentrate instead on articulatory differences between, say, [p] and [k], two segments whose differences are distinctive. The major segments of English and their symbols are listed with examples in Table 5–1.

The most basic division among these segments is between consonants and vowels. Consonants are formed by constricting part of the mouth to a complete or near closure. This stops or impedes the rush of air through the mouth and produces a distinctive sound. Vowels, on the other hand, are formed by letting the vocal cords vibrate as air moves through the mouth in an open static configuration. The shape of the "resonators"—the various cavities in the mouth—is what gives different vowels their distinctive sounds. Despite this clean dichotomy, many segments do not fall readily into either category. The "liquid" [l] is at once both consonant-like and vowel-like, and the "semivowels" [w] and [y] lack important properties of both consonants and vowels. Speech is carried along by a succession of syllables, and at the center of each syllable stand one or more vowels. Consonants are pronounced as the tongue and mouth move from the vowel of one syllable to the vowel of the next. The consonants hang off one or both sides of each vowel, so to speak, and depend for their very existence on the pronunciation of the vowel.

Consonants

The consonants differ from one another in three major ways—in the part of the mouth that is constricted, in the manner in which it is constricted, and in whether or not this constriction is accompanied by the vibration of the vocal cords.

First, consonants differ in their *place of articulation*. In English there are seven major points at which the mouth can be constricted, and these are shown in Figure 5–1. They are:

(1) the two lips together (called *bilabial*)
(2) the bottom lip against the upper front teeth (*labiodental*)
(3) the tongue against the teeth (*dental*)
(4) the tongue against the alveolar ridge of the gums just behind the upper front teeth (*alveolar*)
(5) the tongue against the hard palate in the roof of the mouth just behind the alveolar ridge (*palatal*)
(6) the tongue against the soft palate, or velum, in the rear roof of the mouth (*velar*)
(7) the glottis in the throat (*glottal*)

This division breaks up the consonants into seven major groups:

(1) *bilabial:* p, b, m, w
(2) *labiodental:* f, v
(3) *dental:* θ, ð
(4) *alveolar:* t, d, s, z, n, l, r
(5) *palatal:* š, ž, č, ǰ, y
(6) *velar:* k, g
(7) *glottal:* h

Consonants also differ in their *manner of articulation*, the mechanical means by which the sound is produced. The six main categories are as follows:

FIGURE 5–1

POSITIONS OF ARTICULATION IN THE MOUTH

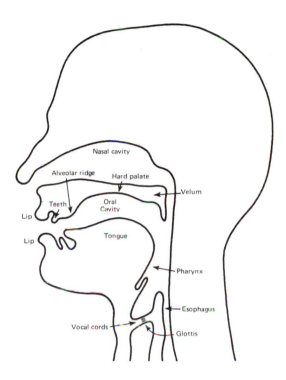

(1) *stops:* p, b, t, d, k, g
(2) *fricatives:* f, v, θ, ð, s, z, š, ž, h
(3) *affricates:* č, ǰ
(4) *nasals:* m, n, ŋ
(5) *laterals:* l
(6) *semivowels:* w, r, y

The *stops,* the most "consonantal" of the consonants, are produced by a complete closure at a point of articulation. Thus [p] is produced by a closure of the two lips and the release of a slight rush of air that has built up with the closure. The *fricatives* are produced by a constriction at the point of articulation, which sets up turbulence as the air rushes through. So [f] gets its character from air rushing between the almost complete closure of the bottom lip against the upper front teeth. Unlike stops, which necessarily have a brief duration, fricatives can be sustained as long as there is air in the lungs. The *affricates* are produced by a sequence of complete closure followed by a fricative-like rushing of air through a constriction. Some linguists consider affricates to be an amalgamation of a stop and a fricative, writing [č] and [ǰ] (in **church** and **judge,** respectively) as [tš] and [dž]. The *nasals* are formed by a complete closure of the mouth at some point of

TABLE 5–2

THE ENGLISH CONSONANTS

Symbols on the left side of each column are voiceless, those on the right side are voiced

	BI-LABIAL	LABIO-DENTAL	DENTAL	ALVEO-LAR	PALA-TAL	VELAR	GLOT-TAL
STOPS	p b			t d		k g	
FRICATIVES		f v	θ ð	s z	š ž		h
AFFRICATES					č ǰ		
NASALS	m			n		ŋ	
LATERAL				l			
SEMIVOWELS	w			r	y		

articulation along with the opening of the nasal cavity (by lowering the velum) to let the air rush through the nose. (Note that the nasals, [m], [n], and [ŋ], cannot be produced with the nose held shut.) Nasals can be held indefinitely too, as in humming. Finally, *laterals* and *semivowels* are produced by shaping the tongue in different ways. The main opening is at the sides of the tongue for the lateral [l] and in the middle for the semivowels [w], [r], and [y]. Each of these different mechanical means leads to a different quality of sound, so manner of articulation is very important in the specification of phonetic segments. The classification of consonants by place and manner of articulation leads to the consonant chart shown in Table 5–2.

Consonants in English—though not in all languages—can also be divided in a third way: by the feature called *voicing*. Compare the [s] in **sip** and the [z] in **zip**. The [s] is pronounced without any accompanying vibration of the vocal cords, while the [z] is pronounced like [s] but is accompanied by a vibration of the vocal cords. The voicing of the [z] can be felt by placing the fingers on the Adam's apple of the throat. The [s], then, is said to be *voiceless* (or unvoiced) and the [z] *voiced*. As the chart in Table 5–2 shows, many pairs of English consonants are identical in place and manner of articulation and differ only in voicing: [p]–[b], [t]–[d], [k]–[g], [f]–[v], [s]–[z], [θ]–[ð], [š]–[ž], and [č]–[ǰ]. All the nasals, laterals, and semivowels are voiced and [h] is voiceless.

Vowels

Vowels are produced by articulatory gestures mainly associated with the position of the tongue. The highest part of the tongue can be in the front, as in **pit**, in the center, as in **putt**, or in the back, as in **put**. And the height of the tongue can be high, as in **pit**, "mid," as in **pet**, or low, as in **pat**. The jaw tends to open more and more too as the vowels are formed lower and lower in the mouth. This two-way classification of vowels, according to the dimensions of front-central-back and high-mid-low, forms the classic "vowel chart" shown in Table 5–3.

TABLE 5–3
TWO-WAY CLASSIFICATION OF ENGLISH VOWELS

| HEIGHT OF TONGUE | PART OF THE TONGUE INVOLVED | | |
	FRONT	CENTRAL	BACK
HIGH	i beet		u boot
	ɪ bit	ɨ marry	ʊ put
MID	e bait		o boat
	ɛ bet	ə sofa	ɔ bought
LOW	æ bat	ʌ but	a pot

Within several cells of this chart there are two vowels that differ in whether they are formed with a slower, more deliberate "tense" motion—the [i] in **heed**—or with a more "lax" motion—the [ɪ] in **hid**. In addition, the four back vowels [u], [ʊ], [o], [ə] are all formed with some rounding of the lips. Although in English none of the front vowels is "rounded," some are in German, as in **grün**, and in French, as in **tu**.

The mid central vowel [ə], the final vowel of **sofa**, is called the *schwa* and has a special status among vowels. It is a neutral "reduced" vowel that appears only in syllables that do not have stress (or accent). In the phrase **the beautiful telephone**, the **e** in **the**, the **i** in **beautiful**, and the second **e** in **telephone** are all pronounced as schwas. It is as if vowels without stress tend to be formed with the tongue in its resting position, with no special effort or movement, and these appear as the neutral schwas. Other vowels are deliberate shifts away from this resting position.

Intonation and Stress

Phoneticians have also attempted to describe the *suprasegmental* aspects of speech—those aspects, like intonation and stress, that stretch over more than one segment. The sentence **You're going home**, for example, takes on different intonation patterns depending on whether it is an inquisitive question (**You're going home?**), a question evincing surprise (**You're going home!?**), a stern command (**You're going home—right this minute**), a statement stressing one of the three words (**YOU'RE going home**, or **You're GOING home**, or **You're going HOME**), or simply a neutral statement of fact (**You took the right turn— you're going home**). The intonation contour in each version arises mainly from variations in the pitch of the voice. Most English assertions begin with a raised pitch near the beginning of the sentence, and the pitch falls at the end. With questions, the pitch rises slightly at the end of the sentence, giving a "question intonation."

Closely tied to intonation is stress, the difference in emphasis given to different syllables in a sentence. Compare **black board** with **blackboard**. In the adjective + noun expression **black board**, **black** gets "secondary" stress and **board** "primary" stress. In the compound noun **blackboard**, on the other hand, **black** gets primary stress and **board** "tertiary" stress. The difference in meaning between **black board** and **blackboard**, then, is signaled in the stress pattern. Besides primary, secondary, and tertiary stress, there is also "weak" or zero stress, as in the second syllable of **telephone**. Stress is produced by making the vowel in a syllable louder, higher in pitch, or longer, and so stress is a property of the vowel center of each syllable. There is no such location for intonation, of course, for it arises from the overall "melody" of the sentence. Intonation is much more difficult to characterize than stress.

These two suprasegmental features—intonation and stress—are important in speech because they tie the individual segments and syllables together. For this reason they should play a significant role in the perception of speech.

Acoustic Phonetics

Phonetic segments can also be studied acoustically, just as car horns, violin notes, or pure tones can be studied for their acoustic properties. For this purpose phoneticians have made extensive use of the *spectrogram* (Figure 5–2). This is a

FIGURE 5–2

A SPECTROGRAM

The words **bab**, **dad**, **gag** spoken with a British accent.

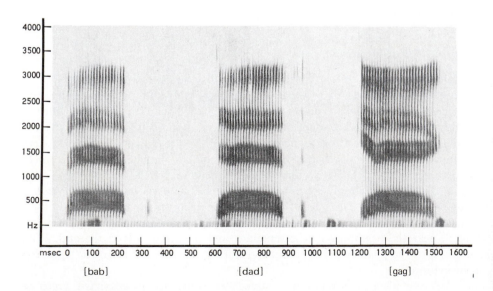

From Ladefoged (1975).   Reproduced by permission.

graphic representation of the frequencies of the voice. The horizontal axis shows time from the beginning of speech in thousandths of a second (milliseconds), while the vertical axis shows the frequency of the speech sounds in Hertz, or cycles per second. The lighter and darker smudges show how loud the sound is at each frequency and at each point in time. So there are loud sounds around the frequency of 300 to 700 Hertz for about 200 milliseconds in the pronunciation of the [æ] in **bab**. Spectrograms have made it possible to study the acoustic properties of phonetic segments in all types of sentences.

Interpreting Spectrograms

But what do the smudges on the spectrogram mean? The answer lies in the nature of the voice and the mouth cavities. The voice begins in the throat with the vibration of the vocal cords, which is very much like the vibration of a guitar string. In men they vibrate about 80 to 200 times a second, and in women they can go up to 400 times a second (Ladefoged, 1975). This results in the *fundamental* pitch of the voice. Imagine that the vocal cords vibrate at 128 times a second. This gives a fundamental pitch of 128 Hertz, which is the C one octave below middle C on the piano. At the same time, the voice produces harmonics of this fundamental pitch—that is, pitches at multiples of the fundamental at 256, 384, 512 Hertz, and so on. As the vibrations produced pass through the pharynx and the oral cavity (see Figure 5–1), some of these harmonics are enhanced and others are diminished, and this leads to a particular pattern of sound. The spectrogram for **bab**, for example, shows that the frequencies have been enhanced in a band around 500 Hertz, in a band around 1450 Hertz, and in several other bands at higher frequencies. These bands of enhanced sound are called *formants*. The lowest is the first formant, and the next lowest the second formant. These two formants correspond to the two major cavities in the speech system—the pharynx and the oral cavity.

  Since the shapes of these two cavities are responsible for the first and second formants, any change in these shapes should change the first and second formants. And indeed, this is what distinguishes one vowel from another. Here, for example, are some average frequencies for the first two formants in two vowels (from Ladefoged, 1975):

Vowel	*As in*	*First formant*	*Second formant*
[i]	heed	280 Hertz	2250 Hertz
[æ]	had	690 Hertz	1660 Hertz

Of course, only pure vowels have this character. They are produced from a static configuration of the vocal tract, and so their formants do not change during the production of the sound. This is not true of consonants, which are characterized by abrupt changes in the formants, sometimes accompanied by wide bands of sound spread over the whole frequency range. For example, the fricatives [s] and [š], as in **see** and **she**, yield a broad smear of energy up and down the spectrogram that reflects their buzzing quality. Other consonants produce other patterns on the spectrogram.

Distinctive Features

Phonetic segments, therefore, fit into a classification scheme with articulatory gestures at its base. From around 1940 on, linguists began to think of this scheme in terms of the distinctive oppositions it contained. The segments [p] and [b], for example, differ only in whether or not they are voiced: [p] is voiceless and [b] is voiced. The attribute of voicing is therefore a *distinctive feature* of these two segments, and they contrast in the value of the distinctive feature they contain. The [b] is said to be [+voice] and the [p] is said to be [−voice]. The plus denotes the presence of voicing, and the minus its absence. The rest of the classification scheme can be broken up into binary distinctive features as well. Each segment is uniquely characterized by its values on thirteen or so distinctive features. In this system, a segment is said to be a bundle of distinctive features.

The distinctive features of most English segments are listed in Table 5–4, based on the work of N. Chomsky and Halle (1968). Some explanation of these features is in order. The main two features are Vocalic and Consonantal. Just as one would suppose, all true consonants are [+consonantal] and [−vocalic], and all true vowels are [−consonantal] and [+vocalic]. But the few segments that have aspects of both consonants and vowels, namely the liquids [r] and [l], are [+consonantal] and [+vocalic], and the segments [y], [w], [h], which lack certain consonantal and vowel properties, are classified as [−consonantal] and [−vocalic]. The distinctive feature Anterior determines whether the segment is made in the front ("anterior") or back of the mouth, and Coronal, whether it is made in the top center (the "crown" or "corona") or the periphery of the mouth. The feature Continuant classifies segments according to whether they are produced with a continuous sound or not, and the feature Strident, whether or not there is a buzzing quality involved. The features Voice and Nasal are self-explanatory. Height in vowels is reflected in the features High and Low, and the front-back dimension in the features Back and Round. Finally, vowels can be [+tense] or [−tense] according to whether they are "tense" or "lax."

After a moment's reflection, it is easy to see that the matrix in Table 5–4 is exceptionally wasteful of distinctive features. With thirteen different features, each with two values, it is possible in theory to construct 2^{13} or 8192 different phonetic segments by combining the features in every possible way. Instead there are less than forty segments. What this means is that the values on some distinctive features are predictable from others. To take one example, if a segment is [+nasal]—that is, it is [m], [n], or [ŋ]—then it must also be [+consonantal], [−vocalic], [+voice], [−continuant], and [−strident]. This type of predictability can be captured in phonological rules. When all the entries in the matrix that can be reconstructed on the basis of such rules are eliminated, the matrix contains only a scattering of pluses and minuses, namely those values not pre-

TABLE 5–4

DISTINCTIVE FEATURES FOR ENGLISH CONSONANTS AND VOWELS

CONSONANTS AND LIQUIDS

DISTINCTIVE FEATURE	p	b	t	d	č	ǰ	k	g	f	v	θ	ð	s	z	š	ž	r	l	m	n	ŋ
CONSONANTAL	+	+	+	+	+	+	+	+	+	+	+	+	+	+	+	+	+	+	+	+	+
VOCALIC	−	−	−	−	−	−	−	−	−	−	−	−	−	−	−	−	+	+	−	−	−
ANTERIOR	+	+	+	+	−	−	−	−	+	+	+	+	+	+	−	−	−	+	+	+	−
CORONAL	−	−	+	+	+	+	−	−	−	−	+	+	+	+	+	+	+	+	−	+	−
VOICE	−	+	−	+	−	+	−	+	−	+	−	+	−	+	−	+	+	+	+	+	+
NASAL	−	−	−	−	−	−	−	−	−	−	−	−	−	−	−	−	−	−	+	+	+
STRIDENT	−	−	−	−	+	+	−	−	+	+	−	−	+	+	+	+	−	−	−	−	−
CONTINUANT	−	−	−	−	−	−	−	−	+	+	+	+	+	+	+	+	+	+	−	−	−

VOWELS AND GLIDES

DISTINCTIVE FEATURE	i	ɪ	e	ɛ	æ	ɨ	ə	ʌ	a	u	ʊ	o	ɔ	y	w	h
VOCALIC	+	+	+	+	+	+	+	+	+	+	+	+	+	−	−	−
CONSONANTAL	−	−	−	−	−	−	−	−	−	−	−	−	−	−	−	−
HIGH	+	+	−	−	−	+	−	−	−	+	+	−	−	+	+	−
BACK	−	−	−	−	−	+	+	+	+	+	+	+	+	−	+	−
LOW	−	−	−	−	+	−	−	−	+	−	−	−	+	−	−	+
ROUND	−	−	−	−	−	−	−	−	−	+	+	+	+	−	+	−
TENSE	+	−	+	−	−	−	−	−	+	+	−	+	−	−	−	−

dictable from other features. The notion of predictability is fundamental to the study of phonology.

Phonology

In phonology, linguists have been interested in two things: (1) an abstract representation that captures the true "essence" of the sounds in words and sentences; and (2) a set of rules that tells how to change and fill in this representation to make the phonetic segments that specify how words are actually pronounced. The backbone of the phonological enterprise is the phonological representation. It consists of a series of phonological segments, each of which is a bundle of distinctive features. But in this representation, the only features included are those not predictable from other features. Added to this is a set of phonological rules that fills in the predictable distinctive features that are missing. Once the rules have been applied, the result is a phonetic representation that corresponds to the pronunciation of the word.

This abstract picture of phonology can be brought down to earth with a concrete example. At the top of Table 5–5 is the phonological representation for the word **spin**. It consists of a series of four segments—the four segments in [spɪn]—with the distinctive features arranged vertically in square brackets. This phonological representation doesn't list all the features of each segment. The [s], for example, has only one feature, namely [+consonantal]—hardly enough to specify it as an [s]. How could this be? What keeps this segment from being confused with the other twenty segments that are [+consonantal]? Here is where the phonological rules come in. In English, whenever a word begins with two "true" consonants, the first must be an [s]. English doesn't allow such sequences as **fpin** or **mpin** or **rpin** (although other languages may). To reflect this fact, phonologists have developed a phonological rule that goes like this: If a segment at the beginning of a word is [+consonantal] and is followed by a segment marked [+consonantal] and [−vocalic], then the first segment is also [−vocalic], [+anterior], [+coronal], [−voice], [+continuant], [−nasal], and [+strident]. This bundle of features, of course, uniquely specifies the segment [s]. The other three segments of **spin** are expanded by similar rules, and the result is the "final phonetic representation" shown in the lower part of Table 5–5.

Word Formation

Phonologists have worked hard to write rules for the addition of prefixes and suffixes. Take the word **electric**, whose phonological representation (symbolized in segments instead of features) is [ɛlɛktrɪk]. Add the suffix **-ity** and the phonological representation becomes [ɛlɛktrɪk + ɪti]. With no changes in the phonological representation, this would be pronounced "electrickity," with a [k] instead of an [s] just before the suffix. This is clearly wrong. What is needed is a rule to capture the fact that in English the final [k] in words like [ɛlɛktrɪk] "softens" to an [s] just before any suffix (like **-ity**) that begins with an [ɪ]. This is accomplished by

TABLE 5–5
UNDERLYING PHONOLOGICAL REPRESENTATION AND FINAL
PHONETIC REPRESENTATION FOR **SPIN**

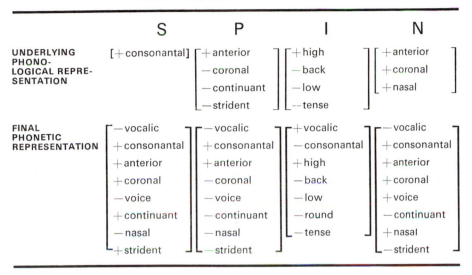

	S	P	I	N
UNDERLYING PHONO- LOGICAL REPRE- SENTATION	[+consonantal]	⎡+anterior −coronal −continuant −strident⎤	⎡+high −back −low --tense⎤	⎡+anterior +coronal +nasal⎤
FINAL PHONETIC REPRESENTATION	⎡−vocalic +consonantal +anterior +coronal −voice +continuant −nasal +strident⎤	⎡−vocalic +consonantal +anterior −coronal −voice −continuant −nasal −strident⎤	⎡+vocalic −consonantal +high −back −low −round −tense⎤	⎡−vocalic +consonantal +anterior +coronal +voice −continuant +nasal −strident⎤

the Velar Softening Rule. This rule also accounts for the softening of [k] to [s] in **medic** to **medicine, elastic** to **elasticity, critic** to **criticize,** and many other changes. In all, there are many phonological rules that together capture the regularities in the sound structure of English.

Certain aspects of pronunciation that at first appear odd and quite irregular have been shown to fit neatly into regular phonological rules. Take the formation of plural nouns in English with the addition of **-s.** On close scrutiny, we find there are actually three different phonetic manifestations of the **-s:**

bats: [bæt] + [s]
bags: [bæg] + [z]
batches: [bæč] + [əz]

That is, **-s** appears phonetically as [s], [z], or [əz], depending on the just preceding consonant. With the proper phonological rules, this apparent irregularity disappears. The following three rules, when applied in order, will do the job:

Rule 1. Add [z].

Rule 2. If the segment preceding [z] is the same as [z] in all features except Anterior, Voice, and Continuant, insert a schwa [ə] before the [z].

Rule 3. If the segment preceding [z] is [−voice], change the [z] to [−voice], namely to [s].

With these three rules, here are the successive changes made for **bag**, **bat**, and **batch**:

Original word	bæg	bæt	bæč
Rule 1	bægz	bætz	bæčz
Rule 2	——	——	bæčəz
Rule 3	——	bæts	——
Final form	bægz	bæts	bæčəz

The final form brought about by Rules 1, 2, and 3 is the correct pronunciation for all three words.

What is significant here is that roughly the same three rules are needed to account for other facts of English too. Without change, Rules 1, 2, and 3 account for the formation of singular verbs like **eats**, **needs**, and **reaches** and the formation of possessive nouns like **Pete's**, **Bob's**, and **George's**. With slight changes, they also account for the formation of past tense verbs:

bagged: [bæg] + [d]
batched: [bæč] + [t]
batted: [bæt] + [əd]

Here Rule 1 would add [d]. Rule 2 would check whether the [d] was too similar to the preceding consonant and if so insert a schwa [ə]. Rule 3 would check whether the preceding segment was voiceless and if so change the [d] to a voiceless [t]. Rules 2 and 3 happen to be very general rules in English.

Phonology Versus Phonetics

Why should phonologists go to all the bother of building abstract phonological representations and devising rules that lead to phonetic segments that can be pronounced? Why not stop with the concrete phonetic representations themselves? The critical arguments for phonological representations are ultimately psychological in character. Here are two of them:

(1) Phonological rules characterize regularities all speakers implicitly know. The rules for the formation of plurals with **-s**, for example, characterize our ability to make plurals of words we have never heard before, like **glitches** or **ruks**. Other rules characterize our ability to judge that **grat** and **bluck** are possible English words while **fpat** and **mluck** are not.

(2) Phonological rules enable us to see universal properties of pronunciation and word formation across all languages. Although the world's languages exhibit great variety in pronunciation, they still fall within certain limits. These limits are best described in relation to phonological rules. The sounds of languages change over the centuries, and these changes are often best described in relation to phonological rules too. If we are ever to discover the mental limits on pronunciation and the mental processes that lead to language change, phonological rules will be critical.

Like syntactic rules, however, phonological rules were not meant to describe the mental processes people actually use in speaking and listening. They merely capture the regularities of language. For theories about the mental processes used in speech perception, we turn first to the identification of isolated speech sounds.

IDENTIFICATION OF ISOLATED SPEECH SOUNDS

The study of speech perception is necessarily indirect. In articulatory phonetics, the mouth is visible and open for study, and in acoustic phonetics, so is the spectrogram. In speech perception, however, the ear is immobile and the brain inaccessible, and so new methods have had to be invented. One method is to analyze the acoustic properties of speech sounds that people identify as one or another phonetic segment. A second method is to create artificial speech sounds on the computer for people to identify. Still another is to have people identify speech sounds under conditions of noise or other distortion. From these methods it is possible to infer a lot about what people do in taking in and identifying speech sounds. Yet the conclusions one reaches about speech perception are different depending on whether the speech sounds are heard in isolation or as part of continuous speech. The first task is to see what is known about the identification of isolated speech sounds.

A Preliminary View

The main issue was posed in 1955 by George Miller and Patricia Nicely in their monumental study of perceptual confusions among sixteen English consonants. They had five people try to identify a long series of consonant-vowel (CV) syllables heard in the presence of noise or some other distortion. Each CV syllable consisted of one of the sixteen consonants followed by the vowel [a] of **father**. The consonants were: p, t, k, f, θ, s, š, b, d, g, v, ð, z, ž, m, n. Over several months, Miller and Nicely asked for 68,000 identifications of the sixteen CV syllables. Of interest here are the seven conditions in which the syllables were spoken in the presence of "white noise," an electronic hiss similar to that emitted by an unused channel of a television set. The noise was always at one level of loudness, and the speech varied from session to session over seven levels of loudness, from very soft to very loud. At its softest, the speech was about $\frac{1}{12}$ as loud as the noise (-18 decibels signal-to-noise ratio), and at its loudest, it was about 12 times as loud as the noise ($+18$ decibels signal-to-noise ratio). The louder the speech, of course, the fewer confusions these listeners made in their identifications. With the softer conditions, they made many errors.

Patterns of Confusions

The misidentifications fell into a strikingly regular pattern, one that is generally explicable by the articulatory features of the consonants. Examining these confusions is a complicated business, but it can be facilitated with a spatial display Shepard (1972) made of the data, shown in Figure 5–3. Although the way Shepard arrived at this layout is just as complicated to explain, the display

FIGURE 5–3

SIXTEEN CONSONANTS

Representation of the Effect of Signal-to-Noise Ratio
on Confusions among Miller and Nicely's Sixteen Consonants.

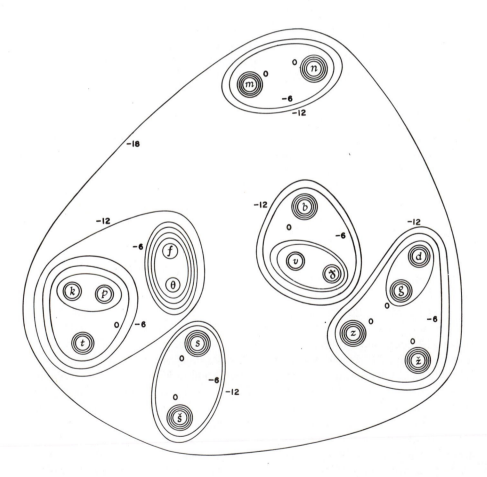

itself has a simple interpretation. The closer together two consonants are in the display, the more often they were confused with one another. On top of this spatial layout is superimposed a series of circles labeled with the loudness level of the speech, from −18 decibels (very soft) to +18 decibels (very loud). The consonants enclosed by each circle were all highly confused in the speech of that loudness level. So when speech was at its softest (−18 decibels), all consonants were highly confused; when it was equal to the noise in loudness (0 decibels), some consonants were confused; and when it was at its loudest (+18 decibels), almost no consonants were misidentified.

Two consonants were most likely to be confused when they were similar in their articulatory features. Here are the highly confused pairs in Figure 5–3:

m–n   f–θ   v–ð   p–t–k   d–g   s–š   z–ž

The two or three segments within each group are virtually identical in pronunciation. Within the first five groups, the two or three segments differ only in place of articulation, and within the last two, they differ only in manner and place of articulation. Another way to view this display is to see what consonants were least likely to be confused. The sixteen consonants in Figure 5–3 fall roughly into three well-differentiated groups:

voiceless consonants: p, t, k, f, θ, s, š (lower left)

voiced consonants: b, d, g, v, ð, z, ž (lower right)

nasals: m, n (upper right)

Two consonants were least likely to be confused when they differed only in voicing or nasality. In short, the noise was most detrimental to distinguishing place of articulation, less so to manner of articulation, and least of all to voicing and nasality.

Perception of Consonant Pieces

All this suggests that people perceive the separate features of the sixteen consonants relatively independently of each other. They take in each segment, not as a unitary whole, but as a collection of separate pieces of a pattern. If they had perceived each segment as a unitary whole, then on making a mistake, they should be as likely to guess one segment as any other. Perception would be "all or none." But this does not happen. They sometimes get partial information about the segment, identifying it as voiced and non-nasal, for example, without identifying it as bilabial. On the basis of such partial identifications, the errors that they make are systematic ones. They select only segments that are voiced and non-nasal.

One can think of people as having five different "channels" through which they take in five separate pieces of each consonant simultaneously. The five

TABLE 5–6

CHANNELS

Five hypothetical channels for perceiving the sixteen consonants in the Miller-Nicely study.
The groups of segments distinguished by each channel are listed at the right.

CHANNEL	SEGMENTS DISTINGUISHED
1 : Voicing	[b d g v ð z ž m n] vs. [p t k f θ s š]
2 : Nasality	[m n] vs. the rest
3 : Stridency	[f θ s š v ð z ž] vs. [p t k b d g m n]
4 : Duration	[s š z ž] vs. the rest
5 : Place of articulation	[p f b v m] vs. [t θ s d ð z n] vs. [k š g ž]

channels Miller and Nicely proposed are shown in Table 5–6. Each channel accepts only one piece of information, but this piece is enough to enable people to identify which of two (and in one case three) groups of segments the heard segment belongs to. By putting all five channels together, people can uniquely identify the correct segment. Take [p]. It would lead to these values on the five channels:

Channel 1: voiceless
Channel 2: not nasal
Channel 3: not strident
Channel 4: short duration
Channel 5: front consonant

Taken together, these values uniquely specify the segment as [p]. Imagine, however, that Channel 5 had been turned off. Now the segment heard would have no specification for place of articulation and could be [p], [t], or [k]. When forced to guess, people will be wrong about two-thirds of the time. In Miller and Nicely's study, these were just the misidentifications the listeners made. They often misidentified [p] as [k] and [t], and vice versa. Other distortions that were used selectively knocked out, or turned off, different ones of the five channels. When low frequencies of the speech were eliminated, for example, it was as if Channel 1 had been turned off, and there were many confusions between consonants, like [p] and [b], that differed only in voicing.

By now it should be obvious that at least four of Miller and Nicely's five channels correspond to single distinctive features or a combination of two features. Here is the correspondence:

Channel 1: Voice
Channel 2: Nasal
Channel 3: Strident
Channel 4: No direct correspondence
Channel 5: A combination of Anterior and Coronal

Speech perception appears to be closely linked to phonetics and phonology. The parts of a segment people perceive are with few exceptions the same as the features in a phonetic and phonological analysis of that segment.

This part of the Miller-Nicely study, then, provides a preliminary answer to the question of how people identify speech sounds in isolation. It suggests that people take in phonetic segments in pieces, put the pieces together, and identify the segments from the combined pattern. But further questions remain. Exactly what are the pieces people perceive? How are they put together into a whole pattern? How is this pattern used in the identification of a segment? More recent research has tried to answer these questions and fill in other details about speech perception.

The Auditory Stage

Many investigators have argued that speech sounds are identified in roughly three stages: an auditory stage, a phonetic stage, and a phonological stage (see Pisoni and Sawsch, 1975; Studdert-Kennedy, 1974u, 1975).

During the *auditory stage*, listeners take in short stretches of the raw acoustic signal reaching the ear, make a preliminary auditory analysis of the signal, and place the result in an "auditory" memory. So far no speech segments have been identified.

During the *phonetic stage*, listeners examine the contents of this auditory memory for "acoustic cues," put these cues together, and identify each pattern of cues as a particular phonetic segment such as [s]. These identifications are placed in a "phonetic" memory that is categorical in nature. It preserves the identification of a sound as [s], but does not preserve the acoustic cues upon which this identification was made.

During the *phonological stage*, listeners consult the constraints English places on sequences of phonetic segments and adjusts the preliminary identifications to conform to these constraints. The phonological stage, for example, might alter the phonetic sequence from [fpɪn] to [spɪn], since [fpɪn] is an impossible sequence in English. The final product is stored in the familiar short-term memory (see Chapter 4) whose contents can be rehearsed to preserve for later use.

Only the last of these three stages, unfortunately, is open to conscious inspection. Most experiments are designed to get people to reveal the products of their phonological stage. Examining the contents of the auditory and phonetic stages takes a special experimental ingenuity that will become apparent in our look at the auditory stage.

Acoustic Cues

The aim of the auditory stage is to analyze raw speech into the "pieces" the Miller-Nicely study suggested are used in the identification of phonetic segments. These pieces have been called *acoustic cues*. In this view the auditory stage takes in short stretches of raw speech, one stretch at a time, and analyzes each stretch for the presence of acoustic cues (see Massaro, 1972). But what are these acoustic cues? It would be convenient for us if they fit the following ideal: Each stretch of speech corresponding to a phonetic segment—for example, [d]—would consist of, say, eight acoustic cues. These eight cues would be the same for every [d] and would be enough by themselves to enable the phonetic stage to identify that stretch of sound as a [d]. But nothing is ever so simple. The cues are not the same for every [d]. Nor are the cues from that stretch of sound alone sufficient to identify it as a [d]. This poses a major problem for speech perception.

The problem has been nicely illustrated by Liberman and his colleagues (1967), who showed that the acoustic cues for the [d] in [di] are radically different from those for the [d] in [du]. To demonstrate this, they synthesized the syllables [di] and [du] on the computer. They drew some artificial spectrograms, as in Figure 5–4, and programmed a computer to produce the sounds corresponding to these spectrograms. Note that this is the reverse of the usual procedure. Typically, phoneticians make spectrograms from actual speech, and not vice versa. But by this reverse procedure, Liberman and his colleagues could make phonetic segments with any acoustic cues they chose and then see how the segments were identified. As Figure 5–4 shows, their spectrograms contained only the first two

FIGURE 5–4
TWO ARTIFICIAL SPECTROGRAMS

Artificial spectrograms for [di] and [du], showing the first and second formants

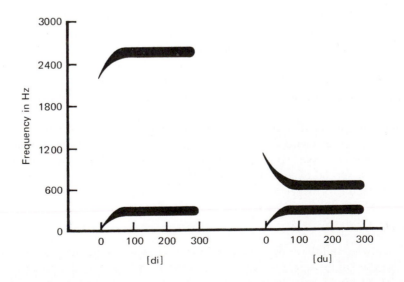

From Liberman, Cooper, Shankweiler, and Studdert-Kennedy (1967). Reproduced by permission.

formants. Normally these are enough to distinguish one vowel from another.

The two spectrograms in Figure 5–4 are the ones that were identified as [di] and [du]. First, consider the sustained vowels [i] and [u], the last two-thirds of each syllable. They differ only in the position of their second formant. For both [i] and [u], the first formant, the lowest bar, is around 300 Hertz, or just above Middle C on the piano. For [i], the second formant, the upper bar, is at 2700 Hertz, more than three octaves above the first formant. For [u], in contrast, the second formant is at 600 Hertz, only one octave above the first formant. The difference in the second formant is the acoustic cue that distinguishes [i] from [u].

What is striking, however, is that there is no single spectrographic pattern associated with the [d]s. The [d] in [di] is signaled by a short quick sweep of the second formant up to its final level for the [i], whereas the [d] in [du] is signaled by a quick sweep of the second formant down to its final level for [u]. The two [d]s are signaled by the transition of the formants from silence to the following vowels, and the transitions take different forms. Put another way, the acoustic cue that signals the [d] depends on the vowel that follows: it has one form before [i] and another before [u]. To identify the [d]s, the phonetic stage must look at acoustic cues from the transition and following vowel together.

This demonstration suggests that the acoustic cues made available to the phonetic stage are of two broad types: context-independent and context-dependent. These can be illustrated for consonants:

(1) *Context-independent cues*. The hissing sound in [s] occurs no matter what segments precede and follow the [s]. And [z] is invariably distinguished from [s] by an additional low pitch caused by the voicing. Consonants that can apparently be identified on the basis of their context-independent cues alone are [s], [z], [š], [ž], [č], [ǰ] (Cole and Scott, 1974).

(2) *Context-dependent cues*. For many segments, the acoustic cues depend on the segments that precede or follow. This was true of the [d]s in the syllables [di] and [du]. The time course of transitions can also be critical. For example, when a short silence is introduced between the [s] and [l] of **slit**, the word is suddenly heard as **split**. And increasing the silence between the syllables of **rabid (ra-bid)** and **topic (to-pic)** leads to perception of the words **rapid** and **top pick**. Context-dependent cues like these appear to be far more usual than the context-independent cues.

Voice Onset Time

One important context-dependent cue in English is what has been called *Voice Onset Time*. In the pronunciation of [b] and [p], two things happen: the closed lips are released, and the vocal cords begin vibrating. In [ba], the release usually occurs simultaneously with the beginning of the vibration, while in [pa], the release occurs about 0.06 seconds after the vibration begins (Lisker and Abramson, 1964; W. Cooper, 1975). That is, the Voice Onset Time for [b] is 0 and for [p] +0.06

seconds. The difference is shown in Figure 5–5. It is this small 0.06-second difference in Voice Onset Time that distinguishes [ba] from [pa] and gives us the impression that [b] is voiced and [p] is voiceless. A similar difference in Voice Onset Time distinguishes other voiced consonants from their voiceless counterparts, for example, [d] and [t]. As an acoustic cue, Voice Onset Time is partially context-dependent. The time relation between voicing and release changes slightly from one consonant to the next and from one context to the next.

FIGURE 5–5

VOICE ONSET TIME

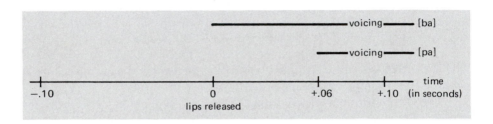

It is easy to see how acoustic cues like Voice Onset Time might be the "pieces" used by the five channels in Miller and Nicely's model of consonant perception. Channel 1, Voicing, would make use of the acoustic cue of Voice Onset Time. As long as the sound of the vocal cords and the sound of the release are audible, people should be able to distinguish a voiced consonant from its voiceless counterpart. This is just what happened in Miller and Nicely's "white noise" experiment. Channel 3, Stridency, on the other hand, would make use of the acoustic cue of whether or not there are certain high frequency hisses in the consonant. If white noise obliterates this cue without affecting Voice Onset Time, people should get stridency wrong and voicing right. This, too, often happened in Miller and Nicely's experiment. Thus, since the acoustic cues themselves are relatively independent of each other—but only relatively—people can make mistakes on one channel and not on another, yielding the pattern of confusions Miller and Nicely found (but see P. Smith, 1973; P. Smith and Jones, 1975).

Auditory Memory

The acoustic cues are stored in auditory memory, but what is the character of this memory? According to Crowder and Morton (1969; Crowder, 1971a, b; 1972), this memory, which they call the "precategorical acoustic store," lasts a very short time (up to a few seconds) and its contents can be obliterated during that time by certain types of new acoustic input. In one experiment people listened to nine digits in a row and then tried to recall all nine. In some lists, they heard an additional word, called the "suffix," immediately after the ninth digit. For example:

List: 4 7 1 5 9 3 8 6 2   *List and suffix:* 4 7 1 5 9 3 8 6 2 *rosy*

Although people knew beforehand they were supposed to ignore the suffix (the word **rosy** here), it had the effect of partially obliterating the ninth digit in auditory memory. When the suffix occurred, it greatly reduced their ability to recall the ninth digit.

The suffix, then, degrades what is already in auditory memory (although an argument could be made that it degrades phonetic memory instead). Over many experiments, Crowder and Morton tried out different suffixes and found some more debilitating than others. Here is a list of the most to the least debilitating of suffixes:

(1) a word (like **rosy, uh,** or even the nonsense word **orez**) spoken in the same voice as the previous digits

(2) a word spoken in a different voice or to the opposite ear

(3) a buzzer or burst of white noise of the same duration and intensity as a real word

This suggests that the auditory stage is selective in what it analyzes and stores. It is tuned to analyze speech, and not other sounds, from one person at one location at a time. This selectivity has an obvious value, a point that will come up again in selective listening.

The Phonetic Stage and Categorical Perception

The main purpose of the phonetic stage is to identify speech segments. During this stage listeners implicitly consult the acoustic cues provided by the auditory stage and attempt to *name* the segments they were meant to signal. The phonetic stage is faced with two problems. It must identify each segment, and it must put them in the right order. It must see that [di] consists of the segments [d] and [i], and that they come in this order. As noted before, the naming process is not simple. To identify [d], the phonetic stage must examine the acoustic cues of the whole syllable [di], not just the first "segment" of the syllable, because the cues for [d] differ depending on the following vowel. Even though phonetic segments are perceived to be in a linear order, the cues on which the perception is based do not necessarily come in that order. It is usually enough to examine cues one syllable at a time, but sometimes the cues for a segment may be even more distant.

Categorical Perception

The most important property of the phonetic stage is that its naming of most segments is categorical. Acoustically, speech segments can vary infinitely in their properties, with one segment shading off into another. Yet the phonetic stage forces these segments into discrete categories. Consider [b] and [p], which differ mainly in Voice Onset Time, the time between the release of the lips and the onset of the voicing. For [b], Voice Onset Time was 0 seconds, and for [p], it was +0.06 seconds. These time intervals represent averages for [b] and [p] spoken carefully and in isolation. In running conversation, [b] and [p] vary a great deal in Voice Onset Time, yet are still identified as [b] and [p]. How extreme can this variation become? How would a consonant halfway between the [b] and [p] be identified? Would it be identified as [b], or [p], or as neither?

The answers to these questions may be surprising. Lisker and Abramson (1970) used a computer to synthesize artificial syllables that began with a bilabial stop, [b] or [p], followed by the vowel [a]. By this method they were able to vary the Voice Onset Time of the stop from −0.15 seconds to +0.15 seconds in steps of .01 seconds. This procedure gave them thirty-one distinct syllables that differed only in Voice Onset Time. These thirty-one syllables were then presented to people in random order for identification. The results are shown in Figure 5–6. When Voice Onset Time was less than +0.03 seconds, the consonants were almost invariably identified as [b], but when it was greater than +0.03 seconds, they were identified as [p]. Throughout most of the continuum, people agreed 100 percent on what they heard: some consonants were [b] for everyone, and others were [p]. Only at the boundary were there disagreements about the identifications.

The boundary between [b] and [p] in Figure 5–6 is strikingly sharp. The area in which people's judgments were not 100 percent spans only 0.04 or 0.05 seconds. The same is true for the boundary in Voice Onset Time between [d] and [t], and between [g] and [k]. Sharp boundaries are typical of continua defined by other acoustic cues too, although the boundaries are usually much sharper for consonants than for vowels (Pisoni and Tash, 1974). It is as if the bilabial stops are sorted on the basis of Voice Onset Time into two adjacent pigeonholes, one labeled [b] and the other labeled [p]. The partition between them is so thin that very few bilabial stops hit the partition and do not make cleanly it into one of the two pigeonholes.

What the phonetic stage does, in effect, is map the continuum of Voice Onset Time onto the two phonetic features [+voice] and [−voice]. All those bilabial stops with Voice Onset Time below +0.03 seconds get the feature [+voice], and all those with Voice Onset Time above +0.03 seconds get the feature [−voice]. There are similar cutoffs on Voice Onset Time to mark the

FIGURE 5–6

BILABIAL CONSONANTS

Identification of Bilabial Consonants with Different Voice Onset Times As [b] or [p]

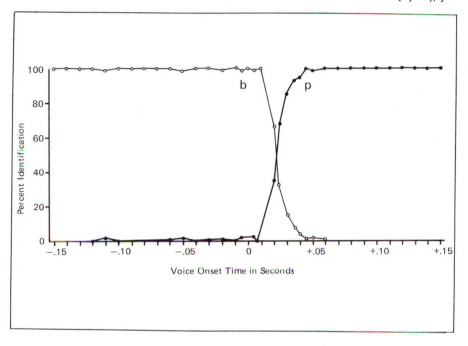

From L. Lisker and A. Abramson (1970). Reproduced by permission.

dental stops [d] and [t] as [+voice] or [−voice] and to mark the velar stops [g] and [k] as [+voice] or [−voice]. But is [+voice] truly the same feature in [b], [d], and [g]? Is [+voice] handled by the same mechanism no matter what the consonant? Somewhat surprisingly, the answer appears to be yes. This has been demonstrated in an ingenious set of experiments on "selective adaptation."

Selective Adaptation

When the back of the hand is tapped repeatedly over several minutes, that spot becomes less sensitive to the touch, even though other spots nearby will remain just as sensitive as before. This is called *selective adaptation*. On the basis of this phenomenon, Eimas and Corbit (1973) reasoned that repeated presentations of the syllable [ba] ought to make people much less sensitive to the various features of [ba], in particular the feature [+voice]. To show this, Eimas and Corbit had people listen to repeated presentations of [ba] and then, using Lisker and Abramson's technique, had them determine the boundary between [ba] and

[pa]. They assumed that when the [b] is fatigued, fewer of the bilabial stop consonants would be identified as [b] and more would be identified as [p], hence the boundary between [b] and [p] should move closer to 0 seconds. This is precisely what happened. It was as if the partition between the pigeonholes for [b] and [p] had moved slightly to one side, shrinking the pigeonhole for [b] and enlarging the one for [p].

[b]	[p]

[+voice]   [−voice]

But as Eimas and Corbit realized, the shrinking of the [b] pigeonhole could have arisen because the repeated [b]s fatigued the perception of [b] as a whole, not just the feature [+voice]. So they also determined the boundary between [b] and [p] after repeated presentations of [d], which is also [+voice]. There too they found that the boundary had moved left—that the pigeonhole for [b] had shrunk. W. Cooper and Blumstein (1974) were able to achieve the same effect along another dimension by repeated presentations of the other bilabial consonants [p], [m], and [w]. Selective adaptation has been demonstrated for many other phonetic features too (W. Cooper, 1975). These demonstrations are of considerable interest. They show, for example, that the perceptual analysis of [b] consists in part of the separate analysis of Voice Onset Time, an acoustic cue, into [+voice] or [−voice], a phonetic feature. At present, it appears that what is selectively adapted is the phonetic feature, although adaptation also occurs in acoustic cues (W. Cooper, 1975).

Phonetic Memory

The names arrived at in the phonetic stage are stored in phonetic memory, which is quite different from auditory memory. Recall that auditory memory stores acoustic cues for a segment. It therefore distinguishes among all the [b]s and [p]s that have different Voice Onset Times. Phonetic memory, on the other hand, stores only the names of the segments, the labels on the pigeonholes the segments have been sorted into. So while it distinguishes the [b]s from the [p]s— they have different names—it does not distinguish among the various [b]s or among the various [p]s, as auditory memory does. This difference between auditory and phonetic memory has turned up in many experiments since the original demonstration by Liberman and his colleagues in 1957.

In one study Pisoni (1973) drew four bilabial stop consonants from Lisker and Abramson's thirty-one synthetic consonants that varied only in Voice Onset Time (see Figure 5–6). These four consonants—call them C_1, C_2, C_3, and C_4—had Voice Onset Times as follows:

Voice Onset Time	0.00	+0.02	+0.04	+0.06	(seconds)
Auditory Memory	C_1	C_2	C_3	C_4	
Phonetic Memory	[b]	[b]	[p]	[p]	

Since the boundary between [b] and [p] is at +0.03 seconds on this continuum, C_1 and C_2 would be called [b], and C_3 and C_4 would be called [p]. In this configuration, auditory memory should contain Voice Onset Time information that would distinguish all four consonants, while phonetic memory should only distinguish C_1 and C_2 from C_3 and C_4—the [b]s from the [p]s. These consonants were combined with [a] into consonant-vowel syllables. People were presented two such syllables, one right after the other, and were asked to judge whether the two were the "same" or "different" in sound (not in name).

Different outcomes should arise depending on whether people make this judgment using auditory or phonetic memory. The critical comparisons are on these three pairs:

Pair 1: C_1 and C_2 Two [b]s
Pair 2: C_2 and C_3 A [b] and a [p]
Pair 3: C_3 and C_4 Two [p]s

Note that within each pair the two consonants differ by exactly 0.02 seconds in Voice Onset Time. Ideally, the three pairs should be judged to be "different" equally often. But will they? Imagine that people could consult auditory memory only. Since all three pairs have the same difference in Voice Onset Time and since that is what is stored in auditory memory, the three pairs should be equally discriminable. Imagine instead that people could consult only phonetic memory. Since C_1 and C_2 both have the same name and since that is what is stored in phonetic memory, they should not be distinguishable. People should do no better than chance in judging Pair 1, or in judging Pair 3. But since C_2 and C_3 have different names—[b] and [p]—they should be distinguishable, and people should be right on Pair 2 all of the time.

Pisoni found that phonetic memory was all people could generally consult. They were virtually perfect on Pair 2 and near chance on Pairs 1 and 3. This was typical of consonants on other acoustic continua too. For vowels, however, Pisoni noted that people could often consult auditory memory as well and make some discriminations on pairs analogous to 1 and 3. However, the longer the time interval between the presentation of the two vowels, the more people lost from auditory memory and the more they relied on phonetic memory instead. To Pisoni, this suggested that auditory memory fades rapidly, and more rapidly for consonants than for vowels. In short, the auditory and phonetic stages seem to work in sequence. Auditory memory lasts just long enough for the phonetic stage to identify the segments, while phonetic memory is able to store names for considerably longer periods of time.

Whenever two segments are classified under the same label in phonetic memory, they should be difficult, if not impossible, to tell apart. This point has been demonstrated in another way by Miyawaki and several American and Japanese colleagues (1975) in an experiment based on the fact that there is no phonetic contrast between [l] and [r] in Japanese. English [l]s and [r]s are all identified by Japanese listeners as the same sound. So while English listeners would have no trouble making fine discriminations between [l] and [r], Japanese listeners would. In a study like Pisoni's, Miyawaki and his colleagues included three critical pairs:

Pair 1:	C_1 and C_2	Two [l]s
Pair 2:	C_2 and C_3	An [l] and an [r]
Pair 3:	C_3 and C_4	Two [r]s

As predicted, the English listeners did well on Pair 2 and badly on Pairs 1 and 3. The Japanese listeners did equally badly on all three pairs. The role of phonetic memory, then, is critical to discriminating speech sounds, and what gets distinct labels in phonetic memory depends crucially on one's experience with a language.

The names in phonetic memory, however, are not single units that disappear in an all-or-none fashion. Rather, they seem to be amalgamations of distinctive features, and each feature can be lost from memory relatively independently of other features. Wickelgren (1965, 1966) demonstrated this point by examining the errors people made in trying to recall lists of six different CV syllables—like **ba, ka, ta, sa, ra, ma**. Since people tried to recall each list of syllables immediately, they were presumably tapping their short-term phonetic memory of the syllables. The errors they made in recall tended to preserve as many distinctive features of the original syllable as possible. Take the syllable [ba]. The three most frequent errors were these:

[pa]	Differs from [ba] only in voicing
[va]	Differs from [ba] only in manner and place of articulation
[ga]	Differs from [ba] only in place of articulation

These and other findings suggest that names are stored in phonetic memory as bundles of distinctive features, and that these features are preserved relatively independently of each other (but see also P. Smith, 1973; P. Smith and Jones, 1975).

The Phonological Stage

Every new English word people hear is expected to fit the phonological rules for English. Since phonological rules disallow [fp] at word beginnings, [fpar] wouldn't be expected to crop up as a new English word. Indeed, people are very accurate in judging which phonetic sequences are possible in a language and which are not. Greenberg and Jenkins (1964) presented English listeners with four-segment strings such as [stɪk], an actual English word, and [žyɪk], which is very un-English, and asked them to rate each for "how far this seems to be from an English word." Their ratings were in excellent agreement with predictions from the phonological rules of English. The more segments that needed altering before the word fit the English phonological rules, the more un-English it was rated. There is little doubt that people can judge phonetic sequences for their fit to phonological rules.

It is more remarkable, however, that these phonological rules affect what people actually hear. In a demonstration of this point by Day (1968, 1970), people were simultaneously presented with, for example, **banket** in the left ear and **lanket** in the right ear. Although some people heard **banket** and **lanket** separately, others "fused" the two sequences and heard **blanket**. For **sin** and **pin**, these people heard **spin**. What is remarkable is that these people never heard [lbæŋkɪt] or [psɪn], two sequences that are excluded by the phonological rules of English. When **lanket** was presented as much as 0.15 seconds before **banket**, these people still fused the two words into the phonologically correct **blanket**. Thus, while they were perfectly able to hear **tak** and **tass** as either **tacks** or **task**, they were constrained to hear **banket** and **lanket** only as **blanket** (see also Cutting, 1975, 1976).

But how do phonological rules influence what people actually hear? Here are two views—though not the only possible views. Under the first, the phonological stage comes after the phonetic stage. Given **lanket** and **banket**, it would take the contents of phonetic memory, [lbæŋkɪt], change it to [blæŋkɪt] to fit the phonological rules of English, and place this result in "short-term memory." Under the second view, the phonetic and phonological stages work simultaneously to form the contents of a single memory, a short-term memory. For [bæŋkɪt] and [læŋkɪt], the phonetic stage would interpret the acoustic cues for the initial consonants as [b] and [l], and the phonological stage would constrain them to be stored in the order [bl]. At no time would [lbæŋkɪt] per se be stored in memory. At present there is little reason to choose one of these views over any other.

Analysis by Synthesis

So far speech perception has seemed straightforward. The auditory stage analyzes raw speech into acoustic cues. These cues are used in the phonetic stage for the naming of phonetic segments. These in turn are adjusted in the phonological stage. There are complications because acoustic cues do not come neatly packaged in tight bundles. They must often be assembled from several stretches of speech taken together, like the [d] before a vowel. But these complications don't seem so great that they cannot be solved with more precise knowledge of the contingencies among neighboring segments. For every segment there is a pattern, a *template*, and to identify a segment it is all a matter of finding the template that matches the available acoustic cues.

But there is one problem that this view of the identification process can't deal with: there is more than one speaker in the world. The mapping of acoustic cues onto phonetic segments—call it the *acoustic-phonetic mapping*—is highly variable from one speaker to the next, and even from one utterance to the next within the same speaker. People differ in fundamental pitch, speed, quality of articulation, dialect, speech impediments, and general style. A single person sounds different depending on whether he is excited or calm, speaking with or without food in his mouth, shouting or whispering, talking to adults or to children, and so on. Each of these differences leads to a different acoustic-phonetic mapping, and the variation is potentially infinite. So phonetic segments cannot be identified by the finding of matching templates, because there would have to be an infinite number of such templates.

To solve this problem, many investigators (e.g., Halle and Stevens, 1962; Stevens, 1960) have proposed an active theory of speech perception called *analysis by synthesis*. It works like this. Listeners are assumed to have an internal production system by which they can generate or "synthesize" speech sounds for themselves. When they hear a stretch of speech, they synthesize a succession of speech sounds until they find a set that matches the incoming acoustic cues in every way. The speech sounds that are found to match are taken to be the segments the speaker meant to produce. Imagine listeners trying to identify **lass**. They might synthesize **race**, find it didn't fit in the first consonant and vowel, synthesize **loss**, find it didn't match in the vowel, synthesize **lass**, find it matched everywhere, and accept it as what the speaker said. In this procedure, the "analysis" of **lass** was brought about by the internal "synthesis" of a matching **lass**, hence the name analysis by synthesis. The internal synthesizer, of course, doesn't generate phonetic segments at random—it would never find matching speech sounds if it did that. Rather, it relies on the acoustic cues themselves to give it a start in the right direction and tries then to minimize the difference between the just synthesized segment and the actual segment, as in the succession **race**, **loss**, **lass**.

The important advantage of analysis by synthesis here is that it can handle variability both within and between speakers. The internal synthesizer can be adjusted to fit all the different speeds, pitches, voice qualities, dialects, and speech impediments thrown its way. From just a few moments of speech, listeners are able to adjust their synthesizers until the synthesized speech closely approximates the characteristics of the speaker. This way the synthesizer retains all the important phonetic and phonological distinctions inherent in language, but makes allowances for the precise qualities of the speaker's speech at this place and time.

Ladefoged and Broadbent (1957) have demonstrated just how immediate and compelling listeners' adjustments to a speaker can be. They presented people with one of six artificially generated versions of **Please say what this word is** followed by one of four artificially synthesized "test words." The task was to say whether each test word was **bit**, **bet**, **bat**, or **but**. The short introductory sentence had a striking effect on the following test words. When the introductory sentence was spoken in a relatively high-pitched voice, the first test word, for example, was identified as **bit** 87 percent of the time. However, when the introductory sentence was spoken in a low-pitched voice, the very same test word was identified as **bet** 90 percent of the time. The influence of the introductory sentence on the other three test words was just as large. Ladefoged and Broadbent were able to show that people used the introductory sentence to determine the characteristics of the "speaker" and adjust their perception to fit these characteristics. The identifications they made were fully predictable on this basis.

An even more important advantage of analysis by synthesis is that, at least in theory, it makes contact with the more global properties of speech. First, the synthesizer is programmed so that it will only synthesize segments that fit the phonetic and phonological properties of the language being spoken. This auto-matically brings in the phonological rules that make **blanket** possible and **lbanket** not. Second, it synthesizes segments within the suprasegmental structure appropriate for sentences. It brings in intonation, stress, and syllable structure. Note that the acoustic-phonetic mapping changes depending on the stress level of a syllable, the intonation contour, and the nature of the preceding and following syllables. Analysis by synthesis is capable of handling this kind of variability too. Third, the synthesizer will only synthesize speech that makes good sense syntactically and semantically. Here, then, is a place where the "later" stages of comprehension—the construction and utilization processes—can make contact with the process of identifying individual sounds. This point will become very important later on.

The Motor Theory of Speech Perception

But what is our internal speech synthesizer like? How does it adjust for differ-ences in the speaker's speed, dialect, voice quality, and speech impediments? One theory often proposed (Halle and Stevens, 1962; Liberman, Cooper, Shankweiler, and Studdert-Kennedy, 1967; Stevens, 1960; Stevens and House, 1972) is that it models the articulatory gestures the other person makes when speaking. Metaphorically speaking, our internal speech synthesizer contains a model of a mouth, which it adjusts to fit the size and shape, speed of gesture, impediments, and so forth, of the speaker's mouth. Since this theory conceives of the internal speech synthesizer as a model of the motor movements of the other person's speech mechanisms, it is called the *motor theory of speech per-ception.*

One piece of evidence for the motor theory lies in the way sounds are classified. Note that the [d]s in [di] and [du] are given the same name in English even though they are quite different acoustically, perhaps no more similar than [d] is to [b] in the syllables [di] and [bi]. Why are they classified together? Perhaps it is because they are pronounced with the same articulatory gesture: the closure of the tongue against the alveolar ridge accompanied by voicing. Listeners infer that the speaker must have intended to convey [d] in both instances since the same articulatory gesture was used. The fact that they do not sound exactly the same is more or less irrelevant—just as voice quality, speech impedi-ments, hesitations, and speed are irrelevant. Many other segments have analo-gous characteristics: the name they are given corresponds more directly to the way they are produced than to the way they sound. As Liberman et al. (1967, p. 453) put it, "This supports the assumption that the listener uses the inconstant sound as a basis for finding his way back to the articulatory gestures that pro-duced it and thence, as it were, to the speaker's intent."

Another type of evidence for the motor theory is illustrated by Lehiste and Peterson's (1959) study of the perception of loudness in vowels. As they noted, vowels spoken with the same effort differ widely in the amount of acoustic energy they contain. For example, when spoken with the same effort, the [i] in **beat** contains much more acoustic energy than the [o] in **boat**. Lehiste and Peterson had some speakers produce vowels such as these so that they all had the same physically measured acoustic energy and then presented these vowels to other listeners for judgments of relative loudness. Even though the amounts of acoustic energy were the same, the [o] was judged to be much "louder" than the [i]. Listeners apparently judge two vowels as being equally loud, not when they have the same acoustic energy, but when they are thought to have been pronounced with the same effort. Thus, the listener's model of the speaker's mouth and articulatory gestures is critical. Perception follows the inferred articulatory gestures, not the acoustic characteristics they are inferred from (see also Lieberman, 1967).

The Strong and Weak Versions

The motor theory, however, is only plausible in a weak version. Taken literally— the "strong" version—it suggests that listeners use their own speech production mechanism to "say" words to themselves that match the incoming words. There is considerable evidence that this doesn't happen. For one thing, there is no evidence that people "talk" to themselves subvocally while listening to other people talk. During listening there is no patterned activity in the speech muscles. Secondly, if the speech production mechanism were necessarily involved, people who for neurological reasons cannot speak should not be able to understand either. Yet Lenneberg (1962) and Fourcin (1975a) have reported cases of people without speech who could apparently understand speech perfectly well. More generally, the strong view would imply that people could not understand speech they themselves could not produce. This is clearly incorrect. We can all understand stutterers, members of the opposite sex, children, people with extreme dialect differences or foreign accents, and many other people whose speech we could not remotely reproduce.

The motor theory, therefore, has to be thought of more abstractly as a perceptual mechanism that determines how the speaker would have to say what he said. Regrettably, this weakening of the motor theory saps it of much of its original vitality. In the weaker version, the predictions are less compelling and often have alternative explanations (see Fant, 1967; Fourcin, 1975b). Some investigators have even argued that the weak version has no predictive power at all. For many, however, the motor theory still provides a way of looking at speech perception, a way of thinking about the indirect correspondences between the acoustic signal and the segments people actually perceive. Time will tell whether this theory can be given enough muscle to tackle all the facts of speech perception.

A Recapitulation

In summary, the identification of isolated speech sounds is a complicated process. The auditory stage analyzes the incoming speech stream into acoustic cues; the phonetic and phonological stages identify the intended phonetic segments and their order from these acoustic cues. The use of acoustic cues in this identification

process, however, is indirect. The cues leading to a particular identification, say a [d], are not all found together in a single stretch of speech, but come distributed along the speech stream and change with the presence of other cues. Moreover, there is an enormous variation in acoustic-phonetic mapping with changes in speakers, situations, and even intonation and stress. To handle this, people are often assumed to have an internal production system that synthesizes speech sounds to match the incoming acoustic cues. According to the motor theory of speech perception, this synthesis is based on a model of the articulatory gestures the speaker goes through in producing the speech.

For many investigators, analysis by synthesis is a critical part of this process. It is the internal synthesizer that introduces phonetic and phonological constraints, takes intonation and stress into account, and brings meaning and use into play. To see how meaning and use *do* seem to influence speech perception, however, we must turn to the perception of continuous speech and examine processes that work mainly from the top down—from meaning and use toward the speech stream.

PERCEPTION OF CONTINUOUS SPEECH

Speech normally occurs in conversations with meaning and substance, and people listen for the message, not the sounds. This is quite unlike the situations just reviewed in which people identified single syllables heard in isolation for sound rather than message. This disparity should make us wary. Are the theories of isolated speech sounds adequate for continuous speech? The answer turns out to be no. Then what is the relation between these two types of perception? One possibility is that the perception of continuous speech uses all the processes of the perception of isolated speech sounds and then some. A more troublesome possibility is that the two kinds of perception are in certain ways fundamentally different. Although the verdict is not yet in, the second of these two possibilities is still too real to dismiss out of hand.

Consider the hypothesis that the perception of continuous speech is *identical* to the perception of isolated speech sounds. This hypothesis is demolished by some of the earliest work on speech perception. G. Miller, Heise, and Lichten (1951) had people try to identify words in various amounts of white noise. The words were presented to some people in five-word sentences and to others in isolation. At all levels of noise, the words heard in sentences were identified more accurately. When the speech and noise were equally loud, for example, the difference amounted to 70 percent versus 40 percent words correctly identified. Miller and his colleagues attributed this difference to the greater predictability of the words in sentences where syntactic and semantic constraints helped people rule out what words could occur where. As further evidence for this view, they showed that people were much more accurate in identifying words from a known list of 2, 4, or 8 words than from a known list of 32, 256, or 1000 words. The smaller the list, the more predictable the words, and the more predictable the words, the more accurately they were heard and identified.

Later G. Miller and Isard (1963) demonstrated that syntax and semantics make separate contributions to the identification of words in sentences. They had people listen to three different types of sentences:

(1) Grammatical sentences, like **Accidents kill motorists on the highways.**
(2) Anomalous sentences, like **Accidents carry honey between the house.**
(3) Ungrammatical strings, like **Around accidents country honey the shoot**.

Note that grammatical sentences adhere to both syntactic and semantic constraints, anomalous sentences to constraints on word order but not meaning, and
ungrammatical strings to neither. The sentences were specially constructed so
that the same words occurred in all three types of sentences equally often. No
matter what the level of noise in which the sentences were heard, people were
most accurate on grammatical sentences, a little less accurate on anomalous
sentences, and least accurate on ungrammatical strings. Once again, the more
predictable the word, the more often it was identified correctly.

The Active View of Speech Perception

How are these findings to be accounted for? There are two models one might
turn to, the active and the passive. In actuality they lie at the ends of a continuum of models. Under the simplest passive model listeners try to identify
each word as if it were an isolated word, and whenever they fail, they guess. The
more predictable the word is from syntax and meaning, the more likely they are
to guess it correctly. Under this view, listeners make use of word predictability,
not in the actual perception of the words, but only in their guesses when their
perception has failed. The problem with this model is that listeners do much
better than it predicts they should (see G. Miller and Isard, 1963). Listeners could
not guess correctly often enough to identify sentences as accurately as they do.

The active end of the continuum has more appeal. Under the active view
listeners use linguistic constraints in the actual perception of the sentence. It is
as if they listen for some words or phrases and not others, as if they are optimally
ready to perceive some sounds and not others. The analysis by synthesis model is
one active model of speech perception. Listeners synthesize words to match
what they hear and succeed when they synthesize a word that truly matches.
Linguistic contraints aid this process by narrowing down what they synthesize.
They thereby come up with the correct match more often. The appeal of the
active view is that it accounts quite naturally for a series of quite extraordinary
perceptual phenomena.

Unintelligibility in Normal Speech

The first phenomenon is perhaps the most surprising. Although normal conversational speech seems lucid and unexceptionable, it is in actuality quite
unintelligible when taken word by word. This has been demonstrated by Pollack
and Pickett (1964). They surreptitiously recorded several people in a spontaneous conversation and then played single words excised from these tape recordings
to other people for identification. Single words like this were correctly identified
only 47 percent of the time—a surprisingly low percentage. To show that this
wasn't peculiar to spontaneous conversations, Pollack and Pickett had other

people read passages at a normal rate. Single words excised from this speech were correctly identified only 55 percent of the time. When the passages were read quickly, this percentage fell to 41 percent. To the causal listener, however, all of this speech, when heard intact, sounds quite intelligible. People don't have the impression they are guessing at words, filling in for the sloppy speech where intelligibility is nil.

Although Pollack and Pickett presented single words first, they then added on larger and larger segments of the tape following each word. As the stretch of speech was gradually increased, people became more and more accurate. They were able to use more and more of the acoustic, syntactic, and intonational setting in which the first word had appeared. The compelling subjective impression, however, is not one of gradually increasing intelligibility. Instead, the word remains unintelligible until a certain point is reached—at which time it suddenly becomes perfectly clear. Lieberman, who listened to these tapes, noted that this impression is consistent with an active view of speech perception in analysis by synthesis (1967, p. 165):

> Some of the distinctive features that specify each phonetic segment probably can be determined from the available acoustic signal. Other distinctive features cannot be uniquely identified. The listener therefore forms a hypothesis concerning the probable phonetic content of the message that is consistent with the known features. However, he cannot test this hypothesis for its syntactic and semantic consistency until he gets a fairly long segment of speech into his temporary processing space. The speech signal therefore remains unintelligible until the listener can successfully test a hypothesis. When a hypothesis is confirmed, the signal abruptly becomes intelligible. The acoustic signal is, of course, necessary to provide even a partial specification of the phonetic signal. However, these experiments indicate that in many instances the phonetic signal that the listener "hears" is internally computed.

According to Lieberman, much of the speech people hear is ultimately what they themselves have synthesized, and not what the speaker has produced. The reason this speech is clear is because it is self-generated. In this sense the clarity of speech is normally an "illusion."

Illusions

Another such "illusion" is one G. Miller (1956) devised in conjunction with the Miller and Nicely study. In one of their listening conditions, speech was put through a "low-pass filter," one that eliminates all the high frequencies in the auditory signal. This filter had the effect of reducing the consonants perceptually to five groups:

p, t, k   f, θ, s, š   b, d, g   v, ð, z, ž   m, n

Nearly all the confusions were within these groups and only a few were between groups. Using this knowledge Miller devised examples of what he called "elliptic speech," improper sentences that should not be distinguishable from proper sentences with this low-pass filter. One such sentence was **Pooh kluss free soub eatwull size** for **Two plus three should equal five**. As Miller (1956, p. 358) described it:

> With a little practice these elliptic passages can be read with normal speed and intonation. When heard without distortion, the elliptic speech can be followed with some difficulty, but the talker seems to have a crippling defect of speech. Now we introduce a low-pass filter to recreate the conditions under which the confusions were observed and the speech defect suddenly disappears; the speech is muffled and booming, but the ellipsis cannot be detected.

It is as if the listener fills in synthetically what isn't there and "hears" the speech as perfectly normal but through a distorting transmission line.

An even more provocative "illusion" of this kind was demonstrated by Warren and his colleagues (Warren, 1970; Warren and Warren, 1970; Warren and Obusek, 1971; Obusek and Warren, 1973) with their discovery of the *phonemic restoration effect*. The phenomenon is illustrated by Warren's first study. He presented twenty people with a recording that said: **The state governors met with their respective legi*latures convening in the capital city.** The asterisk indicates a 0.12 second portion of the recorded speech that had been excised electronically and replaced with an ordinary cough. When asked if there were any sounds missing from this recording, nineteen of the twenty people said no, and the remaining person selected the wrong sound. As Warren (p. 392) reported it, "The illusory perception of the absent phoneme [s] was in keeping with the observation of others (graduate students and staff), who, despite knowledge of the actual stimulus, still perceived the missing phoneme as distinctly as the clearly pronounced sounds actually present." When asked to locate the cough in the sentence, none of the twenty people could do so accurately. Half of them judged the cough to have occurred beyond the boundaries of the word **legislature**. The same illusion was created with a tone or buzz in place of the cough and when even more of the word **legislature** (**le***lature**) had been replaced. The illusion disappeared, however, when the [s] was replaced by silence. In that case the silence was located very accurately. The illusion, then, is of a normally pronounced sentence coexisting with an extraneous sound occurring somewhere alongside it. There is no sense that the sentence is interrupted by a cough, buzz, or tone, or that a part of the sentence is missing.

How does the listener know what to fill in? With the word **legi*lature**, there is little choice, but Warren and Warren (1970) argued that in other instances people rely on syntactic and semantic constraints far beyond the missing segment itself. In one study they reported, people were presented with one of these four recorded sentences:

It was found that the *eel was on the *axle*.
It was found that the *eel was on the *shoe*.
It was found that the *eel was on the *orange*.
It was found that the *eel was on the *table*.

The only difference among the four was the word spliced onto the end—**axle**, **shoe**, **orange**, or **table**. Again the asterisk indicated a segment replaced with a cough. Depending on the version people listened to, *eel was "heard" as **wheel**, **heel**, **peel**, and **meal**, respectively. Here the restoration of the missing sound was based on semantic considerations alone, and indeed, the constraining element occurred four words *after* the sound to be restored. Phonemic restorations appear to be effected over quite some distance and from constraints at all levels of language.

Misperceptions

Misperceptions in everyday conversations reveal similar processes. Consider these errors in hearing Garnes and Bond (1975) collected from casual speech:

Original	Misperception
wrapping service	wrecking service
meet Mr. Anderson	meet Mr. Edison
I'm covered with chalk dust	I'm covered with chocolate
get some sealing tape	get some ceiling paint

Most of the misperceptions bear some phonetic relation to the original. In the first example [p] is misperceived as [k], which is also a voiceless stop (see also R. Cole, 1973). In the other examples, the relation is far more complex. Virtually all the misperceptions Garnes and Bond found, however, fit the original syntactically and semantically as well. Many of the changes went beyond explicable phonological changes—like **chalk dust** to **chocolate**—and seem as much determined by sense as by sound. These misperceptions are not mere guesses. According to Garnes and Bond, "The listener hears something definite, although it does not correspond to what was said. He does not hear an unintelligible stream of speech and wonder, or guess, what may have been said (214)." These misperceptions are also a sort of illusion.

The case for an active view of speech perception is quite compelling. Speech is normally heard under noisy conditions. Doors slam, typewriters clack, telephones ring, and other people talk, all of which obliterate portions of ongoing speech. The obliterated portions are filled in automatically and without effort. Even without extraneous noise, ordinary speech is so badly articulated that it isn't possible to identify more than half of the words accurately. Yet the speech is heard as clear and distinct. People do not see themselves guessing at the indistinct words as if they were reading from print with missing or indistinct letters. The restorations Warren demonstrated may well pervade the perception of normal continuous speech. Misperceptions in casual speech seem to attest to this. Although no one has yet suggested in any detail how such an active process of speech perception would work (but see Nash-Webber, 1975; Reddy, 1975; Woods and Makhoul, 1973), it obviously requires the active intervention of the construction and utilization processes discussed in Chapters 2 and 3. This gives further weight to the argument that much of comprehension works from the utilization of a sentence downwards.

Syllables and Rhythm

Continuous speech has one essential property speech sounds in isolation can never have: rhythm. As many phoneticians have noted, speakers of English speak with accented syllables at roughly equal temporal intervals. They tend to say **lickety split** and **black horse**, both of which begin and end with a stressed syllable, in about the same interval of time, despite the two extra syllables in **lickety split**. To achieve this, people speed up the two unstressed syllables in **lickety split**, and they slow down **black** and **horse**. English is often called a "stress timed" language because stressed syllables tend to come at equal intervals. Other languages, like French, are "syllable timed," because their syllables, not stresses, tend to come at equal intervals.

The carrier of rhythm is the syllable, and listeners are very sensitive to disruption in syllable rhythm. In demonstrating this experimentally, Huggins (1972) electronically added and deleted minute portions of speech from a recorded sentence and asked people whether the result sounded "normal" or not. He found that if he lengthened one phonetic segment, he had to shorten another one nearby to keep the sentence sounding normal. What was critical, he found, was to preserve the timing of the vowels, the centers of the syllables. It was not critical to preserve the timing of adjacent segments if that didn't affect the interval between the vowels. The conclusion is clear. Since disruptions in the timing of syllables are tantamount to disruptions in rhythm, people must be paying close attention to rhythm.

Listening for Stress

What, then, is rhythm good for? Its most obvious function is to enable listeners to get at another piece of information about a word—its stress pattern. If a syllable "falls on the beat" in English, it most probably is a stressed syllable. It is the second syllable of **tomato**, not the first or third. If a syllable "falls off the beat," it is probably without stress. J. G. Martin (1972) has argued that rhythm gives listeners a chance to anticipate what is coming up. Since they know there will be an accented syllable following the last one by a roughly constant interval, they can listen for it. Martin argued, therefore, that listeners organize their perception around the stressed syllables. To demonstrate this, Shields, McHugh, and J. G. Martin (1974) had people listen for a [b] in a sentence like this:

> You will have to curtail any morning sightseeing plans, as the plane to benKIK leaves at noon.

The [b] they were listening for came at the beginning of a nonsense word with stress either on the first syllable (e.g., **BENkik**) or on the second syllable (**benKIK**). The [b] was detected faster when it was in the stressed syllable. By itself, this would not be surprising. But when the same words were heard in a list of nonsense words, where there is no rhythm, this difference disappeared. In ongoing speech, therefore, people listen for stress.

Rhythm and stress may also be important because they point to the syllables with the most phonetic information. Recall that most unstressed syllables contain the neutral central vowel [ə], whereas stressed syllables always contain some other vowel. Unstressed syllables tend to be reduced in other ways too, and in very rapid speech, they are often omitted entirely. In other words, a major portion of the phonetic information in speech is carried by the stressed syllables, and therefore listeners should listen for them.

Rhythm is especially critical to theories of analysis by synthesis. To synthesize segments to match against the incoming speech sounds, listeners must not only get the right segments in the right order, but also place them in the right temporal pattern. If the incoming speech had no temporal pattern, no rhythmic anchor points, it is hard to imagine how they could ever synthesize the right temporal pattern. Rhythm should be a positive aid in this process.

Selective Listening

One phenomenon that poses a special challenge to theories of speech perception is the classic "cocktail party phenomenon." Imagine that George is talking to Jane in a crowded room where there are several other equally loud conversations nearby. Despite the plethora of linguistic signals arriving at his ears, George is able to attend selectively to Jane's conversation and ignore the rest. The challenge posed is this: how does George manage to pick Jane's speech stream out of the others without getting hopelessly lost in the linguistic chaos reaching his ears? The answer reemphasizes the point that the perception of continuous speech is more than the putting together of speech sounds identified in isolation. The cocktail party phenomenon stresses once again how important the construction and utilization processes are in speech perception.

Memory for the Other Message

One of the first to study selective listening was Cherry (1953). Through earphones, he would present people with two spoken messages, one they were to "shadow" and one they were to ignore. Shadowing a message consists of repeating the message back aloud, word for word, while listening to it. To Cherry the critical question was: how easily could people ignore the unattended message? He found they were very good at it. They could easily ignore speech directed to the ear opposite the shadowed speech. They could even ignore speech directed to the same ear and in the same voice and loudness as the shadowed message, though with greater difficulty. The most remarkable fact, however, was that people later had virtually no memory for the unattended message. Although they noticed when the unattended message was changed from speech to a pure tone, from forward to backward speech, or from a male to a female voice, they did *not* notice when it was changed from English to German, nor could they ever recall its contents.

Later studies have amplified Cherry's findings. People in a shadowing task are unable to recognize words that have occurred as many as thirty-five times in the unattended message, even when they have been forewarned they will be asked to do so (Moray, 1959). They don't even notice immediately when without warning in the middle of a shadowing task the shadowed and unattended messages are switched to the opposite ears. They simply go on shadowing the right message for a short time (Treisman, 1964a). Some of the unattended message, however, can get through. People notice about 30 percent of the time when their own name turns up in the unattended message (Moray, 1959). And they notice when the unattended message is identical to the shadowed message but delayed by no more than five to eight seconds (Treisman, 1964b).

Analysis of the Other Message

Do people really "hear" the unattended message? The answer, clearly, is yes. When the two messages come to the same ear in the same voice and amplitude, as in Cherry's study, there is logically no way for people to shadow one and ignore the other without "listening" to both. People must constantly test the shadowed message for its phonological, intonational, syntactic, and semantic continuity and reject anything that doesn't fit. Cherry, for example, showed that when the shadowed and unattended messages consisted of strings of clichés, people often unwittingly switched to the wrong message between clichés. These, of course, are just the points at which semantic continuity is broken and people may therefore follow either message. There is other empirical evidence too. When Norman (1969) interrupted people while they were shadowing, he found that they could repeat short portions of the unattended message just preceding the interruption. From this he argued that the unattended message gets into short-term memory, although it is never stored in a more permanent memory.

If the unattended message is truly heard, it ought to influence the shadowing of the attended message, and it does. First of all, the closer the unattended message is to the shadowed message, the more mistakes it induces in the shadowing. What is critical is the relation of the unattended to the shadowed message.

In a series of investigations of these errors, Treisman (1964a) came up with this ordering of unattended messages from the least to the most disruptive:

(1) A different voice to the opposite ear.

(2) The same voice to the opposite ear but in a different language.

(3) The same voice to the opposite ear but in a second language also known to the listener.

(4) The same voice to the same ear.

Generally, the more spatial, acoustic, and semantic differences between the unattended and shadowed messages, the fewer errors people made in shadowing. Second, the unattended message, though never conscious, can bias shadowers toward one or the other of two interpretations of an ambiguous sentence they are shadowing (Lackner and Garrett, 1972; MacKay, 1973a). In Lackner and Garrett's experiment people were more likely to interpret **The spy put out the torch as our signal to attack** in one way when the unattended message contained **extinguished**, but in the other way when it contained **displayed**. The rejected message has to be processed at least a little to have this influence on the shadowed message (see also Corteen and Wood, 1972).

Speeded Shadowing

The process of shadowing itself, without a competing message, suggests that speech perception involves more than auditory, phonetic, and phonological processes. Marslen-Wilson (1973) was able to find people who could shadow continuous speech at a distance of only 0.25 seconds. That is, they lagged behind the speech they were repeating by only a syllable. This is so fast that it is hard to imagine they were not anticipating and identifying the speech on the basis of syntax and meaning too. Indeed, the errors they made were almost always appropriate to the syntax and meaning of the original sentence. For example, in **It was beginning to be light enough so I could see**, some shadowers inserted **that** after **so**. This error could only have come from an awareness of the meaning and syntax of the sentence. In another study (Marslen-Wilson, 1975), the sentences that were shadowed contained deliberate anomalies, like **tomorrance** instead of **tomorrow**, and **already** instead of **envelope**. These anomalies were often corrected in shadowing. Strikingly, the words that were anomalous for syntactic and semantic reasons, like **already** for **envelope**, were corrected faster, if anything, than the words that were anomalous for phonological reasons, like **tomorrance**. These findings reinforce the argument that the construction and utilization processes play a central role in the perception of continuous speech from the very beginning.

Limits on Speech Perception

Although selective listening seems quite distant from the more basic phenomena in speech perception, it nevertheless sets important limits on theories about the perception of running speech. Some of the limits are these:

(1) *Running speech is not perceived as a series of isolated segments.* An analogy should make this clear. Imagine two typists at the same typewriter at the same time. Typist A types one or two letters, then Typist B does a few, and so on at random. If Typist A and Typist B use red and black ink respectively, then readers might just be able to follow A's message, rejecting the other message on the basis of its physical characteristics. In shadowing too, people can most readily ignore an unattended message with distinctive physical characteristics—for example, a voice of a different sex in a different location. But if both typists use black ink, readers will find the task virtually impossible, especially at normal speeds. In one of Cherry's experiments, however, people were quite successful at the analogous speech task, shadowing one of two identical voices to the same ear. This suggests that the perception of continuous speech cannot be viewed as the successive identification of phonetic segments, as is required in the typewriter analogy.

(2) *Perception of running speech normally involves the construction and utilization processes.* Cherry found that people could follow a message as long as it was semantically coherent. As soon as it consisted of clichés strung together, people would switch from one message to the other. People attempt to interpret and utilize speech as they go along, and this affects what sounds they pick out for identification. The sounds have to make sense before they are accepted as part of the speech stream.

(3) *The early stages in speech perception can be accomplished without awareness.* The unattended message must be analyzed before it can be rejected. Indeed, it may be analyzed as far as the meaning of its words—as is demonstrated by the biases in interpreting ambiguous sentences. Yet all this is normally done without awareness.

These and other possible lessons from selective listening dovetail with what else is known about the perception of running speech. It is one more phenomenon that suggests that the perception of running speech differs in certain fundamental ways from the perception of speech sounds in isolation.

SUMMARY

The identification of isolated speech sounds is an intricate process. The raw sounds are analyzed at the auditory stage into acoustic cues. These cues are used in the phonetic stage as a basis for the naming or classification of phonetic segments. These segments are constrained and adjusted at the phonological stage to fit the phonological rules of the language. However, three factors complicate this picture considerably. First, there is not a one-to-one mapping of stretches of the speech stream onto phonetic segments. The American pronunciations of **writer** and **rider** differ in the vowel, not the consonant. Second, a single phonetic segment has different cues in different contexts. The [d]s in [di] and [du] are not the same. The acoustic cues for [d] are context-dependent. Third, the mapping of acoustic cues onto phonetic segments varies a lot with the speaker and the situation. To handle these problems, some investigators have proposed that speech is perceived by analysis by synthesis, which works according to the motor theory of speech perception. Listeners identify speech sounds by matching them against sounds they have synthesized internally by modeling the speaker's articulatory gestures.

The perception of running speech, however, shows that these auditory, phonetic, and phonological processes aren't enough. Ordinary speech is too full of missing and unintelligible words to be perceived accurately this way. Instead, there may be an active process that tries to make its perception consistent with rhythm and intonation and with the way the speech is to be interpreted and utilized. Such a view seems to be needed to account for the clarity of ordinary speech, the phonemic restoration effect, people's misperceptions in casual speech, and even selective listening, people's ability to follow one conversation out of many.

Further Reading

There are many excellent introductions to phonetics and phonology. These include Abercrombie (1966) and Ladefoged (1975) on articulatory phonetics, Denes and Pinson (1973) and Ladefoged (1971) on acoustic phonetics, and Hyman (1975) and Schane (1973) on phonology. Surprisingly, there are few broad reviews of speech perception itself. Among the exceptions are Pisoni (1977) and Studdert-Kennedy (1974, 1975), who both review large portions of the field. For reviews of special topics within speech perception one can look at Liberman et al. (1967) on categorical perception, W. Cooper (1975) on selective adaptation, Warren and Warren (1970) for speech illusions, and Moray (1969) for selective listening. In addition, there are several collections of specialized articles on speech perception, including Cohen and Nooteboom (1975) and Fant (1975). The start made on identification of speech by computer is well represented in Reddy (1975).

part **3**

PRODUCTION

"Then you should say what you mean," the March Hare went on.
   "I do," Alice hastily replied; "at least—at least I mean what I say—
that's the same thing, you know."
   "Not the same thing a bit!" said the Hatter.
"Why, you might just as well say that 'I see what I eat'
is the same thing as 'I eat what I see'!"

Lewis Carroll

Plans for What to Say

Talking seems to require little thought or effort. In most conversations the words flow with just the least bit of mental urging. People think about what they want to say and their tongues seem to take care of the rest, automatically putting their thoughts into words. But the effortlessness of speaking is deceptive. This becomes obvious when people attempt something difficult—like telling a story, explaining a joke, instructing someone on how to tie a tie, or describing an apartment. They find themselves planning where to start, what to include and what to omit, what words to use, and what route to take. For professional writers this is part of a highly skilled craft. That these decisions are often difficult is apparent in every-day speech. Speakers may hesitate midsentence to pick just the right word, pause between sentences to plan what to say next, and correct phrases they have just spoken. Even when they know what they want to say, they may stutter, produce spoonerisms (saying **queer old dean** for **dear old queen**), and give other evidence of intricate processes at the phonetic level. What at first glance appears so effortless and automatic is in fact riddled with complicated processes of decision, articulation, and correction. The goal of this chapter and the next is to lay out these processes and see how they fit together in the unified activity we call speaking.

WHAT IS SPEAKING?

Speaking is fundamentally an instrumental act. Speakers talk in order to have some effect on their listeners. They assert things to change their state of knowledge. They ask them questions to get them to provide information. They request things to get them to do things for them. And they promise, bet, warn, and exclaim to affect them in still other ways. The nature of the speech act should therefore play a central role in the process of speech production. Speakers begin with the intention of affecting their listeners in a particular way, and they select and utter a sentence they believe will bring about just this effect.

Planning and Execution

Speaking, therefore, appears to be divided into two types of activity—planning and execution. Speakers first plan what they want to say based on how they want to change the mental state of their listeners. They then put their plan into execution, uttering the segments, words, phrases, and sentences that make up the plan. The division between planning and execution, however, is not a clean one. At any moment speakers are usually doing a little of both. They are planning what to say next while executing what they had planned moments before. It is impossible to say where planning leaves off and execution begins. Is deciding on the exact articulatory gestures to make for each word a part of planning or of execution? Despite this problem, planning and execution are convenient labels for the two ends of speech production. The considerations that go into planning an utterance can generally be distinguished from those that go into its execution.

How is speech planned and executed? In rough outline the process looks like this:

(1) *Discourse plans.* The first step for speakers is to decide what kind of discourse they are participating in. Are they telling a story, conversing with other people, giving instructions, describing an event, or making a pledge? Each kind of discourse has a different structure, and they must plan their utterances to fit. Each utterance must contribute to the discourse by conveying the right message.

(2) *Sentence plans.* Given the discourse and their intention to produce a sentence with the right message, speakers must select one that will do this. They must decide on the speech act, what to put as subject, and given and new information, and what to subordinate to what. They must also decide how they want to convey their message: directly, by means of the literal meaning of a sentence, or indirectly, by means of irony, understatement, or other indirect rhetorical devices.

(3) *Constituent plans.* Once they have decided on the global characteristics of a sentence, they can begin planning its constituents. For this they must pick the right words, phrases, or idioms to inhabit each constituent and put them in the right order. Although they may have planned the global form of a sentence, they normally select specific words only phrase by phrase.

(4) *Articulatory program.* As specific words are chosen, they are formed into an "articulatory program" in a memory "buffer" capable of holding all the words of a planned constituent at once. It contains a representation of the actual phonetic segments, stresses, and intonation pattern that are to be executed at the next step.

(5) *Articulation.* The final step is to execute the contents of the articulatory program. This is done by mechanisms that add sequence and timing to the

articulatory program, telling the articulatory muscles what they should do when. This step results in audible sounds, the speech the speaker intended to produce.

This rough outline, of course, needs elaboration and justification. That is the purpose of this chapter, which takes up the diverse decisions that go into the planning of speech, and the next, which deals more with the mechanics of executing utterances and how these lead to hesitations, corrections, and other speech errors. Historically, the study of speaking has confronted investigators with very tough problems. One of the toughest is that because it is difficult to exert control over what people say, it has been difficult to conduct experiments to study it. This has led to the relative neglect of the study of speaking. Yet investigators have discovered indirect and often ingenious methods for the study of speech production. Indeed, it is surprising how much can be said about planning and execution.

One word of caution. It is easy to fall into the trap of thinking that speaking is simply listening in reverse. In speaking, meaning is turned into sounds, and in listening, sounds are turned into meaning. The parallels are there, of course, but the differences are much more striking. At the sound end, speaking requires the motor activation of the speech organs, while listening consists of an auditory analysis of the speech signal. These two activities involve different organs—the mouth versus the ear—and distinct mental faculties—motor activation versus auditory analysis. At the meaning end, speakers begin with the intention of affecting listeners and turn this intention into a plan of an utterance; at the other end, listeners recognize the speakers' plan and infer their intentions. Again, these two activities are quite distinct. In these two chapters the differences will become more evident. The illusion of similarity is engendered by the fact that speaking and listening both deal with the same structural units: phonetic segments, words, constituents, sentences, speech acts, and discourse structure. But just because speaking and listening have a medium in common, they need not involve similar processes. The tools, skills, materials, and procedures used in speaking are plainly different from those used in listening.

Planning Speech as Problem Solving

In planning what to say, speakers implicitly have a problem to solve: "What linguistic devices should I select to affect the listener in the way I intend?" The solution to this problem is not easy. It requires a battery of considerations, including these five:

(1) *Knowledge of the listener*. Depending on what speakers think listeners know, they will refer to a third person as **she**, **my next door neighbor**, or **the woman over there**.

(2) *The cooperative principle*. Speakers expect their listeners to assume that they are trying to be cooperative—that they are trying to tell the truth, be informative, be relevant, and be clear. They can therefore say **What a glorious day out!** on a rainy day, for example, and be confident their listeners will catch the irony.

(3) *The reality principle*. Speakers expect their listeners to assume they will talk about comprehensible events, states, and facts. Thus the invented compound **alligator-shoes** will be construed as "shoes made from alligators," not as "shoes for alligators," an unreal possibility analogous to the legitimate **horseshoes**.

(4) *The social context*. Different social contexts lead to different vocabularies. Depending on a listener's status, speakers will address him as **Floyd** or **Mr. Thursby**, and depending on the formality of the situation, they will refer to police as **policemen** or **cops**.

(5) *The linguistic devices available*. Many things speakers may want to talk about have no ready linguistic expression. To refer to an odd-looking house one may have to use a circumlocution like **ranch-style cottage with California gothic trim** simply because no better single expression is available. These considerations—and others—each play a role in what speakers eventually decide to say.

For many problems, speakers have available to them ready-made, or conventional, solutions—but usually only partial ones. To take an example, people in conversations have to work out with each other how to coordinate their speaking: who talks when, for how long, and about what. As a partial solution to this problem, there are ready-made rules people conventionally follow in conversations—for example, rules about turn taking. Nevertheless, speakers have choices to make. The rules go only partway toward specifying what they should say at any particular moment, and they may even want to flout the rules for their own devious purposes. The point is, speakers always have choices and they resolve them on the basis of their goals in talking plus the side considerations just listed.

The problem speakers have to solve is different depending on the unit being planned—for example, whether it is the discourse, the sentence, or the constituent. In discourse, the main problem is to organize the flow of information so that by the end all the pertinent information has been expressed and understood. In sentences, the problem is more tactical. It is to design a sentence that fits into the discourse at this point and accurately conveys just the right piece of information. In constituents, the problem is still more local. It is to find expressions that pick out for this listener the objects, events, and facts this sentence is meant to convey. These levels, of course, are not strictly separable. Yet it is convenient to consider each level in turn for the problems it poses to speakers and for the processes by which they appear to arrive at their solution.

For many, the term "problem solving" may suggest that people are consciously weighing alternatives and making explicit choices. It need not do so. In mathematics, problem solving involves countless decisions and processes that are not open to conscious inspection. In the planning of what to say, too, the problem solving is usually accomplished so quickly and easily that people aren't aware of what they are doing. Planning is a process with choices, heuristics, and a goal to be accomplished; it is open to mistakes and corrections; and it takes time. With these and other characteristics, it is appropriately viewed as a kind of problem solving.

DISCOURSE PLANS

Each sentence people utter is carefully designed to fit into the discourse they are taking part in. Take stories, as described in Chapter 4. Conventionally, a story consists of a setting followed by an episode, the episode consists of one of several possibilities, and so on. In telling a story, people must follow this structure or they will be accused of not having told the story properly. Telling stories is a skill, its techniques have to learned. Young children may tell the end of a story before its beginning, get events out of sequence, or fail to provide the right setting. Either they don't yet know the conventional structure for stories or they aren't yet able to plan their speaking to conform to this structure. And even though most adults can recognize a story when they hear one, they may not have the skill to tell one well.

Although it is obvious that stories have structure, it is not so obvious that other kinds of discourse do too. At first glance conversations, descriptions, explanations, and other "natural" talk seem spontaneous and devoid of deliberate planning. Yet nothing could be further from the truth. Each of these situations has an intricate structure and requires careful planning—problem solving—on the part of speakers. Very generally, these situations divide into two categories: dialogues (two or more people talking together) and monologues (one person talking alone). These two categories confront speakers with rather different problems. In dialogues, they must coordinate their talk with the talk of others, and in monologues, they have to plan the whole discourse without the intervention of others. It is useful to take up examples of these two categories in some detail. Together they will show us more clearly how speakers plan the overall course of their speaking.

Conversations

Most conversations seem simple enough—they begin with "Hello," end with "Goodbye," and have a lot of talk in between. But in reality, the planning of conversations is complex. Each participant comes to a conversation with a particular goal in mind—which may be specific or diffuse—and is aware that the other participants have goals of their own. The problem they have to solve is how to coordinate their speech so that they can jointly reach their respective goals. This process has been investigated in great detail by Sacks, Schegloff, and Jefferson (1974; Schegloff, 1968; Schegloff and Sacks, 1973), who have analyzed spontaneous conversations in natural settings. Three of the problems they have taken up are how participants take turns in talking, how they open a conversation, and how they close a conversation.

Turn Taking

If the participants in a conversation are ever to achieve their goals jointly, they must agree implicitly on an orderly method for talking. The major requirements of this method are obvious:

> Each participant should have a chance to talk.
>
> Only one person should talk at a time (so that he or she can be heard).
>
> The gaps between turns should be brief (for efficiency).
>
> The order of speakers, and the amount they say, should not be fixed ahead of time.
>
> There must be techniques for deciding who should speak when.

Together, these requirements lead to a system of *turn taking*, the orderly passing of the conversational ball from one person to the next. In a two-part conversation, the turns alternate between A and B as in ABABABAB, but with more people, turn taking becomes much more involved.

The problem of coordinating talk is solved, according to Sacks, Schegloff, and Jefferson, by the conventions captured in these three rules:

> *Rule 1.* The next turn goes to the person addressed by the current speaker.
>
> *Rule 2.* The next turn goes to the person who speaks first.
>
> *Rule 3.* The next turn goes to the current speaker, if he resumes before anyone else speaks.

These three rules are ordered. Rule 1 takes priority over Rules 2 and 3. If the current speaker A asks B a question, B is obliged to speak next, and C is not allowed to take the next turn merely by speaking first. And Rule 2 takes priority over Rule 3. Note that these three rules accomplish the requirements listed earlier. Each participant normally gets a chance to talk (Rule 2). Only one person talks at a time. The gaps between turns will be small since the next speaker has to start quickly to preempt anyone else who may want to speak (Rule 2). The order of speakers, and how much they say, is not fixed ahead of time, although two or three participants could conspire to exclude the rest by addressing only each other (Rule 1). The rules themselves constitute a technique for deciding who should speak when. The important point is that these rules solve the problem of how to coordinate talk efficiently. Surely they have evolved this way for just that reason.

Adjacency Pairs

A significant proportion of turn taking is coordinated by Rule 1, where one speaker addresses a second, and the second responds. Together the two turns constitute an *adjacency pair*. These pairs come in many varieties, a few of which are listed here with examples:

Question-answer:
> A: What do you want for dinner?
> B: Steak will be fine.

Greeting-greeting
> A: Hi.
> B: Hi.

Offer-acceptance/rejection
> A: Let's go to the movie tonight.
> B: Okay.

Assertion-acknowledgment
> A: Bill didn't even come home the next night.
> B: Oh, yeah?

Compliment-acceptance/rejection
> A: I'm glad I have you for a friend.
> B: Ah, go jump in a lake.

Request-grant
> A: I don't want to see *Monkey Business* again.
> B: Okay, let's go to *A Night at the Opera.*

As these examples suggest, adjacency pairs serve a function beyond the mere coordination of two turns. Each has a specific purpose. Questions are used for eliciting information. Greetings are used to indicate formal contact. Offers show a willingness to do something. And so on. But the adjacency pairs are much more than that. When A asks B a question, A is not only asking for information, but also indicating that B could cooperate by answering the question immediately. For his part, B, by answering the question, not only provides the information A wants, but signals to A his willingness to cooperate at that point in the conversation. B's answer usually carries with it an implicit invitation for A to continue the conversation. Adjacency pairs are devices for A and B to coordinate their talk through a series of reciprocal obligations.

Adjacency pairs are themselves organized into larger sections in service of more global aims. They may help to open conversations, negotiate deals, relate facts, change topics, and close conversations. They are especially important when it is critical to gain the explicit cooperation of the other speakers. Two examples of their use come in the opening and closing of telephone conversations.

Opening Conversations

To start up a conversation, one person must get another's attention and signal the desire for a conversation, and the other person must show willingness to take part. For this purpose there is the *summons-answer sequence*. One person says "Hey, Bill," and the other says "Yes?" Or the first says "Pardon me, sir" to a stranger, and the stranger says "What?" Or the first taps the second on the shoulder, and the second says "Oh, hi, Sally!" By answering the way he has, the second person has not only signaled his willingness to talk with the first—he could have walked away, ignored her, or not answered—but also turned the conversation back over to the first. In such summons-answer sequences, it is the summoner who is obligated to provide the first topic of conversation. It would be silly or rude for her to summon a second person and yet not provide the first topic of conversation, even if it is only a simple "Hello." After all, why did the summoner bother the second person if she didn't have a topic she wanted to take up?

Telephone conversations, like all other conversations, begin with a summons-answer sequence, but here the telephone ring is the summons and the "Hello" or "Extension 2889" or "Clark Kent speaking" is the answer. In telephone calls, the ring from A has the same function as "Hey, Bill" or a tap on the shoulder. It is a way of getting B's attention, a summons that A wants B to acknowledge. By answering the telephone and saying "Hello," B shows his willingness to converse. B's answer itself invites A to continue and to introduce the first topic of conversation.

As with violations of other rules, violations of the rules implicit in summons-answer sequences have their consequences. Imagine that A had summoned B with "Hey, Bill" and that B had turned away without answering. A would infer, and B would normally intend A to infer, that B was trying to snub A, insult A, or otherwise be uncooperative. For telephone calls, the matter is more complicated. If B did not answer the phone, A would most likely infer that B was away or asleep. But if A knew B was there and could reasonably expect the call to be from A, A would infer that B was trying to snub him, insult him, or otherwise be uncooperative. In a summons-answer sequence, after the summons has been made, the second person must answer. The same goes for telephone openings. When B answers the phone, he must speak first. If A spoke first instead, or if B waited for A to speak, the conversation would go awry. B would have to start over again in the first instance, and A would think B rude in the second. Furthermore, B must allow A to introduce the first topic of conversation. If B started right in with the first topic of conversation, he would be considered to be out of turn.

Closing Conversations

It is still more complicated to close a conversation. In a simple telephone conversation, the participants A and B have to figure out some way to coordinate their conversation so that it ends by mutual agreement. To solve this problem, as Schegloff and Sacks demonstrate, they close in two main steps. First, A and B agree to close. Second, they actually close. It is the first step that poses the most difficult problem, and it is solved by use of yet another conversational device: the *pre-closing statement* and its response. When carried out properly, this statement initiates the *closing section* of the conversation, which ends with the classical terminal exchange, "Goodbye," "Goodbye." Once again, adjacency pairs play a central role in the solution of how to get a conversation to work.

Closings in telephone conversations come about when one of the two conversants suggests a point at which it might close, and the other takes up the suggestion and agrees to the closing. Imagine that A and B have conversed for some time, and A thinks the present topic has just about run dry. He could say "We-ell" or "Okay" or "So-oo" to signal to B that he thought the topic was closed. This constitutes a pre-closing statement, which signals to B the possibility of ending the conversation with that just-finished topic. The statement actually invites B to do one of two things:

(1) Bring up a topic that hasn't been mentioned before.

(2) Agree to participate in the closing of the conversation.

Thus B could respond by bringing up a new topic of conversation, "So let me tell you what happened to *me* yesterday" or "Say, did I tell you about the book I just read?" Or B could agree to close the conversation with a simple "Yes" or "Okay." The loquacious people who cannot close a conversation are those who always select option 1 instead of option 2, as if they can never take the hint that the conversation should be ended. If A wanted to insist more strongly on the second option, his pre-closing statement could be "Well, I've got to go now" or "Well, I'll let you get back to work now." When B accepts the invitation to close the conversation, A is then obliged to go on with the closing section proper.

The closing section begins with a pre-closing statement plus response and ends with the terminal exchange. In its simplest form, it might look like this:

A. O.K.
B. O.K.
A. Bye.
B. Bye.

More often, even after A and B have agreed to end the conversation, they still have preparations to make. They may make arrangements: "See you Wednesday." A may reinvoke the reason for calling in the first place: "Well, I just wanted to hear what happened." Or they may wish each other well: "Have a good time in London." Schegloff and Sacks (1973, p. 318) quote this "modest" example of a closing section:

A. Yeah.
B. Yeah.
A. *Al*righty. Well, *I'll* give you a call before we decide to come down. O.K.?
B. O.K.
A. *Al*righty.
B. O.K.
A. We'll see you then.
B. O.K.

A. *Bye* bye.

B. Bye.

Although closing sections can become elaborate, A and B recognize throughout that the conversation is being closed. They cannot bring up a new topic of conversation, for example, without explicit justification. For B to bring up a new topic, he would have to signal he was doing so with "By the way" or "Incidentally" or "I forgot to tell you," making it explicit that he is interrupting the closing section for a piece of information he should have introduced earlier.

It is extraordinary how powerful these conventions are. In any telephone conversation, the caller, A, must first have some purpose for calling. Imagine he wanted to tell B about an accident he had just witnessed. Nevertheless, he must open the conversation in the conventional way, for if he does not, he may never succeed in telling B about the accident without considerable loss in time or without offending B. After the opening, he must bring up the topic in a conventional manner, getting B to agree with the course of conversation at virtually every point. Once finished with the topic, he must provide a pre-closing statement and only when B agrees, close the conversation according to the rules for closings. Each step of the way is governed by tacit agreements and obligations between A and B. These agreements cannot be breached without cost or without some excellent reason, such as an emergency. Furthermore, these conventions have to be learned. Three- and four-year-old children learn quickly how to begin conversations ("You know what?" "What?"), but not generally how to proceed or how to end. When children this age run out of a topic, they simply stop. Unlike adults, they don't fill in or tie topics together to minimize the gaps between successive turns. And when they want to end a conversation, they don't bother with an elaborate closing. They simply walk away from each other (Umiker-Sebeok, 1976).

Descriptions

In describing a landscape, novelists are faced with a series of problems:

(1) *Level*. At what level should they describe it? Should they merely say, "I saw a beautiful landscape," or should they mention every last leaf and pebble?

(2) *Content*. Given the level, which parts should they include and which should they omit? Normally, the landscape will be too complicated to include everything, so they must pick and choose.

(3) *Order*. Given the parts they have decided to include, what order should they put them in? Should they describe them from left to right, from nearest to farthest, from most to least important, from largest to smallest, or how?

(4) *Relations*. For the given level, content, and order, how should they relate the parts to each other? Is it enough for the parts to be listed as present, or should each be given a precise location with respect to the rest?

The novelists' solution to these problems hangs ultimately on their purpose. Do they want the reader to be able to recreate the objective details of the scene? Do they want to highlight one object and describe its relation to everything else? Or do they want to evoke a diffuse mood?

Describing Apartments

Descriptions come in many shapes and sizes, but all demand this kind of planning. This point is nicely illustrated in a study by Linde and Labov (1975) on the description of apartments. They tape-recorded about one hundred New York City apartment dwellers as they answered the question, "Could you tell me the layout of your apartment?" Linde and Labov chose this kind of description for several reasons. The respondents have to plan their discourse on the spot from scratch. They cannot simply recall something they have said or heard before. They are being asked to describe something they know well, but probably have never verbalized before. As an added bonus for the researcher, their descriptions can be checked for accuracy against the actual apartments. And the descriptions elicited are linguistically natural since they were recorded as part of a general sociological survey of attitudes toward urban life.

The problem the respondents attempted to solve was this: "How can I describe every room in my apartment in such a way that the listener can imagine where everything is?" Note that they had already assumed the appropriate level to be at the detail of rooms, not, say, of furniture or of the shape of the perimeter. The important parts left to solve, then, were the contents (which rooms to include and which to omit), their order (which order to describe them in), and their relations (how to relate the rooms to each other).

The Tour

What is extraordinary is that virtually everyone solved these problems in the same way. A very few of them (less than 3 percent) described a map of the apartment and filled in the details—for example, "I'd say it's laid out in a huge square pattern, broken down into four units . . ." The rest (over 97 percent), however, described a *tour* of the apartment (p. 927):

> You walked in the front door.
> There was a narrow hallway.
> To the left, the first door you came to was a tiny bedroom.
> Then there was a kitchen,
> and then bathroom,
> and then the main room was in the back, living room, I guess.

The tour solves the problems of content, order, and relation all at once. It hits every main room, in a particular order, and places each room in relation to every other. Of course, it does not give a complete picture of the apartment. Only rarely, for example, could even an approximate floor plan be drawn from these respondents' descriptions. Little information was provided about the shapes and sizes of the rooms or about the way the rooms fit into the perimeter of the apartment. But all this arose because of decisions the respondents made about content: size and exact shape were not deemed important enough to describe in detail.

The tour, it was found, proceeded according to a strict set of rules (p. 930):

(1) The imaginary tour begins at the front door of the apartment.

(2) If the visitor comes to a one-room branch, he does not enter it.

(3) If he comes to a branch with rooms beyond the first room, he always enters.

(4) When he reaches the end of a branch, and there are other branches to be traversed, he does not turn around and go back; instead he is brought back instantaneously to the fork point where the other branches originate.

By Rules 1, 2, and 3, the visitor takes in every room, and by Rule 4, he does not describe a cul-de-sac twice, once going in and once going out. By another rule he describes one-room branches first. These rules, of course, lead to an efficient description. The respondents know they will describe every room, each only once, and that they need not refer back in their description to see what there is left to describe. The solution most respondents discover for this problem is indeed optimal. That may be why they were all led to it.

Rooms and Vectors

The problems of content and relations tended to have uniform treatment too. The basic units in these descriptions consisted of two parts: a vector and a room. An example of such a unit is the following: "And on your left, you would find the master bedroom, which is a very large bedroom." The vector is that part of the unit that places the room in some direction relative to the tour. It came in two types, static and mobile. The static type was like the following:

> to the right . . .
> straight ahead of you . . .

The mobile vectors, on the other hand, described motion through a room, a part of the touring itself:

> you keep walking straight ahead . . .
> now if you turn right . . .

The static and mobile vectors were used for different purposes. When the visitors looked into a room but did not enter it, they normally used a static vector. They said where the room was, statically, in relation to the tour. But when they entered a room to get to another room beyond, they used a mobile vector, indicating their motion through the room. The visitors therefore distinguished the path from the sights they saw from the path.

Drawing by Stevenson; © *1976 The New Yorker Magazine, Inc.*

In solving the problem of contents, Linde and Labov's respondents treated some rooms as major and others as minor. The major rooms were the kitchen, dining room, living room, and bedrooms. The minor rooms were the study, den, laundry room, and so on. The major rooms were normally introduced by a definite article—**the kitchen**—as if the listener expected them to be present, while the minor rooms were introduced with indefinite articles—**a closet**. The major rooms were typically placed in the subject position of sentences, and minor rooms only in the predicates. The respondents always started a new sentence on entering a branch with a major room, "And on the right side, straight ahead of you again, is a dining room which is not too big." But they were more likely to tag the minor rooms on at the ends of sentences with such phrases as "with a little dressing room off that," "with a foyer at the front," and "with a bathroom on the right." Clearly, these respondents judged some rooms to be more important and tended to introduce them in a manner befitting their status.

Orderly Solutions

Linde and Labov's respondents, in short, solved the problems of level, content, order, and relations in a relatively uniform way. They toured the apartment by the most efficient route, only *looking* into rooms if there were no rooms beyond, and dwelled on major rooms, slighting minor ones. It is no mystery why they should all have reached similar solutions. They judged that the questioner wanted to know about the apartment's functional equipment—its rooms—and, to describe them in relation to each other, they thought of only a few optimal solutions.

Not all descriptions yield to such a uniform and orderly solution. This may explain why Linde and Labov chose apartment descriptions. Nevertheless, for many problems there is one solution most people will discover to be optimal. For example, when asked to describe events that happen in time, like car accidents or tennis games, people will normally take up the events in chronological order. Time gives them a quick and ready solution to the otherwise difficult problem of order. But the most severe problem people are faced with is how to chop up the thing being described into verbalizable chunks. Apartments have natural divisions that correspond to names readily available in the language—**kitchen, dining room, bathroom**. Events that happen in time do not. It is difficult to describe in detail a woman strolling down the street. There are few if any natural divisions in her strolling, and what divisions there are do not have ready names. Problems like these have yet to be studied in any detail.

The Structure of Discourse

Although discourse has structure—conversations and descriptions attest to that —it has two kinds of structure: hierarchical and local. In both examples the hierarchical structure grows out of the speaker's purpose for talking in the first place. In telephone conversations, A calls B for a particular purpose—for information, advice, a favor, or something else. The opening of the call revolves around A's introduction of this purpose and all the back and forth exchanges help bring this goal about. The conversation ends with the closing section. In apartment descriptions, people mean to inform their audience about the layout of their apartment, and they do so in the most efficient way possible. This goal dictates the hierarchical structure: where to begin, how to proceed, what to make prominent, and where to end. No matter whether the discourse is a dialogue or monologue, speakers have an overall hierarchical plan that they try to abide by throughout.

Yet each sentence has to be planned locally. In conversations the next sentence is dictated by the momentary agreement the speaker has made with the other participants. This agreement is often carried by adjacency pairs— question plus answer, greeting plus greeting, and so on. A participant cannot select the next utterance without paying heed to the last thing said. In apartment descriptions, speakers could conceivably design the whole discourse before saying the first word, but they don't. What they plan beforehand is the tour, not their description of the tour. It is the tour that enables them to decide what to say next at each point in the discourse.

Discourse also varies in how much of its structure is conventional and how much is planned anew each time by problem solving. Stories, for example, have a conventional hierarchical structure, whereas descriptions of a series of events do not. Classroom discussions have a conventional hierarchical structure that is probably more confining than the structure for barroom conversations. As

Sacks and his colleagues have noted, conversations lie at the end of a continuum of structured dialogues: (1) casual conversations; (2) discussions headed by a chairperson who selects who is to speak next according to parliamentary rules; (3) debates in which the "pro" and "con" sides are allotted turns and times in advance; and (4) rituals in which each participant's turns and words are completely specified in advance. In all but the most structured discourse, speakers have at least some problem to solve. At the very least they have to select the sentence they will say, and that brings us to the next topic.

SENTENCE PLANS

In planning a sentence, a speaker has many options. As described in Chapter 1, these fall into three categories: propositional content, illocutionary content, and thematic structure. First, what states or events does the speaker want to talk about? A boy hitting a ball, a dinosaur romping through swamps, Julia discovering a virus? These come under the heading of propositional content. Second, how does he want to deal with it? Does he want to make an assertion, a request, a promise, or what? This is a question of illocutionary content, and reflects the speech act the speaker intends to make. Third, what does the speaker want as subject, what does he think the listener does and does not know, and what framework does he want to set his utterance in? These are questions that have to do with thematic structure. The speaker must decide on all three aspects before he can compose a sentence.

Planning sentences—deciding on these three aspects—requires problem solving that is just as complicated as planning discourse. The problem to be solved remains the same: what linguistic devices should speakers select to have the intended effect on the listener? But speakers have new considerations to take into account. These include: How are states and events to be conceived of? What are their precise intentions in uttering a sentence at this time? And how much can they assume the listener knows of what is being talked about? The problems encountered by speakers are different for propositional content, illocutionary content, and thematic structure, and so they will be taken up separately.

Propositional Content

At the core of the sentence to be planned are its propositions—units of meaning that reflect the ideas speakers want to express. Before speakers can assert, ask questions, promise, or command, they have to have something to assert, ask questions, promise, or command about. An apartment description, for example, might break down into a series of propositions such as these:

> you enter the door
> the door is at the front
> the bedroom is left of the hallway

and so on. Before these unadorned propositions can be realized as sentences they must be usefully combined and given illocutionary content and thematic structure. The result might be an assertion, **You are entering the front door**, or a request, **Enter the front door**. And the result can vary in frame and insert, as in **A bedroom is on the left** versus **On the left is a bedroom**.

Experiential Chunking

The first problem that speakers have to solve might be called the *problem of experiential chunking*, a problem alluded to in discourse plans. Imagine that Charlotte has just watched a movie clip of a knight slaying a dragon and is asked to describe it. In planning this short discourse, she has to decide on the level, content, order, and relations of her description. The propositions underlying her description might be these:

> The knight watched the dragon. The knight approached the dragon. The knight picked up a sword. The knight swung the sword. The sword pierced the dragon. The dragon fell. The dragon died.

It is as if she divided the film clip into seven segments and found a proposition to characterize each segment. But how did she arrive at these divisions? How did she happen to chunk her experience in just this way?

Experiential chunking appears to depend on two closely related factors, conceptual salience and verbalizability, and what is described depends also on pertinence to the discourse.

(1) *Conceptual salience.* Episodes like the dragon slaying are not experienced, or conceived of, as uniformly smooth happenings. They have "joints," points of rapid change from one state to another, and "intervals" in between those joints. To take one example, the dragon was upright for much of the film clip and, after a sudden change, it was down for the remainder. The sudden change is a joint and corresponds to the proposition **the dragon fell**. The interval between the beginning of the clip and the knight's first movement toward the dragon was filled by a static period in which the knight watched the dragon. This interval corresponds to the proposition **the knight watched the dragon**. People are also aware of states that continue with no change at all. One such state corresponds to a proposition like **the dragon was ugly**. What gets turned into propositions are the joints, intervals, and states that people experience.

(2) *Verbalizability.* But not all joints, intervals, and states correspond to propositions that can be expressed in the language. Although English has propositions designed for the major chunks of experience people might want to refer to, it certainly doesn't have propositions for all. Many chunks take a complex conglomeration of propositions to describe, and even then the description won't be that precise. Imagine describing the sudden twists and turns of the dragon as it fell. Essentially, these things are unspeakable, unverbalizable, and hence do not become part of people's descriptions. Other things, while not entirely unverbalizable, would require many difficult words to describe, hence they too are

generally not described. In short, speakers are guided in their experiential chunking partly by what propositions are available in the language.

(3) *Pertinence*. Charlotte, however, did not choose to describe all of the joints, intervals, and states she saw in the film clip. She took up only the most pertinent ones. For example, although the death of the dragon may not have been very significant visually, it was highly pertinent to the episode as a whole. That was a good enough reason for including the proposition **the dragon died**.

What do these joints, intervals, and states—these chunks of experience— consist of? And how are they turned into propositions? These questions have no firm answers—they have hardly been broached in the psychology of language. A plausible view, however, is this. Each chunk of experience is conceived of as some action or state, with one or more participants. The dragon's falling, for example, consists of the action of falling, and the dragon is the one participant in this action. If this is the way all such chunks are conceived of, then it is a short step to propositions. For the dragon's falling, the action corresponds to the predicate **Fall(x)**, and the participant to the argument **x**, the dragon. Together, they make up the proposition **Fall(dragon)**.

The Simplicity Criterion

Even within these constraints, speakers often have the choice of several propositions. For example, a nut and its shell could be described as either **the nut is in the shell** or **the shell surrounds the nut**. In these instances, people appear to apply what might be called the simplicity criterion:

> *Simplicity criterion:* Build the simplest proposition available unless there are reasons to do otherwise.

This criterion is illustrated in a study by H. Clark and Chase (1974) of descriptions of vertical arrangements. People were shown configurations in which one geometrical figure, say A, was placed above another, B. These people were asked to describe each configuration with a simple sentence. The A's and B's were of various sizes and shapes. Since each configuration could be described in two ways, **A is above B** and **B is below A**, the question was how people implicitly selected which proposition to use. Their descriptions were found to conform to these three ordered rules:

> *Rule 1.* If you want to describe the position of A, use **A is above B**; if you want to describe the position of B, use **B is below A**.

> *Rule 2.* If A is a perceptually salient, stable point of reference, use **B is below A**; if B is a prominent, stable point of reference, use **A is above B**.

> *Rule 3.* If Rules 1 and 2 don't apply, use **A is above B** by default.

Rule 1 is tried first; if it doesn't apply, Rule 2 is tried; and if it doesn't apply, use Rule 3.

These three rules show how the simplicity criterion works. Clark and Chase argued a priori that **A is above B** is a "simpler" proposition in certain respects than **B is below A**. This is reflected in Rule 3, which prescribes the use of **A is above B** when A and B are of equal prominence and there are no other constraints. But as the simplicity criterion allows, this "default" rule is preempted when other factors become important. When A is large and prominent, people are apt to choose **B is below A** (Rule 2), making A the point of reference in the proposition. And when asked **Where is B?**, regardless of whether A or B is more prominent, people choose **B is below A** (Rule 1), since this is the proposition that fits the question and represents B in relation to A.

As this example illustrates, there is often a "natural" or "simple" order for coding objects and events into propositions. Some of these follow the speaker-listener agreements discussed in Chapter 2; others have a more perceptual basis (see Chapter 14). Here are several well-attested examples:

(1) *Vertical arrays*. These are normally coded from top down, as in **A is above B**, not bottom up, as in **B is below A** (H. Clark and Chase, 1972, 1974; DeSoto, London, and Handel, 1965; Osgood, 1971).

(2) *Temporal sequences*. These tend to be coded from first to last, as in **A is before B**, not last to first, as in **B is after A**. E. Clark (1970a) found that children begin describing events in time by successively mastering these four constructions:

The boy jumped. The dog barked.   (*two sentences*)

The boy jumped and the dog barked.   (*coordination*)

The boy jumped before the dog barked.   (*subordination with* **before**)

The dog barked after the boy jumped.   (*subordination with* **after**)

The first three constructions describe the two events in chronological order, from first to last, and only the one mastered last does not. H. Clark and E. Clark (1968) and Osgood (1971) confirmed that adult descriptions tended to go from first to last too.

(3) *Comparisons*. These tend to be coded from the positive end down, not the negative end up. For example, people normally describe two objects as **A is larger than B** in preference to **B is smaller than A** (Flores d'Arcais, 1970).

(4) *Affirmation and negation*. People prefer to code experience in terms of positive rather than negative propositions. An object is more likely to be represented as **A is inside B** than as **A is not outside B**, that is, as **Inside(A,B)** rather than as **False(Outside(A,B))**.

As with **A is above B**, each of these "simpler" propositions can be preempted by other factors. Take affirmatives and negatives. Virtually every study in which people have been asked to describe things has yielded the exclusive use of affirmative sentences. Yet there are situations where the use of negation becomes necessary (see H. Clark, 1974a; Osgood, 1971; Wason, 1965). Consider these two logically equivalent assertions:

The police chief here is a woman.

The police chief here isn't a man.

The affirmative sentence asserts a simple fact about the police chief: that she is a woman. The denial, however, adds the assumption that listeners may well believe that the police chief is a man, and they are being disabused of this belief. Thus, if speakers want explicitly to deny some prior expectation, they will use the negative coding, which preempts the affirmative one. This has been demonstrated by Osgood (1971), who asked people to describe two situations, one in which an expectation that several objects would be present was fulfilled, and another in which the same expectation was not fulfilled. People described the first situation exclusively with affirmative sentences, but overwhelmingly described the second situation with denials.

The more complicated negative representation may sometimes even be the simplest way of coding a situation. Imagine a couple out to buy a car that isn't red. Surely they would not say to the car dealer, "We want a car that is blue or brown or white or gray or tangerine or . . ." Rather they would say, with great efficiency, "We want a car that isn't red." By use of just one extra negative they have avoided the long list of colors that would be acceptable. They have therefore followed the simplicity criterion and have represented this situation in the simplest propositional form available.

Illocutionary Content

In planning a sentence, speakers also have to decide on its illocutionary content —on what speech act they intend to make and how. Take the proposition expressed in **John will be here**. It can be dressed up as many different speech acts:

John will be here.   (*an assertion*)

Will John be here?   (*a yes/no question*)

I warn you that John will be here.   (*a warning*)

I bet you that John will be here.   (*a bet*)

and so on. The choice, clearly, is critical to the course of the discourse. Furthermore, any one of these speech acts can be dressed up in different ways. The yes/no question can be expressed directly:

Will John be here?

or indirectly:

Do you know whether John will be here?

Tell me whether or not John will be here.

Please let me know whether John will be here or not.

Thus, speakers have two problems to solve. First, which speech act do they intend to convey? Second, in which form should they express it?

Felicity Conditions

For a speech act to come off properly, the speaker must assure himself that certain conditions have been fulfilled. To get some idea of their complexity, consider Searle's (1965) list of conditions for the uttering of a promise. Imagine that Alan says to Ben **I promise you that I will go home tomorrow**. The rules Alan must adhere to are these:

(1) *Propositional content rule.* The propositional content **I will go home tomorrow** must predicate a future act of Alan (which it does).

(2) *Preparatory rule.* Alan must believe that Ben would prefer Alan's going home tomorrow to his not going home tomorrow; and Alan must also believe that it is not obvious to Alan or Ben that Alan would go home tomorrow in the normal course of events.

(3) *Sincerity rule.* Alan intends to go home tomorrow.

(4) *Essential rule.* By uttering this sentence, Alan undertakes an obligation to go home tomorrow.

If any one of these rules is not fulfilled, Alan could be said to be making an "infelicitous" promise. Hence these rules are often called the *felicity conditions* of a promise.

Consider some of the ways in which Alan's promise can become infelicitous. If he had said **I promise you that it rained yesterday**, he would be violating Rule 1. Although this sentence is legitimate as an emphatic assertion, it is not really a promise. If Alan had said **I promise you that I will breathe tomorrow**, he would be violating Rule 2. Promises have to be about something Alan might not necessarily do. If Alan had said **I promise you that I will go home tomorrow** but had no intention of doing so, he would be violating Rule 3. He would be making an insincere promise. And if Alan had made this promise but did not think he had obligated himself to go home tomorrow, he would be violating Rule 4.

Every other type of speech act has analogous felicity conditions. From Chapter 3 recall that there are five major categories of speech acts:

Category of speech act	*Example*
Representatives	John is home. (*an assertion*)
Directives	Go home. (*a command*)
Commissives	I promise you I will go home. (*a promise*)
Expressives	I apologize for going home. (*an apology*)
Declarations	You are fired. (*a dismissal*)

For each category, there are generally different felicity conditions. The essential rule, for example, varies from category to category. With a representative, speakers commit themselves to the truth of the proposition, here **John is home**. With a directive, they attempt to get the listener to do something, here to go home. With a commissive, they commit themselves to some future action, here the act of going home. With an expressive, they express their own psychological state about something, here their sorrow about going home. And with a declaration, they alter some state over which they have control, here the listener's employment.

Choosing Illocutionary Content

Although the speakers' choice of speech act has to take account of these felicity conditions, little is known about how they make this choice. Take Alan's promise to Ben **I promise you that I will go home tomorrow**. Does Alan begin with the intention of going home (Rule 3) and then make sure the other conditions hold? Do the preparatory conditions (Rule 2) have to hold before Alan ever even thinks of intending to go home (Rule 3)? Does Alan ever commit himself before realizing that he intends to go home tomorrow (Rule 3)? There may be no uniform procedure by which speakers make their selection of a speech act. Different circumstances may lead by different routes to the same end. Whatever the process, speakers must solve the problem: what speech act will accomplish the intended ends in the present circumstances?

In many circumstances, however, the solution to this problem is virtually foreordained. Most monologues, designed as they are to impart information, consist of uninterrupted sequences of representatives. Most of Linde and Labov's apartment descriptions had this character. Dialogues, on the other hand, abound in all types of speech acts, many of which are heavily determined by the preceding sentence. When one speaker utters the first half of an adjacency pair, the person he has addressed normally utters an appropriate second half. When asked a question, the second speaker answers with an assertion, a representative. When given a greeting, he returns with a greeting, an expressive. When requested to do something, he returns with a commitment, a commissive. And so on. A large part of what Schegloff, Sacks, and Jefferson said about conversations consisted of specifying what speech act speakers select to utter when.

Yet even the first half of an adjacency pair does not guarantee which speech act will come next. Take this example of a question-answer sequence from Schegloff (1972):

A. Are you coming tonight?
B. Can I bring a guest?
A. Sure.
B. I'll be there.

Before B answers A's question, he needs more information. Thus, he inserts his question **Can I bring a guest?** and gets A's answer **Sure** before he attempts to answer A's original question. B's question and A's answer together are called an *insertion sequence*. But since this insertion sequence can itself contain insertion sequences, and so on, the answer to the original question can become delayed by many sentences, although it is rarely forgotten, as in this illustration (p. 79):

A. Are you coming tonight?
B. Can I bring a guest?
A. Male or female?
B. What difference does that make?
A. An issue of balance.
B. Female.
A. Sure.
B. I'll be there.

Note that B's original insertion sequence served as an attempt to satisfy certain conditions on his promise **I'll be there**. Although B could satisfy Rules 1 and 2 for this promise, he didn't intend to go (Rule 3) and wouldn't commit himself to go (Rule 4) unless he could bring a guest. After determining that he could, he could then commit himself and sincerely intend to go. In this example part of B's problem solving in deciding on his promise is made explicit. B is assuring himself of Rules 3 and 4 before promising he'll be there.

Direct and Indirect Speech Acts

Once speakers have decided on a particular speech act, they have to decide what form it should take. In asking whether or not John is there, they could select **Is John there?**, **Could you tell me if John is there?**, **Please let me know whether or not John is there**, or one of many other possible forms. One basis on which they make the selection is efficiency. Some forms are shorter and less cumbersome than others. A more usual basis, however, is interpretation. The indirect ways of expressing a speech act usually carry slightly different interpretations.

The varieties of indirect requests provide a good illustration. They differ mainly in their politeness:

1. Open the door.

2. I would like you to open the door.

3. Can you open the door?

4. Would you mind opening the door?

5. May I ask you whether or not you would mind opening the door?

These run the gamut of politeness from 1, which is normally rude and authoritarian, to 5, which is usually overly polite. R. Lakoff (1973) has argued that this variation comes about from two rules of politeness:

Rule 1: Don't impose.

Rule 2: Give options.

Sentence 1 is the most imposing and therefore the least polite. Because it doesn't give options, it assumes the speaker has considerable authority over the listener. Sentence 2 gives the listener the option of whether or not to please the speaker. That isn't very much of an option, and so it too imposes, though not as much as 1. As a question, 3 gives an explicit option, for the listener can answer yes or no to the question about the possibility of opening the door. It assumes little authority, imposes very little, and is therefore more polite than 1 or 2. Sentence 4 goes one step beyond 3 and gives the listener the option of saying whether or not opening the door would be an imposition. And 5 is ultra polite, for it requests permission even to ask the listener whether or not opening the door would be an imposition.

So to choose among 1 through 5, speakers have to decide on several questions. What is their authority relative to the listener? Do they want to be rude or polite, and if so, to what degree? Should they give options? In an emergency, as during a fire, they wouldn't want to give options and would always yell **Open the door**. Once again, however, although it is possible to spell out the conditions under which they might select one version or the other, little is known about the process by which they make that selection.

Thematic Structure

The third set of options speakers have open to them are concerned with thematic structure. They have to decide what is to be subject and predicate, what is to be given information and new information, and what is to be frame and insert. Recall that subject and predicate specify what is being talked about and what is being said about it. Given and new information specify what the listener is expected to be able to identify uniquely and what he doesn't yet know. Frame and insert specify the framework of the utterance and its contents. Normally these three pairs of functions roughly coincide. What is being talked about is known to the listener, as is the setting within which the predicate and new information are placed. Nevertheless, they can be separated. The problem speakers have to solve is which options they should select to further their aims.

Frame and Insert

Frame and insert were important in the apartment descriptions given by Linde and Labov's New Yorkers. Recall that the frame of a sentence is its first main phrase. In **During the summer, Alison lives in Scotland**, the phrase **during the summer** is the frame, the setting within which one can understand the information that Alison lives in Scotland. In the apartment descriptions, people selected frames with great consistency. Some took the tour itself as the organizing center of their descriptions and produced sentences like: **To the left we see the kitchen**. The frame **to the left** relates the information conveyed to the route of the tour. Other people organized their descriptions around the rooms being toured and produced sentences like: **The kitchen is on the left**. The frame **the kitchen** relates the information conveyed to the list of rooms. Although these two types of description have identical propositions and impart the same facts, they are distinct in their organizing principle and result in a slightly different impression.

Given and New Information

Given and new information normally come in that order. As described in Chapters 1 and 3, given and new are conveyed in the stress pattern. In one interpretation of **Mr. Fields juggled the BOXES**, the given information is **Mr. Fields juggled X**, and the new information **X = boxes**. In monologues this ordering is particularly prominent. In dialogues, however, there are many reasons for altering this order. Take this question and answer as an example:

> Sue: Who gave you that beautiful flute?
> Dan: HILARY did.

In an appropriate answer, the wanted fact should appear as new information, and in Dan's answer it does. **Hilary** is pronounced with heavy stress. In addition, however, answerers usually try to preserve the syntax of the question too. Dan's answer is an elliptical version of **HILARY gave me this beautiful flute**, not **This beautiful flute was given to me by HILARY**, and in it the new information comes first. The same thing happens when Dan corrects what Sue has said:

> Sue: I hear that Evelyn gave you a beautiful flute.
> Dan: No, HILARY did.

To use given and new information properly, speakers have to assess what their listener does and doesn't know. In the last set of examples, Dan knew precisely what Sue did and didn't know because of her question and her mistake. He could therefore express the identifiable information as given and the unknown information as new. In other circumstances his assessment wouldn't be so easy. What he must do, metaphorically, is keep a mental diary of what Sue knows. Each time she is told something new, he adds a new entry to this diary. When he selects a sentence, he consults the diary, determines what she knows, builds the given information to refer to this knowledge, and builds the new information to contain information not yet in the diary. This metaphor seems straightforward, but in practice, little is known about how speakers make this kind of assessment.

Subject and Predicate

The subject and predicate of a sentence should reflect what one is talking about and what one is saying about it. Metaphorically, the subject names the place in memory where the propositions being conveyed are to be stored. **Connie owns a horse** is a fact to be stored about Connie, while **The horse is Connie's** is a fact to be stored about the horse. Virtually every fact can be expressed in more than one way, and so speakers are always forced to decide on subject and predicate.

All other things being equal, however, they will select the given information, the frame, or both, as subject. And when these factors do not apply, they will select the agent of the action (saying **Connie bought the horse** in preference to **The horse was bought by Connie**) or the experiencer (saying **Connie saw the house** in preference to **The house was seen by Connie**). How they make these decisions, however, is not at all clear.

There are two different ways to view the choices of subject and predicate, given and new information, and frame and insert. In the context of speakers and listeners, subject-predicate and frame-insert are speaker oriented and given-new is listener oriented. Speakers place what *they* want to talk about as subject and state the framework *they* want to place it in as frame. But at the same time they place what they judge the *listeners* already know as given information and what the *listeners* don't yet know as new. These orientations are quite distinct. Viewed as elements in an ongoing discourse, on the other hand, subject-predicate and frame-insert are forward looking, while given-new is backward looking. Subject and predicate reveal the direction speakers are expecting to go in the discourse, and frame and insert, the framework within which they are going to talk. These tell listeners what to pay attention to. Given and new information, in contrast, are adjustments speakers must make to what has already been said, since the given information must refer directly or indirectly to known material and they can be certain that what has been said before is known. Although there is little hard evidence on these decisions, participants in spontaneous conversations appear to make these selections with considerable care. They may stumble and hesitate in talking, but they pay close attention to the thematic choices they make.

Tannenbaum and Williams (1968) have demonstrated how important these thematic distinctions are in the production of sentences. In their study people were shown a picture and asked to describe it as quickly as possible in either an active or a passive sentence. For example, they were shown a picture of a train hitting a car. In the upper left-hand corner of the picture there was either an A or a P. They were to produce 6 if there was an A and 7 if there was a P:

6. The train is hitting the car.

7. The car is being hit by the train.

Before people were shown this picture, however, they read a preamble, a short paragraph, that was about trains and their importance, about cars and their function and importance, or about neither. Schematically, there were three types of preamble: (A) about trains, (B) about cars, (C) neutral.

The times people took to produce the complete sentences suggest that one or more of the three thematic distinctions affect speed of sentence production. Sentence 6 was fastest for Preamble A, next fastest for Preamble C, and slowest for Preamble B. On the other hand, 7 was fastest for Preamble B, next fastest for Preamble C, and slowest for Preamble A. That is, it was easiest to produce a sentence whose subject, frame, and given information referred back to the preamble. Apparently, the preamble sets up the theme of the discourse and states what is known. The next sentence, to be produced quickly, has to carry on the theme with the subject and frame and refer back to what is known with the given information. It is impossible to tell, however, how many and which ones of the three thematic functions were critical.

In sum, the planning of an individual sentence is not easy. Speakers have to decide on the propositional content, illocutionary content, and thematic structure of what they want to say and then select a sentence to fit. Imagine they have made the following choices:

Propositional content: **Hit(Harry, Bill)** = S

Speech act: I request you to tell me whether S is true.

Thematic structure: **Harry** is subject and frame; **X hit Bill** is given.

Taken together, these choices lead to **Did HARRY hit Bill?** or **Was it HARRY who hit Bill?** The difficult problem, however, is how to make the three selections in the first place. It is fairly clear what considerations speakers must pay attention to, but it is far from clear what mental processes are involved or how the final decision is arrived at. The study of sentence planning has barely begun.

CONSTITUENT PLANS

Planning has so far been discussed as if speakers decide on each sentence all at once—as if they select every last adjective, adverb, and article before they utter their first word. Common sense tells us that this cannot be right, and there is evidence to this effect. It seems equally outrageous to maintain the opposite extreme—that speakers wait until they have said one word before selecting the next. The truth lies somewhere in between. Speakers plan more than one word at a time, but not the whole sentence at once.

The obvious candidate for planning at this level is the constituent. In a noun phrase referring to a specific person, the choices of adjective and noun are interdependent. The same person could be referred to as **an immense happy man** or as **a happy giant**, but not as **an immense happy giant** (thus making him too big). At the same time, these choices do not greatly affect word choices in the preceding or following constituents—at least not if the overall skeleton of the sentence has already been planned. Drastic changes in the first noun phrase of **the happy giant decided to buy himself a sandwich** have little effect on word choices in the rest of the sentence.

The selection of specific words, therefore, might go like this. As part of the discourse, a speaker has built a skeleton plan for the whole sentence. He has chosen:

(a) to talk about some entity E_{92} hitting another entity E_{44},

(b) to place E_{92} as subject and frame and E_{92} **hit X** as given information, and

(c) to ask a yes/no question of this content.

The next step is to flesh out the skeleton with words. For example, he must decide whether to express E_{92} as **Bob**, **Mr. Smith**, or **the sorry-looking man over there in the blue suit**, all of which correctly describe E_{92}. His decision will depend on which one he thinks will pick out E_{92} for the listener uniquely, and that will depend on many things. Strictly speaking, of course, the content of these noun phrases is part of the propositional content of the sentence. After all, noun phrases express propositions of various sorts. But the idea here is that people generally plan the skeletal propositions before planning the propositions to be packed into each successive constituent. They plan to talk about someone hitting someone before they plan to describe the first someone as **the sorry-looking man over there in the blue suit**.

Just as the planning of discourse and sentences confronts speakers with difficult problems to solve, so does the planning of constituents. Each type of constituent, however, poses its own problems. Since it would be impossible to consider every different type of constituent, it will be convenient to focus on just one, the noun phrase. In its planning, speakers have to solve the problem of how to get the listener to think of the entity or class of entities they want to refer to. In solving this problem, they have to pay special attention to previous mention, implicit alternatives, and social formality, factors that are directly involved in the selection of articles, adjectives, nouns, and pronouns.

Articles

In English every noun phrase is either definite or indefinite. Speakers would use a definite noun phrase, like **the jack rabbit**, if they thought the entity being referred to was something their audience knew of and could uniquely identify from the noun phrase. They would use an indefinite noun phrase, like **a jack rabbit**, if they were mentioning the existence of this entity for the first time. Thus, speakers select the articles **a** and **the** on the basis of what they think their listeners do and don't know.

It is easy to demonstrate that speakers will make the right selection depending on the circumstances. Grieve (1973) showed people film clips in which the same person or object reappeared several times. These people were asked to describe the film clips as if they were giving eyewitness testimony. On their first reference to an object, virtually 100 percent of them used an indefinite noun phrase, like **an envelope**, and on the second mention, 100 percent of them used a definite noun phrase, **the envelope**. They dealt with unknown people that appeared twice in exactly the same way, first with an indefinite article and second with a definite article (see also Osgood, 1971; Warden, 1976). There is little doubt that adult speakers know how to select the articles **a** and **the** in the most obvious cases.

The choice of **a** versus **the**, however, is much more subtle than it first appears. Speakers have to assess not just what their audience knows, but what they will be able to figure out. Note, for example, that since there is only one sun, moon, and president that people normally think of, one can refer to them as **the sun, the moon**, and **the President**, even when they haven't been mentioned before. The same goes for steering wheel in **I stepped into a car and grabbed hold of the steering wheel**. Since cars have but one steering wheel, it can be referred to as **the steering wheel**, even though it hasn't been mentioned before either (Chafe, 1972). What is critical in the use of **the** is that listeners can figure out uniquely what entity is being referred to.

The choice of **a** versus **the** often induces listeners to draw inferences beyond the direct meaning of the noun phrase, and clever speakers exploit this device to the full (H. Clark, 1977; H. Clark and Haviland, 1977). Compare 8 and 9:

8. The man had been murdered. A knife lay nearby.

9. The man had been murdered. The knife lay nearby.

In 8, there is no necessary implication that the knife had anything to do with the murder, but in 9, there is. Because **the knife** is definite, listeners know they are expected to be able to identify this knife uniquely. To do that, they find it easiest to assume that the knife was the murder weapon that caused the man's death. In other words, they draw the implicature in 9′:

9′. The man was stabbed to death with a knife.

For another example, compare 10 and 11:

10. I went to the cupboard and took out a bottle of wine there.

11. I went to the cupboard and took out the bottle of wine there.

In 10, it is implied that there was more than one bottle of wine in the cupboard, while in 11, it is implied that there was only one (unless a special bottle of wine had just been mentioned). To get listeners to draw such inferences, speakers can make judicious use of **a** and **the**.

Nouns and Modifiers

Recall that speakers would use a definite noun phrase "if they thought the entity being referred to was something their audience knew of and could uniquely identify from the noun phrase." An important word here is "uniquely." Speakers cannot refer to someone as **Dr. Baker** or **my next door neighbor** or **she** unless they are confident the listener can pick her out of all other conceivable referents. The problem speakers have to solve—and it often requires careful thought—is this: what combination of nouns and modifiers will enable the listener to pick out the intended referent uniquely and, for efficiency, in the simplest and least number of words?

TABLE 6–1

MODIFICATION IN THE NOUN PHRASE

Four arrays of figures and the noun phrases that
could be used to describe the left-hand circle in each.

	ARRAY	DESCRIPTION
Set A	○ □	the round one
Set B	○ ○	the small one
Set C	○ ○ □ □	the small round one
Set D	○	the circle that is about 1mm in diameter

Descriptions and Arrays

One approach to this problem is to think of the referent as belonging to an array
of objects, and the goal as finding a noun phrase that will distinguish the referent
from the rest of the array. This approach has been discussed by D. Olson (1970).
He invites us to imagine people who are asked to refer to the left-hand circle in
each of the four arrays of circles and squares in Table 6–1. For Set A, they will
say **the round one**, since that is enough to distinguish it from the square one. In
Set B, they will say **the small one** to distinguish it from the remaining large one.
For Set C, they must go to two modifiers, **the small round one**, to distinguish it
from the other three figures. Set D is probably the most complicated set, for
people have to infer the alternatives from which this figure is to be distinguished.
If they take the figure in Set D as the lone alternative, they should say simply
that one or **it**; but if they include all possible geometric figures, they might say
the circle about 1mm in diameter drawn in black ink. In short, people will refer
to the same figure with very different noun phrases depending on what they take
to be the array of objects it is to be picked out of.

The modifiers people choose should depend not only on the number of
alternatives in the array, but also on their distinguishability. It will take more
modifiers to pick an object out of an array of very similar than of very different
objects. This has been demonstrated by Krauss and Weinheimer (1967). They
presented people with four patches of color, numbered 1 through 4, and asked
them to describe the patches so that someone else, sitting opposite and hearing
only the description, could put corresponding patches into the same order. Half
the arrays consisted of four very similar colors (for example, various shades of
red), and the other half consisted of four very dissimilar colors (for example,
red, orange, yellow, and green). As expected, the number of words in each

noun phrase (excluding the article) averaged 3.5 for the "similar" arrays and only 2.3 for the "dissimilar" arrays. These people were highly sensitive to which noun phrases would succeed and which wouldn't.

Shorthand Expressions

With repeated references to the same object, however, speakers can often simplify their noun phrases drastically. They may first refer to **my cousin Harriet from Central City in the heart of the Rocky Mountains** to distinguish her from many other people, but thereafter refer to her simply as **Harriet**. The use of such shorthands has been investigated by Krauss and Weinheimer (1964) too. In a task like the previous one, people were given an array of four figures and asked to describe them so that another person could put them into the same order. The figures used were all abstract configurations, like Figure 6–1, that are difficult to describe in a few words. On successive trials, some figures came up repeatedly, giving people the opportunity to use shorthands. Although long names were invariably used at first, they were soon shortened. On first reference, the noun phrases (excluding articles) averaged 7.8 words, but by even the sixth

FIGURE 6–1
ABSTRACT FIGURE

Abstract configuration used in a
communication task.

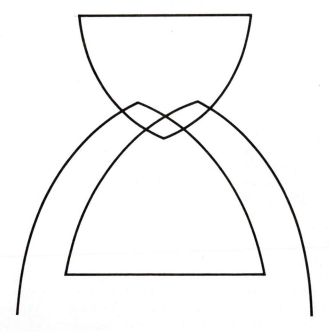

Based on R. M. Krauss and S. Weinheimer (1964).

reference, they averaged only a little over one word. Repeated references to the shape in Figure 6–1, for example, went like this: **the upside-down martini glass in a wire stand**, **the inverted martini glass**, **the martini glass**, and eventually **the martini**. Efficiency of expression is clearly an important criterion in the choice of noun phrases.

To be able to use such a shorthand, however, speakers must be sure it does what it is supposed to do: pick out the intended referent for the listener uniquely. In making this judgment, they rely heavily on feedback from the listener. Listeners who are present can indicate with a "Right" or "What?" or "Which do you mean?" whether or not they understood a particular shorthand. But if the listeners are not present, speakers can never be sure whether they will be understood. This point was demonstrated by Krauss and Weinheimer (1966) in a third study. They redid the experiment with the repeated abstract figures, once with people talking to responsive listeners and once with them talking into a tape recorder for some future listener. When there were responsive listeners, the noun phrases reduced dramatically, as before. But with an unresponsive tape recorder, the noun phrases reduced hardly at all. Feedback from listeners is apparently critical for the use of shorthands, since it is them they are meant to help.

Basic Level Nouns

Most of what has been said about choosing modifiers also goes for choosing nouns. Imagine redoing Olson's demonstration with these three arrays.

A.

B.

C.

The task here is to refer to the left-hand member of each array. Following the earlier example, each additional distinction should add a modifier. The girl should be referred to as **the human one** in Set A, **the nonadult human one** in Set B, and **the female nonadult human one** in Set C. These phrases, however, are unnecessarily cumbersome, for in English **human one** is equivalent to **person**, **nonadult human one** to **child**, and **female nonadult human one** to **girl**. Thus, just as the modifiers one selects depend on the array the referent is being picked out of, so do the nouns. And just as finer and finer distinctions can be made by adding more and more modifiers, so can they be made by increasing the specificity of the noun—for example, from **person** to **child** to **girl**. Indeed, the information carried by the adjectives and nouns of a noun phrase are often interchangeable, as in **immense person** and **giant**, or **unmarried man** and **bachelor**.

People's choice of nouns, however, doesn't always follow the simple principle "Be only as specific as necessary," as R. Brown (1958) has noted. Take this array:

D.

The item on the far left wouldn't normally be referred to as **the animal**, but as **the dog**, or even **the terrier**, two nouns that are far more specific than they have to be. Even in Sets A, B, and C, the critical item would normally be called **the girl**. As Brown has argued, there appears to be an optimal level of utility for references to objects, a level Rosch and her colleagues (1976) have called the *basic level*. This level is not too abstract (like **the thing** or **the animal**) and not too specific (like **the Airedale terrier**), but just right (like **the dog** or **the terrier**). A noun phrase at this level gives as much information as is necessary for most references, but not so much that it takes time and effort to find or understand the right word. Brown has pointed out that the optimal level of utility is less specific for children than for adults. Where **the terrier** or **the pigeon** would be used with adults, **the dog** or **the bird** would be used with very young children. The basic level is a topic that will be taken up again in Chapter 14.

Pronouns

The sparsest noun phrases of all are the definite pronouns, like **I**, **you**, **he**, **she**, and **it**. They are simply definite noun phrases stripped of the power to distinguish objects along any dimension except "person" (**I** versus **you** versus **he**), "sex" (**he** versus **she**), and "number" (**he** versus **they**). Because of their sparseness, they can pick out referents uniquely only when the set of alternatives is small and of just the right kind. They are most useful when there is for all practical purposes only one alternative, as in the use of **she** here:

12. The woman stepped forward. Then she stopped.

It has been proposed by Chafe (1974) that speakers will only use a pronoun when they are certain its referent is at that moment in the listener's consciousness. Note, for example, that because the speaker and listener can always be assumed to be in consciousness, they are invariably referred to as **I** and **you**. And since a person or thing mentioned in the just-preceding sentence can also be assumed to be in consciousness, it too will be referred to with a pronoun—unless, of course, the pronoun won't pick the referent out uniquely, as in this example:

13. Two women stepped forward. Then she stopped.

Indeed, when the referent is clearly in consciousness and there would be no ambiguity, the use of the pronoun is almost obligatory. Compare:

14. Julia skied past the first flag. Then Julia fell.

15. Julia skied past the first flag. Then she fell.

The second appearance of **Julia** in 14 is decidedly odd, whereas the pronoun **she** in 15 is perfectly natural. Chafe's proposal also explains why it is obligatory in most cases to use a pronoun for the second mention of a person or object within a single sentence. One must say 16 and not 17:

16. My pregnant neighbor decided that my pregnant neighbor should move.

17. My pregnant neighbor decided that she should move.

In actuality, there are other complex and poorly understood constraints on pronominalization within sentences (P. Cole, 1974; Kuno, 1975; Langacker, 1969; Ross, 1967). Nevertheless, they appear roughly compatible with the notion that pronouns are used to pick out objects immediately available in in consciousness.

Personal Pronouns and Terms of Address

In an earlier period of English, speakers also had to decide between the "familiar" **thou** and the "formal" **you** in referring to a listener, and in many other languages, they still have to make the familiar-formal choice. In French, the two terms are **tu** and **vous**, in German **du** and **Sie**, in Italian **tu** and **lei**, and in Spanish **tu** and

Usted. To take French as a paradigmatic example, one generally speaks to friends and close family with familiar **tu** and to others with formal **vous**. Close family and friends use **tu** in return, and the others use **vous**. On the other hand, one always speaks to children with **tu**, and they always return with **vous** unless they are close members of the same family. And there are other situations in which **tu** is used in one direction and **vous** is used in the other. It is clear that the choice of **tu** and **vous** is not simple. It often depends on subtle judgments about the social situation.

The Power Semantic and Solidarity Semantic

R. Brown and Gilman (1960) have argued persuasively that the choice of **tu** versus **vous** depends on two social factors, the *power semantic* and the *solidarity semantic*. The power semantic works like this. In most social systems some people have power over others by virtue of their rank, status, or age. This power is asymmetrical, and the use of **tu** and **vous** reflects this asymmetry. The more powerful person uses **tu** with an inferior, whereas the less powerful person uses **vous** with a superior. The solidarity semantic, on the other hand, is concerned with social distance. Some people are close to each other because they attend the same school, belong to the same family, or practice the same profession, and other people are distant. People can be said to vary on the dimension of solidarity. Two people with close solidarity will use **tu** with each other, while two people without will use **vous**. As Brown and Gilman have shown, the power semantic has been giving way over the centuries to the solidarity semantic, so that by now the power semantic enters into only a few pronoun choices, like that between adults and children. What remains is the solidarity semantic, and with the rise of social egalitarianism, even that has been liberalizing over the years. More and more people are included among those to whom one uses the familiar **tu**.

One area where power and solidarity play a role in English is in the choice of address terms (R. Brown and Ford, 1961). Two people in close solidarity address each other by their first names—**Sally** and **Bob**—whereas two people with more distance address each other by a title and last name—**Miss Jones** and **Mr. Horowitz**. In some instances, a social superior can address a social inferior by his first name, while the social inferior must use title and last name back. This is the case with adults and children (unless they are members of the same family). As it happens, there is a series of address terms in English, and they vary in their formality:

(1) *Title alone:* sir, madam, doctor, professor

(2) *Title and last name:* Miss Jones, Professor Smith, Dr. Wills

(3) *Last name alone:* Jones, Smith, Wills

(4) *First name alone:* Sally, Janet, Bob

(5) *Pet names:* honey, dear, Bobbie

The farther down the list one goes, the more familiar one must be with the addressee. Nevertheless, the two most common address terms are 2 and 4. So terms of address are chosen in much the same way as familiar and formal pronouns except that there are more than two ways someone can be addressed.

All in all, the planning of noun phrases is complicated. Speakers must assess their listeners for their knowledge of the possible referents of the noun phrase, for the contents of their "consciousness" at the time of utterance, and even for the power and solidarity relationship holding between them. It is hardly surprising that the planning of other types of constituents is just as complicated and that it depends on similar assessments. What is remarkable is how little is known about the process of planning itself. Our discussion has centered on *what* one plans—the particular articles, adjectives, and nouns selected for a particular purpose—but not *how* one plans it. The *process* of planning constituents is still largely a mystery.

SUMMARY

In planning what to say, speakers are faced with a series of interrelated problems. These are solved at the level of the discourse, the sentence, or the constituent.

At the grossest level, speakers have to give structure to the discourse. The goal is to order the flow of information so that the discourse achieves the ends each intended for it. In dialogues, the goal may be to negotiate a deal, dig out information, or exchange gossip; in monologues, it may be to describe a scene, explain how something works, or tell a story. In either case, speakers must plan the level, content, order, and relations among the pieces of information. This results in a global plan that specifies how to begin, what route to follow, and where to end. In dialogues, the participants have to coordinate their routes as they go along.

Within discourse, each sentence is nevertheless planned locally, roughly one at a time. The problem speakers have to solve at this level is this: which sentence will lead the discourse in a direction that fits the global structure? In choosing a sentence, speakers have to decide on propositional content, illocutionary content, and thematic structure. They have to pick propositions that mirror the ideas they want to get across. They have to focus on salient verbalizable events and states and their participants and find propositions to fit them. They also have to decide on a speech act with felicity conditions that fit the planned discourse and then settle on one way of expressing that speech act. And they must design each sentence so that its subject and predicate, given and new information, and frame and insert fit where they are going and mesh with the listener's knowledge.

The words within a sentence, however, are not all planned at once. Speakers appear to work from a skeleton plan of a sentence and select the words roughly constituent by constituent. For noun phrases, the problem is to find the noun phrase with which the listener can pick out the intended referent uniquely and efficiently. Speakers select **a** versus **the** based on their judgment of what the listener does and doesn't know. They select the head noun and its modifiers based on a judgment of the implicit array the referent belongs to and whether the referent is in the listener's consciousness at the time. And they select the level of familiarity and formality based on judgments of social factors.

Further Reading

Although little has been written on the actual planning of utterances, a bit more has been said about the choices speakers make. Sacks, Schegloff, and Jefferson, in the papers already cited, provide a fascinating account of certain phenomena in conversations; still other essays on the topic can be found in Sudnow (1972). J. Sinclair and Coulthard (1975) take up talk in the classroom and illustrate with many fully analyzed conversations. Labov (1972) discusses the structure of narratives. As for sentences, Halliday (1970, 1973) gives a thorough discussion of their functions—especially their thematic functions. Searle (1969) gives a clear account of the prerequisites for promising and other speech acts. Osgood (1971) describes a naturalistic study of people's choices of certain constructions in context. Finally, many of the choices people make depend on social factors. Trudgill (1974) discusses many of these.

For instance, take the two words "fuming" and "furious." Make up your mind that you will say both words, but leave it unsettled which you will say first. Now open your mouth and speak. If your thoughts incline ever so little towards "fuming," you will say "fuming-furious"; if they turn, even by a hair's breadth, towards "furious," you will say "furious-fuming"; but if you have that rarest of gifts, a perfectly balanced mind, you will say "frumious."

Lewis Carroll

7

Execution of Speech Plans

It is one thing to plan what one is going to say and quite another thing to execute that plan. As described in the last chapter, speakers build up a general structure for the discourse, form a skeleton for the sentence to be uttered, and select words to fit this skeleton constituent by constituent. Their next task is to execute this plan, to get their articulatory organs—larynx, mouth, and tongue—to emit the sounds they intended. The process of executing these plans is the subject of the present chapter.

At first glance the execution of speech seems unexceptionable. In speaking, people take already formulated plans and execute them. But not all goes well in everyday speech. In practice they have fundamental problems. First, they have not always formulated their plans fully before they begin their execution. For this reason they often speak in fits and starts and make a variety of speech errors. Second, in final preparation for execution, they must build an "articulatory program," a plan in working memory that tells the articulatory muscles what to do when. In forming this program they also make errors. Thus, there are two fundamental issues to examine in the execution process: the alternation between planning and execution, and the formation of the articulatory program for pronunciation.

What are the units of the execution process, and at what levels are they dealt with? Recall that in planning, the concepts of units and levels were critical. Speech is planned at the level of the discourse, the sentence, and the constituent. What is planned at these levels generally are chunks of discourse, skeletons of sentences, and individual words. It would be surprising if these same units and levels didn't turn up in execution too. Indeed, they do. For example, just as speakers try to plan a single constituent all at once, they try to execute this plan in a single uninterrupted train of speech. In executing speech plans, however, there are several more levels to attend to—principally the levels of word formation and phonetic segment formation. These additional levels add some surprising complications to the execution of speech.

Virtually all information about speech execution comes from speech errors. These errors are roughly of two kinds. Some are the result of gross difficulties the speaker has in trying to plan and execute speech at the same time. These include hesitations, corrections, **uh**s, and many other indications that speakers are interrupting the execution to do further planning. Other errors are the result of more localized difficulties speakers have in forming the articulatory program to guide the articulatory muscles in the production of sounds. These include all the "slips of the tongue," which multiply when speakers are tired, in a hurry, or under pressure. What is astonishing is how much has been learned about the execution of speech from these two sources alone. The first topic to be taken up is the alternation of planning and execution.

PLANNING AND EXECUTION

When people speak spontaneously, they hem and haw, repeat and correct themselves, and stutter and stammer. Spontaneous speech in the raw can be very raw indeed, as in this example from Maclay and Osgood (1959, p. 25):

> As far as I know, no one yet has done the / in a way obvious now and interesting problem of [pause] doing a / in a sense a structural frequency study of the alternative [pause] syntactical [uh] / in a given language, say, like English, the alternative [uh] possible structures, and how / what their hierarchical [pause] probability of occurrence structure is.

This is a genuine example, replete with pauses, **uh**s, and false starts. (The false starts are marked by the slashes where the speaker has backed up and begun again.) The speaker obviously didn't have everything planned before he talked. Otherwise he wouldn't have had to stop or retrace his steps before going on.

How do planning and execution intermix to produce these errors? From the study of speech errors, there is an outline of an answer that dovetails with the outline of planning discussed in the last chapter. There it was suggested that speakers generally select their words constituent by constituent, where the constituent may vary in size from two words (as in **the man**) up to seven or eight words (for example, a short clause). In the execution process, their main goal is to execute the planned constituent and to do so as fluently as possible. Sometimes, however, they have to commit themselves to begin speaking before they have a constituent completely planned. In these cases they have to stop, plan, and try again to say the constituent fluently. There is good evidence for this outline from speech errors alone. They show that:

(1) speakers try to produce each constituent fluently;

(2) they try to plan each constituent as a unit;

(3) when they do have to stop, they often offer a brief explanation before correcting themselves and going on; and

(4) it is the selection of words that makes them stop when they do.

The Ideal Delivery

For there to be a speech "error" there must be a "correct" way of executing a sentence, and this will be called the *ideal delivery*. When people know what they want to say and say it fluently, they are giving an ideal delivery. Actors saying their lines, except when making deliberate errors, come close to the ideal delivery, and so do practiced readers and orators. For theories of speech production the ideal delivery is of central importance. They all assume that people strive for the ideal delivery, and every deviation points to something that has gone wrong in planning or execution.

In the ideal delivery, most types of clauses are executed in a single fluent speech train under one smooth intonation contour. On the other hand, the "grammatical junctures" between these clauses may contain momentary pauses. Language has been designed this way so that speakers may breathe without interrupting fluent speech. In the ideal delivery they can breathe at junctures, but not within clauses. Henderson, Goldman-Eisler, and Skarbek (1965) examined the speech of people reading a passage fluently and of people speaking spontaneously. The readers, who were presumably close to an ideal delivery, breathed *only* at grammatical junctures, whereas the others, falling short of the ideal, breathed within clauses as well. This is not to say that there cannot be pauses within clauses. Some, which can be called *conventional pauses*, are obligatory, since they serve a specific linguistic purpose. Compare:

1. Her brother the dentist is as ugly as a mule.

2. Her brother, the dentist, is as ugly as a mule.

The "comma pauses" in 2 give it a different interpretation from 1 and must therefore be present to signal this interpretation. So the ideal delivery has these characteristics. The execution of each clause between junctures takes a fixed amount of time; any pauses that appear within the clause are obligatory and vary little from one execution to the next. But the junctures themselves may vary considerably in length depending on whether or not the speaker takes the opportunity to breathe or to stop momentarily.

Why should speakers try for an ideal delivery? One reason is to make themselves better understood. Speech with breaks that are not at constituent boundaries is difficult to understand (see Chapter 2). In the ideal delivery, all breaks will be at grammatical junctures between sentences or major clauses, where they will help, not hinder. Another less obvious reason is that people who speak fluently are very likely judged cleverer, abler, and more effective than people without the same fluency. Moreover, it isn't considered polite to speak unless one has something definite to say, and every hesitation, **uh**, and false start adds to the impression that one does not have something definite to say. So it is only natural, in most circumstances, to strive for the ideal delivery.

Common Speech Errors

The most common disruption in the ideal delivery is the hesitation pause— either the *silent pause*, a period of no speech between words, or the *filled pause*, a gap filled by **ah**, **er**, **uh**, **mm**, or the like. Speed of talking is almost entirely determined by the amount of such pausing. People who speak slowly hesitate a lot, and when they speed up their rate of words, they do it by eliminating the pauses, not by shortening the words. Goldman-Eisler (1968), who made these observations, found that pauses took up from 5 to 65 percent of the total speaking time of people she interviewed or had describe pictures; most people paused between 40 and 50 percent of the time. Apparently, people spend a large proportion of their speaking time *not* speaking. Maclay and Osgood (1959) showed that it is these pauses that distinguish fast from slow speakers. Fast speakers are fluent because they do not hesitate much, and slow speakers are not as fluent because they hesitate a great deal. Other speech errors do not distinguish between the two types of speakers. It is hardly surprising that people differ widely in their native fluency. Yet it is significant that this fluency resides mostly in a speaker's propensity for hesitations.

The common types of speech errors, including silent and filled pauses, are listed and illustrated in Table 7–1. Although most are self-explanatory, repeats, unretraced false starts, and retraced false starts are more complicated. *Repeats* are repetitions of one or more words in a row, whereas *false starts* are corrections of a word. *Retraced false starts* also include the repetition of one or more words before the corrected word, whereas *unretraced false starts* do not. The category called *corrections* is like false starts, except that they contain an explicit **I mean**, **or rather**, or **that is** to mark the phrase as a correction. As it happens, the different speech errors in Table 7–1 characteristically arise at different points in the execution process. Where they occur tells us much about the nature of the process itself.

Constituents in Execution

In the last chapter, it was suggested that speakers plan the skeleton of a sentence first and its constituents later. Consider the following sentence, whose constituents are enclosed in parentheses:

TABLE 7–1
COMMON TYPES OF SPEECH ERRORS

NAME OF SPEECH ERROR	EXAMPLE
Silent pause	Turn on the // heater switch.
Filled pause	Turn on, uh, the heater switch.
Repeats	Turn on the heater / the heater switch.
False starts (unretraced)	Turn on the stove / heater switch.
False starts (retraced)	Turn on the stove / the heater switch.
Corrections	Turn on the stove switch—I mean, the heater switch.
Interjections	Turn on, oh, the heater switch.
Stutters	Turn on the h-h-h-heater switch.
Slips of the tongue	Turn on the sweeter hitch.

((The (neighbor (of (my brother))))(visited (the (main (judge (of Minot)))) (on Tuesday)))

According to the skeleton + constituents notion, the speaker first plans the skeleton:

E_{47} visited E_{93} Time$_{33}$

Once the skeleton is fixed, he plans E_{47} to be **the neighbor of my brother**, goes on to **visited**, next plans E_{93} to be **the main judge of Minot**, and finally plans **Time$_{33}$** to be the adverbial **on Tuesday**. Another possibility is that the speaker plans a less complete skeleton first, say:

E_{47} Action$_{85}$

Then, as he plans E_{47}, he expands **Action$_{85}$** into its three parts, giving:

The neighbor of my brother [visited E_{93} Time$_{33}$].

The initial plan specifies just a rough outline of the propositional content, say, that E_{47} did a particular something, **Action$_{85}$**. It is only as the sentence is being executed that **Action$_{85}$** is planned in more detail. This view was originally proposed, in more or less this form, by Yngve (1960).

According to the skeleton + constituent notion, the constituent is an important unit of planning. But what about execution itself? It would be convenient if the constituent were also a major unit of execution, since once a unit is planned it could be uttered in one fluent speech stream. The speaker who has planned E_{47} to be **the neighbor of my brother** could execute it fluently while planning the next constituent. But recall that speakers strive ultimately for the ideal delivery, which demands that each constituent be executed in one fluent stream. So even if they should run into difficulty planning a constituent, they should try to execute it as much as a single unit as they can.

There is evidence that this is precisely what speakers try to do. Maclay and Osgood (1959) recorded the spontaneous discussions of a small group of scholars at a psycholinguistics conference and later combed the recordings for speech errors. It comes as no surprise that there were thousands of errors, but Maclay and Osgood showed they were highly systematic. For repeats and false starts, the pattern was this (illustrated with simplified examples). Fully 89 percent of all words repeated were function words, like articles (**the / the neighbor**), prepositions (**in / in the garden**), conjunctions (**and / and the neighbor**), and pronouns (**he / he didn't go**). On the other hand, most of the words corrected in the false starts were content words: nouns (**the man / the woman**), adjectives (**the silvery/ the shiny tray**), verbs (**can be seen / can be viewed**), or adverbs (**the very / the rather nice house**). What was striking, however, was that when content words were corrected, the speaker usually (77 percent of the time) retraced one or more words before them, as in **the silvery / the shiny tray**, where **the** is repeated along with the replacement word **shiny**. In the rare cases when function words were corrected, the speaker usually (78 percent of the time) did not retrace any of the previous words, as in **under / behind the sofa**, where **under** is corrected to **behind** without any retracing.

These errors suggest that speakers try hard to preserve constituents in their execution. Imagine someone trying to say **those dirty cups**, but having difficulty at various points. According to Maclay and Osgood's findings, there are three characteristic patterns of errors:

> those / those dirty cups (*a repeat*)
> these / those dirty cups (*an unretraced false start*)
> those clean / those dirty cups (*a retraced false start*)

What these three patterns have in common is that the speaker, after all corrections and hesitations, executes the whole constituent **those dirty cups** in one uninterrupted movement. If he runs into a problem, he stops to deal with it, but then he goes back and executes the constituent from the very beginning.

The speech errors called corrections prove much the same point. These errors consist of a "correction phrase," like **I mean**, **that is**, or **well**, followed by the "corrected words," the words to replace what was said earlier. As DuBois (1975) has shown, the corrected words always begin at a constituent boundary. Compare:

3. The doctor looked up Joe's nose—that is, up Joe's left nostril.

4. *The operator looked up Joe's address—that is, up Joe's apartment number.

TABLE 7–2

SILENT PAUSES AND REPEATS

The most frequent silent pauses (///) and repeats (/)
in twelve types of constituents.

COMMONEST SILENT PAUSES	TYPICAL REPEATS
the // house	the / the house
the // big house	the / the big house
the // manor house	the / the manor house
in // houses	in / in houses
in // big houses	in / in big houses
in // manor houses	in / in manor houses
in the // house	in the / in the house
in the // big house	in the / in the big house
in the // manor house	in the / in the manor house
may // go	may / may go
may have // gone	may have / may have gone
in // going home	in / in going home

Based on Maclay and Osgood (1959).

In 3 the corrected words begin at a constituent boundary, at the beginning of the prepositional phrase **up Joe's left nostril**. In 4, however, they begin in the middle of a constituent, since in this sentence **up** is part of the verb **look up** and does not combine with **Joe's apartment number** to form a prepositional phrase. This is why the corrected words in 4 sound wrong. (The asterisk in 4 indicates an unacceptable sentence.) After examining many examples like this, DuBois concluded that the corrected words cannot include fragments of previous constituents.

Repeats, false starts, and corrections, therefore, provide excellent evidence that speakers consider the constituent a basic unit of execution. They attempt, to the best of their ability, to execute constituents as complete wholes. When for some reason they do stop, make a false start, or correct themselves, they tend to return to the beginning of the constituent.

Constituents in Planning

But what about planning? Do speech errors provide any evidence that the constituent is a unit of planning too? At first glance, they seem to go against this assumption. Maclay and Osgood (1959) classified the silent and filled pauses in their data by their position of occurrence within various types of constituents. Table 7–2 lists twelve different types of constituents they looked at. For example, **in the manor house** consists of preposition + article + noun + noun.

In constituents of this type, silent pauses could have occurred at any one of five points in the constituent from before the word **in** to after the word **house**. Most silent pauses, however, occurred just before the word **manor**, as in **in the // manor house**. For comparison, the table also lists the typical kind of repeat that would occur with each type of constituent.

The striking feature of these silent pauses and repeats is that speakers tend to stop just before the first content word of the constituent, just before the first adjective or noun. After they have stopped, either they hesitate and go on, or they hesitate, return to the beginning, and repeat. It is as if speakers execute the first one or two function words of the constituent—the article, preposition, or verbal auxiliaries—and then stop to plan the rest of the constituent—the adjectives and nouns. This seems to go directly against the idea that speakers plan each constituent all at once. If they had, they should have paused just before the constituent—but never halfway through, as they often did.

Syntactic and Semantic Planning

The resolution of this apparent problem is to posit two levels of planning, one syntactic and the other semantic (see Maclay and Osgood, 1959; Goldman-Eisler, 1968). Indeed, this is the essence of the skeleton + constituent model. Consider the example used earlier:

The neighbor of my brother visited the main judge of Minot on Tuesday.

The speaker begins with a skeleton, namely:

E_{47} visited E_{93} Time$_{33}$

By this point he has planned the *syntactic form* of his utterance. But even before he plans that E_{47} should be **the neighbor of my brother**, he knows that E_{47} is a noun phrase, even a definite noun phrase. He can therefore start in on the execution of E_{47} with no further planning, since it will most likely begin with **the**. This **the** can be viewed as part of the syntactic planning, since it is predictable from the skeleton alone. But once he has executed **the**, he may have to stop, since he has not decided on the exact form of E_{47} at the semantic level of planning. Eventually, he selects **the neighbor of my brother** and executes the rest of the constituent, namely **neighbor of my brother**, fluently. He would thereby produce either a silent pause or a repeat:

The // neighbor of my brother . . .
The / the neighbor of my brother . . .

It sometimes happens, however, that the first word **the** may actually be wrong, and then of course it has to be corrected, as in:

The / my brother's neighbor . . .

These three patterns are among those that appeared most regularly in Maclay and Osgood's speech errors.

Boomer (1965) provided more evidence for these two levels of planning. In his samples of spontaneous speech, he first identified what he called *phonemic clauses*, stretches of speech spoken under one intonation contour between two successive grammatical junctures. Phonemic clauses typically consist of a single independent clause or a sentence with a subordinate clause. Boomer then identified the points at which pauses occurred within these phonemic clauses. What he found was that his speakers executed over half of these phonemic clauses without a pause. When they did pause, they were most likely to pause after the very first word. (Although Boomer didn't analyze his phonemic clauses further, the first word in most of them was probably a function word: an article like **the** or **a**, a preposition, a conjunction, or a pronoun.) So these findings coincide with those of Maclay and Osgood: speakers tend to pause after the first function word of a major constituent. But Boomer showed in addition that the constituent within which speakers are most likely to pause is first in the sentence. The remainder of the sentence is most often uttered fluently.

An even more important finding in Boomer's study was that speakers paused at grammatical junctures as well. In fact, they were more likely to pause *before* a phonemic clause than *within* one. And when they did pause, the pauses at grammatical junctures averaged more than a third longer than the pauses within phonemic clauses:

Average pause length at grammatical junctures: 1.03 seconds
Average pause length within phonemic clauses: 0.75 seconds

Juncture pauses, of course, are not usually considered speech errors, since they occur at points where the speaker in an ideal delivery is allowed to breathe. For this reason they don't appear in Maclay and Osgood's data at all. Yet given their length and frequency, they are surely points at which speakers do a lot of planning. Speakers also appear to plan at other constituent boundaries. Maclay and Osgood (1959) found that filled pauses—as distinct from silent pauses—tended to appear at constituent boundaries other than junctures—for example, at the left and right ends of the constituents listed in Table 7–2.

Three Hesitation Points

What all this evidence suggests is that there are three major points at which speakers are liable to stop for planning:

(1) *Grammatical junctures.* This is the logical place to stop to plan the skeleton and first constituent of the upcoming sentence. Pauses at these junctures tend to be long and frequent.

(2) *Other constituent boundaries.* Within sentences these boundaries are the appropriate place to stop to plan details of the next major constituent—

precisely what noun phrase, prepositional phrase, verb phrase, or adverbial phrase is to fit next into the sentence skeleton. This stopping place is typically marked by a filled pause.

(3) *Before the first content word within a constituent.* This is a point after speakers have committed themselves to the syntactic form of the constituent being executed, but before they have planned the precise words to fill it out. This stopping place, like the previous kind, gives speakers time to plan the very next major constituent. It is typically marked by a silent pause (**the //dirty cups**) or by a repeat of the beginning of the constituent (**the / the dirty cups**).

These pauses reveal how speakers are pulled by two opposing forces: the ideal delivery and the press of the conversation. In their efforts to produce an ideal delivery, they would like to pause until they have fully planned the next sentence, or at least the next major constituent. This tendency leads to pauses of Types 1 and 2. On the other hand, there is the press of conversation. If they wait too long at these points they know other people will think they have finished their contribution and will begin to take their turns. To avert this possibility, speakers must boldly start in on the first function words of the next constituent, especially when it begins a sentence, and only then stop to plan the constituent in detail. In this way they can signal to their audience that they are not yet finished with their contribution, but in so doing, they will produce a pause of Type 3.

Interjections and Corrections

There are many reasons why speakers may stop in midsentence. They may have forgotten something they wanted to refer to; they may be searching for just the right word; or they may be selecting which of several examples they could mention. English has two remarkable devices by which speakers can signal just why they are stopping, the interjection (**oh**, **ah**, **well**, **say**, etc.) and the correction (**I mean**, **that is**, **well**, etc.). Moreover, these two devices provide further evidence that the constituent is an important unit of planning.

Interjections

Interjections, like hesitation pauses, indicate that speakers have had to stop to think about what to say next, and as James (1972, 1973a, b) has noted, they select a particular interjection to signal why they have had to stop. The interjections **oh**, **ah**, **well**, and **say** are illustrated in the following sentences.

5. John would like, oh, carrots.

6. John would like—ah, carrots.

7. John would like, well, carrots.

8. John would like, say, carrots.

According to James's analysis, each interjection here "refers to" the word **carrots**. The functions of these interjections are these:

5'. oh: *referent selection*

6'. ah: *memory success*

7'. well: *word approximation*

8'. say: *exemplification*

In 5 the **oh** indicates the speaker has stopped to pick out **carrots** as just one of several possibilities he could mention. In 6 the **ah** indicates that the speaker had forgotten and has just managed to remember what it was that John would like. In 7 the **well** indicates that the speaker thinks that **carrots** is only an approximate description of what John would like. In 8 the **say** indicates that the speaker is giving an example of what John would like. In other instances, **say** could mean instead "let's imagine." Finally, consider these two examples:

9. John would like // carrots.

10. John would like, uh, carrots.

James noted that the silent pause in 9 and the filled pause in 10 lead to still other interpretations of why the speaker has stopped, but these are not nearly so specific as the other interjections. Thus speakers use interjections when they deem it important to let the listener know just why they are pausing.

According to James, however, interjections always refer to whole constituents. Note the alternatives implied by the **oh** in this sentence:

11. John was expected to buy, oh, carrots by his parents.

Oh signals that the speaker is choosing the word **carrots** from among a set of alternatives—say, **carrots**, **radishes**, and **cucumbers**. It cannot signal that the speaker is choosing the words **carrots by his parents** from among a set of alternatives—say, **carrots by his parents**, **radishes by his sister**, and **cucumbers by his cousin**. The reason is that **carrots** is a constituent of Sentence 11, **carrots by his parents** is not, and **oh** can only refer to whole constituents. Along the same vein, take this sentence:

12. After eating thirty green apples, John suddenly threw, oh, up.

Oh indicates that the speaker is choosing from a set of alternatives, but it can't be so in this case. **Threw up**, an idiom meaning "vomit," is a single constituent, so after saying **threw**, and meaning "vomit," the speaker has no choice but **up**. It is for this reason that Sentence 12 sounds decidedly odd.

This evidence alone is enough to reinforce our assumption that the constituent is the unit of planning, but James has argued the same thing about silent and filled pauses. Consider 13 and 14:

13. John was expected to buy, uh, carrots by his parents.

14. After eating thirty green apples, John suddenly threw, uh, up.

The filled pause in 13 behaves just like the **oh** in 11 and indicates that the speaker is trying to decide on **carrots**, not on **carrots by his parents**. Likewise, the filled pause in 14 is just as odd as the **oh** in 12, since the speaker really has no choice and thus no reason to hesitate. Replace the filled pauses by silent ones and the conclusions don't change. With this and the other evidence James has amassed on this issue, it seems particularly clear that the constituent is a major unit of planning and that interjections and hesitation pauses signal choices being made for single constituents.

Correction Phrases

Correction phrases, like interjections, signal why speakers are interrupting themselves. DuBois (1975) has noted that the correction phrases **that is, or rather, I mean**, and **well** signal distinctly different errors speakers are about to correct:

15. He hit Mary—that is, Bill did—with a frying pan.

16. I'm trying to lease—or rather, sublease—my apartment.

17. I really love—I mean, despise—getting up in the morning.

18. I'll be done immediately—well, in a few minutes.

As illustrated in these sentences, the correction phrases have roughly these functions:

15'. that is: *reference editing*

16'. or rather: *nuance editing*

17'. I mean: *mistake editing*

18'. well: *claim editing*

In 15, **that is** is used to specify further the referent of **he**. In 16, **or rather** is used to provide a word that is slightly closer to what the speaker meant to say. In 17, **I mean** is used for correcting an out-and-out mistake in wording, one that would have left the utterance with a significantly wrong meaning. And in 18, **well** is used to soften a claim the speaker decides is too excessive. These correction phrases are not interchangeable. Sentence 15 means something entirely different with **that is** replaced by **well**, and 17 becomes nonsense with **I mean** replaced by **well**. Speakers, then, know not only when they have made a mistake, but what kind of mistake it is, and they use these correction phrases to "explain" why they are making the corrections.

Here again the constituent emerges as a major unit of planning. In each correction, speakers replace certain old words with new ones, indicating that the old words had been misplanned. Typically, this means correcting one word, but sometimes it means correcting more than one. When more than one word is changed, the words almost invariably belong to a single constituent, not to parts of two successive but unlinked constituents. And if the constituent is the unit of misplanning, then it is also the unit of planning.

So planning and execution, at the level of the actual delivery, work by constituents. Speakers plan a constituent and then execute it while planning the next. When planning is disrupted or needs correcting, they still try to execute the constituent as a whole, and this often means retracing their steps. What is perhaps most extraordinary is that speakers, at some level of consciousness, know the word choices and corrections they are making, for they often signal their reasons for them to the listener. These interjections and correction phrases are comments on why speakers happened to say what they said and are not part of the direct message itself. Speakers know a good deal about how they select the words they are going to say.

Sources of Planning Difficulty

Planning takes time—and more time on some occasions than others. Presumably, the more difficult the planning, the more time it should take, and the more likely speech itself will be disrupted. From the research on speech errors, planning can become difficult for cognitive reasons, from anxiety, and for social reasons (see Rochester, 1973).

Cognitive Difficulty

The first source of planning difficulty could be called *cognitive difficulty*. Take a study by Taylor (1969) in which people were asked to produce, as quickly as possible, a sentence on a topic like "car," "joy," "kaleidoscope," or "dominance." Some of these topics were concrete objects (like car and kaleidoscope), and others were abstract concepts (like joy and dominance). It took people longer to produce the first word of the sentence for an abstract than for a concrete topic. Apparently, it took them longer to develop a sentence skeleton for an abstract topic—to think of anything to say at all. Or take a study by Goldman-Eisler (1968), who presented people with *New Yorker* cartoons and asked them to talk about each one. One group was asked to describe each cartoon, while another was asked to explain why each one was funny. There were more hesitations scattered through the explanations than through the descriptions, presumably because it was harder to come up with explanations and the right words to express them (see also Levin, Silverman, and Ford, 1967). If these suggestions are correct, topics that are tough to talk about affect two levels of planning. They delay the planning of the sentence skeleton, and they delay the selection of the words to fit each constituent of the skeleton.

An even more global level of planning—the structuring of discourse—is also reflected in hesitations. It had been noticed by Henderson, Goldman-Eisler, and Skarbek (1966) that spontaneous monologues tend to go in cycles (though see Jaffe, Breskin, and Gerstman, 1972). Each cycle begins with a hesitant phase—a relatively large number of hesitations and slow rate of words—and is followed by a fluent phase—relatively few hesitations and a fast rate of words. What is the source of these cycles? To answer this question, Butterworth (1975) made transcripts of spontaneous monologues and had special judges pick out the points at which there was the beginning of a new idea. One two-hundred-word monologue, for example, was divided up into twelve sections this way. Remarkably, the beginning of each new idea coincided roughly with the beginning, or slow phase, of a cycle. This finding has a ready interpretation. Each new section in discourse takes special global planning in the beginning, and this reveals itself in a hesitant output. As the section proceeds, the global plans becomes complete, there is less need to hesitate, and the result is a fluent output.

At the level of word selection, hesitations should appear when the speaker has difficulty finding just the right word. This has been demonstrated by Goldman-Eisler (1968) and Tannenbaum, Williams, and Hillier (1965). First, they collected samples of spontaneous speech and examined them for their hesitation pauses. Next, they made transcripts of this speech, gave them to other people with some of the words deleted, and asked them to guess what the original words were. The words that immediately followed a hesitation pause in the original speech were found to be harder to guess than words elsewhere in the speech. That is, the original speaker had paused immediately before uttering a word that was not very predictable from what had been said before. It was a hard word. What remains to be answered, of course, is what made these words hard. This is a topic that will be taken up in Chapter 12.

Social Factors

A second source of speech errors is *situational anxiety*. When people talk about topics they are anxious about, they tend to produce more silent pauses and certain other speech errors (Mahl, 1956; Siegman and Pope, 1965). Why? One possibility is that anxiety disrupts the planning and execution processes generally. Speakers become tense, and their planning and execution become less efficient. Another possibility is that what people talk about when they are anxious is simply more difficult cognitively. It may be very difficult to verbalize the abstract anxiety states they want to express, and so they spend more time planning, groping for just the right words. Under this alternative the anxiety pauses have the same source as the pauses of any other cognitively difficult talk. It is safest to assume that situational anxiety affects planning and execution in both of these ways.

The final source of difficulty is *social*. Under the press of a conversation, speakers must make clear when they still have something to say and when they are finished. If they hesitate too long at any point, someone else may take over the conversation. Earlier it was noted how this might push speakers into starting the first word of the next constituent before having the constituent all planned out. It might also push them to use more filled pauses—**uh**, for example—to fill spaces where other speakers might possibly take over. Indeed, speakers do tend to use more **uh**s in dialogues than monologues (see Rochester, 1973). On the other hand, people telling stories to a passive audience are likely to increase silent pauses (Levin and Silverman, 1965)—perhaps because they are being more careful in selecting their words or because they are executing more slowly to make themselves more comprehensible. So speakers are concerned about their audience. A concern with how intelligible they are encourages the use of silent pauses to plan and to assure comprehensibility, and a concern with finishing their contribution leads to the use of filled pauses to signal their intention to continue.

Not all speakers are alike in the speech errors they produce. As Maclay and Osgood (1959) found, some consistently go the **uh** route, with more filled than silent pauses, while others go their silent way, with more silent than filled pauses. And some prefer repeats to false starts, while others prefer false starts to repeats. Each of us, apparently, has a style, a small battery of strategies for overcoming our limited ability to plan and execute at the same time. Some are simply more fluent than others. These observations come as no surprise—we all know orators and stumblers, **uh**-sayers and silent types—but they do point up one important fact. The very same planning difficulty may result in different patterns of speech errors. One person may plan all of a constituent before starting it, another may plan it after the first word, and a third may forge ahead, make a mistake, and then return to repair the mistake. Although they all strive for the ideal delivery, how they try to achieve it varies from person to person.

THE ARTICULATORY PROGRAM

Planning and execution, so the evidence suggests, are interleaved in a complex way so that extra planning may lead to delays in execution. Ultimately, however, speech consists of a sequence of articulatory gestures, a coordinated succession of muscular contractions in and around the mouth. Years ago, Lashley (1951) argued that speech execution like this requires a plan—a plan to direct the order and timing of these articulatory gestures, a plan to command what muscles to move when. This plan will be called the *articulatory program*. From the speech errors discussed so far, there is already much that can be said about the articulatory program, but that is not enough. In the articulatory program there are several lower, finer levels of planning and execution that deal with the formation of words, syllables, and sounds. What is the articulatory program? How is it formed? How is it executed?

Slips of the Tongue

As Lashley himself suggested, the answers to these questions can be found in part in an extraordinary source of evidence: slips of the tongue. Over the years

TABLE 7–3
COMMONEST TYPES OF TONGUE-SLIPS

NAME	ATTESTED EXAMPLES
Anticipations	take my bike → **b**ake my bike
Perseverations	pulled a tantrum → pulled a **p**antrum
Reversals	Katz and Fodor → **f**ats and **k**odor
Blends	grizzly + ghastly → grastly
Haplologies	Post Toasties → Posties
Misderivations	an intervening node → an interven**ient** node
Word substitutions	before the place opens → before the place **closes**

Based on Fromkin (1973).

there has been a sporadic but abiding interest in tongue-slips. A number of assiduous investigators—notably Meringer and Mayer (1895), Freud (1966), Boomer and Laver (1968), Nooteboom (1969), Fromkin (1973), and Garrett (1975)—have risked the patience and good will of their friends and family to collect tongue-slips from conversations around them. Not only have they taken careful note of tongue-slips—a difficult job itself because of their rarity—but also they have often interrupted the speaker to ask what he or she meant to say and was thinking about. Whatever their personal sacrifice, these investigators have done us a grand service, for their collections of tongue-slips have led to important discoveries about the nature of the articulatory program.

The major types of tongue-slips that have been catalogued are listed in Table 7–3. Consider *anticipations*. In the example in Table 7–3, the speaker intended to say **take my bike**, but said instead **bake my bike**, "anticipating" the **b** at the beginning of **bike** in his pronunciation of **take**. (The arrow means "was mispronounced as.") In this example **take** is said to be the *target word*, and **bike** is said to be the *origin* of the error (since that is where the **b** came from). For anticipations the tongue-slip comes before the origin, and for *perseverations* it comes after. For *reversals*, two segments are interchanged, and so the origin of one error is the target for the other, and vice versa. These errors are also known as spoonerisms, after William A. Spooner, an English clergyman who is reported to have made such errors often, wittily, but probably deliberately. *Blends* have two target words, here **grizzly** and **ghastly**, which the speaker "blends" together by taking the first half of one and the second half of the other. In *haplologies*, the speaker leaves out a short stretch of speech. In *misderivations*, the speaker somehow attaches the wrong suffix or prefix to the word. And finally, in *word substitutions*, the speaker produces a word that is wrong, but typically related either semantically or phonologically to the word intended.

From even these few tongue-slips, there is the suggestion that the articulatory program is planned and formed at several levels. Very likely, word substitutions occur at a different level from anticipations, perseverations, and reversals.

WILLIAM SPOONER

You have hissed all my mystery lectures.

I saw you fight a liar in the back quad; in fact, you have tasted the whole worm.

I assure you the insanitary spectre has seen all the bathrooms.

Easier for a camel to go through the knee of an idol.

The Lord is a shoving leopard to his flock.

Take the flea of my cat and heave it at the louse of my mother-in-law.

And very likely, misderivations occur at yet another level, possibly in between the other two. The first task, then, is to examine the evidence for these different levels. Knowing these levels, however, doesn't say how the articulatory program is formed. Are the words inserted in order of articulation, in order of importance, or in some other order? This is the second task to be tackled. The available evidence suggests a natural extension of the skeleton + constituent model already discussed. The articulatory program is first endowed with an outline, filled in with nouns, verbs, and adjectives, and then filled out with function words, prefixes, and suffixes. And finally, the articulatory program must also be fitted out with rhythm and timing and adjusted to the speed of the speech. This is the third task to be taken up.

Units in the Articulatory Program

In comprehension there was need to posit a hierarchy of units, which from smallest to largest looked like this:

distinctive features, like Voicing
phonetic segments, like [b]
syllables, like [bro]
words, like [brokən]
larger constituents, like **the broken promise**

And so on up the line. But what about speech production? Conceivably speakers could store in memory a complete motor pattern for every possible phrase. To utter **in the manor house,** they would initiate the appropriate stored motor pattern and let it play to the finish like a tape recorder. But if **in the manor house** were programmed as a whole unit, there would be no possibility of hesitations occurring within it, as in **in the // manor house,** and there wouldn't be smaller units in the articulatory program. Even from planning, one must conclude that the phrase is too large to be the ultimate unit in the articulatory program. Planning often deals in words and perhaps even smaller units. What, then, are the ultimate units? How are they formed within larger units? Slips of the tongue suggest that the units of the articulatory program are just those units listed above: distinctive features, phonetic segments, syllables, words, and larger constituents.

Segments and Features

The articulatory program must deal in at least phonetic segments, since they are frequently interchanged in tongue-slips. The argument is this: If words were indissoluble units, then phonetic segments could not be interchanged as parts of those units. Consider the following reversals (attested examples from Fromkin, 1973):

19. with this ring I thee wed → with this **w**ing I thee **r**ed

20. left hemisphere → **h**eft **l**emisphere

21. pass out → pa**t** ou**s**

22. David, feed the pooch → David, f**oo**d the p**ea**ch

23. brake fluid → b**l**ake f**r**uid

In each case there are two segments interchanged: [r] and [w] in 19, [l] and [h] in 20, [t] and [s] in 21, [i] and [u] in 22, and [r] and [l] in 23. From 19 alone we might think that the final product had to consist of genuine English words; however, that isn't true of 20, 21, or 23, nor is it true in general, although there is some tendency in this direction (Baars, Motley, and MacKay, 1975). The segments interchanged can be initial consonants, as in 19 and 20, final consonants, as in 21, consonants between vowels (no examples here), vowels, as in 22, and even parts of consonant clusters, as in 23. There is little doubt that phonetic segments are available for switching in the articulatory program.

While speech is divided "horizontally" into phonetic segments, each phonetic segment is divided "vertically" into distinctive features (like Voicing, Nasality, and Stridency). There are many striking examples of tongue-slips that indicate that the articulatory program deals with distinctive features too. Consider this reversal (from Fromkin, 1973):

Terry and Julia → **D**erry and **Ch**ulia

Here what has been reversed are not two intact segments, [t] and [j], but rather only the voicing of the two segments, [−voice] and [+voice]. Originally, [t] is voiceless, and [j] is voiced. In the reversal, [t] is voiced to become [d], and [j] is deprived of its voicing to become [č]. In all other respects the two consonants have remained unchanged. A reversal of [−voice] and [+voice] is evident in this example too (Fromkin, 1971):

clear blue sky → glear plue sky

There are many examples of other features being anticipated, perseverated, and reversed as well. Thus, as Fromkin argued, the articulatory program must have these distinctive features, these vertical components of the phonetic segment, available as units. If phonetic segments were programmed as indissoluble units, these switches in features could never have occurred.

Syllables

The syllable is the next obvious unit. Reversals of segments almost always take place between the "homologous" parts of two syllables. The first consonant of one syllable gets interchanged with the first, not final, consonant of another, and so on. Fromkin gives as examples of these within-word reversals:

harp-si-chord → carp-si-hord

a-ni-mal → a-mi-nal

In both examples the two segments that reverse are first in the syllable (where the syllables are separated by hyphens). In all the reversals given earlier, the segments reversed were also of homologous parts of syllables. The syllable must therefore be part of the articulatory program, for it specifies which segments can be anticipated, perseverated, or reversed and which segments cannot.

The syllable itself, according to Hockett (1967) and MacKay (1972), consists of an initial consonant group and a final vowel group. The one syllable found apparently in all languages is the consonant-vowel (CV) syllable on the pattern of **ba**. Some languages allow more than one initial consonant, as in English **spla** and **shra**, some allow deletion of the initial consonant group, as in English **I**, and some allow the vowel to be followed by one or more consonants, as in English **bests** and **limps**. The structure, nevertheless, is of an initial consonant group followed by a vowel group, as in **bl** + **imps**, forming **blimps**. As evidence, note that many initial consonant groups, or clusters, reverse as a whole, as in **coat thrutting** and **clamage dame**. And blends most often switch from one target word to the next between the initial consonant group of the first word and the vowel group of the second (MacKay, 1972), as in:

shout + **yell** → sh/ell

grizzly + **gh**astly → gr/astly

Note also that Western rhyme (as in **beast-feast**) requires a repeated vowel group and alliteration (as in Hopkins' **dragonflies draw flame**) uses a repeated initial consonant group. And Ig-pay Atin-lay, the children's language Pig Latin, breaks off the initial consonant group of each word and places it at the end followed by **-ay**.

Larger Units

Whole words are involved in anticipations, perseverations, and reversals too, as in these examples from Fromkin (1973):

a tank of gas → a **gas** of **tank**

a lighter for every purse → a **purse** for every **lighter**

wine is being served at dinner → **dinner** is being served at **wine**

So the articulatory program deals at least in words.

But as Fromkin (1971) has argued, it must handle larger units as well. For **gas** and **tank** to have been reversed in the first example, they must both have been present in the articulatory program at the time of the reversal. What was there were the rudiments of **tank of gas**, a constituent, or probably **a tank of gas**, also a constituent. As a collection of such examples shows, the origin and target words are almost invariably in the same constituent, usually both stressed, and within six or seven words of each other. The general conclusion, then, is that the articulatory program handles constituents no more than six or seven words in length. This conclusion, if correct, is extraordinarily important, for it dovetails with the earlier conclusion that constituents of this size are the main units of planning and execution.

Formation of the Articulatory Program

From clues like these, Fromkin (1971, 1973) has pieced together a picture of how the speaker forms the articulatory program in memory before executing it. Garrett (1975) has proposed a similar model. The process has roughly five steps:

(1) *Meaning selection.* The first step is to decide on the meaning the present constituent is to have.

(2) *Selection of a syntactic outline.* The next step is to build a syntactic outline of the constituent. It specifies a succession of word slots and indicates which slots are to get primary, secondary, and zero stress.

(3) *Content word selection.* The third step is to select nouns, verbs, adjectives, and adverbs to fit into the appropriate slots.

(4) *Affix and function word formation.* With the content words decided on, the next step is to spell out the phonological shape of the function words (like articles, conjunctions, and prepositions), prefixes, and suffixes.

(5) *Specification of phonetic segments.* The final step is to build up fully specified phonetic segments syllable by syllable.

By Step 5, the articulatory program is complete and can be executed. Typically, however, people monitor what they actually say to make certain it agrees with what they intended it to mean. Whenever they detect an error, they stop, correct themselves, and then go on. It seems likely that the more attention is required elsewhere—in planning of various sorts—the less likely they are to detect an error. Indeed, many tongue-slips go unnoticed by both speakers and listeners.

Note, incidentally, that these steps are a natural continuation of the skeleton + constituent model. Speakers begin with an intended message, build an overall skeleton for the sentence, and finally set about planning each constituent to fit this skeleton. According to Fromkin's proposal, they then build a syntactic outline for each major constituent—not unlike the skeleton built for the sentence as a whole—fill in the content words, and finally spell out the phonological shape of the function words, suffixes, and prefixes.

Analysis of a Word Reversal

What is the evidence for such a model? To see, it is instructive to work through a reversal attested by Fromkin (1973):

a *weekend* for MANIACS → a *maniac* for WEEKENDS

Here capital letters indicate primary stress and italics secondary stress.

At *Step 1*, the speaker decides to build a constituent referring to a time period, $Time_{41}$.

At *Step 2*, the speaker builds a syntactic outline for this constituent:

indefinite-article + noun + [2 STRESS]
+ preposition + noun + [PLURAL] + [1 STRESS]

This outline specifies a succession of elements, among them [1 STRESS] for primary stress, [2 STRESS] for secondary stress, and [PLURAL] for a plural. These three elements will eventually be incorporated into the words just preceding them. Along with this outline, the speaker knows, semantically, that the first *article + noun + [2 STRESS]* denotes an indefinite two-day period, and the *preposition + noun + [PLURAL] + [1 STRESS]* characterizes the time period as "fit for crazy people."

At *Step 3*, the speaker, using his semantic plan, selects **weekend** and **maniac** to fit into the two noun slots. But he makes a mistake and inserts them into the wrong slots:

indefinite-article + maniac + [2 STRESS]
+ preposition + weekend + [PLURAL] + [1 STRESS]

Here, then, is where the actual tongue-slip occurs.

At *Step 4*, the speaker spells out the phonological shape of the function words, suffixes, and stresses. The result looks like this:

a + *maniac* + for + WEEKEND + [z]

At *Step 5*, he specifies the individual phonetic segments in terms of their distinctive features.

The Order of Steps

In this example alone, there is strong evidence that Step 3 comes after Step 2. The basic idea is that **maniac** and **weekend** have been interchanged while everything else—articles, plurality, and stress—have stayed put. Take stress. When **maniac** and **weekend** were interchanged, the stress didn't go with them. If it had, the tongue-slip would have been "a MANIAC for *weekends*," with primary stress still on **maniac**. In most other interchanges the stress pattern is left unchanged too. Or take the article and the plural suffix. When **maniac** and **weekend** were interchanged, the **a** and **-s** did not go with them. If they had, the tongue-slip would have been "*maniacs* for a WEEKEND." The prefixes and suffixes have stayed put in these examples as well (from Garrett, 1975):

McGovern favors **bust**ing **push**ers → McGovern favors **push**ing **bust**ers

She's already **pack**ed two **trunk**s → She's already **trunk**ed two **pack**s

in**stall**ing **telephone**s → in**telephon**ing **stall**s

The evidence that Step 4 comes after Step 3 is just as strong. The basic idea is that when the articles, prefixes, and suffixes are spelled out at Step 4, they are accommodated to the words already inserted at Step 3. Consider the pronunciation of [PLURAL] in **a maniac for weekends**. In the original phrase **a weekend for maniacs**, [PLURAL] turns into an [s] sound, because of the [k] sound at the end of **maniac**. If [PLURAL] had been specified as an [s] before **weekend** and **maniac** had been interchanged, it would have been attached to **weekend** to form **weekence**. But it did not. Instead, [PLURAL] was realized as a [z] sound appropriate to the [d] at the end of **weekend**. Thus, [PLURAL] couldn't have been specified as [z] until *after* **maniac** and **weekend** had been selected and reversed. Fromkin has noted a similar accommodation with **a** and **an** to what has been inserted at Step 3. Take these two tongue-slips:

a history of **an** ideology → **an** istory of **a** hideology

a current argument → **an** arrent curgument

In the second example, the article has been accommodated to **an** to agree with **arrent**, not to **a** to agree with **current**, the word "originally" in that position. Accommodations like these show that Step 4 must come after Step 3.

Very broadly, as Garrett (1975) has argued, some tongue-slips involve content words, some involve function words, but virtually none involve both. For example, when two words are interchanged, they are most often in the same word class—both nouns, for instance—and virtually always both content words. Tongue-slips like this never occur:

the **pot of** gold → the **of pot** gold

On the other hand, suffixes can be interchanged, as in:

Sing**er** sew**ing** machine → Sing**ing** sew**er** machine

Or they can be shifted, as in:

he goes back to → he go back**s** to

In either case, the changes occur without affecting the content words. If the tongue-slips involving content words and function elements are distinct, then this is further evidence that Steps 3 and 4 are distinct.

Errors in Word Selection

Blends make it clear that at Step 3 speakers often sift through many possible words before settling on the one with just the right meaning. Sometimes they discover simultaneously two equally suitable words, such as **slick** and **slippery**, find themselves unable to decide between them, and program a blend from elements of both words, here **slickery**. The following are more examples (again from Fromkin, 1973):

spank + paddle → spaddle

stomach + tummy → stummy

she + Fromkin → Shromkin

In all these examples the two source words are alternatives for the same slot, although not always synonyms, such as **she** and **Fromkin**. Thus, the semantic plan specifies only the denotation of the word to be selected: it doesn't specify the exact words.

Word substitutions reveal the same phenomenon. Sometimes speakers enter the right semantic domain but select a word that is incorrect for the meaning intended, as in these examples (from Fromkin, 1973):

my dissertation is too short—long

you'll have to call earlier—later

don't burn your fingers [intended: toes]

For these substitutions to occur, the speaker must have simultaneous access to several words closely related to his intended meaning.

Phonetic Similarity

Phonetic patterns, nevertheless, wield a powerful influence on the words being programmed. Most blends combine two words that are similar not only semantically, but also phonetically. **Slick** and **slippery**, for example, both begin with [slɪ] followed by a voiceless stop consonant. It is easy to imagine how a speaker might begin programming **slick** but finish out with **slippery**, switching from one to the other on phonetically similar segments (see also MacKay, 1973a). Indeed, most anticipations, perseverations, and reversals of phonetic segments occur in phonetic environments that are identical or nearly identical. In the reversal **heft lemisphere**, for example, the [h] and [l] both come just before an [ɛ] in a stressed syllable.

Word substitutions sometimes fall completely under the spell of phonetic similarity. Fromkin (1973) has heard examples such as these:

like wild fire → like wild flower

sesame seed crackers → Sesame Street crackers

in our academic ivory tower → in our academic ivy league

In each instance the substitution bears little relation to the meaning of the intended word or phrase, yet has an obvious relation to its sound. It is as if the speaker, in trying to program **wild fire**, switched over to **wild flower**, which was so available and so similar phonetically that it took precedence. As Fromkin noted, it may be critical that the interfering word be highly available. A flutist, about to play in a concert, was heard to say:

the Art of the Fugue → the Arg of the Flute

This example is both a reversal and a substitution. First, the [g] and [t] have been reversed, giving **arg of the fute**, and then **flute** has been substituted for **fute**, probably because it was so available to the flutist. In another example, a linguist studying suffixes said:

you and David are automatic suspects → you and David are automatic suffixes

Again the word substituted was both phonetically similar and highly available. In his *Psychopathology of Everyday Life*, Freud documented many other such substitutions and attempted to explain their special availability in psychodynamic terms.

Availability

MacKay (1970b) has argued for a similar principle of availability in explaining why phonetic tongue-slips occur most commonly in stressed words. The phenomenon to be accounted for is this. Nooteboom (1969), in a careful count of phonetic tongue-slips, found that anticipations far outnumbered perseverations and reversals, with examples like **bake my BIKE** occurring about three times as often as examples like **pulled a PANTRUM**. MacKay pointed out that what was usually being anticipated in such cases was a segment from a stressed word, one more highly stressed than the target word. Now in Fromkin's scheme, the most highly stressed words are inserted into the constituent outline first and so are most available for intrusion. In the anticipation *bake* **my BIKE**, the word **bike** is selected before **take**, allowing **bike** to force an error on **take**. Note too that the most highly stressed word in a constituent conveys the new information. That may explain both why it is inserted into the outline first and why it is especially available for intrusion. The speaker is anticipating the central force of his message—its new information.

In short, tongue-slips arise because words other than the target word are too readily available at the time it is being programmed. The intrusive word may be a semantic alternative but phonetically unrelated to the target word, giving a word substitution like **short** instead of **long**. Or it may be both a semantic alternative and phonetically related to the target, resulting in a blend like **slickery**. Or it may be a word unrelated to the target semantically but both phonetically related and conceptually available, as in Fromkin's example **the Arg of the Flute**. Nevertheless, most tongue-slips come from words being programmed simultaneously in other slots in the constituent. This leads to anticipations, perseverations, and reversals of segments or words. Among them, the commonest tongue-slips anticipate words with the highest stress. These words are selected first and are especially available for intrusion.

Word Formation

There is a fundamental question here that is still to be answered. How are words represented in permanent memory? In building up an articulatory program, speakers obviously draw on their phonological knowledge of words in memory. Consider the verb **act**. At some level in memory it is surely represented as a single unit, with a coherent meaning, as a string of phonological segments ready to be inserted into the articulatory program. But what about **acted**, the past tense of **act**? There at least two ways it might be represented. It might be a single unit, **acted**, to which is attached the semantic information that it is the past tense of **act**. Or it might consist of two units, *act* + [PAST], which some later process turns into the articulatory program [æktɪd]. In the extreme these two views might be called the concrete and abstract theories of word formation.

The Abstractness of Words

Just how abstract, then, is the representation of words? The tongue-slips already examined suggest it is fairly abstract. Recall that in **a maniac for weekends, maniac** and **weekend** were interchanged while the features [1 STRESS], [2 STRESS], and [PLURAL] stayed put. The speaker did not dredge up **MANIACS**, complete with [1 STRESS] and [PLURAL], to insert at this point, but rather **maniac**, to which [1 STRESS] and [PLURAL] would have been added in the normal course of events. This procedure makes good sense. Under the concrete theory, **maniac**, **maniacs**, **MANIAC**, and **MANIACS** would all be stored in memory, and so would the forms with other stress levels. Under the abstract theory, just the one form, **maniac**, is stored in memory. By later word formation rules [1 STRESS], [2 STRESS], or [PLURAL] are added to it. The form **maniac** may also be used in the formation of **maniacal**, which has yet another stress pattern. So the abstract theory is efficient. It requires one form in memory instead of four, or more, and it makes use of word formation rules that apply across the board.

Less obvious word parts may also be specified in an abstract form. Fromkin (1973) has argued that words like **imprecise**, **disregard**, **unclear**, and **nothing** may be represented with the abstract negative prefix [NEG], that is, as [NEG] + **precise**, [NEG] + **regard**, [NEG] + **clear**, and [NEG] + **anything**. As evidence she cited the following tongue-slips:

I regard this as **im**precise → I **dis**regard this as precise

if there was anything that was **un**clear → if there was **nothing** that was clear

In the first example it wasn't **im-** that was transposed, for that would have resulted in **imregard**. Instead, it was [NEG] that was moved from in front of **precise** to in front of **regard**. Later, [NEG] + **regard** was changed by word formation rules to **disregard**. In the second example [NEG] appears to have been moved too. For a tongue-slip requiring [PAST], consider this example (from Fromkin, 1973):

Rosa always dated shrinks → Rosa always date shranks

This tongue-slip must have taken place at the following abstract stage of the process:

date + [PAST] + shrink + [PLURAL]
$$→ date + shrink + [PAST] + [PLURAL]$$

Before [PAST] was moved, **date** + [PAST] would have formed **dated**. But after the shift, **shrink** + [PAST] combined to form **shrank**, which with [PLURAL] became **shranks**. This byzantine tongue-slip makes good sense once [PAST] is assumed to be an abstract feature.

The Source of Wrong Word Formations

Abstract features are also revealed in "misderivations" (see Table 7–3). In these tongue-slips, the speaker had an abstract feature in mind, but programmed the wrong realization for it, as in these examples from Fromkin (1973):

peculiarity → peculiar**acy**

specializing in → special**ating** in

swam → swimm**ed**

For the first error, imagine that **peculiarity** had been programmed as **peculiar** + [NOMINAL], where the feature [NOMINAL] means that **peculiar** should be nominalized, turned into a noun. Now in English, adjectives can be nominalized by adding, for example, **-ity, -acy, -ness**, or **-ation**. Yet the one appropriate for **peculiar** is **-ity** and not any of the others. In this tongue-slip, the speaker mistakenly chose **-acy** and programmed **peculiaracy**. For this to have happened, **peculiarity** must have been retrieved from memory, not as an unanalyzed word, but rather as **peculiar** + [NOMINAL]. Then, with incorrect word formation rules, it came out as **peculiaracy**. The abstract feature [NOMINAL] is a necessary ingredient here. The other examples reveal such abstract features as [VERBAL] and [PAST].

To have produced **swimmed**, the last example, the speaker must have begun with **swim** + [PAST], applied the regular past tense formation rule, and programmed **swimmed**. He must have failed to realize that **swim** is irregular, an exception to the rule, and that it demands a vowel change instead of an added **-ed**. These errors are so common that MacKay (1976) was able to study them experimentally. People were read a series of verbs, one at a time, and were required to produce the past tense for each as quickly as they could. Indeed, they produced regular past tense verbs, like **kissed**, reliably faster than irregular ones, like **taught**. To MacKay, this suggested that people were applying rules of word formation in their production of past tense verbs. Since irregular verbs require more complex rules than regular verbs, they should take longer to program, just as MacKay found.

Evidence for word formation, however, was most convincingly revealed in the many errors. Most of these came from attempts to produce irregular past tense forms like **swam**. These forms were often regularized, so **digged** was produced instead of **dug**, and **teached** instead of **taught**. To produce **digged**, people must have begun with **dig** + [PAST] and applied the regular past tense rule. In other instances, people didn't quite complete the changes required by irregular rules. One person, given **catch**, produced **cat** instead of **caught**, changing the final consonant from [č] to [t], but failing to change [æ] to [ɔ]. Generally, the more changes required by the rules, the less likely people were to complete them all. In still other instances people applied an irregular rule appropriate to some other verb. One person, given **ride**, said **rid** instead of **rode**, probably on the pattern of **hide-hid** and **slide-slid**. From all these errors, MacKay argued that past tense verbs are represented in an abstract form—as the infinitive plus [PAST] —and that the final articulatory program is built by processes of word formation.

Although some word features appear to be stored separately, how many and which ones are hard to estimate. **Maniacs** seems to be stored as **maniac** + [PLURAL], **imprecise** as [NEG] + **precise**, **peculiarity** as **peculiar** + [NOM-INAL], and **swam** as **swim** + [PAST]. But it isn't certain that even these features are always stored and retrieved in their abstract form. As MacKay cautioned, both abstract and concrete forms may be available for use in the articulatory program. He found that people could give **swam** as a rhyme to, say, **ram**, just as quickly as they could give **swim** as a rhyme to **rim**. If **swam** always had to be produced by way of past tense formation rules applied to **swim, swam** should have taken longer than **swim**. Since it didn't, people must have had direct acess to **swam**. Furthermore, some word formation rules seem so exotic or specialized that it is doubtful they are ever used (Steinberg, 1973). For example, although **sign** and **signature** are related by a rule, it seems unlikely that **signature** is ever stored as **sign** + [NOMINAL]. So even though the representation of words can be abstract, it has yet to be determined how abstract and when.

Word Representations

The problems of word formation aside, not all words are equally accessible for insertion into the articulatory program. This is demonstrated most vividly by the "tip-of-the-tongue" phenomenon. Imagine asking someone for the name of a Chinese flat-bottomed boat. He may immediately realize that such a word exists and that he "knows" it. It is just that he can't quite think of it. Very often a word will spring to mind—like **sandal, sanddab,** or **tincan**—that he recognizes as sounding like the word he is trying to think of. Later, after a few minutes or even days, he may suddenly think of the word **sampan** and recognize it as the word he was searching for. The tip-of-the-tongue experience is familiar and has been described in detail by such careful observers as Bolinger (1961). A typical part of these experiences is that the experiencer comes up with a word that sounds like the target word yet is recognized as different from it. For this to happen, he must be able to access some of the phonological information in memory, but not all.

Tip-of-the-Tongue Experiences

What phonological information is accessible? To study this problem, R. Brown and McNeill (1966) induced tip-of-the-tongue experiences in people by reading them definitions of rare words and asking them to try to think of the word being defined, the target word. One definition they used was this:

> A navigational instrument used in measuring angular distances, especially the altitude of sun, moon, and stars at sea.

Some people knew the target **sextant** immediately. Others couldn't think of any word at all. The remaining few people had a tip-of-the-tongue experience and were asked four questions about the word they had on the tip of their tongue:

(1) How many syllables does it have?

(2) What letter does it start with?

(3) What words does it sound like?

(4) What words are similar in meaning?

The people with tip-of-the-tongue experiences generally had a relatively accurate outline of the target word. On number of syllables, they were correct 57 percent of the time, where by chance they should be correct only 20 percent of the time. On initial letters they were correct 62 percent of the time where chance is only 8 percent. As for sound-alikes, people trying to get **sextant** came up with such words as **secant, sextet,** and **sexton.** Note that all three of these words have two syllables, stress on the first syllable, [sɛk] at the beginning, and [n], [t], or [nt] at the end. As Brown and McNeill noted, it is as if people had an incomplete phonological representation of **sextant**—for example, [sɛk*-**t], where the asterisks indicate lack of information. With time, some of these people came up with the right word and recognized it as such. So even these asterisks are misleading. They should be replaced perhaps by faint copies of the right phonological segments, which are then available for eventual recognition or recall of the right word (see also Rubin, 1975).

Word Storage and Access

The tip-of-the-tongue phenomenon suggests two things. First, the phonetic patterns of words differ in the speed with which they can be accessed in memory. Second, the syllable structure, stress pattern, and phonetic segments of these patterns may be stored somewhat independently. If correct, these suggestions have three interesting consequences.

(1) In spontaneous speech, the difficulty in finding a word may have two sources. One is that speakers may have trouble planning precisely what meaning they want to convey. But the second is that they may find it difficult, once they have their semantic plan, to retrieve the phonetic pattern for the word they are thinking of. When they hesitate before a word, they could be doing so for either reason.

(2) When speakers do program a word like **sextant**, they may do so in several steps. Note that while **swam** divides morphologically into **swim** + [PAST], **sextant** is a "unified" word of only one morpheme. Nevertheless, it may be built from its shell inwards. Here is one possibility. The syllable structure and stress pattern are inserted first. The phonetic segments for the stressed syllables are added next. And the phonetic segments for the unstressed syllables are added last. It may take steps like these to explain why anticipations, perseverations, and reversals in slips of the tongue occur most often between homologous parts of syllables and words, especially stressed syllables.

(3) When speakers program a single word, because of incomplete phonetic information they are prone to make mistakes. These mistakes commonly take the form of *malapropisms*, a type of speech error named for Mrs. Malaprop, a character in one of Sheridan's plays who tried to use high-sounding words but couldn't quite get them right. She would say **reprehend** for **apprehend, derange-**

MRS. MALAPROP
The Rivals

I am sure I have done everything in my power since I exploded the affair; long ago I laid my positive conjunctions on her, never to think on the fellow again; I have since laid Sir Anthony's preposition before her; but, I am sorry to say, she seems resolved to decline every particle that I enjoin her.

ment for **arrangement**, and **epitaphs** for **epithets**. With the many Mrs. Malaprops of this world, these errors are common. Hockett quotes an army officer at a formal hearing who said:

We should be *reminisce* in our duty if we did not investigate.

And a woman who was hungry who said:

I'm simply *ravishing*.

The substitution of **reminisce** for **remiss** and **ravishing** for **ravenous** may have come about because the speakers had incomplete phonetic representations of the words they were thinking of and so they selected the first word that sounded right. Note that the syllable structure and stress pattern of **reminisce** and **ravishing** don't differ much from **remiss** and **ravenous**, and it is the stressed syllables in both that remain intact. At present, however, too little is known about malapropisms and their origins.

Rhythm and Timing

Since speech occurs in real time, the articulatory program has to specify not only the phonetic segments and their order, but also their timing and rhythm. In English, a "stress timed" language, the major carriers of rhythm are the stressed syllables. They should therefore play a central role in speech production, and they do. The unit planned at a single time in the articulatory program is the constituent, and most constituents have a single primary stress. Furthermore, in Fromkin's scheme, the first parts specified in the articulatory program are the word slots and their stress patterns, and the first words inserted are those with stress. But stress plays an important part in two other aspects of the articulatory program too: its regularities and its speed. First, it is easier to build an articulatory program when there are regular patterns associated with successive stressed syllables than when there are not. This is demonstrated by the disruptive effects of tongue twisters. Second, when people talk fast, they have to have some way of deciding which segments to retain and which to give short shrift to. The principles they use are intimately connected with rhythm and stress too.

Rhythm and Regularity

As anyone who has stumbled through tough tongue twisters can attest, regular articulatory patterns are easier to pronounce than irregular ones, What tongue twisters do is sabotage the articulatory program by mixing regular with irregular patterns in a way that confuses (Schourup, 1973). Take these short tongue twisters:

24. she sells sea shells

25. six thick thistle sticks

26. rubber baby buggy bumpers

In 24 the final vowel groups fit a regular alternating pattern ABAB (**ee**, **ells**, **ee**, **ells**), but the initial consonants, just to confuse, fit the so-called mirror-image pattern ABBA (**sh**, **s**, **s**, **sh**). Because the ABAB pattern conflicts with the ABBA pattern, the twister is difficult to say quickly. The same happens in 25. In 26 the initial consonants fit the pattern ABBB, the next vowels ABAA, the middle consonant groups AABA (that is, labial **b**, labial **b**, velar **g**, labial **mp**), and the final vowel group ABBA. With four independent and conflicting patterns, it is no wonder this tongue twister tangles tongues.

The mistakes people make in trying to say twisters further attest to the importance of regularity. What people do typically is regularize the broken patterns. So 24 often emerges this way:

24'. She sells she sells

The initial consonants have been forced into the same ABAB pattern that is found in the final vowels. And 26 often comes out this way:

26'. rubber baby buggy bu*n*kers

The middle consonant group AABA has been turned into the regular AABB by changing the last middle consonant group from labial [mp] to velar [ŋk] to agree with the velar [g] in **buggy**.

A critical ingredient in 24 through 26, as Schourup argued, is the regular stress pattern. In 24 and 25 there are four heavily stressed syllables in a row. In 26 there are four identical trochees. These drumming stress patterns "drive" the process along and reinforce any regularities that exist around them. Any irregularities, by the same token, are highly disruptive. Just as homologous parts of stressed syllables are vulnerable to anticipations, perseverations, and reversals in slips of the tongue, so are they easy to regularize in tongue twisters. The rhythm here seems to be a crucial ingredient.

Rhythm, however, is not critical to all tongue twisters. In many there is something that might be called phonetic compatibility. Some segments, such as [s], [f], and [θ], are simply difficult to program in close proximity to each other:

> The sea ceaseth and it sufficeth us.

> The Leith police beseecheth us.

Regularity and phonetic compatibility join up to make this next tongue twister almost impossible:

> Miss Smith's fish sauce shop seldom sells shellfish.

Shortcuts

The next aspect of the articulatory program in which rhythm is important is speed. When people try to talk fast, they have to cut corners, and the way they cut corners involves rhythm. In formal situations, or in talking to foreigners, people tend to speak slowly and articulate every phonetic segment as it is "supposed" to be pronounced. They would say:

> I want to get you on his catamaran.

But in casual everyday speech people speed up and have to take shortcuts. The first shortcut is to reduce the vowels in unstressed syllables to schwa [ə], the neutral **uh**. They would say:

> I wanta get ya on his catamaran.

The **to** and **you** have been replaced with **tuh** and **yuh**. With further shortcuts, they leave out certain consonants and coalesce others and say:

> I wanna gecha oniz catamaran.

Here the [t] in **wanta** and the [h] in **his** disappear, and the [t] and [y] in **get ya** coalesce into [č]. There are still other shortcuts they can take. Still, there is one word that manages to remain relatively untouched, namely **catamaran**. Since it is not predictable from the rest of the sentence, people pronounce it carefully no matter how sloppy they are on the rest, just to make sure it is intelligible (Lieberman, 1967).

At the core of these shortcuts are the stressed syllables and the rhythm they carry. In Fromkin's scheme, the first aspect of a constituent to be specified is its stress pattern. In these shortcuts, speakers apparently squeeze these stresses together, but leave the pattern otherwise unaltered. The result is the same rhythm pattern but greater speed. The shortcuts first applied simplify the unstressed syllables. They neutralize their vowels and delete their consonants. This preserves the stressed syllables, which carry most of the information. Further shortcuts may drop syllables altogether, but these are always unstressed syllables of little importance. Thus, speakers tacitly adhere to an important principle. Stressed syllables carry the main semantic content of the sentence, and they should be preserved at all costs.

Articulation

The final step in executing speech is the actual articulation of the phonetic segments. MacNeilage (1970) has argued that the commands sent to the articulatory organs, presumably by the articulatory program, specify "ideal targets," places where the articulatory organs ought to be in the pronunciation of some phonetic segment. MacNeilage makes an analogy to the positioning of a door. If one wants to have a door open at an angle of forty-five degrees, one moves it one way if the door is closed or if it is open less than forty-five degrees, but another way if it is open more than that amount. And one moves it different distances depending on the discrepancy between the starting position and the target position. The same goes for articulation. The articulatory program specifies the target position of the articulatory organs, and the articulatory muscles compute the discrepancy between their present position and the target position and initiate a ballistic movement to eliminate that discrepancy. When speech is speeded up, it becomes more and more difficult to attain each of the successive targets, and so it becomes sensible to omit certain "distant" targets (like the [t] in **wanta**) and to coalesce certain adjacent targets (like the [t] and [y] in **get ya**) into a single movement.

In casual speech, certain phonetic segments are often mispronounced, apparently because of their complexity. Cairns, Cairns, and Williams (1974) examined school children's pronunciations of a variety of common English words and found they occasionally mispronounced certain segments. For example, [ð], as in **that**, was often mispronounced as [d], which is phonetically less complex than [ð]. Similarly, the complex affricates [č] and [j], as in **match** and **rage**, were sometimes simplified to [t] or [š] and to [d], respectively. MacNeilage's notion of target position may help account for these occasional errors. The children may have planned the more complex target, but could reach only the simpler articulatory target instead.

So rhythm, timing, and shortcuts in articulation are all bound to each other. Rhythm is a fundamental organizing force in the articulatory program, as shown in slips of the tongue, which typically involve stressed syllables, and in tongue twisters, which superimpose irregular phonetic patterns over regular rhythmic patterns. And when speech is speeded up, the speaker tends to simplify the un-stressed portions of the articulatory program, but to preserve the stressed portions that carry the rhythm. At the most detailed level, the program appears to specify a series of "target" gestures for the articulatory organs to make. The speaker attempts to hit every target, but in speeded speech may leave some out, treat others in combination, and mispronounce still others.

SUMMARY

The planning and execution of spontaneous speech are interleaved in a complicated pattern. The reason is that speakers are trying to do two things as they talk. They are trying to select the words for each major constituent all at once, but at the same time, they are trying to execute each constituent in a single fluent ideal delivery. They are often prevented from accomplishing these two goals by various difficulties they run into. They may begin executing a constituent before they have it fully planned and be forced to stop, usually before the first content word. Once they have it planned, they have two choices. They can go on, leaving a noticeable silent pause at mid-constituent, or return to the beginning and execute the complete constituent fluently. Different speakers take different options. The factors that make planning hard and lead to these hesitations, repeats, and corrections include difficulties in planning the discourse, planning each sentence, and finding the right words.

In the execution of speech itself, speakers have to form an articulatory program to tell the articulatory muscles where to move when. The articulatory program is apparently formed one major constituent at a time and in several steps. The first step is to build a syntactic outline of the constituent. This consists of a succession of word slots with a stress pattern superimposed on them. The second step is to select the nouns, verbs, adjectives, and adverbs and insert them into the appropriate slots. The third step is to insert the function words into their slots and finish off the content words with the right prefixes and suffixes. The final step is to fill out the phonetic segments themselves and add timing and rhythm. Each step is vulnerable to mistakes, and these appear as slips of the tongue, like **out of the glear plue sky** and **he's a laving runiac**.

Further Reading

This chapter has focused on speech errors, and although there aren't many discussions, the available ones are excellent. For hesitations and pauses, Maclay and Osgood's (1959) early paper gives a clear introduction, while Goldman-Eisler's (1968) monograph is a more thorough exposition of her own fifteen years of research on the subject. For slips of the tongue, the best source is a set of readings collected by Fromkin (1973). It contains the major writings on slips of the tongue from Freud's *Psychopathology of Everyday Life* up to present-day work. Best of all, it contains a fascinating collection of speech errors from which one can build one's own theories.

part **4**

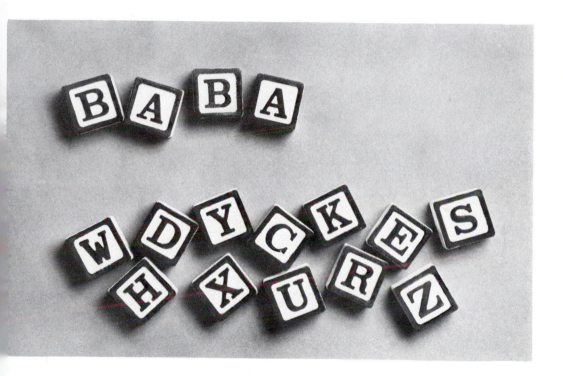

ACQUISITION

8

First Steps in the Child's Language

9

Later Growth in the Child's Language

10

First Sounds in the Child's Language

When I was a little girl I could go "geek-geek"
like that. But now I can go "This is a chair."

Child aged two years ten months

First Steps
in the Child's Language

Everyone knows that six-month-old babies can't talk whereas four-year-old
children can. Even in the first year or so of language development, children
change dramatically. Take some typical utterances from children between the
ages of 1;0 (i.e., one year) and 2;8 (i.e., two years and eight months). At first
they use single words, as in 1:

1. 1;3 years: More. [reaching for a cookie]

No. [resisting being put to bed]

Ball. [pointing to doorknob]

Within a few months, they begin to combine two or more words to produce
longer utterances like those in 2 and 3:

2. 1;8 years: Allgone lettuce. [looking at empty plate]

More read. [holding up book]

Mommy sleep. [of mother lying down]

3. 2;1 years: Andrew that off. [wanting to turn off light]

Where go car? [holding toy car]

Pants change. [wanting to change his pants]

And, by two and a half or so, they sound even more advanced:

4. 2;8 years: What he can ride in?

He not taking the walls down.

I want to open it.

The utterances in 1 through 4 show an enormous increase in sophistication: they go from single words to combinations five or six words long. Yet none, except the last, sounds quite adultlike. The children omit words and word endings, use word orders different from the adult ones, and combine words in a way adults would not. Why do children produce utterances like these? How do they go from very simple utterances to more complicated ones? And, more generally, how do children master their first language?

COMMUNICATING WITH LANGUAGE

From the outset children are faced with two general problems. First of all, they have to figure out how to *map* their ideas and general knowledge onto propositions that they can then express as single words or groups of words, e.g., **More**, **Ball**, **Two shoe**. Second, they have to find out how to *communicate* speech acts and thematic information along with the propositional content of their utterances. For this too they have to look for ways to map their intention—to assert or request something, for instance—onto appropriate linguistic forms, e.g., **That car** as an assertion in contrast to **Want car** as a request. *Mapping* and *communication* go hand in hand: both are fundamental to the process of acquisition.

Once children have started to map ideas onto propositions, they can start on the arduous task of working out rules for combining words into sentences. These sentences can then be used to express single propositions or combinations of propositions. In speaking, children have to work out ways of combining words to build up sentences intelligible to others. And in listening, they have to work out ways of analyzing what other people say by breaking utterances down into their constituents. Here, then, children have to focus on the structure of the language they are acquiring.

At the same time, children have to work on finding out the rules for carrying on conversations. They have to figure out which linguistic devices best convey different speech acts and what conditions should apply when one asserts, requests, or promises something. They also have to work out how to convey thematic information and identify the devices for indicating to a listener what is given and what is new in each utterance. In essence, they must focus on the function of language in order to figure out the cooperative principle and all that goes along with it.

From the very first children have to work at mastering the sound system too. They have to find out how to produce the appropriate sounds and combinations of sounds that will be intelligible to others. And to do this, they have to work out which sounds are used in their language and come to recognize them when they are pronounced by others.

The present chapter takes up the earliest stages of language acquisition and follows children as they go from no language to one- or two-word utterances. It is followed by three further chapters on acquisition. Chapter 9 takes up later stages in the acquisition of language structure and language function. Its main emphasis is on the principles children appear to apply in the acquisition of structure. Chapter 10 examines the acquisition of the sound system—how children perceive and produce the sounds of their language at different stages, and how these sounds might be represented in memory. Finally, the question of how children map ideas onto language is taken up in much greater detail in Chapter 13, which focuses on the acquisition of meaning.

The present chapter is organized around three separate strands that are woven together in language: ideas, speech acts, and thematic information. Each strand will be discussed in turn as children go from no words to single words and then to combinations of words. We look first, therefore, at *what* young children say—the propositional content of their one- and two-word utterances—and at *how* they say what they say—the speech acts they use and their presentation of thematic information. Then we turn to the role adults play and examine the ways in which they tailor their speech so young children can best understand what they are talking about.

Issues in Language Acquisition

There have been numerous controversies among psychologists, philosophers, and linguists about how children acquire language. Three of these issues are critical for a general theory about the acquisition of language.

Continuity in Development

What are the connections between earlier and later points in development? This question is as important for language acquisition as it is for other kinds of development. In language, one can argue for continuity at several levels. For example, children may show continuity in some of the words they use as they move from single words like **more** or **cookie** to combinations of words like **more read** or **want cookie**. Or, to take another example, children may show continuity in the gestures they use in early communication: at first they use the gestures on their own and later accompany them with words.

Is there such a thing as discontinuity? The emergence of the child's first words, for example, seems to mark a discontinuity, a change from no words to words. Even so, one could argue that there is continuity in the child's ideas at both "stages" and that it is some of these ideas that are first mapped onto words. One could also argue that there is continuity between the child's babbling and the first words. The first words, then, could simply be viewed as a combination of elements already present at an earlier "stage" of development.

Can one talk about continuity from one *stage* to the next, or do stages necessarily mark discontinuity? In development, the notion of *stage* has been used in at least two ways: to mark the emergence of some new behavior that may or may not be related to earlier developments, and to break up large time spans into more manageable portions by using criteria like children's ages or the average length of their utterances. Stages, then, are not necessarily marked by discontinuity in the strict sense, but they often pinpoint the emergence of new combinations of behaviors. In language acquisition, it is continuity rather than discontinuity that appears to be the rule.

Innateness in Language

How much of language is innate and how much learned? Nativists propose that language acquisition is the result of innate capacities specific to language and is thus found only in human beings. Empiricists, on the other hand, propose that language, like other skills, is learned as a result of experience. The strict opposition between nativism and empiricism presents the issue as if it were an all-or-none affair. In fact, it is much more a matter of degree. At the very least, there must be some innate mechanisms that allow one to learn in the first place. At the same time, children will not acquire language unless they are exposed to it. The real question, then, concerns the nature of the innate mechanisms and the constraints they place on what is learned. Several candidates for innate mechanisms will be considered in the course of these chapters (e.g., the ability to pick out subjects and predicates). However, there appears to be little evidence that such grammatical distinctions per se are either innate or central to the process of acquiring language.

Comprehension and Production

The process of comprehension requires that listeners take in an utterance, analyze it, construct an interpretation, and utilize what they have understood in the way the speaker intended (Chapters 2 and 3). In production, on the other hand, speakers have to come up with a way of conveying information to someone else. They must plan what they want to say, choose the right words and the appropriate speech act, and then produce their utterances (Chapters 6 and 7). There is an asymmetry between these two processes even for adults. People understand many words they never use themselves, and they also understand people who speak quite different dialects of their language (speakers from New England, Scotland, and Texas, for example). In other words, people understand many things that they can't produce, but they rarely produce anything they don't understand.

This asymmetry also appears quite early in acquisition. Children often seem able to understand more than they can actually say. The question this raises is whether the asymmetry between comprehension and production itself plays any role in the *process* of acquisition.

These issues—continuity, innateness, and the gap between comprehension and production—have directly or indirectly motivated much of the research on acquisition and will appear in various guises in these chapters.

Methods of Studying the Child's Language

Investigators of early language acquisition have relied mainly on naturalistic observations. The usual method has been to follow a child and write down each utterance, noting the pronunciation and apparent meaning. Many investigators have kept diaries of how their children's language developed from the first word on (see Leopold, 1939–1949, for a very careful record). Nowadays, tape recorders and video-tape systems have either supplemented or replaced paper and pencil. Children are usually recorded for set periods of time in their homes while the observer keeps additional notes on the context and each child's activities. Tape-recordings have two advantages over a paper-and-pencil method: first, they record what others say to the child as well as what the child says, and second, the tapes can be checked and rechecked afterwards for accuracy in their transcription. Although video-tapes record the context and the children's activities as well as their utterances, this method of observation is harder to use in the home because video cameras are much more intrusive than tape recorders.

The next step has been to take each utterance and by drawing on its context decide what it meant. The context normally includes what is known about the children, their routines, their toys, and their activity at the time of the utterance as well as what others may have been saying. This use of context in interpreting what children most probably meant is known as *rich interpretation* (Bloom, 1970; R. Brown, 1973). Essentially, it assumes that children intended to communicate something by their utterances and it allows the investigator to make an interpretation appropriate to the context.

The third step is to use these data to make inferences about the nature of the acquisition process. In addition to the utterances produced by the child, investigators may take into account the child's cognitive and social development; the eventual goal of acquisition (attainment of an adultlike use of language); and the information available to the child about language (primarily information from the speech of others).

Naturalistic observations are generally complemented by experimental studies to follow up the observations and test specific predictions (Chapter 1). In language acquisition, experiments have been used mainly to study children's comprehension—to find out how much they really understand and to what degree they rely on contextual clues. A few experiments have concentrated on production and have used various techniques to elicit speech from children. However, the younger the children, the harder it is to collect experimental data. Most studies discussed in this chapter, therefore, are based on naturalistic observations of what children say.

WHAT YOUNG CHILDREN TALK ABOUT

The first strand to be followed through language acquisition is that of the ideas that children express in their early utterances. In the space of a few months, children advance from using no words at all to using single-word utterances and then two- or three-word combinations. By the time they reach the age of two, many children have begun to combine words to talk about a variety of objects, attributes, relations, and events. But although two-year-olds can produce longer utterances than younger children, they still talk about roughly the same things as one- or one-and-a-half-year-olds.

Children seem to talk about what they already know, and they begin by talking about their surroundings. This is not surprising since they usually spend a year or more actively taking in information about their surroundings before using a single word. Investigators like Slobin (1973) and Sinclair-de Zwart (1973) have assumed that children build directly on this knowledge when they come to the formidable task of mapping ideas and communicative intentions onto language. We begin, therefore, by looking at what one- or one-and-a-half-year-olds know, and then turn to what they talk about, first with single-word utterances and then with two-word utterances.

Precursors to the First Utterances

What do one-year-olds know? From early infancy they have looked at the things around them: rattles, mobiles, soft toys, their blankets, and people's faces. From three or four months on, people have shown them new things and encouraged them to touch, hold, and mouth new objects. Before long, they can reach for what they want and adjust their hands to grasp whatever is in reach. With crawling and walking they steadily enlarge their horizons, exploring and manipulating toys, blocks, household utensils, and anything else in sight and in reach, people included. They know by the age of one that people sleep in beds, sit on chairs, drink from cups, and so on. They know their own routines for feeding, dressing, playing, changing, bathing, and sleeping. The precise course of their development from birth to one or one and a half years has probably been most carefully traced by Piaget (1951, 1955). He called this period the *sensori-motor* stage of development, and argued that children acquire knowledge during this stage by acting on their surroundings, by touching, grasping, looking at, and manipulating the objects around them.

The Sensori-Motor Stage

Toward the end of the sensori-motor period, between about 1;0 and 1;6 years, children begin to reproduce events from memory a day or so later. One of Piaget's examples of this comes from his daughter Jacqueline, aged 1;4. One afternoon she saw a small boy having a temper tantrum as he tried to get out of his playpen.

He screamed and stamped his feet as he tried to move the pen. The next day, Jacqueline herself for the first time screamed and stamped one foot as she tried to move her playpen (Piaget, 1951). Piaget argued that deferred imitations like this showed that the child could by then *represent* events and objects in memory.

The last part of the sensori-motor period is marked by at least three other related developments: the establishment of object permanence, the discovery of tools, and the emergence of symbolic play. Children have acquired what Piaget calls object permanence when they not only recognize objects but also realize that objects remain in place even though out of sight. For example, if a toy is hidden from young children by a cloth being put over it, they turn away and act as if the object is no longer there. By the age of one, though, they will look for the object under the cloth, and even remember later where it was hidden. Children discover tools, according to Piaget, when they start to use an intermediary to get what they want. The intermediary can be a person or an object. For example, children may tug at an adult's hand and point at something out of reach, or they may get hold of an object by pulling the cloth it is on toward them. Symbolic play is "pretending": a one-year-old picks up a pebble and pretends it is a car, running it across the floor and making car noises. Another child may pretend to go to sleep, lying on the floor with her favorite blanket, or she may pretend to eat with a stick instead of a spoon, and so on. All these developments depend on children's being able to *represent* to themselves actual objects and events (Piaget, 1951, 1955; Bruner, 1973; D. Edwards, 1973).

Piaget has suggested that the ability to represent objects and events is a necessary prerequisite for the acquisition of any system of symbolic representation for knowledge and experience. The child's first words, then, should not appear until the child reaches the part of the sensori-motor stage that is marked by deferred imitations, object permanence, tool use, and beginnings of symbolic play. In fact, children consistently begin to use their first words at about this point, usually sometime between the ages of 1;0 and 1;8 (Piaget, 1951; Bates, 1976; Bates, Benigni, Bretherton, Camaioni, and Volterra, 1976).

Role of Objects

By one or one and a half, children have amassed specific knowledge about many of the objects around them. They know, for example, about their shape, size, and texture, how they move, and what noises they make. And children by this time have also begun to build up some general knowledge about the roles these objects play in different events:

(1) *Movers.* This group consists of those objects able to move on their own or pick up other objects. Children probably include both adults and themselves in this group: both can move and manipulate things (Piaget, 1951). They may also include pets and other animals, and possibly even cars, since those too seem to move on their own.

(2) *Movables.* These are objects that can be moved and manipulated, but cannot move on their own. Children probably begin to pick out movables

fairly early even though they do not achieve object permanence until age one or so (Piaget, 1955; T. Bower, 1974). Examples of movables are toys, building blocks, bottles, cups, and cookies.

(3) *Places.* Places are also objects but they are not usually movable, at least not for a child. Places are where other objects are normally kept or where particular routines like feeding or sleeping are carried out. Toyboxes, playpens, cribs, kitchen drawers, and coat closets are all examples of places.

(4) *Recipients.* Recipients are people acting as places. For example, children show things to recipients, put objects in their hands or on their laps, and give things to them for safekeeping (see Rheingold, 1973). Recipients, then, are very like places, and may not be fully distinguished from them at this age. But children do not show objects to chairs or beds.

(5) *Instruments.* These are objects used as tools, to take Piaget's term, in achieving particular goals—for example, a spoon used for eating or a stick used to knock down a tower of building blocks (Piaget, 1951). Children's symbolic play often shows that they know how to use instruments like spoons by this time, but the class of instruments is probably still rather limited.

These general classes or groups may be very small to begin with and include only a few of the objects that might be included by the adult. This is because children at age one know only a fraction of what adults know, and their view of the world is a much more restricted one. At the same time, these classes represent one way of starting to organize children's specific knowledge about objects, properties, and relations. This becomes more and more important as they begin to map their ideas onto words.

Single-Word Utterances

What do children talk about first? They talk about the objects around them and therefore show considerable agreement in their first words. Animals, food, and toys were the three categories referred to most frequently in the first ten words of eighteen children studied by Nelson (1973). By the time these children had vocabularies of fifty words (somewhere between the age of 1;3 and 2;0, depending on the child), most of them used some words for food, body parts, clothing, animals, household items, vehicles, and people. The words in these categories that occurred most frequently were **juice, milk,** and **cookie** for food; **ear, eye,** and **nose** for body parts; **shoe, hat** and **sock** for clothing; **dog, cat,** and **duck** for animals; **clock** and **light** for household items; **ball** and **block** for toys; and **car, boat,** and **truck** for vehicles. The people named most often were **mama, dada,** and **baby.** Some children also used words like **bottle** and **cup,** classed by Nelson in the category of utensils connected with eating. The categories each child talked about were very similar although few children used exactly the same words.

Yet a list of the objects that the child's first words refer to does not tell us much about what the child is talking about. When children say **Truck,** for example, they might be talking about it because it is a mover, a movable, or a place. What is important is the *role* the truck plays in the event being talked about. Greenfield and Smith (1976) have argued that children's one-word

Darling! Justin verbalized!

utterances name particular roles, not just the objects themselves. For example, they name movers, usually the agents or instigators of an action, as in **Dada** said as someone opens the door, or **Mama** said as she puts on a child's shoes. They also name movables, objects affected by an action, as in **Ban** ("fan") said when a child wanted the fan turned on or off. And they name recipients and places too. In addition, they may talk about an action or the state resulting from an action. For example, they may use **Down** after sitting down themselves, or when they put something else down on the floor.

Children use words not just to name objects, then, but also to pick out the roles those objects play in whatever event is being described. The frequency with which some objects are named suggests that some roles may be more salient than others. The children Nelson studied appear to name mostly movers (e.g., people, vehicles, animals) and movables (e.g., food, clothing, toys), with a few recipients (people). They hardly ever named places or instruments.

Greenfield and Smith (1976), in fact, looked at the order of acquisition of these different roles. They found that the two children they followed both began by naming movers or agents, then movables or objects affected by an action, and finally places or locations, and possessors or recipients. Table 8–1 illustrates this order of acquisition with data from one child between the ages of

TABLE 8–1

ROLES AND ACTIONS TALKED ABOUT IN ONE-WORD UTTERANCES

ROLE OR ACTION*	UTTERANCE	CONTEXT
Agent	Dada	Hears *someone* come in
Action or state resulting from action	Down	When sits *down* or steps *down* from somewhere
Object affected by action	Ban	When wants *fan* turned off
State of object affected by action	Down	When *shuts* cabinet door
Object associated with another object or location	Poo	With hand on *bottom* after being changed, usually after bowel movement
Possessor	Lara	On seeing *Lauren's* empty bed
Location	Bap	Indicating location of feces on *diaper*

* Roles are listed in the order, from top to bottom, in which the child began to talk about them.
Based on Greenfield and Smith (1976).

1;1 and 1;7. It lists the different roles and the actions or states that the child talked about in the order (from top to bottom) that they emerged in his speech.

Case Relations

The roles children pick out appear to be precursors to the semantic roles expressed in adult utterances. These semantic roles have been studied in most detail by Fillmore (1968, 1971a) in his analysis of propositions into case relations. Although incomplete in certain respects, his analysis provides a way of looking at the insides of propositions—which are the basic units of meaning—and identifies roles that may prove fundamental in how humans think.

As noted in Chapter 1, every proposition consists of a verbal unit and one or more nouns. Within each proposition, however, the nouns each play distinct roles. Consider 5:

5. a. The leaf moved.
   b. The man moved the leaf.
   c. The stick moved the leaf.
   d. The man moved the leaf with a stick.

Consider **the leaf**. Although it is the subject in 5a and the direct object in the other three sentences, it plays the same "semantic" role in all four: the leaf is the thing that moves. For this reason, Fillmore classified all these instances of **the leaf** under one label. To take another example, **the stick** plays the same semantic role in 5c and 5d: it names the instrument involved in the action of moving, and so it too has a single label. Or compare 5b and 5c. Even though both **the stick** and **the man** are sentence subjects, they play different semantic roles. **The man** refers to the agent of the action of moving, but **the stick** refers to the instrument through which the action is carried out.

In Fillmore's account, each noun in a proposition fills one of a limited number of *case roles*, or *case relations*, with respect to its verb. The same few case roles appear in all languages. The six major case relations Fillmore identified are the following:

(1) *Agentive case* (*A*). A noun in the Agentive case, like **the man** in 5b and 5d and the italicized nouns in 6, names the instigator (the "agent") of the action described by the verb:

> 6. a. *Dirk* hit the ball.
>   b. The door was opened by *Roy*.

In 6, as in most instances, the instigator is animate.

(2) *Instrumental case* (*I*). A noun in the Instrumental case stands for an inanimate force or object (the "instrument") involved in the action described by the verb. This is illustrated by **the stick** in 5c and 5d, and by the nouns in italics in 7:

> 7. a. *The key* opened the door.
>   b. The burglar forced the door with *a crowbar*.

(3) *Experiencer case* (*E*). A noun in the Experiencer case is a being affected (the "experiencer") by the psychological state or action named by the verb. Here are several quite different examples of nouns in the Experiencer case:

> 8. a. *Jane* heard the donkey.
>   b. *The carpenter* has a hammer.
>   c. John told *Mary* a story.
>   d. *The president* is sick.

In 8a, **Jane** is a being affected by hearing something. Since hearing is not a deliberate or voluntary action, she is the experiencer. If she had *listened* to the donkey, that would be considered a deliberate action, and then **Jane** would be in the Agentive case. The distinction between **hear** and **listen** is a subtle one. Similarly, having a hammer, being told a story, and being sick are experiencer roles, so **the carpenter**, **Mary**, and **the president** are each said to be in the Experiencer case.

(4) *Goal case* (*G*). A noun in the Goal case stands for an object or state

(a "goal") that results from the action or state named by the verb, as illustrated in 9:

9. a. Julia made *a bookcase.*
   b. Olaf turned the field into *a farm.*
   c. The king gave the reward to *the lieutenant.*

The bookcase in 9a and **the farm** in 9b did not exist before Julia and Olaf carried out their actions, and so they are the results of actions and therefore in the Goal case. In 9c, **the lieutenant** is the literal goal of the king's reward and so it too is in the Goal case.

(5) *Locative case (L).* A noun in the Locative case denotes a location or orientation for the action or state named by the verb:

10. a. The vase was on *the shelf.*
    b. James was *here.*

(6) *Objective case (O).* This case is a neutral, catchall category for any noun whose role in the state or action depends on the meaning of the verb. Many such nouns have appeared in examples already considered:

11. a. Dirk hit *the ball.*
    b. The key opened *the door.*
    c. The carpenter has *a hammer.*
    d. The king gave *the reward* to the lieutenant.

These examples show how the roles of the italicized nouns depend critically on the verb. The action of opening, for example, has to happen to some object no matter how the action came about. In 11b there wouldn't be an action of opening without the door. **The door** is therefore in the Objective case. Similar considerations apply to the other examples as well.

Now that case relations have been defined, it is possible to make several important observations about propositions. First, no proposition contains more than one instance of any case role. There can be one noun in the Agentive case, but never two, one noun in the Objective case, but never two, and so on. Second, each proposition can be characterized as a verb (V) plus one or more of the case roles. **Break**, for example, requires the Objective case (O), but it also allows the Agentive case (A), the Instrumental case (I), or both, as these examples show:

12. a. The cup broke.   (V + O)
    b. Michael broke the cup.   (V + A + O)
    c. The hammer broke the cup.   (V + I + O)
    d. Michael broke the cup with the hammer.   (V + A + I + O)

Hear requires two nouns, one in the Objective case and one in the Experiencer case (E):

    13. Jack heard the bell.   (V + E + O)

Other verbs take other patterns of cases. The point is that verbs, and the propositions they occur in, can be characterized in part by the case relations they can or must occur with.

    Case relations like these appear to play an important role in the acquisition of language. At the one-word stage, movers seem to correspond to the Agentive case, movables to the Objective case, recipients to the Experiencer case, places to the Locative case, and instruments to the Instrumental case. However, the child's notion of mover is not yet the exact equivalent of the adult's Agentive case: mover applies to a smaller group than the Agentive and at the same time may include things like cars or trains that are not agentive (see Schlesinger, 1974; Bowerman, 1974a; Braine, 1976). Nonetheless, from now on we will use the names of case relations like the Agentive or Locative case whenever we describe the roles that children express.

Two-Word Utterances

Within a few months of their first one-word utterances, children begin to combine single words into two-word utterances. Two-word utterances are often preceded by a brief period in which the child produces strings of single words in succession, with separate intonation on each one and pauses in between (Leopold, 1949; Bloom, 1973). In fact, children at this intermediate point often use "precisely the words in succession which they could be expected to combine in two-word utterances" (Bloom, 1973, p. 55). For example, a child might produce two single-word utterances in succession:

Baby.   Chair.

and later on produce the two-word utterance:

Baby chair.

These chains of single words signal the imminent appearance of longer utterances.

    Table 8–2 contains some two-word utterances from a two-year-old girl called Kendall (Bowerman, 1973a). Her utterances have been arranged according to the case relation used in verb-and-noun combinations (1–5) and the pairs of cases used in noun-and-noun combinations (6–8). The first thing to notice is that the cases are not always expressed with consistent word order. For example, in the Verb and Objective case combinations in 5 and the Locative and Objective case combinations in 8, Kendall sometimes placed the Objective case first, as in **Kimmy** kick ("kick Kimmy") or **Towel** bed ("the towel's on the bed"), and

TABLE 8–2

CASE RELATIONS IN KENDALL'S TWO-WORD UTTERANCES

1. **Verb and Agentive** (28) *	Kendall pick up [pick up K]
Kendall swim	pillow fell
Kimmy come	6. **Agentive and Objective** (5)
Mommy read	Kendall spider [is looking at]
doggie bark	Kendall book [is reading]
2. **Verb and Experiencer** (1)	7. **Experiencer and Objective** (14)
see Kendall [K sees]	Kimmy bike
3. **Verb and Goal** (1)	Papa door
writing book	Kimmy pail
4. **Verb and Locative** (3)	Kendall turn
play bed	8. **Locative and Objective** (13)
sit pool	Kendall bed
5. **Verb and Objective** (23)	Kendall water
look Kendall [look at K]	towel bed
Kimmy kick [kick K]	pillow here
shoe off	there cow

* Frequency of each kind of combination in Kendall's corpus.
Based on Bowerman (1973a).

sometimes second as in **Look *Kendall*** ("look at Kendall") or **There *cow*** ("there's the cow"). But in her Agentive and Objective case combinations in 6 and her Experiencer and Objective case combinations in 7, Kendall always placed the Objective case in second position, e.g., **Kendall *book*** ("Kendall is reading a book") or **Kimmy *bike*** ("Kimmy's bike"). The Agentive case always went in first position, whether combined with a verb as in 1, or combined with another noun as in 6. The Locative case always followed when it was combined with a verb as in 4, but either preceded or followed when it was combined with a noun in the Objective case as in 8. Kendall used only one instance each of a verb combined with the Experiencer case as in 2 or with the Goal case as in 3, too few instances to tell whether she used a particular word order or not.

A second point is that the two-word utterances in Table 8–2 are not the only utterances Kendall produced the day these were recorded. She also used many single-word utterances, six other two-word utterances of the form **That hole** ("that's a hole"), and some three-word utterances that combined a verb and an Agentive case with either an Objective or a Locative case, e.g., **Kimmy ride bike** and **Ben swim pool**. Children at the two-word stage use more than just two-word utterances. The two-word stage, therefore, is marked by the appearance of two-word utterances where before the child had only used single words.

In her two-word utterances, Kendall talked about four roles: the Agentive, the Objective, the Locative, and the Experiencer. The Agentive cases in 1 and 6 of Table 8–2 clearly correspond to movers or agents; the Objective cases in 5, 6, 7, and 8 correspond to movables or objects affected by an action; the Locative cases in 4 and 8 correspond to places, and the Experiencer cases in 2 and 7 correspond to recipients or possessors. These roles are the same ones that appear in one-word utterances (see Table 8–1). It therefore looks as if children continue to talk about what they talked about at the one-word stage, but now use more complex utterances. Instead of naming only one object with a role in an event, they begin to mention an object and an action together, or two objects each playing a role.

But how typical is the propositional content of Kendall's two-word utterances? Braine (1976) looked at two-word combinations in the speech of ten children (five acquiring English, two Samoan, one Finnish, one Hebrew, and one Swedish) and found that all the children talked about the roles of mover (the Agentive case), movable (the Objective case), and place (the Locative case), just as Kendall did. However, only some children talked about recipients or possessors (the Experiencer case), and practically none talked about instruments or goals. Kendall did talk about possessors (the Experiencer case), but like most other children she did not yet talk about instruments and she only used one instance of the Goal case (see Table 8–2).

Braine pointed out that many of the differences between children at the two-word stage can be put down to variations in how each child decides to combine two words to express the relationship between an action and a role or between two roles. He argued that children pick on a *formula* to express a particular relationship. For instance, some children pick on the formula of talking about the location of an object by first naming the object and then naming the place, in that order (**Baby chair**, **Daddy car**). Other children may opt for the opposite formula, naming the place first and then the object (**Here book**, **There doggie**). Not all children choose the same word order in their first formulae, and when they add other word orders for the same relationship, these may be used with a slightly different meaning.

Bloom, Lightbown, Hood (1975), and Nelson (1975) described another source of variation in two-word utterances. They found that the children they studied fell into two groups. One combined content words with content words in two-word utterances (**Build house**, **Lois cup**). The other combined content words with pronouns: these children typically used a pronoun like **I** for a mover (**I finish**, **I do**); a pronoun like **it** or the demonstrative **this** for movables (**Pull it**, **Try this**); and pro-forms like **here** for places (**Tape here**). The second group of children, therefore, talked about relationships with many fewer nouns for particular roles. Within a few months, though, the first group began to use some pronouns in their word combinations, while the second began to produce combinations of content words. Children may vary, then, in their choice of formulae for expressing particular relationships and in the kinds of words they first combine.

We can conclude that children talk about the same kinds of things as they move from single-word utterances to their first combinations of words. But now they express more than one role or action at a time when they describe an event. They may name both the mover and the action, for instance, as in **Doggie bark**, or the mover and the movable affected by the action, as in **Kendall book**, or both the movable and its place, as in **Towel bed**. Some children also talk about recipients or possessors together with the object possessed, as in **Kimmy pail**. The way different children choose to combine their first words, however, varies considerably from child to child.

Early Analyses of Two-Word Utterances

Previous analyses have stressed the *structure* of two-word utterances rather than their propositional content. This is because many investigators have assumed that children, like adults, rely on grammatical relations like subject, predicate, or direct object in the expression of propositional content. Once children begin to combine single words into longer utterances, one can look at how they use these grammatical relations. The first step, though, is to find out whether children show any consistency in their use of a relation like "subject of."

Pivotal Structures

Several investigators began by examining the possible arrangements of words in two-word utterances. By looking at the position of each word (first or second) and at the words it occurred with, they were often able to distinguish two classes. Consider the words **allgone**, **my**, and **it** in the following utterances:

allgone shoe	my mommy	push it
allgone vitamins	my daddy	close it

Allgone and **my** were used only in first position, and **it** was used only in second position. Braine (1963) called these words "pivot words" and the rest "open words." A particular pivot word occurs in the same position in every sentence, but some only occur in first position, and some only in second position. Pivot words are a very small class compared to open words, and their number grows very slowly. Lastly, pivot words, unlike open words, are rarely used on their own as single-word utterances. Under this analysis, the majority of early two-word utterances seemed to have the structure Pivot + Open or Open + Pivot (Braine, 1963; W. Miller and Ervin, 1964; R. Brown and Fraser, 1964).

The notion of pivotal structures soon came under fire. First, analyses of pivotal structure ignore the apparent meanings of two-word utterances. For instance, the utterance **Mommy sock** said while the mother was putting on the child's sock seems to express the roles of Agentive and Objective whereas **Mommy sock** said when pointing at a sock belonging to the mother seems to express the role of Experiencer (the possessor) and Objective (Bloom, 1970). A pivotal analysis does not distinguish between them. Secondly, pivotal structures bear no obvious relation to adult grammatical relations: pivot words are drawn from several different classes, e.g., demonstratives (**that**), pronouns (**it**), quantifiers (**more**), prepositions (**off**), and verbs (**want, do**). It is therefore difficult to account for the child's transition from pivotal structures to grammatical relations like subject and predicate. Finally, as data from more and more children were examined, it became apparent that only some children used pivotal structures in their two-word utterances. Bloom (1970) found that only 17 percent of the two-word utterances for two of the children she studied were pivotal, compared to 75 percent in Braine's data (see also Bowerman, 1973a).

Grammatical Relations

Some investigators have assumed that since grammatical relations are universal, they must form part of the child's innate knowledge about language (McNeill, 1966a, 1970). However, these relations can only be studied once children begin to combine two or more words in a single utterance. While not all investigators have subscribed to the innate view of grammatical relations, many have assumed that by the time children start combining words, they are aware of these grammatical relations, and that it is therefore quite reasonable to use adult grammatical relations like subject, predicate, and direct object to label the various parts of children's utterances (e.g., Bloom, 1970). However, other investigators have argued that children start by talking about a limited number of different roles (case relations) and only later learn the more abstract grammatical relations of subject, predicate, or direct object (e.g., Schlesinger, 1971, 1974).

What evidence is there that children at the two-word stage use grammatical relations? One place to look is in the constituent structure of their utterances. Sentences are made up of two separate constituents: a noun phrase as subject and a verb phrase as predicate. The verb phrase may consist of a verb alone, as in **The man** *walks*, a verb and direct object, as in **The man** *dropped the stick*, or a verb and locative phrase, as in **The man** *sat on the chair*. McNeill (1970) argued that if the predicate was a constituent for the child, one should find more verb + noun combinations (i.e., *verb* + *object*) like **Drop stick** or **Sit chair**, than noun + verb combinations (i.e., *subject* + *verb*) like **Man drop** or **Man sit**, among children's two-word utterances. Both Bloom (1970) and R. Brown (1973) in fact found that verb + noun combinations were more frequent than noun + verb ones. However, as Bowerman (1973b) has pointed out, the frequency argument cuts both ways: if children did use more noun + verb combinations, one would be compelled to argue that they were using the combination of *subject* + *verb* as a constituent, and this does not correspond to any grammatical relation. Unfortunately, Bowerman (1973a, b) found just this situation in three children she studied (one acquiring English and two Finnish): noun + verb strings were more frequent than verb + noun ones. The relative frequency of verb + noun strings versus noun + verb strings, therefore, at best provides inconclusive evidence of children's having identified the predicate as a constituent.

Braine (1971) used children's "replacement sequences" to argue that many two-word utterances consisted of predicates with optional subjects. A replacement sequence consists of a short sentence without a subject followed by the same sentence with a subject, as in **Chair**—*Pussycat* **chair**, and **Go nursery**—*Lucy* **go nursery**. Bowerman (1973b), however, found that some children just as often produced replacement sequences that went against Braine's hypothesis, as in **Chick**—**Chick** *sings*, and **Kristin**—**Kristin** *sit chair*. Replacement sequences, then, seem to be no more conclusive than frequency in providing evidence that the predicate is a constituent of children's two-word utterances.

The usual criteria for identifying a noun phrase as the *subject* of a sentence cannot really be applied to two-word utterances (Bowerman, 1973b). First, children do not use the word endings that might indicate number agreement between subject and verb—for example, **The dog barks** versus **The dogs bark**. And second, they do not distinguish subject pronouns from object pronouns—**I** versus **me** or **he** versus **him** (Chapter 1). The only criterion that might be applied is word order, and this is the criterion most investigators have relied on: in English, for example, they would identify the noun phrase just before the verb as the subject. But in practice, they have actually relied on what they consider the subject would be in the equivalent adult utterance. Utterances like **Ball hit**, **Apple eat**, or **Chair kick** are not analyzed as subject + verb sequences. Instead, it is simply assumed that children sometimes use the "wrong" word order (see also Matthews, 1975). In effect, we are forced to conclude that there is no reliable evidence so far that children use the notion of *subject* in their two-word utterances.

HOW YOUNG CHILDREN USE THEIR UTTERANCES

One-year-olds act on their world in countless ways: they are constantly exploring new objects and finding out new things about old ones as they handle them, move them around, and play with them. By about one, they enlist the aid of others in their acts. They get adults to open boxes for them, take off unwanted shoes or gloves, peel oranges, hand out cookies, and play games. But to achieve this, children have to be able to communicate, using their first words to convey both speech acts and thematic information. Speech acts and thematic content are as integral a part of children's utterances as propositional content, the first strand we followed in language acquisition.

Precursors to Speech Acts

Parents and children start communicating well before the children can use language. Their first communicative exchanges are mainly gestural, and these are initiated by adults from very early on. Escalona (1973) observed that adults begin to offer and show things to infants, naming them and talking about them as they do so, from the time infants are three or four months old. By six or seven months, infants begin to reciprocate by picking things up and spontaneously showing them to adults. From seven or eight months on, adults start to use pointing gestures to direct the infants' attention in addition to showing and offering new or potentially interesting objects. Again, within three months or so, infants begin to reciprocate: they start to use pointing gestures to pick things out instead of just gazing fixedly at new or attractive objects. When infants show, offer, and point things out for a "listener," they are using a primitive form of communication (see also M. Lewis and Freedle, 1973; D. Stern, 1974).

One major function of the adult's gestures, and of the child's, is to capture the attention of the other—the "listener"—and then focus it on a particular object or event. By the age of one or so, children use gestures communicatively in the sense that they check to see whether adults are attending or not. For example, a child will point at something and then turn to check that his mother is looking in the right direction. If she isn't he will try to attract her attention by tugging at her hand, for example, and then point again (see Bates, 1976). By one, children also respond to pointing as a communicative gesture: they know they are meant to look in the direction pointed rather than at the adult's hand or face as younger children tend to do (Lempers, Flavell, and Flavell, 1977). Pointing, then, serves communicatively both to get the attention of the "listener" and to indicate what it is the child or adult "speaker" is interested in (Bruner, 1974/5; E. Clark, 1977b).

Children use other gestures besides pointing for communication. For instance, they commonly use openhanded reaching or grasping gestures to signal that they want something (Ingram, 1971; Carter, 1974). These reaching gestures are often accompanied by the child's looking alternately at what he wants and at his adult "listener." Children also use more specific gestures or combinations of gestures to show what they want. Carter (1975) observed a little boy "ask for" a drink of juice in the following way. He went over to his mother who was holding a cup, stationed himself right in front of her, opened his mouth, thrust his chin forward, and then stared at her till she looked at him, asked if he wanted some juice, and held the cup out. Children often actively solicit the attention of their "listeners," by tugging at their hands or clothes, before they try to indicate what they want. And they wait, often staring at the "listener" until they get some response.

Overall, children's gestures seem to fall into two groups: first, they use pointing gestures that seem to communicate "Look at X" or "Tell me about X." In these cases, children are usually satisfied as long as their "listener" looks too, and maybe names the object or says something about it. Second, children use reaching gestures that seem to communicate "Give me X" or "Let me see (touch, play with) X." In these cases, children may be more insistent about getting a response. They repeat the gesture and sometimes accompany it by whining. They usually seem to expect the "listener" to hand them whatever it is they want. Several investigators have argued that these two types of gesture are precursors to the speech acts of asserting and requesting, respectively. Pointing is used to *assert* the presence of something, and reaching is used to *request* something (Bates, 1976; Bates, Camaioni, and Volterra, 1975; Bruner, 1975; Dore, 1973). That is, gestures and speech acts are parallel in function: pointing gestures require acknowledgment from the listener just as assertions do, and

TABLE 8–3
ASSERTING AND REQUESTING WITH SINGLE WORDS

CHILD	SPEECH ACT	UTTERANCE	CONTEXT
Nicky	Assertion	**Ba** + look	Looking at ball
	Request	**Mama** + whine + reach	Reaches toward any object desired
Matthew	Assertion	**Dada** + look	Looking at father
	Request	**Ma** + whine + point	Pointing at microphone

Based on Greenfield and Smith (1976).

reaching gestures require an action or an answer just as requests do. This hypothesis gains added support from the fact that children continue to use pointing and reaching gestures together with single words and even combinations of words.

Early Speech Acts

The very first words children produce often seem to be an integral part of the gestures they accompany, as, for example, "**Bye-bye** + hand wave" or "**Boo** + peeping from behind hand." These very early gesture and word combinations tend to be part of a routine or game that adults insist on in certain contexts, rather than primitive speech acts. The speech acts of asserting and requesting, though, emerge very shortly. The first assertions of presence usually consist of a general deictic or "pointing" word (like **there** or **that**) combined with a gesture, as in "**Da** + point," and the first requests usually consist of a general request word combined with reaching, as in "**Ma** + reach" (e.g., Leopold, 1949). Shortly afterwards, children start to name the objects designated in their assertions and requests. Greenfield and Smith (1976) found that their two children first used words in conjunction with pointing or looking toward the objects picked out or named. Then two or three months later, they began to use words with reaching gestures as well. Their request word, some form of **ma** or **mama** at first, was usually used with a whining intonation. These early assertions and requests are illustrated in Table 8–3. As the children acquired more words, they began naming the objects they talked about in their assertions and requests.

Children at this stage continue to use mainly two types of speech acts: assertions and requests. These two belong to the classes Searle (1975a) characterized as representatives and directives (Chapter 3). Roughly speaking, representatives are used to convey to the listener the speaker's belief in the truth of a proposition, and directives are used to get the listener to act in response to the speaker's request for action or information. Children may also use one or two primitive expressives, greeting someone with **hi** or expressing dismay with **oh-oh**. But at this stage, they do not promise things (commissives) nor do they say things that bring about a particular state of affairs like "I resign" (declarations).

TABLE 8–4

ASSERTIONS AND REQUESTS AT THE TWO-WORD STAGE

SPEECH ACT	UTTERANCES
Assertions	
Presence of object	See boy. See sock. That car.
Denial of presence	Allgone shoe. No wet. Byebye hot.
Location of object	Bill here. There doggie. Penny innere.
Possession of object	My milk. Kendall chair. Mama dress.
Quality of object	Pretty boat. Big bus.
Ongoing event	Mommy sleep. Hit ball. Block fall.
Requests	
For action	More taxi. Want gum. Where ball?
For information	Where doggie go? Sit water?
Refusal	No more.

Based on data from Slobin (1970), Bowerman (1973a), and R. Brown (1973).

They do not add to their repertoire of speech acts until they are considerably older, but they do elaborate the kinds of assertions and requests they use as soon as they start to produce longer utterances.

Once children begin to combine words, the actual words they select often indicate the function of the utterance—the speech act intended. Antinucci and Parisi (1973) examined utterances produced by a young Italian girl called Claudia. They found that in requests she consistently named either the speaker (**Claudia** or **me**) or the listener (e.g., **Mamma**) in combination with words like **dai** or **tazie** (= give) or **oio** (= want). In assertions, though, Claudia rarely referred to speaker or listener, and never used **give** or **want**. Slobin (1970) observed similar consistencies in two-word utterances from children acquiring several different languages (English, German, Finnish, Luo, Russian, and Samoan). For example, words like **here**, **there**, **see**, and **that** were very common in assertions, while requests were more likely to contain words like **more**, **want**, and **give** (see also Gruber, 1973, and Halliday, 1975). Some examples of assertions and requests used at the two-word stage are shown in Table 8–4.

Assertions

The first kind of assertion listed in Table 8–4 is the assertion of the presence of an object in context. Assertions like this typically contain words like **see** or **that** and are usually accompanied by pointing gestures. These assertions are elaborated versions of earlier one-word naming or labeling. Children at this stage also assert that objects are in particular places, belong to particular people, or have particular qualities. These have been labeled as assertions of location, possession, and quality in Table 8–4. Lastly, children make assertions about ongoing events, often simply to point out that something is happening.

Children also produce negative assertions at the two-word stage. The examples listed in Table 8–4 are called "denials of presence" because children assert that an object they expected to be there is not present (e.g., **No ball**), or an object that was there earlier has now vanished or is vanishing (e.g., **Allgone lettuce**). Denials of presence appear to be the first negative assertions to be used (Bloom, 1970). Negatives as a whole, though, pose rather a problem at the two-word stage. When children use only a single word with a negative like **allgone** or **no**, it is often hard to tell whether they are denying that an object is in its usual location, belongs to a particular person, or possesses a particular property.

Requests

Requests seem to fall into two groups at this stage: requests for action and requests for information. Requests for action may simply name the object the child wants to be given, as in **Give *candy*** or **Want *milk***, or they can take the form of a **where** question, as in **Where ball?** In fact, **where** questions are frequently used in requests for action addressed to young children. For instance, **Where's your nose?** and **Where's your ball?** are both requests for action, the first for showing and the second for getting (Holzman, 1974). Requests for information are not very common at this stage: children may ask questions demanding a simple "yes" or "no" answer by using rising intonation, as in **Sit water?** or by staring at the listener after the utterance, or both. Other requests for information tend to take the form of **where** questions, as in **Where doggie go?** Children also make some negative requests, and these may be identical in form with negative assertions. For example, **No more** could be a request equivalent to "Don't do that any more" or an assertion equivalent to "There isn't any more left," but their intonation may not be a very reliable guide at this stage (Weir, 1962). When children actively push something away, though, their utterances can be considered as negative requests.

Thematic Information in One- and Two-Word Utterances

Adults use a number of different syntactic devices to convey to their listeners what they assume to be *given* information—facts already known to the listener—and what they assume to be *new* in each utterance. For them, new information is indicated by focal stress (Chapter 1). Children at the one-word stage have the option of talking either about what is given or about what is new. In fact, they typically talk about what is new, but what is new tends to be what is new to the children themselves. With the two-word stage, they begin to combine given and new information in the same utterance. What they pick out as new information still seems to be what is new for them rather than what is new for their listeners. This rarely impairs understanding, for children's conversations are usually limited to the "here and now." Later on, children learn to take their listeners more fully into account.

New Information

Single-word utterances could supply either given or new information, but there is nothing intrinsic to single words that allows one to decide which kind of information a child intended to convey. Greenfield and Smith (1976) have suggested that at this stage children talk about what is new *for them*. Consider the following utterances and their contexts:

14. A child is playing with his toy bear on the floor when he notices a block lying under the edge of the sofa. He points to it and says **Block**.

15. A child is standing at the basin holding a piece of soap in her hands. As her mother turns on the tap, she says **Hot**.

16. A child comes into the room, looks at one of the lights that happens to be on, and says **Light**.

In each of these situations the children seem to be talking about what is new to them: in 14, the block that had just been noticed; in 15, the tap being turned on; and in 16, the light's being on rather than off. What is new to the children as speakers, of course, may or may not be new to the listeners (see also M. Miller, 1975; Weisenburger, 1976).

The conversations children have at the one-word stage also suggest that they concentrate on new information. For example, most children at the one-word stage can supply new information in answer to questions. Greenfield and Smith reported several exchanges between Nicky, aged 1;6, and his mother, among them:

17. *Mother:* What do you want?
    Nicky: Shovel.

18. *Mother:* Do you want some milk?
    Nicky: [Ba]nana.

In each case Nicky supplied information that was new to the listener, his mother. Appropriate answers to questions are by definition new information.

Children clearly convey new information with single words, but what about given information? They often start a conversation in the following way: they introduce something new in a one-word utterance, and then wait for the listener to acknowledge it, usually by repeating the word. This has the effect of making the original utterance into *given* information. Once this has been achieved, children can add *new* information with their next utterance.

Scollon (1974) reported several examples of conversations initiated by Brenda, aged 1;3, in just this way:

19. *Brenda:* Fan. [looking at the electric fan]
          Fan.
    Mother: Hm?
    Brenda: Fan.
    Mother: Bathroom?
    Brenda: Fan.
    Mother: Fan! Yeah.
    Brenda: Cool!
    Mother: Cool, yeah. Fan makes you cool.

Brenda persisted in repeating **Fan**, changing her pronunciation each time, until her listener understood and acknowledged it. In fact, Brenda nearly always repeated herself until the adult acknowledged what she said, usually through repetition. When an adult misunderstood her, she sometimes tried again with another word.

Focal Stress

Although it is often difficult to decide which information is new and which is given in one-word utterances, once children begin to combine words, they can put both given and new in the same utterance. Children could use word order to do this, either mentioning what is given first and then what is new, or providing what is new first and then anchoring it by adding some relevant given information. Or instead, they could add focal stress to whatever is new in each utterance.

Children often use heavier stress on one word than the other in two-word utterances. Wieman (1974, 1976) got independent judges to decide which word carried the heavier stress in each of the two-word utterances from five children. She then looked at the context of each utterance for what other people had said just before each child utterance and concluded that children at the two-word stage use focal stress systematically to indicate new information.

The five children Wieman studied usually used the order given-new, but this order could be reversed when answering certain questions, when adding further information to some initial utterance, or when producing a series of utterances that described ongoing events. For example, David, aged 2;1, used the order new-given in 20:

20. *Mother:* What's in the street?
    David: FIRETRUCK street.

Seth, aged 1;9, usually used the order given-new, with heavier stress on new, but he tended to reverse this order when adding further information, as in 21:

21. a. Man. [pause] BLUE man.
    b. Ball. [pause] NICE ball. [pause] ORANGE ball.

Each attribute—**blue** in 21a and **nice** followed by **orange** in 21b—provided new information. These words were more heavily stressed than **man** or **ball**. Another example of variable given-new order comes from Mark, aged 2;5, as he played with some marbles:

> 22. MORE marbles [picks up another marble]. Marble DOWN [drops it]. One marble MISSING. SEE marble [finds marble on floor].

Marble is always given information in these utterances, and what is new depends on what he does as he plays.

Getting the Listener's Acknowledgment

Children at the two-word stage start conversations much as they did at the one-word stage. They first get their listener's attention, usually with some acknowledgment of the topic, and then they add some new information. By now, though, the new information is usually conveyed in an utterance that contains both given and new. E. O. Keenan (1974) found this was true even of children talking to each other. The listener has to acknowledge the topic before the first speaker will continue. Consider a conversation she recorded between twin boys, aged 2;9:

> 23. *David:* [alarm clock rings] Oh oh oh, bell.
> *Toby:* Bell.
> *David:* Bell. It's Mommy's.
> *Toby:* [mumbles indistinctly]
> *David:* Was Mommy's alarm clock. Was Mommy's alarm clock.
> *Toby:* Alarm clock.
> *David:* Yeah. Goes ding dong. Ding dong.

The listener repeats the first utterance by way of acknowledgment, and this, of course, indicates for sure that he is listening (see also Mueller, 1972; Umiker-Sebeok, 1976).

The way Toby and David built up patterns of given and new information seemed to result from how they expected a speaker and listener to take turns (Chapter 6), so David waited for Toby to acknowledge the topic in 23 by repeating the word **bell**. As listeners, these children seemed to assume that they should acknowledge what the speaker is talking about, and as speakers, wait for that acknowledgment before going on. Even very young children seem to make the same assumptions. Turn taking, then, appears to play a central role in the buildup of given and new information.

Children clearly use their one- and two-word utterances to full effect. They build their first speech acts on what they already know about communicating with gestures. They start with single words combined with pointing or reaching to assert or request things. Later they use words like **see** or **that** in two-word utterances intended as assertions and words like **want** or **give** in utterances intended as requests. At the one-word stage, children typically talk about what is new, and as soon as they can combine two or more words, they combine given and new in the same utterance. The assignment of information as given or new depends partly on children's ability to take turns in conversations. To find out more about this, however, we have to look at who children talk to and who talks to them during the early stages of language acquisition.

HOW ADULTS TALK TO YOUNG CHILDREN

When people talk to one another, their general goal is to get listeners to understand what they are saying (see Chapter 3). This applies just as much when listeners are young children as when they are adults. The problem is that young children know very little about the structure and function of the language adults use to communicate with each other. As a result, adult speakers often have to modify their speech to make sure that children understand them.

What adults say to children provides them with information about the structure and function of the language they are to acquire. One reason for studying adult speech to children is to find out what *model of language* young children are exposed to. Several recent studies, for example, have shown that adults tend to use very short grammatical sentences when talking to young children. These observations contradict earlier claims that the language children hear contains numerous ungrammatical forms, hesitations, changes of construction, and mistakes. Exposure to a simple, error-free model of language would presumably make acquisition easier for children, but very little is known about whether such information is a *necessary* ingredient for acquisition to take place. Although error-free models are evidently available to most children, there are virtually no studies of the effect this has on acquisition. As it is, we can only describe what children say, compare it to what adults say to children, and assume that there is some connection between the two.

A second reason for looking closely at how adults talk to young children is that what adults say provides an indirect measure of how much children understand. Since adults want to make children understand, they will modify their speech to the point where children give some evidence of listening, taking in what is said, and responding appropriately. It is instructive, therefore, to look both at what adults say to young children and at how they talk when they really want to make sure children will understand.

How adults talk to children is influenced by three things. First, adults have to make sure that children realize an utterance is being addressed to them, and not to someone else. To do this, they can use a name, a special tone of voice, or even get their attention by touching them. Second, once they have a child's attention, they must choose the right words and the right sentences so the child is likely to understand what is said. For example, they are unlikely to discuss philosophy, but very likely to talk about what the child is doing, looking at, or playing with at that moment. Third, they can say what they have to say in many different ways. They can talk quickly or slowly, use short sentences or long ones, and so on. How adults talk also has certain incidental consequences: children are presented with a specially tailored model of language use, adjusted to fit, as far as possible, what they appear to understand.

How Adults Get Children to Attend

Speakers depend on their listeners being cooperative and listening when they are spoken to (Chapter 6). But when the listeners are children, adult speakers normally have to work a bit harder. They use *attention-getters* to tell children which utterances are addressed to them rather than to someone else, and hence which utterances they ought to be listening to. And they use *attention-holders* whenever they have more than one thing to say—for example, when telling a story.

Attention-getters and attention-holders fall into two broad classes. The first consists of names and exclamations. For example, adults often use the child's name at the beginning of an utterance, as in **Ned, there's a car**, and even four-year-olds know that this is an effective way to make two-year-olds attend (Shatz and Gelman, 1973). Or, instead of the child's name, adults use exclamations like **Look!** or **Hey!** as a preface to each utterance. Again, children as young as three or four use the same devices to make sure their listeners are attending (Mueller, 1972; Umiker-Sebeok, 1976; Garvey, 1975). Names or exclamations may be repeated at intervals to make sure the child is still listening, and sometimes adults repeat part or all of what they have just said, again apparently to recapture or hold the child's attention (see Snow, 1972).

The second class of attention-getters consists of modulations that adults use to distinguish utterances addressed to young children from utterances addressed to other listeners. One of the most noticeable is the high-pitched voice adults use for talking to small children. When Garnica (1975a) compared recordings of adults talking to two-year-olds, five-year-olds, and adults in the same setting, she found that the pitch of the adults' voices was highest to the youngest children, next highest to the five-year-olds, and lowest to other adults.

Another modulation adults use is whispering. If children are sitting on their laps or standing right next to them, adults will speak directly into their ears so it is clear they are intended to listen. Garnica observed that all the mothers in her study on occasion whispered to two-year-olds, a few whispered to five-year-olds, but none whispered to adults.

Adults also exaggerate the intonational ups and downs in talking to young children. Garnica found that they used a three- to four-octave range to two-years-olds. This is twice the normal range used in adult-to-adult conversations. Sachs, Brown, and Salerno (1976) also noted that adults frequently raise the pitch of their voices at the ends of utterances when telling stories to young children. Normally, this kind of rising pitch is used to signal a question, but with children it seems to be used as an attention-holder, with the general function "Give me confirmation that you're listening and have understood." The child's continuing to look at the speaker is usually confirmation enough.

Not all attention-getters and attention-holders are linguistic. Speakers often rely on gestures as well, and may touch a child's shoulder or cheek, for example, as they begin talking. They also use gestures to hold a child's attention and frequently look at and point to objects they name.or describe (Collis, 1975, 1977; Garnica, 1975b).

What Adults Say to Young Children

Adults both observe and impose the cooperative principle when they talk to young children. They make what they say relevant, talking about the "here and now" of the child's world. They encourage children to take their turns and make their contributions to the conversation. And they make sure that children make their contributions truthful by correcting them.

The " Here and Now"

Adults talk to young children mainly about the "here and now." They make running commentaries on what children do, either anticipating their actions— for example, **Build me a tower now**, said just as a child picks up a box of building blocks—or describing what has just happened—**That's right, pick up the blocks**, said just after a child has done so. Adults talk about the objects children show interest in: they name them (**That's a puppy**), describe their properties (**He's very soft and furry**), and talk about relations between objects (**The puppy's in the basket**). In talking about the "here and now"—usually whatever is directly under the child's eyes—adults are usually very selective about the words they use. They seem to be guided by the following assumptions:

(1) Some words are easier for children to pronounce than others.

(2) Some words are more useful for children than others.

(3) Some words are hard to understand and best avoided.

Most languages contain "baby talk" words that are considered appropriate in talking to very young children. For example, adult speakers of English often replace the words for animals by words for their sounds—**miaow, woof-woof**—or by a diminutive form of the adult word—**kitty, doggie**. As one would expect, the domains in which baby talk words are found overlap considerably with the domains young children first talk about. They include kinship terms and nick-names, such as **mommy, daddy**; the child's bodily functions and routines, **wee-wee, night-night**; names of animals; games and the occasional toy, **peek-a-boo, choo-choo**; and a few general qualities, **uh-oh**! (disapproval), **teenie** (Ferguson, 1964; Snow and Ferguson, 1977). Adults appear to use baby talk words because they seem to be easier for children to pronounce. This assumption may well have some basis in fact since in many languages baby talk words seem to be modeled on the sounds and combinations of sounds that young children tend to produce when trying their first words (see Chapter 10). At the same time, baby

talk words provide yet another signal that a particular utterance is addressed to a child rather than anyone else.

R. Brown (1958) argued that the words parents use in speaking to young children anticipate the nature of the child's world. This seems to be true not only of baby talk words but also of the other words used in speaking to young children. Adults select the words that seem to have the most immediate relevance to what their children might want to talk about. For instance, they would not point to an Irish wolf hound and say to a one- or two-year-old, **That's an Irish wolf hound**. They would be much more likely to say **That's a dog**. They supply words for different kinds of fruit the child might eat, such as **apple** or **orange**, but not the word **fruit**. They likewise supply the names of animals, but not the word **animal**. In other domains, though, they provide more general words—like **tree**—and do not use the more specific words for different kinds of tree—like **oak**, **ash**, or **birch**. Some of the words adults select are very frequent in adult-to-adult speech, others are not. The criterion adults seem to use can be characterized by what Brown called "level of utility": the judgment that one word is more likely to be useful than another in the child's own utterances (see Chapter 7).

Adults are selective in another way too: they omit some words and word endings and avoid other words. Snow (1972) found that adults used fewer word endings (e.g., plural **-s** or possessive **-'s**) and articles (**the, a**) when speaking to two-year-olds than to ten-year-olds, and fewer to ten-year-olds than to adults. Adults seem to leave out function words and word endings because they think this simplifies what they are saying. In fact, they do the same thing when talking to foreigners (Ferguson, 1971). Adults also try to avoid certain words. Instead of using pronouns like **he, she,** or **they,** they often repeat the antecedent noun phrase instead, as in **The boy was running, the boy climbed the tree,** where the second instance of **the boy** would normally be changed to **he** (Snow, 1972). Where **I** and **you** would be used in adult-to-adult speech, adults often use names instead, as in **Mommy's going to lift Tommy up** for **I'm going to lift you up,** or **Daddy wants to brush Julie's hair** for **I want to brush your hair.** Adults often use names in questions addressed to children too, for example, **Does Jennie want to play in the sand today?** addressed to Jennie herself. Adults seem to realize that pronouns are complicated for young children and so they try to avoid them.

Taking Turns

From very early on, adults encourage children to take their turns as speaker and listener in conversation. Even when adults talk to very small infants, they thrust "conversational turns" upon them. During the first months of life, adults respond to small infants *as if* their burps, yawns, and blinks count as turns in conversations (e.g., Snow, 1977). This is illustrated in the following proto-dialogue:

> 24. *Mother:* Hello. Give me a smile then [gently pokes infant in the ribs].
>   *Infant:* [yawns]
>   *Mother:* Sleepy, are you? You woke up too early today.
>   *Infant:* [opens fist]
>   *Mother:* [touching infant's hand] What are you looking at? Can you see something?
>   *Infant:* [grasps mother's finger]
>   *Mother:* Oh, that's what you wanted. In a friendly mood, then. Come on, give us a smile.

Whatever the infant does is treated as a conversational turn, even though, at this stage, the adult carries the entire conversation alone. As infants develop, adults become more demanding about what "counts" as a turn. Yawning or stretching may be enough at three months, but by eight months babbling is what really counts. And by the age of one year or so, only words will do.

Once children begin to use one- and two-word utterances, adults begin to provide both implicit and explicit information about conversational turns. For example, they may provide model dialogues in which the same speaker asks a question and then supplies a possible answer to it (Ervin-Tripp, 1970):

> 25. *Adult:* Where's the ball?
>   [picks up ball] THERE'S the ball.

26. *Adult:* [looking at picture book with child]
          What's the little boy doing?
          He's CLIMBING up the TREE.

These model dialogues also give the adult speaker the opportunity to show how new information can be combined with given information in the answers to questions. On other occasions, adults expatiate on whatever topic the child introduces:

27. *Child:* Dere rabbit.
    Adult: The rabbit likes eating lettuce.
          Do you want to give him some?

By ending with a question, the adult offers the child another turn, and in this way deliberately prolongs the conversation. In fact, when necessary they also use "prompt" questions to get the child to make a contribution and so take his turn as speaker:

28. *Adult:* What did you see?
    Child: [silence]
    Adult: You saw WHAT?

Prompt questions like **You saw what?** or **He went where?** are often more successful in eliciting speech from a child than questions with normal word order (R. Brown, Cazden, and Bellugi, 1969).

Making Corrections

Adults seldom correct what children have to say, but when they do, they only seem to do it to make sure the child's contribution is true (R. Brown and Hanlon, 1970). They may correct children explicitly, as in 29 and 30, or implicitly, as in 31:

29. *Child:* [points] Doggie.
    Adult: No, that's a HORSIE.

30. *Child:* That's the animal farmhouse.
    Adult: No, that's the LIGHTHOUSE.

31. *Child:* [pointing to picture of bird on nest]
          Bird house.
    Adult: Yes, the bird's sitting on a NEST.

In each instance, the adult speakers are concerned with the truth of what the children have said, with whether they have used the right words for their listeners to be able to work out what they are talking about.

The other corrections adults make are of how children pronounce certain words. If a child's version of a word sounds quite different from the adult version, a listener may have a hard time understanding what the child is trying to say (see Chapter 10). Getting children to produce recognizable words is a prerequisite for carrying on conversations. What is striking, though, is that adults do not correct any other "mistakes" that children make when they talk. For example, Brown and Hanlon observed that even blatant grammatical errors go uncorrected as long as what the child says is true. As a result, utterances like **He a girl**, said by a child of her mother, are received with approval. In correcting children's language, adults seem to be primarily concerned with the ability to communicate with a listener.

How Adults Talk to Children

Just as adults select what they say to young children by restricting it to the "here and now," so they alter the way they say what they say when talking to children. They do this in three ways: they slow down, they use short, simple sentences, and they repeat themselves frequently. Each of these modifications seems to be geared to making sure young children understand what adults say.

Speech addressed to two-year-olds is only half the speed of speech addressed to other adults (Remick, 1971; Broen, 1972). When adults talk to children aged four to six, they go a little faster but still speak more slowly than they do to adults. To achieve a slower rate, adults put in pauses rather than stretch out each word. Broen (1972) found that almost 100 percent of the utterances addressed to children aged two were followed by a pause, compared to about 75 percent for children between four and six, and only about 25 percent for adults. With the youngest children, 75 percent of the pauses occurred at the ends of utterances, and 25 percent after single words. Broen found a similar pattern in speech to the older children, but in speech to adults, only 50 percent of the pauses occurred at the end of utterances and 50 percent occurred within utterances (see also Chapter 7). By speaking slowly and pausing between utterances, adults separate out each sentence and presumably make it easier to understand.

Adults also use very short sentences when talking to young children. Phillips (1973), for instance, found that adult utterances to two-year-olds averaged less than four words each, while adult utterances to other adults averaged over eight words (see also Broen, 1972). These short sentences are generally very simple ones. For example, Sachs et al. (1976) found that adults used much simpler constructions in telling a story to a two-year-old than in telling it to another adult. With the two-year-old, they used only a few coordinate and subordinate clauses, and hardly any relative clauses, complements, or negative constructions.

There is a great deal of repetition in adult speech to children. One reason for this is the adults' use of "sentence frames" like those in the left-hand column of 32:

32.
$$\left.\begin{array}{l} \text{Where's} \\ \text{Let's play with} \\ \text{Look at} \\ \text{Here's} \\ \text{That's a} \\ \text{Here comes} \end{array}\right\} + \left\{\begin{array}{l} \text{Mommy} \\ \text{Daddy} \\ \text{[the] birdie} \\ \ldots \\ \ldots \\ \text{etc.} \end{array}\right.$$

Broen (1972) found that parents tended to use one or two frames very frequently, usually with exaggerated intonation and heavy stress on the word following the frame (see also Ferguson, Peizer, and Weeks, 1973). These frames mark off the beginnings of new words by placing them in familiar slots, and one of their main uses besides attention-getting seems to be to introduce new vocabulary.

Adults also repeat themselves when giving instructions. Snow (1972) found that repetitions like those in 33 are three times more frequent in speech to two-year-olds than in speech to ten-year-olds:

33. *Adult:* Pick up *the red one*. Find *the red one*. Not the green one. I want *the red one*. Can you find *the red one*?

These repetitions provide structural information about the kinds of frame the repeated unit (here **the red one**) can be used in. Snow also argued that repetitions allow children more time to interpret adult utterances because they don't have to try to remember the whole sentence.

When all these modifications are put together, it is clear that adults adjust what they say to make themselves better understood. They first get children to attend, then select the appropriate words and the way to say them. This suggests that young children are able to understand only short sentences and need to have the beginnings and ends of sentences identified. In addition, the sentences used are about the "here and now" since children rely heavily on the context to guess whenever they don't understand. But as children show signs of understanding more, adults modify the way they talk less and less. The shortest sentences and the slowest rate are reserved for the youngest children; both sentence length and rate of speech increase when adults talk to older children.

Incidental Consequences of Adult Speech

When adults are intent on making children understand, the modifications they use may have some important incidental consequences for children, providing "language lessons in miniature." These language lessons cover several different aspects of language use. There are lessons on how to take part in conversations, on how to map ideas onto language—words, phrases, and sentences—and on how to segment the stream of speech into words, phrases, and sentences.

Conversational Lessons

The *conversational lessons* all tend to converge on the cooperative principle for carrying on conversations (Chapter 3). Before children can take turns, they must first work out which utterances are addressed to them, and which to others. Adults make sure they know this by using attention-getters such as the child's name and attention-holders such as high pitch or whispering. These devices are signals that the utterance is intended for the child alone. Adults encourage children to take turns, switching from listener to speaker, and back, both by expatiating on the child's utterances and by asking follow-up and prompt questions. They occasionally correct what children say, but only where the listener might be led astray. They correct for truth value—that is, they make sure the child uses the appropriate words for the situation—and they correct for pronunciation.

Mapping Lessons

The *mapping lessons* provide children with clues on how to map ideas onto language. Adults usually pick out objects, actions, and events that are immediately accessible to the children they are talking to. Their focus on the "here and now" allows children to make full use of any contextual clues to what the words might mean. For instance, even one- and two-year-olds may get a long way in dealing with such indirect requests as **Can you shut the door?** just by knowing the word **door** and using their knowledge of the context—namely, the fact that the door is open and that the speaker is looking at it (see Shatz, 1974). The "here and now" provides children with an initially limited setting in which to start working out how ideas map onto language (see Chapter 13).

Conversational interchanges also provide mapping lessons. When adults expatiate on what children say, they provide them with other words for different facets of the context. Thus, if a child starts a conversation by talking about his ball, the adult may expatiate by using words for properties of balls (**big, bouncy, round**) and actions associated with balls (**throw, play, catch**). In this way, adults build up children's vocabulary in different conceptual domains. The corrections adults make are also important: they help children to be more precise in picking the "right" words so the listener will understand (Chapter 6).

Segmentation Lessons

Many of the utterances addressed to young children contain *segmentation lessons*, lessons that suggest how utterances ought to be divided up into words, phrases, and clauses. For example, adults speak very slowly and pause at the end of each utterance. With one-word utterances, this serves to pick out the boundaries of each word. Adults also help children identify boundaries by placing new words in familiar frames such as **Look at**——— or **There's a**———. Finally, when adults repeat themselves, they repeat single words, phrases, and occasionally whole sentences. These repetitions provide further information about the constituents of each utterance. Table 8–5 summarizes the contributions different types of adult modification may make to these language lessons on conversations, mapping, and segmentation.

TABLE 8–5
ADULT SPEECH TO YOUNG CHILDREN

ADULT MODIFICATIONS:	POSSIBLE ROLES IN ACQUISITION:		
	IDENTIFYING CONVERSATIONAL TURNS	MAPPING IDEAS ONTO LANGUAGE	IDENTIFYING LINGUISTIC UNITS
Name of child	X		
Exclamations	X		
High pitch	X		
Whispering	X		
Exaggerated intonation	X		
Baby talk words		X	
Selection of vocabulary		X	
Omission of word endings		X	
Avoidance of pronouns		X	
Model dialogues	X		X
Expatiations	X	X	
Prompt questions	X		
Corrections for truth		X	X
Slow speech			X
Pauses			X
Short sentences		X	X
Frames		X	X
Repetitions		X	X

How Necessary Is Adult Speech?

The fact that adults systematically modify the speech they address to very young children forces us to ask two questions. First, are the modifications adults make *necessary* for acquisition? Second, even if they are not necessary, are they at least helpful? Some exposure to language is obviously necessary before children can start to acquire it. But it is quite possible that any kind of language might do. Unfortunately, there have been virtually no studies of this aspect of acquisition. We need to know, for example, whether children could learn language if their only information came from speech they overheard between adults, or from what they heard on the radio or television. If they could, it would be clear that adult modifications are not necessary, even though they might be helpful. On the other hand, if children could not, it would be clear that some adult modifications are not only helpful but necessary. Further investigations would then be needed to find out *what* was necessary: the conversational lessons, the mapping lessons, the segmentation lessons, or all three.

Experiments on these topics are difficult if not impossible to devise, but occasionally a naturalistic situation presents itself in a way that provides a glimpse of the answers to these questions. For example, the hearing children of deaf parents who only use sign language sometimes have little spoken language addressed to them by adults until they enter nursery school. The parents' solution for teaching their children to speak rather than use sign language is to turn on the radio or television as much as possible. Sachs and Johnson (1976) reported on one such child. At 3;9, Jim had only a small vocabulary that he had probably picked up from playmates plus a few words from television jingles. His language was far behind that of other children his age. Although he had *overheard* a great deal of adult-to-adult speech on television, no adults had spoken to him directly on any regular basis. Once Jim was exposed to an adult who talked to him, his language improved rapidly. Sachs and Johnson concluded that exposure to adult speech intended for other adults does not necessarily help children acquire language.

Exposure to a second language on television constitutes another naturalistic situation in which children regularly hear adults talking to each other. However, Snow and her colleagues (1976) reported that young Dutch children who watched German television every day did not acquire any German. There are probably at least two reasons why children seem not to acquire language from radio or television. First, none of the speech on the radio can be matched to a situation visible to the child, and even on television, people rarely talk about things immediately accessible to view for the audience. Children therefore receive no clues about how to map their own ideas onto words and sentences. Second, the stream of speech must be very hard to segment: they hear rapid speech that cannot easily be linked to familiar situations. All this suggests that one ingredient that might prove necessary for acquisition is the "here and now" nature of adult speech to children.

Questions about what is necessary for the process of acquisition to take place, and about what is helpful to children during that process, will ultimately be critical for theories about acquisition. At this stage, however, far too little is known about either.

SUMMARY

When children use their first words, sometime between the ages of one and two years, they begin by talking about what they already know. In effect, the "here and now" provides the *propositional content* of one- and two-word utterances. Children also rely on what they know about communicating *without* language when they start to communicate *with* language. Their first *speech acts*—assertions and requests—are built on what they know about conveying interest (e.g., by pointing) and conveying desires (e.g., by reaching). Children also seem to convey *thematic information* with their earliest utterances. At the one-word stage, for example, children may introduce a topic to start a conversation and then treat it as given when they go on to provide further new information. By the two-word stage they often combine given and new in a single utterance and use focal stress to indicate what is new.

What young children say is complemented by what they appear to understand. This is usually harder to assess because they rely on all kinds of non-linguistic cues—direction of gaze, gestures, and the context itself—in trying to interpret what adults say to them. At the same time, adults systematically modify their speech in an effort to tailor it for children whose understanding of language is still very limited. The adults' goal is to make sure children understand as much as possible. The modifications they make to this end have the incidental side effect of providing children with miniature language lessons on how to talk about the "here and now" and how to carry on conversations.

Further Reading

There are useful introductions to child development in J. Turner (1975)—a brief but clear overview—and in Mussen, Conger, and Kagan (1974). Ginsburg and Opper (1969) give a useful introduction to Piaget that can be supplemented by Flavell (1963). In Piaget's own writings, there is a clear and relatively non-technical account in Piaget and Inhelder, *The Psychology of the Child* (1969). For the early stages of language acquisition, the reader might consult Leopold (1949) and Bloom (1973). Halliday (1975), Bates (1976), and Greenfield and Smith (1976) all focus on the communicative aspects of early language. Bloom (1970), Bowerman (1973a) and R. Brown (1973) contain extensive discussions of the two-word stage, while McNeill (1970) offers a different view. There is a useful collection of articles on mother-infant interactions in Schaffer (1977), and on adult speech to children in Snow and Ferguson (1977). And finally, there are collections of articles on children's language edited by Bar-Adon and Leopold (1971), by Ferguson and Slobin (1973), and by Rogers (1975).

Child: My teacher holded the baby rabbits
and we patted them.
Mother: Did you say your teacher held the
baby rabbits?
Child: Yes.
Mother: What did you say she did?
Child: She holded the baby rabbits and we
patted them.
Mother: Did you say she held them tightly?
Child: No, she holded them loosely.

Child aged 4;0 years.

Later Growth
in the Child's Language

Once children have reached the two-word stage, their next step is to start elaborating the structure of the utterances they use. One of the first things they do is begin to fill in the function words and the word endings that show how the content words are meant to be related. They add some syntactic "glue" in the form of articles, prepositions, auxiliary verbs, pronouns, and noun and verb endings, going from utterances like **Want off** or **Daddy ball** to **I want to get this lid off** or **He's throwing the ball to Daddy**. The puzzle is how children move from two-word utterances to much more complicated structures. To solve it, we have to look not only at how children might go about learning language, but also at what factors seem to determine the course children follow as they elaborate the structure of what they say say—what it is, in other words, that makes some structures easy to acquire and others difficult.

This chapter takes up the same three strands that were followed in Chapter 8: ideas and how they are mapped onto language, speech acts, and thematic information. The first half of the chapter is concerned with children's acquisition of *language structure*. It begins with their acquisition of the function words and word endings that glue content words together in each sentence, and then goes on to look at negatives and questions, and other more complex sentences: relative clauses, adverbial clauses, and complement constructions. The second half of the chapter takes up children's acquisition of *language function*: their speech acts and their use of thematic information. It begins with the order in which different speech acts are acquired and the devices children use to convey them, and goes on to consider how children get across thematic information.

LEARNING, COMPLEXITY, AND PROCESSING

Before the three strands are taken up, we must consider some general questions about the actual process of acquisition—how children learn, what complexity is, and what processing strategies children might bring to language.

(1) How do children go about learning a language? Do they imitate what they hear, are they reinforced by their parents for saying things "right," or do they form and test different hypotheses about what they have heard? It will be argued that children play an active role in acquisition and appear to learn about the structure of language by hypothesis-testing. This accounts for the many systematic errors children make during acquisition.

(2) What is complexity in language? Why are some structures and functions harder to learn than others? At least two kinds of complexity seem to play a role in acquisition: first, the complexity of the ideas children are trying to map onto language, and second, the complexity of the devices available in a specific language for the expression of those ideas.

(3) What processing strategies or "operating principles" do children apply to language in the early stages of acquisition? Some operating principles seem to dispose children to find some structures easier to learn than others. Operating principles, then, may provide another way of looking at complexity in language.

Theories of Learning

Traditionally, many people have assumed that children learn language by *imitating* what adults say. For imitation to provide a mechanism for the acquisition of language, though, children must imitate structures that are more complex than those they can already produce. These imitations would be *innovations* from the child's point of view and could therefore provide the next step to be taken in acquisition. However, studies of acquisition have found that children's imitations show no evidence of innovation.

Imitation

Ervin-Tripp (1964) found that children's imitations never contained new structures. When children at the two-word stage tried to imitate longer utterances, they typically produced only two-word sentences, as in 1:

   1. a. *Adult:* I'll make a cup for her to drink.
         Child: Cup drink.

      b. *Adult:* Mr. Miller will try.
         Child: Miller try.

Their imitations were either on a par with their spontaneous speech or even simpler. They usually retained only the most recent, stressed, content words, and omitted all the elements like articles, prepositions, and auxiliary verbs that were absent from their own utterances. In other words, when children imitate, they tend to be very systematic about what they imitate. Rather than trying to reproduce all they hear, they seem to put each utterance through some kind of "filter" that corresponds to what they themselves already know about the structure of their language.

Other studies have shown that children vary considerably in the amount that they imitate. Bloom, Hood, and Lightbown (1974) found that some children hardly ever imitated while others did so frequently. Like Ervin-Tripp, however, they found that the children they studied only imitated structures that had already begun to appear in their spontaneous speech: their imitations, therefore, offered no mechanism for acquiring new and more complex structures. Imitation was used primarily for the acquisition of new vocabulary: children imitated new words.

It may be easier for a child to imitate a sentence that reflects the child's intention to communicate a particular piece of information. Slobin and Welsh (1973) found that the child they studied could not always imitate sentences she herself had produced spontaneously on other occasions. For example, Echo, aged 2;5, said the sentence in 2 at breakfast one morning:

2. *Echo:* If you finish your eggs all up, daddy, you can have your coffee.

Her father asked her to imitate it immediately afterwards, which she did fairly successfully, as shown in 3a. Ten minutes later, however, when asked to imitate it again, she had much more difficulty, as shown in 3b:

3. a. *Father:* If you finish your eggs all up, daddy, you can have your coffee.
   Echo: After you finish your eggs all up then you can have your coffee, daddy.

   b. *Father:* If you finish your eggs all up, daddy, you can have your coffee.
   Echo: You can have coffee, daddy, after.

Since children are rarely asked to imitate sentences that reflect their communicative intentions, as Slobin and Welsh pointed out, imitation would not normally provide a way of learning devices that express their own intentions.

Overall, children do not imitate new structures, even though some of them do imitate new words. Imitation per se, therefore, does not seem to involve a mechanism through which children might learn to produce more complicated sentences. Other evidence against imitation, to be more fully explored later, is that children consistently produce many forms they have never heard from adults, such as **mans** and **tooths** alongside **shoes** and **coats**, or **putted** and **goed** alongside **jumped** and **walked**.

Reinforcement

Another way children might learn language is by *reinforcement*. Under this view, children would learn by being encouraged positively for any utterances that conformed to adult structure and function. At the same time, they would be discouraged and corrected whenever their utterances were at variance with the adult's. Unfortunately, this view of learning receives little support from the available evidence. Adults do not seem to be at all attentive to *how* their children say things as long as they are comprehensible. Parents encourage children to talk but they rarely correct anything they say, except occasionally for truth or for pronunciation (Chapter 8). In fact, R. Brown and his colleagues (1969) found no evidence that parental approval and disapproval were contingent on the syntactic correctness of their children's utterances.

Reinforcement, therefore, does not appear to provide any mechanism whereby children might learn the more complicated structures used by adult speakers of the language. Adult approval is not contingent on the grammaticality of what children say, and adults do not correct their children's grammar in the early stages of acquisition. On the rare occasions when they have been observed trying to correct a child's syntax, their corrections appear to be quite ineffective. McNeill (1966a) reported an example of this in an exchange between a small boy and his mother:

> *Child:* Nobody don't like me.
> *Mother:* No, say "nobody likes me."
> *Child:* Nobody don't like me.
> [eight repetitions of this dialogue]
> *Mother:* No, now listen carefully; say "nobody likes me."
> *Child:* Oh! Nobody don't LIKES me.

Correcting children's syntax is very hard work.

Hypothesis-Testing

A third approach to how children learn language might be called *hypothesis-testing*. Under this view, children use what people say to form hypotheses about how different ideas are expressed in the language they are acquiring. For example, children acquiring English might form the hypothesis that the idea of "more than one object" is expressed by the addition of **-s** at the end of the word designating the object. This hypothesis might be expressed in the form of a rule written roughly as:

> Noun + "more than one"   →   Noun + **s**

They then apply this rule to produce plurals like **shoes**, **cats**, and **dogs**, as well as plurals like **mans**, **mouses**, and **tooths**. Systematic "errors" like **mans** or **mouses** provide some of the strongest evidence that children learn language, at least in large part, by testing their hypotheses about structure and function and by finding out how well they are understood by others when doing this. The evidence for and against this approach will be examined as we consider stages children go through in the acquisition of more and more complex structures.

Complexity in Language

Most speakers of a language share the intuition that some structures are more complicated than others. Long sentences, for instance, are usually more complex than short ones. Negative sentences are harder than positive ones. Sentences with relative clauses are more complicated than sentences without, and so on. These judgments tend to be borne out by the modifications adults make when talking to young children (Chapter 8). They deliberately try to reduce the complexity of what they say and with the youngest children use the simplest language possible.

As children advance from very simple one- and two-word utterances, they gradually elaborate the way they say things by adding more and more detail to their utterances. From the two-word stage on, for example, they begin to add word endings like the plural or past tense to nouns and verbs, use the articles **a** and **the**, and also use an occasional preposition like **on**. Shortly after that, they produce their first coordinate sentences as well as a sprinkling of relative clauses and complements. And by the age of five or six, many of their utterances are indistinguishable from the adult's. The course of acquisition children follow appears to be much the same, regardless of the language being acquired.

All the proposals investigators have made start, naturally enough, with the same assumption, that children learn the simplest structures and functions first and work up to more complex ones later. Investigators have identified two interrelated sources of complexity: *cognitive complexity*—the complexity of the child's ideas being mapped onto language—and *formal complexity*—the complexity of the linguistic devices available in each language.

Cognitive Complexity

Children's ideas about their world, its organization, and its structure are clearly far from complete at the age of one or two years. Their ideas about objects, properties, relations, and events continue to develop for many years to come (see Flavell, 1963). The complexity of these ideas appears to affect the order in which children acquire different structures. The simpler an idea is, the earlier children are able to map it onto language and so talk about it. More complex ideas take much longer to get mapped onto language.

It would appear that cognitive complexity sets the pace for acquisition, at least in part. Support for this view comes from two sources. First of all, children tend not to use words and word endings for which they have no meaning. Second, children acquiring quite different languages tend to start talking about the same ideas at about the same time. Take the notion of "more than one" as an example. It is only when children have an idea in mind that they look for a way to express it. Children acquiring English usually start by using a word like **more** or **'nother**, or even a numeral, in combination with a noun that refers to the object being talked about, e.g., **More shoe**, **'Nother cookie**, **Two kitty**. They very rarely hit on the exact device adults use (the suffix **-s** on nouns). And children acquiring Egyptian Arabic, for example, start to express the notion "more than one" at virtually the same age and stage of development as children acquiring English.

However, even though English and Arabic children start on plurality at about the same age, they master the appropriate adult devices at strikingly different ages (Omar, 1973). English-speaking children master the plural by age six and Arabic-speaking children by age fourteen or fifteen. Differences such as these have led investigators like Slobin (1973) to argue that cognitive complexity must be distinguished from formal complexity—the complexity of the linguistic devices each language has for the expression of ideas.

Formal Complexity

Although formal complexity is not yet very well defined, roughly speaking a system within a language is formally complex whenever it contains rules with exceptions. For example, the past tense in English is formally more complex than the expression of possession. The past tense is usually expressed by the suffix **-ed** but there are numerous exceptions where **-ed** may not appear at all, as in **took**, **came**, or **bought**. Possession, on the other hand, is expressed by the suffix **-'s** that in principle can be added to any noun whatever. Its application is completely regular. The irregularity in the past tense, then, makes for greater formal complexity. Within a language, different devices may vary a great deal in complexity. One language, for example, might have a simple device for indicating past tense and plural on verbs alongside a complicated set of devices for expressing plural on nouns, while another language might have just the reverse. It seems reasonable to suppose that the more complex a linguistic device is, the longer children will take to learn it.

Differences in formal complexity between languages can be illustrated by comparing noun plurals in English and Egyptian Arabic. In English, the usual way to form plurals is to add the suffix **-s**. This morpheme takes one of three forms depending on the last sound in the noun stem it is added to: [s] as in **sticks**, [z] as in **roads**, and [əz] as in **watches** (Chapter 5). In addition to this large class of regular plurals, English has a small number of nouns that form their plurals differently, e.g., **man-men**, **goose-geese**, **child-children**. Egyptian Arabic, in contrast, uses many more devices for expressing plurality. First, there is a small class of nouns with regular plural endings, but this class is outnumbered by the many classes of nouns with irregular plurals, each forming the plural in a different way. Arabic not only makes a singular-plural distinction in nouns, but also uses a special form for pairs of objects—the dual. On top of this, nouns that denote a collection of objects take a different plural form depending on whether the objects are being regarded as individuals or as a group. (In English, the use of **trees** versus **forest** is somewhat analogous). And finally, when counting things, adults use the dual with 2, the plurals of nouns with numerals 3 to 10, and, for some reason, the singular with 11 and up.

Since the Egyptian Arabic system of plurals is much more complex than the English one, it is correspondingly harder for children to master. Both Arabic and English children start to express the idea of "more than one" at much the same age, but the gap between the first expressions of plurality and mastery of the adult devices is much greater in the case of children acquiring Arabic. In general, the more complex the linguistic device to be acquired, the greater this gap should be (Slobin, 1973).

In studying formal complexity *within* a language, there is a danger of falling into circular argument: Children acquire certain structures in a particular order, so this order must reflect their relative formal complexity. This formal complexity is then used to explain the children's order of acquisition. What is needed is an independent criterion of formal complexity. Some investigators have relied on grammars and have used the linguist's account of how certain sentences are related as a basis for predicting an order of acquisition (e.g., R. Brown and Hanlon, 1970). But not all linguists agree on how best to describe the relations between sentences of a language, so one grammar might make accurate predictions while another might even predict the opposite order of acquisition (see Watt, 1970a,b).

Another criterion of formal complexity is the degree of "fit" between children's *operating principles* and the linguistic devices to be acquired. Investigators like Slobin (1973) have argued that children come to the task of language acquisition armed with various operating principles or processing strategies. These operating principles "fit" some linguistic devices, but not others. For example, children seem to attend to suffixes before prefixes or prepositions, regardless of the language they are acquiring. As a result, they find it easier to acquire suffixes. So, because of the absence of fit between this operating principle and prefixes and prepositions, these two devices can be regarded as formally more complex than suffixes.

Operating Principles

Children seem to acquire some structures before others because of the operating principles they apply to language. These operating principles seem to be used at first for discovery: children use them to begin finding out about the structure of the language they are acquiring. The early operating principles are gradually replaced by more specific strategies designed to deal with the particular language being acquired—strategies like those adults seem to rely on as they listen to other people talk (see Chapter 2).

After comparing the patterns of acquisition for some forty languages, Slobin (1973) was able to suggest a number of such operating principles. Some are listed in Table 9-1. They can be divided into roughly two groups: those concerned with semantic coherence and those concerned with the surface forms of utterances. The first three principles, labeled A, B, and C, are concerned with the mapping of ideas onto language, and they depend crucially on a tacit hy-

TABLE 9–1
OPERATING PRINCIPLES USED BY YOUNG CHILDREN

SEMANTIC COHERENCE:

    A. Look for systematic modifications in the forms of words.

    B. Look for grammatical markers that indicate underlying semantic distinctions clearly and make semantic sense.

    C. Avoid exceptions.

SURFACE STRUCTURE:

    D. Pay attention to the ends of words.

    E. Pay attention to the order of words, prefixes, and suffixes.

    F. Avoid interruption or rearrangement of linguistic units.

Based on Slobin (1973).

pothesis that all children seem to subscribe to from the time they begin to speak —that language should make sense. In essence, this is the child's version of the reality principle adults adhere to—the belief that speakers will only refer to situations or ideas that their listeners will be able to make sense of (Chapter 2). The other three operating principles, labeled D, E, and F, are mainly concerned with the segmentation problem, with how to divide up the speech stream and keep track of different linguistic units (see Chapter 8).

Semantic Coherence

Principle A captures children's early recognition that the forms of words may vary. This is obviously a prerequisite for the acquisition of any kind of addition to the word stem—prefixes, suffixes, or even morphemes inserted into the stem (as in some American Indian languages). Context is critical to the application of this operating principle. Adults, for example, use both **shoe** and **shoes** to pick out the same objects, so children can safely conclude that the mapping for both sequences of sounds is somehow "the same." And context will stop children from relating sequences like **free** and **freeze**, or **pat** and **patch**, because adults do not use these pairs of words in the same situations, or to pick out the same objects or events.

    The second operating principle, B, again relates to the mapping of ideas onto language, but this time the focus is on such grammatical morphemes as the function words and suffixes of English. In their quest for semantic coherence, children tend to look for one-to-one mappings between ideas and linguistic units. English-speaking children, for example, go through a stage of using only the suffix **-s** to mark the plural of nouns, and only **-ed** to mark the past tense of verbs. Children acquiring other languages do much the same. Russian-speaking children, for instance, go through a stage of using only the suffix **-om** to mark the instrumental case although adults use a number of different suffixes (Slobin, 1966b, 1973). This operating principle is closely allied to Principle C: "Avoid exceptions." In effect, children look for regular patterns, preferably with a simple mapping between ideas and linguistic units.

Surface Form

The second group consists of operating principles designed to segment the surface forms of utterances in both production and comprehension. The first principle, D, helps children identify suffixes that alter the meaning of word stems, for example, the plural morpheme **-s** on nouns in English. Because of the linear nature of language, children presumably have to listen for recurring sequences of sounds, matching them from the initial segments on until they reach the end of a matching sequence. They are then ready to pay attention to what happens at the end of the sequence. Evidence from many different languages, in fact, suggests that suffixes are much more salient for young children than prefixes and tend to be acquired earlier (Slobin, 1966b; Mikeš, 1967). Thus, children's attention to surface form and their mapping in context allow them to isolate the final sound in sequences like **dogs** or **books**, and to work out its relation to the idea of "more than one." The processes of segmentation and mapping must proceed hand in hand if children are to learn which word forms are variants of one another, and what alterations can be made in the form of each word.

Operating Principle E comes into play for keeping track of the order of elements within words, and, for example, of whether a grammatical morpheme is a suffix or a prefix. Children rarely, if ever, make the mistake of having a preposition follow the noun it goes with or of adding a suffix to the beginning of a word. Operating Principle E is also important for keeping track of the order of words within sentences. In languages like English, for example, word order provides the main clue for identifying grammatical relations such as subject and predicate of the sentence.

Operating Principle F helps children keep track of the different relationships being talked about in each sentence. Notice, for example, that in a sentence like **The man who was running fell down**, the relative clause (**who was running**) interrupts the main clause (**The man fell down**). Children avoid producing structures like this, and if asked to imitate them, often leave out the relative clause altogether. This operating principle appears to play an important role when children first start trying to express several propositions in a single sentence.

These operating principles, then, provide some preliminary guidelines to what should be easy to acquire and what should be hard. Structures that are more acceptable to these operating principles should be easier to acquire, and those that do not may define the structures that are formally more complex. And, the operating principles children use at the age of two clearly differ from those they may rely on at age eight. Their operating principles interact at each stage with whatever they have already learned about the structure of their language. In this way, their operating procedures gradually evolve into the kinds of strategies adults use for processing language (Chapter 2).

ELABORATIONS OF LANGUAGE STRUCTURE

Children first elaborate the propositional content of their utterances by adding function words and word endings—the grammatical morphemes that help tie all the content words together. Then, typically, they elaborate the sentence structure proper and begin to combine several propositions into a single utterance. In doing this, they have several options to choose from. They could combine propositions by simply juxtaposing them in succession; they could incorporate one proposition into another; or they could use both these operations—juxtaposition and incorporation. What all children have to learn to deal with, in effect, is the linearization inherent in speech.

Grammatical Morphemes

Children go through several stages in the acquisition of most suffixes and function words (Cazden, 1968). What they do at certain stages suggests that they actively construct rules for the use of different grammatical morphemes, and in the process they often overregularize the system. These stages, shown in Table 9–2, can be illustrated by the acquisition of the past tense by children acquiring English.

The Past Tense Ending

In English, the past tense of most verbs is formed by the addition of the suffix written **-ed** (e.g., **jump** becomes **jumped**). There is also a group of strong or irregular verbs where the addition of the past tense morpheme may involve changes in the stem as well as in the suffix (e.g., **bring** becomes **brought**). During the one- and two-word stages children hardly ever use any past tense suffixes. This is shown as Stage 1 in Table 9–2.

Next, children begin to use several irregular past tense forms such as **went** or **broke**. Although these forms generally seem to be appropriate in context, a few children may pick up a past tense form like **went** without realizing that it is related to **go**. **Went**, for example, might at first be used with the present tense meaning of "move." Children do not use any regular past tense forms at this stage. Presumably, though, they are beginning to apply several operating principles to the verbs they hear. Principle A (Look for systematic modifications in the forms of words) and Principle D (Pay attention to the ends of words) are both critical at the next stage.

At the third stage, children add the regular past tense suffix to the verbs they use. They therefore produce appropriate past tense forms for all regular or weak verbs (e.g., **jump-jumped, pick-picked**) but make mistakes on the irregular

TABLE 9–2

PAST TENSE

Stages in the acquisition of the past tense suffix in English.

STAGE 1   Little or no use of past tense forms.

STAGE 2   Sporadic use of some irregular forms (examples: **went**, **broke**).

STAGE 3   Use of regular suffix **-ed** for all past tense forms (examples: **jumped, goed, breaked**).

STAGE 4   Adultlike use of regular and irregular forms (examples: **jumped, went**).

---

verbs they used to get right. **Goed, buyed,** and **breaked,** for example, now replace **went, bought,** and **broke.** Occasionally, one even hears **went-wented**—evidence that **went** is not always treated as part of the verb **go.** These overregularizations suggest that children have formed the hypothesis that the idea of an event occurring "earlier in time" maps onto the suffix **-ed** in English. This hypothesis would be a natural outcome of Operating Principle B (Look for grammatical markers that indicate underlying semantic distinctions clearly) used in conjunction with Principles A and D. The hypothesis provides the basis for the rule children apply when they want to talk about past events:

Verb stem + "earlier in time"   →   Verb stem + **-ed**

The fact that children apply this rule to regular and irregular verbs alike suggests that operating Principle C (Avoid exceptions) also plays a role at this stage.

Finally, at the fourth stage, children manage to sort out their verbs and from then on apply their rule only to the regular verb forms. By this time, they have realized that **went** is the past tense form of **go,** so **go** must belong to a different class from verbs like **jump, kick,** or **walk,** all regular verbs in English. New irregular (strong) verbs may have to be learned on a one-by-one basis from then on since there are very few in English that form their past tenses in exactly the same way (e.g., **ring-rang, buy-bought, eat-ate, light-lit, hit-hit**).

Other suffixes and function words are acquired in roughly the same stages. For grammatical morphemes with only one form, like the preposition **in,** children do not have to sort out different classes of words, but they still go through several stages in acquisition. The first is a period of no use, just as for the past tense suffix. This is followed by a period of occasional use where children may use **in** correctly but also make mistakes in meaning. For example, they may use it to signal any kind of spatial proximity between two objects. At the third stage, it is used appropriately for the idea of "containment" in an increasing number of contexts.

These stages in the acquisition of suffixes and function words—the grammatical morphemes—are not unique to children acquiring English. Stages roughly equivalent to those summarized in Table 9–2 are also found in the acquisition of very complicated systems of suffixes in languages like Russian (Slobin, 1966b), Latvian (Rūķe-Draviņa, 1973), Serbo-Croatian (Radulović, 1975), Hungarian (MacWhinney, 1974), and German (Leopold, 1949) among many others. In each of these languages children try to map particular ideas onto particular word endings. And in each instance their systematic overregularizations reveal that they are actively constructing rules on the basis of their hypotheses.

Use of Rules

The active role that children play in constructing rules has also been examined in an ingenious study by Berko (1958). She hypothesized that if children were using rules for the addition of different word endings, they ought to be able to add appropriate endings to words they had never heard before. To elicit word endings, Berko used a series of nonsense syllables to name drawings of strange animals and people doing odd actions. For example, she would point to a drawing of a birdlike creature, tell the child "This is a wug," then point to a second picture and say, "Now, there's another one. There are two of them. There are two _____." The child, usually cooperative, would fill in the plural form **wugs**.

   With this technique Berko showed that five- and six-year-olds consistently added the appropriate suffixes to new words. On request, they could add the plural, **two wugs**, the past tense, **he ricked yesterday**, the third person singular present, **he ricks every day**, and the possessive, **the bik's hat**. This ability to add the right suffixes to completely new nonsense words shows very clearly that they do construct rules for using grammatical morphemes and, in doing this, they make a strong generalization about the structure of the language they are acquiring (but see Keeney and Wolfe, 1972).

Order of Acquisition

English contains few grammatical morphemes compared to many other languages, but even so children have to learn how to express a number of different ideas that map onto various function words and word endings. R. Brown (1973) looked at the acquisition of fourteen grammatical morphemes in a longitudinal study of three children—Adam, Eve, and Sarah. These morphemes are listed in the left-hand column of Table 9–3, with their appropriate meanings in the center, and examples of their use on the right. Brown followed each grammatical morpheme from its first appearance up to the point where the children used it in 90 percent of the contexts in which an adult would have used it. Brown found that the three children were remarkably consistent with each other: the order in which all three acquired the fourteen morphemes, with only a few minor variations, is the one listed on the left of Table 9–3. In fact, the same order of acquisition has been found in less detailed studies but with much larger numbers of children (J. de Villiers and P. de Villiers, 1973).

TABLE 9–3

SUFFIXES AND FUNCTION WORDS
Fourteen suffixes and function words in English.

FORM	MEANING	EXAMPLE
1. Present progressive: **-ing**	Ongoing process	He is sitt*ing* down.
2. Preposition: **in**	Containment	The mouse is *in* the box.
3. Preposition: **on**	Support	The book is *on* the table.
4. Plural: **-s**	Number	The dog*s* ran away.
5. Past irregular: e.g., **went**	Earlier in time relative to time of speaking	The boy *went* home.
6. Possessive: **-'s**	Possession	The girl'*s* dog is big.
7. Uncontractible copula **be**: e.g., **are, was**	Number; earlier in time	*Are* they boys or girls? *Was* that a dog?
8. Articles: **the, a**	Definite/indefinite	He has *a* book.
9. Past regular: **-ed**	Earlier in time	He jump*ed* the stream.
10. Third person regular: **-s**	Number; earlier in time	She run*s* fast.
11. Third person irregular: e.g., **has, does**	Number; earlier in time	*Does* the dog bark?
12. Uncontractible auxiliary **be**: e.g., **is, were**	Number; earlier in time; ongoing process	*Is* he running? *Were* they at home?
13. Contractible copula **be**: e.g., **-'s, -'re**	Number; earlier in time	That'*s* a spaniel.
14. Contractible auxiliary **be**: e.g., **-'s, -'re**	Number; earlier in time; ongoing process	They'*re* running very slowly.

Based on R. Brown (1973).

Semantic Complexity

What factors might predict the order of acquisition Brown found? Two possibilities are semantic complexity—the complexity of the ideas mapped onto each morpheme—and the frequency of each morpheme in parental speech. The approximate meanings of the morphemes are listed in the center column of Table 9–3. Some have a unitary meaning: **in**, for example, means "containment," while the plural **-s** on nouns means "number." Others combine two or more ideas in their meaning, e.g., the copula **be** ("number" + "earlier in time") or the auxiliary **be** ("number" + "earlier in time" + "ongoing process"). Wherever there was an overlap in meaning, Brown predicted that the morpheme with the simpler meaning of the two should be acquired earlier. Meaning X should be acquired before X + Y, and X + Y in turn, should be acquired before

X + Y + Z. For example, one would predict that the plural -s on nouns ought to be acquired before the copula be, which in turn ought to be acquired before the auxiliary be. These predictions accounted for the data very well. In essence, Brown was using a rough measure of cognitive complexity: the more ideas that had to be mapped onto the morpheme, the later it was acquired.

Frequency

Brown also examined the frequency of the fourteen morphemes in parental speech on the tape-recordings of their children's speech. He found that the three different sets of parents were very consistent with each other, and all three used the fourteen morphemes with approximately the same relative frequencies. However, when the children's order of acquisition was compared with the parental frequencies, Brown found virtually no relation between them. For example, the articles (a and the) and the contractible copula be were the two most frequent morphemes for all the parents, but they were acquired seventh and eighth out of the fourteen by the children. The least frequent morpheme in parental speech was the third person irregular (e.g., has, does), yet this was consistently acquired by the children *before* one of the two most frequently used parental morphemes —the contractible copula be. Parental frequency, therefore, did not predict the order of acquisition Brown found.

This is an important conclusion because most imitation and reinforcement theories of learning have assumed that frequency of exposure to any behavior is a critical factor in learning: the more frequently children hear a word, the sooner they should learn it. Yet here is a case where children's order of acquisition appears to bear no relation to the frequency of usage by parents. Brown scrutinized the pattern of acquisition in even greater detail for the two morphemes in and on in Eve's speech. If she was attentive to these prepositions being used in particular phrases by her parents, her first uses of in and on would presumably occur in the phrases she heard most frequently. However, once Eve began to use these prepositions, she showed no signs of using them only in selected phrases, much less in those phrases that had been most frequent in her parents' speech. Brown concluded that frequency had no discernible role beyond simple exposure in the acquisition of these grammatical morphemes. Children have to hear a morpheme before they can acquire it, but those morphemes they hear most frequently are not necessarily the ones they acquire first.

All this evidence suggests that children add function words and suffixes to their utterances with great consistency: different children acquire grammatical morphemes in virtually the same order. Moreover, during acquisition, they consistently go through several stages in constructing rules for the use of each morpheme. Their reliance on rules shows up in their overregularization of word endings like the past tense -ed (added to regular and irregular verbs alike) or the plural -s on nouns (added to all nouns). Eventually they refine these overgeneral rules till they match those used by adults, but may take several years to complete the details.

Negative and Interrogative Sentences

As children start to combine words and fill in grammatical morphemes, they also have to find ways of expressing more than one proposition in each utterance. Consider the sentences in 4–7:

4. a. Katherine is sitting down.
   b. Katherine isn't sitting down.

5. a. I wanted some soup.
   b. I didn't want any soup.

6. a. Why can Justin pick it up?
   b. Why can't Justin pick it up?

7. a. Jan could climb over the wall.
   b. Jan couldn't climb over the wall.

The negative element, **not**, is really a shorthand version of "It is not the case that" inserted into the positive sentences in 4a–7a to form the negative ones in 4b–7b. The negative proposition has not simply been juxtaposed to the positive proposition in each case: it has been incorporated so that the negative marker, **not**, immediately follows the first auxiliary verb (**is**, **can**, and **could** in 4b, 6b, and 7b). Where there is no auxiliary verb in the positive clause, the verb **do** has to be supplied, the tense and number suffixes transferred to it, and the negative **not** made to follow it, as in 5b. These are only a few of the changes that accompany the incorporation of a negative into an utterance. The process is not a simple one.

Interrogative sentences also involve an extra proposition—one that is not found in assertions—which can be expressed roughly as "Tell me." However, this proposition takes quite different forms on the surface depending on what kind of question it is. Consider the pairs of sentences in 8–11:

8. a. Hilary was carrying a pack.
   b. Was Hilary carrying a pack?

9. a. The baby finished the bottle.
   b. Did the baby finish the bottle?

10. a. Bevis can paint something.
    b. What can Bevis paint?

11. a. The boy saw somebody.
    b. Who did the boy see?

Yes/no questions—expecting the answer **yes** or **no**—are marked as questions by inversion of the subject and verb from the affirmatives in 8a and 9a to the interrogatives in 8b and 9b. If there is no auxiliary verb like **be**, **have**, or **can**, then **do** has to be supplied, together with tense and number suffixes, as in 9b. Yes/no questions are also marked by the use of rising pitch toward the end of the sentence. The questions in 10 and 11 are marked by the interrogative words **what** and **who**. In WH- questions, not only are subject and verb inverted, but the WH- word has to be placed first in the sentence as well.

The surface structures used to express both negatives (roughly, "it is not the case that") and questions (roughly, "tell me") are very complex. Not surprisingly, it takes children a long time to work out exactly which devices are used in each language for the expression of a negative or an interrogative. In English, children go through rather similar stages in the acquisition of these two structures. In both, they appear to apply certain operating principles to the earliest forms they use and later relinquish these principles in favor of rules more specific to the structures being acquired.

Negatives

Children express negation in several ways during the very earliest stages of acquisition. A negative gesture like shaking one's head or frowning may be combined with single words, a gesture may be used alone, or the word **no** used alone. A few children mark one- and two-word utterances as negative by using a different intonation pattern (Lord, 1974). At the one- and two-word stages negation is often expressed by words like **byebye**, **allgone**, or **off**, as in **Byebye man**, **Allgone shoe**, and **Boot off**, as well as by **no** or **not**.

Bloom (1970) found that the three children she studied first used utterances with **no** or **not** to indicate that a particular object was not in its usual place (see also Greenfield and Smith, 1976)—for example, **No cookie**, said when the child noticed there were none in the jar. Next they extended **no** and **not** to cover the rejection of a suggestion or an offer, as in **No car**, said as the child pushed away a toy he was offered. Finally, they extended **no** and **not** to situations in which they denied or contradicted a positive assertion, for example, **Not a truck**, said as the child pointed to a bicycle. Bloom argued that these three types of negation—nonpresence, rejection, and denial—are semantically distinct. However, the differences in meaning between them are generally obscured in English because they all have the same negative form (but see McNeill and McNeill, 1973).

Children at the two-word stage place the negative word at the beginning or end of their utterance, combining the negative proposition with the rest of the clause by juxtaposition alone. Klima and Bellugi (1966) took this as their starting point for examining the explicit negatives **no** and **not** produced by three children over a fairly long period of development—up to sixteen months beyond the two-word stage. They were able to identify three main stages in the acquisition of negative structures in English.

Stage 1 utterances consisted of a "nucleus" (the positive proposition or propositions) either preceded or followed by a negative. Table 9–4 lists some typical examples from the three children. All three were using a variety of two-word utterances and were beginning to use some grammatical morphemes like **-ing**.

TABLE 9–4

NEGATIVES IN CHILDREN'S SPEECH

THE FIRST STAGE

No . . . wipe finger	No sit there
Not . . . fit	Wear mitten no
No the sun shining	Not a teddy bear!
No mitten	No fall!

THE SECOND STAGE

No pinch me	Don't bite me yet
Book say no	Don't wait for me . . . come in
No square . . . is clown	
	That no O, that blue
I can't catch you	That no fish school
You can't dance	There no squirrels
I don't sit on Cromer's coffee	He no bite you
I don't know his name	I no want envelope

THE THIRD STAGE

Paul can't have one	This not ice cream
This can't stick	They not hot
	Paul not tired
I didn't did it	It's not cold
You don't want some supper	
I didn't caught it	I not crying
Paul didn't laugh	He not taking the walls down
I gave him some so he won't cry	Don't put the two wings on
Donna won't let go	Don't kick my box
No, I don't have a book	I not see you anymore
That was not me	I not hurt him
I isn't . . . I not sad	Ask me if I not made mistake

Based on Klima and Bellugi (1966).

Children at this stage are probably using two of the operating principles that focus on semantic coherence: B and C (see Table 9–1). The result is that they use **no** and **not** consistently for negation in all sorts of utterances and contexts. At the same time, they observe Principle F and avoid interrupting the nuclear sentences with **no** or **not**, always placing the negative at the beginning or, less commonly, at the end. Further evidence for F comes from the children's comprehension: they usually ignored negative words that interrupted a clause, as in **You're not to touch that**, and were more likely to respond to negative sentences prefaced by **no**, as in **No, don't touch that**.

At Stage 2, the children began to incorporate their negatives into affirmative clauses. They used both **can't** and **don't** as internal negatives (as in **You can't dance** and **I don't want it**), but these seemed to be unitary negative words, not **can** and **do** with the negative **-n't** attached. They also inserted **no** into clauses (**There no squirrels** and **He no bite you**). The fact that **no** is inserted in front of verbs like **bite** and **want** suggests that all the negative elements—**no**, **not**, **can't**, and **don't**—are being used in a similar way, although they may have subtly different meanings. And, as Table 9–4 shows, the children still used some Stage 1–type negatives, for example, **No pinch me**. They also used negative commands like **Don't leave me** or **Don't wait for me**, with **don't** instead of **no** in first position. On their own, though, these negative commands would not be evidence for the incorporation of the negative into the clause. **Don't** could simply be attached at the beginning just as **no** was at Stage 1.

From the point of view of semantic coherence, the children at Stage 2 appear to have added to their repertoire of possible negative elements. **Can't** and **don't** have been added to **no** and **not**, so any one of them can be used to mark a clause as negative by Operating Principle B. As far as surface form is concerned, children at this stage seem to pay special attention to the word order in each utterance (Principle D). Once they start to insert negatives into clauses, they consistently do so in the right place, between the subject and verb. Their earlier reliance on the principle of not interrupting the clause with a negative, then, gives way to the principle of keeping track of word order.

By Stage 3, the children always incorporated the negative into negative utterances. The examples in Table 9–4 show that **don't**, **can't**, **won't**, and **not** appeared as internal negatives. Since the children by then also used **do**, **can**, and **will** in affirmative sentences, **don't**, for example, from now on can be analyzed as **do** + **not**. This allows a closer look at where children place the negative element. Whenever they use an auxiliary verb (**do** or a modal like **can** or **will**) they correctly place the negative **not** immediately after it (e.g., **I gave him some so he won't cry**). They also used **not** internally without an auxiliary (**They not hot**) and no longer used **no** in this context.

By Stage 3 all three children appeared to understand most of the negatives addressed to them and no longer had difficulty picking out the negative element inside a clause (but see further J. de Villiers and Tager Flusberg, 1975). But in their own speech they still made mistakes. For example, all three omitted the copula **be** and auxiliary **be**, two grammatical morphemes that are acquired relatively late (Table 9–3) and said things like **Paul not tired** instead of **Paul isn't tired** or **I not crying** rather than **I'm not crying**. They also had some difficulty with the past tense suffix at times and would add it to both the auxiliary and main verb (e.g., **I didn't caught it**). They still didn't know when to alternate **some** with **any** and would say **I didn't see something** instead of **I didn't see anything**. Lastly, they still hadn't worked out how negatives such as **no one** or **nothing** are used, and often came up with double negatives by using **not** as well, saying **No one didn't come in**. These details are mastered later still.

Which operating principles are still being applied at Stage 3? At this point, children are very close to having acquired the adult system for negation. They have clearly mastered **not** as the sentence-internal negative element and generally produce it appropriately in combination with **do** or a modal verb. Principle C, avoiding exceptions, still applies, however. Children overregularize their system of negation by placing **not** in all their negative sentences, even those that begin with a negative like **nothing**, **nobody**, or **nowhere**. This overregularization is analogous to the overregularization of the plural or past tense in English. As far as surface form is concerned, attention to the order of different elements is still very important, so Principle E is apparently also still operating. By this time, however, children are probably using a much more sophisticated version of this operating principle, a version specifically built for negative sentences to keep track of the order of subject, auxiliary verb, main verb, and so on (see Chapter 2).

At this point it ought to be made clear how these stages in the acquisition of negatives are related to children's ages. R. Brown (1973) found that in the early stages of language development, the average length of children's utterances is often a better guide to the stage they are at than their actual age. At Stage 1, for example, Eve was 1;6, Adam 2;2, and Sarah 2;3, but all three children were in the two-word stage of development. The mean length of their utterances, counted in morphemes to give them credit for any suffixes they used, was 1.75 morphemes. By Stage 2, their mean length of utterance (or MLU) had increased to 2.25 morphemes, while in terms of age, Eve was 1;10, Adam about 2;6, and Sarah about 2;7. By Stage 3, their utterances averaged 3.5 morphemes. Eve was aged 2;0, Adam 3;0, and Sarah 3;5. The rate at which different children go through such stages, then, may vary considerably. This is also true for the acquisition of other grammatical morphemes as well as of different kinds of sentence structure.

Children, then, appear to go through at least three stages in the acquisition of the adult devices used for negation. To begin with, they combine a negative element, **no** or **not**, with other propositions by placing it at the beginning of the sentence. At the second stage, they begin to incorporate the negative into the sentence and use negatives like **can't** and **don't** in addition to **not**. By the third stage, they appear to have mastered the essentials of the adult system for English, although they still have to work out many of its subtler details, which will take them years to learn. Children acquiring negation in Italian and German seem to go through similar stages (e.g., Volterra, 1972; Antinucci and Volterra, 1975; Grimm, 1973).

Questions

The stages children go through in the acquisition of interrogative sentences are roughly parallel to the stages for negatives. At the first stage, they use some yes/no questions and a few WH- words. Some examples of Stage 1 questions from Klima and Bellugi (1966) are shown in Table 9–5. The yes/no questions are indistinguishable in structure from assertions, but they were usually uttered with rising pitch toward the end and accompanied by the children's looking intently at the adult as they waited for some response. The WH- questions, rather like the early negatives, seem to consist of a WH- word attached to the beginning of a nuclear sentence.

The main WH- words the children used were **where** and **what**, but the only WH- question they seemed to understand at this stage was **where**. When their parents asked **what** questions, they usually got irrelevant answers (see also Ervin-Tripp, 1970). **Where** questions, in fact, are those most frequently asked by adults: they made up 80 percent of the WH- questions put to Adam, Eve, and Sarah by their parents (R. Brown, Cazden, and Bellugi, 1969; Savić, 1975). Whether parents ask a lot of **where** questions because children appear to understand them, or whether children come to understand them because those are the WH- questions most frequently addressed to them, we cannot tell.

Children seem to rely on Operating Principle B for semantic coherence at this stage (Table 9–1). In production, they consistently mark WH- questions with **where** or **what**, both WH- words. And in comprehension, they seem to assume that any WH- word at this stage should be treated as if it means **where** (Ervin-Tripp, 1970). In yes/no questions, there is nothing directly equivalent to the WH- word, but some children consistently use rising intonation. Others resort instead to gestural cues: prolonged eye contact, reaching, and so on. Children may also be observing Principle E (pay attention to the order of words) in their WH- questions since they regularly attach the WH- word to the beginning of the sentence.

At Stage 2, the children's questions had become more complex. For example, they asked **why** questions as well as **where** and **what** questions, and used a greater variety of verbs. However, in comprehension, most **why** questions still tended to be treated as if they were **where** or **what** questions (Ervin-Tripp, 1970). The spontaneous use of a new WH- word, then, does not necessarily mean it is correctly understood.

There is comparatively little change in the forms of yes/no questions. They were still marked by intonation alone. The children still had not mastered the copula **be** or the auxiliary **be** (see Table 9–3), and the only modal verb they used was the negative form **can't**, which they used in yes/no questions (**You can't fix it?**) but never in WH- questions. In negative yes/no questions at this stage, the negative word is incorporated into the clause, as in **You can't fix it?**, but in WH- questions it still remains outside the clause or nucleus sentence, as in **Why not me drink it?** Overall, children's questions differ from adults' at this stage in never inverting subject and verb.

By Stage 3, the children regularly inverted the subject and verb in both positive and negative yes/no questions, for example, **Will you help me?** and **Can't you get it?** As the examples in Table 9–5 show, however, they still made mistakes with the tense and number suffixes on the auxiliary verb, for example, **Did I caught it?** where the past tense suffix has been added to both **do** and **catch**.

TABLE 9–5
CHILDREN'S QUESTIONS

THE FIRST STAGE

Fraser water?   Where Ann pencil?

See hole?   Where Mama boot?

Sit chair?   Where kitty?

No ear?   Where horse go?

                                 Where milk go?

What(s) that?

What cowboy doing?   Who that?

THE SECOND STAGE

See my doggie?   What book name?

Dat black too?   What me think?

You want eat?   What the dollie have?

I have it?   What soldier marching?

You can't fix it?   Why?

This can't write a flower?   Why you smiling?

                                 Why not?

Where baby Sarah rattle?   Why not me sleeping?

Where me sleep?   Why not me drink it?

THE THIRD STAGE

Does lions walk?   What I did yesterday?

Oh, did I caught it?   What he can ride in?

Are you going to make it with me? What did you doed?

Will you help me?   Sue, what you have in your mouth?

Can I have a piece of paper?

                                 Why he don't know how to pretend?

Can't it be a bigger truck?   Why kitty can't stand up?

Can't you work this thing?   Why the Christmas tree going?

Can't you get it?

                                 Which way they should go?

Where small trailer he should pull? How he can be a doctor?

Where the other Joe will drive? How they can't talk?

Where my spoon goed?   How that opened?

Based on Klima and Bellugi (1966).

The devices used to express yes/no questions in English appear to be formally less complex than those used to express WH- questions. WH- questions lag behind yes/no ones at each step in acquisition. For example, children first use negative auxiliary verbs in yes/no questions, and only later use them in WH-questions. They first invert the subject and auxiliary verb in yes/no questions, and only later do so in WH- questions as well. Bellugi (1971) also found that subject-verb inversion seemed to be acquired earlier for positive WH- questions than it was for negative ones where children presumably have to think about the negative word too. She discovered this by eliciting different questions with the aid of a puppet, as in the following two examples:

12. *Adult:* Adam, ask the Old Lady [puppet] what she'll do next.
    Adam: Old Lady, what *will you* do now?
13. *Adult:* Adam, ask the Old Lady why she can't sit down.
    Adam: Old Lady, why *you can't* sit down?

The operating principles children apply to questions are similar to those they apply to negatives. Most children seem to make special use of Principle B and attempt to find a grammatical marker to indicate that a question is a question. With yes/no questions, they usually start with rising intonation, and later supplement that by inversion of the subject and auxiliary verb. With WH- questions, they pick a WH- word. Moreover, comprehension studies suggest that new WH-words are often equated at first with ones already known. For example, children often treat **what** as **where**, **when** as **where**, and **why** as **what** in their answers to WH- questions (Ervin-Tripp, 1970; E. Clark, 1971). Children also pay attention to word order (Principle E) and avoid rearrangements (Principle F). For example, they first place auxiliary verbs between the subject and main verb, just as in positive or negative assertions. Only later do they start to rearrange the subject and auxiliary to mark questions by inversion. They invert on yes/no questions by Stage 3 (Table 9–5), but do not manage it on WH- questions until later. WH- questions may be more difficult because they require two rearrangements: movement of the WH- word from where it would have been to initial position in the sentence and inversion of the subject and auxiliary verb (see R. Brown, 1968).

Children, then, go through very similar stages in the acquisition of both negatives and questions. They begin combining the negative or question proposition with others by simple juxtaposition: **no** or **where**, for example, attached to the beginning of an utterance. Then they go on to slip one proposition inside another. Structurally, this is achieved in both negatives and questions with the acquisition of the auxiliary verb: first in negative form only (**can't, don't**), and only in yes/no questions. Next, the auxiliary appears in both negative and positive form (**can't** and **can**) and is used in both yes/no and WH- questions. At Stage 3, the auxiliary and subject are regularly inverted in yes/no questions, but have not yet reached that point in WH- ones. There remain a large number of structural details for children to work out in negation and in questions before they can be said to have mastered the adult system.

Complex Sentences

At around three, children begin to use the first complex sentences that combine propositions into clauses through *coordination, relativization,* and *complementation* (Chapter 1). They start to link two or more ideas in coordinate sentences like 14:

14. Susan chopped some wood and Annie put up the tent.

They start to modify ideas with relative clauses attached to noun phrases like **the man** in 15, or attached to main clauses, as in 16:

15. The man who was wearing a black beret jumped onto the deck.

16. They ran away when they caught sight of the dog.

And they start to fill in ideas by using complement structures in place of empty nouns like **something** in **He wanted something**, as in 17:

17. He wanted to see a heron.

In acquiring complex sentences like these, children seem to begin by choosing structures that conform to some of the operating principles discussed earlier. The three principles that seem to influence them most are B (Look for grammatical markers that indicate underlying semantic distinctions clearly), C (Avoid exceptions), and F (Avoid interruption or rearrangement of linguistic units).

Relative Clauses

In English, relative clauses can be attached to the subject of a main clause (as in 18 and 19) or to its object (as in 20 and 21):

18. The girl *who hit the boy* came to the party.

19. The girl *who the boy hit* came to the party.

20. The girl caught the dog *that ran after the boy.*

21. The girl caught the dog *that the boy ran after.*

In addition, the subject of the main clause may be identical with the subject of the relative clause, as in 18 and 20, or with the object of the relative clause, as in 19 and 21. Finally, the relative clause can be marked as a relative by the relative pronouns **who, which,** or **that.** In some cases, the relative pronoun can be omitted. For example, **who** could be omitted from 19 and **that** from 21, but they can't be omitted in 18 or 20. Note that children's operating principles should lead them to find relative clauses with explicit relative pronouns easier than those without. The relative clauses in 18 and 20 should therefore be easier than 19 or 21 because the relative pronoun can never be omitted. Furthermore, the relative clauses that do not interrupt main clauses (namely 20 and 21) ought to be easier to acquire than those that do interrupt (18 and 19). These two operating principles, then, would predict that forms like 20 should be the easiest type of relative clause for children to acquire.

The first relative clauses children use largely conform to these predictions. Limber (1973) found that children began by attaching relative clauses to the objects of main clauses, as in 20 and 21. He recorded sentences like **I want the ones you've got**, but heard no sentences like **The ones you've got are bigger** where the relative clause interrupts the main clause. In their spontaneous speech, therefore, these children were clearly following Principle F: they were careful not to interrupt the main clause with a relative clause.

The earliest relative clauses Limber recorded were attached to empty nouns like **kind**, **one**, or **thing**. But they were attached without any relative pronoun: the children simply juxtaposed two clauses, as in **There's the thing I saw** and **Look at the ones Mommy got**. This goes against the prediction made by Operating Principle B since the relative clauses (**I saw** and **Mommy got**) are not overtly marked as relatives. It is possible that at this early stage, children have not yet identified any device to mark relativization. Within a month or two, they begin to use the relative pronoun **that** and to attach relative clauses to nouns like **ball**, **chair**, and **dog** (e.g., **See the ball that I got**). **Who** and **which** did not appear as relative pronouns until several months later, after being used as WH- words in WH- questions. With utterances like **See the ball that I got**, the children conformed to Operating Principle B (overt marking) as well as Principle F (no interruptions).

These predictions receive further support from data on children's imitations of relative clause constructions. Slobin and Welsh (1973) asked a child called Echo to imitate sentences containing relatives that interrupted the main clause. Some of these appear on the left of Table 9–6. Echo's imitations provide strong support for Principle F since she consistently avoided interrupting the main clause. Either she left out the relative clause and reproduced only the main clause, as in her imitation of 1 in Table 9–6 (see also C. Smith, 1970); or she reproduced the original sentence as two clauses coordinated by **and**, as in 2 through 5 of Table 9–6.

The principle of overt marking (Operating Principle B) also showed up very clearly in Echo's imitations. Most of the relative clauses she imitated were overtly marked as relatives by **who** or **that**, but on several occasions Slobin and Welsh gave her some where the pronoun had been omitted, as in 22 and 23 with the relative clauses in italics:

22. The boy *the book hit* was crying.

23. The house *the boy hit* was big.

Except for the absence of relative pronouns, 22 and 23 have the same structure as Sentences 4 and 5 in Table 9–6, sentences that Echo appeared to understand

TABLE 9–6
SOME IMITATIONS OF RELATIVE CLAUSES

ADULT MODEL	ECHO'S IMITATION (AGED 2;4)
1. Mozart who cried came to my party*	→ Mozart came to my party
2. Mozart who cried came to my party	→ Mozart cried and he came to my party
3. The owl who eats candy runs fast	→ Owl eat a candy and he run fast
4. The man who I saw yesterday got wet	→ I saw the man and he got wet
5. The man who I saw yesterday runs fast	→ I saw the man and he run fast

* Mozart is the name of the child's bear.
Based on Slobin and Welsh (1973).

perfectly. Her imitations of 22 and 23, however, were usually incoherent and she had clearly not understood the originals:

22'. Boy the book was crying.

23'. Boyhouse was big.

H. Brown (1971) also found that relative clauses were hard for children to recognize unless they were marked by relative pronouns; four- and five-year-olds did much better in a comprehension test when the relative clauses were introduced by relative markers like **that** (see also Chapter 2).

Adverbial Clauses

Some relative clauses, commonly called adverbial clauses, modify the main verb rather than a noun phrase. Some examples of these are listed in 24–27:

24. When they were small, they lived in the mountains.

25. He opened the door before he turned on the lights.

26. He put on his coat because he was cold.

27. If you fall off, you'll hurt yourself.

Each adverbial can be paraphrased in the form of a prepositional phrase introducing a relative clause. **When**, for example, can be paraphrased as "at the time at which," **before** as "before the time at which," **because** as "for the reason that," and **if** as "on condition that." Adverbial clauses can move around more freely than relatives attached to noun phrases. Most of them can either follow or precede the main clause they go with, although some tend to be used more in one position than the other. **Because** adverbials, for instance, usually follow the main clause, while **if** and **when** tend to precede it (Quirk et al., 1972).

Since adverbial clauses are always overtly marked by conjunctions and almost never interrupt main clauses, there are no cases of mismatch with Operating Principles B (Look for grammatical markers) and F (Avoid interruption). However, there are two other principles that do make predictions about the acquisition of adverbial clauses. The first of these is closely related to an adult strategy discussed earlier (see Chapter 2, Strategy 7):

Assume the first clause is the main clause.

This principle predicts that adverbial clauses that follow the main clause (as in 25 or 26) should be easier to acquire than adverbials that precede the main clause (as in 24 or 27). The second principle children seem to use is the principle of order of mention (see Chapter 2, Strategy 13):

Look for the first of two clauses to describe the first of two events, and the second clause the second event.

This principle derives from the "order of mention contract" (Chapter 3):

Mention two events in the order in which they occurred.

The second principle predicts that children should find constructions where order of mention is the same as order of occurrence (as in 24 or 25) easier to understand than constructions where order of mention doesn't follow order of occurrence (as in 26). This principle also predicts that, in production, children should begin by trying to describe events in their order of occurrence.

In accordance with these principles, the first adverbial clauses children use are consistently attached to the end of the main clause (E. Clark, 1970a, 1973c). The top half of Table 9–7 lists some typical examples from three-year-olds. Children soon begin to use some adverbial clauses in first position as well, preceding the main clause (see Table 9–7B). The commonest conjunctions, starting with the most frequent, are **when**, **if**, and **'cos** (because). Only a few children used **before**, **till** (until), and **after** at this stage.

The main-clause-first principle takes precedence over order of mention. Prior to using adverbial clauses, children describe events in their order of occurrence, with a separate sentence for each event or else a series of clauses joined by **and** or **and then** (E. Clark, 1973c). This reliance on order of mention gives way to the main-clause-first principle with the first adverbial clauses. Later on, children start to use adverbial clauses in first position as well and thus regain the option of using an order of mention that coincides with the order of occurrence. This pattern of acquisition appears to hold for each new conjunction children acquire.

Children also rely on the order of mention principle in comprehension. When E. Clark (1971) asked children between 3;0 and 5;0 to act out a series of

TABLE 9–7

ADVERBIAL CLAUSES

Adverbial clauses in the speech of three-year-olds.

CONJUNCTION	UTTERANCE
A. When	I was crying *when* my mummy goed away.
	I'll pick it up *when* I've made this. [book on floor]
If	Somebody will paint them *if* we leave them up there.
	You'll have to knock at the door *if* you want to get in.
'Cos (because)	Take it off *'cos* I'm going to paint on it. [wants clean paper put on easel]
	They can't come here *'cos* we're sweeping up.
Before	We'd better get down *before* she comes.
Till	I'll leave the shapes *till* I put this away.
After	You can have one of my shoes *after* I've finished. [dressing up]
B. When	*When* I've cut out something, I know how to flatten it again. [clay]
	When I was a baby, I got washed in a basin.
If	*If* you're bad, I'll not bring them back.

Based on E. Clark (1970a, 1973c).

two events with toys, the young children found the task much easier after hearing descriptions like 28a and 28b than they did with 28c or 28d:

28. a. The boy patted the dog before he kicked the rock.
    b. After the boy patted the dog, he kicked the rock.
    c. Before the boy kicked the rock, he patted the dog.
    d. The boy kicked the rock after he patted the dog.

When the order of mention coincided with the order of occurrence, as in 28a and 28b, the younger children responded correctly 93 percent of the time. But when the order of mention did not coincide with the order of occurrence, as in 28c and 28d, they responded correctly only 18 percent of the time. Older children were able to pay attention to the conjunctions, and by the age of five or six, most of them understood the order of the events correctly for all four types of description (see also H. L. Johnson, 1975).

Children acquiring other languages such as French and German also rely heavily on the order of mention principle. In comprehension tasks, they make the same mistakes as children acquiring English and treat the first clause in each sentence as if it described the first event (Ferreiro, 1971; Schöler, 1975).

Complements

Complements of various kinds can replace the empty noun **something** in sentences like **I want something** (Chapter 1). The main verb **want**, for example, could be followed by the complements, in italics, in 29:

> 29. a. I want *to go home*.
>   b. I want *Bill to go home*.

In 29a, the subject of the complement verb **go** is the same as the subject of the main verb, but in 29b, the subjects of **go** and **want** are different. In both sentences, however, the subject of the complement verb is the most recent noun phrase before the verb in the complement: **I** in 29a and **Bill** in 29b. The subject of any complement following a verb like **want** is the nearest noun phrase to the left. This general rule has been called the *minimal-distance principle* (C. Chomsky, 1969). It works for many English verbs, but not for all.

Children seem to apply two general operating principles in the acquisition of complement structures. They look for grammatical markers that indicate the underlying semantic relations (Principle B) with markers like **that, for . . . to**, or a WH-word, and they avoid exceptions: they begin by assuming that all complements work the same way (Principle C). In addition to these general principles, children rely heavily on the minimal-distance principle to identify the subjects of complement verbs: they consistently choose the most recent noun phrase before the verb, for example, **I** in 29a and **Bill** in 29b. Because they want to avoid exceptions, they treat all complements alike and apply the minimal-distance principle everywhere. Complements that are clearly marked as complements, therefore, should be acquired before those that are not, and complements that conform to the minimal-distance principle should be acquired before those that don't.

The earliest complements in children's speech conform to the minimal-distance principle. Limber (1973) noted that children between 2;6 and 3;0 typically started by using verbs that could have either a noun phrase or a complement as their object. One such verb is **want**, which in the earliest utterances appeared only with noun phrase objects: **Want juice, Me want ball**. The first complement structures used with **want** tended to have the same subject for the main verb and the complement, for instance, **I want to go out**, and hence automatically conformed to the minimal-distance principle. By the age of three, the children used a variety of verbs with complements including **want, hope, make, guess, like, show**, and **remember**. The complements continued to conform to the minimal-distance principle, as in **I don't want you read that book, Watch me draw circles, I see you sit down**, and **Lookit a boy play ball**.

Most of these early complements also conformed to Operating Principle B. They were overtly marked as complements by **to** or a WH- word like **what**, for example, **I want to get out, Look what I got**. However, when the subject of the complement was different from the subject of the main verb, the children often left out the complement marker, as in **I don't want you read that book** (with

Child acting out instructions like: **Donald promises Bozo to stand on the book. Make him do it.**

to omitted) or **I guess she's sick** (with optional **that** omitted). This suggests that other factors may override Principle B in production. For example, children may try to avoid interruptions in the complement itself and therefore prefer to omit **to**, as in **you read that book**. But even so, Principle B plays a very important role in comprehension.

Several investigators have looked at how children interpret different complement structures, particularly those that do *not* conform to the minimal-distance principle. Since the minimal-distance principle applies to most verbs of communication (e.g., **say, tell, order, command**), C. Chomsky (1969) predicted that children would also apply it to verbs like **promise**. Compare 30 and 31:

30. Kevin told Will to go out.

31. Kevin promised Will to go out.

In 30 it is the nearest noun phrase (**Will**) that is the subject of the complement verb, but in 31, it is the subject of **promise** (the farthest noun phrase) that is the subject of the verb in the complement. Chomsky therefore predicted that children would begin by assuming, for 31, that **Will** was the subject of **go out**.

Chomsky tested this prediction by asking children to make toys called Donald and Bozo do various actions. The instructions appeared with either **tell** or **promise**, as shown in this typical dialogue between Peter, aged 6;9, and Chomsky herself:

TABLE 9–8

WHEN **ASK** IS TREATED LIKE **TELL**

Errors in children's interpretations are in italics.

| COMPLEMENT WITH ASK | I | INTERPRETATION STAGE | | | |
		II	III	IV	V
Ask X what time it is.	*tell*	ask	ask	ask	ask
Ask X his last name.	*tell*	*tell*	ask	ask	ask
Ask X what to feed the doll.	*tell*	*tell*	*tell*	ask*	ask

* Ask was treated as a question at this stage, but children assigned the wrong subject to the complement verb, and asked: **What are *you* going to feed the doll?** instead of **What should *I* feed the doll?**

Based on C. Chomsky (1969).

Adult: Donald tells Bozo to hop across the table. Can you make him hop?
Peter: [making Bozo hop] Bozo, hop across the table.
Adult: Bozo promises Donald to do a somersault. Can you make him do it?
Peter: [making *Donald* do the somersault] I promised you you can do a somersault.
Adult: Would you say that again?
Peter: I promised you you could do a somersault.

Peter's interpretation of the complement of **tell** was quite correct, but when it came to **promise**, he made the wrong toy—Donald—do the somersault. He treated **promise** as if it too conformed to the minimal-distance principle. What he clearly didn't realize yet was that the person making a promise is the one who has to carry it out. Few children under eight succeeded on instructions with the verb **promise**.

The verb **ask** (a question) behaves like **promise**. It doesn't conform to the minimal-distance principle either. In 32, for example, the subject of the complement verb **do** is the same as the subject of **ask**, as shown in 32′:

32. Kevin asked Will what to do.

32′. Kevin asked Will: What shall I do?

If children apply the minimal-distance principle to the complement of **ask**, as in 32, they should come up with the wrong subject for **do**—**you** rather than **I**—because **Will** (the person addressed) is the nearest noun phrase before the complement. Chomsky therefore asked each child the following series of questions with either **ask** or **tell**:

33. a. Ask Chris [another child] what time it is.
    b. Tell Chris what time it is.

34. a. Ask Chris her last name.
    b. Tell Chris your last name.

35. a. Ask Chris what to feed the doll.
    b. Tell Chris what to feed the doll.

Chomsky found that children went through five stages, summarized in Table 9–8, before responding appropriately to all six instructions. At the first stage, the youngest children (five-year-olds) consistently treated all the instructions as if they contained **tell**: they told Chris what the time was (33a and 33b), they told Chris her last name (34a) and their own last names (34b), and they told Chris what she should feed the doll next (35a and 35b). The confusion between **tell** and **ask** was gradually sorted out, first for 33 at Stage 2, then for 34 at Stage 3. Next, at Stage 4, children differentiated **ask** from **tell** in 35, but they applied the minimal-distance principle to 35a and consistently asked Chris **What are you going to feed the doll?** instead of **What should I feed the doll?** Finally, at Stage 5, the oldest children (nine- and ten-year-olds) got even 35a correct and responded like adults. One final point: all the children who succeeded with **ask** also succeeded with **promise**, but not the reverse.

Why should the different complements with **ask** be mastered in the order they are? Here is where Operating Principle B (Look for grammatical markers) seems to play a part. The complements in 33 and 35 are both clearly marked as complements by the WH- word **what**, but both 34 and 35 have been condensed. The complement in 34a, for example, is a condensed version of **Ask Chris what her last name is**, a structure identical to 33a. The complement in 35a has also been condensed so as to omit the subject of **feed**. A priori, there is no reason to expect the complement in 35a to cause children more difficulty than the one in 34a, but there is a second factor here as well. The minimal-distance principle cannot possibly be applied to 33a or 34a, but it can to 35a even though it should not be. And, as Chomsky's study showed, children did apply it there and got the subject wrong. The complement in 35a, then, seems to be the most difficult, one, because it lacks explicit markers, and two, because children have to learn *not* to apply the minimal-distance principle (see also Cromer, 1970).

Although children begin to elaborate the structure of their utterances very early in acquisition, the elaboration is rather slow. Eight or ten years is probably an underestimate of the time children require to master the structures of their first language. From the age of two and a half or three, they begin to combine propositions into single sentences through coordination, relativization, and complementation. But they use only a limited number of devices to express the link between two ideas, the modification of one idea by another, or the filling in of an idea. The operating principles children apply to language lead them first to acquire those structures that fit their operating principles, for instance, structures that show a clear relation between grammatical markers and underlying semantic relations, structures that do not interrupt other linguistic units, and structures that fit regular rules. It takes much longer to acquire structures that do not conform to these general operating principles.

ELABORATIONS OF LANGUAGE FUNCTION

Just as children elaborate language structure, so they also elaborate language function. With function, the problem is that different structures can be used with the same function and different functions can be conveyed by means of the same structure. Compare the directives (requests) in 36 with the representatives (assertions) in 37:

36. a. Can I have some chocolate ice cream?
    b. Chocolate ice cream tastes really good.

37. a. I did a somersault.
    b. Did you see me do a somersault?

In 36a, the interrogative conveys a request but in 37b it conveys an assertion. Similarly, the statement in 36b can be used to convey a request while the statement in 37a conveys an assertion. Although structure and function go hand in hand, there is rarely a one-to-one relationship between them. Some speech acts are direct, as in 36a or 37a, and others are indirect, as in 36b and 37b (see Chapter 3). Children are exposed to both from very early on. Holzman (1974) found that mothers used almost as many indirect as direct requests when talking to their children.

Children at the two-word stage seem to use only two types of speech acts: representatives, such as **That Mommy** or **Doggie bark**, and directives, such as **More milk** or **Want cookie** (Chapter 8). And they have only a limited repertoire of structures for expressing these speech acts. Over the next few years they add enormously to this repertoire and expand it to include other speech acts too. By six or seven, they know several ways of conveying threats and promises (both commissive speech acts) and they also use a number of expressives, like **Thank you** or **I'm sorry**. However, it is still very rare to find them using any explicit performative verbs such as **tell**, **order**, or **promise** to introduce the relevant speech act. And it is rarer still to hear children of this age making declarations such as **I quit**.

Speech Acts

Children elaborate their speech acts along two dimensions. First of all, as they get older they add new types of speech acts to their repertoire. They start off with representatives and directives, and then add commissives and expressives, with declarations coming in last of all. Second, they constantly add new ways of expressing each speech act both directly and indirectly. These two dimensions will be explored in turn.

Directives and Commissives

Grimm (1975a) used an ingenious technique to elicit various directives—asking, ordering, forbidding, and permitting—and a commissive—promising. She told

TABLE 9–9

SPEECH ACTS IN CONTEXT

Percentages of adequate utterances for speech acts required in context.

| AGE | ask | DIRECTIVES: | | permit | COMMISSIVE: |
		order	forbid		promise
5;0–5;6	82	92	86	51	57
7;0–7;6	95	92	93	86	55

Based on Grimm (1975a).

children of five and seven a brief story designed to get them to convey particular speech acts to Felix, a large toy cat for whom the experimenter acted as mouthpiece. To get a child to *ask* for something, for example, Grimm used the story in 38:

38. You are at a playground with Felix. He is sitting on the swing and you're sitting on the slide. Now you'd like Felix to let you swing too. What do you say to Felix?

To get a child to *forbid* something, she used the story in 39:

39. You want to visit someone and you've put on your best clothes. Felix is smearing paint all over and would like to smear some on you too. You don't want him to put paint on you. What do you say to Felix?

At each attempt to get Felix to comply with the directives, Felix refuses with increasing emphasis until the child has produced four versions of the relevant speech act. A dialogue typical of those that followed 38 is shown in 40:

40. *Child:* Felix, will you let me swing too, just once, please?
    Felix: I don't want you to swing.
    Child: But then you can slide down the slide.
    Felix: I'd rather not let you swing.
    Child: I'd like to swing once too, not you all the time.
    Felix: I'd still rather not let you swing.
    Child: But you must!

Grimm found that five-year-olds managed very well when asking Felix for something, ordering him to do something, and forbidding him to do something, but they had some difficulty producing suitable utterances for permitting Felix to do something. This shows that not all directives are equally easy: five-year-olds still have something to learn about how to convey permission. They also had considerable difficulty with the commissive. Only 57 percent of the utterances meant to be promises were adequate to convey that speech act. As Table 9–9 shows, the seven-year-olds did rather better. They managed very well on all four directives—asking, ordering, forbidding, and permitting—but they still had a lot of difficulty in making promises.

One difference between directives and commissives that might help explain Grimm's findings is that directives place an obligation on the listener whereas commissives place one on the speaker. With directives, the listener is expected to answer a question, carry out some action, or refrain from some action. The speaker, therefore, has simply to wait for the listener's response. With commissives, however, the speaker places *himself* under an obligation. When he makes a promise, *he* is the one who is expected to carry it out, *not* his listener (see Chapter 6). Grimm's results suggest that children find it much easier to work out the conditions under which the listener is expected to do something than the conditions under which the speaker is. For some reason, the speech acts that place an obligation on the speaker all tend to be acquired later than those that place the obligation on the listener.

These findings fit in fairly well with the comprehension studies of directives and commissives. C. Chomsky (1969), for example, found that children understood **tell**, a directive, long before they understood **promise**, a commissive. In fact, children under eight often assumed that the verb **promise** was a directive and consistently took what was promised as something for the listener to do:

> *Adult:* Bozo promises Donald to do a somersault. Can you make him do it?
> *Child:* [making *Donald* do the somersault] I promised you you can do a somersault.

Grimm and Schöler (1975), in a similar experiment with German-speaking children, found that directives like **order** and **allow** were better understood by children of seven than the commissive **promise**. The mistake children usually made was to ask their listeners to do something rather than doing it themselves, as speakers.

Expressives and Declarations

After representatives, directives, and commissives, children still have to acquire expressives and declarations. Expressives constitute one part of language that adults seem to teach by rote. Once children reach the age of two or three, their parents begin to insist they say **Please, Thank you, You're welcome, I'm sorry,** and so on in the appropriate social contexts. Expressives place no obligations on either speaker or listener, but they are often essential to the smooth functioning of society. They may or may not reflect the speaker's feelings about someone or something, but they express the feeling expected within a particular society for that particular situation. As such, expressives are often hard to explain or justify to small children, and parents don't usually try. Their concern is usually a purely social one: **Say "Please" to your grandmother, Have you said "Thank you" to your uncle?, I hope you said "I'm sorry" to Mr. Stone**, and so on (Berko Gleason, 1973; Berko Gleason and Weintraub, 1976). As a result, it is usually many years before children fully understand the social role of expressives.

The few studies available suggest that the different types of speech acts are acquired in the following order: representatives and directives, then commissives, then expressives, then declarations. This order is necessarily tentative, but it is supported so far by studies of both production and comprehension.

Indirect Speech Acts

But what of the actual devices children use to convey these speech acts? Very little attention has been paid to this. Children seem to use positive or negative statements for their assertions from very early on, but as they get older, they must also learn how to convey assertions less directly and how to indicate the strength of their belief in the fact asserted. They learn to assert something indirectly by attributing it to someone else, as in **Martin said it was snowing**, or by asking a question, **Did you know it was snowing?** They also begin to hedge what they assert and even at four will "soften" their claims by saying **I think the piece fits here** rather than **That piece fits here** (see Gelman and Shatz, 1976).

The requests young children make are usually direct, but as they get older, they use more and more indirect ones as well (Ervin-Tripp, 1974, 1977). Garvey (1975), for example, found that both four- and five-year-olds used direct requests like **Give me the hammer** or **Don't touch my car**. And both could justify their requests, e.g., **Stop it—you hurt my head** or **Gimme, gimme that—I need it**. Five-year-olds, though, used over twice as many indirect requests as four-year-olds. Some examples are given in 41 and 42:

41. *Child A:* Wanta get on my new car? Wanta get on my new car? Want to?
    Child B: Oh, I'm coming. [climbs on car without enthusiasm]

42. *Child A:* Why don't you tickle me?
    Child B: Okay. [does so]

In 41, A makes the indirect request by asking B whether he wants to do something, and in 42, A asks if B has a reason for not doing something—both classic devices for making indirect requests.

Grimm (1975a) found that the trend continued with even older children. Seven-year-olds, for example, would *permit* someone to swing by saying **I don't mind your swinging** where five-year-olds simply said **You can swing**. And when *forbidding* someone to swing, seven-year-olds would say **I'd rather you didn't swing** while five-year-olds would say baldly **You MUSTN'T swing**. The older children were also more likely to offer reasons why one should or shouldn't do something and to use words like **please**. In reporting similar findings for Italian children, Bates (1974, 1976) also examined their judgments about the different degrees of politeness implicit in the uses of different structures. **Could you give me a candy?** and **Please could I have a candy?**, for example, are both considered more polite (in English and Italian) than **Give me a candy**. While three-year-olds knew which one was more polite only about 50 percent of the time, six-year-olds knew 80 percent of the time. In effect, the older children usually picked the most indirect form of request as the politest one.

Even less is known about the expression of other types of speech acts—commissives, expressives, and declarations. If children follow the same route they appear to follow in the acquisition of representatives and directives, the number of devices they use to convey a speech act should increase as they acquire more sentence structures. The expression of different speech acts clearly goes hand in hand with the acquisition of syntax.

Thematic Information

At the one- and two-word stage children use focal stress to indicate what is new information in their utterances. But as their repertoire of language structures expands, they begin to indicate what is given and what new in other ways as well. They begin to use the definite and indefinite articles—**the** and **a**—and they also show increasing evidence of both producing and understanding a variety of different sentence structures that can be combined with focal stress to convey given and new information.

First and Second Mention

Roughly speaking, adults use the indefinite article **a** to introduce new information and the definite article **the** for given information (Chapter 3). One result of this distinction is that in conversation, the first mention of something is usually marked by use of the indefinite article, while subsequent mentions have the definite one, as in 43:

> 43. *Speaker A:* I saw a man on the roof yesterday.
> *Speaker B:* Well?
> *Speaker A:* The man climbed all the way up to mend those tiles that fell off.

Children begin to use **the** and **a** soon after the two-word stage (see Table 9–3), and by age three or so, most of them seem to use the articles where adults would. But several investigators have found that their pattern of usage for **the** and **a** is different from the adult one. Children overuse the definite article at the expense of the indefinite one. In other words, they seem to treat some information as given that ought to be treated as new for their listeners.

TABLE 9–10

FIRST AND SECOND MENTION

Percentage of definite and indefinite articles used in a storytelling context.

AGE	FIRST MENTION: Definite	Indefinite	SECOND MENTION: Definite	Indefinite
3 years	54	46	92	8
5 years	38	62	90	10
7 years	39	61	100	0
9 years	18	82	100	0
adults	0	100	100	0

Based on Warden (1976).

Warden (1976), for example, got children between three and nine to tell each other a short story while seated at opposite ends of a table with a screen across the middle. The story each child told was based on a sequence of three cartoon pictures, visible only to the storyteller:

Each child was expected to use the indefinite **a** with his first mention of each new object in the pictures, and the definite article with subsequent mentions since the objects would then be given information for the listener.

Warden's findings are summarized in Table 9–10. In contexts that called for the definite **the**, with second mention, he found virtually no differences between three-year-olds and adults telling the story. But in contexts that called for the indefinite **a**, with first mention, he found that three-year-olds used **the** 54 percent of the time (see also Maratsos, 1974, 1976). Even nine-year-olds sometimes made the mistake of using **the** with the first mention of an object. The conventions for using the indefinite article for first mentions in a conversation or a story, then, seem to take a long time for children to work out.

Children acquiring French seem to have much the same difficulty in acquiring the indefinite article. The French system is even further complicated by having several forms of the article: **un** or **une** for the singular and **des** for the plural. Bresson and his colleagues found that six-year-olds used the definite article, **le** or **la**, instead of **un** or **une** 38 percent of the time where adults always used the indefinite article. With the plural form of the indefinite **des** they did even worse and used the definite article **les** instead 76 percent of the time (Bresson, 1974; Bresson, Bouvier, Dannequin, Depreux, Hardy, and Platone, 1970).

In consistently overusing the definite article for information that is actually new to their listeners children incorrectly assume that whatever is known to them is also known to their listeners and can therefore be presented as given. This failure to take listeners fully into account is nothing new. When children acquiring English first start to talk, they tend to pick out what is new for them as speakers, rather than what is new for their listeners (Chapter 8). They take their own point of view as speakers in much the same way when they begin to use **the** and **a**.

Focal Stress and Sentence Structure

With their increase in knowledge about language structure, children can begin to combine focal stress with different syntactic structures to convey given and new information. But when do children become aware that subjects of sentences, for example, usually coincide with given information and predicates with what is new? At age four they still seem to rely mainly on focal stress to indicate what is new and make little attempt to manipulate syntactic structure in presenting thematic information (Hornby and Hass, 1970). For example, they usually opt for 44 with stress on the new information in the subject rather than 45 where the new information appears in the predicate:

44. The BOY picked up the ball.

45. The ball was picked up by the BOY.

By seven, however, children seem to be aware that, in English, subject and predicate usually convey given and new information respectively. To establish this, Hornby, Hass, and Feldman (1970) asked five- and seven-year-olds to change sentences like 46 into their opposites:

46. The man is running across the field.

They reasoned that making a sentence into its opposite was analogous to negating it. And a negation always applies to the new information, not to what is given (Chapter 3). Five-year-olds, they found, were just as likely to change the information in the subject (e.g., changing **the man** to **the woman**) as they were information in the predicate. But seven-year-olds always changed words in the predicate (e.g., **run** to **walk**, **field** to **road**)—part of the new information.

Hornby (1971) also looked at children's understanding of the relationship of given and new information to various syntactic structures. To do this, he showed six-, eight-, and ten-year-olds pairs of pictures like the following:

A.   B.

and asked them which picture he was talking about when, for example, he said 46:

46. The one who is riding the horse is the boy.

Since 46 didn't fit either picture completely, Hornby assumed that the children would choose whichever one matched the given information in 46. Thus, if the children took as given the fact that the boy was riding something, they should choose Picture A, but if they took as given the fact that someone was riding the horse, they should choose Picture B. One problem with this technique is that children may not necessarily use what they think is given when they choose one of the two pictures. Hornby used several types of sentences with each pair of pictures so as to vary the order of given and new information and the syntactic structure that accompanied focal stress. Some of the sentences used with the pictures are shown in 47:

47. a. The horse is being ridden by the boy. (*passive*)
    b. It is the boy that is riding the horse. (*cleft*)
    c. The one who is riding the horse is the boy. (*pseudo-cleft*)

In each instance it is given that someone is riding the horse. This information matches Picture B. After the children had chosen a picture, Hornby asked them to tell him what he should have said about the picture they chose. In this way, he was able to look at some of the syntactic structures they themselves might use to convey given and new information.

Children were more likely to use the given information of a sentence in choosing a picture as they got older. On sentences like 47c, six-year-olds chose Picture B, which matched the given information, almost as often as ten-year-olds, but on sentences like 47a and 47b, the older children chose Picture B much more often than the younger ones. Ten-year-olds also did better than six-year-olds on active sentences like 48:

48. The boy is riding the horse.

In fact, 48 was the hardest kind of sentence for all the children when it came to choosing between two pictures. This should not be surprising since the thematic information in 48 can be divided up in several ways. The whole event can be new (in answer to the question, **What's happening?**), the action can be new (**What is the boy doing?**), or the object affected by the action can be new (**What is the boy riding?**). Even the oldest children chose the subject (**the boy**) as given only 61 percent of the time.

When the children were asked to "correct" Hornby's description of the picture they had chosen, 93 percent relied on focal stress to indicate new information in the sentences they offered as descriptions. Regardless of age, they indicated given and new information appropriately in over 90 percent of their "corrections." From the younger children, most corrections consisted of simple active sentences with stress on the new information whether it was in the subject, verb, or object. The ten-year-olds used more passive sentences, like 47a, than the younger children did:

47. a. The horse is being ridden by the boy.

And both eight- and ten-year-olds used more cleft and pseudo-cleft sentences— like 47b and 47c—than did the six-year-olds:

47. b. It is the boy that is riding the horse.
    c. The one who is riding the horse is the boy.

The older children, then, seemed to possess a larger repertoire of sentence types for the expression of given and new information. But the younger ones made good use of their more limited means and nearly always conveyed given and new information appropriately.

As children add to their stock of sentence structures, they acquire more and more ways of setting off what is given information from what is new. The new information still carries focal stress, but it can either precede or follow the given information, and it can appear in a variety of different syntactic structures. Precisely how and when children relate these different syntactic structures to given and new information remains to be discovered. Again, it is a place where the elaboration of function goes hand in hand with the elaboration of structure.

SUMMARY

Once past the two-word stage, children begin to elaborate both the structure and function of their first language. In the case of language structure, they start to add function words and word endings to "fill in" their utterances, combine two or more propositions in a single sentence to express negation and ask questions, use relative clauses to modify one idea by another, and use complement structures to fill in ideas. These elaborations seem to follow a route laid down by the operating principles children bring to language. They first learn those structures that conform to their operating principles and only later acquire more complex structures that do not fit them.

Children also elaborate language function. They extend their repertoire of speech acts beyond representatives and directives to commissives and expressives. They also add to their repertoire for conveying each speech act and learn how to express them indirectly in more and more ways. As they get older, they also become more sensitive to what their listener knows when deciding what to present as given and what as new. For example, their earlier overuse of the definite article **the** gives way to a more precise use of the definite article for what is given and the indefinite article **a** for what is new. Within each utterance, children also start to combine focal stress on new information with an increasing number of different sentence structures to convey even more precisely what is given and what is new information.

Children have to build up structure and function at the same time. As they learn more about structure, they acquire more devices with which to convey different functions. And as they learn more about function, they extend the uses to which different structures can be put. But even at age seven or eight, children still have a long way to go. Acquiring a language is a long and complicated process.

Further Reading

A general account of the later stages in language acquisition can be found in Menyuk (1971) and in Bloom and Lahey (1977). Cazden (1972) and Rosen and Rosen (1973) consider various aspects of the language children use in school. R. Brown (1973) contains an excellent discussion of the acquisition of grammatical morphemes. For more complex sentence structures, the reader can consult articles in the collections edited by J. Hayes (1970), Flores d'Arcais and Levelt (1970), Ferguson and Slobin (1973), Moore (1973), and Bloom (1977). C. Chomsky's (1969) monograph provides a very readable account of her comprehension studies. The operating principles children seem to use in the acquisition of language structure have been discussed in some detail by Slobin (1973, 1975). J. Sinclair and Coulthard (1975) present an analysis of language functions used by children and teachers in the classroom. It follows on, to some extent, from Halliday's (1975) discussion of language function in very young children.

Father: What does [maus] mean?
Child: Like a cat.
Father: Yes: what else?
Child: Nothing else.
Father: It's part of you.
Child: (disbelief)
Father: It's part of your head.
Child: (fascinated)
Father: (touching child's mouth) What's this?
Child: [maus]

Neilson Smith

10

First Sounds in the Child's Language

In the dialogue above, between a father and his four-year-old son (N. Smith, 1973), the child is being asked to identify the phonetic sequence [maus]. Although the child himself pronounces both **mouse** and **mouth** as [maus], he identifies his father's [maus] only with **mouse** ("Like a cat"). Why? Imagine that the child has different mental representations for **mouse** and **mouth**, and therefore recognizes the difference when he hears them pronounced. Yet he himself can't pronounce -th and usually says -s instead. This would explain why he doesn't recognize [maus] as **mouth** when his father says it. At this stage, the child's pronunciation seems to be less well developed than his perception.

The exchange between father and son illustrates a central issue in children's acquisition of the sound system: the nature of the relation between speech as they perceive it and the speech that they themselves can produce. For adults, perception and production are assumed to be closely linked: adult listeners rely on their own representation of the phonetic form of a word to recognize it in the speech of others, and when speaking themselves try to match their production to the same representation so that their listeners will recognize what they are saying. For example, the adult quoted above pronounces the word **mouse** differently from **mouth**, and these two pronunciations match two different representations, one for each word. And since the child also distinguishes **mouse** from **mouth** in the speech of others, he too must have distinct representations for these two words. But at this stage, he has only one pronunciation: both words are [maus].

What, then, is the relation between children's representations of a word and their own pronunciations of it? Are their representations based directly on adult pronunciations, and if so, how close are they? Do their representations change over time? And how do they use their representations of words when they themselves try to pronounce them? The answers to these questions all hinge on the relationship between what children can perceive and what they can say. This chapter takes up both sides in the acquisition of the sound system: first the *perception* and then the *production* of speech.

PERCEPTION OF SPEECH SOUNDS

In the course of acquisition children learn to recognize the sounds of their language. To do this, they must first distinguish the sounds made by human voices from other sounds. Next they must detect differences between the sounds humans produce. Finally, they must identify those sounds that are important for the language they are acquiring and work out which sounds can be combined with which.

How do children manage such a complicated task? First, they build on what they already know and can do. They only begin to discriminate differences between sounds, for example, after they have learned to pick out human voices. And they have to be able to discriminate differences before they can begin to identify particular sounds and sequences of sounds. Second, they tend to begin with the simplest distinctions. For example, they learn to discriminate consonants from vowels before they learn to discriminate among consonants or vowels. They learn to perceive more complex distinctions later.

Children apply the same procedures to intonation and stress as they do to sounds or phonetic segments. They build on what they learned to perceive at an earlier stage. They have to discriminate differences between intonation contours or stress patterns before they can learn to identify them. They learn the simplest intonations and stress patterns first and may take many years to master the more complex details of these suprasegmental properties of the sound system.

Precursors to Speech Perception

Infants attend to speech sounds, or at least to the human voice, very early indeed. By the age of two weeks, they seem to be capable of distinguishing the human voice from other sounds—from bells, rattles, and whistles, for instance. They will stop crying if someone speaks, but not if someone rings a bell or shakes a rattle (Wolff, 1966). But what is it that infants discriminate when they stop crying? Are they attending to the frequency range of the human voice? To the intonational contour superimposed on what is said? Or are there particular acoustic properties they are sensitive to? Ultimately, they have to learn to perceive differences between speech sounds, and there is evidence that they can do this well before they learn to talk. The ability to discriminate differences is a prerequisite for the acquisition of specific speech sounds from twelve months on.

Most studies of what very young children perceive about speech have depended on observations of what they seem to attend to at different ages (E. Kaplan and Kaplan, 1970). One of the first things is the location of sounds: infants turn their heads toward the source of a sound within the first few days of birth. Within a couple of weeks, they seem to discriminate voices from other sounds. By about two months, they seem to respond differentially to the emotional quality of human voices: angry voices tend to induce crying while friendly ones elicit smiling and cooing. By four months, they seem able to distinguish male and female voices, and at six months or so, observers have claimed, they begin to pay attention to intonation and rhythm in speech since they then start to produce babbled sequences of sound with a melodic contour.

Researchers have devised ingenious ways of studying the infant's ability to discriminate sounds. Some have used a non-nutritive sucking measure of the following kind: Infants are given a nipple to suck on that contains a recording device to measure their rate of sucking. Then they are played a sound over and over again until their sucking rate stabilizes. Then the sound is changed. If they notice the change, their sucking rate increases abruptly and then gradually slows down again as they get used to the new sound. This technique has been widely used to study which changes in speech sounds very young infants can perceive.

As described in Chapter 5, adults are able to place speech sounds in discrete categories. For example, they can pay attention to the acoustic cue of Voice Onset Time, the time between a stop being released and the vocal cords starting to vibrate, and classify it as the phonetic feature [+ voice] or [− voice]. The question is whether infants pay attention to the same acoustic cues and, if they do, whether they divide them into categories in the same way adults do. If so, one might say that children have "built-in feature detectors," that is, their perceptual apparatus is designed to discriminate certain sounds, sounds that adults use as part of the sound system of the language.

Eimas and his colleagues (1971), using the non-nutritive sucking technique, showed that one-month-old infants could discriminate between two syllables that differed only on the feature of voicing in the consonant sound, [ba] versus [pa]. Moreover, they showed that this discrimination appeared to be categorical. They gave infants two synthetic speech syllables each that differed by 0.02 seconds in voice onset time. For one group, this difference occurred across the boundary of the adult categories [ba] and [pa]. For a second group, this difference occurred within the adult category [ba], and for a third, within the adult category [pa]. If infants make categorical distinctions, only the first group should show an increase in sucking rate when the sound they are listening to is changed—and this was what Eimas and his colleagues found.

When infants discriminate [pa] from [ba], are they doing the same thing as adults? Adults who hear a phonetic segment have a fully developed phonological system to refer to in identifying that segment. This system plays an important role in their discrimination of one segment from another. But one-month-old infants can hardly have acquired much knowledge of this system and cannot be referring to it in discriminating [p] from [b], sounds from two separate adult categories. Eimas (1975) has argued, therefore, that infants must be using feature detectors that are sensitive to certain acoustic properties of speech. These detectors are what allow even one-month-olds to make quasi-categorical discriminations among speech sounds (see also Cutting and Eimas, 1975).

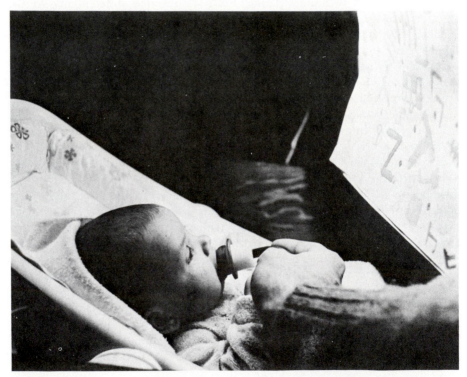

An infant sucking on nipple while listening to a recording of different syllables. The picture keeps the infant's head oriented toward the loudspeaker.

Infants can discriminate not only between such voiced and voiceless segments as [b] and [p], but also between different places of articulation. Morse (1972) examined their ability to discriminate [ba] from [ga]. He also looked at their ability to discriminate between the transitional "chirps"—the onset portions of the syllables [ba] and [ga]—when these were isolated from the rest of the syllable. Infants seven weeks old could discriminate a difference in place of articulation (see also Moffitt, 1971), but when it came to the chirps, the infants, just like adults, failed to make any discriminations. This finding provides further evidence that infants perceive some speech sounds in a quasi-categorical way from very early on. They seem to notice only those differences between two sounds that involve possible category boundaries for adults.

Discrimination is only the first step in learning which differences between sounds are relevant to the acquisition of a particular language. Children have to learn to distinguish just those sounds that play a role in the phonological system —all the phonetic segments that they would expect to hear from adult speakers of the language they are acquiring. Part of this task involves learning which oppositions among sounds are systematic and have to be discriminated, and which can safely be ignored. For example, stops in English contrast on two dimensions: voicing and place of articulation. Voiced [d] is in opposition to voiceless [t], and also in opposition to [b] and [g], segments pronounced at different places of articulation (see Fodor, Garrett, and Brill, 1975).

Phonetic Segments and Sequences

In 1948 Shvachkin published a detailed study of the stages children go through in learning to perceive contrasts between segments in Russian. What he discovered was that children go through systematic stages, mastering what seem to be the simplest contrasts first and more complex ones later. What remains to be discovered is a metric for predicting complexity—from acoustic cues, phonetic properties, or some combination of the two.

Perception of Segments

Shvachkin argued that children learn a sound contrast only when it makes a difference to meaning. To study the acquisition of contrasts, therefore, he taught very young children (aged from ten months up to two years) names for geometric shapes and unusual toys, things for which the children had no names. He first taught them the name of each toy separately, then presented them with two toys whose names contrasted on only one or two features, such as voicing (**bak** versus **pak**) or nasality and manner (**bak** versus **mak**). The names were all nonsense syllables with the form Vowel + Consonant (VC) or Consonant + Vowel + Consonant (CVC). Shvachkin found that the initial position in the word seemed to be most salient, so he used as names syllables in which initial vowels contrasted, as in **ek** and **ok**; syllables in which a vowel contrasted with a consonant, as in **ek** and **mek**; and syllables in which the initial consonants contrasted, as in the pairs **mak-nak**, **mak-bak**, and **dak-tak**. Children's ability to discriminate and recognize the right names was tested by asking them to choose the toy named **bak**, say, in a situation where there were two toys present, **bak** and **mak**. They had to point to, pick up, or move the toy asked for. If they had not already learned that the segment [b] contrasted with [m], say, they should choose the right toy only half the time. The testing itself took place over a period of eight months.

Shvachkin found that children learned to recognize the different oppositions in Russian in a distinct order. The twelve stages he identified have been summarized in Table 10–1. The first distinctions perceived were those among VC syllables, and the children did best in distinguishing [a] from all other initial vowels. Next, they acquired the oppositions between front and back vowels, and between high and low vowels. This progression from a gross distinction ([a] versus all other vowels) to finer and finer ones was also apparent in the consonants. They first distinguished some gross oppositions, for example, the presence versus absence of an initial consonant. This was followed by discrimination of stops and fricatives from nasals, liquids, and glides (see Stage 3). And this in turn was followed by progressively finer distinctions among the remaining consonants. The opposition between voiced and voiceless segments, surprisingly, was one of the last to be acquired (Stage 10). But since the children Shvachkin was working with were mostly under the age of two, this is not really a very late acquisition.

The ordering of the twelve stages shown in Table 10–1 was very consistent from child to child among those children Shvachkin tested, and he concluded that this order of acquisition might well be universal. In fact, it does appear to be very close to the order in which children generally learn to produce the same contrasts (Jakobson, 1968). Any claim about universality, however, must be tested on more than one language.

In follow-up studies of this research, investigators have generally supported Shvachkin, but have reported much more variability across children in their order of acquisition. M. Edwards (1974), for example, found some variation in the acquisition of fricatives and glides in English. She concluded that while the overall order of acquisition tended to be uniform (e.g., stops were acquired before fricatives, and voiceless fricatives before voiced ones), the details for each child might vary considerably. Some children, for example, acquired an opposition for a single pair of segments at a time, rather than for the whole class (see also Garnica, 1973). From Shvachkin's account, it is impossible to tell whether each opposition was tested with only a single pair of segments or with all pairs showing that contrast.

Perception of Sequences

Children not only learn to perceive and identify different phonetic segments, they also learn the phonological rules for combining segments into sequences. Recall that each language allows only certain combinations or sequences within syllables, words, and even at the boundaries between words (Chapter 5). Our knowledge about these phonological rules of English allows us to judge which words

TABLE 10–1

PHONOLOGICAL ACQUISITION

Stages in the acquisition of phonological oppositions for Russian children.

STAGE	OPPOSITION
1a	[a] *vs.* other vowels
1b	[i] *vs.* [u], [e] *vs.* [o], [i] *vs.* [o], [e] *vs.* [u]
1c	[i] *vs.* [e], [u] *vs.* [o]
2	Presence *vs.* absence of initial consonant, e.g., [bok] *vs.* [ok], [ek] *vs.* [vek]
3	Nasals, liquids, and glides *vs.* stops and fricatives e.g., [m] – [b], [r] – [d], [n] – [g], [y] – [v]
4	Palatalized * *vs.* non-palatalized consonants, e.g., [n'] – [n], [b'] – [b], [v'] – [v], [r'] – [r]
5a	Nasals *vs.* liquids and glides, e.g., [m] – [l], [m] – [r], [n] – [l], [n] – [r], [n] – [y], [m] – [y]
5b	Intra-nasal distinctions, e.g., [m] – [n]
5c	Intra-liquid distinctions, e.g., [l] – [r]
6	Nasals, liquids, and glides *vs.* fricatives, e.g., [m] – [z], [n] – [ž]
7	Labials *vs.* non-labials, e.g., [b] – [d], [b] – [g], [v] – [z]
8	Stops *vs.* fricatives, e.g., [b] – [v], [d] – [ž]
9	Alveolars *vs.* velars, e.g., [d] – [g], [t] – [k]
10	Voiced *vs.* voiceless, e.g., [b] – [p], [d] – [t], [g] – [k], [v] – [f], [z] – [s], [ž] – [š]
11	"Hushing" *vs.* "hissing" sibilants e.g., [ž] – [z], [š] – [s]
12	Liquids *vs.* glides, e.g., [r] – [y], [l] – [y]

* Palatalization does not occur as a distinctive opposition in English. Palatalized consonants are pronounced as if very closely followed by an *i*.
Based on Shvachkin (1973).

are possible English words and which are not. For example, as adults, we accept Lewis Carroll's **slithy** and **toves** as possible, but reject sequences like **mvaq** or **dvorn** (Greenberg and Jenkins, 1964). Since children start out not knowing the phonological rules for possible words, they inevitably produce some "impossible" ones. One child used the initial cluster **sr-**, an impossible cluster for

English, at the beginning of words like **thread**, to produce **sred** (N. Smith, 1973). They may also segment words wrongly, as in the following interchange reported by Garnes and Bond (1975):

> Mother: Natives of New Guinea go out lumbering every day.
> Child: What's *tlumbering*, Mommy?

Children presumably learn which sequences are and are not permissible only after they have learned to perceive the phonetic segments of the language they are acquiring.

Children show some evidence of knowing which sequences are possible in English by their fourth year. Messer (1967) looked at the choices made by children between 3;1 and 4;5 of potential names for toys. He presented each child with several pairs of names and, for each pair, asked which name would be better. The names Messer used either conformed or did not conform to the sequence rules for English. For example, in the pairs [klek] – [dlek] and [frul] – [mrul], the first word in each conforms to English, while the second does not. In Messer's study English-speaking children were much more likely to choose possible English sequences than impossible ones. They also tended to mispronounce impossible sequences more often than possible ones in their spontaneous repetitions of what the experimenter said. Their mispronunciations usually changed the impossible sequences minimally but consistently in the direction of possible sequences. For example, the non-English sequence [tšluf] became [šluf] and [škib] became [skib] (see also Menyuk, 1968).

Messer's findings suggest that by their fourth year children have learned at least some of the phonological rules for identifying a sequence of segments as possible in the language they are acquiring. Their recognition not only guides their choices of "names" but also leads them to mispronounce some impossible sequences with predictable distortions—distortions that go in the direction of possible sequences.

Intonation and Stress

It has long been the contention of investigators like M. M. Lewis (1951) that infants perceive intonation—the melody of an utterance—before they learn to perceive phonetic segments. He based his claim on the fact that infants begin to babble with intonation-like rises and falls from about the age of six or eight months. This precedes the production of segments by some six months. Yet the work of Eimas, Morse, and others has shown that infants as young as six weeks can perceive differences between certain segments. This suggests that segmental information *and* intonation may be discriminated very early. In fact, Morse (1972) presented seven-week-old infants with a syllable, [ba], on which he imposed either a rising tone, [ba↑], or a falling one, [ba↓], and found that they were able to detect the difference (see also E. Kaplan, 1969).

Stress

Children probably perceive stress fairly early too, but this is difficult to determine. Diary study reports suggest that it is rare for children between one and three to place primary stress on the wrong syllable in their spontaneous speech, but they may make occasional mistakes with compound words and say **pull-óver**, for example, instead of **púll-over**, where the primary stress is shown by the accent. In general, stressed syllables appear to play an important role in how children first pronounce words in their own speech. Word stress is nearly always correctly reproduced in their imitations of words and whole sentences. This suggests that it must be stored as part of the mental representation for each word. Stress is also used as a device to pick out new information as soon as children begin to combine two or more words (Chapters 8 and 9). By the age of five or so, some word-stress assignments appear to be rule-governed. Berko (1958) found that five-year-olds could produce compound nouns like **bírdcage** and **wúghouse** with primary stress correctly placed on the first word of the compound and tertiary stress on the second word.

However, a study by Atkinson-King (1973) suggests that it may take children many years to learn how to interpret certain contrasting stress patterns, even if they perceive them from very early on. She looked at children's comprehension of "minimal pairs" like **gréenhouse** and **green hoúse**, **hótdog** and **hot dóg**, and **récord** (noun) and **recórd** (verb). She presented children aged five to twelve with two pictures at a time, one of a frankfurter sausage and one of a dog panting, for example, and asked which was the **hótdog**, or which was the **hot dóg**. The five-year-olds did very badly, but the older the children the better they did in choosing the appropriate picture. Five-year-olds undoubtedly perceive the differences in stress pattern but they seem uncertain how to interpret them consistently (see also L. Gleitman and Gleitman, 1970). Identifying particular stress patterns on compounds may be made more difficult in part because "contrastive" stress can be used freely, anywhere, to correct misunderstandings and provide new information, as in 1:

1. I didn't say the YÉLLOW house, I said the GRÉEN house.

Here **green** receives primary stress because it is being marked as new information (in capitals) despite the fact that it is *not* part of a compound noun. Stress and its use in English clearly take years to acquire.

Intonation

Intonation isn't mastered quickly either. The discrimination of different patterns is only the first step. Children must then go on to recognize different intonation contours—the patterns of rise and fall—and identify their linguistic functions. Several investigators have noticed that two- and three-year-olds do not use intonation reliably and at times come out with the wrong melody (Weir, 1962). To add to this, Cruttenden (1975) looked at the ability of seven- and nine-year-olds to predict football scores (win, lose, draw) from the intonation patterns used on the first half of British Broadcasting Corporation radio announcements of match results. Adults are able to do this very reliably, but the nine-year-olds still made errors, and the younger children did very poorly. From this, Cruttenden concluded that some suprasegmental information may take many years to acquire. Overall, intonation and stress have been largely neglected in the study of language acquisition. The handful of studies that have been carried out can hardly answer all the questions that arise (Crystal, 1973).

Representations of Words

The first words children say often bear little apparent relation to the adult words they are based on. For example, adult **dog** may be pronounced **da** or even **ga** by a very young child. Children generally simplify their pronunciations. Given the gap between the adult word and children's pronunciation of it, the question is how children represent the words they hear during acquisition.

There are two main possibilities. The first is that children could base their representations of a word on what they perceive when they hear it spoken by an adult. If they perceive any distinctions they can't produce themselves, then their representations for that word should incorporate all the distinctions they perceive as relevant. In the beginning they shouldn't necessarily pick out the same distinctions as the adult, but they would probably include at least some distinctions they themselves cannot produce. Because their representation for a word would be more similar to the adult's pronunciation than to their own, it might be called an *adult-based* representation. The second main possibility is that children might represent only those distinctions that they themselves can produce at a given stage (Waterson, 1971). In this case, children might be said to have a *child-based* representation since it would be closer to their own pronunciation than to the adult's. One immediate problem with child-based representations is that they provide no clue as to (a) how children identify the words they hear from other speakers, or (b) how children ever change their pronunciations.

The "Fis" Phenomenon

A critical factor in deciding between these two possibilities is whether children can identify words they themselves cannot pronounce. The answer is that they can. Their ability to do this is clearly illustrated in what Berko and Brown called the "fis" phenomenon, shown in the following examples:

> 2. One of us, for instance, spoke to a child who called his inflated plastic fish a *fis*. In imitation of the child's pronunciation, the observer said: "This is your *fis*?" "No," said the child, "my *fis*." He continued to reject the adult's imitation until he was told, "That is your fish." "Yes," he said, "my *fis*." (Berko and Brown, 1960, p. 531)

3. An example of this was provided in the author's experience by a child who asked if he could come along on a trip to the "mewwy-go-wound." An older child, teasing him, said "David wants to go on the mewwy-go-wound." "No," said David firmly, "you don't say it wight." (Maccoby and Bee, 1965, p. 67)

4. Father: Say "jump."
   Child: *Dup.*
   Father: No, "jump."
   Child: *Dup.*
   Father: No, "jummmp."
   Child: Only Daddy can say *dup*! (N. Smith, 1973, p. 10)

In 2, the child is clearly aware of the adult opposition between [s] and [š] even though he cannot produce it himself, and he "corrects" the adult. The little boy cited in 3 can discriminate [r] from [w] and rejects the pronunciation based on his own production. Elkonin (1974) and Jakobson (1968) give similar examples from Russian and French. And the child in 4 can distinguish between his own pronunciation of the cluster **-mp** and the adult's. The common ingredient in these examples is the child's rejection of his own pronunciation. This suggests that the child's representation for the word **fish** is much closer to adult **fish** than to **fis**, the version actually produced by the child.

Adult-Based Representations

Children can also distinguish pairs of adult words that they themselves pronounce alike. N. Smith (1973) noted that his son could perceive the difference between **mouse** and **mouth** long before he could produce it: he regularly fetched the appropriate drawing on a card from an adjoining room. After he began to talk, he continued to perceive this distinction although he himself said [maus] for both. He also pronounced **card** and **cart** alike, as **gart**, and **jug** and **duck** alike, as **guck**. Yet he always distinguished between the two adult words when his comprehension was tested.

The child's perception of the adult distinction between words like **mouse** and **mouth** led Smith to argue that the child must have stored fairly adult-like representations of these words. These adult-based representations also seemed to take priority in word identification over any representations based on the child's own pronunciations (Morton and Smith, 1974). As a result, whenever the child's own production coincided with his representation of some adult word, the child came up with the meaning of the adult word first. For example Smith asked his son, aged 4;2, about his pronunciation of the words **shirt**, **shoe**, and **ship**. At the time, his son used [s] in place of [š] in all three:

Father: What is a sirt? (using [s] instead of [š] in *shirt*)
Child: (immediately points to his shirt)
Father: What's a soo? (using [s] instead of [š])
Child: (immediately points to shoe)
Father: What's a sip?
Child: When you drink. (imitates action)

Father: What else does sip mean?
Child: (puzzled, then doubtfully suggests *zip*, though pronouncing it quite correctly)
Father: No: it goes in the water.
Child: A boat.
Father: Say it.
Child: No. I can only say *sip*.

(N. Smith, 1973, pp. 136–137).

The child identified his own forms immediately in the case of **shirt** and **shoe**, but he had difficulty with [sɪp] because the first meaning he retrieved was for the adult verb **sip**. As in the case of [maus] for **mouth**, it was only with prompting that he was able to come up with the meaning "ship."

The child's difficulty in identifying **ship** and **mouth** from the pronunciations [sɪp] and [maus] seems explicable if his representations of words are closer to adult words than to his own pronunciations. These adult-based representations, of course, need not be identical to the adult's representations, but they must be close enough for the child to identify a meaning based on the adult pronunciation instead of his own. This is reasonable given what children are trying to do as they acquire language. They are trying both to work out what different words and phrases mean (the mapping problem) and to produce words themselves in such a way that they make themselves understood. If they did not store representations based on the more complex adult pronunciations, they would have no way to identify what was said in the speech addressed to them by adults.

Although Morton and Smith (1974) hypothesized that children store both adult-based representations and child-based ones, with the former taking priority in recognition, it looks as though they may only sometimes store their own pronunciations. Dodd (1975) found that three-year-olds were usually much worse at recognizing their own versions of words than the same words said by an unfamiliar adult. When they heard a tape-recording of their own "mispronunciations," they failed to identify the words correctly 52 percent of the time compared to only 6 percent of the time when they listened to a tape of an adult saying the same words. Dodd also played the tape of each child to a second child unfamiliar with the first. These children failed to identify the mispronunciations 48 percent of the time compared to only 4 percent when listening to the adult tape of the same words. The words the children failed to identify were consistently farther from the adult pronunciation than the words they did identify. Some examples from her tapes are listed below:

Target word	Identifiable pronunciation	Unidentifiable pronunciation
umbrella	ʌmbələ	nənʌ
skipping	škɪpɪŋ	kɪpɪŋk
giraffe	dəræf	raft
zebra	zɛvrʌ	jɛbrʌ
shoe	su	sə
flower	fæ:ə	æ:ə

Dodd concluded that children do not store their own deviant pronunciations for recognition in the same way they store adult pronunciations.

New Sounds in Old Words

If children's representations are based on adult pronunciations, their knowledge about the adult versions should be observable elsewhere as their sound system develops. Consider children who still cannot pronounce [s] when it is followed by another consonant and pronounce **stick** and **stop** as **tick** and **top**. But suppose that the same children perceive the [s] and include it in their representations for such words. Later, when they master the [s], they should be able to put the new sound into just those words where it belongs on the basis of their representations. Thus, initial [s] should appear in words like **stick**, **spider**, and **stand**, but not in words like **peel**, **table**, or **can**. This very phenomenon has been observed by many investigators. Children may spend a few days or weeks alternating between their old and new pronunciations before they settle for the more adultlike one. But once the change is introduced it spreads to all the words in which it would be found in adult speech (N. Smith, 1973, 1975).

The "fis" phenomenon in children's speech, their identification of word meanings, and their across-the-board innovations all provide convincing evidence that young children perceive and store words in a more complex form than they themselves can produce. From the very beginning, their representations of words in memory appear to be closer to adult forms than to their own pronunciations. This is not to say that these representations are fixed. A number of details may change as children learn to perceive and store all the phonetic contrasts relevant to the sound system they are acquiring. It may take some time to work out which phonetic details can be ignored and which are essential. By age three or so, their representations of most words are probably very close, if not identical, to the adult's. These representations in memory play an important role in acquisition: they provide a model of what children should be aiming for when they speak. The closer they get to an adult pronunciation, the better they make themselves understood.

PRODUCTION OF SPEECH SOUNDS

The young child's ability to talk and make himself understood is at first very limited. It is often difficult to identify [dus] as **juice**, [doti] as **doggie**, or [dot] as either **coat** or **don't** without help from the context and knowledge of the child. Table 10–2 contains some of the first words recorded from two children by Leopold (1949) and Menn (1971). Their pronunciations illustrate how wide the gap is between the adult words and children's early pronunciations. The children's versions in Table 10–2 are highly simplified: each one typically consists of a single syllable that to begin with may be pronounced in several ways.

TABLE 10–2

EXAMPLES FROM THE FIRST RECORDED FORMS FOR TWO CHILDREN

HILDEGARD			DANIEL		
AGE	ADULT MODEL	CHILD'S PRONUNCIATION	AGE	ADULT MODEL	CHILD'S PRONUNCIATION.
0;10	there	[dɛi]	1;4	byebye	[bab]
		[dɪi]			[bæbæ]
		[de]	1;6	hi	[hæ]
0;11	there	[dɛ]			[hay]
	ticktock	[tak]	1;7	no	[oⁿo]
1;0	ball	[ba]			[no]
	Blumen	[bu]			[nu]
	da	[da]		hello	[hwow]
	papa	[pa-pa]		squirrel	[gæ]
	pipe	[pi]			[gow]
		[pip]	1;8	nose	[o]
1;1	ball	[ba]		boot	[bu]
	bimbam	[bɪ]	1;9	light	[ay]
	da	[da]	1;10	car	[gar]
	Gertrude	[dɛda]		Stevie	[iv]
		[dədi]		apple	[æp]
	kick	[ti]		up	[ʌf]

Based on Leopold (1949) and Menn (1971).

Variability in Pronunciation

The variability in these children's forms is typical of early child speech. Hildegard, for example, used at least two versions of the words **there**, **pipe**, and **Gertrude**, while Daniel used at least two forms for **byebye**, **hi**, **no**, and **squirrel**. Ingram (1974) analyzed data from two diary studies and reported as many as five versions of some words. One child, Philip, used five different forms for **blanket** within a month, and another, Fernande, used five forms for the French **chaise** (chair). In all, Philip at age 1;9 had multiple versions for 50 of his 125-word repertoire, while Fernande at age 1;5 had multiple versions for 47 of her 114 words.

This variability in pronunciations appears to have at least two sources. First, children are continually trying to match their production to the representations they have for the adult words. However, because they have only a few sounds under control, their "approximations" may fluctuate considerably. Second, children are concerned with making themselves understood, and they may have to try out several different versions of a word before they succeed. As their productions get closer to the adult model, the number of different versions for a word decreases, and at the same time, they become more comprehensible.

Although the gap between the adult and child pronunciations is often large, children make systematic, rather than accidental, approximations to the adult words. These result from simplifications in their versions of the adult words. When children start out, they can make only a few consistent contrasts between segments, and so they may produce a form simpler than the one they have stored in memory. As they master new sounds, though, they restructure the relevant words by adding the new sounds where needed. They are guided in this by the representations of adult words they have stored in memory. They are also guided by these representations in their spontaneous practice of new sounds when they repeat newly mastered segments and correct their old pronunciations.

Infant Babbling

During their first days of life, infants make crying sounds. Soon they add different kinds of crying as well as cooing sounds to their repertoire (Wolff, 1966). Despite this, parents of three- to five-month-olds have great difficulty telling apart cries of pain, hunger, and surprise heard without any contextual clues to what is happening (Müller, Hollien, and Murry, 1974). By seven or eight months, however, parents accurately identify different cries as requests, greetings, hunger, and surprise (Ricks, 1975). At the age of five or six months, infants start to babble. This babbling gives the impression of being much more language-like than their cries, with vowels and consonants combined into syllable-like sequences such as **bababa**, **memememe**, or **gugugu**. These sequences may be produced with something of a monotone or have some kind of intonational rise and fall superimposed on them. Babbling characteristically lasts for six or eight months, but starts to decrease after children produce their first identifiable words. Many small children "babble" in play long after they begin to talk, pretending to talk to toys or to read a newspaper or a book.

Continuity Versus Discontinuity

Is there any connection between this early babbling and the later acquisition of the adult sound system? Opinion on this has been divided between the *continuity approach*—that babbling sounds are the direct precursors of speech sounds—and the *discontinuity approach*—that babbling bears no direct relation to later development. Advocates of the continuity hypothesis such as Mowrer (1960) have argued that in babbling infants produce all the sounds to be found in the world's languages. Their repertoire is then gradually narrowed down, as a result of selective reinforcement by parents and caretakers, to just those sounds that occur in the language spoken around them. However, when babbling is examined closely, this hypothesis does not seem to fit the facts.

In the first place, careful observations have shown that there are many sounds infants do *not* produce when babbling. And there are also many groups of sounds used at the beginnings and ends of syllables (e.g., consonant clusters like **str-** in **string** or **-ngth** in **strength**) that do not appear in babbling at all.

Second, parents don't seem to be in the least selective about the sounds they want their babies to produce. They encourage all vocalization indiscriminately.

And finally, when children start to use their first words, they no longer seem able to produce some of the very sounds they used when babbling. One striking example can be found in their use of **l** and **r**: although these are very frequent in babbling, they rarely appear in children's first words and are among the latest sounds that children master. The facts, then, do not lend much support to a continuity approach.

The discontinuity approach, in contrast, posits that there are two distinct stages in the production of sounds. Jakobson (1968) argued that infants first go through a period of babbling and produce a fairly wide range of sounds. These sounds don't emerge in any particular order, and so they don't seem to be related in any obvious way to children's later development. The onset of the second stage is marked by the disappearance of many sounds previously frequent in their repertoires, for example, the **l** and **r** sounds. Some sounds are dropped permanently and others temporarily, and the latter may take months or even years to re-emerge. It is characteristic of this second stage that children gradually master the different contrasts in the language they are acquiring, and they do this in a relatively invariant manner. Jakobson argued that only the second stage is critical in the development of the sound system, and that this stage begins only when children realize that certain sounds have a distinct linguistic value.

Although Jakobson made a strong case for an actual break between the first babbling stage and the later build-up of the sound system, there are several troublesome facts to account for.

First, many children continue to babble after the onset of speech and there are often several months of overlap when they both babble and talk (Menn, 1976).

Second, investigators like Oller and his colleagues (1976) have argued that the phonetic content of babbling exhibits many of the preferences for certain kinds of phonetic sequences that are later found in meaningful words.

And finally, some children seem to use babbling to "carry" particular intonation patterns used for requesting or rejecting, for example. And they do this even after they have begun to use some words (Menn, 1976; Halliday, 1975). This suggests that there is continuity, at least at the suprasegmental level.

Neither continuity nor discontinuity fully accounts for the facts. The relation between babbling and speech is probably an indirect one. For example, experience with babbling could be a necessary preliminary to gaining articulatory control of certain organs in the mouth and vocal tract. Babbling would give children practice in producing sequences of sounds and in adding a melodic contour—intonation—to those sequences. If babbling simply provided exercise for the vocal apparatus, there would be little reason to expect any connection between the sounds produced in babbling and those produced later on (but see Oller et al., 1976). Still, there is at least some discontinuity. Mastery of some phonetic segments only begins when children start to use their first words.

Segments and Syllables

Once past the babbling stage, children begin to work on phonetic segments—the building blocks used in pronouncing words. They also learn how to pronounce sequences of segments, that is, syllables and words. Their mastery of phonetic segments is closely allied to their mastery of the systematic contrasts found in each language. In English, for example, voiced stops like [b] and [d] contrast with voiceless [p] and [t]. Learning to produce the right segment involves learning which contrasts are systematic.

Mastering Segments

Children produce their first words with recognizable meanings somewhere between age one and one and a half. Yet the sounds they use are restricted in number and do not even include all those present in earlier babbling. One conceivable explanation for this is that children focus on each segment in turn and practice it until they get it right. Only then do they go on to tackle another segment. One problem with this "one-at-a-time" theory is that it cannot easily explain why the pronunciation of a particular word, **doggie** say, might change from **do** to **dodi**, to **goggie**, and finally **doggie**. For example, if a child has really mastered [d], there are two questions to be answered. First, why does he pronounce the adult [d] in initial position in a word, as in **dodi** for **doggie**, but not in final position, as in **buh** for **bird**? Second, why does he substitute [g] for [d] at a certain stage in development, as in **goggie**, after a period of apparently "correct" usage?

An alternative to the one-at-a-time theory is the *hypothesis-testing theory*. According to this, children try out different hypotheses about how to produce the right sound. When they have only a few segments under control, they sometimes hit on the right way to produce a particular segment, as in the case above of the initial [d] in **dodi**. Later, when they add other stop consonants to their repertoire, they may find it difficult at first to produce two different stops in the same word. They therefore focus on the newest one, say [g], and end up producing it in both places, as in **goggie**. Later still, they sort out the right articulatory gestures to produce the adult form **doggie**. In testing their hypotheses about particular segments, children slowly build up a set of "articulatory programs" for producing segments that match the distinctions they can perceive (Menn, 1976; Kiparsky and Menn, 1977). In the course of doing this, they work out which contrasts between segments are systematic in the language being acquired. In fact, one influential theory about the acquisition of the sound system, proposed by Jakobson, focuses almost exclusively on the acquisition of contrasts.

Acquisition of Contrasts

Jakobson (1968) hypothesized that the way children master the sounds of their language is closely related to properties all languages have in common. He proposed that:

(1) Children gradually acquire the ability to pronounce sounds by mastering the contrasts of the adult language.

(2) The order in which children acquire these contrasts is universal.

(3) This order of acquisition is predictable from the contrasts found in the languages of the world. Those that are most widespread are acquired earliest, while those that occur in only a few languages are among the last to be acquired.

(4) Children go on elaborating their own set of contrasts until it matches the set found in the adult language.

To evaluate this hypothesis, Jakobson examined the diary records for children acquiring a variety of different languages. In these diaries, observers had written down as accurately as possible the way their children pronounced words at different stages during acquisition.

Consonant Contrasts

Jakobson found that contrasts were learned in a highly consistent order. The first one to appear was that between vowel and consonant. The first vowel sound was generally a low front vowel, produced with a wide open mouth and fairly flat tongue, represented by [A]. This sound was used in opposition to a consonantal sound, usually a bilabial stop that was voiced or voiceless, or fluctuated between the two. This sound is represented by [P-B]. Because children's segments are extremely variable at this stage, they will be represented by capital letters in square brackets. From the articulatory point of view, this vowel-consonant contrast is maximal. In a syllable like [pa], for example, the vocal tract is completely closed at the lips to start with and then opened wide for the vowel (see Jakobson and Halle, 1956). The next contrast to emerge within the system of consonants, according to Jakobson, was the one between oral and nasal consonants, between [P-B] and [M]. (Here again, [M] represents the first nasal segment but its phonetic form may vary considerably from one occasion to the next.) By that stage, a very early one, children had several potential "word forms" at their disposal: **ba**, **pa**, **ma**, **baba**, **papa**, and **mama**. The vowels in these forms varied somewhat, but they tended to be open and front. The next contrast was that between bilabial and dental consonants. Each member of the earlier oral-nasal opposition split in two: [P-B] contrasted with [T-D], and [M] with [N]. This set of consonantal oppositions can be pictured as a "tree" with children starting at the top and gradually working their way down as they manage to produce more contrasts:

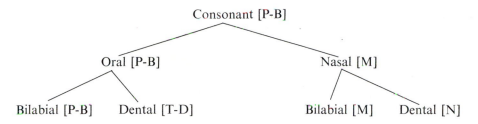

This set of contrasts actually constitutes the smallest number of consonantal oppositions possible in a language (Jakobson, 1968). With these contrasts, children could produce words like **papa**, **baba**, **tata**, **dada**, **mama**, and **nana**, not to mention one-syllable words and words with other vowels.

Incidentally, Jakobson (1960) argued that these early developments in the sound system provide an explanation for why words like **mama** and **papa** are so widely used in unrelated languages as words for "mother" and "father" (or vice versa). The sequences **mama** and **papa** are among children's earliest "words" regardless of the language being acquired. Because parents are vain, Jakobson argued, they attribute to these words the meanings "mother" and "father," and have adopted them as baby talk words in many languages. But in actuality, **mama** is typically used to indicate that a child needs something and it is addressed to anyone who might be able to meet the child's need. **Papa** is often used for both parents and may be extended to all men before being restricted to "father" (see Chapter 13).

Vowel Contrasts

The vowels were differentiated in much the same way as consonants. Children's first vowel was usually [A] as in **papa** or **cat**. The first contrast to emerge was between one produced with the tongue flat in the bottom of the mouth, as in the open [A] in **papa**, and one where the tongue was raised as close to the roof of the mouth as possible without friction, for example, the closed vowel [I] in **pipi**. Both these vowels are made with the tongue at the front of the mouth. The next opposition to be added took one of two forms. Some children added a back vowel in contrast to the two front vowels, usually some kind of back rounded vowel, [U] as in **boot**, say. This vowel system, with [A], [I], and [U], constitutes a minimal vowel system. That is, there are languages in which these are the only vowels. Other children added a third front vowel, [E] as in **bet**, placed somewhere between [A] and [I]. This too is a minimal vowel system: open [A] contrasts with closed [E], and then relatively open [E] contrasts with closed [I]. The stages of elaboration among vowels, then, looked similar to the gradual unfolding of the contrasts among consonants: children added contrasts and each addition led to a change in the system as a whole.

Word Structures

As Jakobson's theory predicts, children's words are generally very simple compared to the adult's. Two structures—consonant + vowel (CV) and consonant

TABLE 10–3

WORDS AND SYLLABLES

Percentages of different syllable structure types in children's early words.

AGE	CV	CVC	SYLLABLE STRUCTURE: CVCV(C)*	CVCV†	Other
1;2	18	6	21	31	24
1;4	44	20	5	16	15
1;6	34	16	9	28	13

* Optional final consonant on a reduplicated syllable; both consonants *and* both vowels identical, e.g., **papa**, **mimi**.

† *Either* both consonants *or* both vowels are the same in CVCV structure, e.g., **gegu**, **tiki**.

Based on data from Winitz and Irwin (1958).

+ vowel reduplicated (CVCV)—accounted for 85 percent of the early words examined by M. M. Lewis (1951). Winitz and Irwin (1958) counted the different word structures that appeared in the speech of ninety-three children between the ages of 1;2 and 1;6. Their findings, summarized in Table 10–3, agree strongly with Lewis's observations. None of the words had complicated beginnings or endings, so there were no initial or final clusters like **str-** in **stripe** or **-sp** in **wisp**. In fact, final consonants were often left out altogether, as in [da] for **dog** or [hə] for **home**.

Children's use of consonants is asymmetrical. Note that many consonants in English occur initially (at the beginning of a syllable), medially (between the two vowels), and finally (at the end of a syllable), like the segment [p] in **pod**, **tipping**, and **stop**. Jakobson, in putting forward his hypothesis, apparently considered only initial position consonants, but how children pronounce segments seems to depend in part on their position in the adult word. They use many more different consonants initially than either medially or finally, and their pronunciation of medial consonants shows much more variation than initial ones (Moskowitz, 1970; Ferguson and Farwell, 1975). It is unclear, therefore, whether Jakobson's theory about contrasts applies equally well to segments in all three positions, with the contrasts simply emerging somewhat later with medial and final consonants.

Order of Acquisition

Jakobson related different stages in acquisition to his work on the universal characteristics of sound systems. He had observed that although the precise inventory of segments differed from language to language, certain relations remained invariable. For example, if a language contained any velar stops, such as [g], it also contained some bilabial and dental stops, such as [b] or [t]. If a language contained fricative consonants like [v] or [s], it invariably had some stop consonants as well. And if a language contained affricates such as [č] or [j], it had some stops and fricatives too. Jakobson predicted that these interdependencies should be reflected in the order in which children acquire contrasts. The contrast between bilabial and dental stops should therefore be acquired before the one between bilabial and velar or dental and velar stops. Stops should also be acquired before fricatives, and both stops and fricatives before affricates. Liquids and glides should emerge later still, given their place in the sound systems of the world.

This order of acquisition is generally borne out by the data. Children usually master stops like [b] and [d] before fricatives like [f] or [s]. In fact, they often replace a fricative with its corresponding stop—the stop made at the same point of articulation. For example, [f] is produced as [p], so a word like **fish** becomes [pɪš], and [s] is produced as [t], so **suit**, for example, becomes [tut]. The same thing is frequently observed with affricates: children substitute the corresponding stop or even the corresponding fricative for the affricate. The sound [č] becomes [t], with **chase** pronounced as [teis] and **cherry** as [tɛri] (see N. Smith, 1973). Liquids and glides, as predicted, emerge rather later, and to begin with children may use a segment that fluctuates between [l], [y], [r], and [w]. **Red** often comes out as [wɛd] or even [lɛd], while **yellow** may become [lɛlo]. The contrasts between liquids and glides are among the last parts of the sound system English-speaking children master.

Olmsted (1971) used recordings of 100 children between the ages of 1;3 and 4;6 to analyze the frequencies of individual segments, errors in their production, substitutions for them, and variability in their pronunciation. The typical phonetic inventory used by four-year-olds is summarized in Table 10–4. He found they still mispronounced segments like [t] between two vowels and the nasal [ŋ]. Among fricatives, [θ], as in **thistle**, and its voiced counterpart, [ð], as in **this**, are probably not fully mastered until age six. Both [z] and [ž], as in **zoo** and **leisure**, are also mastered later, as are affricates like the [č] in **churn**, and the voiced [ǰ] in **juice** (see Ingram, 1976). Many children master [l] and [r] last of all. The inventory in Table 10–4 only covers single consonants. Clusters of consonants like **st-** or **pl-** may take even longer to master. For example, initial **st-** is usually reduced to [t]: a word like **sticky** may be pronounced first as [tɪti], then as [tɪki], and only later as **sticky**.

Some Problems

An important weakness of Jakobson's theory, however, is that it deals only with the acquisition of contrasts. To account for children's production of individual sounds, one needs a theory about the mastery of particular phonetic targets (Kiparsky and Menn, 1977). This weakness shows up in several phenomena Jakobson's theory does not predict or account for.

(1) Even when children can control the contrast between one voiced-voiceless pair of consonants, for example, [b] and [p], and the contrast between a labial and velar consonant, such as [p] and [k], they often cannot combine these two contrasts to produce the voiced velar consonant [g]. In other words, although children learn contrasts, they also have to learn how to articulate each

TABLE 10–4

ENGLISH CONSONANTS USED BY FOUR-YEAR-OLDS

The position of each segment is shown by a dash. For example, initial **t** is **t-**, medial **t** would be **-t-**, and final **t** is **-t**. Where no position is indicated, children already use the segment appropriately in all three.

	BILABIAL	LABIO-DENTAL	DENTAL	ALVEOLAR	PALATAL	VELAR
STOPS:	p b			t- -t d		k g
FRICA- TIVES:		f v	-θ- θ-	s	š -ž- -ž	
AFFRI- CATES:					č ǰ	
NASALS:	m			n		
LATERAL:				l		
SEMI- VOWELS:	w			r	y	

Based on data from Olmsted (1971).

individual phonetic segment. Furthermore, when they learn to produce a contrast between two segments, they do not immediately make that contrast in all the contexts where it is required (Ferguson and Farwell, 1975; Menn, 1976).

(2) Some children appear systematically to avoid saying certain words because of the phonetic segments they contain. Ferguson and Farwell (1975) reported one child who for some months avoided words containing [p], but freely tried words containing [b], a sound she could pronounce. Menn (1976) reported further examples from a child who avoided [b] but said words with [d]. Later on, when he began to produce words containing [b], he avoided words with [p]. The fact that children deliberately avoid some words provides further evidence that they can perceive an opposition—for example, between voiced and voiceless consonants—before they learn how to make that contrast themselves.

(3) Several investigators have noted occasional but striking exceptions to the systematic simplifications children use in pronouncing words. Leopold (1949), for example, reported that his daughter Hildegard could say **pretty** perfectly at a time when she simplified all her other words, as in Table 10–2, and used no other consonant clusters like **pr-** at all. These "advanced" pronunciations of words are evidence that children's simplifications do not result from an inability to perceive or pronounce certain sequences accurately (Kiparsky and

Menn, 1977). Rather, they probably result from the specific articulatory pro-grams children construct for producing particular words and sounds (Menn, 1976).

Phenomena like these have led investigators to emphasize the need to look at how children master phonetic segments—the targets provided by adult pronunciations—and not just at how they master the contrasts between seg-ments. Children do not aim at single segments pronounced in isolation: they aim at words and phrases—whole sequences of phonetic segments.

Children, it can be concluded, have a clearly defined goal from the very start: they are trying to learn how to say recognizable words. They have to learn not only how to produce a sound close to the adult target, but also just how close they have to be before others can identify the segment they are aiming at. Just as in the acquisition of syntactic structure, they probably try out different hypotheses about how to produce the right segments before they eventually hit appropriate articulatory programs (Ferguson and Farwell, 1975; Kiparsky and Menn, 1977).

Children's Simplifications

While learning adult pronunciations, children consistently simplify the words they say. When we compare the adult and child versions of the words in Table 10–2, for instance, it is often hard to recognize the adult word in the child's pronunciation. Adult **squirrel** became [gæ] or [gow] in Daniel's earliest attempts to pronounce it. Similarly, the German **Blumen** (flower) in Hildegard's speech was reduced to the single syllable [bu]. Children shorten adult words, often drastically. They reduce clusters of consonants, like the [skw-] in **squirrel** or [bl-] in **Blumen**, to a single segment—[g] and [b]—and often omit certain segments altogether, such as [l] and [r]. These simplifications, because they are highly systematic, provide further evidence that children's pronunciations are directly related to their adult-based representations. But precisely why children simplify their words is not yet clear, although it may be because there are certain limits on what children can pronounce.

N. Smith (1973) has described four general ways children simplify adult words. They omit final consonants, reduce consonant clusters, omit unstressed syllables, and reduplicate syllables. The first three procedures have the effect of shortening the adult word, often to a single syllable, and all four reduce the complexity of the consonantal structure of the word or syllable children are attempting to say.

Omission of Final Segments

This procedure is very common in young children's speech, as Table 10–2 shows for Hildegard and, to a lesser extent, for Daniel. The word **ball** became [ba], **Blumen** [bu], **pipe** [pi], **kick** [ti], and **boot** [bu]. Most of Hildegard's early words had a simple CV structure even where the adult model ended in a consonant. Daniel made rather more use of final consonants, as in [iv] for **Stevie**, [æp] for

apple, and [ʌf] for **up**, but even so he used relatively few during his first year of talking (Menn, 1971). The omission of final consonants by young children is typical, but does not last very long. By the age of three, children omit fewer than 10 percent of the final consonants found in adult words (Templin, 1957; Irwin, 1951). It is during the period in which children omit final consonants (roughly from their first words up to age three) that they master most of the segments that are used in first position.

Shvachkin (1973) found that initial position seemed to be very salient in perception too: young children could discriminate and recognize sounds more easily at the beginning of CVC syllables. Presumably, this is because people have to process speech as it impinges upon the ear: they cannot start with the last segment they heard and go backward. It is the initial segment that is usually the most critical in identifying which word was said. In producing their first words, therefore, young children seem to be following a principle much like this:

> Get the first segment right so it will be easier for the listener to work out which word is being said.

A principle of this type would give initial position just the priority it seems to enjoy in the child's emerging sound system.

Reduction of Consonant Clusters

Children consistently simplify consonant clusters by reducing them to fewer segments. They may do this by deleting the entire cluster so that an English word like **cry** would become [ai], by reducing the cluster to a single segment so that **cry** might become [kai], or by substituting some other sound for one member of the cluster so that **cry** might become [kwai].

The commonest simplification of a cluster is to reduce it to a single segment. N. Smith (1973) reported many instances of this procedure applied to the clusters listed below. In each case, the child systematically simplified the cluster:

a. *Cluster:* [s] + consonant
   Rule: Omit [s].
   Examples: stop   (2;8)   [tʰɔp]
   small   (2;4)   [mɔ]
   slide   (2;7)   [laid]
   desk   (2;8)   [dɛk]

b. *Cluster:* stop + liquid
   Rule: Omit liquid.
   Examples: clock   (2;2)   [gɔk]
   milk   (2;2)   [mɪk]
   bring   (2;5)   [bɪŋ]

c. *Cluster:* fricative + liquid or glide
    Rule: Omit liquid or glide.
    Examples: from   (2;10)   [fɔm]
              few   (2;11)   [fu]

d. *Cluster:* nasal + stop
    Rule: Omit nasal.
    Examples: bump   (2;2)   [bʌp]
              tent   (2;2)   [tɛt]

The rules in *a* through *d* were applied very generally by Smith's child and are typical of other young children's speech. But the other member of a cluster may also occasionally be omitted instead. For example, in *a* the [s] is sometimes retained and the stop omitted, as in [sɔp] for **stop**, and in *c* the liquid may be retained instead of the fricative, as in [li:] for **three**. Smith also noted an alternative to the rule in *d*. When the final stop was voiced in such clusters, his child regularly omitted the stop rather than the nasal, for example, [mɛn] for **mend**. These alternatives were rare, though, compared to all the instances accounted for by rules *a* through *d*.

The way consonant clusters are reduced appears to be closely linked to the order of acquisition noted by Jakobson (1968). Roughly speaking, the order in which children master segments is: stops, nasals, fricatives, and then liquids and glides. This order of acquisition is also reflected in children's rules for reducing clusters. The higher on the list a segment is, the more likely it is to be retained from a consonant cluster. Consider the rules children apply: *a*, *b*, and *d* involve a stop combined with a fricative, a liquid or glide, or a nasal. In each case, the stop is the segment normally retained, and the other segment is the one omitted:

a. fricative [s] + stop   →   stop

b. stop + liquid   →   stop

d. nasal + stop   →   stop

Rule *c* involves a fricative followed by a liquid or glide, and here it is the fricative that is retained:

c. fricative + liquid/glide   →   fricative

The order of acquisition observed for single segments, therefore, seems to reappear in the acquisition of clusters.

Omission of Unstressed Syllables

Up to the age of two or so, most of the words children produce consist of single syllables, even though they hear two- and three-syllable words as well. In the early stages, children often cope with two-syllable words by reducing them to one syllable (see Table 10–2), omitting whichever syllable is unstressed. They rarely even attempt to pronounce longer, three-syllable, words at this stage (Ingram, 1976).

Next, children produce some two-syllable words as well as one-syllable ones. They may attempt some three-syllable words as well, but they continue to omit most unstressed syllables. In two-syllable words they retain both syllables from the adult model but usually reduce unstressed vowels to the neutral vowel schwa, [ə]. This pattern of omission with three-syllable words and reduction with two-syllable ones soon gives way to more complicated rules for simplifying adult words. For example, children may start to retain all the syllables with the exception of unstressed initial syllables, which they systematically omit whatever the length of the word. Thus, the name **Robbie**, with initial syllable stress, would be produced as [wɔbi], but the word **away**, with stress on the second syllable, would emerge as [we]. Similarly, a three-syllable word like **telephone** with initial stress, retains all three syllables, [dewibun], but the three-syllable **tomato**, with stress on the second syllable, appears as [mado] (see N. Smith, 1973).

The three early "stages" sketched here show children tackling progressively more complicated adult words. At first, they attempt only one- and two-syllable words, and their own productions generally consist of only one syllable. Next, they produce some two-syllable words as well and then attempt one-, two-, and three-syllable ones. At the third stage, children manage to produce some three-syllable words as well, but still omit certain syllables. The favorite candidate for omission is an unstressed syllable in initial position in the adult word.

Reduplication

Some children simplify words with two distinct syllables by choosing a single syllable and reduplicating it. To produce **kitchen**, they may choose the syllable [kɪ] and reduplicate it to make [kɪkɪ]. Similarly, the word **away** may appear as [baba] and **daddy** as [dada] (Velten, 1943; Ingram, 1976). In early reduplications, both consonants and both vowels are usually the same. This procedure later gives way to reduplications in which only the consonants remain the same, as in [babi] for **blanket**, or only the vowels remain the same, as in [lɪdɪ] for **little**. This type of consonant or vowel "harmony" is characteristic of the earlier stages of word acquisition (N. Smith, 1973). The degree to which children reduplicate whole syllables varies from child to child. Some never do so, although they do show this kind of consonant and vowel harmony in their word forms, while others reduplicate the majority of their first words. In some cases, children seem to use reduplication in order to keep two word forms separate that might otherwise sound the same. For example, Ingram (1975) reported one French child who used [koko] for **cocotte** (dish), which would otherwise have been confused with [ko] for **corde** (string).

These four types of simplification represent the major options young children take as they learn to produce recognizable words (N. Smith, 1973). Both the omission of final consonants and the reduction of clusters simplify the structure of the syllable, while the omission of unstressed syllables and the use of reduplication reduce the amount of syllable structure to be tackled in each word. These simplifications are systematic: adult models are usually discernible in the child versions of adult words. As children gain greater mastery over different segments, they become more ambitious until eventually they are able to pronounce the adult words accurately.

Why Simplify?

Why do young children make any simplifications at all? Few investigators have tackled this question, but the following hypotheses have been offered, though not explored in depth:

(1) *Limited memory span.* Young children have limited memory compared to older children and adults. They therefore have difficulty keeping the whole adult word in mind as they try to say it. This explanation has also been offered to account for the apparent limits on utterance length: why children start with single words and only gradually work up to utterances of two words or more.

(2) *Limited representational ability.* Young children are unable to represent complicated sequences of sounds (or words). They therefore store a simplified representation, close to their own pronunciations of adult words. This is the view, taken up earlier, under the label of child-based representations.

(3) *Limited articulatory skill.* Children take a long time to develop the articulatory skill required to produce a match between their own pronunciations and the adult versions they have represented in memory.

There are convincing arguments against the first two hypotheses. In the case of the first, G. Olson (1973) has argued that since memory capacity does not appear to change with age, that alone is not an adequate explanation of why children move from very short utterances to longer ones, or, as here, from reducing all words to one syllable to pronouncing them in an adult fashion. The evidence against the second hypothesis—that children have only a limited, child-based, representational ability—has already been discussed. What is critical is that children clearly do have representations in memory for sounds and sequences that they themselves cannot pronounce (N. Smith, 1973; Dodd, 1975). The simplifications that they make cannot, then, be a direct result of their representations of adult words. The third hypothesis, that children have limited articulatory skill in the early stages, is somewhat more plausible. Even when children have found out how to pronounce a particular segment or sequence of segments, it may take them months of practice before their articulation becomes automatic (Menn, 1976). Consider how long it takes to master a particular stroke in tennis: we may know perfectly well how we ought to hit a backhand—we have a very accurate "mental picture" of it—but the motor skill required to match that picture takes a long time to build up. Overall, the first two hypotheses have little to offer, and there is evidence against them. The third may have more to contribute, but there is still no adequate theory about the relation between children's simplified pronunciations and the adult-based representations they rely on in speech perception.

Practice and Sound Play

Young children don't wait for the right occasion to use new words. They often practice them too. They practice newly mastered segments, play with sound patterns that seem alike in some way, substitute one segment for another, and as they get older make up rhymes by changing the segments on the ends of words. They also practice words and phrases: they string words together and then play substitution games, taking out one word and putting in another, adding on phrases to build up longer sentences, and systematically changing the forms of sentences to make them into questions, or negatives, and back again into statements (Weir, 1962). Sound play and substitution "drills" are common among young children. They provide additional evidence that children use adult-based representations of words. Without such representations, they would have no "model" against which to practice newly acquired segments or from which to correct former pronunciations.

Weir (1962, 1966) recorded bedtime monologues from one child and noted many instances of daytime sound play in the speech of several others. The children in 5 and 6, for example, are both practicing particular classes of consonants. The child in 5 (Weir, 1966, p. 160) seems to be concentrating on bilabials, mainly [b] and [w], while the child in 6 (Weir, 1962, p. 104) seems to be focusing on the velar consonants [g] and [k]:

5. I go dis way / way bay / baby go dis bib / all bib / bib / dere.
6. Like a piggy bank / like a piggy bank / had a pink sheet on / the grey pig out.

Another common form of sound play is to substitute one segment for another, as in 7 (Weir, 1966, p. 166):

7. Fumbelina / tumbelina / lumbelina / thumbelina.

Although many of Weir's examples are from children aged two to three, practice and sound play are also frequently observed in nursery school children (Chukovsky, 1963; H. M. Johnson, 1972; Cazden, 1974).

Sound play allows children to practice both newly mastered segments and complicated sequences of segments. For example, Weir (1966, p. 163) observed one child, David, practicing the segment [r] in the word **story**. He had just begun to produce [r] in his spontaneous speech where before he had always used the segment [l] for both [r] and [l]:

8. Stoly / stoly here / want a stoly / Dave, stoly / story, story / story's de hat / story's de big hat / story's a hat.

Another child, Anthony, practiced a newly acquired contrast between two vowels in much the same way (Weir, 1962, p. 108). The event that triggered this practice was Anthony's having been given some raspberries. That evening, he produced the following sequence:

9. Back please / berries / *not* barries / barries, barries, *not* barries / berries / ba ba.

These observations show that young children are often aware that what they actually say doesn't match the words offered by other speakers. They try out particular segments, and sequences of segments; they practice till they have real mastery of the distinctions they perceive. Their goal is to produce words recognizable to others. Achieving this brings its own reward: it becomes easier and easier for children to make themselves understood to those around them.

SUMMARY

Children have to learn both to perceive and to produce the sounds of their language. In doing this, they set up some form of representation in memory for the words they hear. They then use these representations in identifying words spoken by others and in trying to pronounce words in the way adults do. These representations play a central role in children's acquisition of the sound system.

In the perception of speech sounds, two-month-olds appear able to make discriminations very similar to the categorical distinctions made by adults. This presumably aids children when they come to discriminate and recognize the different phonetic segments of the language they are acquiring. They start to identify adult words early on and soon show evidence of being able to distinguish adult words that differ by a single segment, such as **ship** and **sip** or **mouse** and **mouth**. The representations for these words must therefore differ, even though children do not yet pronounce them differently. The "fis" phenomenon, the identification of adult words, and the restructuring of the child's sound system after mastery of a new segment all suggest that children's representations of words in perception are based on adult pronunciations. These representations guide children in word identification and in progressively "correcting" their own pronunciations of the words.

In the production of speech sounds, children produce their first recognizable words around the age of one. At first their mastery of different segments is very unsure and some words may be pronounced in several different ways. As they master more segments and oppositions and start to build up more complicated syllables and words, their words begin to sound more like the adult's and are therefore more easily identified. In the early stages of acquisition, children usually produce simplified versions of adult words by omitting final consonants, reducing consonant clusters to single segments, omitting unstressed syllables, and sometimes reduplicating simple syllables. These simplifications fade out as children master more segments and sequences of segments. Children also practice newly acquired segments and may correct themselves when they pronounce a word incorrectly. Practice and self-correction provide additional evidence that children rely on adult-based representations of what words *should* sound like.

Further Reading

For a general overview of the acquisition of the sound system, see Ferguson and Garnica (1975), who review some of the main theories, and Ingram (1976), who gives a general account of the stages children go through on their way to mastery of the adult system. Jakobson (1968) provides an intriguing theory about the possible relations between language universals and children's acquisition of sound contrasts. For another perspective—one that emphasizes phonetic segments rather than phonetic contrasts—see Ferguson and Farwell (1975) and Kiparsky and Menn (1977). Finally, N. Smith (1973) raises some very important theoretical questions about the relation between perception and production in his case study of how one child mastered the sound system of English.

part 5

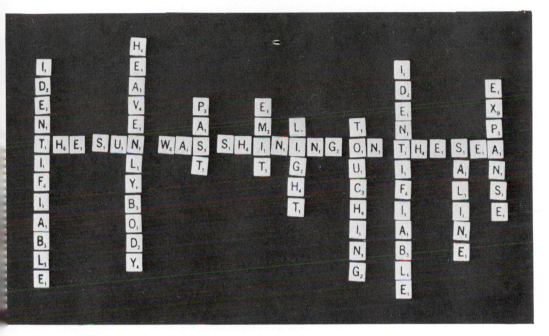

MEANING AND THOUGHT

"There's glory for you!"

"I don't know what you mean by 'glory,'" Alice said.

Humpty Dumpty smiled contemptuously. "Of course you don't—till I tell you. I meant there's a nice knock-down argument for you!'"

"But 'glory' doesn't mean 'a nice knock-down argument,'" Alice objected.

"When *I* use a word," Humpty Dumpty said, in rather a scornful tone, "it means just what I choose it to mean—neither more nor less."

"The question is," said Alice, "whether you *can* make words mean so many different things."

"The question is," said Humpty Dumpty, "which is to be master—that's all."

Lewis Carroll

11

The Representation of Meaning

The end of language is the communication of meaning. People talk in order to express the meaning of their thoughts, and they listen in order to discover the meaning of what others say. Without meaning there would be no real point in language. But what is meaning? And what is its role in comprehension, production, and acquisition? These two questions are basic enough that they form the foundation for this and the next three chapters. They are among the most difficult and controversial questions in the psychology of language and have anything but clear answers. Yet they are also among the most important questions, for they confront basic issues in the study of the mind.

Of these two questions, "What is meaning?" may seem more basic; for if it had a clear answer, the second question, "What is the role of meaning in language processing?" would become much easier to answer. Within the psychology of language, however, the two questions are interlocked. It would be futile to try answering "What is meaning?" without simultaneously worrying about "How is it used?" The first task, then, is to lay out some of the main issues that bear on the relation between meaning and its use.

THE NATURE OF MEANING

The only unit of meaning introduced so far is the proposition. Recall that each sentence was said to have an underlying representation that consisted of propositions combined in a particular pattern. **The old man lit his awful cigar**, for example, consisted of roughly these eight propositions:

$$Known(E_{57})$$
$$Man(E_{57})$$
$$Old(E_{57})$$

$$Known(E_8)$$
$$Cigar(E_8)$$
$$Awful(E_8)$$
$$Belong(E_8, E_{57})$$

$$Light(E_{57}, E_8)$$

These propositions played a central role in comprehension and production. In comprehending, it was argued, listeners try to identify constituents, like **the old man**, and try to build the propositions appropriate to each. And in speaking, people plan propositions and later form an articulatory program for words that express them.

How does the analysis of sentences into propositions help illuminate meaning? In effect, it tells us how the meaning of a sentence is put together from the meanings of its words. It turns the problem of sentence meaning into one of the combination of word meanings. Note that in **The old man lit his awful cigar**, each word signals the presence of one, or possibly two, propositions. **Old** signals the presence of **Old(x)**, **man** the presence of **Man(x)**, **lit** the presence of **Light(x, y)**, and so on. It is then the syntax that signals how these propositions are combined to create the meaning of the whole sentence. It is because **the old man** is the subject of **lit** that it picks out the first argument in **Light(x, y)**.

Still, what are propositions like **Old(x)**, **Man(x)**, and **Light(x, y)**? Or put more traditionally, what are the meanings of words like **old**, **man**, and **light**? The answer so far has been rather vague. It was pointed out that propositions correspond roughly to events (like lighting) or states (like being old or being a man), and each state and event has one or more participants (like the man and cigar in the event called lighting). Yet this doesn't go very far. It should be possible to be more precise. For that, it is instructive to look at meaning more closely.

The Study of Meaning

The study of meaning has traditionally been called *semantics*. Over the years semanticists have tried to set minimum standards for what a theory of meaning should be able to do. According to Bierwisch (1970), for example, it should be able to account for at least five things:

(1) *Anomaly*. Why is **His typewriter has bad intentions** meaningless or anomalous?

(2) *Self-contradiction*. Why is **My unmarried sister is married to a bachelor** self-contradictory?

(3) *Ambiguity*. Why is **John was looking for the glasses** ambiguous?

(4) *Synonymy*. Why is **The needle is too short** synonymous with **The needle isn't long enough**?

(5) *Entailment*. Why does **Many of the students were unable to answer your question** entail **Only a few of the students grasped your question**?

For other semanticists, a theory of meaning should do still more. As far as the psychology of language goes, it should specify how word meanings fit into the processes of comprehension and production. It should also relate word meanings to other things people know and should specify how word meanings are organized in memory.

The Referential and Picture Theories of Meaning

These minimal requirements immediately rule out several theories of meaning that often occur to the layman and have sometimes been entertained within the psychology of language. Two of these theories are the referential theory of meaning and the image, or picture, theory of meaning.

The *referential theory* is that the meaning of a word is what the word refers to, or is the relation of a word to what it refers to. So the expression **the old man** "means" the entity that the speaker of **The old man lit his awful cigar** was referring to with these words. The first problem is that not all words refer to things. It is hard to imagine what is referred to by **and, although, if, the, not, is,** and **could**. Second, the theory implies that any two expressions that refer to the same entity are synonymous, but that isn't necessarily so. **The old man, my next door neighbor, the town mayor,** and **Adam Schwartz,** for example, could all refer to the same person, yet they clearly don't have the same meaning. Conversely, one word can refer to different objects at different times and yet have the *same* meaning. One such word is **I,** which refers to John when he uses it, but to Mary when she uses it. The theory fails to account for synonymy. Thus, treating meaning as reference seems to capture only part of its essence.

The *image theory* is that the meaning of a word is the image it evokes (see, for example, Paivio, 1971). The problem with this theory is that images, or mental pictures, are particular and not general (Alston, 1964; Fodor, Bever, and Garrett, 1974). **Dog** might evoke an image of a particular beagle lying down, but so might **hound, beagle, beagle lying down,** and **man's best friend**. That is, many expressions may evoke the same image even though they aren't synonymous. On the other side of the coin, **dog** might evoke the image of a beagle one time, a spaniel another, and a Great Dane another. Yet we wouldn't say that **dog** means something different each time. And if the meaning of **dog** was an image of a particular beagle lying down, how is it that a Great Dane standing up is called a dog, while a wolf lying down is not? Surely the image for dog is pictorially closer to the wolf than to the Great Dane. The image theory, therefore, fails to account for synonymy too. And what is the image for **and, if, because, the**, and other such function words? So thinking of meaning as images doesn't get us very far either. Although words often do evoke images, the images are not themselves meaning, but something built on the basis of meaning.

Sense and Reference

The central problem with these two theories is that they do not separate knowledge of the language from knowledge of the world. People can know what a word means without knowing what it refers to. This problem has traditionally been handled with a distinction between two aspects of meaning: sense and reference. The *sense* of a word, its *intension*, is the "concept" associated with the word. The *reference* of a word, its *extension*, is the set of things the word applies to in any real or imaginary world—the objects, states, events, or processes in that world. The sense of **dog** is one's concept of what it is to be a dog, while the possible referents of **dog**—its extension—is the set of all real or imaginary dogs that fit this concept. This distinction helps solve some of the problems just encountered. Take **the old man** and **my next door neighbor**, which both referred to Adam Schwartz, a particular individual. The two expressions have different senses—for one's concept of an old man and a next door neighbor are different—but the same referent, namely Adam Schwartz. Or take **I**. It has a single sense— the concept of the speaker of the sentence now being uttered—but a different referent depending on who utters it.

Returning to the question of meaning, one way to proceed is to see what it is that speakers try to do with propositions. Take the expression **the old man** in **The old man lit his awful cigar** as spoken by Ann to Bill. What Ann is trying to do is get Bill to understand who is being referred to as the lighter of the cigar. Ann thinks that Bill can identify this entity uniquely if he is told that it falls under the concepts of man and oldness. Put differently, Ann thinks that Bill can identify the referent of **the old man** by means of the senses of **the, old**, and **man** in the right combination. For his part, Bill infers that Ann is trying to do this and therefore searches for a unique entity fitting his concepts of man and oldness. That is, he searches for a unique referent that fits the senses of **the, old**, and **man** in the right combination. This leaves us with two principal questions. What are Ann's and Bill's concepts of man, oldness, and other such things? And how do they decide whether or not some real world entity fits such a concept? Before these questions can be answered, however, it is necessary to take up a central problem in semantics, the dictionary-encyclopedia problem.

The Dictionary and the Encyclopedia

For people to be said to "know" the word **dog**, they would generally have to know three things: its pronunciation [dɔg], its syntactic properties (it is a noun), and its meaning. Because these three things look remarkably like the entry in the dictionary for **dog**, the dictionary has often been used as an analogy for the mental storehouse of one's word knowledge. **Dog** is said to have a *lexical entry* in long-term memory with roughly this form:

Pronunciation: [dɔg]

Syntactic category: noun

Meaning:

Every word has a lexical entry, and together, these entries form the *mental lexicon.* The question of what goes in the slot headed "meaning" will be taken up later.

People also have in memory what could be called a *mental encyclopedia.* It stores all the facts and generalizations they know about objects, events, and states in the world around them. For example, it might have an entry for the category of objects called dog:

appearance: is generally four-legged, two-eyed, furry, etc.

function: is used as pet, in hunting, tracking, guarding, etc.

typical behavior: can run, likes to chase cats, is territorial, etc.

origins: is animal, born live, mammal, of different breeds, etc.

history: was domesticated by early man, developed into pet, etc.

dated facts: George has a dog named Rover, Rin-Tin-Tin ate caviar, etc.

Everything people know about the world would be stored in entries like this, and together the entries would constitute the mental encyclopedia.

Is the Encyclopedia the Same as the Lexicon?

An obvious first hypothesis is that the mental encyclopedia is the same thing as the mental lexicon. However, there are several reasons why this cannot be so.

(1) Many entries in the mental encyclopedia will not correspond to names in the mental lexicon. Take the category dogs of California. It is distinguished from other categories and may have a separate encyclopedic entry. Yet it corresponds to no single lexical entry (in English). There is the expression **dogs in California**, but it is composed of three separate words, and its meaning is determined by the meaning of the three in combination. Although the category could conceivably have a name, like **caldog**, it happens not to. Examples like this suggest that the mental encyclopedia covers far more categories of experience than the mental lexicon.

(2) People who for various reasons have never acquired language or who have lost language through brain damage still have mental encyclopedias. They are often able to function normally as long as they don't need to communicate by language. They would know, for example, what dogs are and would recognize

a new member of the class when they saw one. All they would lack is the information people normally get from talking or reading, like the history of dogs. The congenitally deaf, with only sign language, probably have a mental encyclopedia that differs little from the rest of us. Encyclopedic knowledge isn't limited to humans. Chimpanzees, dogs, horses, and the rest all categorize the world and store generalizations and specific facts about these categories. So do pre-linguistic children. Language is hardly necessary for thinking beings to categorize, gather information, and form mental encyclopedias (see Fodor, 1975; Lenneberg, 1967).

Organization in the Encyclopedia

The mental encyclopedia, it has often been argued, is organized into categories that are a product of a system for classifying experience. Physical objects, for example, are organized according to such properties or attributes as size, shape, color, uses, and origins. These properties cut up the domain into categories—chairs, horses, trees, bottles, and so on—just as the lines on a map cut up a terrain into regions. Yet the boundaries for most categories are fuzzy. There is no clean boundary between trees and bushes; one category shades off into the other. And there is a complicated system of cross-references. The entry for dog mentions fur, which is indirectly a cross-reference to the entry for fur. Unfortunately, not very much can be said about the mental encyclopedia. Only recently have there been serious attempts to discover its internal organization. Some of these studies will be taken up later.

All this suggests that the mental encyclopedia is basic, and the mental lexicon is somehow grafted onto it. The encyclopedia contains an enormous amount of information, specifying many categories of all sizes and descriptions. The lexicon contains words denoting only a few of these categories. As a result, while categories like dogs, jumping, oldness, and truth can be talked about with single words, others require word combinations, like **dogs in California**, **quickly jump**, **extremely old**, and **logical truth**. Still other categories cannot be talked about at all. This is the problem faced by poets, novelists, and scientists who in striking out into unexplored territories come upon categories of experience with no ready descriptions. This is also a reason why new words are invented. They are needed for talking about previously unnamed categories.

The Lexical Entry

The question that still remains is, What fills the meaning slot in the lexical entry for **dog**? At present there is no clear single answer. As pointed out earlier most philosophers, linguists, and psychologists distinguish sense from reference and assume that it is the sense of **dog**, for example, that leads people to dogs as its referents. The sense of **dog**, in turn, is one's "concept" of what dogs are. One's concept of dog, in turn, is found in, or is parasitic on, the information about dogs in the mental encyclopedia. Even if all investigators agreed on this much—and they don't—there are still several ways to proceed. The three major ways are these.

The Encyclopedic View

In the *encyclopedic view*, the meaning slot in the lexical entry for **dog** would be filled with the complete encyclopedic entry for dog. The assumption is that everything in the encyclopedic entry for **dog** is pertinent to one's concept of dog. It is all part of what it means to know the meaning of the word **dog**. This view is implicit in many psychological studies that will be taken up later.

There are at least two problems with this view. First, it implies that everyone's meaning of **dog** is different, for no two people have the same facts and generalizations about dogs. This goes counter to what a speaker normally assumes about meaning. One assumes that even though other people possess different facts about dogs, they nevertheless have the same *meaning* for **dog**. Without this assumption, one could never be sure **dog** was conveying what it was meant to convey. Second, it implies that the meaning of **dog** changes every time one learns something new about dogs—like "Dogs often have fleas" or even "Mary's dog Fido won the Dog of the Year Award on July 4." If meaning changes constantly, how is it ever possible to decide on synonymy, semantic anomaly, and self-contradiction? These two problems are akin to the failure to distinguish sense from reference, and for many, the consequences are just as undesirable.

The Componential View

In the *componential view*, the lexical entry for **dog** contains merely a list of those properties dogs must have to be dogs. To take a simple example, the lexical entry for **man** might list three properties: the object must be human, male, and adult. This entry contains only a small part of the full encyclopedic entry for man—that is, only the necessary attributes of man. This view is especially common among linguists (for example, Bierwisch, 1970; Katz, 1972).

Although this view circumvents some problems of the encyclopedic view, it introduces others. In the componential view, **dog** will have more or less the same meaning for everyone, since most people will store the same necessary attributes. **Dog** won't change meaning with each newly discovered fact about dogs. But as later discussion will bring out, not all concepts are definable in terms of necessary attributes. **Dog** may be a case in point. It is not easy to specify the essence of doghood with a list of necessary attributes. Furthermore, component attributes—like being human, being adult, and being male in the entry for **man**—themselves have encyclopedic entries with lists of necessary properties, so it is not clear where the list should stop (Bolinger, 1965).

The Nominal View

In the *nominal view*, the lexical entry for **dog** contains no information about dogs at all. It merely "names" the category dog, which itself is defined as part of the encyclopedic entry for dog. Consider first the proper name **San Francisco**. It picks out a particular California city not because of any properties that city *has* to have, but because it is an individual entity that has been named **San Francisco**. A similar argument can be made for names of natural categories. **Dog** picks out a member of the category dog not because of any properties that dogs have to have, but because it is an already existing category that happens to be named **dog** (see Kripke, 1972; McCawley, 1975; Putnam, 1975). The lexical entry for **dog** might therefore look like this:

Pronunciation: [dɔg]

Syntactic category: noun

Meaning: a member of the category dog

So far this view has been put forward only for names of natural categories—animals, plants, minerals, and the like—but it may be extendable to other words too.

This view solves many problems, but largely by consigning them to the encyclopedia. It says, for example, that two expressions (like **male adult human** and **man**) are synonymous if they name the same category. It matters little, therefore, what facts are associated with the category as long as both expressions name it. Yet what counts as the "same category"—and that is no easy problem—is left entirely to the encyclopedia. It also gets around listing necessary attributes of things like dogs (which may not have necessary attributes anyway) and leaves the job of what dogs are to the encyclopedia as well. Depending on what the mental lexicon itself is to account for, these are either virtues or drawbacks.

The view one prefers rests ultimately on one's goals in studying meaning. The goal here is to account for the role meaning plays in comprehension, production, and acquisition, and the three views should be judged in this light. In practice there have been three approaches to meaning, but unfortunately they do not correspond exactly to the three views just described. The first two approaches—the componential and quantificational approaches—conform roughly to the componential and encyclopedic views of meaning. But the third, the functional approach, could be placed either within the componential or the nominal view of meaning.

SEMANTIC COMPONENTS

For many investigators, the sense of a word has three fundamental characteristics. First, it is a bundle of elementary semantic components. Second, the components themselves are propositions—each consisting of a predicate and one or more arguments. And third, these propositions are formally identical to those used for the representation of sentence meaning. That is, there is a continuity between sentence and word meaning. Just as sentences consist of propositions, so do words, and the propositions are essentially the same kind. The arguments for these three characteristics are important and should be examined carefully.

The first characteristic is that word senses consist of components. Imagine being asked what **boy** means. One might answer by giving the paraphrase "male non-adult human." Or one might answer by listing the attributes that seem to be necessary for something to be a boy, say, "male," "non-adult," and "human." In either case the sense of **boy** has been broken up into the components "male," "non-adult," and "human." This is the basic idea of the componential approach. Investigators have argued for this position from many different points of view, calling the components minimal units of content, semantic features, semantic components, semantic markers, semantic primitives, prelexical predicates, and semantic nodes (see Bierwisch, 1967, 1970; Hjelmslev, 1953, Katz, 1972; Katz and Fodor, 1963; Kintsch, 1974; G. Lakoff, 1972b; Lyons, 1968; McCawley, 1971; Norman and Rumelhart, 1975; Postal, 1966; Rumelhart and Ortony, 1977; Schank, 1972). Behind the diversity of names, however, is the same basic idea: the sense of a word is a bundle of components. For many investigators the ultimate hope is that there is a set of atomic components that cannot be decomposed any further. There should be fewer atomic components than words, and they should encompass all words in all languages.

These components, as many have argued, are propositions. The argument hangs on the idea that sense is a characteristic not of words, but of the propositions they express. This is illustrated with **boy** in the sentence:

1. John is a boy.

At first glance, it seems possible to characterize the sense of **boy** independently of the sentence it is in. **Boy** is "male," "non-adult," and "human." But these three components are not disembodied ideas in some vague relation to 1. They are properties specifically being predicated of John. The mental representation for the sense of **boy** must reflect this fact.

The solution is to treat each component as a proposition. Recall that **boy** itself signals the proposition **Boy(x)**, which predicates "being a boy" of some x. In 1, **x** is specified to be **John**, and this gives the full proposition **Boy(John)**. It is a simple step from here to realize that the three components of **boy** have the same character. In 1, John is predicated as "being male," "being non-adult," and "being human," notions that are denoted by the three propositions **Male(John)**, **Non-adult(John)**, and **Human(John)**. Furthermore, these three propositions must be fulfilled jointly, in conjunction. Thus, the sense of **boy**, or rather **Boy(x)**, is this:

$$Boy(x) = Male(x) \ \& \ Non\text{-}adult(x) \ \& \ Human(x)$$

As a consequence, the meaning of 1 would be something like this:

1′. Male(John) & Non-adult(John) & Human(John)

More complex sentences would have correspondingly more complex semantic representations.

These points lead directly to the third characteristic of sense in the componential approach: there is a continuity between word meaning and sentence meaning. Compare 1 to 2:

1. John is a boy.

2. John is a male non-adult human.

These two sentences are virtually synonymous, and what is more, would both be represented by 1'. The sense represented by **Male(x) & Non-adult(x) & Human(x)** may surface in English either as a single noun **boy** or as the phrase **male non-adult human**. **Boy** is essentially a phrase compressed into a single word. Many other words, though not all, have a similar character. The propositions that serve as the components of a word's sense can usually be expanded out into a phrase. Indeed, it is often useful to search for phrases (like **male non-adult human**) that mean the same as single words (like **boy**), for they suggest what the component propositions in the single words should be.

These three characteristics of sense are basic to a method of semantic analysis called *componential analysis* (see Lounsbury, 1956; Romney and d'Andrade, 1964; Goodenough, 1965). It was first used mainly by anthropologists to analyze the kinship terms—**father, mother, uncle, aunt**, etc.—of many languages; but it was later extended to many other domains as well. Over the years it has developed a more precise notation, yet the main principles have remained unaltered. It is worthwhile examining these principles, their justification, and their application to a few semantic domains.

Componential Analysis

At the heart of componential analysis is the notion that semantic components reveal themselves in analogies among words. The method involves three steps, with the investigator's intuition important at each step:

(1) Select a domain of words that all seem interrelated.

(2) Form analogies among the words in the domain.

(3) Identify the semantic components on the basis of the analogies.

Deriving Components

The method of componential analysis can be illustrated for the domain consisting of **man, woman, boy**, and **girl**. One analogy that could be formed is this:

man : woman : : boy : girl

If this analogy is valid, the argument goes, the difference in meaning between **man** and **woman**, the first two terms, is the same as that between **boy** and **girl**, the second two terms. The difference in both pairs, of course, is one of sex. **Man** and

boy might be said to be $+$Male, and **woman** and **girl** $-$Male. The four words fit into a second analogy too:

$$\text{man} \quad : \quad \text{boy} \quad : : \quad \text{woman} \quad : \quad \text{girl}$$

By the same logic, **man** and **boy** differ in the same way as **woman** and **girl**, on a dimension that might be called adultness. **Man** and **woman** would be $+$Adult, and **boy** and **girl** $-$Adult. The result for the four words looks like this:

Man	*Woman*	*Boy*	*Girl*
$+$Male	$-$Male	$+$Male	$-$Male
$+$Adult	$+$Adult	$-$Adult	$-$Adult
Remainder	Remainder	Remainder	Remainder

The component called Remainder, what is left over once $\pm$Male and $\pm$Adult have been extracted from the four terms, could be called $+$Human, but it would take further analogies to justify this component properly.

In this illustration, the semantic components have been denoted in a traditional way, writing "being male" as $+$Male. This notation, however, is equivalent to writing "being male" as **Male(x)**, and so these two representations of the sense of **boy** are the same:

Boy	*Boy*
$+$Male	Male(x) & Non-adult(x) & Human(x)
$-$Adult	
$+$Human	

Nevertheless, the propositional notation has distinct advantages over the plus-minus notation. This is demonstrated in the following example.

The domain of words **father**, **mother**, **son**, and **daughter**, like the domain **man**, **woman**, **boy**, and **girl**, has two valid analogies and leads to a set of plus-minus components like this:

Father	*Mother*	*Son*	*Daughter*
$+$Male	$-$Male	$+$Male	$-$Male
$+$Parent	$+$Parent	$-$Parent	$-$Parent
$+$Human	$+$Human	$+$Human	$+$Human

Indeed, all that has been changed is $+$Adult to $+$Parent. But something is missing. Note that **man** expresses an attribute about one person alone, "x is a man," while **father** expresses a relation between two people **x** and **y**, "x is the father of y." More formally, **man** expresses the one-place proposition **Man(x)**, "x is a man," and **father** the two-place proposition **Father(x, y)**, "x is the father of y." This difference is not reflected in the plus-minus notation. On close scrutiny, it is clear that +Parent is the part of **father** that expresses the relation between **x** and **y**, but the simple +Parent doesn't make clear whether **x** is the parent of **y**, or **y** is the parent of **x**. Furthermore, +Male and +Human aren't specific as to whether they apply to **x**, or to **y**, or to both **x** and **y**.

For **father, mother, son,** and **daughter**, therefore, the propositional notation is more precise. The four senses would be represented this way:

x is the father of y: Male(x) & Parent(x, y) & Human(x) & Human(y)

x is the mother of y: Female(x) & Parent(x, y) & Human(x) & Human(y)

x is the son of y: Male(x) & Parent(y, x) & Human(x) & Human(y)

x is the daughter of y: Female(x) & Parent(y, x) & Human(x) & Human(y)

In this notation, **Male(x)**, **Female(x)**, and **Human(x)** are attributional and it is clear whether they apply to **x** or **y**. **Parent(x, y)** is the only relational component. Note too that the relation **Parent(x, y)** denotes both "being a parent of" and "being a child of" simply by a reversal of the arguments **x** and **y**.

The components that fall out of this method depend crucially on the domain of words selected for analysis. **Man** and **woman** would have come out differently within the domain **man, woman, bull,** and **cow**. Ideally, **man** should be analyzed in relation to all other words, although of course in practice this is impossible. Instead, one tries to include all the relevant vocabulary, the words in the "semantic field" immediately surrounding the word of interest. This tack has been useful, for investigators have been able to proceed by small steps that are easily handled.

Taxonomies

Despite its disadvantages, the plus-minus notation handled one important fact: something cannot be both +Male and −Male at the same time. To deal with this, the propositional notation needs supplementation by devices that will be called *taxonomies* (see Leech, 1974). **Male(x)** and **Female(x)** can be said to form a binary taxonomy, to be denoted this way:

[Male(x), Female(x)]

This carries the information that some **x** can be male, or female, but not both. Other possible binary taxonomies include these two:

[Open(x), Closed(x)]

[Alive(x), Dead(x)]

In addition, some components belong to multiple taxonomies in which there are more than two components incompatible with each other. Two examples of multiple taxonomies are of colors and metals:

[Red(x), Green(x), Yellow(x), Blue(x), ...]

[Copper(x), Gold(x), Iron(x), Mercury(x), ...]

If something is red, it cannot be another color at the same time—although it may have parts of various colors. The same goes for metals.

Many pairs of components that appear to belong to binary taxonomies should instead be denoted as one component and its negative. The features ±Adult, for example, appear as if they belong to a binary taxonomy:

[Adult(x), Non-adult(x)]

But this hides the fact that **Non-adult(x)** is really the negative of **Adult(x)** and should be written **Not(Adult(x))**. In this way **woman** would be **Adult(x)** and **girl** **Not(Adult(x))**. Similarly, McCawley (1971) has argued that **Dead(x)** is really **Not(Alive(x))**.

Redundancy Rules

Another device that has been introduced in componential analyses is the *redundancy rule* (see Bierwisch, 1970). It specifies the properties an entity must have before it can serve as the argument for a proposition. One such redundancy rule is this:

Parent(x,y) → Adult(x) & Animate(x) & Animate(y)

According to this rule, if **x** is the parent of **y**, then **x** must be an adult and both **x** and **y** must be animate beings. The rule reflects the encyclopedic fact that non-adults and inanimate objects cannot bear children. With redundancy rules, the semantic components of a word can be extended to indicate how it is related to many other words in the vocabulary. The extra "redundant" components, like **Animate(x)** in the above example, are often written in "angle" brackets to distinguish them from the rest, as in this expanded version of the sense of **father**:

Father(x, y) = Parent(x, y) & Male(x) & Human(x) & Human(y) &
⟨Adult(x) & Animate(x) & Animate(y)⟩

Here are several more possible redundancy rules (Bierwisch, 1970):

Human(x) → Animate(x)   Male(x) → Animate(x)
Female(x) → Animate(x)

Formal Advantages of Componential Analyses

An important use to which semantic components have been put is in the characterization of why some sentences are necessarily true, some necessarily false, and some semantically anomalous (see Katz, 1972; Leech, 1974). An assertion that is necessarily true is said to be *analytically true*, or simply *analytic*, as illustrated here:

3. That man is male.

4. My mother is adult.

5. Our pregnant neighbor is a woman.

An assertion that is necessarily false is said to be *self-contradictory*, as illustrated here:

6. That man is female.

7. My mother isn't an adult.

8. Our pregnant neighbor is a man.

Still other sentences are odd, or *semantically anomalous*, as illustrated here:

9. That rock is male.

10. My mother assembled.

11. Our pregnant neighbor is geometric.

The Logic of Components

Semanticists such as Bierwisch (1970), Katz (1972), and Leech (1974) have devised logical systems in which semantic components are used to "prove" that sentences 3 through 5 are analytic, 6 through 8 are self-contradictory, and 9 through 11 semantically anomalous. Informally, the proofs go like this. In 3 **man** expands out into the components **Male(x) & Adult(x) & Human(x)**, and so the subject of the sentence is male. But the rest of 3 asserts that the subject is male—that the entity that is male is male. Since this is a tautology and must always be true, 3 is necessarily true. The claim is that all sentences judged to be analytically true—necessarily true by their wording alone—can be "proved" true by the same analysis.

Self-contradictions and semantic anomalies can be "proved" in much the same way. The self-contradictions in 4 through 6 make use of negation or taxonomies in their proofs. In 6, as in 3, the man is male, yet in 6 he is asserted to be female. But since **Male(x)** and **Female(x)** belong to a binary taxonomy, something cannot be both male and female simultaneously. So asserting that something that is male is female is self-contradictory. The semantic anomalies in 9 through 11 are ruled out via redundancy rules. In 9, the rock is asserted to be male, but **Male(x)** has the following redundancy rule associated with it:

$$Male(x) \rightarrow Animate(x)$$

KINDLY DISREGARD
THIS NOTICE

Drawing by Chon Day; © 1975 The New Yorker Magazine, Inc.

So before something can be asserted to be male, it has to be animate. Since one component of rock is **Not(Animate(x))**, rocks cannot be **Animate(x)**, and therefore maleness is something that cannot be asserted of them. This, of course, excludes metaphorical uses as in **That electric plug is male**.

Semantic components can also be used formally to show why certain sentences imply others. In the following sentences, the first implies the next two:

12. Her secretary is a man.

13. Her secretary is an adult.

14. Her secretary is male.

In 12, **man** contains the components **Male(x) & Adult(x) & Human(x)**. So if something is asserted to be a man, it is automatically asserted to be an adult too. It follows that if 12 is true, so is 13. The same holds for 12 and 14. The idea is, simply, that with the right set of logical principles, semantic components can be used to explain the intuitions people have about analyticity, self-contradictoriness, semantic anomaly, and implication.

Meaning Relations

Semantic components have also been used to account for meaning relations among words within the vocabulary. Five familiar types of meaning relations

TABLE 11–1

FIVE COMMON MEANING RELATIONS

RELATION	EXAMPLE
Synonymy	**big** is a synonym of **large**
Antonymy	
1. Contradictoriness	**male** is the contradictory of **female**
2. Contrariness	**large** is the contrary of **small**
Converseness	**parent** is the converse of **child**
Hyponymy	**father** is a hyponym of **parent**

are listed in Table 11–1. Formally they are defined in this way:

(1) *Synonyms* have identical sets of semantic components.

(2) *Antonyms* contrast on only one component. The two components that differ belong either to a binary taxonomy, like **Male(x)** and **Female(x)**, or to a positive-negative pair,-like **Alive(x)** and **Not(Alive(x))**. Thus, **man** and **woman**, **boy** and **girl**, **male** and **female**, and **dead** and **alive** are all antonyms. But antonyms come in two types. *Contradictories* exhaust the options on a scale, whereas *contraries* do not. Someone is either male or female; no one can be neither male nor female. But things do not have to be either large or small; they could be neither large nor small. Thus, **male** and **female** are contradictories, while **large** and **small** are contraries. Whether a pair of antonyms is contradictory or contrary depends on the place of the contrastive component among all the other components. The contrastive component in certain contraries will be taken up later.

(3) *Converses* differ in only one component, and that component has merely a switch in arguments. Recall that both **parent** and **child** contain the component **Parent(x, y)**. But whereas **x is the parent of y** comes out **Parent(x, y)**, **x is the child of y** comes out **Parent(y, x)**, in which **x** and **y** have been switched.

(4) The *hyponym* of a word contains all the components of the second word plus one or more extra. **Father**, which is **Male(x) & Parent(x, y)**, contains the components of **parent**, which is **Parent(x, y)**, plus the extra component **Male(x)**.

For some semanticists (e.g., Katz, 1972), these formal consequences have become the *raison d'être* for studying meaning. The goal of semantics is to account for analyticity, self-contradictoriness, semantic anomaly, implication, synonymy, antonymy, converseness, hyponymy, and certain other judgments about meaning. Semantic components are needed to account for these judgments. Thus, there are good formal reasons for thinking of sense as consisting of semantic components. It remains to be seen whether they ought to be part of the mental lexicon.

TABLE 11–2

STATE AND CHANGE

Pairs of words in the relation of state to change-of-state.

STATE : CHANGE-OF-STATE	STATE : CHANGE-OF-STATE
x was warm : x warmed	x was higher : x rose, ascended
x was longer : x lengthened	x was lower : x descended, dropped, fell
x was hard : x hardened	x was in y : x entered y
x was solid : x solidified	x was at y : x arrived at y
x was liquid : x liquefied, melted	x was not at y : x left y
x was dead : x died	x had y : x got y

APPLICATIONS OF COMPONENTIAL ANALYSIS

Although only a few examples of semantic components have been provided so far, they have been important ones. **Male(x)** and **Female(x)** turn up not only in **father-mother** and **boy-girl**, but also in **king-queen, bachelor-spinster, bull-cow, actor-actress**, and many more. **Adult(x)** and **Not(Adult(x))** turn up in **rooster-chick, tomcat-kitten**, and others. And **Parent(x, y)** is found in **grandfather, uncle**, and even **brother** and **sister** (Bierwisch, 1970)—as well as **sire, orphan, offspring**, and many others. Still, these components are all limited to animate objects.

There are three semantic components, however, that have especially broad applicability because they are not tied to narrow classes of objects or events. They are the components that represent change, cause, and negation. They are also of interest because they may be a reflection of three fundamental human concepts (to be dealt with further in Chapter 14).

Change and Causation

Verbs that denote change, of which there are many, make use of the component to be written **Come-about(x)**. Consider the word pairs in Table 11–2. They have been arranged so that analogies can be formed between any two pairs, for example:

> x was hard   :   x hardened   : :   x was dead   :   x died

It follows that **hard** and **harden** differ in the same way as **dead** and **die**. Intuitively, **hard** and **dead** denote the states **x** being hard and **x** being dead, while **harden** and **die** denote the process of changing into that state, of **x** becoming hard or of **x** becoming dead. It is natural to assume, then, that **harden** and **die** are simply **hard** and **dead** with an extra component denoting the change. Take 15 and 16:

15. The steel was hard.

16. The steel hardened.

If **hard** in 15 is represented as **Hard(x)** as in 15′, then **harden** in 16 can be represented as a combination of **Come-about(x)** and **Hard(x)**, as in 16′:

15′. Hard(the steel)

16′. Come-about(Hard(the steel))

Note that 16′ is not written as a conjunction of **Come-about(x)** and **Hard(x)**; rather the second component is inserted as the argument for the first. What came about was not the steel, but the hardness of the steel. Thus, 16′ could be paraphrased as **it came about that the steel was hard**.

In many pairs in Table 11–2, the two words are morphologically related. **Harden** consists of **hard** plus **-en**, and **solidify** of **solid** plus **-ify**. These are just two suffixes that historically have been exploited in English to form change-of-state verbs from adjectives or verbs for states. Note that just as **harden** is formed morphologically from **hard** plus a suffix, the sense of **harden** is formed from the sense of **hard** plus **Come-about(x)**. The suffix signals the presence of the additional semantic component. However, two words do not need to be related historically to be related semantically. Next to **liquefy**, which has the sense of **liquid** plus **Come-about(x)**, is **melt**, which also has the sense of **liquid** plus **Come-about(x)**. Word morphology may hint at the contemporary sense of a word, but it won't usually give the complete story.

Causation is another common component of verbs, and it will be denoted by the proposition **Cause(x, y)**. Compare 16 and 17:

16. The steel hardened.

17. The process hardened the steel.

Although both sentences contain **harden**, 16 is intransitive (without a direct object) and 17 is transitive. Because of the extra process involved, **harden** in 17 has a different sense from **harden** in 16. Yet as the identity of their surface forms suggests, they are related. Loosely paraphrased, 17 means "the process caused the steel to harden," which has two parts: the process caused something and what was caused was the occurrence of 16. This suggests that 17 can be written this way:

17′. Cause(the process, the steel hardened)

Cause(x,y) is a two-place proposition whose first argument **x** denotes a causing event, here **the process**, and whose second argument **y** denotes the resulting

TABLE 11–3

CHANGE AND CAUSE

Pairs of verbs in the relation of change-of-state to causation of that change-of-state.

CHANGE-OF-STATE : CAUSATIVE		CHANGE-OF-STATE : CAUSATIVE	
x warmed	: y warmed x	x rose	: y raised x
x lengthened	: y lengthened x	x dropped	: y dropped x
x hardened	: y hardened x	x got y	: z gave y to x
x solidified	: y solidified x	x left	: y expelled x
x liquefied	: y liquified x	x lay down	: y laid x down
x melted	: y melted x	x came	: y brought x
x died	: y killed x	x learned y	: z taught y to x

event, here **the steel hardened** (which is simply 16). Since 16 should be written as 16′, and since it is a part of 17, the meaning of 17 is this:

17″. Cause(the process, Come-about(Hard(the steel)))

That is, **harden** in its transitive sense has this representation:

Harden(x,y) = Cause(x, Come-about(Hard(y)))

Table 11–3 lists word pairs consisting of an intransitive verb denoting change of state and a transitive verb denoting the causation of this change of state. As before, analogies can be formed between any two pairs on the list. For the pairs with counterparts in Table 11–2 (like **harden**), there are three related senses, as in 18, 19, and 20:

18. *x is warm:* Warm(x)

19. *x warmed:* Come-about(Warm(x))

20. *y warmed x:* Cause(y, Come-about(Warm(x)))

All that changes from triplet to triplet is the state, whether it is **Warm(x)**, **Liquid(x)**, **Dead(x)**, or whatever. The states that already are two-place predicates, like **Have(x, y)**, end up with three arguments as in 23:

21. *x had y:* Have(x, y)

22. *x got y:* Come-about(Have(x, y))

23. *z gave y to x:* Cause(z, Come-about(Have(x, y)))

Negation

Negation is a common component in word senses too. It is easy to find instances of positive-negative contrast, as in this analogy:

> x is present : x is absent : : x is there : x is not there

This analogy suggests that **absent** is the negation of **present** just as **not there** is the negation of **there**. If **x is present** is written as **Present(x)**, then **x is absent** would be **Not(Present(x))**. Here are two other simple instances:

24. a. *x and y are the same:* Same(x, y)
    b. *x and y are different:* Not(Same(x, y))

25. a. *x and y agree:* Agree(x, y)
    b. *x and y disagree or conflict:* Not(Agree(x, y))

Some positive-negative pairs are related morphologically, as in **agree-disagree**. The extra component **Not(x)** is often reflected in a prefix, as in **able-unable**, **activate-deactivate**, and **moral-amoral**. Yet in other pairs, the morphology gives no hint of the positive-negative relationship, as in **often-seldom**, **remember-forget**, and **have-lack**.

    The component **Not(x)** may be lodged deep in among the other components of a word sense. Take **persuade** and **dissuade** in 26 and 27, where the sentence in *a*, with its paraphrase in *b*, has the semantic representation in *c* (G. Lakoff, 1970):

26. a. x persuaded y to do z
    b. x caused it to come about that y intended to do z
    c. Cause(x, Come-about(Intend(y, Do(y, z))))

27. a. x dissuaded y from doing z
    b. x caused it to come about that y intended not to do z
    c. Cause(x, Come-about(Intend(y, Not(Do(y, z)))))

Note that **dissuade** doesn't mean simply "not persuade," for **I dissuaded Vivien from leaving** doesn't mean the same as **I didn't persuade Vivien to leave**. Rather, as 27c shows, the negative component **Not(x)** in **dissuade** is buried deep within the other components, attached to the second argument of **Intend(y, Do(y, z))**. If it weren't attached just there, **dissuade** wouldn't have the right interpretation. This is typical of many negative words.

Unmarked and Marked Adjectives

The component **Not(x)** is perhaps least visible in such antonyms as **long-short**, **high-low**, and **happy-sad**. Take **long** and **short**, which denote opposite ends of the scale called length. This scale has a positive and a negative direction. To make a board long, one has to *add* to its length, while to make it short, one has to *sub-*

tract. **Long** therefore denotes the positive end of the scale, and **short**, the negative end. Likewise, **high** and **happy** are positive, and **low** and **sad** are negative. The negative is sometimes signaled in the prefix, as in **unhappy** and **unkind**.

. Negativity in antonyms is often tied to a phenomenon called *markedness* in adjectives (Sapir, 1944; Greenberg, 1966; Lyons, 1968; Vendler, 1968; H. Clark, 1969; Givón, 1970). It can be illustrated with **long** and **short**. In certain contexts **long** "neutralizes" in meaning to denote the whole scale of length, not just the positive end. **Short**, on the other hand, never neutralizes. The neutralization of **long** shows up in three constructions. First, compare these two questions:

28. a. *Neutral:* How long is the movie?
    b. *Non-neutral:* How short is the movie?

To ask about the length of a movie one would normally use 28a, not 28b. Question 28a is neutral and doesn't prejudge the movie's length, whereas 28b presupposes the movie is short and asks *how* short. Second, compare these two scale names:

29. a. *Full scale:* length
    b. *Half scale:* shortness

Length names the full scale on which **long** and **short** lie, whereas **shortness** names only the negative end. **Length**, of course, is morphologically related to **long**, and **shortness** to **short**. Now, third, compare these two "measure phrases":

30. a. *Possible:* two hours long
    b. *Impossible:* two hours short

In 30a, **long** covers the whole scale of length and does not presuppose the movie to be long. **Two hours long** is equivalent to the neutral expression **two hours in length**. Expression 30b is impossible and shows that **short** does not neutralize. Because **long** neutralizes in these ways, it is said to be "unmarked" and **short** is said to be "marked with respect to **long**." Other antonyms, when one neutralizes, at least in questions like 28a, are also called marked and unmarked.

What are the components of **long** and **short**? The answer is complex and can only be hinted at here (see Bartsch and Vennemann, 1972). First, **long** and **short** are implicitly comparative. **The play is long** means "the play is long compared to some standard." The standard is usually given by the context, but is sometimes explicit, as in **The play was long for a Shakespearean tragedy**, meaning "the play was long compared to the typical Shakespearean tragedy." Second, **long** implies measurement in the normal, or positive, direction from that standard, while **short** implies measurement in the non-normal, or negative, direction. This point is examined more closely in Chapter 14. In sum, **long** and **short** signal the two-place propositions **Long(x, y)** and **Short(x, y)** with these paraphrases:

x is long for a y: x has a length that is some distance from the length of the typical y in a direction that is normal *x is short for a y:* x has length that is some distance from the length of the typical y in a direction that is not normal

Once again, the negative **Not(x)** is buried deep within the other components. Whereas the direction of measurement from the standard for **long** is normal, that for **short** is *not* normal.

Complex Nouns and Adjectives

Many nouns are built from verbs or adjectives. For example, the agentive noun **baker** is a morphological combination of the verb **bake** and the suffix **-er**. It is natural to suggest that **x is a baker**, or **Baker(x)**, consists of these components:

$$\text{Baker}(x) = \text{Human}(x) \ \& \ \text{Professional}(\text{Bake}(x, y))$$

That is, a **baker** is a "human who bakes things (y) professionally." Not all verbal components are so transparent. Take the following analogy:

$$\text{baker} \ : \ \text{bake} \ : : \ \text{author} \ : \ \text{write}$$

It suggests that the relation of **author** to **write** is the same as that of **baker** to **bake** even though **author** does not divide into **auth + or**. **Author** might therefore be written this way:

$$\text{Author}(x) = \text{Human}(x) \ \& \ \text{Professional}(\text{Write}(x, y))$$

That is, an **author** is a "human who writes things (y) professionally." Other agent nouns like **baker** with their component verbs apparent in the morphology are **worker, banker, farmer, teacher, actor, writer, inventor,** and **manager,** and other agent nouns like **author** are **mechanic, butcher, grocer, poet,** and **doctor.**

Agent nouns are just one of many types that have verbs or adjectives as immediate components. For some nouns the immediate components are obvious. **Persuasion** contains **persuade, stinginess** contains **stingy,** and **ability** contains **able.** The verbs or adjectives themselves may contain further components, as does **persuade.** For other nouns, the immediate components are not so obvious, for example, the **few** in **paucity,** the **free** in **liberty,** and the **mind** in **mentality.** Most abstract nouns have this character.

Some adjectives are built on verbal components too. Take **x is literate,** or **Literate(x).** Someone is literate if he is able to read, so:

$$\text{Literate}(x) = \text{Able}(x, \text{Read}(x, y))$$

Its opposite, **illiterate,** would contain a negative:

$$\text{Illiterate}(x) = \text{Not}(\text{Able}(x, \text{Read}(x, y)))$$

Or consider **x is deaf**, **Deaf(x)**. To be deaf is to be unable to hear:

$$Deaf(x) = Not(Able(x, Hear(x, y)))$$

Words like **literate** and **deaf** that "contain" other verbal components are numerous.

Representing Sentences

In Chapter 2, it was noted that the meaning of a sentence can be represented as a set of propositions combined with each other in a particular pattern. Thus, 31 would be represented as 32:

31. The boy's father killed the illiterate baker.

32. $Boy(E_{13})$
    & $Father(E_9, E_{13})$
    & $Baker(E_4)$
    & $Illiterate(E_4)$
    & $Kill(E_9, E_4)$

For convenience, certain subsidiary propositions have been omitted, the entities have been given arbitrary labels, and each proposition has been put on a separate line. In the componential approach, each of these propositions consists of semantic components that are themselves propositions. From the analyses illustrated so far, each line of 32 expands into the propositions of 33:

33. $Male(E_{13})$ & $Not(Adult(E_{13}))$ & $Human(E_{13})$
    & $Male(E_9)$ & $Human(E_9)$ & $Parent(E_9, E_{13})$
    & $Human(E_4)$ & $Professional(Bake(E_4, things))$
    & $Not(Able(E_4, Read(E_4, things)))$
    & $Cause(E_9, Come\text{-}about(Not(Alive(E_4))))$

In the componential approach, 33 represents what it is people understand of 31. The meaning of a sentence is represented in terms of its primitive semantic components.

Limitations of the Componential Approach

Many word domains have been analyzed into semantic components. Some of those studied in English are listed in Table 11–4. In other languages, they have included kinship terms, pronouns, disease names, plant names, color terms, and names for meals (see Burling, 1970). These analyses have been useful, especially for the comparison of semantic systems in different languages. Yet the componential approach has certain inherent limitations as a theory about what goes into the mental lexicon.

TABLE 11-4

SOME SEMANTIC FIELDS STUDIED BY COMPONENTIAL ANALYSIS

SEMANTIC FIELD	EXAMPLES OF WORDS STUDIED	INVESTIGATORS
Kinship terms	mother, son, aunt, step-sister	Romney & d'Andrade (1964), Wallace & Atkins (1960), Goodenough (1965)
Containers	pot, bottle, glass, tub	Lehrer (1970)
Possession verbs	get, find, keep, borrow	Bendix (1966), Fillmore (1969)
Motion verbs	go, ride, lift, escape	G. Miller (1972)
Cooking verbs	boil, roast, sauté, poach	Lehrer (1969)
Judging verbs	accuse, credit, praise, condemn	Fillmore (1971b), Osgood (1970)
Spatial terms	high, down, front, shallow	Bierwisch (1967), Teller (1969), H. Clark (1973a)
Temporal terms	hour, after, next, often	Leech (1969)
Sound terms	noise, din, loud, shrill	Lehrer (1974)

What is the Nature of Semantic Components?

Many semantic fields do not break down into neat semantic components. Roughly speaking, semantic fields lie between two extreme types, paradigms and taxonomies, as illustrated here:

Paradigm: man, woman, boy, girl

Taxonomy: copper, lead, zinc, gold, silver, . . .

Note that both the humans and the metals are mutually exclusive hyponyms of a single superordinate term, **human** and **metal**. Despite that, the two domains differ in their susceptibility to componential analysis. The humans have two clear cross-classifiable dimensions, sex and maturity, and fit into well-formed analogies like **man : woman :: boy : girl**. The metals do not have such clear dimensions, if they have any at all. Nor do they fit into well-formed analogies. So while componential analysis is ready-made for human names, it is not very illuminating for metals. With them one has to be content with a "multinary taxonomy" like this:

[Copper(x), Lead(x), Zinc(x), Gold(x), Silver(x), . . .]

Any further analysis would get into chemical properties: their color, state, density, and texture at different temperatures. The trouble is, most domains are a mixture of paradigms and taxonomies, and natural categories like the plant and animal names are mostly taxonomic. Leech (1974), among others, has argued that for the latter there are rarely any components at all. **Horse** is left unanalyzed as **Horse(x)**.

The status of the semantic components themselves is rather unclear. Note that the sense of **man** is given by the proposition **Man(x)**, which divides up into the propositions **Male(x) & Adult(x) & Human(x)**. Do these divide further? If not, what is their sense? This question is especially urgent for those terms that do not seem to have components, such as **Red(x)**, **Copper(x)**, **Horse(x)**, and the like. It doesn't get us very far to say that the sense of **red** is given by the proposition **Red(x)**. Indeed, this solution looks very much like that of the nominal approach in which **red** names the category red and does nothing more. The category red, in turn, would be part of the mental encyclopedia and dependent on the ability of the human perceptual apparatus to analyze light into colors. If this is so, what is gained by analyzing any term into components?

Can Components Represent All of Meaning?

For many investigators (like Katz, 1972), the sense of a word is a listing of the necessary properties of the entities the word can refer to. This list is a set of semantic components. For example, **Man(x)** should be divided into **Male(x) & Adult(x) & Human(x)** to show that man is necessarily male, adult, and human. Philosophers like Putnam (1975), however, have argued that there are virtually no properties that are necessarily true for something to be in a named category. For example, there are no properties that a thing must have to be a tiger or a lemon, although there are properties most tigers or lemons would be expected to have. These properties define the stereotype of a tiger (a striped animal of the cat family with four legs and a long tail) and the stereotype of a lemon (a small yellow citrus fruit with a distinctive flavor), but not the concepts tiger and lemon themselves.

According to Wittgenstein (1953, 1958), Ryle (1951), and others, there are some named categories that couldn't conceivably be defined in terms of necessary properties. Wittgenstein's famous example is **game**, and Ryle has added **work**, **thinking**, **fighting**, **trading**, and **playing**. According to Wittgenstein, there are no properties that are common to all games—card games, board games, ball games, Olympic games, children's games, and so on. Rather, the things called games belong together only because they bear a "family resemblance" to each other. Each has properties in common with some other games, but no properties in common with all of them. If this is so, it is futile to look for semantic components for **game**, for there aren't any.

Finally, by their very nature, semantic components leave out many subtleties of meaning. **Bachelor**, for example, might be represented as "an adult man who has never married" and **spinster** "an adult woman who has never married." Yet **bachelor** and **spinster** differ in ways this analysis doesn't capture. **Bachelor** applies more readily to a young man at a marriageable age, and **spinster**, to a woman past the usual age of marriage. **Girl**, to take another example, has been represented as **Female(x) & Not(Adult(x)) & Human(x)**. Yet it is commonly used to refer to adult female humans, as in **the girls at the office** and **the girls in the bridge club**. If these senses are to be accounted for, we must look beyond semantic components.

QUANTIFICATIONAL REPRESENTATIONS
OF MEANING

In psychology there has been a relatively independent tradition that we will call the quantificational approach to meaning. It is distinguished mostly by its methods. Many people, typically fifty or more, may be asked to judge some aspect of the meanings of words in a semantic field—for instance, the color terms in English. These judgments are then submitted to one of several highly sophisticated mathematical methods of analysis, like "factor analysis," "multidimensional scaling," or "cluster analysis." What emerges is a "quantificational representation" of the meanings of these words. Over the years these methods have been applied to broad sections of the English vocabulary. The question is: what has the approach discovered about the nature of the mental lexicon?

The quantificational approach resembles the componential approach in several ways. It is concerned with word sense. It assumes that word sense consists of components, in this case called "factors" or "dimensions." And it assumes that the more components two words have in common, the more similar they are in meaning. The major difference between the two approaches is in the role of the investigator's own semantic judgments. In the componential approach, it is typically the investigator who judges which analogies are well formed and which are not. In the quantificational approach, other people make the judgments and the investigator merely extracts the components latent in their judgments. The quantificational methods were developed for three reasons. First, it was felt that these methods would be more "objective" and less open to the investigator's own biases. Second, it was possible to investigate semantic fields about which the investigator had no clear intuitions. And third, these methods were able to handle components of meaning that were continuous, like age, where the componential approach could handle only components that were discrete, like adult versus non-adult.

Semantic Factors

In an early quantificational approach to meaning, Osgood, Suci, and Tannenbaum (1957) tried to measure "affective" meaning—the emotional reactions words elicit—by a paper-and-pencil test they called the *semantic differential*. People were asked to rate each of many words on twenty bi-polar adjective scales such as the following:

happy:____:____:____:____:____:____:____:____: sad

hard:____:____:____:____:____:____:____:____: soft

slow:____:____:____:____:____:____:____:____: fast

The word **mother**, for example, might be rated impressionistically as quite happy, very soft, and neither fast nor slow. These ratings were then analyzed by a method called factor analysis. Roughly speaking, it showed that the twenty bi-polar scales fell into three groups. A word was given similar ratings on each scale within a group, but different ratings on scales not in the same group. Thus, each group of bi-polar scales seemed to reflect a different "factor" or aspect of affective meaning. The three factors were called:

Evaluation (reflected in **good/bad**, **happy/sad**, and **beautiful/ugly**)

Potency (reflected in **strong/weak**, **brave/cowardly**, and **hard/soft**)

Activity (reflected in **fast/slow**, **tense/relaxed**, and **active/passive**)

Two words were most likely to differ on the scales for Evaluation. This reflects the basic positive/negative reaction people have toward objects, states, and events. With the semantic differential, Osgood and others have demonstrated the applicability and stability of the Evaluation, Potency, and Activity factors in the words of many languages.

As a complete representation of word senses, however, the semantic differential has limitations (see Carroll, 1959; Weinreich, 1958). The most serious is that it measures the affective reactions a word elicits, but not the concept it denotes. It tells us that **mother** elicits a reaction of very good, somewhat strong, and slightly passive, but not that **mother** denotes an adult human female that is a parent of others. That is, it appears to tap one part of people's encylopedic knowledge of such things as mothers, Wednesdays, cups, or marriage, but not the part that is pertinent to the senses of **mother**, **Wednesday**, **cup**, or **marriage**. Although the semantic differential has been useful in studying attitudes and emotional reactions, it has had little success in explaining how word sense is involved in comprehension, production, and acquisition.

Semantic Space

In more recent quantificational methods, word meanings are often represented by means of a *semantic space*. The meaning of a word is taken to be a location in physical space in which each dimension represents one of the word's semantic components. The basic idea is illustrated in Figure 11–1 for the words **man**, **woman**, **boy**, **girl**, **child**, **buck**, **doe**, and **fawn**. Each word is represented as a point in three-dimensional space in which the dimensions represent Sex, Maturity, and Species. The horizontal dimension called Sex has **boy**, **man**, and **buck** at the male end, **woman**, **girl**, and **doe** at the female end, and **child** and **fawn** in the center indicating an unspecified sex. The vertical dimension of Maturity,

FIGURE 11–1

HYPOTHETICAL SEMANTIC SPACE FOR EIGHT TERMS

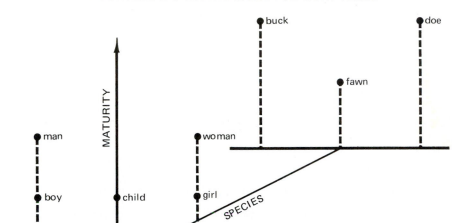

on the other hand, is continuous, varying from zero maturity to full maturity. **Boy**, **girl**, **child**, and **fawn** are relatively immature, and **man**, **woman**, **buck**, and **doe** are relatively mature. The horizontal dimension into the graph, Species, is for illustrative purposes binary, with humans at one end and deer at the other. This fragment of semantic space represents the sense relations among these eight words in a systematic and comprehensible way.

In semantic space, the closer two words are, the more similar they are in meaning. In Figure 11–1, **child** is closer to **boy** and **girl** than to **man** or **woman**, showing that **child** is more similar in meaning to **boy** and **girl** than to **man** or **woman**. **Child** is equidistant from **boy** and **girl** showing it is equally similar in meaning to the two. In every comparison throughout the figure, physical proximity in the semantic space is a faithful reflection of semantic similarity.

Multidimensional Scaling

Seizing on this relation, Shepard (1962) and Kruskal (1964) developed a method, called multidimensional scaling, by which they could work backward from people's judgments of similarity to the semantic space. In applying this method, one typically shows people all possible pairings of words within a semantic domain—for example, the twenty-eight possible pairings of the eight words in Figure 11–1. For each pair they rate how similar the two words are on a scale of 1 to 10. The average ratings for the twenty-eight pairs are then submitted to a special computer program. It is designed to find a semantic space in which the more similar two words are rated on the average, the closer they are in the space. The goal is to find the best spatial representation that fits all pairs simultaneously. With this technique, people make simple judgments—"How similar are these two words?"—yet from the judgments one can discover the complex semantic space on which the judgments are presumably based.

Multidimensional scaling methods have been applied to many semantic domains, including color terms, kinship terms, pronouns, emotion names, prepositions, conjunctions, judgment verbs, possession verbs, trait names, occupation names, and others (see Fillenbaum & Rapaport, 1971; Romney, Shepard, and Nerlove, 1972). Although the technique seems most appropriate for paradigms, like the one in Figure 11–1, it has actually been more revealing for taxonomies, like the color terms, where the investigator's intuitions are of little value.

As an illustration, consider the semantic space in Figure 11–2 for animal names as studied by Rips, Shoben, and Smith (1973). Each local part of the space fits our intuitions. The more similar two animals are, the closer they are in space. But as the global picture brings out, the animals lie on two dimensions. The horizontal dimension reflects size, with small animals on the left and large animals on the right. The vertical dimension reflects "ferocity" or "predacity." The farther down the animal is, generally the more ferocious or predatory it is. The two superordinate terms **animal** and **mammal** fell near the center

FIGURE 11–2
SEMANTIC SPACE FOR MAMMALS

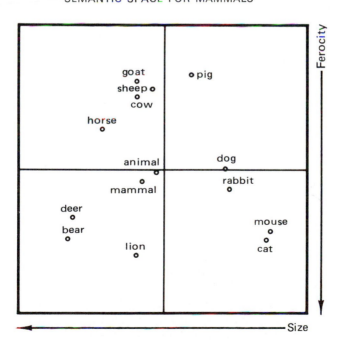

From Rips, Shoben, and Smith (1973). Reproduced by permission.

of the space, as one might expect. Semantic spaces, however, are often much messier than this. It is usually not as easy to label the dimensions (even here, the dimension of ferocity or predacity isn't exactly right). And when there are more than three dimensions, as there often are (unlike real space), they are not as easy to visualize or interpret. Still, these semantic spaces do show the continuous nature of such dimensions as size and ferocity.

Semantic Clusters

Word domains that do not fit into neat semantic spaces may instead divide into word clusters. For these S. Johnson (1967) has devised a method called hierarchical cluster analysis. Once again people are asked to rate all word pairs within a domain for their similarity in meaning, but what is produced is a hierarchical arrangement of clusters. The words within a cluster are all closely related, and the clusters themselves are related to each other in a hierarchy.

For illustration consider the clusters of English pronouns in Table 11–5 as analyzed by Fillenbaum and Rapaport (1971). At the left are the sixteen pronouns. They fall first into semantic clusters 1 through 6. These make obvious sense, with 1 containing the first person singular pronouns (**I**, **me**, and **my**), 2 containing the first person plural pronouns (**we**, **us**, and **our**), and so on. These six clusters themselves combine at the next level up in the hierarchy as clusters 7, 8, and 9. These too make good sense, with 7 containing the first person pronouns, 8 the third person singular pronouns, and 9 the rest. At the next level up, clusters 8 and 9 combine into a single cluster, 11. At this level, 10 contains the first person pronouns, and 11 the rest. Thus, the cluster analysis brings out some of the structure within the pronouns with considerable clarity.

As this example shows, however, cluster analysis can miss certain relationships and be misleading on others. Note that English pronouns are nominative (**I**, **we**, **he**, **she**, **they**), accusative (**me**, **us**, **him**, **her**, **them**), or possessive (**my**, **our**, **his**, **her**, **their**, **your**). Cluster analysis cannot represent this fact because it does not extract cross-classifications from clusters. Note also that some levels in the hierarchy are improper, and without other evidence, it is difficult to tell which. Clusters 7, 8, and 9 are one example. Cluster 7 contains the singular and plural first person pronouns, 8 only the singular third person pronouns, and 9 the rest—a combination of second person singular or plural pronouns and third person plural pronouns. Cluster analysis is limited to discovering only certain types of relationships (see Fillenbaum and Rapaport, 1971).

Limitations of the Quantificational Approach

Within psychology, quantificational methods were taken up because they were felt to be more "objective." They used simple judgments from naive people and relied on mechanical procedures for extracting the semantic spaces and clusters latent in the judgments. But this objectivity was bought at the cost of certain limitations. Some were in the methods themselves, and others were in the notions of semantic space and semantic clusters.

TABLE 11–5
MAJOR CLUSTERS FOR THE ENGLISH PRONOUNS

WORDS

I
me   } 1
my
                    } 7   } 10
we
us   } 2
our

he
him   } 3
his
                    } 8
she
her   } 4
                              } 11
they
them   } 5
their
                    } 9
you
your   } 6

Based on Fillenbaum and Rapaport (1971).

Are the Methods Adequate?

Ironically, the objectivity in the methods constitutes one of their chief weaknesses. When people distill their knowledge of two words into a 1-to-10 rating of how similar the words are, they gloss over the subtleties of word meaning. And averaging over many such ratings only obscures any subtleties that may be there. Even more troubling is the unavoidable tendency for people to change their criterion for "semantic similarity" as they go from one word pair to the next. This was cleverly demonstrated by Fillenbaum and Rapaport (1974). The linguist Charles Fillmore (1971b) had already done a detailed componential analysis of such "verbs of judging" as **criticize**, **accuse**, **praise**, and **credit**. He was asked by Fillenbaum and Rapaport to make similarity judgments of the same words as if he were a subject in a psychological study, and his judgments were analyzed by quantificational methods. If the methods were adequate, they should have brought out the same components Fillmore himself had uncovered. However, while they revealed some aspects of these words, in general they displayed little of Fillmore's own subtle and complex analysis. The quantificational methods, sophisticated as they are, are too clumsy, too insensitive to nuances in meaning, to give more than a gross representation for most semantic domains.

For many investigators, another drawback is that these methods tacitly take the encyclopedic view of meaning. When people make a 1-to-10 judgment of word similarity, they are not asked to distinguish what they know about dogs from what they know about the word **dog**. They do not distinguish their mental encyclopedia from their mental lexicon. Imagine that people without language but knowledgeable about animals were asked to judge similarity among all types of animals. They would probably yield the same "semantic space" as people who judged similarity among the animal names. If the sense of a word is to be distinguished from general encyclopedic knowledge, then the quantificational methods may be inherently limited.

Is a Semantic Space Enough?

Even in the ideal, the notion of semantic space has inherent limitations. One problem is that its dimensions have incomplete interpretations. In the kinship terms, for example, one dimension of semantic space would be "parent-child," a dimension that distinguishes **parent** from **child**, **father** from **son**, and **mother** from **daughter**. What the semantic space does not tell us is that **parent** and **child** are relational, specifying the relation between two people **x** and **y** as in **x is the parent of y**. Nor does it tell us that **parent** and **child** are converses, that if **x is the parent of y**, then **y is the child of x**. In verbs, to take another example, one dimension of semantic space would correspond to the contrast between **die-kill**, **rise-raise**, and **get-give**—between verbs of change of state and verbs of cause of change of state (see Table 11–3). The space does not show that the former verbs, all with **Come-about(x)**, are "embedded" in the latter verbs, all with **Cause(y,z)**, and that **Come-about(x)** is the second argument of the relation **Cause(y,z)**. Semantic space cannot represent relational information of this kind.

A related problem is that while this approach may reveal the meaning of single words or simple phrases, it cannot deal with sentences. It cannot in principle tell how word meanings fit together to form sentence meanings. For many investigators, this is the central goal in studying meaning—to explain how **man** is just a compressed version of **male adult human** and how **man**, **bite**, and **dog** go together to form **man bites dog**.

For our purposes, the last two defects are crippling. The lexical entry for **parent** has to say that it is a relation between two things. If it does not, it cannot specify how **parent** combines with other words to form phrases like **Robert's parent** or to form sentences like **Jane is a parent of Robert**. If **parent** is entered into the mental lexicon simply as a set of numbers reflecting its place on the dimensions of semantic space, the relational information will not be available. Thus, despite the insights the quantificational approach has brought for some semantic and encyclopedic domains, it is not really up to the job of filling in lexical entries.

THE FUNCTIONAL APPROACH TO MEANING

When a speaker uses the word **dog**, as in **The dog jumped**, he does so to get the listener to attend to certain parts of his encyclopedic knowledge about dogs. **Dog** is a tool the speaker uses to point to the encyclopedic knowledge that is pertinent to the assertion he is trying to make. How does **dog** accomplish this goal? This is the fundamental question in the functional approach to meaning. Instead of asking what **dog** means, the functional approach asks how **dog** does what the speaker intended it to do.

One view is that **dog** accomplishes what it does via the concept dog. Recall that in the nominal view of meaning, **dog** is merely the name for the category dog, which is defined by one's concept of dog. But what is a concept? For many it is a rule for deciding whether or not an object is a member of a category. The concept of even number is this rule: a number is even if it is divisible by two. Traditionally, the rules for concepts come in two main forms: the *conjunctive rule* and the *disjunctive rule*. Within a deck of cards, the queen of hearts is defined by a conjunctive rule: a card is a queen of hearts if it is *both* a queen *and* a heart. Each member of the category fits a conjunction of the two properties being a queen and being a heart. Another concept, call it "queen-or-heart," is defined by this disjunctive rule: A card is a queen-or-heart if it is *either* a queen *or* a heart *or both*. Each member of the category queen-or-heart has at least one of the two properties. Rules for concepts may take other forms as well.

Within the functional approach, concepts are defined by rules, but the rules correspond to mental operations by which people actually decide whether or not an object belongs to a category. This assumption has been made concrete in the approach called procedural semantics.

Procedural Semantics

The basic idea behind procedural semantics is that the sense of a word is a procedure—a set of mental operations—for deciding when a word applies to a thing. Consider the procedure for **man** in Table 11–6. Its goal is to decide for some object x whether or not **man** would apply to it. The procedure is written as if it were a computer program with a series of steps. In this approach, it is the procedure for **man** that occupies the lexical entry for **man**. As something that can be put into execution, it is the sense of **man**. Once put into execution, it can pick out the possible referents of **man**.

Components as Procedures

No one will have missed the obvious resemblance of the procedure for **man** to the semantic components of **man**, namely **Male(x) & Adult(x) & Human(x)**. The procedure, it seems, is just the three components of **man** strung out in a serial order. Yet in principle, semantic procedures are more general. One criticism of semantic components is that not all words can be defined in terms of necessary conditions. Some words require disjunctive rules, and others some combination

TABLE 11–6

A SAMPLE PROCEDURE

Semantic Procedure for **man**, or **Man(x)**

Step 1. Is x human?

If so, continue to 2

If not, go to 5

Step 2. Is x adult?

If so, continue to 3

If not, go to 5

Step 3. Is x male?

If so, continue to 4

If not, go to 5

Step 4. The procedure succeeds: x is a man

Step 5. The procedure fails: x is not a man

---

of conjunctive and disjunctive rules. The judicious choice and ordering of steps can enable a procedure to handle these more complex instances. At the same time, procedural semantics can draw on all the useful analyses carried out by the componential approach, wherever the analyses work. Thus, our examination of semantic components has not been useless, for they correspond, typically, to the components of semantic procedures.

Each procedure itself relies on other procedures in its operation. In the procedure for **Man(x)**, Step 1 is really another procedure called **Human(x)**, which is able to decide whether or not something is human. **Human(x)** in turn makes use of other more elementary procedures, and so on. The procedure **Man(x)** itself may be used as part of other procedures, like that for **King(x)** and **Bachelor(x)**. The advantage of this system is that the sense of a word like **man** calls on the same mental operations that are required for the senses of many other words. Elementary procedures can be combined in various ways to form the procedures for complex words.

In illustration of this last point, consider the six motion verbs studied by Johnson-Laird (1977), listed at the bottom of Table 11–7. Imagine a line with two marbles on it labeled K and Q, and imagine that K is moving toward Q. How should this motion be described? That depends on what Q is doing— whether it is also moving, and if so which direction, and whether it then touches K. (The symbols t_0 and t_1 used in the table are two successive points in time). Steps 1 to 4 are part of the procedures for all six verbs, but which verb is appropriate depends on the outcomes of these four steps. The six patterns of outcomes shown form a "decision table" for the choice of verb. When the answer is *yes* for all four steps, as it is under test outcome 1, the appropriate verb is **meet**. Under test outcome 2, where the answer is *yes* for Steps 1 through 3 and *no* for Step 4, the appropriate verb is **converge**. And so on. The x's in parentheses show

TABLE 11–7

A DECISION TABLE FOR SIX MOTION VERBS

PROCEDURE STEPS	TEST OUTCOMES					
	1	2	3	4	5	6
Step 1: Is K moving toward Q at t_0?	yes	yes	yes	yes	yes	yes
Step 2: Is Q moving at t_0?	yes	yes	yes	yes	no	no
Step 3: Is Q moving toward K at t_0?	yes	yes	no	no	no	no
Step 4: Do K and Q touch at t_1?	yes	no	yes	no	yes	no

VERBAL DESCRIPTIONS FOR THE SIX TEST OUTCOMES						
K and Q *meet*	x					
K and Q *converge*	(x)	x				
K *catches up with* Q			x			
K *gains on* Q			(x)	x		
K *joins* Q	(x)		(x)		x	
K *moves toward* Q	(x)	(x)	(x)	(x)	(x)	x

Based on Johnson-Laird (1977).

that, for example, **converge** is also appropriate for test outcome 1, but it is pre-empted by **meet**, which describes the action more completely.

This example shows that the same component procedures—Steps 1 through 4—are used in combination for a number of related words. Indeed, the words are seen as related because of the component procedures they have in common. This has its parallel in the componential approach, where the words in a semantic field—like **man**, **woman**, **boy**, and **girl**—were related to each other by the semantic components they had in common.

Procedures as Mental Operations

This example also illustrates how semantic procedures go beyond semantic components in relating words to encyclopedic knowledge. Semantic components have often been criticized as being merely another "language" or symbol system into which words are translated. Decomposing **man** into **Male(x) & Adult(x) & Human(x)** is no more revealing than translating **man** into the French **male adulte humain**. These components may show how one word is related to another, but they have no substance themselves. Although investigators such as Bierwisch (1970) have argued that semantic components correspond to basic perceptual and cognitive operations, the analysis itself doesn't require this or make it explicit. Procedural semantics does. Each procedure is an actual mental operation that links up directly with the primitive mental operations used in perceiving, attending, deciding, and intending. In Step 2 of the last example, the procedure **Move(x)**, "Is x moving?," is assumed to contain primitive procedures used by the human perceptual system for detecting movement. A linkage between language and perception has been proposed for many English words by G. Miller and Johnson-Laird (1976).

In the functional approach, therefore, semantic components have a natural explanation. They are those basic mental operations in the human cognitive system that are used for classifying encyclopedic knowledge—for categorizing immediate perceptions and past recollections. If this is right, then **Male(x)**, **Female(x)**, **Cause(x,y)**, **Come-about(x)**, and **Not(x)** denote fundamental classificatory schemes by which people see and conceive of the world around them. This in turn makes word meanings anything but arbitrary. They are constrained to follow the classifications of experience by the human conceptual apparatus, which is there independent of language. This view of word meaning has several important implications. First, the categories that are named in a language should depend on the way its users conceive of the world. Second, children should build their first attempts in using words on the conceptual components already available to them. And third, these components should be apparent in all languages. These implications will be considered, respectively, in Chapters 12, 13, and 14.

Limitations of Procedural Semantics

Because procedural semantics is in its infancy, its strengths and weaknesses are not easy to judge. Most procedures proposed so far have been taken directly from componential analysis, and where that is successful, so is procedural semantics. Yet procedural semantics has made some progress beyond componential analysis. Winograd (1972) and Woods (1968) have shown how semantic procedures might fit within comprehension and production, and G. Miller and Johnson-Laird (1976) have given some substance to the claim that many procedures are ultimately perceptual in origin.

The toughest words have yet to be tackled. Category names such as **dog**, **lemon**, and **bluejay** pose as severe problems for procedural semantics as for componential analysis. Subjective terms such as **good**, **pain**, and **hurt** will be hard to relate to basic mental operations. And work has only begun on such difficult words as the conditional **if**, the hypothetical **would**, and the possible **can** (see Isard, 1975). More serious are the logical problems to be solved. If two words have the same procedure, are they necessarily synonymous? If two words have different procedures, are they necessarily different in meaning? Can a single word have different procedures and still mean the same thing? And can all procedures be written in a finite number of steps—a finite number of mental operations (see Hempel, 1950)?

Are Procedures Flexible Enough?

Because the procedures designed so far are fairly inflexible, they run into difficulties where flexibility is called for—as in contextual variation, received knowledge, conversational adjustments, and fuzzy boundaries.

As illustration of contextual variation—how one person's procedures must change with context—take Ann's procedure for **Male(x)**, "Is x male?" As part of the word **man**, the procedure might check clothing, haircut, pitch of voice, or gender of name. As part of **baby boy**, it would check other details. As part of **rooster**, **cock**, or **drake**, it would check plumage—and different plumage for different birds. And as part of **bull sea elephant**, it would take still a different form. Yet the characteristics it checks are only outward clues as to whether x is male. What really counts is Ann's theory about what it means to be male. It is her theory that dictates what superficial clues count as evidence for maleness. The procedure for **Male(x)** must therefore have access to any clues that are pertinent. Just how it would exploit this wide range of Ann's knowledge is hard to see.

Semantic procedures must also be flexible enough to deal with received knowledge. For example, a zircon that was well cut and mounted might be taken for a diamond. Yet as soon as one is told by a jeweler that it is a zircon, that received knowledge preempts all other knowledge, and the engagement would be off. Likewise, people rely on chemists to say whether something should be called gold or fool's gold, and on biologists to say whether a whale should be called a mammal or a fish. Knowledge received from experts may be pertinent for the moment only, as with the zircon, or over the long term, as with whales. It is hard to see how such knowledge would be introduced into semantic procedures.

Another problem is how to adjust procedures to the speaker and listener. An adult speaking to a child may refer to a wolf as a **doggie** to accommodate to the child's conception of wolves. And a scientist talking to a layman might use **science** to include astrology and numerology (despite the scientist's own meaning for the term) to accommodate to the layman's understanding of **science**. Semantic procedures don't yet allow for such conversational adjustments.

The categories words name typically have fuzzy boundaries, putting an even greater strain on semantic procedures. Because tomatoes lie on the boundary between fruit and vegetables, they may sometimes be called **fruit** and other times **vegetable**. And because a sixteen-year-old female lies on the boundary between adolescence and adulthood, she may be called a **girl** or a **woman**, depending on the circumstances. Semantic procedures must be able to show that these objects are on the boundary and be flexible enough to name them differently depending on the context. But how this is to be done is not yet clear.

The limitations of inflexible procedures, however, are not necessarily limitations of semantic procedures in general, nor are they limitations on the broader functional approach to meaning. It could be argued instead that one strength of the functional approach is that it draws out these issues and tries to address them.

COMPLICATIONS IN THE
REPRESENTATION OF MEANING

So far, each word has been treated as if it had one and only one sense. This is incorrect for three reasons. First, almost all words are *polysemous*—they have more than one sense. Second, there are expressions called *idioms*, like **kick the bucket** meaning "die," which do not get their meaning directly from the words they contain. And third, some words can be used for conveying senses never before associated with them. This phenomenon will be called *lexical creativity*. These three complications raise important issues for the mental lexicon.

Polysemy

Although words almost always have more than one sense, these multiple senses are of two kinds: *homonymy* and *polysemy*. Consider these three senses for the phonological sequence **ear**:

> *Sense 1:* the visible organ of hearing, as in **floppy ears**.

> *Sense 2:* the sense of hearing, as in **good ear for jazz**.

> *Sense 3:* the spike that bears corn, as in **three ears of corn**.

The *American Heritage Dictionary* classifies the first two senses together under a dictionary entry labeled **ear**[1], and the third sense under another labeled **ear**[2]. In this way, it claims that **ear**[1] and **ear**[2] are two different words. By historical accident they happen to be pronounced (and spelled) alike, but are otherwise as different as **nose** and **stalk**. **Ear**[1] and **ear**[2] are therefore called homonyms. Senses 1 and 2, in contrast, are claimed to be different senses of the same word. They are historically related, with sense 2 thought to be an "extension" of sense 1. **Ear**[1] is therefore said to be polysemous, to show the property of polysemy.

How should senses 1, 2, and 3 be represented in the mental lexicon? Here are three rough possibilities:

> *Model A:* Every sense has a separate lexical entry.

> *Model B:* Every homonym has a separate lexical entry. The many senses of a single word, however, are represented together under one lexical entry.

> *Model C:* Every homonym has a separate lexical entry. Within a single entry, however, some senses are basic and others built by rule from the basic senses.

In Model A, senses 1, 2, and 3 would each appear in a separate lexical entry. The disadvantage with this is that it does not show that senses 1 and 2 are related. In Model B, senses 1 and 2 would appear together in the lexical entry for **ear**[1] and sense 3 in that for **ear**[2]. This is how the *American Heritage Diction-ary* does it. In Model C, sense 1 would appear under **ear**[1], and sense 3 under **ear**[2], but sense 2 would not exist as a ready-made sense of **ear**[1]. Rather, sense 2 would be built when needed from sense 1 using a "lexical rule" like this: a word that picks out a sense organ may also pick out the function of that organ. In Model C, "derivative" word senses, like sense 2 of **ear**[1], are built on the spot by an active mental process.

Are Some Senses Built on the Spot?

How plausible is Model C? Take **actor**, which means either "male person who acts" (**This part requires an actor, not an actress**) or just "a person who acts" (**This play requires actors, not hacks**). These two senses might be represented as semantic components this way:

Sense 1: Actor(x) = Human(x) & Professional(Act(x)) & Male(x)

Sense 2: Actor(x) = Human(x) & Professional(Act(x))

But which sense is basic, and how can one tell? One lexical rule might build sense 2 from sense 1 by dropping **Male(x)**. Another might build sense 1 from sense 2 by adding **Male(x)**. The first rule seems more plausible for **man, father, son,** and **brother,** which like **actor** neutralize in some contexts. The second rule seems more plausible for **lion, tiger,** and **heir,** which like **actor** take on maleness in some contexts. Neither rule works everywhere. **Uncle, step-brother, grandfather,** and **steward,** for example, never lose their component **Male(x)**, and **cat, elephant,** and **hippopotamus** never add the component. Indeed, **duck** and **nurse** add the component **Female(x)**. At present there is no evidence that one sense is built from the other in speaking and listening.

In a study of **line**, Caramazza and Grober (1976) demonstrated that people at least see some senses as more central than others. **Line** has five relatively distinct senses:

Sense 1: A physical mark, as in **Two parallel lines never meet**.

Sense 2: A demarcation, as in **His bags were checked at the state line**.

Sense 3: A continuous arrangement, as in **Line up the blocks**.

Sense 4: A continuous sequence of words, as in **Actors learn lines**.

Sense 5: A sequence of constructs, as in **What is your line of work?**

Through a variety of quantificational techniques, it was shown that people view sense 1 as most central, sense 2 as next most central, and so on. Caramazza and Grober argued that **line** had a core meaning, approximately "an exten-sion," and the five senses were all realizations of this core meaning. Sense 1 was the most concrete, and sense 5 the most abstract, and this led to people's judgments of centrality. These findings make clear that the senses of a single word are tightly organized. However, they do not say whether all five senses are built on the spot from a core meaning (Model C) or come ready-made for use when they are needed (Model B).

Idioms

Idioms are phrases with special meanings. Note that **kick the dog** gets its sense from **kick** ("strike with one's foot") and **dog** ("canine animal"), for it means "strike the canine animal with one's foot." Not so with the idiom **kick the bucket** in the sense of "die." It does not mean "strike the pail with one's foot." It is a peculiar fact that **kick the bucket** as a whole means "die." For this fact to be represented, the phrase **kick the bucket** must have a lexical entry all its own, one unrelated to those for **kick** and **bucket**. It is also true of other idioms, such as **hit the sack, put one's foot in one's mouth,** or **be in hot water**.

Drawing by O'B. ; © 1976 The New Yorker Magazine, Inc.

"you're a fine one to talk!"

Most idioms are the petrified remains of dead metaphors. **Kick the bucket** may once have suggested a vivid metaphor for dying, but it has since become so petrified that the metaphor is unrecognizable. With petrification also comes a tightening in syntactic options. **Abel kicked the bucket** can mean that Abel died, whereas **The bucket was kicked by Abel, It was the bucket Abel kicked,** and **Abel's bucket kicking saddened Adam** can only be interpreted literally. This is typical of idioms. New metaphors, however, are being created every day. At any moment some metaphors have just been born, some are old and familiar, some are dying, and some are dead and petrified. There is no sharp dividing line between idioms and non-idioms. How then should idioms like **hit the sack, hit the trail,** and **hit the books** be entered in the mental lexicon? As half-comprehensible dying metaphors, they may sometimes be understood as true metaphors and sometimes not. Perhaps people have both options available.

Lexical Creativity

People are not content to leave language alone. When it leaves them too little room to maneuver efficiently, they invent new uses for old words and sometimes invent new words altogether. Some innovations are so natural that they go unnoticed: **This mountain is jeepable**, **The player had to be stretchered off the field**; and **The rocket faltered at lift-off**. Others hit us as innovations, even though they are perfectly comprehensible: **Margaret 747'd to San Francisco, Ned Houdini'd his way out of the closet**, and **This music is very Beethoveny**. But where do the senses of **jeepable, stretchered, lift-off, 747'd, Houdini'd**, and **Beethoveny** come from? The mental lexicon does not contain them ready-made in this form. They must be created on the spot as a normal part of speaking and listening.

The functional approach suggests a natural way of handling innovations, for it allows semantic procedures to be built on the spot. Take **Margaret 747'd to San Francisco**. On hearing **747'd**, listeners realize they must come up with a procedure for an action. The action the speaker must be suggesting with **747** is the one associated with the normal function of 747's, namely flying with a 747 as an instrument. They would then build a procedure for "fly by means of a 747" just as the speaker intended. What makes the functional approach especially suitable is that it views word senses as dynamic, not static.

SUMMARY

Word meanings have two parts. The sense of a word is the concept it denotes; **dog** denotes the concept of dog. The reference of a word is the set of things to which it applies; **dog** applies to all real and imaginary entities that belong to the category dog. The common view is that because the sense of a word is what allows it to refer, sense should be the main object of study. The problem then is to distinguish what people know about words—the mental lexicon—from what they know about the world—the mental encyclopedia. The encyclopedic view is that the lexical entry for **dog**, say, contains everything people know about dogs. The componential view is that it contains only the necessary conditions for something to be a dog. The nominal view is that it merely names the category dog, which is nevertheless part of the mental encyclopedia. All three views present problems.

In practice, word meaning has been approached from three directions. In the componential approach, the sense of a word divides into components, propositions that reflect the necessary conditions for something to be the word's referent. **Man(x)** divides into **Male(x) & Adult(x) & Human(x)**. This approach accounts for analytic statements, self-contradictions, meaning relations, and the like, but runs into difficulty with ill-defined components like **Red(x)** and with concepts like game that lack necessary conditions. In the quantificational approach, word meanings are represented as locations in a semantic space or in semantic clusters, locations that are determined mechanically from people's judgments about word pairs. Although often revealing, this approach tends to miss nuances in meaning and cannot represent the relational nature of meaning. In the procedural approach, word meanings are represented as procedures, mental operations able to determine whether or not a word applies to an object, event, or state. These procedures have a natural psychological interpretation, but are at present too inflexible to handle such problems as contextual variation, received knowledge, conversational adjustments, and fuzzy boundaries. No single approach seems ideal.

Further Reading

There are several broad introductions to semantics, including, in increasing complexity, Palmer (1976), Ullmann (1962), Leech (1974), and Lyons (1977). There are also discussions of the separate approaches to semantics. The componential approach is introduced in a highly readable chapter by Bierwisch (1970) and developed in more detail by Katz (1972). Critical discussions of various aspects of this approach can be found in Bolinger (1965), Kempson (1975), and Wilson (1975). As for applications of componential analysis, Burling (1970) takes up semantic fields analyzed by anthropologists and Lehrer (1974) ones analyzed mainly by linguists. Discussions and examples of the quantificational approach can be found in Fillenbaum and Rapaport (1971) and Romney, Shepard, and Nerlove (1972). Procedural semantics has been thoroughly discussed by G. Miller and Johnson-Laird (1976).

Words are not crystal, transparent,
and unchanged; they are the skin of
living thoughts, and may vary greatly
in color and content according to the
circumstances and time in which they
are used.

Oliver Wendell Holmes

12

Uses of Meaning

For people concerned with language, the dictionary is more than an ornament for their bookshelf. It is a source of information about the use of words in everyday speaking and listening. It tells them which words can be selected to convey a particular idea and how words can be construed when heard from someone else. The same is true of the mental lexicon, except that it has to be consulted for every word that is spoken or understood. But how is it consulted? That is, what role does it play in speaking and listening? This is the main question to which this chapter is addressed.

Before this question can be discussed, however, there is an important problem to be resolved. In the last chapter, several ways of approaching the mental lexicon were taken up, but none of them was ideal. For the purposes of this chapter one must be chosen. It seems reasonable to suggest that the approach selected should satisfy three criteria. First, it ought potentially to be able to represent the meanings of all types of words. Second, the lexical entry ought to be in a form that is compatible with its use in comprehension and production. And third, the lexical entry ought to make contact with the basic mental operations people use in taking in, classifying, and recollecting experience. By these criteria, the optimal approach is the functional approach, in which the sense of a word is a procedure. It is the only approach that has explicitly set out to satisfy the second and third criteria, which are central to the aims of this chapter.

MEANING AND PROCESS

Although word meanings are used in both interpreting and planning utterances, their roles in these two processes are quite different. In comprehension, they fill out the details of how an utterance is to be utilized. For **Is your sister a virologist?**, the semantic procedures for **your** and **sister** further spell out the place in memory to be searched for the referent of **your sister**, while the semantic procedure for **virologist** further spells out what information is to be checked there. In production, word meanings are critical at the planning stage. In planning **Is x a virologist?**, the speaker has to decide which of many possible expressions—say, **the woman**, **your sister**, **your older sister**, or **my neighbor**—will get the listener to pick out the intended referent correctly. The semantic procedures for these words are critical in deciding which will and which won't. Because meaning plays such different roles in listening and speaking, these two areas will be taken up separately.

Although meaning plays an obvious role in comprehension and production, this role has been largely neglected in the psychology of language. One reason is that it is intrinsically difficult to study. There are few satisfactory experimental techniques for getting at the use of meaning, and the ones that exist are restricted to certain classes of words. Another reason is that it is difficult to make sense of experimental findings without a framework in which to view meaning, and so far there is anything but unanimity about such a framework. With these handicaps, this chapter must be read with caution. The six topics we take up—three in comprehension and three in production—cover only selected uses of meaning and do not fall together in a neat pattern. These topics might best be read as six puzzles. Tentative solutions will be offered for each, but they are really hints or guesses at proper solutions. Still, the puzzles are intrinsically interesting, and they give at least a glimpse of the role of meaning in speaking and listening.

COMPREHENSION

In comprehension, word meaning should play its major role in the utilization process. You will recall that comprehension is accomplished in several steps. In the "construction" process, the listener builds an interpretation for a sentence. Given **The deaf man left**, he builds **Man(x) & Deaf(x) & Leave(x)**, representing its interpretation as a collection of propositions. In the "utilization" process, he utilizes this representation in the way it was meant to be utilized. Since **The deaf man left** is an assertion, he uses the given-new strategy. First, he divides the sentence into given and new information, with **Man(x) & Deaf(x)** as given and **Leave(x)** as new. Second, he searches memory (his mental encyclopedia, in effect) for the antecedent for the given information, for the referent of **the deaf man**. Third, on finding the referent, call it E_{11}, he adds the new information **Leave(E_{11})** to memory. If he were confronted with a yes/no question like

Did the deaf man leave?, a WH- question like **Who left?**, or a request like **Leave quickly**, he would choose other strategies, but they would each consist of steps requiring memory search, comparison operations, and adding or extracting information.

Semantic Procedures as "Mini-Strategies"

From this viewpoint, semantic procedures are merely a further specification of these utilization strategies. For **The deaf man left**, the three propositions **Man(x)**, **Deaf(x)**, and **Leave(x)** were "used" in the given-new strategy. But they are really just the names for three procedures that take part in the strategy. **Man(x)** and **Deaf(x)** name procedures that are instrumental in the search for the referent, E_{11}, of **the deaf man**. They guide the search and terminate it when E_{11} has been found. **Leave(x)** names a procedure that is instrumental in adding the new information, **Leave(E_{11})**, to memory. It creates a new set of concepts attached to E_{11}, and these constitute the new information that is added to memory.

According to this view, semantic procedures are ready-made "mini-strategies" listeners plug into the utilization strategies to make them work. For example, to find the referent for **the deaf man**, listeners have to search memory for a unique entity, E_{11}, that is both a man and deaf. Imagine that the search strategy consists of four stages that test successive entities E_i (where **i** takes successive values) to see if it will fit these two criteria:

Stage 1: Is E_i a man? If yes, continue to 2. If no, go to 3.

Stage 2: Is E_i deaf? If yes, go to 4. If no, go to 3.

Stage 3: Try another E_i and return to 1.

Stage 4: E_i is the referent of **the deaf man**.

It is clear that Stage 1 stands for the procedure **Man(E_i)** and Stage 2 for the procedure **Deaf(E_i)**. But if these are names for procedures, they can each be replaced by the steps of the procedure:

Stage 1:
    Step 1a: Is E_i human? If yes, continue to 1b. If no, go to 3.

    Step 1b: Is E_i adult? If yes, continue to 1c. If no, go to 3.

    Step 1c: Is E_i male? If yes, continue to 2. If no, go to 3.

Stage 2:
    Step 2a: Is E_i able to hear things? Continue to 2b.

    Step 2b: Is the answer to 2a no? If yes, go to 4. If no, go to 3.

Stage 3: Try another E_i and return to 1.

Stage 4: E_i is the referent of **the deaf man**.

In the expanded version of this strategy, Steps 1a to 1c correspond to the components **Human(E$_i$)**, **Adult(E$_i$)**, and **Male(E$_i$)**. They are just the steps found in the procedure for **Man(E$_i$)** in Table 11–6. Likewise, Steps 2a and 2b correspond to the components **Able(E$_i$, Hear(E$_i$, things))** and **Not(y)** in the semantic procedure for **Deaf(E$_i$)**. Of course, the way these procedures have been formulated may not be realistic. It may not be reasonable, for example, to test **E$_i$** first for whether it is human, then for whether it is adult, and finally for whether it is male. The three tests may proceed simultaneously or in some other order. And each of these steps names a procedure that can be expanded still further. In one view of procedures, each step ultimately corresponds to a basic mental operation, like a perceptual operation for detecting movement or a memory operation for detecting whether some fact is true or false. In the end, however, the form a procedure like **Man(x)** takes is an empirical issue. It must have consequences that are consistent with the facts about comprehension. We will take up some of these facts.

What this example suggests is that semantic procedures are much like the utilization strategies examined in Chapter 3. Like strategies, procedures consist of separate mental operations. **Man(E$_i$)** broke down into Steps 1a, 1b, and 1c. Like strategies, procedures should take time to work through, some consuming more time than others. Like strategies, procedures work according to whether a proposition like **Human(E$_i$)** matches information in memory. This is in effect what the question **Is E$_i$ human?** means. And like strategies, procedures may require a good bit of problem solving before they produce the right outcome. The question **Is E$_i$ male?** may be answerable only after drawing inferences from various pieces of encyclopedic information.

It is one thing to suggest that semantic procedures are inserted into utilization strategies and quite another to demonstrate it. One problem is that pertinent evidence is scarce. Another is that when there is pertinent evidence it often has several plausible explanations. Nevertheless, there are three types of words that have been studied that provide some clues about the uses of meaning: inherent negatives (like **absent**, **different**, and **forget**), modifiers (like **tall** and **slightly**), and names for natural and man-made categories (like **bird**, **eagle**, **ostrich**, and **chair**). Each area gives us a look at something different about semantic procedures. The inherent negatives provide evidence that procedures are very much like the more global utilization strategies they are part of. They are often hard to distinguish from the more global strategies. The modifiers give evidence that procedures sometimes consist of relatively independent steps that each take time and effort to carry out. The category names, finally, hint at what encyclopedic information is used in semantic procedures and how it serves to interrelate such categories as birds, robins, ostriches, and bats.

Inherent Negatives

Inherent negatives like **absent**, **different**, **conflict**, **forget**, and **dissuade** illustrate how semantic procedures are "mini-strategies." These procedures look very much like the utilization strategies they are part of. The argument goes like this.

When listeners utilize the assertion **x isn't present**, they have to call upon the procedures for **not** and **present**. And when they utilize the assertion **x is absent**, they have to call upon the procedure for **absent**. But **absent** is merely the phrase **not present** compressed into a single word, and its semantic procedure calls on the procedures for **not** and **present** too. So when expanded out, **x is absent** looks very much like **x isn't present** and is utilized in much the same way.

Procedures for Inherent Negatives

Consider how **x is present** would be judged true or false. In Chapter 3 it was shown that the strategy used for these judgments is the "verification model." The critical part of that model was its "comparison stage." It compares the sentence meaning against the listener's mental representation of reality and computes the judgment true or false. Recast and simplified a little, this comparison consists of a single rule:

> *Rule 1:* Is x present?

When x is present, the sentence is judged to be true, and when x is not present, it is judged to be false. In contrast, **x isn't present**, the same sentence with a negative in it, requires two rules:

> *Rule 1:* Is x present?
> *Rule 2:* Change the answer of 1 to its opposite.

So if x is present, the sentence is judged false, and if x isn't present, it is judged true. On close inspection, these two rules are merely names for semantic procedures, Rule 1 for **Present(x)** and Rule 2 for **False(x)**. Because **x is present** is represented as **Present(x)**, it requires only Rule 1, but because **x isn't present** is represented as **False(Present (x))**, it requires both Rule 1 and Rule 2. Recall that the extra mental operation in Rule 2 makes negative sentences like **x isn't present** take longer to judge than affirmative sentences like **x is present**.

What about **x is absent**? Superficially, it expresses the procedure **Absent(x)** and requires only a single rule:

> *Rule 1:* Is x absent?

But in the last chapter, **Absent(x)** was shown to break down into the semantic components **Not(Present(x))**. This makes it possible to expand Rule 1 into two steps:

> *Step 1:* Is x present?
> *Step 2:* Change the answer of 1 to its opposite.

Here Step 1 calls on the procedure for **Present(x)** and Step 2 on the procedure for **Not(x)**. As before, these two steps lead to the right answers. If x is present, then **x is absent** is judged to be false, while if *x* isn't present, then it is judged to be true.

This example makes explicit the close affinity between **x isn't present**, with its explicit negative, and **x is absent**, with its hidden negative. The two "rules" in the strategy for verifying **x isn't present** are virtually the same as the two "steps" of the first rule in the strategy for verifying **x is absent**. This parallel is remarkable. It suggests that people ought to go through the same mental operations in verifying **x isn't present** as in verifying **x is absent**. Just as Rule 2 adds extra time to the verification of **x isn't present**, Step 2 should add extra time to the verification of **x is absent**.

Verification of Inherent Negatives

There is good evidence for this parallel. In one study people were timed as they judged the truth or falsity of sentences like **The square isn't present** against pictures of either a square or a circle (H. Clark, 1974a). There were four types of sentences (illustrated here for the picture of a square):

> *True Affirmative:* The square is present.
>
> *False Affirmative:* The circle is present.
>
> *False Negative:* The square isn't present.
>
> *True Negative:* The circle isn't present.

These four types are listed in order from the fastest to the slowest. This pattern agrees with the studies of affirmatives and denials described in Chapter 3. Whenever Rule 1 encounters a mismatch instead of a match—a *no* instead of a *yes*—it takes extra time. Hence, false takes longer than true for affirmatives, and true takes longer than false for denials. The extra time taken by Rule 2 causes the denials to take longer than the affirmatives. Together Rules 1 and 2 lead to the ordering that was found.

If Steps 1 and 2 for **absent** are parallel to Rules 1 and 2 for **not present**, then **absent** should yield the same pattern of verification times. It does. In the same study people were asked to judge sentences like **The circle is absent** for truth or falsity too. The four types of sentences, from fastest to slowest, were as follows:

> *True present:* The square is present.
>
> *False present:* The circle is present.
>
> *False absent:* The square is absent.
>
> *True absent:* The circle is absent.

So just as **present** was faster than **not present**, here **present** was faster than **absent**.

And just as false negatives were faster than true negatives, false **absent** was faster than true **absent**. The parallel is complete. Steps 1 and 2 affect people's judgment times in very much the same way as Rules 1 and 2 do.

Although **Not(x)** and **False(x)** are beasts of the same breed, they differ in one important respect. **Not present** took 0.64 seconds longer than **present** to judge, while **absent** took only 0.37 seconds longer. Rule 2, which reflects **False(x)**, took about twice as long as Step 2, which reflects **Not(x)**. This is typical. In most studies inherent negatives have taken less time to deal with than the corresponding explicit negatives, suggesting that it takes less time to represent and carry out the procedure for **Not(x)** than the procedure for **False(x)**. This difference is not explained by the fact that **x isn't present** is one syllable longer than **x is absent** (H. Clark, 1974a; Carpenter & Just, 1975).

Present and **absent** are not the only affirmative and negative words with this pattern of verification times. It has also turned up in the following pairs: **agree-conflict**, **same-different**, **remember-forget**, **thoughtful-thoughtless**, **arrive-leave**, and **find-lose** (H. Clark, 1974b; Just and H. Clark, 1973; H. Clark and Offir, unpublished). For the negative member of each pair, then, there is reason to believe its semantic procedure expands out with an additional step that calls on the procedure for **Not(x)**, and that the extra step takes time and effort to carry out.

Inherently Negative Adjectives

The semantic procedure for **Not(x)** in inherently negative words takes extra time in tasks other than verification. Sherman (1973) studied the comprehension of such positive-negative pairs as **happy-unhappy**, **possible-impossible**, and **tolerant-intolerant**, pairs in which the negative member had a negative prefix like **un-**, **im-**, or **in-**. People were required to read such sentences as **Since she had been laughing/crying for the last hour, we assumed she was happy/unhappy** and decide on their self-evident truth or falsity as quickly as possible. Depending on the choice of **laughing** versus **crying** and **happy** versus **unhappy**, the sentence was either patently true or patently false. Inherently negative words like **unhappy** took about 0.3 seconds longer to deal with than their positive counterparts. Explicit negatives like **not happy** took even longer.

The negative prefix in Sherman's adjectives, however, is not critical, for the same pattern has been observed for positive and negative adjectives like **good-bad**, **high-low**, and **deep-shallow**, pairs of unmarked and marked adjectives without prefixes. In one typical study (H. Clark, 1969), people were required to solve simple problems like **If John is better than Bill, who is best?** and **If John is worse than Bill, who is worst?** These problems were solved faster when they contained the unmarked adjective **good** (in the form of **better**) than when they contained the marked adjective **bad** (in the form of **worse**). As noted in Chapter 11 for unmarked-marked pairs, **bad** calls on the procedure for **Not(x)**, while **good** does not. This predicts that **bad** should take extra time to utilize, just as it does. The superiority of unmarked over marked adjectives has been demonstrated for the following pairs, among others (H. Clark, 1969, 1970c, 1974a; Huttenlocher and Higgins, 1971; Carpenter, 1974; Flores d'Arcais, 1974b):

far-near	thick-thin	good-bad
long-short	wide-narrow	happy-sad
tall-short	old-young	warm-cold
high-low	much-little	many-few
deep-shallow	fast-slow	big-small

And and But

The conjunctions **and** and **but** also contrast in a type of positive-negative relationship. Take these sentences:

> 1. a. Max is old and handsome.
>   b. Max is old but handsome.

The **and** in 1a might be represented as **And(x, y)**, where in this case **x** is **Max is old** and **y** is **Max is handsome**. **But** is related to **and**, for it too says that Max is old and handsome. **But**, however, also says that in this conversation at least, Max's being old suggests that Max would *not* be handsome. **And** and **but** might therefore be represented like this:

> 2. a. And(x,y)
>   b. But(x,y) = And(x,y) & Suggest(x, Not(y))

But is merely **and** with two extra semantic procedures, one of which is **Not(x)**. In one study Osgood and Richards (1973) composed over 200 sentences like 1a and 1b, each with a different pair of adjectives. They presented these to people with a blank in place of the conjunction and asked them to write **and** or **but** in each space, whichever sounded better. In filling in the blanks people were extraordinarily sensitive to the extra procedures in **but**. The less the first adjective suggested or went with the second—as measured on Osgood's semantic differential (see Chapter 11)—the more likely they were to insert **but**.

The extra semantic procedures in **but**, those for **Suggest(x,Not(y))**, should have other consequences as well. Because **but** implies a contrast above and beyond the simple conjunction in **and**, it should be used less often and under more restricted circumstances. In Osgood and Richards' study, **and** was preferred to **but** overall 62 percent to 38 percent. The extra procedures, especially **Not(x)**, should also make **but** take longer to utilize. Hoosain (1973) timed people as they inserted **and** or **but** into sentences that Osgood and Richards had found typically took **and** or typically took **but**. **But** took considerably longer to insert into the appropriate sentences than **and**.

Other Inherent Negatives

If and **unless** also bear a positive-negative relationship to each other, although it is a rather complicated one. The negative nature of **unless** is best seen by comparing 3 with its paraphrase in 4:

3. Twain liked people unless they were hypocrites.
4. Twain liked people only if they were not hypocrites.

Unless means roughly "only if not." With the extra semantic procedure for **Not(x)**, **unless** should take longer to utilize in comprehension than **if**, and it does. In one study, sentences with **unless** took 1.0 second longer to judge for their truth or falsity than the equivalent sentences with **if** (H. Clark and Lucy, 1975).

Even prepositions like **to-from**, **into-out of**, and **on-off** bear a positive-negative relationship to each other (Gruber, 1965). Take **into** and **out of**, for example. If Jane talked Robert *into* going, he went, but if Jane talked Robert *out of* going, he *didn't* go. The semantic procedure for **out of** calls upon the procedure for **Not(x)**, and so do the procedures for **from** and **off**. In tasks requiring verification, **from** has been found to take longer to utilize than **to**, and **out of** longer than **into** (H. Clark, 1974a; Vernon and Gordon, 1975).

The semantic procedure **Not(x)**, therefore, seems real enough. It is called upon in the utilization of inherent negatives in pairs of verbs like **remember** and **forget**, contradictory adjectives like **present** and **absent**, contrary adjectives like **high** and **low**, coordinate conjunctions like **and** and **but**, subordinate conjunctions like **if** and **unless**, and even prepositions like **into** and **out of**. Whenever it is required, it complicates the utilization process in predictable ways. In sentence verification its role is especially clear. The **Not(y)** in **x is absent** calls on a procedure, a set of mental operations, that is very similar to the procedure called upon by the **False(y)** in **x isn't present**. This example illustrates the continuity between semantics and syntax—between semantic procedures and utilization strategies. **Absent** is merely the phrase **not present** compressed into a single word. And the semantic procedure for **Absent(x)** calls upon two procedures, **Not(y)** and **Present(x)**, just as **not present** calls upon **False(y)** and **Present(x)**. In this view, semantic procedures fill in the details of utilization strategies. Procedures and strategies ultimately call on the same mental operations.

Modifiers

If semantic procedures divide into two or more steps, it is important to establish that these steps have truly separate consequences in the utilization process. In effect, that has already been demonstrated for inherent negatives. The semantic procedure for **absent** divides into two steps, **Present(x)** and **Not(y)**, that appeared to affect the utilization process in different ways. Another demonstration is to be found in modifiers—in adjectives like **tall** and adverbs like **slightly**.

The semantic procedures for most modifiers split into two distinct parts. One specifies the dimension the modifier picks out, and the other specifies the value to be assigned to that dimension (Vendler, 1968; Givón, 1970). **Tall**, for example, means roughly "with a height that is great." "Height" is the attribute, and "great" is the value assigned to it. Similarly, **rectangular** means "with a shape that is like a rectangle," **probable** means "with a likelihood that is great," and **wordy** means "with a production of words that is great." Thus, the semantic procedure **Tall(x,y)**, as in **x is tall for a y**, consists of two major steps (each of which, of course, consists of further procedures):

> *Step 1:* Does *x* have height?

> *Step 2:* Is the value of *x* on this dimension greater than the value of the typical *y*?

There is evidence that these two steps play distinct roles in the utilization of adjectives and adverbs. Our discussion will focus on Step 2 first and Step 1 later.

Intensive Adverbs

The modifiers **slightly**, **quite**, **very**, and **extremely** are often called *intensive adverbs* because they focus on the intensity of the adjectives they modify. **Slightly** in the phrase **slightly good** picks out the intensity of goodness and specifies its value to be "slight":

> *Step 1:* Does *x* have an intensity?

> *Step 2:* Is the value of that intensity slight?

At Step 1, **quite**, **very**, and **extremely** all pick out intensity too, but at Step 2 they specify increasingly greater values of this intensity. In a study of these adverbs, Cliff (1959) demonstrated that Step 2 works separately from Step 1. He showed, for example, that the value of intensity that **slightly** specifies at Step 2 is the same no matter whether it modifies **good**, **stupid**, or **green**—no matter whether Step 1 picks out the intensity of goodness, stupidity, or greenness. This finding deserves closer examination.

Cliff argued that intensive adverbs can be thought of as *multipliers* of the adjectives they modify. More precisely, the intensity of a phrase consisting of an adverb and an adjective should be equal to the product of the adverb and adjective like this:

$$\text{Intensity}_{\text{adverb}+\text{adjective}} = \text{Multiplier}_{\text{adverb}} \times \text{Intensity}_{\text{adjective}}$$

If **good** were considered to have an intensity of $+1.0$ and **slightly** a multiplier of 0.5, **slightly good** would have the intensity of $+0.5$ ($= +1.0 \times 0.5$). To determine the adverb multipliers and adjective intensities, Cliff asked people to rate a large number of adverb-adjective phrases like **extremely nice**, **decidedly bad**, **somewhat admirable**, **very lovable**, and **slightly wicked** on a scale of -5 ("most unfavor-

TABLE 12–1

ADVERBS AND ADJECTIVES

Some representative values for adverbs as multipliers and for the intensity of adjectives on a scale of favorable to unfavorable.

MULTIPLIER ADVERB		INTENSITY ADJECTIVE	
——	1.00	wicked	−1.00
slightly	.56	evil	− .99
rather	.89	bad	− .80
quite	1.11	average	− .21
very	1.32	pleasant	+ .97
extremely	1.55	nice	+1.01
		good	+1.08
		admirable	+1.09

Based on Cliff (1959).

able") to +5 ("most favorable"), with 0 being "neither favorable nor unfavorable." In all he had them rate each adjective alone and each adjective modified by each adverb.

Representative values of the adverb multipliers and adjective intensities derived from Cliff's ratings are shown in Table 12–1. They work as expected. The favorable adjectives have positive (+) intensities, and the unfavorable adjectives, negative (−) intensities. The more intense the adjective, the greater the positive or negative value. As for the adverbs, the case of no adverb gets the multiplier of 1 (which would, of course, have no effect on the intensity). Thus the intensity of **good** with no modifier in front of it remains +1.08. **Slightly** and **rather**, with multipliers less than 1, soften the intensity of adjectives. **Slightly good** and **rather good** have intensities of +0.60 and +0.96. **Quite, very,** and **extremely,** with multipliers greater than 1, strengthen the intensity. **Quite good, very good,** and **extremely good** have intensities of +1.20, +1.43, and +1.67. What was most remarkable was that the ratings fit Cliff's equation very accurately. **Slightly bad,** for example, had an average rated intensity of −0.45, and this was equal to the product of **slightly** (0.56) and **bad** (−0.80). Howe (1962) and Lilly (1968a,b, 1969) demonstrated that this multiplicative rule fits other modifiers as well.

Memory Savings

The success of the multiplicative rule is of considerable theoretical interest. Imagine that the intensity of **slightly bad** couldn't be computed from **slightly** and **bad**. The intensity of it and all other adverb-adjective combinations would have to be stored separately in memory, and that would be a tremendous burden. Under Cliff's equation, there would be thirteen numbers to store for the combinations arising from Table 12–1—five adverb multipliers and eight adjective intensities. If the intensity of each combination had to be stored separately, there would instead be forty-eight, one for each of the 6 × 8 possibilities. With Cliff's equations, therefore, there is only 27 percent as much information to store. In practice, the savings are even greater, for there are many more words that fit this scale. So the semantic procedures for modifiers, by dividing into Steps 1 and 2, save a great deal in memory storage.

Given the elegance of this analysis, it is unfortunate that the vast majority of adverbs and adjectives are not multipliers in this simple way. The adjectives **rusty, former**, and **handsome** in the phrases **rusty nail, former mayor**, and **handsome barber** cannot be represented by a single number that multiplies another number inherent in the nouns **nail, mayor**, and **barber**. Yet these and other modifiers surely work separately from the words they modify too, although for them this is harder to demonstrate. Take **handsome**. At Step 1 it selects out a particular aspect of the nouns it modifies, "physical appearance," and at Step 2, it gives that physical appearance the same value, "pleasing and dignified," no matter what noun it modifies. It seems far-fetched to think that the senses of all possible adjective-noun combinations are stored separately. Most are computed on the spot.

This on-the-spot computation is especially plausible for "relative" adjectives like **tall**. A tall elephant does not have the same height as a tall mouse, a tall man, or a tall building. A tall elephant is an elephant that is tall for an elephant. That is why **tall** has been represented as a two-place proposition **Tall(x,y)**, as in **x is tall for a y**. For **tall**, listeners can compute height only after they have seen the noun **tall** modifies—**elephant, mouse, man**, or **building**. However, **tall** is even more relative than that. When **John is a tall man** is used in the context of basketball players, he is probably a seven-footer, but when in the context of jockeys, he is probably only a six-footer. **John is a tall man** means "John is tall for a man considered in this context." With an unlimited variety of such contexts, there can be no ready-made values for height. They must be computed on the spot taking into account all the context that is relevant.

Fitting Adjectives to Attributes

In a phrase like **tall man, tall** can be viewed as adding further steps to the procedure for **man**. Whereas **man** alone picks out adult, male, human objects, **tall man** picks out adult, male, human objects whose height is great. Step 1 is critical here, for it picks out the right attribute to be modified. If the steps before it have picked out an object without the attribute, Step 1 fails. For **tall**, the Step 1 question "Does x have height?" picks out the height of x, and if x has no height, the procedure fails. **Man** always picks out objects with height and so **tall man** always makes sense. **Road**, in contrast, always picks out objects without height, and so **tall road** never makes sense. Step 1 itself consists of further procedures. "Does x have height?" might expand into three questions: "Does x have dimensions?" "Are any of these dimensions physical?" and "Is one of these dimensions vertical?" Roads fail on the third question.

This characterization of Step 1 suggests that it should be more readily applied to some objects than to others. Height, for example, is a prominent dimension of women, buildings, and trees, hence Step 1 should be satisfied quickly in such phrases as **tall women**, **tall buildings**, and **tall trees**. Height is not such a prominent dimension of shoes, loaves of bread, and sparrows, hence Step 1 might take somewhat longer to satisfy in such phrases as **tall shoes**, **tall loaf of bread**, and **tall sparrow**, even though these phrases are perfectly legitimate. This suggestion has been confirmed in several settings.

In a study by Glass, Holyoak, and O'Dell (1974), it was found that the more salient attributes were, the faster they were verified. The salience of attributes was ascertained by having people fill in sentences like **Arrows are** ———— with adjectives. The more people an adjective is produced by, presumably, the more salient an attribute it reflects. For **arrow**, **sharp** was produced often, and **narrow** rarely, and so sharpness is presumably a more salient attribute of arrows than width. A second group of people was then required to judge sentences about arrows true or false as quickly as possible. Sentences about salient attributes, like **Arrows are sharp** (true) and **Arrows are dull** (false), were judged faster than sentences about non-salient attributes, like **Arrows are narrow** (true) and **Arrows are wide** (false) (see also Hampton, 1976). Step 1 in these adjectives was carried out faster the more easily it applied to the objects being modified.

In a demonstration by H. Clark, Carpenter, and Just (1973), people judged the heights or depths of two-dimensional drawings of garbage cans. The height judgments involved the adjectives **tall** and **short**, and the depth judgments, the adjectives **deep** and **shallow**. When the garbage cans were depicted from a side view, height was judged faster than depth. But when they were depicted from a top view, revealing the space inside them, depth was judged faster than height. Apparently, even though the height and depth of a garbage can are equivalent measurements, Step 1 for **tall** and **short** applies more readily to objects with a prominent outside top-to-bottom dimension. Step 1 for **deep** and **shallow**, on the other hand, applies more readily to objects with a prominent inside distance from the top to the bottom.

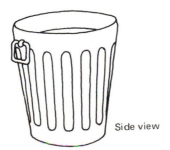
Side view

Top view

In the utilization process, therefore, the semantic procedures for modifiers characteristically expand out into two steps. Step 1 selects the right attribute, and Step 2 assigns a value to that attribute. The evidence suggests that these two steps are separate. Step 1 takes varying amounts of time to apply depending on its fit to the objects being modified. Step 2 yields values that are independent of Step 1. Once more it has been profitable to view semantic procedures as refinements of the grosser utilization strategies.

Category Names

Investigators have made little progress in spelling out the semantic procedures or semantic components for such nouns as **bird**, **furniture**, **robin**, **mouse**, and **oak**, which are names of natural and man-made categories. It is not hard to see why. No one has yet been able to find necessary and sufficient criteria for classifying something as a bird, a piece of furniture, a robin, a mouse, or an oak, and without such criteria, semantic procedures cannot be filled out in any detail. Although some natural categories have scientific definitions, these seem far from what people actually store in their mental lexicons.

There have been two broad approaches to get around these problems. The first, the *network approach*, has been to treat category names not as words with semantic procedures or components, but as members of a network of words. The second and more successful approach, the *featural approach*, assumes that each category name has a semantic procedure that makes use of features of the category being named. The features that emerge are basic to the processes by which people classify the physical world around them into categories. The network approach will be considered first, and the featural approach afterwards.

The Network Approach

In the network approach, each category name is a member of a taxonomy, and the name of this taxonomy is a member of other taxonomies, and so on. In this way each word belongs to a network of words and is defined by its relations to these other words. As an illustration, consider the hierarchy of taxonomies for the animal kingdom proposed by Leech (1974) as pictured in Figure 12–1. What this graph shows is that living things can be divided, subdivided, and then subdivided further. The first division is made according to animacy between plants and animals; further divisions are made on other criteria. At each level, the words belong to a taxonomy. At the level called "kind" the taxonomy consists of **bird**, **fish**, **insect**, **mammal**, and so on—words that denote mutually exclusive categories, just as members of a taxonomy should.

This hierarchy is of considerable linguistic interest, for it can tell us what statements are true and false of the animal kingdom. Statements are true, for example, if they are created by moving up the hierarchy one or more steps, like this: **A spaniel is a dog**, **A spaniel is a mammal**, **A spaniel is an animal**, and so on. Similarly, statements are false if they are created by going up the hierarchy and sideways: **A spaniel is a cow**, **A dog is an insect**, **A dog is a plant**, and so on. This hierarchy can be joined to other hierarchies by relations other than "being a member of." It seems only natural to suggest that this hierarchy, or one like it, might play some role in the comprehension of these terms.

This was the essence of a proposal by Collins and Quillian (1969, 1972a,b)

FIGURE 12–1

A CATEGORY NETWORK

Example of a partial hierarchy of natural categories.

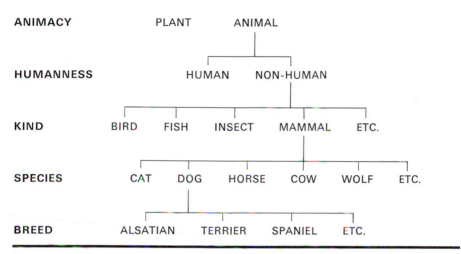

From Leech (1974).

for the verification of sentences like **A dog is an animal**. They proposed that people's "semantic memory" for items like **dog, animal, terrier, insect**, and **cow** is represented in just such a network, and people judge sentences as true or false by moving through this hierarchy. The critical prediction was that the further one has to search through the network, the longer it should take. Compare these two sentences:

A terrier is a dog. (*one step*)

A terrier is a mammal. (*two steps*)

For the first sentence, the search spans one link, while for the second, it spans two. The second should therefore take longer to judge true than the first. There were similar predictions for such sentences as **A terrier has ears** and **A terrier has skin**. In a preliminary study, Collins and Quillian found evidence for their predictions, but in later studies, others have found many sentences that go counter to the predictions (Conrad, 1972; E. Smith, Shoben, and Rips, 1974; E. Smith, 1977). To account for the discrepancies, Collins and Loftus (1975) proposed complicating the networks by adding new links and making some links longer than others. Although the more complicated network model may handle the contrary findings, these and other phenomena seem more naturally accounted for in the featural approach.

TABLE 12–2

TYPICALITY OF CATEGORY MEMBERSHIP

Eight instances from four categories ranked from
most to least typical.

FURNITURE	FRUIT	BIRD	CLOTHING
chair	apple	robin	pants
dresser	plum	swallow	coat
davenport	cherry	eagle	pajamas
footstool	watermelon	crow	slip
lamp	fig	pheasant	boots
cupboard	prune	goose	hat
radio	coconut	chicken	purse
ashtray	olive	penguin	bracelet

Based on Rosch (1975).

The Featural Approach

The featural approach to category names has been developed in the main by Rosch (1973, 1974, 1975, 1977) and her colleagues (Rosch and Mervis, 1975; Rosch, Simpson, and Miller, 1976) and by E. Smith, Shoben, and Rips (1974; Rips, 1975; Shoben, 1976; Smith, 1977). They began by observing that categories have an internal structure that is not captured in hierarchies like that in Figure 12–1. In such hierarchies, robins, eagles, ostriches, and chickens, for example, are all implicitly endowed with equal status as birds. Yet intuitively, they should not be. Some are more typical, more exemplary, of the category bird than others. Robins are typical, and eagles are fairly typical too. But ostriches and chickens would never be selected as "the typical bird." Robins and eagles are "birdier" than ostriches and chickens. Thus, birds can be arranged according to how typical they are of the category bird, and the members of others categories can be arranged in the same way.

Typicality of category membership has been determined for many common categories. In the usual study, people are asked to rate each member of a category for how "typical of" or "exemplary of" or "similar to" the category label it is. For example, they might be asked to order the names of twenty different birds—**robin, eagle, ostrich, chicken**, and the rest—from most to least typical. This is an easy and sensible task, and the judgments obtained are consistent from person to person. Table 12–2 lists eight members from each of four categories, where the eight members are ordered from most to least typical.

If birds vary from highly typical to highly atypical, it is easy to imagine that there is a *prototype* bird that is the most typical of them all. Rosch (1977) has argued that there is, and it is what people generally have in mind when they use **bird** itself. To demonstrate this, she had people compose sentences that contained category names like **bird**, **fruit**, and **vehicle**. For **bird**, three such sentences might be:

I heard a bird twittering outside my window.

Three birds sat on the branch of a tree.

A bird flew down and began eating.

Which bird is the most typical?

Rosch then replaced the category name (here, **bird**) with each member of the category (say, **robin**, **eagle**, **ostrich**, and **chicken**) and asked other people to rate how sensible the resulting sentences were. When **bird** is replaced by **robin**, these three sentences make good sense, but when **bird** is replaced by **chicken**, all three become odd—chickens don't usually twitter, sit in trees, or fly down to eat. This was typical of Rosch's findings. The more typical a category member was, the more easily it could replace the category name. Put another way, the more typical the member, the more similar it is to the prototype of the category.

Verifying Category Statements

Typicality is critical in the process of comprehending category names. The point was demonstrated in studies by Rips et al. (1973) and Rosch (1973), in which people were asked to judge sentences like these true or false:

Sentence true of typical member: A robin is a bird.

Sentence true of atypical member: A chicken is a bird.

Over a wide range of categories and members, the findings were consistent. The more typical the member was of a category, the more quickly it was judged to be a member of that category. Of the above pair, **A robin is a bird** was verified more quickly than **A chicken is a bird**. This was true even when the atypical members tested were as frequent and as familiar words as the typical members.

These findings about typicality, prototypes, and verification time should be accounted for with the right choice of lexical entry for category names. Smith, Rips, and Shoben, and Rosch and her colleagues, have put forward related but distinct suggestions about the nature of these lexical entries. For consistency, we will present these entries here as if they were procedures.

Defining Features and Characteristic Features

According to Smith, Rips, and Shoben, the semantic procedure for a word like **bird** is a collection of tests for what they called the *defining features* and *characteristic features*. All birds possess the defining features of birds or else they wouldn't be members of the category. All birds are feathered, lay eggs, have two legs and two wings, are warm-blooded, and so on. But birds also possess characteristic features. They usually have short legs, are rather small, are able to fly easily, sit in trees, have a musical call, and so on. These features, of course, are not properties of all birds, but they are so common they are thought to be characteristic of birds in general. The semantic procedure for **bird**, in this view, would consist of a long list of procedures testing for defining and characteristic features: Is x warm-blooded? Is x feathered? Does x have short legs? and so on. To be called a **bird**, however, an object need pass only the tests for defining features.

This view provides a natural explanation for typicality. The more characteristic features a member has of its parent category, the more typical it is. So robins, eagles, ostriches, and chickens are viewed as progressively less typical of birds because they have progressively fewer of their characteristic features. Put another way, the semantic procedure for **bird** defines the prototype bird, and this prototype passes progressively fewer of the tests in the semantic procedures for **robin**, **eagle**, **ostrich**, and **chicken**.

This view also provides a basis for saying why typical members are verified faster than atypical members. In verifying **A robin is a bird**, people use the semantic procedure for **robin** to create an object in memory that has all the defining and characteristic features of robins. It is the prototype robin. The task then is to examine this object to see whether it passes all the necessary tests in the semantic procedure for **bird** (see Shoben, 1976). According to Smith et al., the idea is that first impressions count. When two words share a lot of features, it is people's first impression that the second word is synonymous with, subordinate to, or superordinate to the first, enabling them to judge quickly that the second word actually *is* synonymous with, subordinate to, or superordinate to the first. For **A robin is a bird**, people see quickly that robins pass most of the tests for birds, and so they respond "true." But in verifying **A chicken is a bird**, they see that chickens pass only an intermediate number of tests for birds. Only on closer examination do they see that the created object—the chicken—passes all the tests for the *defining* features of birds, and so **A chicken is a bird** is true despite first appearances. Correcting a wrong first impression takes time, making **A chicken is a bird** take longer to verify than **A robin is a bird**.

But just as overlap in semantic procedures speeds up judgments of true, it slows down judgments of false. People quickly judge that bats and birds, for example, share many features, at least in comparison to stones and birds. Hence they are ready to say that **A bat is a bird** is true and that **A stone is a bird** is false. Only on closer examination do they find that their first impression of **A bat is a bird** is wrong. Hence they should take longer to say false to **A bat is a bird** than to **A rock is a bird**. Analogous predictions apply to other false sentences. These predictions have been confirmed by E. Smith et al. (1974) for a variety of category names.

Features and Family Resemblances

In Rosch's view, some categories do not possess defining features—properties an object must have to be a member of the category. In one demonstration by Rosch and Mervis (1975), people were asked to list "the characteristics and attributes . . . common to and characteristic of" members of six categories: vehicles, fruits, weapons, vegetables, pieces of clothing, and pieces of furniture. For the twenty kinds of fruit tested—from apple and orange to coconut and olive—there were no listed features common to all. This was true of other categories too. Yet the features did determine the typicality of each fruit. The more features a fruit shared with the other nineteen fruits, the more typical it was of the category. From these and other findings, Rosch and Mervis argued that fruit coheres as a category not because each member shares any defining features of fruit, but because each member shares a "family resemblance" with the other members of the category. The greater the resemblance, the more central it is to the category.

In the spirit of Rosch's suggestions, the semantic procedure for **fruit** might be thought of as a collection of tests for the features of the prototype fruit. To verify **A plum is a fruit**, people would check that plums possessed a *sufficient number* of the prototype's features to be called a fruit. Since apples would pass more of these tests than coconuts, **An apple is a fruit** would be verified more quickly than **A coconut is a fruit**. One advantage of this proposal is that it explains borderline cases. Olives and tomatoes have about as many features in common with the prototype vegetable as with the prototype fruit. Hence they are sometimes called vegetables and sometimes fruits. Nevertheless, within the semantic procedure for **fruit**, some features would be more salient than others. Some attributes of a category are reliably judged by people to be more important than others, and these are just the attributes people think of first and are more easily able to verify as true of the category (Hampton, 1976).

Features and Encyclopedic Knowledge

In the end, the Smith et al. and Rosch views on category names come down to much the same thing. The semantic procedure for **bird** tests for the features of the prototype bird. It requires that some but not all of those features be present. If a category has defining features, they must be present. But if a category is without many defining features, merely a sufficient number must be present for a close family resemblance. The more features an object shares with the category prototype, the more central it is to that category.

The work on category names brings home the point that semantic procedures are ultimately parasitic on encyclopedic knowledge. In dealing with the world, people have a system for classifying objects into categories. The system makes these classifications on the basis of salient attributes like shape, size, function, and activity. In the featural theories just discussed, this system is simply incorporated into the semantic procedures for category names. The systems for classifying and for naming aren't really distinct. In fact, when Rosch has discussed categories, prototypes, and typicality, she has rarely mentioned word meanings per se. She has tacitly assumed that categories are the product of people's perceptual and cognitive operations, and words like **bird** and **fruit** merely name these categories and call upon the associated mental operations. Described this way, the featural theory fits best within the nominal view of meaning (see Chapter 11). **Fruit** names the category fruit, and the representation of that category belongs to the encyclopedic entry for fruit. The aptness of the nominal view isn't surprising, since it was specially designed to handle names for natural categories.

PRODUCTION

In the planning and execution of an utterance, people have to select words to convey just the right meaning. They begin with a concept they want the listener to grasp, and they select words that will accomplish this. They plan an utterance bit by bit, build an articulatory program according to this plan, and then execute that program. Speaking in general was discussed in some depth in Chapters 6 and 7—however, little was said about the selection of words per se, and that is what we are concerned with here.

Word selection is complicated by what people have to consider in making their selection. First, they must respect the meanings of words. To refer to an uncle, they might use **the man**, **my uncle**, or **the old coot**, but not **the jump**, **my shoe**, or **the old city**. Second, they must take account of their listener. **The man** or **the old coot** might enable the listener to pick the right referent, while **my uncle** would not. Third, they must pay close attention to style, register, and other such matters. In a formal speech, **the man** might be appropriate while **the old coot** would not. Here our main concern is with the first factor: what is the role of meaning in the choice of words? But even this question cannot be addressed without considering the other two factors, especially the second.

Surprisingly little is known about the role of semantic procedures in word selection. What exists is work, concentrated in several disjointed areas, that only hints at the word selection process in general. Still, this work is instructive for its suggestions about semantic procedures. It reaffirms that they are tied into encyclopedic knowledge, consist of separable mental operations, and take time to carry out. The three areas to be taken up here are: the naming of objects, deciding on the order of adjectives before a noun, and the giving of word associations ("Give me the first word you think of when I say **window**").

Naming

Imagine that people are shown a picture of a man in work clothes and straw hat holding a rake and asked to "name" the object. Roughly speaking, what they must do is this. First, they must carry out a visual analysis to identify what they think the picture depicts. They may decide that it is intended to be a male human in work clothes and straw hat holding a rake and from these features infer that it must be a farmer. Next, they must select a "name" that will convey this identification, and for that they have a large choice: **man, laborer, farmer, rustic, raker, man with a rake, farmer with a rake, man in a hat, man in a straw hat,** and so on and on. Which name should they select? That depends on the circumstances. If this were part of a normal conversation, they would try to choose the shortest name that would best enable their listener to pick out the right object from an implicit set of alternatives. They would choose **man** if they thought this picture was to be distinguished from one with a woman in it, or **farmer** if it was to be distinguished from ones with people in other occupations (see Chapter 7).

This example, simple as it is, suggests that people's strategy for selecting names divides roughly into two stages:

Stage 1: Identify the object to be named.

Stage 2: Select a word appropriate to that identification.

This view is more complex than the associationist view that every object has a name associated with it and calls forth that name directly. The present view has distinct advantages over the associationist view. Identification itself occurs in many circumstances other than naming, and an organism doesn't have to talk to be able to identify objects. Children behave appropriately toward bottles, toys, people, furniture, strange rooms, and animals long before they can talk. They expect milk from a bottle but not from a chair and expect to sit on chairs but not bottles. By behaving appropriately toward these objects, they give evidence they have identified them. The same goes for people who have lost the use of language, and for dogs, cats, horses, and other organisms. Even speaking humans often carry out Stage 1, object identification, without Stage 2, word selection. People don't need to name an object, even covertly, to be able to identify it and behave appropriately toward it.

One View of Naming

Although it is impossible to say how Stages 1 and 2 work in any detail, one plausible view goes as follows. The identification of an object at Stage 1 consists of assigning it to categories on the basis of its perceived features. The man with work clothes, straw hat, and rake might be perceived as having the features "being human," "being male," "being adult," "having a hat on," "having work clothes on," "having a rake in hand," and so on. Actually, each of these features is itself a categorization based on more detailed features. The first

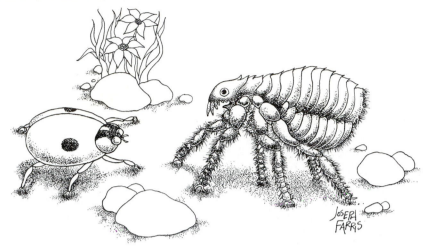

Drawing by Joseph Farris; © 1976 The New Yorker Magazine, Inc.

"*I know who I am but I don't know what I am!*"

three features enable the object to be categorized as a man, and these along with the work clothes and rake enable it to be categorized as a farmer. It can be categorized in other ways too. The selection of a word at Stage 2 then consists of finding a word whose semantic procedure has tests that all pass for the object under consideration. **Man** would work in this example because its procedure calls on the procedures **Male(x)**, **Adult(x)**, and **Human(x)**, and each test—for example, **Is x male?**—is satisfied by a feature of the object. **Farmer** would work too, because its procedure calls on the procedures **Human(x)** and **Professional (Farm(x,y))**, both of which are satisfied by the features of the object. Because both **man** and **farmer** work, Stage 2 must also choose between them, and that is where other factors come into play.

Perhaps the most usual rule for choosing among possible names at Stage 2 is this: choose a basic-level term. In Chapter 6 it was noted that there is an optimal level of utility for naming objects, a level Rosch et al. (1976) have called the basic level. It is a level that is not too general (**animal** or **thing**) and not too specific (**spaniel** or **water spaniel**), but in between (**dog**). Over a large variety of objects and situations, people are most likely to use the basic-level term (**dog**) in preference to the others (**animal**, **thing**, **spaniel**, or **water spaniel**). Why? There are at least two possibilities. As will be taken up in Chapter 14, basic-level categories are in some sense better defined, or tighter, categories than those at other levels. They may be identified faster at Stage 1, hence their names are allotted faster and more often at Stage 2. A second possibility is that the semantic procedures for basic-level terms may have tests that are more readily satisfied at Stage 2 than procedures for terms at other levels (see E. Smith, Balzano, and Walker, 1977). This way basic-level terms would be the ones most readily available.

Object Identification Versus Word Selection

In the empirical studies on naming, there has been some attempt to separate Stage 1, object identification, from Stage 2, word selection. In an experiment by

Oldfield and Wingfield (1965), people were shown a picture of an object and asked to name it as quickly as possible. They were shown common objects, like a book or a drum, and rare objects, like a gyroscope or a xylophone, and responded with what was probably always a basic-level term. As one might expect, the common objects were named over 0.5 seconds faster than the rare ones. But why? Was it because the rare objects were harder to identify at Stage 1? Or was it because their names were harder to select at Stage 2?

On the basis of several further experiments, Wingfield (1967, 1968) argued that the major difficulty came at Stage 2. In one study, people were asked to name the superordinate of each object instead of the basic-level name. In that case, common objects were named no faster than rare ones. A xylophone was named a musical instrument roughly as fast as a drum was. In another study, people were shown a name, like **drum**, followed by a picture, such as one of a drum or a book, and were required to say whether the word named the picture correctly or not. Once again, decisions were no faster on the common than on the rare objects. From these findings, one could argue that people don't necessarily have trouble identifying objects that are rare, but do have trouble selecting words that are rare.

One factor Wingfield did not consider, however, was typicality—how typical an object was of its superordinate category. A superordinate is named faster for typical than atypical members of a category. **Fruit** is given faster to the picture of an apple than to the picture of a coconut (E. Smith, Balzano, and Walker, 1977). By Wingfield's logic, then, the Stage 1 identification process is faster for typical than atypical members of a category. This points up a problem in Wingfield's logic. He implies that identifying an object is the same as identifying its superordinate category, but it is not. A coconut may be easy to identify as a coconut, but not as a fruit. Wingfield's conclusion, however, may still be sound. His evidence at least suggests that rare objects are hard to select names for.

But what determines how quickly a name is selected at Stage 2? One factor is the presence of alternative names. Whenever there is more than one common name available, it takes longer to select any one of them (Lachman, Shaffer, and Hennrikus, 1974). Since a book is always called **book**, it takes little time to name. But since pants may be called **pants**, **slacks**, or **trousers**, more time is needed to select any one of them. The slips of the tongue called blends (discussed in Chapter 7) even show that choices of this sort are sometimes not quite resolved. Something that can be called **draft** or **breeze** may come out **dreeze**. The object has been identified, and more than one name is available, but the choice is inappropriately resolved by producing the first part of **draft** and the second part of **breeze**.

Phonological Accessibility

Perhaps an even more important factor affecting Stage 2 is phonological accessibility. Naming an object requires more than identifying it and then selecting the right word. People may know the right word but not be able to retrieve its phonological shape, as in the tip-of-the-tongue phenomenon discussed in Chapter 7. Confronted with a sextant, someone might say, "I know that I know its name—it's on the tip of my tongue—but I can't quite get it." The same thing happens when one blocks on a friend's name in making an introduction. In both examples, the speakers have completed Stage 1 and identified the object. They can provide many details about it. And at Stage 2 they have even selected the right entry in their mental lexicon. What they cannot do is retrieve the phonological information from that lexical entry.

The tip-of-the-tongue phenomenon suggests that words vary in the accessibility of their phonological representations. The phonological shapes of common words are normally readily accessible, but those for rare words aren't. The latter may be so inaccessible that they result in a tip-of-the-tongue experience. Accessibility of phonological information shows up elsewhere in normal speech. Recall that when other phonological shapes are too accessible, they may intrude on the intended word, resulting in a slip of the tongue. A person from Purdue who tried to say **the conquest of Peru** ended up saying **the conquest of Purdue**; another person who tried to say **in our academic ivory tower** ended up saying **in our academic ivy league**. Inaccessible pronunciations may also force such malapropisms as **ravishing** for **ravenous**, and **reminisce** for **remiss**.

But what makes the phonological shapes of rare words relatively inaccessible? In a detailed examination of naming time, Carroll and White (1973a,b) found that objects were named faster the earlier their names had been learned in childhood. Of course, the earlier a word is learned in childhood, the more likely it is to be a common word, which fits closely with Oldfield and Wingfield's finding that the commoner a word, the faster it is produced. But Carroll and White went further. They demonstrated that age of acquisition predicted naming time even better than did the commonness of words in adulthood. They then argued that common words are produced quickly only because they are learned early in life. What all this suggests is that the phonological shape of a word is more accessible at Stage 2 the earlier in life it was learned. Although this may not be the only reason why rare words take longer to produce, it is probably a potent one.

There are multiple reasons, then, why some objects take longer to name than others. At Stage 1, it may take longer to identify some objects from their attributes than others. At Stage 2, it takes longer to select basic-level terms the rarer they are, probably because the rarer the word, the later it was learned in childhood and the less accessible is its phonological shape. And at Stage 2, it takes longer to select a name if there are several names available for the same object. However, since so little is known about object naming, this characterization should be taken with caution. Yet one thing is certain. The human ability to categorize objects plays a critical role in naming, for it determines what constitutes a basic-level term, which is what people almost always select at Stage 2.

Adjective Order

Naming an object often requires choosing adjectives along with a noun. The adjectives normally narrow down the category the noun picks out. **Car** names a broad category of vehicles, while **red car** narrows this category down to one with a specific color. But how does the speaker decide when to use adjectives, and which ones to use? As discussed in Chapter 6, that depends very much on what the target object is to be distinguished from. If a car is the target and it is to be distinguished from a truck, **car** alone will do. But if it is to be distinguished from another car, speakers must find a dimension along which the two differ—for example, color. They must then determine the target car's value on this dimension (for example, red) and select an adjective that expresses that value (**red**). With that, they have the phrase **red car**. If x is the target object and y is the set of alternatives (excluding x), the speaker's strategy might be put like this:

Stage 1: Select a basic-level term for x.

Stage 2: If that term also describes y, determine a dimension along which x and y differ and select the class of adjectives with that dimension.

Stage 3: Determine the value of x on that dimension and select an adjective with that value.

This strategy, of course, isn't completely general. Yet it is plausible for at least the simplest form of naming objects.

Adjectives fit into this strategy very nicely, for their semantic procedures are a natural elaboration of Stages 2 and 3. Recall that the semantic procedures for adjectives divide into two major steps. The first selects the dimension to be restricted, and the second specifies the value of that dimension. **Red(x)**, for example, has a procedure with two steps:

Step 1: Does x have color?

Step 2: Is the value of that color red?

These two tests are satisfied, respectively, by the dimension determined at Stage 2 and its value determined at Stage 3. In the **red car** example, Stage 2 determines that the dimension the adjective should pick out (Step 1) is color, and Stage 3 that the value it should pick out (Step 2) is red. In this scheme, adjectives are selected by the dimension first and the value second.

The little evidence there is for this strategy is derived from a surprising source—the study of adjective ordering. When x has to be distinguished from y along two dimensions instead of one, the speaker has to repeat Stages 2 and 3 and select a second adjective, as in **fast red car**. There is clear evidence that the adjectives are produced in the order **fast** and then **red** on the basis of their dimensions (Step 1) and not values (Step 2). There is also evidence that the adjectives are decided on in the order **red** and then **fast** on the basis of their dimensions first (Step 1) and values second (Step 2). If this is right, it is evidence that Step 2 is applied relatively separately from Step 1.

Order of Adjectives

The first phenomenon to be accounted for is that in most languages some sequences of adjectives sound right and others don't. Here are two examples that sound right in English:

long Polish word

comfortable upholstered brown mahogany chair

Reverse the adjective order and the sequences sound wrong:

Polish long word

mahogany brown upholstered comfortable chair

The reversed sequences work only with a "broken" intonation that inserts commas and gives contrastive stress to words out of sequence. **POLISH long word**, with stress on **Polish**, sounds fine, but has a special meaning, "a long word that is Polish," that is different from the meaning of **long Polish word**. What is remarkable is that the preferred adjective order seems to differ little from language to language, except for a complete reversal when the adjectives come after the noun (as in French). Compare English, German, and French:

English: the fast red car

German: das schnelle rote Auto (the fast red car)

French: la voiture rouge rapide (the car red fast)

Adjectives order themselves according to the semantic class they belong to. Each semantic class is defined in turn by the dimension the adjective picks out (Step 1). A partial listing of these classes, based on Vendler (1968), is shown in Table 12–3. Items 1 through 4, which are not adjectives, have been included for completeness. Of interest here are items 5 through 17. The dimensions they pick out range from "possibility" and "behavioral characteristics" farthest from the noun, to "origin" and "material" nearest the noun.

Intrinsicality and Ordering

It has often been observed that the semantic classes in Table 12–3 are ordered according to what could be called *intrinsicality* (see Quirk et al., 1972; Vendler, 1968; Ziff, 1960). Intrinsicality has only an approximate definition. As one moves down the list, the dimensions the adjectives pick out tend roughly to be: more intrinsic or inherent to the object being modified; less subjective; less a matter of opinion; less relative to the situation; and more open to objective assessment. For **large gray church**, for example, the suggestion is that grayness is more intrinsic to the church than size. Grayness is more objective an attribute

TABLE 12–3
ORDER OF MODIFIERS
Normal order of modifiers in English noun phrases.

1.	Article	the	the	a
2.	Possessive	city's		
3.	Ordinal number	last	first	
4.	Cardinal number	three		
5.	Possibility		possible	
6.	Behavioral characteristic		able	
7.	Size	large		
8.	Age	old	young	young
9.	Potentiality		electable	undrinkable
10.	Inclination		aggressive	
11.	Past result	abandoned		
12.	Present activity	crumbling		
13.	Shape, texture	square		rough
14.	Color	gray		
15.	Similar object			vinegary
16.	Origin	Gothic	California	
17.	Material	stone		choke-cherry
18.	Head noun	churches	politician	wine

Based on Vendler (1968).

than size—less a matter of opinion and less relative to the situation. In a study by J. E. Martin (1969a), people were asked to rate many adjectives one at a time for their intrinsicality, which was defined for these people in several ways. Their average ratings closely matched the preferred order of adjectives: the more intrinsic an adjective was rated, the closer it was to the noun in the preferred order of adjectives.

But why should the more intrinsic adjectives be placed closer to the noun? According to Danks and Glucksberg (1971), adjectives are ordered to help the listener pick out the referent of a noun phrase most quickly. Imagine that there are two red cars, one German and one Swedish, and the speaker wants to refer to the German one. He would say **GERMAN red car**, not the normal **red German car**, because he means "the one of the red cars that is German." The abnormal adjective order and contrastive stress are used to indicate (a) that the set of things being chosen among are red cars and (b) that the one to be chosen is distinguished on the dimension of origin—it is the German one. The critical point is that here, as in other adjective orders, the most discriminating adjective is placed first. Yet the fact that the adjectives are not in their normal order has to be marked by heavy stress on the misordered one.

To account for the *normal* order of adjectives, Danks and Glucksberg's argument has to go a step further. In everyday contexts, they must assume, it is the least intrinsic adjectives that are on the average the most discriminating. It is more often utilitarian to distinguish objects on subjective properties, like size and age, than on objective properties, like color or material. If listeners are to pick one box out of a set of boxes, they are usually better off being told it is large than that it is wooden, and so **large** is placed before **wooden** to form **large wooden box**. Over the centuries, the most utilitarian order, averaged over all types of situations, has become frozen or conventionalized as the preferred order. In French the most discriminating adjectives are put last, and this has led to the opposite order. So far, however, there is no evidence that the less intrinsic the adjective, the more likely it is on the average to be discriminating. Until such evidence is found, this theory must be considered incomplete.

Adjective Accessibility

Although the words in **fast red car** have this as their normal order, J. E. Martin (1969b) has argued that they are decided on in the reverse order, **car** first, **red** second, and **fast** third. According to this proposal, noun phrases are built from the most "accessible" word to the least, and the more intrinsic the adjective, the more accessible it is. In English, the adjectives and noun happen to be spoken in the reverse of the order in which they are decided on, but in languages like French they are spoken in the same order. The surface order can differ from the decision order, of course, because the articulatory program can hold a fully planned noun phrase before its execution is begun.

As evidence for his proposal, Martin tried to demonstrate that the closer the adjective to the noun in the preferred order, the more accessible it is. He presented people with a placard depicting four figures—for example, a large red circle, a small red circle, a large yellow circle, and a small yellow circle. He would then point to one of the figures and say "Color," or "Size," and they were to give the adjective describing its color, or its size, as quickly as possible. Since people responded faster with the color adjective than with the size adjective, he could argue that color was more accessible than size, fitting the fact that color adjectives are closer to the noun in the preferred order than size (as in **large red circle**). The findings were analogous for other pairs of adjectival dimensions. Yet there is a problem here. The red and yellow circles may have been easier to distinguish perceptually than the large and small circles, and that is why the color was responded to faster than the size. As it stands, accessibility remains a possible though not proven factor in the choosing of adjectives.

Taken together, therefore, these bits of evidence suggest that Steps 1 and 2 in the semantic procedure for adjectives have separate roles in production. Speakers normally select adjectives to help distinguish a target object x from its neighbors y. First they find a dimension along which x differs from y and select a class of adjectives so that Step 1 fits this dimension. From this class they then select an adjective so that Step 2 fits the value of x along that dimension. They repeat these operations if they need more than one adjective. It is the choice of dimension (Step 1) and not its value (Step 2) that determines the order in which they produce two or more adjectives and perhaps also the order in which they decide on them.

Word Associations

"Give me the first word you think of when I say **happy**." "**Sad**." "Now the first word for **blue**." "**Green**." Word associations like these have interested philosophers and psychologists for a long time. Originally, it was thought they revealed how ideas were associated in the mind. Happiness is associated with sadness, and blueness with greenness. By studying them, one could discover how the mind went from one idea to the next—how people thought. Later it was argued that they revealed how words themselves were associated as verbal responses. **Happy** is associated with **sad**, and **blue** with **green**. By studying them, one could discover how people moved from one word to the next in speaking—how they produced sentences. These two views have come under heavy criticism. People's ability to give word associations is surely not basic, but is derived from the more fundamental ability to use language—to speak and understand words in sentences. If word associations are valuable, therefore, it is because they can tell us something about the normal use of language.

Word associations are of interest here because of what they reveal about meaning. In particular, they suggest that semantic components—the steps in the semantic procedure for a word—play a central role in the process of word selection (H. Clark, 1970b; Clifton, 1967; Greenberg, 1966; Marshall, 1969; McNeill, 1966b). This can be illustrated with the word associations given to **man**, **boy**, **long**, and **yellow** in Table 12–4. Responses like these have been collected by psychologists for a variety of stimulus words from large numbers of people (see Postman and Keppel, 1970). In the typical word-association test, a person is asked to give one word in response to each stimulus word. The more people that respond with a particular word, the more indicative of the process that word is taken to be. As even a cursory glance at these associations shows, most of the commonest ones bear an obvious semantic relation to the stimulus word. They are opposites, superordinates, members of the same taxonomy, and the like. As noted in Chapter 11, these relations are readily described in terms of semantic components. Before going any further, however, it is necessary to see what is involved in the process of giving associations.

The Process of Associating

In the word-association task itself, people hear or read a stimulus word, go through some mental process, and produce a response word. Roughly speaking, there are three stages:

Stage 1: Represent the stimulus word.

Stage 2: Alter that representation in some minimal way.

Stage 3: Produce the word corresponding to the altered representation.

TABLE 12–4

WORD ASSOCIATIONS

The five most frequent word associations to the stimulus words
man, **boy**, **long**, and **yellow**. The numbers after each response
are number of people out of 1,008 giving that response.

STIMULUS:	man		STIMULUS:	boy	
RESPONSES:	woman	767	RESPONSES:	girl	768
	boy	65		man	41
	girl	31		scout	37
	dog	18		dog	10
	lady	17		friend	8
	[others]	110		[others]	144
STIMULUS:	long		STIMULUS:	yellow	
RESPONSES:	short	758	RESPONSES:	blue	156
	fellow	11		red	115
	narrow	10		color	106
	John	9		green	89
	time	9		black	73
	[others]	211		[others]	469

Based on Postman and Keppel (1970).

To see how this might work, imagine that people are given the stimulus word
man. At Stage 1, they might represent **man** in terms of, for example, its semantic
procedure, written here in terms of its three components:

Stage 1: **Man** is represented as **Male(x) & Adult(x) & Human(x)**.

At Stage 2, they would alter this representation in some minimal way—say,
by changing the first component like this:

Stage 2: **Male(x)** is changed to **Female(x)**.

By now they have an altered representation, and at Stage 3, they must find an
English word that corresponds to it:

Stage 3: **Female(x) & Adult(x) & Human(x)** is realized as **woman**.

So to the stimulus **man**, they have responded **woman**. Note that Stages 1 and 3
are familiar. Stage 1 represents the sense of a word, setting up its semantic
procedure, just as in normal comprehension. Stage 3 does just the reverse. It
selects a word for production whose semantic procedure fits certain con-

straints. This same selection process is used in naming. What is new and special about the word-association task is Stage 2.

Word associations, however, are not homogeneous—they vary in their "depth." When pushed to respond very quickly, people sometimes give *clang* associations (from the German word for sound), like **man** → **map**, **sister** → **blister**, and **yellow** → **fellow**. **Man**, for example, is represented at Stage 1 in its *phonological* form [mæn], and what is changed at Stage 2 is a phonetic segment—[n] to [p]. When given slightly more time, people tend to give meaning-related associations, like **man** → **woman**, **sister** → **brother**, and **yellow** → **blue**, responses that most other people would give too. In this case **man** is represented at Stage 1 in a *semantic* form, and what is changed at Stage 2 is a semantic component—**Male(x)** to **Female(x)** to give **woman**. When encouraged to take even more time, people will oblige with quite idiosyncratic responses, like **man** → **door**, **sister** → **summer**, and **yellow** → **father**. Here at Stage 1 **man** elicits some particular experience or picture or feeling; after all, words are linguistic devices that are designed to do just that. A minimal change in this *experiential* representation at Stage 2 then leads to words describing other aspects of that personal experience, ones that may reveal special preoccupations and worries. Although these responses may be of interest to the psychiatrist, it is the meaning-related responses that are of interest here. One must step lightly between the clang and the idiosyncratic response and concentrate on the words most people give. They are just the ones listed in Table 12–4.

Rules of Alteration

At Stage 2 in the process, there are many ways in which people can alter their Stage 1 representations minimally. The principal ones can be illustrated with **man**, whose main three semantic components are as follows:

Male(x) & Adult(x) & Human(x).

These components can be changed by one of many different *rules of alteration*. Here are three important rules:

(1) *Replace one or more components.* **Male(x)** can be replaced by **Female(x)** giving:

Female(x) & Adult(x) & Human(x).

The response is therefore **woman**. **Male(x)** and **Female(x)**, of course, belong to the same taxonomy, and taxonomies are the main source of replacement components.

(2) *Delete one or more components.* In **man**, the components **Male(x)** and **Adult(x)** can be deleted, and the result is **Human(x)**. This would lead to a Stage 3 response of **person** or **human**. If only one of these two components were deleted, the result would be:

Adult(x) & Human(x)   *or*   Male(x) & Human(x).

As it happens, no English word corresponds to either of these semantic procedures, and so neither deletion by itself can lead to a response. This illustrates an important point about rules of alteration. If one alteration leads to an impossible word in English, there must be further alterations until a legitimate word is found.

(3) *Add one or more components.* If the component **Not(x)** is added to the second component in **man**, the result is as follows:

Male(x) & Not(Adult(x)) & Human(x).

This is the semantic procedure for **boy** and leads to the Stage 3 response **boy**. The components most often added in Stage 2 are those that apply to many words in the language—those like **Not(x)**, **Come-about(x)**, and **Cause(x,y)**. But more specialized components may also be added, as in the following for **man**:

Male(x) & Adult(x) & Human(x) & Polite(x).

This leads to the Stage 3 response **gentleman**.

Common Types of Associations

Together these three rules account for a remarkable proportion of the most frequent word associations. Consider Rules 2 and 3. Many words come in pairs in which one word differs from the other by a single component. When **Not(x)** is added to **long** by Rule 3, the result is **short**, and when **Not(x)** is deleted from **short** by Rule 2, the result is **long**. In pairs like this, the one member of the pair is almost invariably the most common, or nearly the most common, response to the other. This is illustrated in Table 12–4 for the responses to **long**. **Short** was the response 76 percent of the time, and no other response occurred more than 1 percent of the time. Here are other word pairs with a single contrasting component, and within each pair one member elicits the other by Rules 2 or 3:

Semantic Component	*Examples of Pairs*
Not(x)	deep-shallow, good-bad, arrive-leave, present-absent
Cause(x,y)	kill-die, show-see, teach-learn, feed-eat
Come-about(x)	die-dead, melt-liquid, get-have

Rules 2 and 3 lead to superordinates and subordinates too. For **man**, Rule 2 produced **person**, a superordinate, and Rule 3 produced **gentleman**, a subordinate or hyponym. This often happens when components are added or deleted, respectively, from a semantic procedure. Superordinates and subordinates are among the most common responses to many stimulus words, especially to those that do not have common opposites.

Rule 1 comes into play whenever a component belongs to a binary or

multinary taxonomy. Recall that the color names comprise a multinary taxonomy:

[Red(x), Green(x), Yellow(x), Blue(x), . . .]

By Rule 1, one of these procedures should be replaced by another, and thus one
color name should elicit another. As Table 12–4 illustrates, **yellow** has **blue**,
red, **green**, and **black** among its most frequent responses. The response **color**, of
course, is its superordinate and a result of Rule 2. Other taxonomies that have
analogous patterns include bird names, animal names, dog names, tree names,
fruit names, names of tastes, singular-plural, male-female, and present-past.

In giving word associations, people try to say the first word that comes to
mind. What they assume this means is that they should make the simplest change
at Stage 2 they possibly can. But what is the simplest change? Apparently it is
this: it is simpler to change one component than two or more (H. Clark, 1970b).
In Table 12–4, note that **man** elicited **woman**, **boy**, and **girl**. Whereas **woman** and
boy each come from a change in one component, **girl** comes from a change in
two, and it is also less frequent than the other two responses. This pattern is
typical. It is also simpler to delete than to add components. As a result, superordinates are more frequent responses than subordinates, and they can be
produced more quickly too (Marshall, 1969). And there are more word associations that delete **Not(x)**, **Cause(x,y)**, and **Come-about(x)** than there are ones that
add them. **High** is a more frequent response to **low**, for example, than **low** is to
high (H. Clark, 1970b; Greenberg, 1966; Marshall, 1969). Yet the simplest
changes do not always lead to English words. When that happens, and it
happens often, people have to make as many changes as necessary. The resulting
response may be many components removed from the stimulus. But when
people are cooperative, they try to keep the number of changes to a minimum.

Syntagmatic Associations

These rules, of course, do not exhaust the ways people give word associations.
They account mainly for the so-called *paradigmatic responses*, those that fall in
the same syntactic category as the stimulus word. Another frequent response,
especially for certain types of words, is the so-called *syntagmatic association*,
one that is able to precede or follow the stimulus word in a sentence, as in
whistle → stop, **stove → pipe**, and **so → what**. In Table 12–4, the syntagmatic
associations include **boy → scout**, **boy → friend**, **long → fellow**, and **long → John**.
These responses seem to come from a different source—a different level of
representation—from those accounted for by Rules 1, 2, and 3. **Boy scout**, for
example, is an idiom with its own entry in the mental lexicon. Then it is as if
people take hold of the following rule: "Find an idiom, or a well-known phrase,
that begins with the stimulus word (**boy**) and produce the next main word in the
phrase (**scout**)." Here people are consulting possible phonological representations for lexical entries, a level not as "deep" as that considered by Rules 1, 2,
and 3. There are undoubtedly other such rules.

The components of semantic procedures, therefore, play a central role in many word associations. They are what people consult and alter in coming to many of the commonest responses to stimulus words. But in giving word associations, people aren't tapping a skill they have specially learned for this exotic task. They are dealing with words in some measure as they would in everyday conversations. Once this point is conceded, it is hard not to conclude that the components of semantic procedures are used in ordinary speech production too. Words are selected on the basis of their semantic procedures, and these in turn call upon component procedures that test for the applicability of words to situations. The evidence from word associations suggests that these component procedures are relatively separate mental operations.

SUMMARY

This chapter has dealt with the role of word meanings in comprehension and production. For convenience word meanings have been considered as semantic procedures.

In comprehension, it was argued, semantic procedures spell out precisely how a sentence is to be utilized. The argument was illustrated for inherent negatives (like **absent**), modifiers (like **tall**), and category names (like **bird**), and it went like this. First, the strategy for verifying, say, **The square is absent** is expanded out by the semantic procedure for **absent** into the steps for **Present(x)** and **Not(y)**. These two steps behave very much like the corresponding stages in the strategy for verifying **The square isn't present**, which calls on **Present(x)** and **False(y)** explicitly. Second, a strategy that utilizes an adjective like **tall** is expanded out by its semantic procedure into two steps, one that selects the dimension of the object to be modified (height), and another that specifies its value on this dimension (great). These two steps appear to work separately from each other. Third, strategies for utilizing a category name like **bird** are expanded out by a semantic procedure that specifies the prototype bird. With auxiliary assumptions, this explains why some members of the category are judged to be more typical than others, and why some can be verified as members of the category more quickly than others.

In production, it was argued, semantic procedures are central to the selection of the word that will get the listener to pick out the right concept. This argument was illustrated in three examples. First, in naming an object, people identify it and then select a word, usually a basic-level term, whose semantic procedure fits that identification. The rarer the name, the longer it takes to produce. This may be because the pronunciation of rarer words is less accessible and because their semantic procedures are more complex. Second, people normally select adjectives to narrow down a category and thereby distinguish it from its neighbors. Adjectives appear to be selected in two steps, dimension first and value second. This is necessary to account for the preferred order of adjectives from least to most intrinsic and to account for the order in which adjectives are actually decided upon. Third, in word-association tasks, people hear a stimulus word, change its semantic procedure minimally, and produce the response word corresponding to the altered procedure. The changes people make typically involve the replacement, addition, or deletion of one or more components of the semantic procedure. This gives further evidence that semantic procedures consist of components that can operate separately from each other.

Further Reading

Winograd (1972) and G. Miller and Johnson-Laird (1976) present broad theoretical discussions of semantic procedures, but both stress their logical feasibility rather than their empirical viability. Collins and Loftus (1975), Rosch and Mervis (1975), and E. Smith (1977) review a variety of evidence pertinent to the structure of categories and the verification of statements about them. Vendler (1968) gives a thoughtful discussion of the order of adjectives in English.

Holding a piece of paper above her
sister's head, "I'm gonna just fall
this on her."

Child aged 2 years 9 months

13

Meaning in the Child's Language

In acquiring language, children must learn the meanings of words. Although they begin on this very early, in previous chapters it was taken for granted that they had at least some meaning for the words they used. Recall that children start with single-word utterances. **Doggie** might be used to assert of a particular object "that's a dog," or to request something like "let me pat the dog." Similarly, **more** on its own might be used to assert "there's another one," or to request "give me another." In using these single words, children have already begun on the *mapping problem*: they assume these words convey certain ideas or concepts (Chapter 8). Essentially, they have to *map* what they know about objects, events, and relations onto words, word endings, and word orders. The basic question in this chapter is: how do children acquire these meanings, especially word meanings?

CHILDREN AND MEANING

The words children hear are all new to them—they are not born with a mental lexicon all set up. Building a lexicon is a major part of acquiring language, and to do it, children have to be able to attach meaning to new words. How do people usually find out what a new word means? Adults, faced with words like **inconcinnous** or **widdershins**, have several options. They can go to someone and ask. Or they can go to a dictionary and look up the definitions. Or they can try to guess what these words mean from the context. Adults only meet this problem occasionally, but young children are faced with it all the time. One- and two-year-olds obviously can't take up the first two options open to adults, but they can and do make use of context.

Children may use context in rather unexpected ways. Here are four examples of interpretations made by children between two and five (the last three were observed by E. E. Maccoby):

Situation	*Child's usage*
1. A mother pointed out and named a dog "bow-wow."	The child later applied **bow-wow** to horses, cows, and cats, as well as to dogs.
2. A mother said sternly to her child: "Young man, you did that on purpose."	When asked later what **on purpose** meant, the child replied: *It means you're looking at me.*
3. A nursery school teacher divided her class into teams, spread a small blanket on the floor at one end of the room and said, "This team will start here," and then put another blanket at the other end of the room, saying "This team will start here."	At home, later, a child put down a blanket and set her baby brother on it. He crawled off and the child complained to her mother: *He won't stay on my team!*
4. A mother said "We have to keep the screen door closed, honey, so the flies won't come in. Flies bring germs into the house with them."	When asked what **germs** were, the child said: *Something the flies play with.*

Each child has clearly concluded that something in the context was pertinent to the meanings of the new words **bow-wow**, **on purpose**, **team**, and **germ**. But in each instance the child's first "guess" was quite wrong. In 1, the use of **bow-wow** suggests that the child has hit on only part of its meaning—perhaps "four-legged object" or "moving object," while in 2, the definition of **on purpose** misses the mark completely. In each example the children are clearly trying to work out which concept is being conveyed by the new word. And, given the contexts in which they heard the words, their first inferences are eminently reasonable. These examples raise two critical questions: what do children base their inferences on and how do they go on from there to work out what the *adult meanings* are for new words?

Issues in the Acquisition of Meaning

There are several issues to be kept in mind while studying the acquisition of meaning. Some have already been met in earlier chapters on language acquisition, while others arise specifically from the study of meaning.

Comprehension and Production

Very young children often seem to understand much more than they themselves can say, and they respond appropriately to many words before they even begin to talk. Do they really understand what is said to them? Here one has to be very cautious because young children are very good at interpreting the adult gestures used along with words. As several people have shown, children rely on these gestures to direct their attention and then do what seems most plausible in context. Asked **Why can't you ever shut the door?**, a two-year-old may well act on the adult's accompanying glance toward the door and shut it. But under these circumstances, the child can hardly be credited with a full understanding of the utterance **Why can't you ever shut the door?** One problem then is to find out how much children understand from the words alone at different points during acquisition.

A second problem is that children begin to use words as soon as they have worked out *some* meaning for them. But this meaning is not necessarily the same as the adult one, as the uses of **bow-wow** and **team** have just shown. What children say can often mislead because adults assume that children use their words with adult meanings. The mistakes children do make provide insight into the process of mapping concepts onto words.

To study the child's acquisition of meaning, therefore, we must draw on evidence from carefully designed studies of comprehension—where children have no non-linguistic cues to interpretation—as well as from careful observations of exactly what children say in particular contexts. A first step in the study of meaning acquisition is to identify the semantic hypotheses children entertain and the strategies they derive from them for using new words.

Complexity of Meaning

One of the major issues in Chapter 9 was complexity in language structure and how it affected the order in which children acquired different word endings, function words, and syntactic structures. For example, word endings that expressed a single conceptual component (e.g., "number") were acquired before those that expressed that component plus others (e.g., "number" + "earlier in time"). The complexity of the concepts expressed was one important determinant of the order in which children acquired word endings.

Like word endings, the meanings of some words are more complex than others. One hypothesis is that the more complex meanings include simpler meanings plus other components. For example, the verb **give** means roughly "transfer an object from person A to person B." The verb **sell** contains the same conceptual component plus two others: the notion that there is a transfer of money from B to A and the notion that the two actions are an exchange, that A gets money in return for giving B something. The meaning of **give**, therefore, ought to be easier for children to work out than the meaning of **sell**. Another example is the difference between the meanings of **father** and **great-great-grandfather**. The meaning of **father**, roughly speaking, is "male parent of someone" while that of **great-great-grandfather** is "male parent of a parent of a parent of a parent of someone," a more complicated combination of components that includes the meaning of **father**. Semantic complexity may take other forms as well.

Only some sets of words seem to be related to each other in the way **give** and **sell** or **father** and **great-great-grandfather** are, with much or all of the meaning of the simpler term included in the more complex one. In these semantic fields, the simpler meanings should be worked out first and then the more complex ones. In other domains, the words hardly overlap at all. Consider animals: the meanings of **dog, horse**, and **cow** do not include one another. Conceptual complexity cannot be used to predict which meaning will be easier or harder than others to acquire. The order children learn them in may well be dependent on factors like individual experience and exposure to specific words. In both instances, though, children have to learn how terms fit together in a semantic field.

Hypotheses and Strategies

Children play an active role in the acquisition of meaning by building plausible interpretations for words and utterances from what they know and from cues in the immediate context. In doing this, they appear to start with two assumptions about the function and content of language:

(1) Language is for communication.

(2) Language makes sense in context.

The first assumption probably grows out of their earlier reliance on gestures—gestures that adults always accompany with speech (Chapter 8). The next step, for children, is to infer that language, like gestures, is for communication. Assumption 2 is equally important: children assume that there is a reasonable connection between what the speaker says in a particular situation and the situation itself. They have to work out precisely what these connections are—the mapping between their concepts and the language.

Since they assume that adults are trying to communicate with them about the "here and now," children rely heavily on the "here and now" in working out the meanings of words and utterances. Their first step is to form *hypotheses* about word meanings by drawing on their conceptual knowledge about the objects, events, properties and relations familiar to them (Chapter 8). Take the child who used **bow-wow** for horses and cows as well as dogs. His initial hypothesis might have been that **bow-wow** refers to an object that can move, to an object with a head, body, and four legs (mammal-shaped), to an object that is furry, or to some combination of these. In this way the child ties the supposed meaning of a word to a specific concept—something he already knows about. The next step is for children to derive *strategies* for using and understanding a word like **bow-wow** from the hypothesis they have formed about its meaning. For example, the child's strategy in producing **bow-wow** might be to use it to refer to or request any object that appeared to belong to the category picked out by **bow-wow**. His strategy for understanding **bow-wow** might be to look around for some object that could belong to that category and assume that was what the speaker was referring to.

Children vary in their choice of conceptual information when they form their first hypotheses about the meanings of words. In the case of **bow-wow**, for example, some children seem to pick out four-legged, mammal-shaped objects. Others may pick out furry-textured objects and use **bow-wow** for fur hats and coats as well as dogs. Others still may pick out moving objects. In forming their initial hypothesis, they select a possible meaning from their encyclopedic knowledge and from that derive a strategy for using the word. In effect, children treat what they take to be the meaning of a new word as a rule for how to use it on other occasions. As they find out more about how other people use it and about how well they themselves are understood when using it, they gradually adjust their strategy (their rule) until it eventually coincides with the adult's. The strategies children use at different stages tell us not only about the kind of conceptual information they consider pertinent to different meanings but also about the way their initial hypotheses evolve into the adult meanings.

Conceptual Knowledge and Semantic Knowledge

In Chapter 11, the "mental encyclopedia"—the general knowledge people have about the world—was distinguished from the "mental lexicon"—their knowledge about words. In effect, a concept only takes on linguistic significance once it has been linked to some aspect of language. Some concepts may be expressed universally in languages so they always form part of our semantic knowledge (see Chapter 14). Others may have semantic significance in some languages but not in all. One goal in studying acquisition is to discover how children work out the connections between particular conceptual domains and the linguistic devices available in the language being learned.

For example, children may make a conceptual distinction without having a word for it. They may show that they can perceive the difference between one and more than one shoe, and yet begin by using only the form **shoe**. At this stage, they give no sign of having identified a linguistic device to indicate plurality even though they clearly have the necessary concept available. It is only when children begin to use **More shoe** in contrast to **Shoe** alone or begin to add the suffix **-s** to all nouns in the context of "more than one" that they can be said to have found a linguistic device to express this concept (see Chapter 8). Children's semantic knowledge, then, consists of the lexical entries they have worked out for the linguistic devices used to convey particular concepts. It is only once they have made this mapping that the notion "more than one" can be said to be part of their *semantic knowledge*.

These four issues will come up again and again throughout the chapter. Some of them are linked to more general questions in the acquisition of language. The relations between complexity and order of acquisition, for example, assume continuity from one stage to the next, and the relation between conceptual knowledge and semantic knowledge likewise assumes that children build on what they already know. The hypotheses children try out for word meanings are inseparable from the hypotheses they apply to word endings and word combinations. Word meaning is part of a continuum that includes sentence meaning, and children work on both simultaneously. Scrutiny of the hypotheses and strategies children apply to particular word meanings casts light on the mapping problem as a whole.

The first part of this chapter will examine early word meanings—the meanings children attach to nouns and verbs during the first year or so of speech. The second part will take up strategies used in the acquisition of words for relationships—for example, **in**, **under**, **bigger than**, **before**. And the last part will deal with evidence for the emergence of semantic components based on the notions of *change*, *causation*, and *negation*.

EARLY WORD MEANINGS

When children first attach meaning to a word, they may or may not hit on the adult meaning. In the case of **bow-wow** cited earlier the child could be said to have hit on part of the adult meaning only. In the cases of **on purpose** and **team**, the children "missed" entirely. A priori, there are several possible relations that could hold between adult and child meanings.

Overlap with Over-Extension

The first possibility is that the child's meaning overlaps with the adult's in part but also extends beyond it. An *over-extension* like this has already been illustrated with **bow-wow**: the child over-extended this word to include horses and cows in the same category as dogs. By looking closely at what a child will and won't call **bow-wow** at this stage, it is possible to make inferences about the basis for the over-extension. One common basis is overall shape, here perhaps "mammal-shaped." For example, Perez (1892) found that his own child used the same word, **mou**, for indeterminate drawings of a horizontal line with four downward projections as he did for most animals (see also W. Stern, 1930). Other children may pick on texture and use **bow-wow** for dogs, cats, scarves, and fluffy bedroom slippers. In each of these over-extensions, the children's meaning overlaps in part with the adult's, but many of their uses, from the adult point of view, are "mistakes."

Over-extensions can overlap with the adult meaning in two ways. First, a *pure over-extension* may pick out only one or two properties as criterial for the use of a word. For example, Bowerman (1976) reported that Eva, from the age of 1;3, used the word **moon** to pick out the real moon, grapefruit halves, lemon slices, some tiny flat circular green leaves she had picked, a ball of spinach she was about to eat, a magnetic letter D she was putting on the refrigerator, hangnails she was pulling off, crescent-shaped pieces of paper she had torn off a pad, and so on. The crescent-shaped edge seemed to be criterial for all Eva's over-extensions of **moon**. Over-extensions like this have been widely documented in diary studies.

A second kind of over-extension is the *mixed over-extension*. It is typically based on different characteristics shared by the original referent in different situations. Eva, at 1;5, for example, began to use **kick** first for herself kicking a stationary object, then while looking at a picture of a cat with a ball near its paw, then for a fluttering moth, then for cartoon turtles on TV kicking their legs up, then when she threw something, then as she bumped a ball with the wheel of her tricycle making it roll, and so on (Bowerman, 1976). Each situation is characterized by at least one of three components found in the original "kick" situation: a waving limb (the cartoon turtles), sudden contact with an object (the tricycle wheel), and an object being propelled (the ball). Each situation has something in common with the original, but little overlap with the others. Mixed over-extensions have been reported by a number of investigators too.

Overlap with Under-Extension

Another way in which children's meanings can overlap with those of adults is by *under-extension*. With under-extension, the child's word denotes only a subset of the items included in the adult category. For example, one early talker named Allison used **car** at the age of nine months only for cars moving on the street below as she watched out of the window, not for cars standing still, for cars in pictures, or for cars she rode in herself (Bloom, 1973). She appeared to have identified some characteristics critical to the adult use of **car** but combined them with others that were irrelevant. Because children may fail to use a word for all sorts of reasons—they could simply be sleepy, restless, or attending to something else—under-extensions are often difficult to detect.

Under-extensions, however, might represent the very first stage in the acquisition of each new word. For example, a child might start off using **kitty** only for one specific cat—the family pet. Later on, he could extend **kitty** to include other cats, and possibly then over-extend it to other animals like dogs or sheep (E. Clark, 1973a). Both under- and over-extensions require children to adjust their initial meanings of words until they match the adult's.

Meanings with No Overlap

Another possibility is that the child's first meaning does not overlap at all with the adult meaning. An example cited earlier is the definition of **on purpose**. Another example comes from one of Bowerman's children, Christy. At 1;6 she began to use **hi** in a peculiar way in addition to its normal use as a greeting. She said it, for example, as she balanced tiny toys on the end of a finger, as she slid her hands under a blanket, as she stuck her hand into a mitten-shaped pot-holder, and when a shirt fell over her foot in her crib. Bowerman (1976) suggested that Christy's hypothesis—that **hi** has to do with something resting on or covering her hands or feet—was derived from those occasions when she was shown a finger puppet or pen cap on her mother's finger that "nodded" and said "hi" to her. The child, instead of taking **hi** in its greeting sense, focused on the relationship between finger and finger puppet and from that built her hypothesis about the meaning of **hi**.

What happens to instances of no overlap between adult and child meanings? Because they provide no basis for communication, children presumably abandon such words quite quickly. Several investigators, in fact, have reported that the words some very young children use have a high mortality rate. During their first few months of talking, they often start to use new words for objects and actions only to drop them again almost immediately (Bloom, 1973). These may well be words that have no overlap with the adult meaning. Communication with language is dependent on shared meanings.

Working out the connections between words and concepts is not easy. Since children rarely hit on the exact adult meaning for a word at the very start, they may spend several years adjusting their initial hypotheses to the adult meanings. The "mistakes" children make at different stages provide valuable insights into the processes by which they acquire word meanings. The focus in the next two sections, therefore, is (a) on the mistakes children make, especially with over-extensions, and (b) on the order in which children acquire words related in meaning as they build up semantic fields for various conceptual domains.

Over-Extensions

Recognizable words are produced from about age one onward. In the first year, new words are added slowly and by age two amount to a vocabulary of fifty or so (Nelson, 1973). From then on, words are added much more rapidly. In this early period, over-extensions are common. A word like **stick** is applied to umbrellas and boards of wood as well as to sticks, and a word like **ball** to apples, oranges, and doorknobs as well as to balls. What does each group of objects have in common that might have prompted children to use their words in this way? All the objects picked out by **stick** are fairly long, thin, and rigid. All the objects picked out by **ball** are round and small enough to grasp. Children's concepts of the categories they call **stick** or **ball** contain a number of different components or properties like these. The question is: what components provide the basis for children's first hypotheses about word meanings?

The conceptual component of *shape* is frequently used in deciding whether a particular word can pick out an object. A word like **moon** or **ball** may be used to pick out objects that are round: Eva's use of **moon** for crescent-shaped objects is typical (see E. Clark, 1973a, 1974; Bowerman, 1975). The reliance on shape, illustrated in Table 13–1, appears to spring from children's conceptual organization of objects and relations rather than from anything peculiar to the languages they are acquiring. The over-extensions in Table 13–1 are very similar regardless of whether the language being acquired is English, Serbian, French, or Georgian —all very different languages.

Other conceptual components that provide a basis for over-extension are

TABLE 13-1

SOME OVER-EXTENSIONS BASED ON **SHAPE**

Words were over-extended to other objects in the order listed in the right-hand column.

WORD	FIRST REFERENT	DOMAIN OF APPLICATION
mooi	moon	cakes, round marks on windows, writing on windows and in books, round shapes in books, tooling on leather book covers, round postmarks, letter " O "
nénin	breast, food	button on garment, point of bare elbow, eye in portrait, face in portrait, face in photo
buti	ball	toy, radish, stone spheres at park entrance
ticktock	watch	clocks, all clocks and watches, gas meter, firehose wound on spool, bathscale with round dial
gumene	coat button	collar stud, door handle, light switch, anything small and round
baw	ball	apples, grapes, eggs, squash, bell clapper, anything round
kotibaiz	bars of cot (crib)	large toy abacus, toast rack with parallel bars, picture of building with columned façade
tee	stick	cane, umbrella, ruler, (old-fashioned) razor, board of wood, all stick-like objects
kutija	cardboard box	matchbox, drawer, bedside table
mum	horse	cow, calf, pig, moose, all four-legged animals

Based on E. Clark (1975).

properties of *movement*, *size* (usually rather small size), *sound*, *texture*, and occasionally *taste*. Examples of over-extensions based on these components are shown in Table 13-2. Again, these examples are drawn from children learning a variety of different languages.

Many of the over-extensions in Tables 13-1 and 13-2 appear to be pure over-extensions, where the same component (or components) provides the basis for each over-extension observed. A few appear to be mixed over-extensions, where a component of shape, for example, provides the basis for the first few over-extensions, and then a component of texture or movement takes over. Both types of over-extension occur from very early on.

Identifying the exact basis for an over-extension may be difficult: it depends critically on careful observation of where a child does and doesn't use a word he or she is over-extending. Several investigators have tackled this problem with informal experiments. Some, like Perez (1892) and Stern (1930), looked at their children's ability to name stick-figure drawings and in that way were able to

TABLE 13–2
SOME OVER-EXTENSIONS BASED ON
MOVEMENT, SIZE, SOUND, AND **TEXTURE**
Words were over-extended to other objects in the order listed in the right-hand column.

WORD	FIRST REFERENT	DOMAIN OF APPLICATION
sch	sound of train	all moving machines
ass	toy goat with rough hide, on wheels	a few things that move (e.g., animals, sister, wagon), all things that move, all things with a rough surface
fly	fly	specks of dirt, dust, all small insects, child's own toes, crumbs of bread, a toad
em	worm	flies, ants, all small insects, head of timothy grass
bébé	baby (self)	other babies, all small statues, figures in small pictures and prints
fafer	sound of train	steaming coffee pot, anything that hissed or made a noise
sizo	scissors	all metal objects
bow-wow	dog	toy dog, fur piece with animal head, other fur pieces without heads
wau-wau	dog	all animals, toy dog, soft house slippers, picture of an old man dressed in furs
va	white plush dog	muffler, cat, father's fur coat

Based on E. Clark (1975).

identify some of the conceptual components of shape that were being used. Major (1906) tried a different approach with **mum,** a word his son first applied to horses and then over-extended to various other animals. Major took his son, aged 2;0, to visit a zoological museum and asked him what the different stuffed animals were called. Being mammal-shaped (head, body, and four legs) appeared to be critical. The child used **mum** to name a number of animals he had never seen before, including a hippopotamus, an opossum, a peccary, a tiger, and a wolf. Monkeys, however, were called **babies** and birds **chickens.** Major concluded from this that **mum** served to pick out any four-legged animal for which the child lacked a name. Shape appears to provide the basis for the majority of the over-extensions described in the diary-study literature.

Appearance Versus Function

Although over-extensions based on perceptual information are very common, there may also be over-extensions based on function—the use to which an object

Children's early words for animals are as indeterminate as their later drawings.

is put. Nelson (1974) has proposed that function takes precedence over perceptual attributes when children first work out what a word means. The test of the two positions is what children do when they have a choice between over-extending a word to an object similar in function but not in appearance, versus an object similar in appearance but not in function.

Appearance generally takes precedence over function. In an explicit test of the two positions for her own children's speech, Bowerman (1975) found numerous over-extensions on the basis of appearance but very few indeed that might be attributed to function. She noted that over-extensions based on shared perceptual attributes like shape often *cut across* functional differences that were well known to the children. In the over-extension given earlier, when Eva used **moon** for the moon, grapefruit halves (for eating), a crescent-shaped piece of paper (for drawing on), a crescent-shaped car light, a magnetic capital D, and a hangnail, she clearly knew these objects had different functions. She must have been relying on shape. Another example comes from Christy, who over-extended the word **money** from pennies to buttons, beads, and the circular, flattened copper clapper inside her toy bell, following the appearance rather than the diverse functions of these objects as she knew them. The diary studies back up Bowerman's conclusions with numerous similar examples (E. Clark, 1973a; Anglin, 1976).

Knowledge about perceptual properties, then, plays a major role in children's first hypotheses about word meanings. Children seem to assume that words serve to pick out objects on the basis of shape, size, movement, and so on, and only rarely on the basis of function. They are much more likely to over-extend **ball** to a balloon than to over-extend **car** to a sled. Does knowledge of function play any role in children's early word meanings? There is at least one sense in which it must: children learn very early which objects are movers and which are movables, and the first words they learn tend to pick out movers and movables rather than places, recipients, or instruments (Chapter 8). This functional knowledge, of course, has to do with the *general roles* objects can have in other events or states. More specific functions like the difference between a tea cup and a coffee cup are often defined by the culture and may not be acquired until well after children have learned to name concepts and talk about much of what goes on around them (Andersen, 1975).

Over-Extensions in Comprehension

So far, children's early word use has only been considered in production—in what children say. What happens to their over-extensions in comprehension? Imagine a child who over-extends **doggie** to both cats and dogs. If the conceptual components he picks out are the *only* meaning he has for **doggie**, then he should show no preference for dogs over cats when shown pictures of both and asked **Show me the doggie**. **Doggie** in this case is over-extended both in production and in comprehension. However, mixed over-extensions suggest that the meanings of some words, at least, consist of a core of conceptual components, any one of which can provide the basis for an over-extension. The meaning attached to such a word involves *at least* those conceptual components visible in over-extensions and possibly others as well (E. Clark, 1975; Huttenlocher, 1974). The child who over-extends **doggie** to cats on the one hand and to slippers on the other, should show a preference for dogs over cats when shown pictures of both and asked **Show me the doggie**. In this case, **doggie** would be over-extended in production but not in comprehension.

Some words two-year-olds over-extend in production are not over-extended in comprehension. Thomson and Chapman (1975) studied five children between 1;9 and 2;3, identifying four words that each child over-extended in spontaneous speech. They then tested the children's comprehension of those words by showing them pairs of pictures and saying, for example, **Show me the doggie** where **doggie** was the word that had been over-extended. The pictures consisted of appropriate referents (dogs) paired with inappropriate ones (e.g., horses or cows) to which the word had been over-extended. Four of the five children showed a distinct preference for choosing the *appropriate* adult referent for at least half the words they had over-extended. For example, one child aged 1;11 over-extended **apple** in production to many other spherical and round objects (balls, tomatoes, cherries, onions, biscuits, etc.) yet in comprehension consistently identified the appropriate referent, an apple. Such children clearly know more about the meanings of some of their words than could have been inferred from their productions alone.

One child, however, over-extended all four of her words (**cow, doggie, fish,** and **ketchup**) in comprehension as well as production. She showed no preference for the appropriate adult referent, for example, when asked for a **cow** and shown pictures of a cow and a horse. The other four children also over-extended one or two words each in comprehension. The meanings attached to these words, then, seemed to involve only those conceptual components that could be identified from their over-extensions in production.

These findings suggest that there may be two different steps in children's over-extensions. At the first step, they form a hypothesis about the meaning of a word—that **doggie**, for example, picks out mammal-shaped objects—and use that meaning both in production and comprehension. At the next step, they start gathering more information about the adult referents of **doggie**, aided by the non-linguistic clues adults provide as they talk to young children. For **doggie**, they might add that the animals are furry, bark, and so on, with the result that they learn gradually how to pick out appropriate referents for it. But since they do not yet have words for many of the objects that resemble dogs in appearance, they continue to over-extend **doggie** to point something out or to make a request. They stretch their meager vocabulary to its limits in their attempts to communicate. Adults do much the same when learning a foreign language and when they come across objects they've never seen before. For example, on first seeing a zebra, one might well say **It's a kind of horse**.

So far, children's word meanings have been said to consist of conceptual components. But what is their status? From a componential point of view, they constitute the semantic components being added to the lexical entries for words (Chapter 11). The first components children add seem to be very concrete, for example "mammal-shaped," "furry," "barks," or "moves." Later, these develop into the more abstract ones used by adults, components like **Male(x)** or **Animate(x)**. At present very little is known about how this development takes place.

Semantic Fields

Children usually stop over-extending their words at about the age of 2;6. It is at this point that they start to ask innumerable **What('s) that?** questions and to expand their vocabulary at a much faster rate. It is as though they have just realized that there may be words for all sorts of things for which they, as yet, have no names. As they acquire new words, they narrow down over-extensions and build up semantic fields of words for various conceptual domains.

Children start on semantic fields with their first words: each word picks out part of a conceptual domain and as they add more words to their repertoires, they have to map more concepts in each domain onto words. One domain children tackle early is that of animals. The first steps they take are illustrated in Table 13–3 with data from several different diary studies. At Stage 1, a child begins with a single word, here **bow-wow**, which he may restrict briefly to one particular dog. Other children might start off with a word for cats, or sheep, or some other animal. A little later, **bow-wow** may be over-extended to other animals (Stage 2), but, as more words are acquired, the child works out where each one fits in and narrows down the domain formerly covered by the over-

TABLE 13–3

ADDING WORDS TO THE CONCEPTUAL DOMAIN OF ANIMALS

ORDER OF ACQUISITION	WORD	DOMAIN OF APPLICATION
1	bow-wow	a particular dog
2	bow-wow	dogs, cows, horses, sheep, cats
3	(a) bow-wow	dogs, cats, horses, sheep
	(b) moo	cows
4	(a) bow-wow	dogs, cats, sheep
	(b) moo	cows
	(c) gee-gee	horses
5	(a) bow-wow/doggie	dogs, cats
	(b) moo cow	cows
	(c) gee-gee/horsie	horses
	(d) baa	sheep
6	(a) doggie	dogs
	(b) cow	cows
	(c) horsie	horses
	(d) baa	sheep
	(e) kitty	cats

Based on E. Clark (1973a).

extension of **bow-wow** (Stages 3–6). The schematic outline in Table 13–3 of these stages is probably typical of other domains as well.

Dimensional Terms

In certain semantic fields, there is reason to think that some terms ought to be acquired later than others because of their complexity. Investigators have looked at the acquisition of several fields where the order of acquisition was predicted from the relative semantic complexity of the terms being acquired. Among them are dimensional adjectives and verbs of possession.

The field of *dimensional terms* in English includes adjective pairs like **big-small**, **tall-short**, and **wide-narrow**, which are used to describe the dimensions of different objects. As Bierwisch (1967) and others have pointed out, such adjectives differ in semantic complexity—in the number of restrictions placed on their use. **Big** and **small**, for example, can be used for talking about size in general. They can be used for one dimension only, like height in **He's a big boy**, for two dimensions, like the area in **It's a big field**, and for three, as in **It's a big cube**. **Big** and **small** have few constraints on their use with one, two, or three dimensions. **Tall-short** and **long-short** are more complex than **big-small** because they are restricted to only one dimension. The pair **tall-short** applies only to vertical extent, and **long-short** to nonvertical extent. **Thick-thin, wide-narrow**, and **deep-shallow** also refer to a single, nonvertical dimension, but they are more complex than **long-short** because, Bierwisch argued, they are restricted to secondary dimensions. **Thick** is never used for the most extended dimension of an object, whereas **high, tall**, or **long** are (see Chapter 14). Thus, among these adjectives, the least complex pair is **big-small**, and it is followed by **tall-short, high-low**, and **long-short**—three pairs that pick out a specific dimension. These in turn are followed by **thick-thin, wide-narrow**, and **deep-shallow**, pairs that each pick out a single dimension that is secondary.

Children acquire these terms roughly in the expected order, both in production and comprehension. The first dimensional adjectives, **big** and **small** (or **little**), appear in their speech between the ages of two and three, and the rest follow later, as shown in 5:

5. a. big-small
   b. tall-short, long-short
   c. high-low
   d. thick-thin
   e. wide-narrow, deep-shallow

This order of acquisition reflects the relative semantic complexity of dimensional terms fairly closely (see Donaldson and Wales, 1970; Wales and Campbell, 1970; H. Clark, 1970a; E. Clark, 1972; Brewer and Stone, 1975; E. Bartlett, 1976).

Possession Verbs

Another field where semantic complexity predicts the order of acquisition is the set of *possession verbs* studied by Gentner (1975), namely **give, take, pay, trade, buy, sell**, and **spend**. Semantically, **give** and **take** are the simplest. Roughly speaking, both mean "transfer of an object from one person to another." If the person *with* the object initiates the transfer, one uses **give**, and if the person *without* the object initiates it, one uses **take**. **Pay** and **trade** come next in complexity: they add to the basic meaning of **give** and **take** the notion of an obligation involving money on one side (**pay**) or the notion of a mutual contract for the exchange of objects (**trade**). The most complex verbs are those that combine all these components: a transfer, an obligation involving money, and a mutual contract to exchange one object (the money) against another. These verbs include **buy, sell**, and **spend** (see Bendix, 1966; Fillmore, 1969).

In a comprehension task, children between 3;6 and 8;6 were asked to give, buy, or trade objects according to Gentner's instructions. The simplest verbs were mastered first, and the more complex ones later. The order of acquisition is shown in 6:

> 6. a. give, take
>   b. pay, trade
>   c. buy, spend
>   d. sell

The two simplest verbs, in *a*, were already understood by the youngest children, but the three most difficult ones, in *c* and *d*, had yet to be mastered by most of the eight-year-olds.

Other semantic fields that have been studied include the kinship terms, such as **father**, **sister**, or **cousin** (see Danziger, 1957; Haviland and E. Clark, 1974; Duveen, 1974; Chambers and Tavuchis, 1976); the locative terms, such as **in**, **under**, or **above** (E. Clark, 1972, 1973b, 1977a; Grimm, 1975b); the motion verbs **come**, **go**, **bring**, and **take** (E. Clark and Garnica, 1974), and some verbs of communication like **ask**, **tell**, **allow**, and **promise** (C. Chomsky, 1969; Grimm and Schöler, 1975). In each domain, the greater the complexity of a term, generally the later it is acquired.

Basic-Level Terms

Basic-level categories provide another way of predicting order of acquisition. R. Brown (1958) suggested that children first learned those terms that were most useful to them for talking about their world. The terms were those adults select for their *level of utility*. **Dog**, for example, is more useful to the two-year-old than **animal**, and **tree** more useful than **oak**. These terms are what Rosch called *basic-level terms*. They name a middle level of categorization (see further Chapter 14). Rosch and her colleagues argued that basic-level terms should be acquired before more general or more specific-level terms (Rosch, Mervis, Gray, Johnson, and Boyes-Braem, 1976). **Dog** should therefore be learned before **animal** and **Dachshund** or **red setter**, **tree** before **plant** and **elm** or **oak**, and **car** before **vehicle** and **Volvo** or **Ford**. This prediction was supported by vocabulary data from Eve, one of the three children studied by R. Brown (1973). However, it is not clear whether children learn all the basic-level terms for categories of animals, for example, before learning the more general **animal** or the more specific **cocker spaniel** or **Shetland pony**, or whether, after the first few basic-level terms, they simply add terms from whichever level is appropriate given their experience.

Notice that the basic-level hypothesis makes some predictions that are contrary to those made by the semantic inclusion relations discussed earlier. For example, if a category name like **dog** is treated as if it includes the meaning of **animal**, the semantic complexity hypothesis would predict that **animal** should be acquired first, for simple terms are included in the meanings of more complex ones. But the basic-level hypothesis would predict that **dog** should be acquired first. In this instance, the data conform to the basic-level hypothesis.

However, it is less clear what are basic-level terms and what not when it comes to actions and relations like **give** versus **sell**, and **on** versus **under**.

Can the two theories of complexity be reconciled? One possibility lies in the nature of the terms being acquired. The terms considered under the basic-level rubric are names for concrete objects. Those considered under the semantic complexity rubric are verbs, adjectives, and nouns that pick out more abstract relational information. It may be that semantic complexity of the inclusion type applies to relational terms, and the simpler the relation, the easier it is to acquire. But since category names are not relational in this sense, those predictions do not apply, and basic-level predictions do. Such an explanation, of course, would need considerable justification. Too little is known still about semantic complexity and basic-level terms.

CONTEXT AND STRATEGY

There are two major sources of information that children draw on in forming hypotheses. First, there is their own conceptual knowledge about different objects and the usual or possible relations between them. Children know that cups usually stand upright and hold water, juice, or milk; that people sit *on* chairs, not *under* them; that cars go along *roads*, not across *fields*; and that dogs chase cats. And they are continually adding to this stock of encyclopedic knowledge. Their second source of information is the non-linguistic clues adults provide with the gestures and looks that accompany speech. When an adult says **Put the block on the table**, with a hand gesture toward the block followed by a glance or gesture toward the table, children are successively directed to attend to the block and then to the table. They infer that they are expected to do something with the first object (a movable) in relation to the second (a place). Encyclopedic knowledge and context together help children form semantic hypotheses. These hypotheses, in turn, are used to derive strategies for producing and understanding each new word. This holds in the acquisition not only of object names but also of words for the relations between objects and between events.

Case Relations

One relationship considered earlier was that between a mover or agent and the movable object affected by the agent's action (Chapter 8). Although this relationship can be signaled by word order alone for the adult (for example, **The girl hit the boy** versus **The boy hit the girl**), it is often ignored by young children in favor of what they happen to know about the items named. J. de Villiers and P. de Villiers (1972), for example, found that when two-year-olds were given a sentence like **Teeth your brush**, they immediately pretended to brush their teeth, thereby treating the sentence as if it were quite reasonable (see also Wetstone and Friedlander, 1973). In a study of how children understand active and passive sentences, Strohner and Nelson (1974) found that two-year-olds would get passives right as long as the situation described corresponded to what they expected. They all seemed to understand **The baby is fed by the girl**, but not **The girl is fed by the baby**. For the same reason, passives like **The flower was picked by the boy** are easy for children to understand: there is only one possible relationship between boys, flowers, and the action of picking (see also Slobin, 1966a; H. Sinclair and Bronckart, 1972).

But word order is used in some contexts where children have to form a hypothesis about a new word. Dewart (1975) found that a nonsense word like **huft** placed before the verb in a noun + verb + noun sequence was nearly always taken to be a mover or agent, and hence as animate. After putting twelve toys out on the table—six "animate" ones (a boy, a dog, etc.) and six "inanimate" ones (a chair, a bucket, etc.)—Dewart gave three- and four-year-olds sentences like **The huft broke the chair** and asked them **Which one do you think the huft is?** The children then chose one of the twelve toys. For nonsense words preceding the verb, their choices overwhelmingly favored "animate" toys—the agents of actions. Dewart suggested that order-based choices like this could well be derived from adult clues such as pointing first at the agent and then at the object to be acted on, or first at the object and then at the place where it goes (see Garnica, 1975b). In this way, children gradually learn how different case roles are expressed as well as how to pick out different objects and actions.

Spatial Relations

Children clearly know about different relations in space before they start to talk about them, but they do not use their first spatial prepositions in English until age two or two and a half. Well before this, they show that they know some objects are containers (e.g., cups, boxes), others are supporting surfaces (tables, beds), and many have a normal or usual orientation (a bottle normally stands upright). This knowledge is at work when one-and-a-half-year-olds turn a box with its opening upward, right a glass, or put a doll into a toy crib rather than under it (E. Clark, 1973b, 1974).

The first relations children talk about are between objects and containers or surfaces, and the motion of one object toward another. The first prepositions they produce in English are **in** and **on**, from about the age of 2;0 or 2;6. In German and French, the first are usually **in**, **on**, and **at** or **to**. Later they use other prepositions as well, but sometimes make mistakes, such as using **under** for **in back of**, and often over-extend simpler prepositions in place of more complex ones, such as using **in** rather than **between**, or **on** rather than **above** (Grégoire, 1949; E. Clark, 1972; R. Brown, 1973; Grimm, 1975b). In languages like Hungarian and Turkish, where spatial relations are expressed by suffixes, **in**, **on**, and **to** are again among the earliest relations expressed (Mikeš, 1967; Slobin, 1975). But children's production of different prepositions tells us too little about what they think these words mean.

Containing, Supporting, and Touching

Do children use what they know about containment, support, and motion toward something in forming their first hypotheses about the meanings of spatial

prepositions? The answer seems to be yes. Several studies have shown that young children deal with prepositions by applying a few general strategies. Imagine a one-and-a-half-year-old girl being shown a box lying on a table. She is then given a small toy mouse and allowed to play with it. She will put the mouse *in* the box rather than *on* it. If instead of a box, she is given a toy crib and a mouse, she will put the mouse *in* the crib rather than *under* or *beside* it. Or, given a toy table and a mouse, she will put the mouse *on* the table. In each situation, the child seems to base her action on one of two "rules" about the spatial relations holding between objects and containers or surfaces (E. Clark, 1973b):

Rule 1: If B is a container, A belongs inside it.

Rule 2: If B has a supporting surface, A belongs on it.

Rule 1 takes precedence over Rule 2 since containers always seem to be treated as containers rather than surfaces, even where there is an option.

If these two rules capture children's a priori assumptions about possible spatial relations, they ought to play a role in their first hypotheses about the meaning of spatial prepositions too. E. Clark (1973b) looked at how children between 1;6 and 5;0 dealt with instructions like 7 with **in, on,** and **under:**

7. a. Put the mouse in/on the box.
   b. Put the mouse in/under the crib.
   c. Put the mouse on/under the table.

In instructions like 7a and 7b, even the youngest children appeared to understand **in** correctly, but not **on** or **under**. In 7c, they did appear to understand **on**, but not **under**. The results from the youngest children suggested they were basing their hypotheses about the word meanings on Rules 1 and 2. As a result, their strategies made it look as if they understood **in** all the time, **on** with surfaces but not containers, and **under** not at all. By age three, most children had worked out the meanings of all three prepositions. However, when three- and four-year-olds were faced with instructions containing more complex prepositions like **above**, **below**, **in front of**, or **at the bottom of**, they tended to "revert" to their earlier strategies based on Rules 1 and 2. Given an instruction to place one toy *below* another on a staircase, for example, they would place the toy "on" the staircase instead, usually on the top step, or given an instruction to place one toy *in front of* another, they would place it *on* it instead, usually on the topmost surface (E. Clark, 1975, 1977a). Their first hypotheses about the meaning of spatial prepositions did indeed seem to be based on their a priori conceptual organization of possible spatial relations captured in Rules 1 and 2.

Whenever children put one object in or on another, they always made them touch. Even when trying to copy an array consisting of a block and a mouse an inch apart, they would push the two together (E. Clark, 1973b). If this contact between objects is an essential ingredient in the child's view of spatial relations, it ought to turn up in other situations as well. For example, children ought to find it easier to make one object move *toward* another than to make it move *away*. This was just what Macrae (1976) found. When three-year-olds were asked to move a toy toward or away from another, they consistently moved it *toward* the other. Instructions containing **to** were always acted out correctly and instructions with **from** incorrectly (see also Garman, Griffiths, and Wales, 1970; E. Clark and Garnica, 1974). This preference for putting two objects in contact could be characterized in terms of Rule 3:

> *Rule 3:* If A and B are related to each other in space, they should be touching.

Hypotheses based on this conceptual principle will favor **to** over **from**, **into** over **out of**, and **onto** over **off** during the early stages of acquisition.

Order of Acquisition

The conceptual principles children start with provide them with a basis for acquiring some prepositions before others. Note that their strategies coincide with the adult action based on full understanding in some cases, but not in others. For example, the strategy of placing one object inside another coincides with the meaning of **in**. It could be argued that wherever such strategies "match" the adult meanings, children have very little to learn. Where they do not match, children have more to learn because they have to learn *not* to apply those strategies. Under this view, the meaning of **in** should be easier to acquire than either **on** or **under** because it requires minimal adjustment of the child's strategy.

On should be harder because the child has to learn *not* to apply Rule 1—**on** requires only Rule 2. And **under** should be harder still since the child has to learn *not* to apply either Rule 1 or Rule 2—neither plays a role in the adult meaning. Equally, the meaning of **to** should be easier to acquire than the meaning of **from** because it coincides more nearly with Rule 3.

Deciding whether children truly understand the meanings of words like these can be a complicated business. If a child shows the ability to distinguish **in** from **on** with instructions like 7a, by placing an object either *in* or *on* a box lying on its side, then it is clear that the two meanings—**in** and **on**—contrast. The child can then be credited with at least basic semantic knowledge of both for these contexts. Another test in such instances would be to give small children "impossible" instructions and see whether they realize these are impossible. Given **Put the mouse in the block**, a child who understands the meaning of **in** should reject the instruction. A child who does not yet know the meaning will simply place the mouse *on* the block.

Dimensional Relations

In acquiring dimensional adjectives like **tall** and **short** or **more** and **less**, children generally seem to understand positive terms like **tall** and **more** before the negative ones like **short** and **less**. This could be because they learn the positive meanings earlier or because their conceptual preferences lead them to use a strategy that makes it appear as if they know the positive terms but not the negative ones.

When three-year-olds are asked about two toy apple trees **Does one tree have more apples on it?** or **Does one tree have less apples on it?**, they can correctly answer **yes**, just as adults do. But what happens if they are then asked to point out *which* tree has more or which has less? Donaldson and Balfour (1968) found 91 percent correct answers for **Which one has more?** and 27 percent correct for **Which one has less?** In response to both questions, the children tended to choose the tree with more apples on it, treating questions with **less** as if they contained **more** (see also Palermo, 1973).

Donaldson and Balfour suggested that the children understood the meaning of **more** and that they assumed **less** meant the same. Another possibility, however, is that their answers to both questions reflected some conceptual preference (H. Clark, 1970a). Imagine that children presented with two piles of beads always chose the larger pile—the one with the greater amount—or, presented with two sticks, always chose the longer one—the one with greater extent. Such a preference would explain not only why children seem to get the positive words like **more**, **high**, and **long** correct, but also why they acquire them before negative words (E. Clark, 1973b). This preference would make the acquisition of positive terms easier than the acquisition of negative ones.

To find out whether there is a conceptual preference like this, Klatzky, E. Clark, and Macken (1973) gave children aged 3;6 to 5;0 a concept-learning task in which they had to work out the "meanings" of various nonsense words. For example, they had to learn that nonsense words like **ruk** and **maf** meant "long" and "short." On each trial they were shown a set of five sticks, each a different length. The experimenter chose one of the five sticks as a "standard" and then said **Show me one that is** *ruk*. When the children pointed at one of the other four sticks, their choice was either approved (**That's right**, for the choice of one longer than the standard) or corrected (**No, that's** *maf*, for the choice of one shorter than the standard). Then they went on to the next trial. The children also learned nonsense words for greater and lesser extension in overall size (cubes), height (model doors), and thickness (model "planks"). For each dimension, they learned the "positive" nonsense word more quickly and with fewer errors than the "negative" one despite the fact that both occurred equally often. These results provide support for the view that children do show a conceptual preference for greater extent (see also Carey, 1976).

To return to **more** and **less**, imagine that the children's first hypothesis is that both words denote only "amount." When this partial meaning is combined with a preference for picking objects with greater extent, children appear to understand **more** and misunderstand **less**. In situations where such a preference did not apply for some reason, children should do equally badly on both **more** and **less**, making no consistent choices. The view that both **more** and **less** only mean "amount" to begin with receives some support from what children in Donaldson and Balfour's study said. When asked **Which tree has more on it?**, some children gave answers like **Both of them**, **That one does an' that one does**, and **They two ones** as if they had been asked **Which tree has some on it?** And one child, asked to make the amount less on one tree, objected with **But it IS less on that tree**. In each case, they seem to be using **more** and **less** as if they mean "some" or "an amount."

Temporal Relations

When children talk about events, they stick closely to the "here and now." They focus on what is happening, what has just happened, or what is just about to happen. When they start to talk about events in sequence, therefore, they stick very closely to their actual order of occurrence—they describe the first event first, the second event second, and so on. This parallel between order of occurrence and order of mention appears both in production and in comprehension.

In production, the parallel is particularly apparent. For example, they follow order of occurrence in running commentaries on their own actions, as in 8 (E. Clark, 1970a, 1973c):

8. *Child building a tower with blocks:*
   These ones go here.   [places two large blocks]
   This one goes here.   [as places next block]
   An' this one here.   [as places next block]
   This one goes on here.   [as places next block]
   This one goes here.   [as places next block]
   Watch it fall!   [as tower topples]

They also follow order of occurrence in describing two-event sequences acted out in front of them, like the one in 9 (E. Clark, 1971; Ferreiro and Sinclair, 1971):

9. *Sequence*: Boy jumps fence, boy kicks rock.

    Description: The boy jumped the fence an' then he kicked the rock.

And they find it easier to imitate adult descriptions where the order of mention mirrors the order of occurrence (Keller-Cohen, 1974). For three- and four-year-olds, the sentences in 10, for example, are easier to imitate than the ones in 11:

10. a. The boy came in before the girl did.
    b. After the dog bit him, the man ran away.

11. a. The girl came in after the boy did.
    b. Before the man ran away, the dog bit him.

Children rely on the same strategy in interpreting what others say—they assume that the first event mentioned was the first to occur (see also Chapter 9). E. Clark (1971) found that three-year-olds were able to act out two events in sequence correctly 93 percent of the time after hearing descriptions like those in 12:

12. a. The boy jumped the fence before he patted the dog.
    b. After the boy jumped the fence, he patted the dog.

In both 12a and 12b, the order of mention corresponds to the order of occurrence: the first event mentioned is the first event. But when given the descriptions in 13, the same children got the sequence of events right only 18 percent of the time:

13. a. Before the boy patted the dog, he jumped the fence.
    b. The boy patted the dog after he jumped the fence.

When the order of mention did not match the order of occurrence, the children did not understand **before** and **after**. For both 12 and 13, they relied on their order-of-mention strategy and ignored the contrastive meaning in the conjunctions (see Ferreiro, 1971; Amidon and Carey, 1972; H. Johnson, 1975).

Does this reliance on order of mention play any role in children's hypotheses about the meanings of **before** and **after**? The answer is yes, for children acquiring not only English, but also other languages. Recall that the first adverbial clauses to be acquired are those that follow the main clause (Chapter 9). When the adverbial clause is introduced by **before** in this position, as in 12a, the meaning of **before** "coincides" with the order-of-mention strategy. As a result, the first hypothesis children come up with seems to be that **before** means "prior": the event in the main clause—the first clause—happens *prior to* the event in the subordinate clause introduced by **before**. A strategy based on this hypothesis should produce correct responses to **before** for both 12a and 13a. In fact, Clark found that some children got **before** right while continuing to make mistakes on **after**. These mistakes were of two kinds. **After** was either ignored, so, by order of mention, children got it right in 12b but wrong in 13b, or it was treated as if it too meant "prior," in which case children got both 12b and 13b wrong. Other children—usually older—had worked out the correct meaning.

Children acquiring the French and German equivalents of **before** and **after** follow a similar route. They first rely on order of mention alone, then work out the meaning of **before**, and finally work out the meaning of **after** (Ferreiro, 1971; Schöler, 1975).

Same or Different Routes?

So far, the emphasis has been on the similarities between children acquiring the same language and even different languages. For example, they all seem to pick out the same kinds of properties—shape, texture, and movement—when it comes to over-extensions. These similarities, it has been argued, are due to the way people organize their conceptual knowledge, starting from earliest childhood (E. Clark, 1974, 1976). However, because children may differ in their exposure to particular objects and events and what people say about them, it shouldn't be surprising if their initial hypotheses about meanings are sometimes different. And if their initial hypotheses differ, they may well follow different routes in working out the adult meaning. When are children likely to follow the same routes and when different ones?

Although all young children learn to name movers and movables very early (Chapter 8), there are often differences in the vocabulary they acquire and the style of speech addressed to them (Nelson, 1973; Lieven, 1975). As a result, children may differ in how they use particular words. Some may over-extend **horse** to many other mammal-shaped objects, while others restrict it to one animal or toy and instead over-extend **bird**, say, to anything that moves. Words for relationships between objects also vary in how they are first used. Some children over-extend a word like **off** to cover any situation in which two objects move apart or are moved away from each other, while others may restrict it to the removal of clothes (Bowerman, 1976). There is no guarantee that any child will hit on the same meaning as other children when choosing to try a particular adult word.

Nevertheless, some contexts restrict the meanings children will "guess" much more than others. Adults talking about the "here and now" normally use **in**, for example, when one object is visibly inside another, when one object is conventionally kept inside another, or when containment is a possible relation between two objects in the context. This helps limit children's hypotheses to the domain of spatial relations. Indeed, they all seem to come up with much the same initial meaning and follow the same route in working out the full adult meaning. Other contexts give fewer hints about word meaning and there seems to be much more variability in the hypotheses children come up with. Not only will their initial meanings differ but they may also follow different routes in working out the full adult meaning.

A striking example of different initial hypotheses and different routes in acquisition comes from a study of deictic or "pointing" words like **here**, **there**, **this**, and **that** (E. Clark and Sengul, 1974; E. Clark, 1977b). These words point to the position of an object relative to the speaker: **here** and **this** pick out objects relatively close to the speaker, **there** and **that** objects that are further away. In this study, three- and four-year-olds were shown two identical toy horses standing on a table, were told **This/that horse is jumping up and down** and were then asked **Can you make him do it?** Some always chose the horse nearest themselves, regardless of whether **this** or **that** was used in the description. Since they seemed to assume that both words picked out objects near themselves, their initial hypothesis could be called a child-centered one. Other children always chose the horse nearest the speaker: they seemed to have started with a speaker-centered hypothesis. From these different starting points, the two groups eventually came to contrast **this** and **that**, but how they worked out the contrast depended on whether they began with a child-centered hypothesis or a speaker-centered one. The contexts in which such deictic words are used provide children with very few clues to their meaning.

SEMANTIC COMPONENTS

When children acquire the meaning of a word, they construct an entry for it in their mental lexicon. They start off with a very simple entry containing only a few of the components relevant to its use by an adult. And as they learn more about its meaning and how it contrasts with other words, they may add further components and, if necessary, discard irrelevant ones. Eventually, their entry comes to coincide with the adult entry.

The components used by children in their lexical entries have been discussed mainly from the componential point of view. But they fit equally well into a procedural framework, where each component, be it "mammal-shaped" or "moves," can be regarded as a procedure called up whenever that component forms part of the meaning of a word. Components like "mammal-shaped" or "moves," however, bear little resemblance to adult components like **Male(x)** or **Animate(x)**, and, as was pointed out earlier, very little is known about how children advance from "moves," say, to **Animate(x)**. One advantage of the procedural approach is that it provides for a natural link between children's strategies for producing and interpreting words and the adult semantic procedures called up in production and comprehension. The strategies children use might be regarded as the forerunners of adult procedures. As children find out more about word meanings, they continually adjust their strategies until these eventually coincide with the adult procedures.

Three components that play a very general role in word meanings are **Come-about(x)**, **Cause(x,y)**, and **Not(x)**. Their extensive role in English was described in Chapter 11, and some of the evidence for adult use of **Not(x)** was discussed in Chapter 12. This section takes up evidence for the emergence and subsequent use of these three components by children.

Change and Causation

The first component, **Come-about(x)**, appears only in certain verbs. Verbs in English can be divided into three main groups:

(1) Verbs that describe a state, e.g., **have, want, be red**.

(2) Verbs that describe an activity or process, e.g., **walk, play, sleep**.

(3) Verbs that describe a change of state, e.g., **drop, fix, redden**.

Only the change-of-state verbs, like those in C, contain the component **Come-about(x)**. They describe actions that have a *result*, the state following the change.

Children seem to distinguish change-of-state verbs from the others in a very special way. When English-speaking children begin to use the past tense ending **-ed** at about age two, they go through a stage of adding it only to change-of-state verbs (3). With all other verbs (1 and 2), they use only present tense forms, even when talking about past events. A similar practice is followed by children acquiring Italian, who distinguish change-of-state verbs in much the same way.

From data like these, Antinucci and Miller (1976) have argued that children's use of **-ed** on change-of-state verbs shows that, for them, these verbs contain the component **Come-about(x)**. The argument goes like this. From very early, children name resultant states. For example, in assertions like **Sweater on**, **Light off**, and **Milk allgone**, the words **on**, **off**, and **allgone** describe the end state or result. In requests like **Baby up**, accompanied by a child raising his arms, **up** describes the desired result (Farwell, 1975, 1977; Bronckart and Sinclair, 1973). Then children learn verbs such as **write, walk, spill**, and **break**, and from then on need the option of distinguishing results from actions. To do this, they rely on the **-ed** ending. Notice that the resultant state of milk that one **spills** is **spilled**. In the same way, **breaked** (for **broken**) is the result of **break**, **drinked** (for **drunk**) the result of **drink**, and **falled** (for **fallen**) the result of **fall**. However, the actions described by **write, walk**, and **sleep** do not have results. For this reason, children add **-ed** to change-of-state verbs like **spill** or **fall**, but not to **write** or **walk**. This would explain the fact that at first the **-ed** ending is added only to change-of-state verbs. For children to distinguish change-of-state verbs from the rest, they must have realized that they contain **Come-about(x)**.

Causatives

A change of state often requires an agent to effect the change, and this is expressed by the addition of the component **Cause(x,y)** to the verb describing the action. English makes use of several devices to express the relationship between intransitive verbs and their causative counterparts. For example, the same verb form can be used for both, as in the intransitive **The horse** *walked* **across the moor** and the causative **The man** *walked* **the horse across the moor.** Or one verb form can be used for the intransitive, as in **The cup** *fell* **on the floor**, and another for the causative, as in **He** *dropped* **the cup on the floor.** Or a verb such as **make, get**, or **have** can be used in combination with the intransitive verb to form the causative. Compare the intransitive **His brother** *left*, for example, with the causative **He** *made* **his brother** *leave*.

Children very early become aware of the regular nature of the relationship between pairs of verbs like **walk-walk, fall-drop**, and **leave-make . . . leave**. Bowerman (1974b) found that Christy appeared to grasp the connection between intransitive and causative verbs at about the same time that she mastered the causative expressions that use **make** and **get**. At that point, Christy began to use intransitive verbs like **come** and **fall** as causatives, apparently on the model of **walk-walk**, for example:

Hypothetical intransitive source	*Causative*
The paper falled.	I'm gonna just *fall* it on her.
It came over here.	She *came* it over there.
Will the door stay open?	Mommy, can you *stay* this open?

Christy seemed to have hypothesized that any intransitive verb could be used as a causative, with no change in form. But she went further still: she assumed that transitive verbs like **drink** and **eat**, adjectives like **sharp** and **full**, and locative words like **up** and **round** could also be made into causative verbs. As the examples in Table 13–4 illustrate, Christy used all these forms as if they too contained the component **Cause(x,y)**. These systematic errors show that once she identified the component **Cause(x,y)**, she proceeded to over-regularize the English system, turning many words into causatives that couldn't be used as such by the adult.

These errors are very similar to the over-regularizations observed earlier (Chapter 9). For example, children add the plural **-s** to all nouns: **foot** goes to **foots** instead of **feet**, **man** goes to **mans** instead of **men**, and **sheep** goes to **sheeps**. To be able to over-regularize the plural **-s** ending, children must know that there is a regular relation between the form **-s** and the meaning "more than one." The same argument can be made about the component **Cause(x,y)** in causative verbs. Intransitive **come** goes to causative **come** (as in **She came it over there**) instead of **bring**, intransitive **fall** to causative **fall** instead of **drop**, and so on. This over-regularization of the devices for expressing causation shows that children *know* that certain verbs contain the component **Cause(x,y)**.

In short, from the age of two or two and a half onward, children appear to recognize that the components **Come-about(x)** and **Cause(x,y)** play a role in the meanings of many verbs. The evidence for **Come-about(x)** comes from their selective use of the past tense ending to focus on the result of an action. They add it, to begin with, only to verbs that describe a change of state. The evidence for **Cause(x,y)** comes from systematic over-regularization of the English system

TABLE 13–4

NON-CAUSATIVE TERMS USED IN A CAUSATIVE SENSE

A. Intransitive Verbs

(1) Child: (aged 2;6, trying to hold refrigerator door open, with difficulty): *Mommy, can you stay this open?* [make this stay open]

(2) Child: (aged 2;9, holding a piece of paper above her baby sister's head): *I'm gonna fall this on her.* [make it fall on her; drop it on her]

(3) Mother: (holding broken musical cow; music no longer plays): The cow would like to sing but he can't.

   Child: (aged 3;1, pulling the string that used to make the music play): *I'm singing him.* [making him sing]

(4) Child: (aged 3;1, struggling with sweater): *I wanta be it off.* (Leaning over so her mother can help her take it off): *I wanta put it off.*

B. Transitive Verbs

(5) Child: (aged 3;1. Day before mother squeezed an orange half directly into her mouth; now, handing mother an orange half and waiting expectantly): *Drink me. Uh . . . put it in.* [make, help, let me drink]

(6) Child: (aged 3;3, pretending to feed doll by poking spoon at its mouth): *See, she can't eat.*

   Mother: Just pretend, honey.

   Child: *But I can't eat her!* [make her eat]

C. Adjectives

(7) Child: (aged 2;3, peering with dissatisfaction into her bottle that her mother only partially filled): *Full it up!* [make it full; fill it up]

(8) Child: (aged 2;11, trying to smooth down paper on magic slate)

   Mother: Make it nice and flat.

   Child: (bringing slate to mother): *How would you flat it?* [make it flat; flatten it]

D. Locative Words

(9) Child: (aged 3;0, watching mother use eggbeater; stretching out her hand toward handle): *I wanta . . . wanta . . . wanta . . . round it.* [make it go round; turn it]

(10) Child: (aged 3;3, pushing down on baby sister's flexed knee): *Down your little knee!*

   Mother: What?

   Child: *Down her little knee.* [make your/her little knee go down; put it down]

Based on Bowerman (1974b).

for expressing causation. Adjectives, locative words, and intransitive and transitive verbs may all be treated as if they can express causation on the model of intransitive-causative pairs like **walk-walk**.

Negation

The semantic component **Not(x)** crops up as part of the meaning of many different words in English (Chapter 11), and children seem to find these words harder to acquire than their positive counterparts. Some studies of positive-negative pairs have already been discussed under another guise—in terms of how children's strategies favor the acquisition of positive terms like **into**, **more**, and **long** over negative ones like **out of, less**, and **short**. The positive term is also acquired before the negative one in the case of **same** and **different** (Donaldson and Wales, 1970; Webb, Oliveri, and O'Keeffe, 1974), **always** and **never** (Kuczaj, 1975), and **if** and **unless** (Legum, 1975).

Why should the presence of **Not(x)** make a word more difficult to acquire? An explanation has already been offered for the ease of many positive terms: children start out with conceptual preferences for relationships that correspond to the positive term. For example, they choose the larger of two amounts or the object with greater extension. They move one object toward another, not away, and so on. These situations are taken to be the normal case and the normal case always coincides with the meanings of positive words. Words containing **Not(x)** nearly always describe the other situation—the one that is not normal—and for that reason seem to be harder for children to acquire (see further Chapter 14).

SUMMARY

Children use what they already know together with contextual cues to form hypotheses about what new words might mean. From these hypotheses, they derive strategies for producing and interpreting the words in other situations. Their initial hypotheses often overlap with the adult meaning but their use is over-extended or under-extended compared to the adult's. At other times, they fail to hit on any part of the adult meaning—but with no overlap they have no basis for communication and so soon drop the word. As children find out more about how each word is used, they refine their hypotheses and strategies until their meanings coincide with the adult ones. This process can take years to complete.

In going from their initial simple meaning to the adult one, children have to add, adjust, or even discard components to bring their meaning in line with the adult's and at the same time keep it distinct from other words in their repertoire. An integral part of the acquisition of meaning, therefore, is the filling in of different semantic fields. In some fields, the meaning of the simpler terms may be included largely or wholly in the meanings of more complex ones. In such cases, children work out the meanings of the simpler terms first and then go on to the more complex ones. In other semantic fields, the order in which children acquire different terms may be more a matter of experience and exposure to particular words.

The conceptual preferences children start off with for relating one object or event to another make it easier for them to acquire some word meanings than others. For example, an a priori preference for the larger of two amounts, combined with the initial hypothesis that **more** and **less** mean "amount," may lead them to get **more** "right" and **less** "wrong." In general, their conceptual preferences seem to favor the acquisition of positive terms like **more**, **same**, and **into** over negative ones like **less**, **different**, and **out of**. In some contexts, most children display the same a priori preferences and come up with similar semantic hypotheses. In others, where the context offers fewer clues to a single meaning, their hypotheses are more diverse. In these cases they may follow different routes in the course of working out adult meanings.

As children work out the meanings of words, they could be said to build up entries in their mental lexicon by adding, discarding, or altering components. They start from components of shape, texture, movement, and so on, and move to more abstract components like **Male(x)** or **Animate(x)** as they learn more about the lexicon. Three semantic components that appear in many word meanings, **Come-about(x)**, **Cause(x,y)**, and **Not(x)**, all emerge fairly early in acquisition. **Come-about(x)** is first signaled by a selective use of past tense endings, and **Cause(x,y)** by over-regularization of devices used to express causation. The third component, **Not(x)**, is signaled by added difficulty of acquisition—words that contain it tend to be acquired later than their positive counterparts.

Further Reading

There is a useful introduction to the acquisition of word meaning in E. Clark (1973a) which presents a preliminary theory about acquisition backed by data from diary studies and experiments. Bowerman (1976) provides a helpful review of the literature and relates word meanings to children's early sentence meanings. The cognitive basis for early word meanings is taken up in Bloom (1973) as well as in several papers in Moore (1973) and Macnamara (1977).

Whoever knows grammar in one language also
knows it in another so far as its substance
is concerned. If he cannot, however, speak
another language, or understand those who
speak it, this is because of the difference
of words and their formations which is
accidental to grammar.

Anon., thirteenth century

Language and Thought

Language does not exist in a vacuum. It serves and is molded by other systems in the human mind. Because it is used for conveying ideas, its structure and function must reflect these ideas. Because it must be spoken and understood easily and efficiently, its structure and function are forced to stay within the limits imposed by people's processing capacities. Because it is used for communication within a complex social and cultural system, its structure and function are molded by these forces as well. Yet once people have learned how to use language, it wields a power of its own. It aids them in thinking about some ideas and hinders them in thinking about others. It molds many aspects of their daily affairs.

UNIVERSALS AND RELATIVITY

Over the centuries these forces have been recognized and taken up within two fields of study, linguistic universals and linguistic relativity. If languages are molded in part by the ideas, processing capacities, and social factors all people have in common, they should have certain features in common—linguistic universals. Since people need to refer to objects, every language has nouns. But to the extent that languages are molded by accidental properties of thought, technology, and culture, there will also be features that differ from language to language. Since the Garo of Burma need to distinguish among more kinds of rice than Russians do, their language has more words for rice than Russian does. In the opposite direction, if language molds people's ideas and culture, these language-specific features should lead people who speak different languages to think differently. The Garo may be able to think about rice in ways Russians can't simply because Garo has more words for rice than Russian. This is known as linguistic relativity.

Although linguistic relativity was proposed in the eighteenth century by Johann Herder and later refined by Wilhelm von Humboldt and Edward Sapir, it is most closely associated in the twentieth century with Benjamin Lee Whorf, who stated the hypothesis in its strongest form (1956, pp. 213–14):

> We dissect nature along lines laid down by our native languages. The categories and types that we isolate from the world of phenomena we do not find there because they stare every observer in the face; on the contrary, the world is presented in a kaleidoscopic flux of impressions which has to be organized by our minds—and this means largely by the linguistic systems in our minds. We cut nature up, organize it into concepts, and ascribe significances as we do, largely because we are parties to an agreement to organize it in this way—an agreement that holds through our speech community and is codified in the patterns of our language. The agreement is, of course, an implicit and unstated one, but *its terms are absolutely obligatory*; we cannot talk at all except by subscribing to the organization and classification of data which the agreement decrees.

Here Whorf claims that language influences the very way people perceive and organize the world around them. It is an important hypothesis, then, about the relation between language and thought.

Logic, however, won't let us examine linguistic relativity without at the same time examining linguistic universals. Imagine how people would describe three shirts. They would probably stress their differences. Number one is cotton, two is silk, and three is wool. Or number one is plaid, two is polka-dotted, and three is plain. Or number one has short sleeves while two and three have long sleeves. And so on. But note that each comparison presupposes something universal about the three shirts. Each is made from cloth, and what varies is the kind of cloth. Each has a pattern, and what varies is the kind of pattern. Each has sleeves, and what varies is the length of sleeve. Differences can only be described with respect to constancies. The same goes for languages. Garo may have more nouns for rice than Russian, but to say this presupposes that both languages have nouns. It also presupposes that one can identify that aspect of the conceptual domain, here rice, that the two languages name differently. In short, linguistic relativity presupposes linguistic universals.

Linguistic universals, though of concern for centuries, have recently been taken up with renewed interest. The reasons are clear. The variation that occurs in languages has obvious limits, and these limits ought to tell us something about the nature of language. A priori, every human language must be susceptible of:

(1) Being learned by children.

(2) Being spoken and understood by adults easily and efficiently.

(3) Embodying the ideas people normally want to convey.

(4) Functioning as a communication system in a social and cultural setting.

Consider English and Navaho. One might well be surprised to discover that they have features in common. They are historically unrelated and until recently have not been in contact with each other. The features they have in common, if not accidental, must therefore be there because it is a requirement of a human language that they be there. They are just the features that fulfill the four conditions placed on human languages. Thus, if we knew what is common to all languages, it might be possible to characterize what is inherent in the human capacity to speak, understand, and acquire language.

Linguistic universals, according to Noam Chomsky (1965, 1968), have a special interest because they reflect the human's innate predisposition to learn language. His argument goes like this. In learning a language, children hear a sample of sentences that is quite inadequate for them to acquire the language in all its complexity. Many of its structures are unobservable, and yet they somehow get learned. It must be that children have some "hypothesis" about what language is like, some innate predisposition to look for certain language features and not others. The features they look for will therefore be precisely those that are common to all languages.

> The doctrine of innate ideas is one of the most admirable faiths of philosophy, being itself an innate idea and therefore inaccessible to disproof....
>
> Ambrose Bierce, The Devil's Dictionary

It is not very helpful, however, to stop with the conclusion that linguistic universals spring from innate predispositions. This point has been made by Lehrman (1953), who years ago criticized the widespread use of "innate" explanations for animal behavior. At the time he wrote, many investigators had concluded, for example, that the pecking of the chick immediately after it emerged from the egg was "innate," or "instinctual." After all, the chick didn't have to be taught how to peck. Lehrman noted, however, that on a closer look, pecking consists of a coordinated pattern of dipping the head, opening the beak, and swallowing that develops out of separate behavior patterns that combine while the chick is still in the egg. As Lehrman put it, "The statement that 'pecking' is innate, or that it 'matures,' leads us *away* from any attempt to analyze its specific origins. The assumption that pecking grows *as* a pecking *pattern* discourages examination of the embryological processes leading to pecking. The elements out of whose interaction pecking emerges are not originally a unitary pattern; they *become* related as a consequence of their positions in the organization of the embryonic chick (1953, p. 344)." Lehrman concluded: "The use of 'explanatory' categories such as 'innate' and 'genetically fixed' obscures the necessity of investigating developmental *processes* in order to gain insight into the actual mechanisms of behavior and their interrelations (p. 345)." In this chapter we will try to follow Lehrman's example. Not only will we take up features of language that are thought to be universal, but we will also suggest plausible psychological processes to account for their universality. Linguistic universals may not be as mysterious as the concept of "innate predispositions" makes them seem (Schlesinger, 1967; Levelt, 1975).

In this chapter our goal is to see how thought influences language and how language influences thought. We begin with an examination of human biological specialization for language and, by comparison, the chimpanzee's ability to learn several types of language. We then take up selected linguistic universals and look at the thought processes they might plausibly reflect. These universals are divided into those that derive from perception, general cognition, social systems, and processing capacities—although these divisions are not hard and fast. We conclude by returning to variation in languages and the question of how language may influence thought.

BIOLOGICAL SPECIALIZATION

For centuries it has been a deeply felt conviction that because humans are the only species to have evolved language, they are unique—the only rational animal. This has led to the hypothesis that the human capacity for language is different in kind from the capacities for communication observed in other animals (Lenneberg, 1967). This hypothesis rests on two assumptions. First, that some of the differences between humans and their nearest primate relatives are due to the human's specific innate capacity for language. And second, that human languages are different in kind rather than degree from other systems of animal communication. The corollary is that human languages have some features that are impossible for other species to learn. These two assumptions will be examined in relation to physiological factors in language and to recent experiments on teaching language to chimpanzees.

Physiological Factors in Language

Certain features of the human physiology suggest that humans are especially well suited for communication by vocal language. The critical question is whether these features are specific to language alone or whether they are part of the human's generally greater capacity to think. The major features that distinguish humans from their closest relatives fall into two categories: peripheral and central (Lenneberg, 1967).

Of their peripheral features, the human's main advantage is their superior articulatory apparatus. Humans have evolved a complicated set of facial muscles that allow great mobility of the lips, cheeks, and jaw. They have also evolved a muscular and flexible tongue that can move freely in the mouth cavity, and unlike most other animals, they have teeth set side by side to form a barrier or ridge all the way around the gum. The ridges of the upper and lower jaw meet when the jaw is closed. Finally, the pharynx, the passage from the back of the mouth to the entrance of the lungs, is much longer than in other primates (Lieberman, Klatt, and Wilson, 1969). These features give humans a distinct advantage in producing speech sounds.

Features in the central nervous system also give humans an advantage with language, but these features are not necessarily tied to language per se. Compared to their closest relatives, humans have a larger and heavier brain, a greater degree of cerebral convolution (the extensive fissures on the brain's surface), and larger "associative areas" between the limbic cortex and the auditory and visual areas of the cortex (Campbell, 1971). The larger associative areas may allow closer contact between visual and auditory information (Geschwind, 1964). But humans differ from other animals in many cognitive abilities other than language. It could be that these features give humans deeper cognitive abilities in general, and it is these that allow them to use language. Still, there are two differences in the central nervous system that have often been claimed to be specific to the human's use of language. These are, first, that some language-related abilities appear to be centered on one side of the brain, and second, that there may be a critical period for the acquisition of language.

Brain Lateralization

For most people language appears to be located in the left hemisphere of the brain. Much of the evidence for this *lateralization* comes from studies of injuries to the left hemisphere caused by accidents, strokes, tumors, and certain illnesses. These injuries usually impair some language ability, with the kind and degree of the impairment depending on the site and severity of the injury (Lenneberg, 1967; Geschwind, 1970). Other evidence of lateralization comes from people's speed and accuracy in identifying speech sounds heard in either the left or right ear. Language destined for the left hemisphere through the right ear is processed more quickly than language destined for the right hemisphere through the left ear (Kimura, 1973).

But language is only one of many functions represented asymmetrically in the brain. Various visual and spatial abilities tend to be found in the right hemisphere (Kinsbourne, 1970), while, for example, memory for musical information seems to be located in the left hemisphere for musicians and in the right hemisphere for non-musicians (Bever and Chiarello, 1974). The consensus seems to be that "The left hemisphere is specialized for propositional, analytic, and serial processing of incoming information, while the right hemisphere is more adapted for perception of appositional, holistic, and synthetic relations" (Bever and Chiarello, 1974, p. 537). In short, it may be that humans have a greater capacity for propositional, analytic, and serial processing, and their ability to use language rests on this general capacity. Therefore, humans don't necessarily have a specialized capacity unique to the use of language.

Critical Periods

The second argument for a language-specific capacity is that there is a critical period for the acquisition of language (Lenneberg, 1967). This period is analogous to the critical period for "imprinting" in young birds. For example, geese reared in isolation from the time of hatching react to the first reasonably large moving object they see—even if it is a human—as if it is a parent, and they follow it everywhere. This imprinting, which normally allows the young bird to identify the species it belongs to, takes place only during a brief period after hatching (Lorenz, 1961). In the case of language, Lenneberg has argued for a critical period from studies of recovery of language after injury to the left hemisphere. They showed roughly that adults who hadn't recovered language within five months of their injury were unlikely ever to recover. Children, however, recovered over a longer period, and if they were young enough, they often recovered fully. Some children even reacquired language following removal of the left hemisphere. Lenneberg related the critical period to the process of lateralization. He argued that lateralization takes place gradually between birth and puberty, and the completion of lateralization marks the end of the critical period.

The arguments about the critical period, however, have problems. Many investigators have argued that lateralization occurs long before puberty and may be complete by age two (Kinsbourne and Smith, 1974). Whether or not there is really a critical period hasn't been established with any certainty yet either. Even if there were a critical period, it may be for the capacity for "propositional, analytic, and serial processing" and not for language alone. These arguments, then, do not necessarily suggest that humans have a capacity that is uniquely associated with language.

As a whole, the biological evidence suggests that humans have specialized capacities that give them an advantage in the use of language, but these aren't necessarily tied to language alone. Thus, one might expect to find other species acquiring or using language, but not so sophisticated a language. Bee dancing, bird song, and gibbon calls, for example, are all varieties of communication that are less sophisticated than human language. Some linguists have taken the tack of listing those design features that seem to be characteristic of human languages (Hockett, 1960), and these other systems share some but not all of these features. Yet recent research with chimpanzees hints that they may be able to learn a language that has all the major design features of human languages.

Language in the Chimpanzee

There has long been speculation about whether any of the primates closest to humans could learn to speak. Several investigators have tried unsuccessfully to get chimpanzees to pronounce words (e.g., K. Hayes and Hayes, 1952), not fully appreciating the fact that the chimpanzee's vocal tract is sufficiently different from the human's to make spoken language virtually impossible. The problem of the chimpanzee's vocal tract has been circumvented in recent research through use of a visual language—either "words" in the form of plastic shapes or gestures based on the sign language of the deaf.

Premack (1971a, b) devised an artificial language in which the "words" were metal-backed plastic shapes placed on a magnetic board. Some of these words are shown in Figure 14–1. He used these to teach a chimpanzee, Sarah, a variety of logical and relational functions found in natural languages. Sarah mastered, among other things, the negative particle (as in "Square is-not the-shape-of banana"), "same" and "different," words for shape, size and color in descriptions ("Round is-the-shape-of apple"), the concept "is the name of," and certain spatial relations (e.g., "in," "on"). She showed good understanding of sentences in this language and was able to follow instructions accurately over 75 percent of the time. Her topics of conversation were limited, naturally, by what she had been taught, and there is no evidence that she could use this language spontaneously to produce sentences of her own (see also Rumbaugh et al., 1973).

FIGURE 14–1
SOME PLASTIC SHAPES USED AS WORDS

The bottom row forms the sentence "Red is not the color of chocolate"

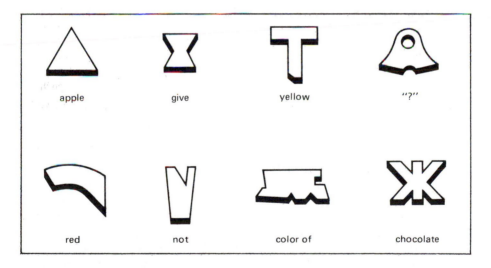

From Premack and Premack (1972).

Sign Language

A natural visual language has obvious advantages over an artificial one, and so other researchers have turned to the American Sign Language (Ameslan), a gestural language used by the deaf. The chimpanzee's manual dexterity is so superior to its vocal dexterity that this language promised to work where spoken

TABLE 14–1

SOME OF WASHOE'S UTTERANCES

Each English word represents a separate sign in Ameslan

Washoe sorry	Out open please hurry	Clothes yours
Baby down	You me in	You hat
Go in	Gimme flower	Roger tickle
Hug hurry	More fruit	You more drink
Open blanket	Baby mine	Comb black

Based on B. Gardner and R. Gardner (1971).

language had failed. B. Gardner and R. Gardner (1969, 1971, 1975), who began this research, started with a one-year-old chimpanzee named Washoe. For three years they communicated with her in nothing but Ameslan and constantly encouraged her to respond in the same language. By age four, she was able to produce 130 different signs and understand even more. She used single signs at first but soon began to combine them to form longer utterances like those in Table 14–1. In this and many other respects, Washoe resembled a young child acquiring language.

As Watt (1974c) has pointed out, Washoe's "speech" meets the criteria proposed by R. Brown (1970, 1973) for what it takes to be a human language. First, her speech made sense. For example, she knew how to pick appropriate verbs to go with particular nouns. Second, many of her utterances formed paradigmatic groups in which the utterances had the same structure. There was, for example, a series of utterances in which she combined the sign for **more** with another sign. Third, in longer, three-sign utterances like **You tickle me** and **I tickle you**, she used the order of signs to distinguish subject from object. In other utterances she tended, like young human children, to put the subject (often animate) before the verb. Fourth, she marked the ends of utterances with the Ameslan equivalent of a "period'" dropping her hands to a rest position. Finally, her utterances were appropriate in context: she answered questions, asserted, requested, and even apologized when scolded for biting.

It is clear, then, that chimpanzees can master some of the complex relationships expressed in natural languages, and, given a gestural language like Ameslan, they begin to acquire language much as a young child does. But these demonstrations leave many questions unanswered: How much language can chimpanzees be taught? Will chimpanzees brought up on Ameslan spontaneously transmit it to their young? Will they use Ameslan to communicate with other chimpanzees brought up in the same way? Will their young "pick up" language in the rather casual way human children do or will they require intensive coaching? Definite answers to these questions may not come for many years.

The hypothesis that the human capacity for language is unique cannot be taken for granted. In the first place, it is not clear that human biological specialization is specific to the capacity for language. The peripheral differences make the vocal tract especially available for language, but gestures like those in Ameslan can serve equally well. The central differences in brain size and specialization go with a general increase in cognitive capacity, but language is only one part of this. Moreover, human language doesn't seem to be beyond the grasp of other species. Chimpanzees can be taught to express many of the major features of human languages, and the limits on what they can learn have yet to be established. All this suggests that natural languages may well lie on a continuum with other systems of communication. Natural languages may differ from them in degree, but not in kind.

PERCEPTUAL CATEGORIES

The work on biological specialization suggests that language may be closely tied to other cognitive abilities, and in earlier chapters, the work on meaning and its acquisition pointed to the same conclusion. But what are these ties? This question is best answered through an examination of language universals. Many of these features are not specific to language per se, but are derived from the human capacity to perceive, categorize, and socialize. The first universals to be taken up are those that probably derive from the human capacity to organize and categorize *perceptual* information. For example, because the human visual apparatus finds certain colors more salient than others, languages are extraordinarily consistent about which few of the infinite number of colors are named. Other aspects of the human perceptual and cognitive system lead to universal ways of treating names for such things as natural categories, names for shapes, and spatial terms.

Complexity of Expression

The features of language that are universal, of course, are not sounds, words, or phrases, but something far more abstract. The first universals to be examined all deal in a commodity called *complexity of expression*. It is central to one of the most important hypotheses about the relation of language to thought:

> *The complexity principle:* Complexity in thought tends to be reflected in complexity of expression.

Broadly speaking, the more complex the expression, the more complex the thought it reflects.

But when is an expression complex? This question has been discussed extensively by Greenberg (1966) under the rubric of *markedness*. He has proposed several criteria for deciding which of two categories of thought—usually two contrasting categories—is given the more complex expression or, in his terminology, is more marked. The following are two of his main criteria.

(1) *Added morphemes.* If expression B consists of expression A plus an added morpheme, then B is more complex than A. The word **dogs**, for example,

consists of **dog** plus an added morpheme, the suffix **-s**, which is said to "mark" **dogs** as plural. **Dogs** is therefore a more complex expression than **dog**. In English generally, plurals are marked by an added morpheme (with exceptions like **deer** and **sheep**), while singulars never are. In Greenberg's terminology, then, the *category* plural is marked with respect to the *category* singular in English: that is, plural is given a more complex expression than singular. In English, added morphemes can be of various kinds, as in these pairs:

happy	unhappy	sleep	will sleep
oak	scrub oak	father	grandfather
blue	light blue	complex	complexity

(2) *Contextual neutralization.* If expression A can neutralize in meaning in contexts that the almost equivalent expression B cannot, then B is more complex than A. In most contexts, for example, **actor** is male and **actress** female. In some contexts, however, **actor** but not **actress** can be neutralized in meaning to cover both males and females. **Actress** is therefore a more complex expression than **actor**. In English generally, the category female is marked with respect to the category male. Note that **actress** would be considered marked by the first criterion too, since it consists of **actor** plus the added morpheme **-ess**. The different criteria for markedness almost always lead to the same judgment of what is simple and what is complex. When they don't, one should be cautious about calling either category marked.

Using these and other criteria, investigators like Greenberg have sifted through many genetically unrelated languages for categories that are universally, or almost universally, given the least complex expression. These criteria have been especially successful in discovering the fundamentals of color terminology.

Basic Color Terms

For many years scholars believed that languages divided up the color spectrum arbitrarily. For these people, it was conceivable that some language had a color term like **binkle** that straddled the English terms **blue** and **red** and had its center in purple. Recently, however, Berlin and Kay (1969; Kay, 1975), two anthropologists, discovered that color naming is far from arbitrary. They did so by examining languages for what they called *basic color terms*. These are the terms in a language that have the least complexity of expression yet cover all parts of the color spectrum. Berlin and Kay used four main criteria to identify the basic color terms of each language, one of which is equivalent to "added morphemes." For a color term to be basic:

(1) It must consist of only one morpheme, like **red**, and not two or more, as in **light red** or **blood-like**.

(2) It must not be contained within another color, as **scarlet** is contained within **red**.

(3) It must not be restricted to a small number of objects, like **blond**, which applies only to hair and a few other objects.

(4) It must be common and generally known, like **yellow** and not **saffron**.

From their survey, Berlin and Kay found that every language takes its basic color terms from the following list of only eleven color names: **black**, **white**, **red**, **yellow**, **green**, **blue**, **brown**, **purple**, **pink**, **orange**, and **gray**. Far from being chaotic, the world's languages are remarkably uniform in their treatment of color.

Even more surprisingly, Berlin and Kay found that these eleven basic color terms formed a hierarchy. Some languages, like English, use all eleven, while others use as few as two. When a language has only two, it picks not just any two at random, but **black** and **white** (sometimes translated as **dark** and **light**). When a language has three colors, it always picks **black**, **white**, and **red**. In general, each language selects its terms from this hierarchy:

$$
\begin{bmatrix} \text{black} \\ \text{white} \end{bmatrix} \longrightarrow \text{red} \longrightarrow \begin{bmatrix} \text{yellow} \\ \text{green} \\ \text{blue} \end{bmatrix} \longrightarrow \text{brown} \longrightarrow \begin{bmatrix} \text{purple} \\ \text{pink} \\ \text{orange} \\ \text{gray} \end{bmatrix}
$$

Thus a language with six color terms will take the first six terms from the left: **black**, **white**, **red**, **yellow**, **green**, and **blue**. To put it another way, if a language has **blue** as one of its basic color terms, it will also have every term to its left in this hierarchy, namely **red**, **black**, and **white**. The terms within brackets can be selected in any order. The hierarchy also carries a historical implication: if a language acquires a new basic color term, it always acquires the next one to the right of the ones it already has. This is a powerful statement about color terminology. If combinations of the eleven basic color terms were random, there would be 2,048 possibilities. The hierarchy restricts that number to thirty-three.

Focal Colors

The hierarchy could not have been constructed if Berlin and Kay had not hit on what they called *focal colors*. To study color terms, they had prepared a chart of 320 small squares of color called "color chips." This chart covered more or less evenly all the saturated hues people can see. Speakers of various languages were asked to point to the color chip that best represented each of the basic color terms in their language. The ones people selected as the best red, green, yellow, and so on were virtually the same from language to language. The major exception came in languages with only two terms. For them, **white** covered all the warm colors and had its focal color in white, red, or yellow, while **black** covered all cool colors and had its focal color in black or brown. Against the high degree of consistency with focal colors, people were not at all consistent in drawing *boundaries* between the basic terms. It is the focal colors that make it possible to match color terms across languages—to say that Japanese **aka** is the same as English **red**, Navaho **lichi**, and Eskimo **anpaluktak**.

Why these particular eleven colors? It must be because they are perceptually the most salient of all colors in the spectrum. Rosch (formerly Heider) set out to demonstrate just that. In one study (Heider, 1971), three-year-old children were presented with an array of color chips and, when the experimenter's back was turned, were asked, "Show me a color." They overwhelmingly preferred focal to non-focal colors. And when four-year-olds were asked to pick from an assortment of color chips the one that matched a test chip, they matched focal colors more accurately than non-focal ones (see also Mervis, Catlin, and Rosch, 1975). In a study with adults from twenty-three different language groups (Heider, 1972), focal colors were named faster and with shorter expressions than non-focal colors. And in a memory task, adults from two language groups were shown a single color chip for five seconds, and after thirty seconds, were presented with 160 color chips from which they were to select the one they had just seen. They matched focal colors more accurately than non-focal colors. In brief, focal colors are easier to remember, named more quickly, given shorter names, and are more "eye-catching"—proof enough of their perceptual salience.

Rosch's most remarkable studies were carried out with the Dani, a New Guinea people whose language has only two basic terms, **mili** ("black") and **mola** ("white") to cover all the colors of the spectrum. Because the Dani had no basic color terms for red, green, yellow, and the rest, it was possible to see how quickly they could learn names for these focal colors. One group was taught arbitrary names for eight *focal* colors, and another group, arbitrary names for eight *non-focal* colors. The first group learned much faster than the second (Rosch, 1973). In a memory study (Heider, 1972), the Dani were found—just like English speakers—to remember focal colors more accurately than non-focal ones. In a study requiring judgments of color similarity (Heider and Olivier, 1972), the Dani were found to represent colors in memory the same way English speakers do, in spite of the great difference between the two systems of color naming. Evidently, focal colors are salient regardless of whether or not people have names for them.

The Visual System

But why the sensitivity to focal colors? The answer undoubtedly lies in the physiology of the human visual system (McDaniel, 1974). The Hering "opponent" theory of color vision holds that the eye has three opponent processes: one for brightness (black-white) and two for hue (red-green and yellow-blue). When light strikes the eye, each opponent pair responds with a value varying from positive to negative, and the combination of the three values produces the sensation of the appropriate color. The system thus has six unique points of response, one for each point at which two of the systems are neutral (with zero response) and the third is maximally positive or negative (Hering,

CONTENTS:
RED and YELLOW

Drawing by Levin; © 1975 The New Yorker Magazine, Inc.

1920; Jameson and Hurvich, 1955; de Valois and Jacobs, 1968). Significantly, these six points correspond to the first six colors of the hierarchy: black, white, red, green, yellow, and blue. It seems likely that the remaining five colors correspond to other "maxima" in the visual system.

The universality of color terms, therefore, has a plausible explanation. The very physiology of the human visual system makes some colors more salient than others. Children find these colors eye-catching and easy to remember. Because of this, they take these colors to be the ones adults talk about whenever they refer to colors and therefore find terms denoting these colors easy to learn (Dougherty, 1976). Adults maintain these preferences for the same reasons. There is more occasion to talk about salient colors, and listeners assume that speakers are more likely to be talking about them. Color terminology is universal because the human visual system is universal.

Basic Category Names

Roger Brown (1958) once observed that although all objects have more than one name, people often talk about *the* name of an object, as if it had just one. An apple is an **apple**, even though it is also a **fruit**, a **thing**, and **object**, a **Golden Delicious apple**, and **Amanda's dessert**. **Apple** is somehow primary, or basic, the name that seems to fit best. But why? According to Brown, **apple** is at a level of abstraction with the greatest utility in most contexts. To call an apple merely a **fruit** would generally do too little, failing to distinguish it from bananas, pears, and other fruit. And to call it a **Golden Delicious apple** would generally do too much, distinguishing it from other minor varieties of apples. But what determines the most useful level of abstraction? What are its origins?

Levels of Abstraction

In their study of "folk biology"—the way people of the world name plants and animals—Berlin and his colleagues (Berlin, 1972; Berlin, Breedlove, and Raven, 1968, 1973) have concluded that all people divide the plant and animal kingdom into categories, each of which is given a name. These categories are hierarchically organized with five (and sometimes six) levels of abstraction:

(1) *Unique beginner:* plant, animal
(2) *Life form:* tree, bush, flower
(3) *Generic name:* pine, oak, maple, elm
(4) *Specific name:* Ponderosa pine, white pine, jack pine
(5) *Varietal name:* northern Ponderosa pine, western Ponderosa pine

At each level, the categories are mutually exclusive—they don't overlap. Nothing is both a pine and an oak. And each category belongs to a category at the next higher level of abstraction. Pines, oaks, maples, and elms are all trees. It is not a foregone conclusion that all peoples should classify and name their world this way.

Berlin and his colleagues argued that the generic level, level 3, is the most basic. For one thing, in each language it has around 500 categories, which is more than any other level. It is more useful than level 2 and better developed than level 4. It is also distinguished from levels 4 and 5 linguistically. Note that in English the generic level uses simple names like **pine**, **oak**, **elm**, and **maple**, whereas the next level down, the specific, uses complex names like **white pine**, **jack pine**, and **Ponderosa pine**. The names at level 4 usually contain more than one word, often a superordinate level 3 term, like **pine**, combined with a modifier, like **Ponderosa**. The same difference between levels 3 and 4 shows up in all languages. Why should level 4 use complex terms? Its categories must belong to a more complex classification system, one in which the divisions are not as natural or as easy to identify. The generic level, with its simple names, represents a relatively natural way of dividing up the world. Indeed, Berlin and his colleagues found that people felt generic names to be primary, and these names were the first ones learned by children in the cultures they studied. The name of an object, in Brown's sense, seems to belong to this basic level of categorization.

Basic-Level Categories

But how do people slice up the world into categories? Rosch and her colleagues have argued that natural categories are a product of the human perceptual and cognitive apparatus for dealing with the world. Objects are perceived in terms of attributes and, in nature, these attributes come in clusters. If an object is feathered, it is a good bet that it sings, flies, has a beak, and a particular shape. It is also a good bet that it doesn't roar, bear live young, or have four legs. Attributes that go together, like feathered, singing, flying, beaked, and bird-shaped, define a natural category, like bird. The objects within a single category share attributes with each other, bear a "family resemblance" to each other. At the same time, they share few attributes with objects in other categories, bear little family resemblance to other objects (see Chapter 12).

Rosch and Mervis (1975) have demonstrated that natural categories are formed by the clustering of perceived attributes. In one study people were asked to list attributes for a variety of objects. As expected, each object shared a good many attributes with other objects in the same category, but few attributes with objects in other categories. Other people were asked to rate each object as to how typical, how good an example, it was of the category. The more typical an object was judged to be, the more attributes it shared with members of the same category—and the fewer attributes it shared with members of other categories. Consider oranges and blueberries, typical and atypical fruits, respectively. Oranges share more attributes with all other fruits than do blueberries, but they share fewer attributes with all vegetables than do blueberries. From these and other findings, Rosch and Mervis have argued that categories are "out there" in nature. The human perceptual apparatus is geared to deal with certain attributes, and in nature those attributes go together to form certain categories (Rosch, 1977).

The reason why Berlin's generic level is basic, Rosch and her colleagues would argue, is because it is the level at which categories are the tightest. Take, for example, the categories furniture, table, and kitchen table. Members of the category furniture (such as chairs, bookcases, rugs, and vases) have few attributes in common. However, members of the category table (dining room tables, kitchen tables, and side tables) have many attributes in common. So do members of the category kitchen table (Aunt Martha's, the neighbor's, and grandfather's), although they have very few more attributes in common than do members of the category table. By the criterion of *common attributes*, table and kitchen table are very good categories. On the other hand, since kitchen tables have many attributes in common with other types of tables, the category kitchen table is hard to distinguish from other categories at the same level, while the category table is easy to distinguish from other categories at the same level. So by the criterion of *distinguishability*, table is a good category and kitchen table a bad one. Table, then, is the "tightest" category. Its members are all very similar to each other yet all very different from members of other categories at the same level. Rosch et al. (1976) have confirmed these impressions for objects in a variety of categories.

Expertise

One caution: not everybody sees the same categories as loose or tight. It depends on how much each person "knows" about the objects in each category. A car novice sees all cars as pretty much the same, but a car fanatic pays attention to all kinds of differences the novice doesn't even notice. The category car is therefore tighter for the novice than for the fanatic, while the subcategories of car are each tighter for the fanatic than for the novice. If the tightness of a category depends on expertise, then so does what people take as a basic category. Rosch et al., for example, found that their city-born subjects treated tree as a basic category, whereas Berlin et al. found that the mainly agricultural peoples they studied treated oak, elm, and pine as basic categories. As Berlin argued (see Rosch et al., 1976), this difference probably reflects a difference in expertise. The English names **oak**, **elm**, and **pine**, all simple generic names, are in the language because at one time most people knew their trees, just as the car fanatics know their cars. Here, then, is a place for cultural relativity. Basic categories will vary with the expertise of the culture or subculture of people naming the objects.

Berlin et al.'s universals of naming categories, therefore, seem to arise from people's perceptual experience with objects. In nature, the attributes people perceive and pay attention to come in clusters and lead people to form natural categories. These categories for most people are tightest at the generic level of abstraction and are called basic categories. When it comes to naming, this level is very useful, and its categories are given simple names. Since these categories will also be among the earliest that children form, they will generally be among the first that children acquire names for (Brown, 1958; Rosch et al., 1976; and Stross, 1973). As for Brown's observation that people think objects have a best name, the name of an object is the name of the tightest category it belongs to, the name of its basic category.

Shape Names

In English some geometrical shapes get named and others do not. The most common one- and two-dimensional shape names (Kučera and Francis, 1967) are these:

Single lines	*Closed figures*
line	square
curve	circle
angle	oval
	triangle
	rectangle

Most other simple shape names are so uncommon that they are virtually technical terms in geometry. How, then, do people describe shapes not covered by this list? One way is to resort to complex expressions like **square with a corner cut off** or **flower-shaped** or **pear-like**. Another is to use the nearest shape name in the above list as an approximation good enough for practical purposes. In any event, there seem to be basic shape names, following Berlin and Kay's (1969) criteria for basic terms, and they correspond to only certain shapes.

Good Figures

To the Gestalt psychologist it is obvious why these are the shapes with basic names. They are just those shapes that form good Gestalts, or "good figures" (see Boring, 1942). A figure has more characteristics of a "good figure" when it is closed, when it is symmetrical, when it has the fewest changes in curvature, and so on. On principles like these, lines, curves, and angles are better figures than squiggles, esses, and ogives. Circles and squares turn out to be the best closed figures followed closely by ovals, triangles, and rectangles. These are all better figures than hexagons, quadrilaterals, and rhombuses, to say nothing of all of the figures that require complex names. Although the shape names have not been systematically studied in various languages, it is difficult to imagine that the same Gestalt principles wouldn't predict what is and isn't named in those languages too.

FIGURE 14–2
TYPES OF GESTALT FIGURES

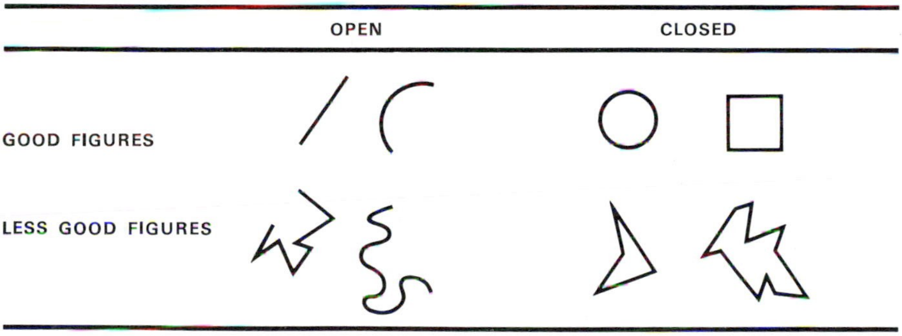

Rosch (1973), however, found that the Dani did not have basic names for the common shapes named in English. To describe geometrical figures, they resorted to circumlocutions like **pig-shaped** or **fence-shaped**. So Rosch had them learn arbitrary names for a variety of shapes. One group of Dani learned one name for a circle and variations of it, another name for a square and variations of that, and a third name for a triangle and variations of that. Other groups learned names for variations of three shapes that are not as good by Gestalt principles. The Dani who learned names for the best figures—the variations of the circle, square, and triangle—did so the fastest. Those who learned names for less good figures did correspondingly less well. So it may not be accidental that English and other languages have basic names for these particular shapes. They are good Gestalts that other people find easiest to learn names for too.

Classifiers

Many languages have a system of so-called *classifiers*, and in them shape plays an important role. To talk about more than one ball in some languages, for example, one cannot use the equivalent of the English **six balls**. One must instead attach **six** to a classifier used with the noun **ball**, as in **six round-things ball**. The classifier (here, **round-thing**) is usually a single word that categorizes the object in some way (Berlin, 1968; Denny, 1976; Greenberg, 1972). There is a comparable categorization in the English expressions **a blade of grass, three sheets of typing paper**, and **three rolls of wall paper**. The words **blade, sheet**, and **roll** help pick out the shape and dimensionality of the objects named. In some languages, the classifier makes up part of the verb instead, as in **he caused-*round-solid-thing*-to-move-upward stone** ("he lifted the stone") and **the man *animate-thing*-moved away** ("the man left"). Classifiers like these are common in languages through Southeast Asia (such as Mandarin Chinese, Vietnamese, and Laotian) and in languages of North and Central America (such as Hopi, Navaho, and Tzeltal).

How do classifiers classify? According to K. Adams and Conklin (1973), they usually distinguish first between animate and non-animate objects and often then divide the animate objects into humans versus animals, with some further subcategorization. More significantly for our purpose, they frequently classify objects on the basis of shape. The shapes most often picked out are *round, long*, and (less frequently) *flat*. Objects are classified by these shapes either alone or in combination with some secondary property like orientation, rigidity, or use. For example, a long object might be classified as a long vertical thing (like a pole) or as a long horizontal thing (like a log), and a flat object might be classified as a flat rigid thing (like a board) or as a flat flexible thing (like a rug). These three shapes—long, flat, and round—are again perceptually simple. *Long* denotes simple one-dimensional extension (as in lines), *flat* simple two-dimensional extension (as in rugs), and *round* simple three-dimensional extension (as in spheres). These are all good Gestalts.

What is remarkable is that the shapes selected by classifiers are most often the very shapes children use in over-extensions of their first nouns (E. Clark, 1976). For example, just as classifier systems commonly categorize objects by their round shape, so do children in their over-extensions. And just as classifiers categorize objects as long (having extension in one dimension), so do children in their over-extensions. These two parallels are illustrated in Table 14–2. There don't seem to be any clear instances of flat objects being grouped together in over-extensions, but this may be because flat is really only a special case of long, as K. Adams and Conklin (1973) suggested. Children also use animacy or movement as a basis for over-extension, and this parallels the non-shape categories of classifier systems. One final note: classifier systems never categorize on the basis of color, and neither do children in their over-extensions.

The shapes people pick out for basic names or classifiers, therefore, have a plausible origin in human perceptual capacities. People have a predilection for good Gestalt figures perceptually, and these are the shapes that are named. Children appear to find some shapes more salient than others and use these in their first hypotheses about what nouns pick out. Names for these shapes will therefore be easy to learn, and with the adult predilection for the same shapes, they will also be maintained in the language. Basic shape names, then, are determined by principles that are built onto the human perceptual system.

TABLE 14–2
PARALLELS BETWEEN CLASSIFIER CATEGORIES AND
CHILDREN'S OVER-EXTENSIONS

SHAPE	CLASSIFIER CATEGORY	CHILDREN'S OVER-EXTENSIONS
ROUND	*Indonesian:* fruit, pea, eye, ball, stone	*English:* moon, cakes, round marks on windows, round marks in books, round tooling on book covers, round postmarks, letter 'O'
	Laotian: sun, moon, plate, pot, eye, stone	
	Thai: bead, stone, seed, globe, fruit	*French:* nipple, point of bare elbow, eye in portrait, face in photo
		Serbian: coat button, collar stud, round light switch, anything small and round
LONG	*Nung:* tree, bamboo, thread, nail, candle	*English:* stick, cane, folded umbrella, ruler, old-fashioned razor, board of wood
	Trukese: tree, canoe, stick, pencil, cigarette	*English:* bars of cot, abacus, columned facade of building

Based on E. Clark (1976).

Spatial Terms

All languages appear to make reference to such spatial dimensions as height, width, distance, and thickness. In English, dimensions are described with adjectives like **high** and **low**, **wide** and **narrow**, **far** and **near**, and **thick** and **thin**. In each pair the first adjective describes extent along the dimension, and the second adjective describes lack of extent. But there is an extraordinary consistency among these adjectives. The terms that describe "having extent" are all linguistically unmarked and positive; the terms that describe "lacking extent" are linguistically marked and negative (see Chapter 11). What is even more remarkable is that, according to Greenberg (1966), this is true in all languages (unless the language treats them equally). In many languages, the terms for "lacking extent" are expressed with an overt negative, the equivalent of **unlong**, **not-deep**, or **non-far**. French, Italian, and Spanish, for example, lack words for **shallow** and are forced to use the equivalent of **little deep**, a more complex expression than **deep**.

One obvious source for this universal is perception. Take length. In nature it is asymmetrical: a line remains a line, for example, as it grows longer, but it eventually decreases to nothing as it grows shorter. It is only natural, then, to conceive of "having extent" as positive and "lacking extent" as negative. Moreover, children seem to attend more to objects that "have extent" than to those that "lack extent" and this appears to explain why they typically learn the words for the positive ends of such dimensions first (see Chapter 13).

TABLE 14–3

DIMENSIONS DESCRIBED BY ENGLISH SPATIAL TERMS

REFERENT OBJECTS	DIMENSION	ADJECTIVES	PREPOSITIONS
Gravity	Verticality	high-low	up-down, above-below
People	Verticality	tall-short	up-down, above-below
	Visibility		front of-back of, ahead-behind
	Laterality		left of-right of, at the side of
	Corpulence	fat-thin	
Directed objects	Verticality	tall-short	up-down, above-below, top of- underneath
	Visibility		front of-back of, ahead-behind
	Laterality	wide-narrow	left of-right of, at the side of
Undirected objects	Length	long-short	at the end of
	Width	wide-narrow	at the side of
	Thickness	thick-thin	
	Size	large-small	
Points	Distance	far-near	at, to-from, near
Containers	Internality	deep-shallow	in-out, inside-outside
Surfaces	Support		on-off

Natural Dimensions

The dimensions languages pick out are far from arbitrary: they appear to be just those dimensions the human perceptual apparatus is tuned to pick out (H. Clark, 1973a). This can be illustrated for the English spatial terms listed in Table 14–3. In nature, there is a dimension defined by the pull of gravity, namely verticality, and there is also a natural plane of reference, namely ground level. When describing spatial relations, it is convenient to use these two perceptual invariants. Gravitational verticality is used in adjectives like **high**, **low**, **tall**, and **short**, in prepositions like **up**, **down, above**, and **below**, and even in verbs like **rise, fall, raise, lower, lift,** and **drop.** Ground level is used in judging something as high or low, unless some other plane of reference supersedes it. It is normally taken to be zero height.

Common objects have natural dimensions as well. The human body has a biologically defined and perceptually obvious plane of symmetry—the sagittal plane that splits the left and right sides of the body in half. This defines the dimension underlying **left** and **right**. The line running from head to toe in the sagittal plane defines another perceptually salient dimension, body verticality, and perpendicular to that plane is **front** and **back.** The terms used with these two dimensions have natural origins. When people are in their normal standing position, body vertical coincides with gravitational vertical, hence it is convenient to use the same terms for both. **Up** and **down**, for example, are used for both gravitational and body verticality, even when these two dimensions don't coincide. English, like so many other languages, builds many of its relational terms for the up-down, front-back, and left-right dimensions around appropriate body parts, such as head, front, back, top, and side, as in **ahead, in front, in back, on top**, and **beside** (see Friedrich, 1970). These terms are then transferred to the vertical, front-back, and lateral dimensions of other "directed" objects like cars, trains, chairs, and houses, objects that all have a normal orientation.

These natural dimensions have natural directions. When people stand, the space in front of them and above the ground is optimal for perception by eye, ear, and touch, hence upward and forward should be "positive" directions. In English, upward *is* positive, as in **high** versus **low opinion**, and so is forward, as in **forward** versus **backward policies**. So even though neither **up** nor **down**, for example, is linguistically marked, **up** denotes movement in a positive direction and should be easier to handle conceptually. Indeed, **up** has been found to take

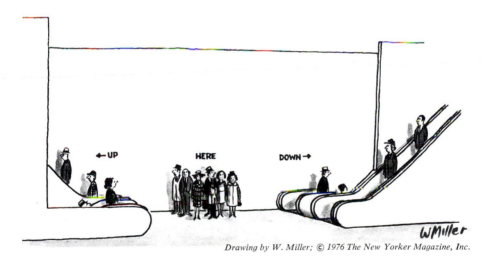

Drawing by W. Miller; © *1976 The New Yorker Magazine, Inc.*

less time to process than **down** (H. Clark and Brownell, 1975), and the same has been found for **above** and **below, in front of** and **in back of, ahead of** and **behind, into** and **out of**, and **to** and **from** (H. Clark, 1974a). Left and right are quite another matter. The left and right sides of the body are symmetrical about the sagittal plane, and that predicts no asymmetry. But since most people are right-handed, right should be positive, as it is in perhaps all languages. For example, **dexterous** comes from the Latin word for right, and **sinister** from the word for left. Consistent with this view, G. Olson and Laxar (1973, 1974) found that right-handers processed **right** faster than **left**, but left-handers processed **left** about as fast as **right**.

Dominance Relations Among Dimensions

In English some dimensions "dominate" others. Height and length, for example, dominate width, and width dominates thickness (Bierwisch, 1967). With a vertically oriented block of wood, the vertical dimension is called height, the more extended of the two remaining dimensions width, and the final remaining dimension thickness. And with an arbitrarily oriented block of wood, the most extended dimension is called length, the more extended of the two remaining dimensions width, and the final remaining dimension thickness.

These dominance relations turn up in children's first perceptual tactics. Very early in life, they pay attention to the natural directions vertical and horizontal, orienting most strongly to the vertical, especially the upper end. As Rudel and Teuber (1963) showed, they are able to learn a contrast between | and —— more easily than between \ and /. Diagonal lines are not natural dimensions for children. In addition, they can learn to distinguish ⊔ from ⊓ more easily than ⊐ from ⊏, showing that they can deal with vertical asymmetries more easily than horizontal ones. These two findings are surely perceptual in origin, for they appear to hold even for octopuses (Sutherland, 1957, 1960). Children also look at the upper parts of figures in preference to the lower parts (Ghent, 1960, 1961). Here, then, the vertical seems to be dominant. In the well-known Piagetian conservation tasks, children are asked to say whether or not the amount of water in two beakers is the same, or whether or not the amount of clay in two rope-like forms is the same. In these judgments, young children attend to the height and ignore the width of the water beakers, and they attend to the length and ignore the width of the clay ropes (Piaget, 1953; Farnham-Diggory and Bermon, 1968; see also Lumsden and Poteat, 1968). In both instances they pick out natural dimensions according to the dominance relations reflected in language.

Unfortunately, unrelated languages have not been systematically examined for the dimensions they make use of. Yet most languages appear to express height, length, distance, depth, and other dimensions, express binary relations with respect to the body's up-down, front-back, and left-right directions, and express verticality in a variety of other terms. It is difficult to imagine a language with a preposition meaning "in a left-ward, upward, and outward direction from," one that does not reflect a natural dimension. Here again it appears that languages pick their terms for perceptual reasons. Dimensions that are perceptually salient are the easiest for children to acquire terms for. They are also the most useful for adults to refer to, hence are maintained better and with greater accuracy.

COGNITIVE CATEGORIES

So far the universals discussed have plausible origins in perception. People have natural, built-in ways of perceiving and representing color, objects, shapes, distances, and spatial relations, and this is reflected in the basic names given them. The universals to be taken up next, the *cognitive* categories, seem to arise from more abstract conceptions of events and relations, although there may be no principled way to distinguish these from perceptual categories. A degree of speculation was often necessary in suggesting accounts for perceptual categories, and this will happen even more often with the cognitive categories. Much remains to be learned about the origins of these universals.

The categories to be examined cover number, negativity, cause and effect, and time. Most of them come from the work of Greenberg (1966), who, using his two criteria for complexity of expression ("added morphemes" and "neutralization"), searched a large number of unrelated languages for regularities in complexity. He concentrated on pairs of categories, one of which he could identify as universally "marked," or more complex, compared to the other.

Number

Most languages have ways of expressing singular and plural in nouns, as in the English **dog** and **dogs**. Some languages even have a "dual" form for denoting two objects, which would mean "two-dogs." (When a language has a dual, its plural means "more than two" instead of "more than one.") As Greenberg noted, in languages where these forms differ in complexity, plural is always marked with respect to singular, and dual is always marked with respect to plural. Or to use a shorthand to denote increasing complexity of expression:

singular : plural : dual

Most languages also distinguish cardinal numbers (**one**, **two**, **three**, etc.) from ordinal numbers (**first**, **second**, **third**, etc.). As Greenberg found:

cardinal : ordinal

In English, this shows up in words like **twentieth**, which consists of **twenty** plus an added suffix **-eth**.

The singular-plural-dual progression very likely derives from the primacy of the individual object in perception. Each object is perceived as an individual with an identity of its own, constant over time. Collections are conceived of as groupings of individual objects in which each object has its own identity. Hence the basic contrast is between an individual and a collection of individuals, between singular and plural. Dual denotes a particular kind of collection—one with exactly two members—and is therefore more complex. Cardinals and ordinals fit another progression of cognitive complexity. Ten objects can be counted in any order, but the ordinal position of each requires two notions: counting and order of counting. Hence cardinals, which are mere counts, depend on less complex conceptual requirements than ordinals, which are ordered counts (see Piaget and Szeminska, 1952).

Negation

One of the most conclusive universals Greenberg found was that negatives are marked with respect to positives:

positive : negative

In English, the complexity of negatives shows up in the material added to sentences (**John is here** versus **John isn't here**), verbs (**tie** versus **untie**), adjectives (**able** versus **unable**), adverbs (**ever** versus **never**), and even pronouns (**one** versus **none**).

Negation is probably expressed in a complex way because it takes more specification to say what something is *not* than to say what something is. The color of a car wouldn't be described in terms of what colors it is not—**blue, yellow, green, orange, black, gray, white**, and **purple**. It would be described positively as **red**. People normally use positive rather than negative representations so that they can represent knowledge as simply and directly as possible. This, of course, is reflected in the representation of **x isn't red** as two propositions: **False(Red(x))**. In the positive case only the specific category, red, is represented, as in **Red(x)**. There is good reason to consider negation complex.

Positive, Good, and Normal

Positive and negative serve to divide domains like color into two parts, such as **red** and **not red**. Many domains divide in half naturally, and then it seems arbitrary to call one half positive and the other negative. Yet there is almost always a conceptual asymmetry between the two halves, and languages often seize on the asymmetry just to be able to express one half positively and the other half negatively. This happens, for example, with dimensional terms like **high** and **low** or **deep** and **shallow**. In all languages, apparently, extent is taken to be positive and lack of extent negative. It also happens with evaluative terms. **Good** is always expressed positively and **bad** negatively, but never the reverse (Greenberg, 1966):

good : bad

The relation between good-bad and positive-negative is very close. In many languages **bad** is expressed explicitly as "not-good" or "ungood." And Zimmer (1964) and Boucher and Osgood (1969) found, for a variety of languages, that it is almost never possible to add negative prefixes or suffixes to bad evaluation words to produce terms like **unbad**, **unsad**, or **unugly**, although these prefixes are often added to good evaluation words to produce terms like **ungood**, **unhappy**, and **unbeautiful**.

Why should goodness be expressed positively and badness negatively? That is, why are good and bad often expressed as **good** and **ungood**, but never as **unbad** and **bad**? Boucher and Osgood (1969) have argued for a "Pollyanna hypothesis":

people tend to "look on (and talk about) the bright side of life (p. 1)." If this is so, words like **good** should occur more frequently in languages than words like **bad**, and this has been amply demonstrated by Zajonc (1968) at least for English and several other European languages. But the Pollyanna hypothesis doesn't explain why good words get positive expression and bad words negative expression. All it implies is that good words should occur more often. Zajonc (1968) has argued for the opposite hypothesis, that frequently encountered objects come to have a positive evaluation, but his hypothesis suffers from the same defect. It may explain why good words occur more often, but not why they get expressed positively and bad words negatively.

The answer more likely lies in the notion of normality. Normal states are conceived of positively, and abnormal states as the absence of normal states, as negative states. Now, as Bierwisch (1967) has noted, goodness itself is conceived of as a normal state, and badness as an abnormal state. Note that milk in its ordinary state is "good milk," but milk in its abnormal state has "gone bad." Goodness is considered normal because it is what is expected—what should be—and so badness is abnormal. Thus, because normal is positive and abnormal negative, goodness is expressed positively and badness negatively. The normality hypothesis is consistent with the Pollyanna hypothesis and Zajonc's findings, but it gives a reason for expressing one state as the negative of the other. Moreover, it accounts for the linguistic form of such pairs as **mortal-immortal**, **usual-unusual**, and **finite-infinite**, words that do not differ in good and bad evaluation (Zajonc, 1968) but do differ in positive and negative expression. Dimensional terms like **high** and **low** fit here too. **High**, the positive term, describes measurement in the normal direction on the height scale, and **low**, the negative term, measurement in the abnormal direction. Whenever possible, languages treat the normal positively and the abnormal negatively, and goodness and badness are just one domain where they do this.

Cause and Effect

According to Greenberg, if a language has expressions that differ in complexity for state, change of state, and cause of change of state, as in **dead**, **die**, and **kill**, then they are given increasingly complex expression:

state : change of state : cause of change of state

In English, change of state often takes an added morpheme as compared to state—as in such pairs as **solid-solidify**, **red-redden**, and **long-lengthen**. The same goes for cause of change of state as compared to state in such pairs as **sharp-sharpen**, **legal-legalize**, and **large-enlarge**. Many languages add a regular "affix" in forming cause of change of state from change of state, as in Turkish **öl** versus **öldür** for "die" versus "kill" (cause to die). French makes causative verbs out of change-of-state ones by adding the verb **faire**, as in **tomber** versus **faire tomber** for "fall" versus "cause to fall."

Why? Intuitively, states are simpler than changes of state. Being solid is a constant state, whereas solidifying involves an initial state, a final state, and a change from the first to the second. Causing a change of state is still more complex. It requires not only an initial state, a final state, and a change from one to the other, but also an event that causes the change to come about. This increase in complexity is reflected quite naturally in the functional notation for these three notions: **Solid(x)**, **Come-about(Solid(x))**, and **Cause(y,Come-about (Solid(x)))**. Children seem to build verbs in this order too, making change-of-state verbs out of state expressions, and causative verbs out of both change-of-state verbs and state expressions (Chapter 13). How these notions develop prior to language is not well understood.

In English two events that occur in succession can be described with the first event subordinated to the second, or with the second event subordinated to the first, as in 1 and 2:

1. John left after Mary insulted Bill.
2. Mary insulted Bill before John left.

But if the first event is the *cause* of the second, one has to use an expression similar to 1 in which the first event (here the cause) is subordinated to the second, as in 3:

3. John left because Mary insulted Bill.

That is, the conjunction **because** is analogous to **after**, and there is no subordinating conjunction expressing cause in English analogous to the **before** in 2. According to Talmy (1976), this asymmetry seems to hold for all languages. Effects are seen and expressed with respect to causes, not vice versa. If true, this is a powerful universal that should be founded in the human conception of cause and effect. It may have its roots in the child's acquisition of notions of causation, but just how is as yet unclear.

Time

All languages have ways of distinguishing among the present, past, and future, but according to Greenberg, the past is usually marked with respect to the present, and the future always is:

present : past   present : future

In English the markedness of past over present shows up in the added morphemes in such pairs as **work** versus **worked** and **work** versus **have worked**, and the markedness of future over present in **work** versus **will work**. In many languages the future is expressed as a hypothetical event, as distinguished from an actual event. Certain linguists (Boyd and Thorne, 1969) have argued that this is the case for English: the auxiliary verb **will** in **will work** expresses an intention to work and hence is a hypothetical. In any case, as Greenberg noted, hypotheticals like **would work** are invariably marked with respect to actuals like **work**:

actual : hypothetical

It is easy to see where these universals might come from. Children begin their speech careers by talking solely about the here and now—objects and events in the present moment. It takes time for them to acquire the notion of non-present. When they do, they first seem to acquire the notion of past, events they have already experienced, and a bit later the notion of future, events they have not yet experienced. For instance, when children begin learning words like **yesterday** and **tomorrow**, they often confuse them (Decroly and Degand, 1913; C. Stern and Stern, 1928). Harner (1975) studied two- to four-year-old children who began by interpreting **yesterday** as both past and future, that is as "not present." Next they got **yesterday** right, then finally learned to use **tomorrow**. The child's understanding of hypothetical events is acquired even later than the notions of present, past, and future (Slobin, 1973).

SOCIAL CATEGORIES

The universals included under the term *social categories* seem to have their roots in the social and cultural conditions in which people live. The two main classes of social categories to be considered probably derive from the universal characteristics of families and human conversations.

Kinship Terms

Kinship terms—the terms used to name one's relatives—have been studied intensively by anthropologists for many languages and cultures. These terms are especially amenable for study because the anthropologist can set out an objective list of the people to which each term applies (Burling, 1970). The English term **uncle**, for example, applies to one's father's brother, one's mother's brother, the husband of one's father's sister, and the husband of one's mother's sister. Once the relatives for each term in each language have been listed, it is relatively straightforward to compare languages in search of the universals of kinship systems. This is precisely what Greenberg (1966) did, and he turned up a number of important universals.

All languages distinguish at least three characteristics in relatives: generation, blood relationship, and sex. All languages keep the generations apart: they have different terms for parents, grandparents, children, and grandchildren, even though they may use only one term for both father and father's brother or one term for all four grandparents. In addition, all languages distinguish between blood relatives and spouse's relatives, as in the English **mother** versus **mother-in-law**. And all languages distinguish the sex of at least some relatives, as in English

mother versus **father** and **sister** versus **brother**. Other characteristics are distinguished in some languages but not others.

But languages treat relatives unequally. They favor ancestors over descendants, near relatives over far relatives, and blood relatives over spouse's relatives. These biases show up in the markedness of kin terms:

ancestor : descendant

one generation away : two generations away : three generations away: . . .

blood relative : spouse's relative

In many languages the terms referring to children and other descendants have more complex expression than the terms referring to parents and other ancestors, although this does not show up in English. As for generations, in English there is a progression from **father** to **grandfather** to **great grandfather** and so on. There is increasing complexity of expression with the addition of **grand** and **great** the more distant the generation the relative belongs to. This applies to descendants as well, as in **grandchild**, **great grandchild**, and **great great grandchild**. As for spouse's relatives, these are clearly marked in English with respect to blood relatives, as in **mother-in-law** versus **mother** and **sister-in-law** versus **sister**. The added morphemes **-in-law** mark a relative as belonging to one's spouse.

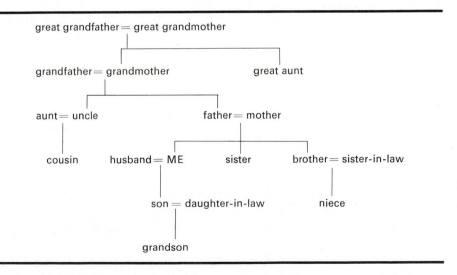

It seems fairly clear why these distinctions and biases should exist. Humans, by their biological nature, have parents and grandparents, and—with the usual systems of stable marriage—they may have brothers and sisters, aunts and uncles, cousins, and children. It seems only natural to distinguish the care-taking generations from those being taken care of, and to give one's ancestors, who are necessarily there, priority over one's descendants, who aren't. The relatives most closely associated with a person, either biologically or as caretakers (and often both), will be near relatives, hence it is the distant relatives who should be marked. In-laws are acquired only by marriage, so they too are out of the ordinary and should be marked. Put simply, languages will develop kin terms useful for everyday purposes, and this favors ancestors, near relatives, and blood relatives.

A widespread though not universal bias in language is the one favoring male over female:

male : female

In English the markedness of female is especially visible. Female terms are formed by the addition of suffixes, as in **actor-actress**, or **major-majorette**, and it is the male term that neutralizes to cover both sexes, as in such terms as **workman**, **chairman**, **forefathers**, **mankind**, and even **he** and **man**. Although one can only speculate here, sexism in language seems to have its roots in society. Men have often been viewed as dominant, and languages have therefore developed simpler terms to denote them. Note how in English-speaking societies, the dominance of men over women varies with profession, and the complexity of expression follows suit. Doctors, judges, and senators are too often assumed to be men, and nurses and secretaries to be women. Newspapers, then, often mark the out of the ordinary people in these professions as **woman doctor**, **lady judge**, **lady senator**, **male nurse**, and **male secretary** where they would never use the terms **man doctor**, **gentleman judge**, **gentleman senator**, **female nurse**, or **female secretary** except under special circumstances. These examples show how complexity of expression follows from the assumptions of society, and so the general markedness of female over male terms in English probably has the same origins (C. Miller and Swift, 1976). Sexism of this sort seems to be widespread in the languages of the world.

Pronouns

Although kin terms arise from family and marriage systems, pronouns are needed in conversation to distinguish the speaker (**I**) from the person or persons addressed (**you**) and from other participants (**he** or **they**). Indeed, pronoun systems universally distinguish among these three roles (Forchheimer, 1953; Ingram, 1971b). And according to Greenberg (1966) and Kuryłowicz (1964), **I** is unmarked with respect to **you**:

speaker : addressee

Pronoun systems also invariably distinguish the number of participants in one way or another, and may have different forms, for example, for singular and plural addressees.

TABLE 14–4
PALAUNG PRONOUNS: AN ELEVEN-FORM SYSTEM

		SPEAKER INCLUDED	SPEAKER EXCLUDED
ADDRESSEE INCLUDED	Singular	——	mi (*thou**)
	Dual	ar (*thou and I*)	par (*he or she, and thou*)
	Plural	ɛ (*thou, I, and he, she, or they*)	pɛ (*they and thou*)
ADDRESSEE EXCLUDED	Singular	ɔ (*I*)	ʌn (*he or she*)
	Dual	yar (*he or she, and I*)	gar (*they two*)
	Plural	yɛ (*they and I*)	gɛ (*they, three or more*)

* *Thou* indicates singular second person pronoun.
Based on Burling (1970).

Languages may have between four and fifteen pronouns. English has only five (if gender distinctions are ignored), namely:

I   you   he   we   they

In this set, **I** and **he** are singular, **we** and **they** plural, and **you** either singular or plural. **I** is used for the speaker, **you** for the addressee, and **he** and **they** for "third persons," other people or objects. **We** can be used either "inclusively" for the speaker and addressee together, or "exclusively" for the speaker and some third person together. **You** can be used either for people addressed or for people addressed plus some other people. English does not distinguish between the two **we**s or the two **you**s, but many languages do. One example is Palaung, a Mon Khmer language spoken in Burma, as shown in Table 14–4. According to Ingram (1971b), this is one of the commonest types of pronoun systems found. Each pronoun specifies whether it denotes one, two, or more than two people, whether one of those people is the speaker, and whether one, two, or more than two of these people are the addressees. The system is perfectly regular and makes good sense.

It seems obvious why languages should universally distinguish role and number in their pronouns. Speech occurs primarily in conversations between a speaker and one or more addressees. It would be highly inefficient to have to refer to these participants with expressions like **John** and **Mary**, **the speaker** and **the addressee**, or **the person here** and **the person there**. Pronouns provide a convenient shortcut. Moreover, the one participant essential to every conversation is the speaker. It therefore makes sense to express **I** in a less complex form than **you**. Significantly, children generally acquire **I** before **you** too (E. Clark, 1977b). In conversations number is less critical than role and it is also less well developed in pronoun systems. Like the kin terms, then, the pronouns take their universal characteristics from the categories people need for the social and cultural system they are a part of.

PROCESSING CONSTRAINTS

At first glance there seems to be no consistency from language to language in the way words are ordered and grouped in surface structure. For example, the verb normally comes first in sentences in Samoan and Tagalog, last in Japanese and Turkish, and in the middle in English and French. This first impression is far from the truth. Only some of the word orders that could conceivably be used in languages actually ever occur, and these have striking characteristics. It appears that the mental processes people have available for speaking and listening exert "forces" on language that favor certain configurations of words over others. The forces to be taken up here have their consequences on the grouping of words, the order of words, and the regularity of paradigms.

Word Groups

It is hard to imagine a language in which an adjective and the noun it modifies are not normally adjacent in the sentence, as in English **red car**, French **voiture rouge**, or German **rotes Auto**. Since **red** and **car** express propositions that make reference to the same entity, they belong together in a single surface constituent. The same goes for other words that reflect closely linked propositions. Indeed, languages appear to conform as closely to this constraint as possible (Greenberg, 1963; Sanders, 1975; Vennemann, 1973, 1974, 1975). The general principle is what Vennemann called Behaghel's First Law:

> *Word groups:* What belongs together mentally is placed close together syntactically.

This principle is nicely illustrated in languages with noun classifiers (Greenberg, 1972, 1975). Recall that these languages refer to objects with noun phrases like **two flat-things book**, in which **two** is a quantifier (Q), **flat-things** is a classifier (C), and **book** is a noun (N). These three constituents "belong together mentally" and always go together to form a single constituent. But as Greenberg argued, the classifier **flat-things** denotes the objective units that are to be counted, much as **grain**, **spoonful**, and **pail** do in the English **two grains of sand**, **two spoonfuls of sand**, and **two pails of sand**. The quantifier therefore goes with the classifier, not with the noun, and should form a surface constituent with the classifier. This is just what Greenberg found. Of the six conceivable orders of Q, C, and N, only four ever occur in languages:

$$(Q + C) + N$$
$$(C + Q) + N$$
$$N + (Q + C)$$
$$N + (C + Q)$$

The two orders that never occur, Q + N + C and C + N + Q, are precisely those in which Q and C do *not* form a natural surface constituent.

Agreement

Another device languages have for linking words in surface structure is "agreement." In English, the verb is made to agree with the subject in number, as in **he works** versus **they work**, and in French, for example, articles and adjectives are made to agree with their nouns in both number and gender, as in **le soleil rond** ("the round sun"), in which all three words are masculine and singular, and **la lune ronde** ("the round moon"), in which all three are feminine and singular. In an extensive survey of unrelated languages, Moravcsik (1971) found that whenever two words agreed like this, they expressed propositions that referred to the same entity. In **he works, he** refers to the same person that the proposition underlying **works** refers to. Thus, rules of agreement function very much like word groups. They are used to indicate that two words denote propositions that "go together mentally."

Word groups and rules of agreement are plausibly accounted for as consequences of the way people produce and understand sentences. In noun phrases —which are word groups *par excellence*—people collect together all the qualifications they want to make about a single entity and pack them into one constituent. In production, they plan all of these qualifications at one time, and so it ought to be easiest to produce them together as a single constituent. In comprehension too it should be easiest to identify the entity referred to when all the qualifications are heard and taken in as part of a single constituent. Most rules of agreement simply reinforce the grouping in noun phrases and underline their coherence as perceptual Gestalts. But rules of agreement can also link words that are compelled by other factors to be widely separated, as with **he** and **works** in **he scarcely ever works**. Here, rules of agreement have an especially critical processing function: they may provide the only way to indicate that two words refer to the same entity.

Word Order

By looking at a diverse sample of the world's languages, Greenberg (1963) discovered a remarkable series of facts about word order. Every language has declarative sentences that express subject (S), verb (V), and object (O), and although many languages (like Latin), allow S, V, and O to occur freely in any order, they all have a preferred, or normal, order for these three elements. In English the order is SVO, as in **Maxine picked the flower**. Greenberg's first discovery was that of the six conceivable orders of S, V, and O, only four occurred in the world's languages, and one of those was exceedingly rare:

VO-Languages		*OV-Languages*	
SVO	35%	SOV	44%
VSO	19%		
VOS	2%		

These percentages, taken from Ultan (1969), are only a rough guide to the relative frequency of these four types. Greenberg found no examples of OVS or OSV languages, a point corroborated by others (Pullum, 1977).

As if this weren't remarkable enough, Greenberg noted that the ordering of many other elements in surface structure generally goes along with having the object before the verb (an "OV-language") or the verb before the object (a "VO-language"):

VO-Languages	OV-Languages
Verb + Object	Object + Verb
Auxiliary + Main verb	Main verb + Auxiliary
Preposition + Noun	Noun + "Postposition"
Noun + Relative clause	Relative clause + Noun
Noun + Possessive	Possessive + Noun
Noun + Adjective	Adjective + Noun
Noun + Demonstrative	Demonstrative + Noun
Noun + Number	Number + Noun

Although these orders generally all go together, the tendencies aren't perfect. English, for example, shows some inconsistency. As a VO language, it displays the first five constructions (**eat apples**, **may go**, **at home**, **man who left**, **leg of chair**), but not the last three (**good man**, **that man**, and **ten men**). This inconsistency may have come about because English, like many other Indo-European languages, used to be an OV language and is still in the process of bringing its constructions into harmony as a proper VO-language (Vennemann, 1974). Lehmann (1972, 1973) has called languages that fit all the VO patterns "consistent VO-languages," and those that fit all the OV patterns "consistent OV-languages." Classical Hebrew and Portuguese are examples of consistent VO-languages, and Japanese and Turkish consistent OV ones.

These consistencies in word order beg for a processing explanation, and that is just what Bartsch and Vennemann (1972; Vennemann, 1973, 1974, 1975) have proposed with their "principle of natural serialization." Each of the orderings in consistent VO languages, they argued, is composed of an "operand" followed by an "operator." In the Verb + Object phrase **eat apples**, for example, **apples** operates on **eat** to specify, or determine, just what it was that was eaten, and in the Noun + Relative Clause **man who left**, **who left** operates on **man** to specify which man is being denoted. In consistent OV languages, the order in all these phrases is just the reverse, with the "operator" before the "operand." So there is a force in languages that might be described like this:

> *Natural Order:* Constituents in surface structure all tend to have the same order, either Operand + Operator, or Operator + Operand.

In essence, this is a processing explanation. The claim is that constituents are produced and taken in according to whether they are operators or operands, and the mental processes involved work best when all the operators and operands are in the same order.

Subjects and Given Information

Another force at work in languages is one that places the subject at or near the beginning of the sentence. Note that the subject (S) comes first in the two commonest language types, SVO and SOV (about 80 percent of Ultan's sample), and it precedes the object in all but the rarest type, VOS (less than 2 percent of Ultan's sample). Why subjects are placed early seems fairly clear. People tend to express given information, what is already known to the listener, before new information, what is not already known. This tendency appears to be universal. Languages overwhelmingly prefer to place definite noun phrases (given information) before indefinite noun phrases (new information). In some instances, the only way to indicate that a noun is definite is to place it before any indefinite noun, or to place it before the verb and to place any indefinite noun after the verb (E. Clark, 1970b; Kuno, 1971; Li and Thompson, 1974). Thus:

> *Given information:* Given information should appear before new information.

In the normal case, however, it is the subject that is preferred as given information (E. L. Keenan, 1976):

> *Subjects:* As given information, subjects are preferred over objects, objects over indirect objects, and indirect objects over other noun phrases.

Together, these two forces lead to subjects being mentioned early in utterances.

The "given-new strategy" discussed in Chapter 3 provides some explanation for the forces called Given Information and Subjects. By that strategy, listeners first search memory for an antecedent to given information—for example, a referent for a definite noun—then attempt to attach the new information to this antecedent. They must find the antecedent in memory before they can attach the new information to it. Thus it is optimal to take in the given information before the new information; otherwise, they have to hold the new information temporarily while they search for the antecedent to which it is to be attached. As for the subject, it is in some sense already formulated when people begin to speak, for it normally reflects the matter that provoked the speech in the first place. And people may even begin speaking before fully formulating the predicate they want to attach to it. It is plausible, then, that because subjects are planned before predicates, they should be expressed first too.

Objective Content

Some words tend to be given more prominence in surface structure than others. In **The man wouldn't have captured the elephant**, the words **man, capture,** and **elephant** are most prominent: they are central syntactically and get major stress. The remaining words are less prominent: they depend on the presence and position of **man, capture,** and **elephant**. Langacker (1974b) has argued that what tends to get prominence is "objective content," the physical objects, events, and attributes being referred to. What gets put in the background are the elements expressing the less tangible content, for example, past tense (**-ed**), completion (**have**), prediction (**would**), negativity (**not**), and definiteness (**the**). These less tangible ideas, of course, can be made prominent, as negation is in **It is not true that the man would have captured the elephant**, but usually they aren't. Languages have various devices for placing these elements in the background. The tendency Langacker described might be characterized like this:

> *Objective Content:* Languages tend to give objective content prominence in surface structure.

As Langacker noted, this force has an obvious function. It places the words that carry the most information, and normally the most important information, in prominent positions. It is natural to suppose that the speaker finds it useful to make this content prominent and that the listener finds it easier to take in and remember this content because it is prominent.

The five "forces" examined so far—Word Grouping, Natural Order, Given Information, Subjects, and Objective Content—each have a relatively independent reason for existence. Each appears to reflect some fundamental process in comprehension and production. Nevertheless, the forces will sometimes be in conflict and have to battle for their effect. At any one time in the history of a language they may collectively compel syntax to take a particular form, but their conflicts may encourage language change. English has undergone a change from SOV to SVO, and because of these natural forces, it is still bringing its subsidiary constructions into line. But as each change is made, other forces come into play that change the language in still other directions. Syntax, and its evolution, may well take the form it does in part because of the forces imposed by the mental processes people rely on for producing and understanding speech.

Paradigms

All languages appear to have "paradigms." In English, the verbs belong to a paradigm in which each verb has a present and a past tense form. The past tense is normally formed by adding **-ed** (in spelling) to the present tense, but there are exceptions.

Regular Past Tense		*Irregular Past Tense*	
work	worked	build	built
bar	barred	eat	ate
add	added	ring	rang

When new verbs are added to the language, like **bicycled**, **helicoptered**, or **blitzed**, they are invariably given the regular past tense **-ed**. This "force" might be described as follows:

> *Paradigms:* Languages favor regular paradigms.

Exceptions tend to be straightened out as languages change historically. The irregular verbs that remain in English come from earlier regular paradigms that have fallen into disuse, and many are being dropped in favor of regular past tense forms. **Work-wrought**, for example, has already become **work-worked**, and in the United States (but not Britain), **spell-spelt** has become **spell-spelled**, and **dream-dreamt** has become **dream-dreamed**.

Regular paradigms have clear advantages in production and comprehension. First, a past tense verb should be easier to plan and produce if all people have to remember is to add **-ed** to the present tense form—and it is (MacKay, 1976). Second, in comprehension a verb should be easier to identify as being in the past tense if there is an invariable signal, the **-ed**, indicating past tense. What makes regular paradigms so advantageous is their economy for memory. Imagine that English had 10,000 verbs. If the present and past tense forms were each as different as **go** and **went**, there would be 20,000 different forms to learn. If, instead, the past tense forms all took **-ed**, there would be only 10,000 forms to learn plus the rule "Add **-ed** to make the past tense." The latter is more economical, and that may be why languages move toward this ideal.

The advantage of regular paradigms shows up clearly in children, for whom the economics of memory are critical. As Slobin (1973, 1975) has persuasively argued (see Chapter 9), children look for suffixes (like **-ed**, **-s**, and **-'s**) that have a systematic mapping into meaning. Once they have found the markers, they try to use them without exceptions. They say **buyed** instead of **bought**, **foots** instead of **feet**, and **hims** instead of **his**, and learn the exceptions only much later. In Turkish, where the major paradigms have virtually no exceptions, children have little trouble learning the complete paradigms, while in English, where there are exceptions, children master the corresponding paradigms rather later. The force called Paradigms, therefore, may have its origin in the strategies children apply in acquisition.

Invented Languages

In many parts of the world, people trading with each other but speaking different languages have had to invent trading languages, technically called *pidgins*, by which they could talk to each other (see DeCamp, 1971). As temporary "contact vernaculars" with restricted purposes, pidgins need only a rudimentary structure. They tend to borrow nouns and verbs from one language —commonly Portuguese, French, Dutch, and English—and to use a highly simplified syntax. They tend not to have subordinate clauses, relative clauses, articles, or grammatical morphemes that mark plurality, present, past, and future tense. They are simplified semantically as well. They often have just a single locative preposition to take the place of **at**, **in**, **by**, **from**, **on**, **to**, and the rest (Traugott, 1974). Pidgins can get by with this simplicity because they are used when the communication requirements are fairly rudimentary.

An extraordinary thing happens, however, when for one reason or another a pidgin begins to be learned as a first language by the children of a culture. Suddenly there are rapid and dramatic changes in vocabulary and syntax, and it becomes what is technically called a *creole*. As a pidgin becomes a creole, it acquires a host of syntactic devices to allow it to distinguish present, past, and future tenses, to distinguish singular from plural, to build relative and subordinate clauses, and to distinguish among all the various locative relations. For example, an English-based creole in New Guinea that is called, appropriately enough, Tok Pisin ("Talk Pidgin"), has evolved a device to allow speakers to build relative clauses, a device that presumably was not there in its pidgin ancestor (Sankoff and Brown, 1976). The relative clause is formed simply by inserting a sentence into the main clause and by "bracketing" it on both sides by the word **ia**, as in this example:

Na pik *ia* ol ikilim bipo *ia* bai ikamap olsem draipela ston.

And this pig *ia* they had killed it before *ia* would turn into a huge stone.

As Slobin (1975) has pointed out, this is just the kind of device that allows speakers to separate main from relative clauses easily and simply, yet is perceptually easy for the listener to take in.

The characteristic ways pidgins turn into creoles may tell us what a linguistic system has to look like for it to be spoken, understood, and learned, and for it to fulfill the communicative functions it is meant to fulfill (Kay and Sankoff, 1974; Slobin, 1975). Many pidgins, for example, are fairly effective communication systems, yet one test they haven't passed is the one that says "To be a human language, a communication system has to be learnable by children as their first language." The changes that occur when pidgins becomes creoles appear to reflect this requirement as much as any. It is as if children demand of their language that it enable them to build relative and subordinate clauses, to indicate present, past, and future tense, to distinguish among locative relations, and the like. Kay and Sankoff (1974) have suggested that the order in which creoles invent linguistic devices will tell us what is "psychologically salient or functionally necessary or both" in language. Indeed, so far as one can tell, the aspects of language that creoles invent first are always among the language universals.

LANGUAGE VARIATION

Despite the emphasis on language universals, it is all too obvious that languages differ. They differ in their sounds, surface structure, grammatical categories, and vocabularies. Just how much can languages vary, in what ways, and why? And what consequences do variations have for the language user?

Language variation has already been examined a little—but under another guise. Many universals discussed earlier define not a standard that languages must adhere to but a range within which they may vary. Berlin and Kay's proposal about basic color terms, for example, really defines thirty-three ways in which languages can select their color terms. They can choose from two to eleven terms, which have to fit the color hierarchy. What Berlin and Kay's proposal does not do is predict how many color terms a language should select. It sets limits on variation in language, but doesn't explain the variation that actually occurs. Much the same could be said of the other universals. What is lacking so far, then, are principles that explain language variation. Unfortunately, there are few firm principles to be found. Probably the most transparent principles—though even these have not yet been carefully formulated—are found in vocabulary.

Variation in Vocabulary

Burling (1970) has compared certain parts of the vocabulary of Garo, a language spoken in Burma, with the corresponding vocabulary in English and has found several obvious differences. Garo, for example, has many words that correspond to the English word **carry**. Their usage depends on how the object is held and conveyed (on the head, on the shoulders, in the hands, by means of a strap or in a basket, and so forth) and on the direction in which it is conveyed. Garo also has many words for the English **basket**, one for each of several kinds of basket found in Burma. Where English has the one word **rice**, Garo has different words for husked and unhusked rice, cooked and uncooked rice, and various varieties of rice. And Garo has names for several different species that would all be called **ant** in English. In the opposite direction, English has eleven basic color terms whereas Garo has only four. English also has many more words for the technical innovations of the last century. Of course, English speakers can describe the different ways of carrying and the different baskets, rice, and ants by use of modifiers as in **uncooked rice**, **wicker basket**, and **red ants**, and Garo speakers can describe the English colors and technical innovations by similar means. It is just that the basic terms, the simple one-word descriptions, do not correspond in English and Garo.

It seems obvious enough why Garo and English should differ in these ways. Rice is critical to the survival of Garo speakers, hence distinctions among kinds of rice are economically and socially important. Baskets are a major aid in transportation, and so baskets and modes of carrying objects are important to distinguish. Ants, although not economically important, have a variety in nature that is more central to an agricultural people than to an industrialized society. Color works the other way around. According to Berlin and Kay (1969), the more industrialized the society (and, presumably, the more artificial dyes used), the more basic color terms it is likely to have. In short, proliferation in the vocabulary of any language reflects utility and hence expertise in concepts.

Expertise Within Subcultures

What is often not appreciated, however, is that expertise varies as much within as between language groups, and vocabulary size varies accordingly. Beekeepers, farmers, carpenters, miners, surgeons, football players, cooks—each group, through its special expertise, has evolved a wealth of special terms. A person off the street might know a handful of names for the internal organs of the body, but the surgeon knows hundreds. Thus, it is misleading to think of vocabulary as characteristic of a language. It is rather a characteristic of the subgroups who speak the language.

The way expertise leads to proliferation in vocabulary is quite simple. Consider a forester's use of **tree** versus **pine**, **oak**, and **elm**, versus **jack pine**, **Ponderosa pine**, and **white pine**. After working closely with trees, he begins to think one level down: in terms of Berlin's levels of abstraction, he treats **tree** as a unique beginner, **pine**, **oak**, and **elm** as life forms, and **jack pine**, **Ponderosa pine**, and **white pine** as generic terms. Because generic terms should be simple one-word names, he speaks of **jacks**, **ponderosas**, and **whites** instead of **jack pines**, **Ponderosa pines**, and **white pines**. He also adds new terms to the specific level, e.g., **Rocky Mountain jacks**, **western ponderosas**, and **short-needled whites**. Anyone familiar with other areas of expertise will recognize this process. Experts distort their worlds by magnifying their own areas of expertise and the words in them out of all proportion.

The process of shortening and proliferation just illustrated makes sense of two observations Zipf (1935, 1949) made some years ago. First, he noted that the most frequent English words have one syllable. Indeed, the less frequent the word, the longer it is likely to be. But note that the most common words— the ones people have most use for—will be just those that denote simpler categories—for example, positive instead of negative, singular instead of plural, and generic instead of specific categories in Berlin's hierarchy—and these are just the ones that have shorter, less complex names. Zipf also noted that as a word becomes more frequent—often because of a technical or cultural change —it tends to get shortened. Most shortening probably reflects a change of levels in Berlin's hierarchy. For example, when the moving picture was a technical gadget in Edison's laboratory, it had a specific level name **moving picture**. But when it became common, it was reclassified as a general level category, and **moving picture** was shortened to **movie**. The same happened with many other technical innovations:

talking picture	⟶	talkie
gasoline	⟶	gas
television	⟶	TV or telly
omnibus	⟶	bus

Both of Zipf's observations ultimately reflect the law that complexity in thought is reflected in complexity of expression.

Another way people adapt vocabulary to their needs is by borrowing and inventing terms. When English speakers were first introduced to the potato, they needed a name and so they adopted the term the Spanish had taken from the Taino Indians. There are similar origins for **dilettante** (Italian), **goulash** (Hungarian), **sabotage** (French), **whisky** (Gaelic), **tomato** (Nahuatl), **Gestalt** (German), and **tomahawk** (Algonquian). The need for new names can also be solved by coining new ones, as English has by using Greek (**pseudopod**), Latin (**quadrilateral**), language mixtures (**Minneapolis** from Dakota **mini** and Greek **polis**), discoverers' names (**Parkinson's disease**), and so on. Apparently, when people lack a word for a useful concept, they soon find one.

How Does Language Affect Thought?

So far language and thought have been looked at from one direction only: from how thought affects language. But perhaps the most celebrated hypothesis in this area—the Sapir-Whorf hypothesis of linguistic relativity—claims just the opposite, that language affects thought. According to Whorf, each language imposes on its speaker a particular "world view." As he put it in the passage cited earlier, "We cut nature up, organize it into concepts, and ascribe significances as we do, largely because we are parties to an agreement to organize it in this way—an agreement that holds through our speech community and is codified in the patterns of our language." He based this view on his comparison of major European languages with such American Indian languages as Hopi, Aztec, Nootka, and Apache. He argued that the world view Indian languages imposed on their speakers was different from the view European languages imposed on theirs.

Most of the evidence Whorf adduced for this hypothesis consisted of anecdotes like this (1956, p. 241):

> We might isolate something in nature by saying "It is a dripping spring." Apache erects the statement on a verb *ga*: "be white (including clear, un-colored, and so on)." With a prefix *nō-* the meaning of downward motion enters: "whiteness moves downward." Then *tó*, meaning both "water" and "spring" is prefixed. The result corresponds to our "dripping spring," but synthetically it is "as water, or springs, whiteness moves downward." How utterly unlike our way of thinking.

It is unlike our way of talking, but is it really so unlike our way of thinking? The Apache word for dripping spring contains elements that denote "white or clear," "moving downward," and "spring," but roughly speaking so does the English **dripping spring**. **Dripping** means "moving downward in drops," and **spring** means "spring." The English expression doesn't happen to mention that the spring is "white" or "clear," although it could. (Perhaps Whorf should have translated the Apache expression as **clear dripping spring**.) What is striking here is that both languages have separate elements for "moving downward," "spring," and "clear." More than that, these elements appear to extend to other domains along similar lines. In his very next sentence, Whorf noted: "The same verb, **ga**, with a prefix that means 'a place manifests the condition' becomes **gohlga**: 'the place is white, clear; a clearing, a plain.'" In English too, one takes the verb **clear**, adding the suffix **-ing**, and forms **clearing**, "a place that manifests the condition of being clear." How utterly *like* our way of thinking!

Unhappily, the evidence for the Sapir-Whorf hypothesis has been equivocal. Whorf's own work suffers all too often from the weaknesses evident in the last example. From his anecdotes it is impossible to tell whether Indian and European languages cut up the world differently or not. Direct tests of the hypothesis have fared no better. Some of the earliest work, for example, examined how perception and memory for colors were affected by different color terminologies (see R. Brown and Lenneberg, 1954; Lenneberg and Roberts, 1956). These studies, however, assumed that the way languages cut up the color domain is arbitrary, and with the work of Berlin and Kay (1969), this assumption is no longer viable. Other tests are difficult to interpret for similar reasons (see Rosch, 1974).

Differentiation of Vocabulary

As evidence that language affects thought, Whorf often pointed to the fact that one language has more words in a particular domain than another language. For example, Eskimo has four words for snow (Boas, 1911) where English and Aztec have only one. But these differences probably reflect differences only in expertise. Eskimos are led by ecological concerns to note and name different kinds of snow, where the Aztecs in Mexico were not. The same variation can occur within a language. In English, expert skiers have specialized words for snow—**powder, corn, ice**, and the like—whereas the rest of us have just **snow**. It cannot be, then, that just because people speak English they cannot notice differences in snow.

Yet becoming an expert may well be aided by a well-differentiated vocabulary. To quote Bross (1973, p. 217):

> How did the surgeon acquire his knowledge of the structure of the human body? In part this comes from the surgeon's firsthand experience during his long training. But what made this experience fruitful was the surgeon's earlier training, the distillation of generations of past experience which was transmitted to the surgeon in his anatomy classes. It has taken hundreds of years and millions of dissections to build up the detailed and accurate picture of the structure of the human body that enables the surgeon to know where to cut. A highly specialized sublanguage has evolved for the sole purpose of describing this structure. The surgeon had to learn this jargon of anatomy before the anatomical facts could be effectively transmitted to him. Thus, underlying the "effective action" of the surgeon is an "effective language."

Bross's illustration is convincing. It would be unimaginable to learn certain fields without learning the special vocabulary developed for them. This does not mean that expertise is always or only gained in this way. In many cases the expertise comes first and the specialized vocabulary, if any, comes later.

The education of the surgeon may be compared to the education of children as they develop into adults. The "highly specialized" language they hear is really a distillation of generations of human experience, and this knowledge is most effectively transmitted to children through this "adult jargon." The process is cumulative. Learning new words enables children to conquer new areas of knowledge, and these new areas enable them to learn new words, and so on. Thus, a well-differentiated vocabulary may be a crucial aid to children in becoming "experts"—adults.

Memory

It is in memory that language has been shown to influence thought most convincingly. In one well-known study by Carmichael, Hogan, and Walter (1932), people were shown a series of line drawings, each accompanied by one of two labels. For example, ○—○ was presented with either the label **eyeglasses** or **barbells**. When later asked to reproduce the line drawings they had seen, those who had seen figure labeled **eyeglasses** tended to distort the figure toward ○~○, and those who had seen the figure labeled **barbells** tended to distort it toward ○——○ (see also Herman, Lawless, and Marshall, 1957; Glanzer and Clark, 1964). Apparently, people remember the label along with some perceptual information and reconstruct the figure in part from the label and what it denotes.

The mere presence of a label aids in the recall and recognition of things. Santa and Ranken (1972) presented people with a large number of so-called nonsense shapes—line drawings of random-looking closed figures drawn from a number of line segments—either with or without arbitrarily chosen labels. The people shown the labeled figures recognized them better at a later time than the ones who were shown the unlabeled ones. Labels help even more when they make sense of a nonsense figure—as, for example, when **star** makes sense of a nonsense figure that looks roughly like a star (Ellis, 1968). What the labels do apparently is help people distinguish among the figures more completely and, if recall is required, help them decide what figures to recall at what times.

Problem Solving

Labeling also affects the way people solve problems. This is nicely illustrated in Duncker's (1945) classic problem in which the solver has to overcome "functional fixedness." In this problem people are each presented with a candle, a box of tacks, and two or three matches. Their problem is to fix the candle to a wall in an upright position so that the candle won't drip. To solve the problem, they must see that the box the tacks are kept in can itself be used as a support for the candle when the box is tacked to the wall. What makes the problem hard is that most people view the box merely as a tack holder and fail to see its possible function as a candle support. In a study by Glucksberg and Weisberg (1966), people tried to solve the problem under one of two conditions—(a) when the objects were each labeled (**box, tacks, candle**, and **matches**) or (b) when there were no labels. When there were labels people averaged 0.61 minutes solving the problem, but when there were no labels, they averaged nearly 9 minutes, almost fifteen times as long. What the labels do, the explanation goes, is encourage people to pay attention to each object separately. This in turn enables them to see the box not merely as a holder but as an object that may figure in the solution to the problem. Interestingly, people who succeeded on the problem talked about **the box**, while those who failed tended to talk about **the box of tacks**.

Although this was a demonstration within one language, in principle it could be extended to compare two languages. Consider the English **thimble** and its German translation **Fingerhut**, literally "finger hat." In German the name itself expresses the object's function as a finger cover, whereas in English it doesn't. A problem that required people to abandon the thimble's function as a finger cover—just as the candle problem requires people to abandon the box's function as a tack holder—may therefore be more difficult when the thimble is labeled **Fingerhut** than **thimble**. Unfortunately, little work of this kind has been carried out.

What can one conclude about the Sapir-Whorf hypothesis? At present, very little. It is easy to find thought processes in which language plays an important role, and we have examined some of these. Certain facts are easier to learn in linguistic than in visual or some other form. Certain visual forms are easier to remember when labeled than when unlabeled. Certain problems are solved more easily expressed one way rather than another. Very generally, language is important whenever people talk to themselves as they try to keep track of where they are in a problem or in a list of things to do. Yet the main thrust of the Sapir-Whorf hypothesis is that differences in languages affect thought. Because one speaks English, Japanese, or Apache, certain concepts are difficult, perhaps impossible, to deal with. So far, however, no convincing examples of these differences have turned up. On the contrary, languages can apparently be stretched and adapted to fit the needs of virtually any group of experts. What this suggests is that language differences reflect the culture, and not the reverse.

SUMMARY

Language is above all a tool, and as a tool it must conform to the uses required of it. Whether the language is English, Hungarian, or Tok Pisin, it must be capable of expressing certain ideas—perceptual experiences, social relationships, and technological facts. At the same time it must conform to people's limitations —to their limited memory and even to the way their ears and mouths are constructed. So language is constrained to take only certain forms, and these are reflected in the universals of language. For example, the basic color terms in all languages are drawn from a hierarchy of only eleven color words. This hierarchy reflects the physiological salience of certain colors in the visual system. The names for natural and man-made objects in all languages belong to hierarchies of categories. These hierarchies reflect the mental processes by which objects are classified according to shared features. The shape names and spatial terms in languages reflect still other characteristics of the perceptual system. Other universals reflect abstract thought processes that favor singular over plural, positive over negative, present tense over past or future tense, and so on. Still other universals, like those of kinship terms and pronouns, reflect invariant social realities. Finally, the universals of word grouping, word order, and paradigms arise from the processes by which people understand and produce ongoing speech.

Languages also differ from each other, but always within limits. In vocabulary, for example, languages tend to multiply words that are useful for the culture, although such proliferation can happen even within subcultures using the same language. The words that are added nevertheless fall within the universal constraints on how objects are categorized according to shared features. But language in its turn affects thought too. A well-developed vocabulary may well aid in learning the concepts the vocabulary covers. For example, surgeons probably learn anatomy quicker by simultaneously acquiring names for all the internal organs. Language also affects how people reconstruct pictures, solve problems, and keep track of things in memory. Thought, therefore, both affects language and is affected by it.

Further Reading

Lenneberg (1967) gives a detailed presentation of the biological basis for language and the evidence for language specialization, while H. Gardner (1974) provides a readable account of the effects of brain injury on one's language and other faculties. Linden (1975) gives a vivid picture of recent research on language in chimpanzees. The linguistic complexity of terms used for talking about perceptual, cognitive, and social categories is discussed by Greenberg (1966). Berlin and Kay's (1969) book still provides the best introduction to focal colors and color terms, and Rosch (1973) gives an overview of her experimental work on this topic. Basic categories and their attributes are discussed in detail in Rosch and Mervis (1975) and in Rosch et al. (1976). Language universals that reflect general processing constraints are described in Greenberg (1963), Lehmann (1973), and Vennemann (1974). Finally, linguistic relativity, both the arguments and the evidence, are clearly presented by Rosch (1974). And, of course, Whorf (1956) himself makes for some fascinating reading.

GLOSSARY

Acoustic cue   A perceptible aspect of the acoustic signal used in distinguishing among phonetic segments, such as Voice Onset Time.

Acoustic-phonetic mapping   The correspondence between acoustic cues in the speech signal and the phonetic segments they are intended to signal.

Adjacency pair   A pair of utterances from two speakers in which the first elicits the second, as in a question-answer or greeting-greeting sequence.

Affix   Any morpheme added to a stem word, including prefixes, suffixes, and internal modifications (infixes).

Affricate   A speech sound consisting of a stop and a fricative, like [ǰ] in **blue jay**.

Agentive case   A case relation that names the instigator (the " agent ") of the action named by the verb.

Agreement   The correspondence of one word to another in gender, number, case, person, and so on, as in **he** and **goes** (singular) versus **they** and **go** (plural).

Alveolar   Pronounced with the constriction of the tip or blade of the tongue against the alveolar ridge, as in [d] in **day**.

Ambiguity   The condition of having more than one possible interpretation, as in **alligator shoes**.

Ameslan   The American sign language for the deaf.

Analytic truth   A statement true by virtue of its wording alone; for example, **Every man is male**.

Anomaly   An expression that is semantically or pragmatically odd; for example, **the thoughtful rock**.

Antecedent   The information in memory some expression refers to.

Anticipation   A slip of the tongue in which part or all of an upcoming word is incorrectly anticipated, as in **cuff of coffee**.

Antonyms   Two words whose meanings differ in only one respect—that of negation or contradiction—as in **man** and **woman**.

Basic-level term   A term that refers to a basic-level category, a category at a level of abstraction that is neither too general nor too specific, but optimal under certain criteria.

Bilabial   Pronounced with the constriction of the two lips, as in [b] in **bonnet**.

Blend   A slip of the tongue that begins with part of one word and ends with part of another, as **grastly**, from **grizzly** and **ghastly**.

Brain   "An apparatus with which we think that we think." (Ambrose Bierce)

Case relations or **roles**   The roles that the noun phrases associated with a verb play with respect to the state, action, or process named by the verb. See **Agentive, Experiencer, Goal, Instrumental, Locative,** and **Objective cases**.

Classifier   A morpheme that in many languages combines with a noun— analogous to **grain** in the English phrase **grain of sand**—classifying that noun by shape, animacy, or other attributes.

Cognitive complexity The complexity of the ideas expressed in language. Compare **Formal complexity**.

Commissive A speech act that commits the speaker to some future course of action.

Complement A proposition that replaces an empty noun argument of a second proposition, as in *that she left* **is possible**. See **Complementation**.

Complementation A way of combining propositions in which one proposition (the "complement") replaces an empty noun argument of a second proposition, as in **that he won was good**. See **Complement**.

Componential analysis A method of breaking up the sense of an expression into semantic components. See **Semantic component**.

Conditional A sentence in which one state of affairs is asserted to be contingent on another, as in most sentences with **if**.

Congruence principle The assumption that it is easier for people to search memory for matching information than for mismatching information.

Conjunction, coordinating **And, or, but,** and their relatives that conjoin two expressions by coordination, as in **Julia and Ken**. See **Coordination**.

Conjunction, subordinating A word that introduces an adverbial subordinate clause; for example, **when, because, before,** and **if**.

Consonant A speech sound that is characterized by constriction in some part of the mouth and is accompanied by audible friction.

Constituent A unit of surface structure that has a single coherent function and generally is replaceable by a single word.

Content word A word that carries meaning over and above its grammatical role in a sentence, including nouns, verbs, adjectives, and most adverbs. Compare **Function word**.

Contradictory antonyms A pair of antonyms for which the negation of one necessarily implies the other; for example, **alive** and **dead**. See **Antonyms**.

Contrary antonyms Two antonyms for which the negation of one does not necessarily imply the other, for example, **good** and **bad**. See **Antonyms**.

Contrastive stress Stress on a word or syllable to mark it as being in contrast with another possible word, as in **KEN found Fido**.

Conversation "A set of two or more monologues carried on simultaneously." (Justin Case)

Converses Two words that differ only in a relational component with two of its arguments reversed, as in **parent** and **child**.

Cooperative principle The assumption speakers and listeners make that speakers try to be informative, truthful, relevant, and clear.

Coordination A way of placing two clauses, generally, on a par with each other by use of a coordinate conjunction such as **and, or,** or **but**.

Creole A pidgin that has developed into a primary language of a speech community. Compare **Pidgin**.

Declaration A speech act that brings about a new state of affairs by the mere utterance of the words.

Deictic term   A word that "points" to places, times, or participants in a conversation from the speaker's point of view; for example, **I**, **you**, **there**, and **yesterday**.

Denial   An assertion with a negative attached to the main verb designed to cancel some supposition held by the listener.

Dental   Pronounced with the constriction of the tongue against the teeth, as in [θ] in **thigh**.

Determiner   The cover term for articles (**a**, **an**, **the**), possessives (**Joe's**, **his**), demonstratives (**this**, **that**), and other words that normally precede attributes in noun phrases.

Directive   A speech act that attempts to get the listener to do something for the speaker.

Discontinuous constituent   A constituent interrupted in surface structure by one or more constituents. See **Constituent**.

Discourse   Any extended stretch of structured language beyond a single sentence.

Distinctive feature   A measurable property used in classifying the speech sounds of a language that make a difference to meaning, such as **Voicing** and **Nasality**.

Ellipsis   The omission of words in surface structure that are otherwise predictable from linguistic or non-linguistic context.

Eloquence   "The prime purpose of eloquence is to keep other people from speaking." (Louis Verneil)

Empty noun   A noun replaced by a whole clause in the formation of a complement, as expressed in this book by **something**.

Epigram   "An epigram is a half-truth so stated as to irritate the person who believes the other half." (Shailer Mathews)

Episodic memory   That part of long-term memory that contains dated facts about episodes. See **Long-term memory**.

Execution of speech   The process of articulating a planned utterance.

Experiencer case   A case role that describes a being affected (the "experiencer") by the psychological state or action named by the verb.

Expressive   A speech act that expresses the speaker's "psychological state" about something.

Extension   The set of entities an expression can refer to. Compare **Intension**.

False start   A correction of one or more words in spontaneous speech, as in **the old / young man**; an **unretraced false start** includes only the corrected word, while a **retraced false start** includes repetition of words prior to the corrected word as well.

Feature detector   A built-in perceptual mechanism postulated to detect single acoustic cues such as Voice Onset Time.

Felicity conditions   The contextual conditions that must be fulfilled before a speech act can be said to have been performed properly. See **Speech act**.

Filled pause   A hesitation in spontaneous speech partly or wholly taken up by a speech sound like **ah**, **er**, **uh**, and so forth. Compare **Silent pause**.

Focal stress   The highest stress in a clause.

Formal complexity   The complexity of the linguistic devices used to express ideas. Compare **Cognitive complexity**.

Formant   A horizontal stripe of acoustic energy, which spectrograms show as horizontal bands, caused by enhancement of the voice by various cavities within the mouth and throat.

Frame and insert   The part of thematic structure that signals the setting or point of departure for a sentence (the frame) and the information that is placed in that setting (the insert). Compare **Given and new information** and **Subject and predicate**.

Fricative   A speech sound pronounced with near closure of part of the mouth, producing a turbulent air flow, as [z] in **zoo**.

Function word   A word, generally unstressed, that expresses a primarily grammatical relationship, for example, prepositions, auxiliary verbs, conjunctions, articles, and pronouns. Compare **Content word**.

Fundamental pitch   The lowest and primary pitch of the voice in speaking.

Given and new information   The part of thematic structure that signals information the speaker believes is identifiable uniquely by the listener (given information) and information the speaker thinks the listener does not yet know (new information). Compare **Subject and predicate** and **Frame and insert**.

Given-new strategy   A strategy by which listeners search memory for the information referred to by the given information of a sentence and then integrate the new information with it. See **Given and new information**.

Glottal   Pronounced with the constriction of the glottis, as in [h] in **hay**.

Glottis   The space between the vocal cords.

Goal case   The case relation that stands for an object or state (a "goal") that results from the action or state named by the verb.

Grammatical juncture   A syntactic break in the surface structure of a sentence at clause or sentence boundaries.

Grammatical relation   The cover term for subject, predicate, direct object, and indirect object—all surface structure relations in a sentence.

Heuristic   A method for discovering the correct solution to a problem through approximations to the correct answer without exploring all possibilities.

Hyponym   The relation of one word to another in which the first is a member of a taxonomy and the second is the name of that taxonomy; for example, **dog** is a hyponym of **animal**.

Ideal delivery   The way a sentence would be spoken under ideal conditions with no speech errors or slips of the tongue.

Idiom   An expression whose interpretation cannot be determined solely from the meanings of its parts; for example, **kick the bucket** meaning "die."

Illocutionary force   The effect speakers intended their utterances to have on their listeners. See **Speech act**.

Immediate constituent   A constituent that is an "immediate" part or division of another constituent. See **Constituent**.

Implicature   An inference speakers intended listeners to draw from their utterances.

Indirect speech act   A speech act expressed by a sentence not primarily designed to convey that type of speech act; for example, a request conveyed by an interrogative sentence. See **Speech act**.

Inflection   An ending to a word stem that expresses grammatical relations; for example, plural **-s**, and past tense **-ed**.

Innate predisposition   An inborn mechanism that leads an organism to acquire certain behaviors but not others.

Instrumental case   The case relation that stands for an inanimate force or object (the "instrument") involved in the action named by the verb.

Intension   The sense of an expression. See **Sense**.

Intonation   The pattern of pitch changes—the melody—that a speaker produces in pronouncing a phrase.

Labiodental   Pronounced with the constriction of the lower lip against the upper front teeth, as in [f] in **fire**.

Language   "The music with which we charm the serpents guarding another's treasure." (Ambrose Bierce)

Lateral   Produced by a deformation of the tongue so that the air stream flows over its sides, as in [l] in **low**.

Lateralization   The specialization of the left or right hemisphere of the brain for different functions. Speech is generally lateralized in the left hemisphere.

Lexicographer   "A writer of dictionaries, a harmless drudge." (Samuel Johnson)

Linguistic relativity   The hypothesis that the language one speaks affects the way one thinks.

Linguistic universal   A feature of language claimed to be common to all possible languages.

Liquid   A cover term for [l] and [r] in English.

Locative case   The case relation that denotes a location or orientation for the action or state named by the verb.

Logic   "The art of thinking and reasoning in strict accordance with the limitations or incapacities of the human misunderstanding." (Ambrose Bierce)

Long-term memory   The relatively permanent part of the memory system. Compare **Short-term memory**.

Main verb   The verb in each clause that denotes the primary action, process, or state being described; it is in contrast to auxiliary (or helping) verbs.

Markedness.   The condition of being morphologically more complex, as in **actress** versus **actor**, or **activate** versus **active**.

Me   "The objectionable case of I. The personal pronoun in English has three cases, the dominative, the objectionable and the oppressive. Each is all three." (Ambrose Bierce)

Mental operation   A hypothetical thought process that "operates" on information in memory, transforming it into other forms.

Mental process   See **Mental operation**.

Mind   "A mysterious form of matter secreted by the brain." (Ambrose Bierce)

Minimal pair   Two words that sound alike in all but one feature; for example, **bin** versus **pin**.

Misderivation   A speech error in which the wrong prefix or suffix is added to a word, as in **swimmed**.

Modal auxiliary   An auxiliary verb that expresses the likelihood, possibility, predictability, or the like, of the event named in the main verb; for example, **can, must, would**, and **may**.

Monitoring task   A task in which people try to understand a sentence while simultaneously listening for a click or specific speech sound.

Morpheme   A minimal unit of speech that is recurrent and meaningful; for example, such word stems as **gentle**, such suffixes as **-ly**, and such prefixes as **un-**.

Nasal   Pronounced with the soft palate lowered so that air goes out through the nose, as in [m] in **may**.

Neutralization   The condition in which a semantic contrast between categories is canceled in certain contexts; for example, **actor** can be neutralized to denote either male or female thespians.

Noun phrase   A constituent of surface structure that expresses the argument of a proposition, such as **the man, what Mary said**, or **that Bill left**.

Objective case   The case relation whose role in the state or action named by a verb depends most closely on the meaning of the verb.

Opposition   The relation between two similar elements of language, such as voiced versus voiceless consonants and present versus past tense.

Oratory   "The art of making deep noises from the chest sound like important messages from the brain." (H. T. Phillips)

Over-extension   The use of a word by children for a category of objects larger than the adult category named by that word, as when a child uses **doggie** for both dogs and horses. Compare **Under-extension**.

Palatal   Pronounced with constriction of the front of the tongue against the hard palate, as in [y] in **ewe**.

Paradigm   A complete set of the conjugational or declensional forms of a word; for example, **jump, jumps, jumping, jumped**.

Parse   Break the surface structure of a sentence into its constituents.

Performative verb   A verb in a sentence that is in the present tense, with **I** as subject and **you** as indirect object, that directly expresses the speech act the speaker is making in uttering the sentence.

Perseveration   A slip of the tongue in which a word or phonetic segment is incorrectly repeated, as in **pull a pantrum**.

Phonetics   The study, analysis, and classification of speech sounds, especially their pronunciation and acoustic properties.

Phonetic segment   A speech sound classifiable by the way it is pronounced; the difference in classification does not necessarily make a difference to meaning. Compare **Phonological segment**.

Phonological segment   A speech sound classifiable by the way it is pronounced; the classification depends on the sound making a difference to meaning. Compare **Phonetic segment**.

Phonology   The study of the system of sound patterns that occur in a language.

Pidgin   A language that arises from casual contact between people having no common speech background, usually characterized by a simplified grammar and a limited and mixed vocabulary.

Pleonasm   "An army of words escorting a corporal of thought." (Ambrose Bierce)

Polysemy   The state of having more than one meaning.

Predicate negative   A negative intended to negate only the predicate of a sentence.

Prefix   A morpheme added to the beginning of a word stem; for example, **pre-**, **un-**, and **dis-**.

Preposition   A word you mustn't end a sentence with.

Prepositional phrase   A constituent of surface structure that begins with a preposition and is completed by a noun phrase.

Procedural semantics   A theory of meaning in which the sense of a word is represented as a procedure, a set of operations for deciding where the word can and cannot apply.

Pronoun   A nominal form that takes the place of a noun phrase; for example, **he**, **she**, **my**, and **one**.

Proposition   A component of the underlying representation of a sentence, a basic unit of meaning; each proposition consists of a propositional function plus one or more fully specified arguments.

Propositional content   The propositions directly expressed by a sentence.

Propositional function   A function, often expressed by a single noun, verb, or adjective, that predicates an action, process, or state that involves one or more participants expressed as the function's arguments, as in **Give(x,y,z)**.

Prototype   The hypothetical member of a category that represents the most typical conceivable member of that category.

Pro-verb   A verb form that stands for a full verb phrase; for example, **do so** and **do it**.

Quantifier   A word that modifies another word and denotes quantity; for example, **two**, **much**, and **several**.

Reading   One interpretation of an expression.

Reality principle   The assumption speakers and listeners make that speakers will normally talk about real or possible states or events.

Recall   A method of testing memory in which people say what they had heard before, often with the prompt of a probe word. Compare **Recognition**.

Recognition   A method for testing memory in which people are given one or more stimuli and are asked to indicate which they had heard before. Compare **Recall**.

Redundancy rule   A rule that expresses how one semantic component necessarily implies another, such as **Human(x)** → **Animate(x)**.

Reference   The set of real world entities or states that an expression may pick out. Compare **Sense**.

Referent   The entity in the real world that an expression is meant to pick out.

Relative clause   A clause introduced by a relative pronoun such as **that, who,** or **which** that expresses a relativized proposition. See **Relativization**.

Relative pronoun   A word such as **who, which,** or **that** that introduces a relative clause, as in **the man that was my uncle**.

Relativization   A way of combining propositions in which the argument in one proposition is restricted or qualified by a second proposition, as in **the man that became my uncle**.

Repeat   An error in spontaneous speech in which one or more words are repeated.

Representative   A speech act that conveys the speaker's belief that some proposition is true.

Research   "When you steal from one author, it's plagiarism; if you steal from many, it's research." (Wilson Mizner)

Response bias   A preference for certain types of responses.

Response latency   The time between some external stimulus and a person's response to it.

Reversal   A slip of the tongue in which two words or two phonetic segments are interchanged, as in **heft lemisphere**.

Sapir-Whorf hypothesis   See **Linguistic relativity**.

Segmentation   The division of the surface structure of a sentence into its constituents and phonetic segments.

Self-contradiction   An expression that contradicts itself by its wording alone; for example, **married bachelor** or **female husband**. Compare **Analytic truth**.

Self-embedded sentence   A sentence with a relative clause inserted between the subject and verb.

Semantic component   A part or aspect of the sense of an expression; for example, **Male(x)** is a semantic component of **man**.

Semantics   The study of meaning.

Semantic space   A geometrical representation of the meanings of a set of related words, each of which is indicated as a point in space.

Semi-vowel   A speech sound produced in the same way as a vowel but unable to form a syllable on its own, as [w] in **way**.

Sense   The aspect of meaning that characterizes the concept denoted by an expression.

Shadowing   The repeating of speech word for word immediately after it is heard through earphones.

Short-term memory   The part of the memory system with limited capacity that maintains information for only a brief period of time with the aid of rehearsal.

Silent pause   A hesitation in speech not filled with any speech sounds. Compare **Filled pause**.

Spectrogram   A graph that plots the intensity of the voice at various frequencies over time.

Speech act   The uttering of a sentence in order to express an intention the speaker wants a listener to recognize.

Stem   A morpheme to which suffixes, prefixes, and inflections are added; for example, **gentle** and **man** in **ungentlemanly**.

Stop consonant   A speech sound pronounced with complete closure of some part of the mouth, as in [p] in **pod**.

Strategy   A method by which people go about solving problems.

Stress   The accent or emphasis on a syllable, generally produced by higher pitch and greater intensity of the voice; stress is classified as primary, secondary, tertiary, or weak, depending on its relative intensity.

Subject and predicate   The part of thematic structure that signals what the speaker is talking about (the subject) and what the speaker is saying about the subject (the predicate). Compare **Given and new information** and **Frame and insert**.

Suffix   A morpheme added to the end of a word stem; for example, **-ly**, **-ing**, and **-s**.

Surface structure   The linear arrangement of sounds, words, phrases, and clauses that specify what is actually spoken.

Syllable   Roughly, a unit of speech with a vowel or diphthong that is surrounded by one or more consonants and is produced and perceived as a unit.

Syllogism   "A logical formula consisting of a major and a minor assumption and an inconsequent." (Ambrose Bierce)

Syntax   The way words, suffixes, and prefixes combine to form sentences.

Taxonomy   A set of words, such as **male** and **female**, that fully cover a conceptual domain—here, sex—but do not overlap with each other.

Tense   The inflectional system that signals whether the process, event, or state denoted by a verb happened in the present or past.

Thematic structure   Those aspects of sentence structure that relate a sentence to the context in which it is uttered.

Ultimate constituent   A constituent that cannot be divided into any further constituents. See **Constituent**.

Under-extension   The use of a word by children for a category smaller than the adult category named by that word, as when a child restricts the use of **doggie** to one specific dog. Compare **Over-extension**.

Underlying representation   The propositions and their interrelations as expressed by a sentence.

Velar   Pronounced with the constriction of the back of the tongue against the velum, or soft palate, as in [g] in **glug**.

Verbal unit   The part of a simple sentence that remains once the noun phrases have been removed; it generally expresses the predication of a proposition.

Verb phrase   A surface constituent that generally contains the verb, its auxiliaries, and its associated noun phrases, except for the subject.

Voice Onset Time   The time between the release of the lips and the onset of voicing (the vibration of the vocal cords), used in distinguishing voiced from voiceless consonants.

Voicing   A feature of consonants produced by vibration of the vocal cords, as in **zip** versus **sip**.

Vowel   A speech sound produced by an unobstructed passage of air through the mouth, which is not constricted enough to cause audible friction.

White noise   A continuous emission of random sounds from all frequencies, like the sound from an unused television channel.

WH- question   A sentence, generally introduced by a WH- word such as **who, which, where, what**, or **how**, that requests the piece of information signaled by the WH- word.

Working memory   A part of memory, probably identical to short-term memory, that holds both the verbatim content of a just spoken sentence and the interpretation constructed for it.

Yes/no question   A sentence, generally signaled by inversion of the subject and auxiliary verb, that requests the confirmation or denial of a proposition, as in **Is this the end of the glossary?**

BIBLIOGRAPHY

Aaronson, D. Stimulus factors and listening strategies in auditory memory: A theoretical analysis. *Cognitive Psychology*, 1974, *6*, 108–132. (a)

Aaronson, D. Stimulus factors and listening strategies in auditory memory: An experimental demonstration. *Cognitive Psychology*, 1974, *6*, 133–158. (b)

Abercrombie, D. *Elements of general phonetics*. Edinburgh: Edinburgh University Press, 1966.

Adams, K. L., & Conklin, N. F. Toward a theory of natural classification. In *Papers from the Ninth Regional Meeting, Chicago Linguistic Society*, 1973, pp. 1–10.

Adams, V. *An introduction to modern English word-formation*. London: Longman, 1973.

Akmajian, A., & Heny, F. *An introduction to the principles of transformational syntax*. Cambridge, Mass.: M.I.T. Press, 1975.

Allport, G. W., & Postman, L. *The psychology of rumor*. New York: Holt, Rinehart and Winston, 1947.

Alston, W. P. *Philosophy of language*. Englewood Cliffs, N.J.: Prentice-Hall, 1964.

Amidon, A., & Carey, P. Why five-year-olds cannot understand *before* and *after*. *Journal of Verbal Learning and Verbal Behavior*, 1972, *11*, 417–423.

Ammon, P. R. The perception of grammatical relations in sentences: A methodological exploration. *Journal of Verbal Learning and Verbal Behavior*, 1968, *7*, 869–875.

Andersen, E. S. Cups and glasses: Learning that boundaries are vague. *Journal of Child Language*, 1975, *2*, 79–103.

Anderson, B. F. *The psychology experiment: An introduction to the scientific method* (2nd ed.). Belmont, Calif.: Brooks/Cole, 1971.

Anderson, J. R. Verbatim and propositional representation of sentences in immediate and long-term memory. *Journal of Verbal Learning and Verbal Behavior*, 1974, *13*, 149–162.

Anderson, J. R., & Bower, G. H. *Human associative memory*. Washington, D.C.: V. H. Winston & Sons, 1973.

Anderson, J. R., & Hastie, R. Individuation and reference in memory: Proper names and definite descriptions. *Cognitive Psychology*, 1974, *6*, 495–514.

Anglin, J. M. Les premiers termes de référence de l'enfant. In S. Ehrlich & E. Tulving (Eds.), *La mémoire sémantique*. Paris: Bulletin de Psychologie, Spécial Annuel, 1976, pp. 232–241.

Anisfeld, M., & Klenbort, I. On the functions of structural paraphrase: The view from the passive voice. *Psychological Bulletin*, 1973, *79*, 117–126.

Antinucci, F., & Miller, R. How children talk about what happened. *Journal of Child Language*, 1976, *3*, 167–189.

Antinucci, F., & Parisi, D. Early language acquisition: A model and some data. In C. A. Ferguson & D. I. Slobin (Eds.), *Studies of child language development*. New York: Holt, Rinehart and Winston, 1973, pp. 607–619.

Antinucci, F., & Volterra, V. Lo sviluppo della negazione nel linguaggio infantile: Un studio pragmatico. *Lingua e Stile*, 1975, *10*, 231–260.

Atkinson-King, K. Children's acquisition of phonological stress contrasts. *UCLA Working Papers in Phonetics*, 1973, *25*.

Austin, J. L. *How to do things with words*. Oxford: Oxford University Press, 1962.

Baars, B. J., Motley, M. T., & MacKay, D. G. Output editing for lexical status in artificially elicited slips of the tongue. *Journal of Verbal Learning and Verbal Behavior*, 1975, *14*, 382–391.

Bach, E. *Syntactic theory*. New York: Holt, Rinehart and Winston, 1974.

Bar-Adon, A., & Leopold, W. F. (Eds.). *Child language: A book of readings*. Englewood Cliffs, N.J.: Prentice-Hall, 1971.

Barclay, J. R. The role of comprehension in remembering sentences. *Cognitive Psychology*, 1973, *4*, 229–254.

Bartlett, E. J. Sizing things up: The acquisition of the meaning of dimensional adjectives. *Journal of Child Language*, 1976, *3*, 205–219.

Bartlett, F. C. *Remembering: An experimental and social study*. Cambridge: Cambridge University Press, 1932.

Bartsch, R., & Vennemann, T. *Semantic structures: A study in the relation between semantics and syntax*. Frankfurt, W. Germany: Athenäum Verlag, 1972.

Bates, E. The acquisition of conditionals by Italian children. In *Papers from the Tenth Regional Meeting, Chicago Linguistic Society*, 1974, pp. 27–36.

Bates, E. *Language and context: The acquisition of pragmatics*. New York: Academic Press, 1976.

Bates, E., Benigni, L., Bretherton, I., Camaioni, L., & Volterra, V. From gesture to the first word: On cognitive and social prerequisites. In M. Lewis & L. Rosenblum (Eds.), *Conversation, interaction, and the development of language*. New York: John Wiley & Sons, 1976.

Bates, E., Camaioni, L., & Volterra, V. The acquisition of performatives prior to speech. *Merrill-Palmer Quarterly*, 1975, *21*, 205–226.

Bellugi, U. Simplification in children's language. In R. Huxley & E. Ingram (Eds.), *Methods and models in language acquisition*. New York: Academic Press, 1971, pp. 95–117.

Bendix, E. H. *Componential analysis of general vocabulary: The semantic structure of a set of verbs in English, Hindi and Japanese*. The Hague: Mouton Publishers, 1966.

Berko, J. The child's learning of English morphology. *Word*, 1958, *14*, 150–177.

Berko Gleason, J. Code switching in children's language. In T. E. Moore (Ed.), *Cognitive development and the acquisition of language*. New York: Academic Press, 1973, pp. 159–167.

Berko, J., & Brown, R. Psycholinguistic research methods. In P. H. Mussen (Ed.), *Handbook of research methods in child development*. New York: John Wiley & Sons, 1960, pp. 517–557.

Berko Gleason, J., and Weintraub, S. The acquisition of routines in child language. *Language in Society*, 1976, *5*, 129–136.

Berlin, B. *Tzeltal numeral classifiers: A study in ethnographic semantics*. The Hague: Mouton Publishers, 1968.

Berlin, B. Speculations on the growth of ethnobotanical nomenclature. *Language in Society*, 1972, *1*, 51–86.

Berlin, B., Breedlove, D. E., & Raven, P. H. Covert categories and folk taxonomies. *American Anthropologist*, 1968, *70*, 290–299.

Berlin, B., Breedlove, D. E., & Raven, P. H. General principles of classification and nomenclature in folk biology. *American Anthropologist*, 1973, *75*, 214–242.

Berlin, B., & Kay, P. *Basic color terms: Their universality and evolution*. Berkeley and Los Angeles: University of California Press, 1969.

Bever, T. G. The cognitive basis for linguistic structures. In J. R. Hayes (Ed.), *Cognition and the development of language*. New York: John Wiley & Sons, 1970, pp. 279–352.

Bever, T. G. Serial position and response biases do not account for the effect of syntactic structure on the location of brief noises during sentences. *Journal of Psycholinguistic Research*, 1973, *2*, 287–288.

Bever, T. G., & Chiarello, R. J. Cerebral dominance in musicians and nonmusicians. *Science*, 1974, *185*, 137–139.

Bever, T. G., Garrett, M. F., & Hurtig, R. The interaction of perceptual processes and ambiguous sentences. *Memory and Cognition*, 1973, *1*, 277–286.

Bever, T. G., & Langendoen, D. T. A dynamic model of the evolution of language. *Linguistic Inquiry*, 1971, *2*, 433–463.

Bierwisch, M. Some semantic universals of German adjectivals. *Foundations of Language*, 1967, *3*, 1–36.

Bierwisch, M. Semantics. In J. Lyons (Ed.), *New horizons in linguistics*. Baltimore: Penguin Books, 1970, pp. 161–185.

Bloom, L. M. *Language development: Form and function in emerging grammars*. Cambridge, Mass.: M.I.T. Press, 1970.

Bloom, L. M. *One word at a time: The use of single word utterances before syntax*. The Hague: Mouton Publishers, 1973.

Bloom, L. M. (Ed.). *Selected readings in language development*. New York: John Wiley & Sons, 1977.

Bloom, L. M., Hood, L., & Lightbown, P. Imitation in language development: If, when and why. *Cognitive Psychology*, 1974, *6*, 380–420.

Bloom, L. M., & Lahey, M. *Language development and language disorders*. New York: John Wiley & Sons, 1977.

Bloom, L. M., Lightbown, P., & Hood, L. Structure and variation in child language. *Monographs of the Society for Research in Child Development*, 1975, *40* (Serial No. 160).

Blumenthal, A. L. Observations with self-embedded sentences. *Psychonomic Science*, 1966, *6*, 453–454.

Blumenthal, A. L. Prompted recall of sentences. *Journal of Verbal Learning and Verbal Behavior*, 1967, *6*, 203–206.

Blumenthal, A. L., & Boakes, R. Prompted recall of sentences: A further study. *Journal of Verbal Learning and Verbal Behavior*, 1967, *6*, 674–676.

Boas, F. Introduction to *Handbook of American Indian languages* (Smithsonian Institution, Bureau of American Ethnology, Bulletin 40). Washington, D.C.: U.S. Government Printing Office, 1911, pp. 1–83.

Bobrow, S. A., & Bower, G. H. Comprehension and recall of sentences. *Journal of Experimental Psychology*, 1969, *80*, 455–461.

Bolinger, D. L. Verbal evocation. *Lingua*, 1961, *10*, 113–127.

Bolinger, D. L. The atomization of meaning. *Language*, 1965, *41*, 555–573.

Bolinger, D. L. *Aspects of language* (2nd ed.). New York: Harcourt Brace Jovanovich, 1975.

Boomer, D. S. Hesitation and grammatical encoding. *Language and Speech*, 1965, *8*, 148–158.

Boomer, D. S., & Laver, J. D. M. Slips of the tongue. *British Journal of Disorders of Communication*, 1968, *3*, 1–12.

Boring, E. G. *Sensation and perception in the history of experimental psychology*. New York: Appleton-Century-Crofts, 1942.

Boucher, J., & Osgood, C. E. The Pollyanna hypothesis. *Journal of Verbal Learning and Verbal Behavior*, 1969, *8*, 1–8.

Bower, G. H. Experiments on story understanding and recall. *Quarterly Journal of Experimental Psychology*, 1976, *28*, 511–534.

Bower, T. G. R. *Development in infancy*. San Francisco: W. H. Freeman, 1974.

Bowerman, M. *Early syntactic development: A cross-linguistic study with special reference to Finnish*. Cambridge: Cambridge University Press, 1973. (a)

Bowerman, M. Structural relationships in children's utterances: Syntactic or semantic? In T. E. Moore (Ed.), *Cognitive development and the acquisition of language*. New York: Academic Press, 1973, pp. 197–213. (b)

Bowerman, M. Discussion summary—Development of concepts underlying language. In R. L. Schiefelbusch & L. L. Lloyd (Eds.), *Language perspectives—Acquisition, retardation and intervention*. Baltimore: University Park Press, 1974, pp. 191–209. (a)

Bowerman, M. Learning the structure of causative verbs: A study in the relationship of cognitive, semantic and syntactic development. *Papers & Reports on Child Language Development* (Stanford University), 1974, *8*, 142–178. (b)

Bowerman, M. The acquisition of word meaning: An investigation of some current conflicts. Paper presented at the Third International Child Language Symposium, London, September 1975.

Bowerman, M. Semantic factors in the acquisition of rules for word use and sentence construction. In D. M. Morehead & A. E. Morehead (Eds.), *Normal and deficient child language*. Baltimore: University Park Press, 1976, pp. 99–179.

Boyd, J., & Thorne, J. P. The semantics of modal verbs. *Journal of Linguistics*, 1969, *5*, 57–74.

Braine, M. D. S. The ontogeny of English phrase structure: The first phase. *Language*, 1963, *39*, 1–13.

Braine, M. D. S. The acquisition of language in infant and child. In C. Reed (Ed.), *The learning of language*. New York: Appleton-Century-Crofts, 1971, pp. 7–95.

Braine, M. D. S. Children's first word combinations. *Monographs of the Society for Research in Child Development*, 1976, *41* (Serial No. 164).

Bransford, J. D., Barclay, J. R., & Franks, J. J. Sentence memory: A constructive versus interpretive approach. *Cognitive Psychology*, 1972, *3*, 193–209.

Bransford, J. D., & Johnson, M. K. Considerations of some problems of comprehension. In W. G. Chase (Ed.), *Visual information processing*. New York: Academic Press, 1973, pp. 383–438.

Bransford, J. D., & McCarrell, N. S. A sketch of a cognitive approach to comprehension: Some thoughts about understanding what it means to comprehend. In W. B. Weimer & D. S. Palermo (Eds.), *Cognition and the symbolic processes*. Hillsdale, N. J.: Lawrence Erlbaum Associates, 1974, pp. 189–229.

Bregman, A. S., & Strasberg, R. Memory for the syntactic form of sentences. *Journal of Verbal Learning and Verbal Behavior*, 1968, *7*, 396–403.

Bresson, F. Remarks on genetic psycholinguistics: The acquisition of the article system in French. In *Problèmes actuels en psycholinguistique / Current problems in psycholinguistics*. Paris: Editions de C.N.R.S., 1974, pp. 67–72.

Bresson, F., Bouvier, N., Dannequin, C., Depreux, J., Hardy, M., & Platone, F. Quelques aspects du système des déterminants chez les enfants de l'école maternelle: Utilisation des articles défini et indéfini. *Centre de Recherche de l'Education Spécialisée et de l'Adaptation Scolaire* (Institut Pédagogique National, Paris), 1970, *2*, 3–40.

Brewer, W. F., & Stone, J. B. Acquisition of spatial antonym pairs. *Journal of Experimental Child Psychology*, 1975, *19*, 299–307.

Broen, P. The verbal environment of the language-learning child. *Monographs of the American Speech and Hearing Association*, 1972, *17*.

Bronckart, J. P., & Sinclair, H. Time, tense, and aspect. *Cognition*, 1973, *2*, 107–130.

Brooks, L. Spatial and verbal components of the act of recall. *Canadian Journal of Psychology*, 1968, *22*, 349–368.

Bross, I. D. J. Languages in cancer research. In G. P. Murphy, D. Pressman, & E. A. Mirand (Eds.), *Perspectives in cancer research and treatment*. New York: Alan R. Liss, 1973, pp. 213–221.

Brown, H. D. Children's comprehension of relativized English sentences. *Child Development*, 1971, *42*, 1923–1936.

Brown, R. How shall a thing be called? *Psychological Review*, 1958, *65*, 14–21.

Brown R. The development of *Wh* questions in child speech. *Journal of Verbal Learning and Verbal Behavior*, 1968, *7*, 277–290.

Brown, R. The first sentences of child and chimpanzee. In R. Brown, *Psycholinguistics*. New York: The Free Press, 1970, pp. 208–231.

Brown, R. *A first language: The early stages*. Cambridge, Mass.: Harvard University Press, 1973.

Brown, R., Cazden, C. B., & Bellugi, U. The child's grammar from I to III. In J. P. Hill (Ed.), *Minnesota symposium on child psychology* (Vol. 2). Minneapolis: University of Minnesota Press, 1969, pp. 28–73.

Brown, R., & Ford, M. Address in American English. *Journal of Abnormal and Social Psychology*, 1961, *62*, 375–385.

Brown, R., & Fraser, C. The acquisition of syntax. In U. Bellugi & R. Brown (Eds.), The acquisition of language. *Monographs of the Society for Research in Child Development*, 1964, *29* (Serial No. 92), 43–79.

Brown, R., & Gilman, A. The pronouns of power and solidarity. In T. A. Sebeok (Ed.), *Style in language*. Cambridge, Mass.: M.I.T. Press, 1960, pp. 253–276.

Brown, R., & Hanlon, C. Derivational complexity and order of acquisition in child speech. In J. R. Hayes (Ed.), *Cognition and the development of language*. New York: John Wiley & Sons, 1970, pp. 11–53.

Brown, R., & Lenneberg, E. H. A study in language and cognition. *Journal of Abnormal and Social Psychology*, 1954, *49*, 454–462.

Brown, R., & McNeill, D. The "tip of the tongue" phenomenon. *Journal of Verbal Learning and Verbal Behavior*, 1966, *5*, 325–337.

Bruner, J. S. Organization of early skilled action. *Child Development*, 1973, *44*, 1–11.

Bruner, J. S. From communication to language—A psychological perspective. *Cognition*. 1974/5, *3*, 225–287.

Bruner, J. S. The ontogenesis of speech acts. *Journal of Child Language*, 1975, *2*, 1–19.

Burling, R. *Man's many voices: Language in its cultural context*. New York: Holt, Rinehart and Winston, 1970.

Butterworth, B. Hesitation and semantic planning in speech. *Journal of Psycholinguistic Research*, 1975, *4*, 75–87.

Cairns, H. S., Cairns, C. E., & Williams, F. Some theoretical considerations of articulation substitution phenomena. *Language and Speech*, 1974, *17*, 160–173.

Campbell, B. The roots of language. In J. Morton (Ed.), *Biological and social factors in psycholinguistics*. London: Logos Press, 1971, pp. 10–23.

Caramazza, A., & Grober, E. Polysemy and the structure of the subjective lexicon. In C. Rameh (Ed.), *Georgetown University round table on languages and linguistics 1976*. Washington, D.C.: Georgetown University Press, 1976, pp. 181–206.

Carey, S. "Less" never means more. Paper presented at the NATO Conference on The Psychology of Language, University of Stirling, Scotland, June 1976.

Carmichael, L., Hogan, H. P., & Walter, A. A. An experimental study of the effect of language on the reproduction of visually perceived forms. *Journal of Experimental Psychology*, 1932, *15*, 73–86.

Carpenter, P. A. On the comprehension, storage, and retrieval of comparative sentences. *Journal of Verbal Learning and Verbal Behavior*, 1974, *13*, 401–411.

Carpenter, P. A., & Just, M. A. Semantic control of eye movements during picture scanning in a sentence-picture verification task. *Perception and Psychophysics*, 1972, *12*, 61–64.

Carpenter, P. A., & Just, M. A. Sentence comprehension: A psycholinguistic processing model of verification. *Psychological Review*, 1975, *82*, 45–73.

Carpenter, P. A., & Just, M. A. Integrative processes in comprehension. In D. LaBerge & S. J. Samuels (Eds.), *Basic processes in reading: Perception and comprehension*. Hillsdale, N. J.: Lawrence Erlbaum Associates, 1977.

Carroll, J. B. (Review of *The measurement of meaning* by Osgood et al.) *Language*, 1959, *35*, 58–77.

Carroll, J. B., & White, M. N. Word frequency and age of acquisition as determiners of picture-naming latency. *Quarterly Journal of Experimental Psychology*, 1973, *25*, 85–95. (a)

Carroll, J. B., & White, M. N. Age of acquisition norms for 220 picturable nouns. *Journal of Verbal Learning and Verbal Behavior*, 1973, *12*, 563–576. (b)

Carter, A. L. *The development of communication in the sensorimotor period: A case study*. Unpublished doctoral dissertation, University of California at Berkeley, 1974.

Carter, A. L. Development of the presyntactic communication system: A case study. *Journal of Child Language*, 1975, *2*, 233–250.

Cattell, N. R. *The new English grammar*. Cambridge, Mass.: M.I.T. Press, 1969.

Cazden, C. B. The acquisition of noun and verb inflections. *Child Development*, 1968, *39*, 433–448.

Cazden, C. B. *Child language and education*. New York: Holt, Rinehart and Winston, 1972.

Cazden, C. B. Play with language and metalinguistic awareness: One dimension of language experience. *Urban Review*, 1974, *7*, 23–39.

Chafe, W. L. *Meaning and the structure of language*. Chicago: University of Chicago Press, 1970.

Chafe, W. L. Discourse structure and human knowledge. In J. B. Carroll & R. O. Freedle (Eds.), *Language comprehension and the acquisition of knowledge*. Washington, D.C.: V. H. Winston & Sons, 1972, pp. 41–69.

Chafe, W. L. Language and consciousness. *Language*, 1974, *50*, 111–133.

Chafe, W. L. Givenness, contrastiveness, definiteness, subjects, topics, and point of view. In C. N. Li (Ed.), *Subject and topic*. New York: Academic Press, 1976, pp. 25–55.

Chambers, J. C., & Tavuchis, N. Kids and kin: Children's understanding of American kin terms. *Journal of Child Language*, 1976, *3*, 63–80.

Chase, W. G., & Clark, H. H. Semantics in the perception of verticality. *British Journal of Psychology*, 1971, *62*, 311–326.

Chase, W. G., & Clark, H. H. Mental operations in the comparison of sentences and pictures. In L. W. Gregg (Ed.), *Cognition in learning and memory*. New York: John Wiley & Sons, 1972, pp. 205–232.

Cherry, E. C. Some experiments on the recognition of speech, with one and with two ears. *Journal of the Acoustical Society of America*, 1953, *25*, 975–979.

Chomsky, C. *The acquisition of syntax in children from 5 to 10*. Cambridge, Mass.: M.I.T. Press, 1969.

Chomsky, N. *Syntactic structures*. The Hague: Mouton Publishers, 1957.

Chomsky, N. *Aspects of the theory of syntax*. Cambridge, Mass.: M.I.T. Press, 1965.

Chomsky, N. *Cartesian linguistics*. New York: Harper & Row, 1966.

Chomsky, N. *Language and mind*. New York: Harcourt Brace Jovanovich, 1968.

Chomsky, N. Remarks on nominalization. In R. A. Jacobs & P. S. Rosenbaum (Eds.), *Readings in English transformational grammar*. Boston: Ginn, 1970, pp. 184–221.

Chomsky, N. *Reflections on language*. New York: Pantheon Books, 1975.

Chomsky, N., & Halle, M. *The sound pattern of English*. New York: Harper & Row, 1968.

Chukovsky, K. *From two to five*. Berkeley and Los Angeles: University of California Press, 1963.

Clark, E. V. How young children describe events in time. In G. B. Flores d'Arcais & W. J. M. Levelt (Eds.), *Advances in psycholinguistics*. Amsterdam: North-Holland Publishing, 1970, pp. 275–284. (a)

Clark, E. V. Locationals: A study of "existential," "locative," and "possessive" sentences. *Working Papers in Language Universals* (Stanford University), 1970, *3*, L1–L36. (b)

Clark, E. V. On the acquisition of the meaning of *before* and *after*. *Journal of Verbal Learning and Verbal Behavior*, 1971, *10*, 266–275.

Clark, E. V. On the child's acquisition of antonyms in two semantic fields. *Journal of Verbal Learning and Verbal Behavior*, 1972, *11*, 750–758.

Clark, E. V. What's in a word? On the child's acquisition of semantics in his first language. In T. E. Moore (Ed.), *Cognitive development and the acquisition of language*. New York: Academic Press, 1973, pp. 65–110. (a)

Clark, E. V. Non-linguistic strategies and the acquisition of word meanings. *Cognition*, 1973, *2*, 161–182. (b)

Clark, E. V. How chidren describe time and order. In C. A. Ferguson & D. I. Slobin (Eds.), *Studies of child language development*. New York: Holt, Rinehart and Winston, 1973, pp. 585–606. (c)

Clark, E. V. Some aspects of the conceptual basis for first language acquisition. In R. L. Schiefelbusch & L. L. Lloyd (Eds.), *Language perspectives—Acquisition, retardation and intervention*. Baltimore: University Park Press, 1974, pp. 105–128.

Clark, E. V. Knowledge, context, and strategy in the acquisition of meaning. In D. P. Dato (Ed.), *Georgetown University round table on languages and linguistics 1975*. Washington, D.C.: Georgetown University Press, 1975, pp. 77–98.

Clark, E. V. Universals categories: On the semantics of classifiers and children's early word meanings. In A. Juilland (Ed.), *Linguistic studies offered to Joseph Greenberg on the occasion of his sixtieth birthday* (Vol. 1). Saratoga, Calif.: Anma Libri, 1976.

Clark, E. V. Strategies and the mapping problem in first language acquisition. In J. Macnamara (Ed.), *Language learning and thought*. New York: Academic Press, 1977. (a)

Clark, E. V. From gesture to word: On the natural history of deixis in language acquisition. In J. S. Bruner and A. Garton (Eds.), *Human growth and development: Wolfson College lectures 1976*. Oxford: Oxford University Press, 1977. (b)

Clark, E. V., & Garnica, O. K. Is he coming or going? On the acquisition of deictic verbs. *Journal of Verbal Learning and Verbal Behavior*, 1974, *13*, 559–572.

Clark, E. V., & Sengul, C. J. Deictic contrasts in language acquisition. Paper presented at the Annual Meeting of the Linguistic Society of America, New York, December 1974.

Clark, H. H. Some structural properties of simple active and passive sentences. *Journal of Verbal Learning and Verbal Behavior*, 1965, *4*, 365–370.

Clark, H. H. The prediction of recall patterns in simple active sentences. *Journal of Verbal Learning and Verbal Behavior*, 1966, *5*, 99–106.

Clark, H. H. Linguistic processes in deductive reasoning. *Psychological Review*, 1969, *76*, 387–404.

Clark, H. H. The primitive nature of children's relational concepts. In J. R. Hayes (Ed.), *Cognition and the development of language*. New York: John Wiley & Sons, 1970, pp. 269–278. (a)

Clark, H. H. Word associations and linguistic theory. In J. Lyons (Ed.), *New horizons in linguistics*. Baltimore: Penguin Books, 1970, pp. 271–286. (b)

Clark, H. H. Comprehending comparatives. In G. B. Flores d'Arcais & W. J. M. Levelt (Eds.), *Advances in psycholinguistics*. Amsterdam: North-Holland Publishing, 1970, pp. 294–306. (c)

Clark, H. H. Difficulties people have in answering the question "Where is it?" *Journal of Verbal Learning and Verbal Behavior*, 1972, *11*, 265–277.

Clark, H. H. Space, time, semantics, and the child. In T. E. Moore (Ed.), *Cognitive development and the acquisition of language*. New York: Academic Press, 1973, pp. 28–64. (a)

Clark, H. H. The language-as-fixed-effect fallacy: A critique of language statistics in psychological research. *Journal of Verbal Learning and Verbal Behavior*, 1973, *12*, 335–359. (b)

Clark, H. H. Semantics and comprehension. In T. A. Sebeok (Ed.), *Current trends in linguistics, Volume 12: Linguistics and adjacent arts and sciences*. The Hague: Mouton Publishers, 1974, pp. 1291–1498. (a)

Clark, H. H. The chronometric study of meaning components. In *Problèmes actuels en psycholinguistique / Current problems in psycholinguistics*. Paris: Editions du C.N.R.S., 1974, pp. 489–505. (b)

Clark, H. H. Inferences in comprehension. In D. LaBerge and S. J. Samuels (Eds.), *Basic processes in reading: Perception and comprehension*. Hillsdale, N.J.: Lawrence Erlbaum Associates, 1977.

Clark, H. H., & Begun, J. S. The use of syntax in understanding sentences. *British Journal of Psychology*, 1968, *59*, 219–229.

Clark, H. H., & Brownell, H. H. Judging up and down. *Journal of Experimental Psychology: Human Perception and Performance*, 1975, *1*, 339–352.

Clark, H. H., & Card, S. K. The role of semantics in remembering comparative sentences. *Journal of Experimental Psychology*, 1969, *82*, 545–552.

Clark, H. H., Carpenter, P. A., & Just, M. A. On the meeting of semantics and perception. In W. G. Chase (Ed.), *Visual information processing*. New York: Academic Press, 1973, pp. 311–381.

Clark, H. H., & Chase, W. G. On the process of comparing sentences against pictures. *Cognitive Psychology*, 1972, *3*, 472–517.

Clark, H. H., & Chase, W. G. Perceptual coding strategies in the formation and verification of descriptions. *Memory and Cognition*, 1974, *2*, 101–111.

Clark, H. H., & Clark, E. V. Semantic distinctions and memory for complex sentences. *Quarterly Journal of Experimental Psychology*, 1968, *20*, 129–138.

Clark, H. H., & Haviland, S. E. Psychological processes as linguistic explanation. In D. Cohen (Ed.), *Explaining linguistic phenomena*. Washington, D.C.: Hemisphere Publishing, 1974, pp. 91–124.

Clark, H. H., & Haviland, S. E. Comprehension and the given-new contract. In R. O. Freedle (Ed.), *Discourse production and comprehension*. Norwood, N.J.: Ablex Publishing, 1977, pp. 1–40.

Clark, H. H., & Lucy, P. Understanding what is meant from what is said: A study in conversationally conveyed requests. *Journal of Verbal Learning and Verbal Behavior*, 1975, *14*, 56–72.

Cliff, N. Adverbs as multipliers. *Psychological Review*, 1959, *66*, 27–44.

Clifton, C. The implications of grammar for word associations. In K. Salzinger & S. Salzinger (Eds.), *Research in verbal behavior and some neurological implications*. New York: Academic Press, 1967, pp. 221–237.

Clifton, C., & Odom, P. Similarity relations among certain English sentence constructions. *Psychological Monographs*, 1966, *80* (No. 5).

Cohen, A., & Nooteboom, S. G. (Eds.) *Structure and process in speech perception*. Heidelberg, W. Germany: Springer-Verlag, 1975.

Colby, B. N. A partial grammar of Eskimo folktales. *American Anthropologist*, 1973, *75*, 645–662.

Cole, P. Indefiniteness and anaphoricity. *Language*, 1974, *50*, 665–674.

Cole, P., & Morgan, J. L. (Eds.) *Syntax and semantics, Vol. 3: Speech acts*. New York: Seminar Press, 1975.

Cole, R. A. Listening for mispronunciations: A measure of what we hear during speech. *Perception and Psychophysics*, 1973, *14*, 153–156.

Cole, R. A., & Scott, B. Toward a theory of speech perception. *Psychological Review*, 1974, *81*, 348–374.

Collins, A. M., & Quillian, M. R. Retrieval time from semantic memory. *Journal of Verbal Learning and Verbal Behavior*, 1969, *8*, 240–248.

Collins, A. M., & Quillian, M. R. Experiments on semantic memory and language comprehension. In L. W. Gregg (Ed.), *Cognition in learning and memory*. New York: John Wiley & Sons, 1972, pp. 117–147. (a)

Collins, A. M., & Quillian, M. R. How to make a language user. In E. Tulving & W. Donaldson (Eds.), *Organization of memory*. New York: Academic Press, 1972, pp. 309–351. (b)

Collins, A. M., & Loftus, E. F. A spreading-activation theory of semantic processing. *Psychological Review*, 1975, *82*, 407–428.

Collis, G. M. The integration of gaze and vocal behaviour in the mother-infant dyad. Paper presented at the Third International Child Language Symposium, London, September 1975.

Collis, G. M. Visual co-orientation and maternal speech. In H. R. Schaffer (Ed.), *Studies in mother-infant interaction*. London: Academic Press, 1977.

Conrad, C. Cognitive economy in semantic memory. *Journal of Experimental Psychology*, 1972, *92*, 149–154.

Cooper, L. A., & Shepard, R. N. Chronometric studies of the rotation of mental images. In W. G. Chase (Ed.), *Visual information processing*. New York: Academic Press, 1973, pp. 75–176.

Cooper, W. E. Selective adaptation to speech. In F. Restle, R. M. Shiffrin, N. J. Castellan, H. Lindman, & D. B. Pisoni (Eds.), *Cognitive theory* (Vol. 1). Hillsdale, N.J.: Lawrence Erlbaum Associates, 1975, pp. 23–54.

Cooper, W. E., & Blumstein, S. E. A "labial" feature analyzer in speech perception. *Perception and Psychophysics*, 1974, *15*, 591–600.

Cornish, E. R., & Wason, P. C. The recall of affirmative and negative sentences in an incidental learning task. *Quarterly Journal of Experimental Psychology*, 1970, *22*, 109–114.

Corteen, R. S., & Wood, B. Autonomic responses to shock-associated words in an unattended channel. *Journal of Experimental Psychology*, 1972, *94*, 308–313.

Craik, F. I. M., & Lockhart, R. S. Levels of processing: A framework for memory research. *Journal of Verbal Learning and Verbal Behavior*, 1972, *11*, 671–684.

Cromer, R. F. Children are nice to understand: Surface structure clues for the recovery of a deep structure. *British Journal of Psychology*, 1970, *61*, 397–408.

Crowder, R. G. The sound of vowels and consonants in immediate memory. *Journal of Verbal Learning and Verbal Behavior*, 1971, *10*, 587–596. (a)

Crowder, R. G. Waiting for the stimulus suffix: Decay, delay, rhythm and readout in immediate memory. *Quarterly Journal of Experimental Psychology*, 1971, *23*, 324–340. (b)

Crowder, R. G. Visual and auditory memory. In J. F. Kavanagh & I. G. Mattingly (Eds.), *Language by ear and by eye*. Cambridge, Mass.: M.I.T. Press, 1972, pp. 251–275.

Crowder, R. G., & Morton, J. Precategorical acoustic storage (PAS). *Perception and Psychophysics*, 1969, *5*, 365–373.

Cruttenden, A. An experiment involving comprehension of intonation in children from 7 to 10. *Journal of Child Language*, 1974, *1*, 221–231.

Crystal, D. Non-segmental phonology in language acquisition: A review of the issues. *Lingua*, 1973, *32*, 1–45.

Cutting, J. E. Aspects of phonological fusion. *Journal of Experimental Psychology: Human Perception and Performance*, 1975, *1*, 105–120.

Cutting, J. E. Auditory and linguistic processes in speech perception: Inferences from six fusions in dichotic listening. *Psychological Review*, 1976, *83*, 114–140.

Cutting, J. E., & Eimas, P. D. Phonetic feature analyzers and the processing of speech in infants. In J. F. Kavanagh & J. E. Cutting (Eds.), *The role of speech in language*. Cambridge, Mass.: M.I.T. Press, 1975, pp. 127–148.

Danks, J. H., & Glucksberg, S. Psychological scaling of adjective orders. *Journal of Verbal Learning and Verbal Behavior*, 1971, *10*, 63–67.

Danziger, K. The child's understanding of kinship terms: A study in the development of relational concepts. *Journal of Genetic Psychology*, 1957, *91*, 213–232.

Day, R. S. *Fusion in dichotic listening*. Unpublished doctoral dissertation, Stanford University, 1968.

Day, R. S. Temporal order judgments in speech: Are individuals language-bound or stimulus-bound? *Haskins Laboratories Status Report*, 1970, SR-21/22, 71–87.

DeCamp, D. Introduction: The study of pidgin and creole languages. In D. H. Hymes (Ed.), *Pidginization and creolization of languages*. Cambridge: Cambridge University Press, 1971, pp. 13–39.

Decroly, O., & Degand, J. Observations relatives au développement de la notion du temps chez une petite fille. *Archives de Psychologie*, 1913, *13*, 113–161.

Denes, P. B., & Pinson, E. N. *The speech chain: The physics and biology of spoken language*. New York: Anchor Books, 1973.

Denny, J. P. The "extendedness" variable in classifier semantics: Universal features and cultural variation. *International Journal of the Sociology of Language*, *3*, 1976.

DeSoto, C., London, M., & Handel, S. Social reasoning and spatial paralogic. *Journal of Personality and Social Psychology*, 1965, *2*, 513–521.

de Valois, R. L., & Jacobs, G. H. Primate color vision. *Science*, 1968, *162*, 533–540.

de Villiers, J. G., & de Villiers, P. A. Early judgments of semantic and syntactic acceptability by children. *Journal of Psycholinguistic Research*, 1972, *1*, 299–310.

de Villiers, J. G., & de Villiers, P. A. A cross-sectional study of the development of grammatical morphemes in child speech. *Journal of Psycholinguistic Research*, 1973, *2*, 267–278.

de Villiers, J. G., & Tager Flusberg, H. B. Some facts one simply cannot deny. *Journal of Child Language*, 1975, *2*, 279–286.

de Villiers, P. A. Imagery and theme in recall of connected discourse. *Journal of Experimental Psychology*, 1974, *103*, 263–268.

Dewart, M. H. *A psychological investigation of sentence comprehension by children*. Unpublished doctoral dissertation, University of London, 1975.

Dodd, B. Children's understanding of their own phonological forms. *Quarterly Journal of Experimental Psychology*, 1975, *27*, 165–172.

Donaldson, M., & Balfour, G. Less is more: A study of language comprehension in children. *British Journal of Psychology*, 1968, *59*, 461–472.

Donaldson, M., & Wales, R. J. On the acquisition of some relational terms. In J. R. Hayes (Ed.), *Cognition and the development of language*. New York: John Wiley & Sons, 1970, pp. 235–268.

Dore, J. *The development of speech acts*. Unpublished doctoral dissertation, City University of New York, 1973.

Dougherty, J. W. D. On the significance of a sequence in the acquisition of colour vocabulary. Paper presented at the NATO Conference on The Psychology of Language, University of Stirling, Scotland, June 1976.

Dreckendorff, H. O. Towards a theory of N-tuple binds. *Sociological Inquiry*, 1977, *47*.

DuBois, J. W. Syntax in mid-sentence. In *Berkeley studies in syntax and semantics* (Vol. 1). Berkeley Calif.: Institute of Human Learning and Department of Linguistics, University of California, 1974, pp. III-1–III-25.

Duncker, K. On problem-solving. *Psychological Monographs*, 1945, *58*, (5, Whole No. 270).

Duveen, G. *The child's conception of kinship: An exploratory study*. Unpublished master of science thesis, University of Strathclyde, Scotland, 1974.

Edwards, D. Sensory motor intelligence and semantic relations in early child grammar. *Cognition*, 1973, *2*, 395–434.

Edwards, M. L. Perception and production in child phonology: The testing of four hypotheses. *Journal of Child Language*, 1974, *1*, 205–219.

Eimas, P. D. Speech perception in early infancy. In L. B. Cohen & P. Salapatek (Eds.), *Infant perception: From sensation to cognition* (Vol. 2). New York: Academic Press, 1975, pp. 193–231.

Eimas, P. D., & Corbit, J. Selective adaptation of linguistic feature detectors. *Cognitive Psychology*, 1973, *4*, 99–109.

Eimas, P. D., Siqueland, E. R., Jusczyk, P., & Vigorito, J. Speech perception in infants. *Science*, 1971, *171*, 303–306.

Elkonin, D. B. Development of speech. In A. V. Zaporozhets & D. B. Elkonin (Eds.), *The psychology of pre-school children*. Cambridge, Mass.: M.I.T. Press, 1974, pp. 111–185.

Ellis, H. C. Transfer of stimulus predifferentiation to shape recognition and identification learning: Role of properties of verbal labels. *Journal of Experimental Psychology*, 1968, *78*, 401–409.

Ervin-Tripp, S. Imitation and structural change in children's language. In E. H. Lenneberg (Ed.), *New directions in the study of language*. Cambridge, Mass.: M.I.T. Press, 1964, pp. 163–189.

Ervin-Tripp, S. Discourse agreement: How children answer questions. In J. R. Hayes (Ed.), *Cognition and the development of language*. New York: John Wiley & Sons, 1970, pp. 79–107.

Ervin-Tripp, S. The comprehension and production of requests by children. *Papers and Reports on Child Language Development* (Stanford University), 1974, *8*, 188–196.

Ervin-Tripp, S. Wait for me, roller-skate! In C. Mitchell-Kernan & S. Ervin-Tripp (Eds.), *Child discourse*. New York: Academic Press, 1977.

Escalona, S. K. Basic modes of social interaction: Their emergence and patterning during the first two years of life. *Merrill-Palmer Quarterly*, 1973, *19*, 205–232.

Fant, G. Auditory patterns of speech. In W. Walthen-Dunn (Ed.), *Models for the perception of speech and visual form*. Cambridge, Mass.: M.I.T. Press, 1967, pp. 111–125.

Fant, G. (Ed.). *Proceedings of the 1974 speech communication seminar*. New York: John Wiley & Sons, 1975.

Farnham-Diggory, S., & Bermon, M. Verbal compensation, cognitive synthesis and conservation. *Merrill-Palmer Quarterly*, 1968, *14*, 215–227.

Farwell, C. B. Aspects of early verb semantics—Pre-causative development. *Papers and Reports on Child Language Development* (Stanford University), 1975, *10*, 48–58.

Farwell, C. B. *The early expression of motion and location: Syntactic, semantic and lexical aspects*. Unpublished doctoral dissertation, Stanford University, 1977.

Ferguson, C. A. Baby talk in six languages. *American Anthropologist*, 1964, *66* (6, Pt. 2), 103–114.

Ferguson, C. A. Absence of copula and the notion of simplicity: A study of normal speech, baby talk, foreigner talk and pidgins. In D. Hymes (Ed.), *Pidginization and creolization of languages*. Cambridge: Cambridge University Press, 1971, pp. 141–150.

Ferguson, C. A., & Farwell, C. B. Words and sounds in early language acquisition. *Language*, 1975, *51*, 419–439.

Ferguson, C. A., & Garnica, O. K. Theories of phonological development. In E. H. Lenneberg and E. Lenneberg (Eds.), *Foundations of language development: A multidisciplinary approach* (Vol. 1). New York: Academic Press, 1975, pp. 153–180.

Ferguson, C. A., Peizer, D. B., & Weeks, T. E. Model-and-replica phonological grammar of a child's first words. *Lingua*, 1973, *31*, 35–65.

Ferguson, C. A., & Slobin, D. I. (Eds.), *Studies of child language development*. New York: Holt, Rinehart and Winston, 1973.

Ferreiro, E. *Les relations temporelles dans le langage de l'enfant*. Geneva: Libraire Droz, 1971.

Ferreiro, E., & Sinclair, H. Temporal relations iu language. *International Journal of Psychology*, 1971, *6*, 39–47.

Fillenbaum, S. Memory for gist: Some relevant variables. *Language and Speech*, 1966, *9*, 217–227.

Fillenbaum, S. Recall for answers to "conducive" questions. *Language and Speech*, 1968, *11*, 46–53.

Fillenbaum, S. On coping with ordered and unordered conjunctive sentences. *Journal of Experimental Psychology*, 1971, *87*, 93–98.

Fillenbaum, S. *Syntactic factors in memory*. The Hague: Mouton Publishers, 1973.

Fillenbaum, S. Pragmatic normalization: Further results for some conjunctive and disjunctive sentences. *Journal of Experimental Psychology*, 1974, *102*, 574–578. (a)

Fillenbaum, S. Or: Some uses. *Journal of Experimental Psychology*, 1974, *103*, 913–921. (b)

Fillenbaum, S., & Rapoport, A. *Structures in the subjective lexicon*. New York: Academic Press, 1971.

Fillenbaum, S., & Rapoport, A. Verbs of judging, judged: A case study. *Journal of Verbal Learning and Verbal Behavior*, 1974, *13*, 54–62.

Fillmore, C. J. The case for case. In E. Bach & R. T. Harms (Eds.), *Universals of linguistic theory*. New York: Holt, Rinehart and Winston, 1968, pp. 1–90.

Fillmore, C. J. (Review of *Componential analysis of general vocabulary* by E. H. Bendix.) *General Linguistics*, 1969, *9*, 41–65.

Fillmore, C. J. Some problems for case grammar. In R. J. O'Brien (Ed.), Linguistics: Developments of the sixties—Viewpoints for the seventies. *Monograph series on languages and linguistics*, 1971, *24*, 35–56. (a)

Fillmore, C. J. Verbs of judging: An exercise in semantic description. In C. J. Fillmore & D. T. Langendoen (Eds.), *Studies in linguistic semantics*. New York: Holt, Rinehart and Winston, 1971, pp. 273–296. (b)

Flavell, J. H. *The developmental psychology of Jean Piaget*. Princeton, N.J.: Van Nostrand Reinhold, 1963.

Flesch, R. *Say what you mean*. New York: Harper & Row, 1972.

Flores d'Arcais, G. B. Linguistic structure and focus of comparison in processing of comparative sentences. In G. B. Flores d'Arcais & W. J. M. Levelt (Eds.), *Advances in psycholinguistics*. Amsterdam: North-Holland Publishing, 1970, pp. 307–321.

Flores d'Arcais, G. B. Is there memory for sentences? *Acta Psychologica*, 1974, *38*, 33–58. (a)

Flores d'Arcais, G. B. Semantic and perceptual factors in the processing of comparative sentences. *Giornale Italiano di Psicologia*, 1974, *1*, 267–303. (b)

Flores d'Arcais, G. B., & Levelt, W. J. M. (Eds.). *Advances in psycholinguistics*. Amsterdam: North-Holland Publishing, 1970.

Fodor, J. A. Recognition of syntactic structures. In D. L. Horton & J. J. Jenkins (Eds.), *The perception of language.* Columbus, Ohio: Charles E. Merrill, 1971, pp. 120–139.

Fodor, J. A. *The language of thought.* New York: Thomas Y. Crowell, 1975.

Fodor, J. A., & Bever, T. G. The psychological reality of linguistic segments. *Journal of Verbal Learning and Verbal Behavior,* 1965, *4,* 414–420.

Fodor, J. A., Bever, T. G., & Garrett, M. F. *The psychology of language: An introduction to psycholinguistics and generative grammar.* New York: McGraw-Hill, 1974.

Fodor, J. A., & Garrett, M. F. Some syntactic determinants of sentential complexity. *Perception and Psychophysics,* 1967, *2,* 289–296.

Fodor, J. A., Garrett, M. F., & Bever, T. G. Some syntactic determinants of sentential complexity, II: Verb structure. *Perception and Psychophysics,* 1968, *3,* 453–461.

Fodor, J. A., Garrett, M. F., & Brill, S. L. Pi ka pu: The perception of speech sounds by prelinguistic infants. *Perception and Psychophysics,* 1975, *18,* 74–78.

Forchheimer, P. *The category of person in language.* Berlin, W. Germany: Walter de Gruyter, 1953.

Forster, K. I., & Olbrei, I. Semantic heuristics and syntactic analysis. *Cognition,* 1973, *2,* 319–347.

Foss, D. J. Decision processes during sentence comprehension: Effects of lexical item difficulty and position upon decision times. *Journal of Verbal Learning and Verbal Behavior,* 1969, *8,* 457–462.

Foss, D. J. Some effects of ambiguity upon sentence comprehension. *Journal of Verbal Learning and Verbal Behavior,* 1970, *9,* 699–706.

Foss, D. J., & Jenkins, C. M. Some effects of context on the comprehension of ambiguous sentences. *Journal of Verbal Learning and Verbal Behavior,* 1973, *12,* 577–589.

Foss, D. J., & Lynch, R. H., Jr. Decision processes during sentence comprehension: Effects of surface structure on decision times. *Perception and Psychophysics,* 1969, *5,* 145–148.

Foulke, E., & Sticht, T. Review of research on the intelligibility and comprehension of accelerated speech. *Psychological Bulletin,* 1969, *72,* 50–62.

Fourcin, A. J. Language development in the absence of expressive speech. In E. H. Lenneberg & E. Lenneberg (Eds.), *Foundations of language development* (Vol. 2). New York: Academic Press, 1975, pp. 263–268. (a)

Fourcin, A. J. Speech perception in the absence of speech productive ability. In N. O'Connor (Ed.), *Language, cognitive deficits, and retardation.* London: Butterworth, 1975, pp. 33–43. (b)

Fraser, C., Bellugi, U., & Brown, R. Control of grammar in imitation, comprehension, and production. *Journal of Verbal Learning and Verbal Behavior,* 1963, *2,* 121–135.

Frederiksen, C. H. Effects of context-induced processing operations on semantic information acquired from discourse. *Cognitive Psychology,* 1975, *7,* 139–166.

Freedle, R. O., & Craun, M. Observations with self-embedded sentences using written aids. *Perception and Psychophysics,* 1970, *7,* 247–249.

Freud, S. Slips of the tongue. In S. Freud [*Psychopathology of everyday life*] (J. Strachey, Ed. and trans.) London: Ernest Benn, 1966, pp. 53–105.

Friedrich, P. Shape in grammar. *Language,* 1970, *46,* 379–407.

Fromkin, V. The non-anomalous nature of anomalous utterances. *Language,* 1971, *47,* 27–52.

Fromkin, V. (Ed.). *Speech errors as linguistic evidence.* The Hague: Mouton Publishers, 1973.

Fromkin, V., & Rodman, R. *An introduction to language.* New York: Holt, Rinehart and Winston, 1974.

Gardner, B. T., & Gardner, R. A. Two-way communication with an infant chimpanzee. In A. M. Schrier & F. Stollnitz (Eds.), *Behavior of nonhuman primates* (Vol. 4). New York: Academic Press, 1971, pp. 117–184.

Gardner, B. T., & Gardner, R. A. Evidence for sentence constituents in the early utterances of child and chimpanzee. *Journal of Experimental Psychology: General,* 1975, *104,* 244–267.

Gardner, H. *The shattered mind.* New York: Alfred A. Knopf, 1975.

Gardner, R. A., & Gardner, B. T. Teaching sign language to a chimpanzee. *Science,* 1969, *165,* 664–672.

Garman, M. A., Griffiths, P. D., & Wales, R. J. Murut (Lun Buwang) prepositions and noun particles in children's speech. *Sarawak Museum Journal,* 1970, *18,* 353–376.

Garnes, S., & Bond, Z. S. Slips of the ear: Errors in perception of casual speech. In *Papers from the Eleventh Regional Meeting, Chicago Linguistic Society,* 1975, pp. 214–225.

Garnica, O. K. The development of phonemic speech perception. In T. E. Moore (Ed.), *Cognitive development and the acquisition of language.* New York: Academic Press, 1973, pp. 215–222.

Garnica, O. K. *Some characteristics of prosodic input to young children.* Unpublished doctoral dissertation, Stanford University, 1975. (a)

Garnica, O. K. Nonverbal concomitants of language input to children: Clues to meaning. Paper presented at the Third International Child Language Symposium, London, September 1975. (b)

Garrett, M. F. Does ambiguity complicate the perception of sentences? In G. B. Flores d'Arcais & W. J. M. Levelt (Eds.), *Advances in psycholinguistics.* Amsterdam: North-Holland Publishing, 1970, pp. 48–60.

Garrett, M. F. The analysis of sentence production. In G. H. Bower (Ed.), *The psychology of learning and motivation* (Vol. 9). New York: Academic Press, 1975, pp. 133–177.

Garrett, M. F., Bever, T. G., & Fodor, J. A. The active use of grammar in speech perception. *Perception and Psychophysics,* 1966, *1,* 30–32.

Garrod, S., & Trabasso, T. A dual-memory information processing interpretation of sentence comprehension. *Journal of Verbal Learning and Verbal Behavior*, 1973, *12*, 155–167.

Garvey, C. Requests and responses in children's speech. *Journal of Child Language*, 1975, *2*, 41–63.

Gelman, R., & Shatz, M. Appropriate speech adjustments: The operation of conversational constraints on talk to two-year-olds. In M. Lewis & L. Rosenblum (Eds.), *Conversation, interaction, and the development of language*. New York: John Wiley & Sons, 1976.

Gentner, D. Evidence for the psychological reality of semantic components: The verbs of possession. In D. A. Norman, D. E. Rumelhart, & the LNR Research Group, *Explorations in cognition*. San Francisco: W. H. Freeman, 1975, pp. 211–246.

Geschwind, N. The development of the brain and the evolution of language. *Monograph Series on Languages and Linguistics*, 1964, *17*, 155–169.

Geschwind, N. The organization of language and the brain. *Science*, 1970, *170*, 940–944.

Ghent, L. Recognition by children of realistic figures in various orientations. *Canadian Journal of Psychology*, 1960, *14*, 249–256.

Ghent, L. Form and its orientation: The child's-eye view. *American Journal of Psychology*, 1961, *74*, 177–190.

Ginsburg, H., & Opper, S. *Piaget's theory of intellectual development: An introduction*. Englewood Cliffs, N.J.: Prentice-Hall, 1969.

Givón, T. Notes on the semantic structure of English adjectives. *Language*, 1970, *46*, 816–837.

Givón, T. Negation in language: Pragmatics, function, and ontology. *Pragmatics Microfiche*, 1975, *1.2*, A2.

Glanzer, M., & Clark, W. H. The verbal loop hypothesis: Conventional figures. *American Journal of Psychology*, 1964, *77*, 621–626.

Glass, A. L., Holyoak, K. J., & O'Dell, C. Production frequency and the verification of quantified statements. *Journal of Verbal Learning and Verbal Behavior*, 1974, *13*, 237–254.

Gleitman, L. R., & Gleitman, H. *Phrase and paraphrase: Some innovative uses of language*. New York: W. W. Norton, 1970.

Glucksberg, S., Trabasso, T., & Wald, J. Linguistic structures and mental operations. *Cognitive Psychology*, 1973, *5*, 338–370.

Glucksberg, S., & Weisberg, R. W. Verbal behavior and problem solving: Some effects of labelling in a functional fixedness problem. *Journal of Experimental Psychology*, 1966, *71*, 659–664.

Goldman-Eisler, F. *Psycholinguistics: Experiments in spontaneous speech*. New York: Academic Press, 1968.

Goodenough, W. Yankee kinship terminology: A problem in componential analysis. In E. Hammell (Ed.), Formal semantic analysis. *American Anthropologist*, 1965, *67*, (5, Pt. 2), 259–287.

Gordon, D., & Lakoff, G. Conversational postulates. In *Papers from the Seventh Regional Meeting, Chicago Linguistic Society*, 1971, pp. 63–84.

Gough, P. B. Grammatical transformations and speed of understanding. *Journal of Verbal Learning and Verbal Behavior*, 1965, *4*, 107–111.

Gough, P. B. The verification of sentences: The effects of delay of evidence and sentence length. *Journal of Verbal Learning and Verbal Behavior*, 1966, *5*, 492–496.

Graf, R., & Torrey, J. W. Perception of phrase structure in written language. *American Psychological Association Convention Proceedings*, 1966, pp. 83–84.

Green, D. W. *A psychological investigation into the memory and comprehension of sentences*. Unpublished doctoral dissertation, University of London, 1973.

Green, D. W. The immediate processing of sentences. *Quarterly Journal of Experimental Psychology*, 1977, *29*, 1–12.

Greenbaum, S. *Studies in English adverbial usage*. London: Longman, 1969.

Greenbaum, S. *Verb-intensifier collocations in English: An experimental approach*. The Hague: Mouton Publishers, 1970.

Greenbaum, S., & Quirk, R. *Elicitation experiments in English: Linguistic studies in use and attitude*. London: Longman, 1970.

Greenberg, J. H. Some universals of grammar with particular reference to the order of meaningful elements. In J. H. Greenberg (Ed.), *Universals of language*. Cambridge, Mass.: M.I.T. Press, 1963, pp. 58–90.

Greenberg, J. H. *Language universals*. The Hague: Mouton Publishers, 1966.

Greenberg, J. H. Numeral classifiers and substantival number: Problems in the genesis of a linguistic type. *Working Papers in Language Universals* (Stanford University), 1972, *9*, 1–39.

Greenberg, J. H. Dynamic aspects of word order in the numeral classifier. In C. N. Li (Ed.), *Word order and word order change*. Austin: University of Texas Press, 1975, pp. 27–45.

Greenberg, J. H., & Jenkins, J. J. Studies in the psychological correlates of the sound system of American English. *Word*, 1964, *20*, 157–177.

Greene, J. M. Syntactic form and semantic function. *Quarterly Journal of Experimental Psychology*, 1970, *22*, 14–27. (a)

Greene, J. M. The semantic function of negatives and passives. *British Journal of Psychology*, 1970, *61*, 17–22. (b)

Greenfield, P. M., & Smith, J. H. *The structure of communication in early language development*. New York: Academic Press, 1976.

Grégoire, A. *L'apprentissage du langage* (2 vols.). Paris: Libraire Droz, 1937, 1949.

Grice, H. P. William James Lectures, Harvard University, 1967. Published in part as "Logic and conversation." In P. Cole & J. L. Morgan

(Eds.), *Syntax and semantics, Vol. 3: Speech acts.* New York: Seminar Press, 1975, pp. 41–58.

Grieve, R. Definiteness in discourse. *Language and Speech,* 1973, *16,* 365–372.

Grimm, H. *Strukturanalytische Untersuchung der Kindersprache.* Bern: Verlag Huber, 1973.

Grimm, H. Analysis of short-term dialogues in 5–7 year olds: Encoding of intentions and modifications of speech acts as a function of negative feedback. Paper presented at the Third International Child Language Symposium, London, September 1975. (a)

Grimm, H. On the child's acquisition of semantic structure underlying the wordfield of prepositions. *Language and Speech,* 1975, *18,* 97–119. (b)

Grimm, H., & Schöler, H. Erlauben—Befehlen—Lassen: Wie gut verstehen kleine Kinder kausativierende Beziehungen? In H. Grimm, H. Schöler, & M. Wintermantel, *Zur Entwicklung sprachlicher Strukturformen bei Kindern.* Weinheim, W. Germany: Julius Beltz Verlag, 1975, pp. 100–120.

Gruber, J. S. *Studies in lexical relations.* Unpublished doctoral dissertation, M.I.T., 1965.

Gruber, J. S. Correlations between the syntactic constructions of the child and the adult. In C. A. Ferguson & D. I. Slobin (Eds.), *Studies of child language development.* New York: Holt, Rinehart and Winston, 1973, pp. 440–445.

Hakes, D. T. Does verb structure affect sentence comprehension? *Perception and Psychophysics,* 1971, *10,* 229–232.

Hakes, D. T. Effects of reducing complement constructions on sentence comprehension. *Journal of Verbal Learning and Verbal Behavior,* 1972, *11,* 278–286.

Hakes, D. T., & Foss, D. J. Decision processes during sentence comprehension: Effects of surface structure reconsidered. *Perception and Psychophysics,* 1970, *8,* 413–416.

Halle, M., & Stevens, K. Speech recognition: A model and a program for research. *IRE Transactions of the Professional Group on Information Theory,* 1962, *IT-8,* 155–159.

Halliday, M. A. K. Notes on transitivity and theme in English: II. *Journal of Linguistics,* 1967, *3,* 199–244.

Halliday, M. A. K. Language structure and language function. In J. Lyons (Ed.), *New horizons in linguistics.* Baltimore: Penguin Books, 1970, pp. 140–165.

Halliday, M. A. K. *Explorations in the functions of language.* London: Edward Arnold, 1973.

Halliday, M. A. K. *Learning how to mean: Explorations in the development of language.* London: Edward Arnold, 1975.

Hampton, J. A. *An experimental study of concepts in language.* Unpublished doctoral dissertation, University of London, 1976.

Harman, G. (Ed.). *On Noam Chomsky: Critical essays.* New York: Anchor Books, 1974.

Harner, L. *Yesterday* and *tomorrow:* Development of early understanding of the terms.

Developmental Psychology, 1975, *11,* 864–865.

Harris, L. J. Spatial direction and grammatical form of instructions affect the solution of spatial problems. *Memory and Cognition,* 1975, *3,* 329–334.

Haviland, S. E., & Clark, E. V. "This man's father is my father's son": A study of the acquisition of English kin terms. *Journal of Child Language,* 1974, *1,* 23–47.

Haviland, S. E., & Clark, H. H. What's new? Acquiring new information as a process in comprehension. *Journal of Verbal Learning and Verbal Behavior,* 1974, *13,* 512–521.

Hayes, J. R. (Ed.). *Cognition and the development of language.* New York: John Wiley & Sons, 1970.

Hayes, K., & Hayes, C. Imitation in a home-raised chimpanzee. *Journal of Comparative and Physiological Psychology,* 1952, *45,* 450–459.

Heider, E. R. "Focal" color areas and the development of color names. *Developmental Psychology,* 1971, *4,* 447–455.

Heider, E. R. Universals in color naming and memory. *Journal of Experimental Psychology,* 1972, *93,* 10–20.

Heider, E. R., & Olivier, D. The structure of the color space in naming and memory for two languages. *Cognitive Psychology,* 1972, *3,* 337–354.

Hempel, C. G. Problems and changes in the empiricist criterion of meaning. *Revue Internationale de Philosophie,* 1950, *11,* 42–63.

Henderson, A., Goldman-Eisler, F., & Skarbek, A. Temporal patterns of cognitive activity and breath control in speech. *Language and Speech,* 1965, *8,* 236–242.

Henderson, A., Goldman-Eisler, F., & Skarbek, A. Sequential temporal patterns in spontaneous speech. *Language and Speech,* 1966, *9,* 207–216.

Hering, E. *Outlines of a theory of the light sense (1920).* Cambridge, Mass.: Harvard University Press, 1964.

Heringer, J. Some grammatical correlates of felicity conditions and presuppositions. *Working Papers in Linguistics* (The Ohio State University), 1972, *11,* 1–110.

Herman, D. T., Lawless, R. H., & Marshall, R. W. Variables in the effect of language on the reproduction of visually perceived forms. *Perceptual and Motor Skills,* 1957, *7, Monograph Supplement 2,* 171–186.

Herriot, P. The comprehension of active and passive sentences as a function of pragmatic expectations. *Journal of Verbal Learning and Verbal Behavior,* 1969, *8,* 166–169.

Herriot, P. *Attributes of memory.* London: Methuen, 1974.

Hjelmslev, L. *Prolegomena to a theory of language.* Bloomington: Indiana University Press, 1953.

Hockett, C. F. The origin of speech. *Scientific American,* 1960, *203,* 89–96.

Hockett, C. F. Where the tongue slips, there slip I. In *To honor Roman Jakobson: Essays on the occasion of his 70th birthday.* The Hague: Mouton Publishers, 1967, pp. 910–935.

Holyoak, K. J. Analogue information and mental size comparison. *Cognitive Psychology,* 1977, *9,* 31–51.

Holzman, M. The verbal environment provided by mothers for their young children. *Merrill-Palmer Quarterly,* 1974, *20,* 31–42.

Hoosain, R. The processing of negation. *Journal of Verbal Learning and Verbal Behavior,* 1973, *12,* 618–626.

Hornby, P. A. Surface structure and topic-comment distinction: A developmental study. *Child Development,* 1971, *42,* 1975–1988.

Hornby, P. A. The psychological subject and predicate. *Cognitive Psychology,* 1972, *3,* 632–642.

Hornby, P. A. Surface structure and presupposition. *Journal of Verbal Learning and Verbal Behavior,* 1974, *13,* 530–538.

Hornby, P. A., & Hass, W. A. Use of contrastive stress by preschool children. *Journal of Speech and Hearing Research,* 1970, *3,* 395–399.

Hornby, P. A., Hass, W. A., & Feldman, C. A. A developmental analysis of the "psychological" subject and predicate of the sentence. *Language and Speech,* 1970, *13,* 182–193.

Howard, J. H., Jr. The attentional demands of negation in a memory scanning task. *Memory and Cognition,* 1975, *3,* 319–324.

Howe, E. S. Probabilistic adverbial qualifications of adjectives. *Journal of Verbal Learning and Verbal Behavior,* 1962, *1,* 225–241.

Huggins, A. On the perception of temporal phenomena in speech. *Journal of the Acoustical Society of America,* 1972, *51,* 1279–1290.

Hupet, M., & Le Bouedec, B. Definiteness and voice in the interpretation of active and passive sentences. *Quarterly Journal of Experimental Psychology,* 1975, *27,* 323–330.

Huttenlocher, J. The origins of language comprehension. In R. L. Solso (Ed.), *Theories in cognitive psychology.* Potomac, Md.: Lawrence Erlbaum Associates, 1974, pp. 331–368.

Huttenlocher, J., Eisenberg, K., & Strauss, S. Comprehension: Relation between perceived actor and logical subject. *Journal of Verbal Learning and Verbal Behavior,* 1968, *7,* 300–304.

Huttenlocher, J., & Higgins, E. T. Adjectives, comparatives, and syllogisms. *Psychological Review,* 1971, *78,* 487–504.

Huttenlocher, J., & Strauss, S. Comprehension and a statement's relations to the situation it describes. *Journal of Verbal Learning and Verbal Behavior,* 1968, *7,* 527–530.

Huttenlocher, J., & Weiner, S. L. Comprehension of instructions in varying contexts. *Cognitive Psychology,* 1971, *2,* 369–385.

Hyman, L. M. *Phonology: Theory and analysis.* New York: Holt, Rinehart and Winston, 1975.

Ingram, D. Transitivity in child language. *Language,* 1971, *47,* 888–910. (a)

Ingram, D. Typology and universals of personal pronouns. *Working Papers in Language Universals* (Stanford University), 1971, *5,* P1–P35. (b)

Ingram, D. Fronting in child phonology. *Journal of Child Language,* 1974, *1,* 233–241.

Ingram, D. Surface contrasts in children's speech. *Journal of Child Language,* 1975, *2,* 287–292.

Ingram, D. *Phonological disability in children.* (Studies in language disability and remediation, 2). London: Edward Arnold, 1976.

Irmscher, W. F. *The Holt guide to English.* New York: Holt, Rinehart and Winston, 1972.

Irwin, O. C. Infant speech: Consonantal position. *Journal of Speech and Hearing Disorders,* 1951, *16,* 159–161.

Isard, S. What would you have done if . . . ? *Theoretical Linguistics,* 1975, *1,* 233–255.

Jackendoff, R. S. *Semantic interpretation in generative grammar.* Cambridge, Mass.: M.I.T. Press, 1972.

Jaffe, J., Beskin, S., & Gerstman, L. J. Random generation of apparent speech rhythms. *Language and Speech,* 1972, *15,* 68–71.

Jakobson, R. Why "mama" and "papa"? In B. Kaplan & S. Wapner (Eds.), *Perspectives in psychological theory.* New York: John Wiley & Sons, 1960, pp. 124–134.

Jakobson, R. *Child language, aphasia and phonological universals.* The Hague: Mouton Publishers, 1968.

Jakobson, R., & Halle, M. *Fundamentals of language.* The Hague: Mouton Publishers, 1956.

James, D. Some aspects of the syntax and semantics of interjections. In *Papers from the Eighth Regional Meeting, Chicago Linguistic Society,* 1972, pp. 162–172.

James, D. Another look at, say, some grammatical constraints on, oh, interjections and hesitations. In *Papers from the Ninth Regional Meeting, Chicago Linguistic Society,* 1973, pp. 242–251. (a)

James, D. A study in the relationship of oh, ah, say, and well to numerous grammatical phenomena. Paper presented at the Annual Meeting of the Linguistic Society of America, San Diego, December 1973. (b)

Jameson, D., & Hurvich, L. M. Some quantitative aspects of an opponent-colors theory. I. Chromatic responses and spectral saturation. *Journal of the Optical Society of America,* 1955, *45,* 546–552.

Jarvella, R. J. Effects of syntax on running memory span for connected discourse. *Psychonomic Science,* 1970, *19,* 235–236.

Jarvella, R. J. Syntactic processing of connected speech. *Journal of Verbal Learning and Verbal Behavior,* 1971, *10,* 409–416.

Jarvella, R. J., & Collas, J. G. Memory for the intentions of sentences. *Memory and Cognition,* 1974, *2,* 185–188.

Johnson, H. L. The meaning of *before* and *after* for preschool children. *Journal of Experimental Child Psychology,* 1975, *19,* 88–99.

Johnson, H. M. *Children in the nursery school.* New York: Agathon Press, 1972.

Johnson, M. K., Bransford, J. D., & Solomon, S. Memory for tacit implications of sentences. *Journal of Experimental Psychology*, 1973, *98*, 203–205.

Johnson, N. F. The psychological reality of phrase structure rules. *Journal of Verbal Learning and Verbal Behavior*, 1965, *4*, 469–475.

Johnson, N. F. The influence of associations between elements of structured verbal responses. *Journal of Verbal Learning and Verbal Behavior*, 1966, *5*, 369–374. (a)

Johnson, N. F. On the relationship between sentence and structure and the latency in generating the sentence. *Journal of Verbal Learning and Verbal Behavior*, 1966, *5*, 375–380. (b)

Johnson, N. F. Sequential verbal behavior. In T. R. Dixon & D. L. Horton (Eds.), *Verbal behavior and general behavior theory.* Englewood Cliffs, N.J.: Prentice-Hall, 1968, pp. 421–450.

Johnson, S. C. Hierarchical clustering schemes. *Psychometrika*, 1967, *32*, 241–254.

Johnson-Laird, P. N. The choice of the passive voice in a communication task. *British Journal of Psychology*, 1968, *59*, 7–15. (a)

Johnson-Laird, P. N. The interpretation of the passive voice. *Quarterly Journal of Experimental Psychology*, 1968, *20*, 69–73. (b)

Johnson-Laird, P. N. Psycholinguistics without linguistics. In N. S. Sutherland (Ed.), *Tutorial essays in psychology* (Vol. 2). Hillsdale, N.J.: Lawrence Erlbaum Associates, 1977.

Just, M. A., & Carpenter, P. A. Comparative studies of comprehension: An investigation of Chinese, Norwegian, and English. *Memory and Cognition*, 1975, *3*, 465–473.

Just, M. A., & Carpenter, P. A. Eye fixations and cognitive processes. *Cognitive Psychology*, 1976, *8*, 441–480. (a)

Just, M. A., & Carpenter, P. A. The relation between comprehending and remembering some complex sentences. *Memory and Cognition*, 1976, *4*, 318–322. (b)

Just, M. A., & Carpenter, P. A. (Eds.). *Cognitive processes in comprehension.* Hillsdale, N.J.: Lawrence Erlbaum Associates, 1977.

Just, M. A., & Clark, H. H. Drawing inferences from the presuppositions and implications of affirmative and negative sentences. *Journal of Verbal Learning and Verbal Behavior*, 1973, *12*, 21–31.

Kaplan, E. L. *The role of intonation in the acquisition of language.* Unpublished doctoral dissertation, Cornell University, 1969.

Kaplan, E. L., & Kaplan, G. A. The prelinguistic child. In J. Eliot (Ed.), *Human development and cognitive processes.* New York: Holt, Rinehart and Winston, 1970, pp. 358–381.

Kaplan, R. Augmented transition networks as psychological models of sentence comprehension. *Artificial Intelligence*, 1972, *3*, 77–100.

Kaplan, R. A general syntactic processor. In R. Rustin (Ed.), *Natural language processing.* Englewood Cliffs, N.J.: Prentice-Hall, 1973, pp. 193–241.

Katz, J. J. *Semantic theory.* New York: Harper & Row, 1972.

Katz, J. J., & Fodor, J. A. The structure of a semantic theory. *Language*, 1963, *39*, 170–210.

Kay, P. Synchronic variability and diachronic changes in basic color terms. *Language in Society*, 1975, *4*, 257–270.

Kay, P., & Sankoff, G. A language-universals approach to pidgins and creoles. In D. DeCamp and I. F. Hancock (Eds.), *Pidgins and creoles: Current trends and prospects.* Washington, D.C.: Georgetown University Press, 1974, pp. 61–72.

Keenan, E. L. Towards a universal definition of "subject." In C. N. Li (Ed.), *Subject and topic.* New York: Academic Press, 1976, pp. 303–333.

Keenan, E. O. Again and again: The pragmatics of imitation in child language. Paper presented at the 73rd Annual Meeting of the American Anthropological Association, Mexico City, November 1974.

Keeney, T. J., & Wolfe, J. The acquisition of agreement in English. *Journal of Verbal Learning and Verbal Behavior*, 1972, *11*, 698–705.

Keller-Cohen, D. The expression of time in language acquisition. Paper presented at the Annual Meeting of the Linguistic Society of America, New York, December 1974.

Kellogg, R. *Analyzing children's art.* Palo Alto, Calif.: Mayfield Publishing, 1970.

Kempen, G. Syntactic constructions as retrieval plans. *British Journal of Psychology*, 1976, *67*, 149–160.

Kempson, R. M. *Presupposition and the delimitation of semantics.* Cambridge: Cambridge University Press, 1975.

Kimball, J. P. Seven principles of surface structure parsing in natural language. *Cognition*, 1973, *2*, 15–47.

Kimura, D. The asymmetry of the human brain. *Scientific American*, 1973, *228*, 70–78.

Kinsbourne, M. The cerebral basis of lateral asymmetry in attention. *Acta Psychologica*, 1970, *33*, 193–201.

Kinsbourne, M., & Smith, W. L. (Eds.). *Hemispheric disconnection and cerebral function.* Springfield, Ill.: Charles C. Thomas, 1974.

Kintsch, W. Notes on the structure of semantic memory. In E. Tulving & W. Donaldson (Eds.), *Organization of memory.* New York: Academic Press, 1972, pp. 247–308.

Kintsch, W. *The representation of meaning in memory.* Hillsdale, N.J.: Lawrence Erlbaum Associates, 1974.

Kintsch, W. Memory for prose. In C. N. Cofer (Ed.), *The structure of human memory.* San Francisco: W. H. Freeman, 1976, pp. 90–113.

Kintsch, W., & Keenan, J. Reading rate and retention as a function of the number of propositions in the base structure of sentences. *Cognitive Psychology*, 1973, *5*, 257–274.

Kintsch, W., & van Dijk, T. A. Comment on rappelle et on résume des histoires. *Languages*, 1975, *9*, 98–116.

Kiparsky, P., & Menn, L. On the acquisition of phonology. In J. Macnamara (Ed.), *Language learning and thought*. New York: Academic Press, 1977.

Klatzky, R. L. *Human memory: Structures and processes*. San Francisco: W. H. Freeman, 1975.

Klatzky, R. L., Clark, E. V., & Macken, M. Asymmetries in the acquisition of polar adjectives: Linguistic or conceptual? *Journal of Experimental Child Psychology*, 1973, *16*, 32–46.

Klenbort, I., & Anisfeld, M. Markedness and perspective in the interpretation of the active and passive voice. *Quarterly Journal of Experimental Psychology*, 1974, *26*, 189–195.

Klima, E. S., & Bellugi, U. Syntactic regularities in the speech of children. In J. Lyons & R. J. Wales (Eds.), *Psycholinguistics papers*. Edinburgh: Edinburgh University Press, 1966, pp. 183–208.

Kosslyn, S. M. Information representation in visual images. *Cognitive Psychology*, 1975, *7*, 341–370.

Krauss, R. M., & Weinheimer, S. Changes in reference phrases as a function of frequency of usage in social interaction: A preliminary study. *Psychonomic Science*, 1964, *1*, 113–114.

Krauss, R. M., & Weinheimer, S. Concurrent feedback, confirmation, and the encoding of referents in verbal communication. *Journal of Personality and Social Psychology*, 1966, *4*, 343–346.

Krauss, R. M., & Weinheimer, S. Effect of referent similarity and communication mode on verbal encoding. *Journal of Verbal Learning and Verbal Behavior*, 1967, *6*, 359–363.

Kripke, S. Naming and necessity. In D. Davidson & G. Harman (Eds.), *Semantics of natural language*. Dordrecht, Netherlands: D. Reidel Publishing, 1972, pp. 253–355.

Kruskal, J. B. Multidimensional scaling by optimizing goodness of fit to a nonmetric hypothesis. *Psychometrika*, 1964, *29*, 1–28.

Kučera, H., & Francis, W. N. *Computational analysis of present-day American English*. Providence: Brown University Press, 1967.

Kuczaj, S. A. On the acquisition of a semantic system. *Journal of Verbal Learning and Verbal Behavior*, 1975, *14*, 340–358.

Kuno, S. The position of locatives in existential sentences. *Linguistic Inquiry*, 1971, *2*, 333–378.

Kuno, S. Functional sentence perspective: A case study from Japanese and English. *Linguistic Inquiry*, 1972, *3*, 269–320.

Kuno, S. Three perspectives in the functional approach to syntax. In *Papers from the Parasession on Functionalism*, Chicago Linguistic Society, 1975, pp. 276–336.

Kuryłowicz, J. *The inflectional categories of Indo-European*. Heidelberg, W. Germany: Carl Winter Universitätsverlag, 1964.

Labov, W. The transformation of experience in narrative syntax. In *Language in the inner city*. Philadelphia; University of Pennsylvania Press, 1972, pp. 354–396.

Lachman, R., Shaffer, J. P., & Hennrikus, D. Language and cognition: Effects of stimulus codability, name-word frequency, and age of acquisition on lexical reaction time. *Journal of Verbal Learning and Verbal Behavior*, 1974, *13*, 613–625.

Lackner, J. R., & Garrett, M. F. Resolving ambiguity: Effects of biasing context in the unattended ear. *Cognition*, 1972, *1*, 359–372.

Ladefoged, P. *Three areas of experimental phonetics*. Oxford: Oxford University Press, 1967.

Ladefoged, P. *Preliminaries to linguistic phonetics*. Chicago: University of Chicago Press, 1971.

Ladefoged, P. *A course in phonetics*. New York: Harcourt Brace Jovanovich, 1975.

Ladefoged, P., & Broadbent, D. Information conveyed by vowels. *Journal of the Acoustical Society of America*, 1957, *29*, 98–104.

Lakoff, G. *Irregularity in syntax*. New York: Holt, Rinehart and Winston, 1970.

Lakoff, G. Structural complexity in fairy tales. *The Study of Man*, 1972, *1*, 128–150. (a)

Lakoff, G. Linguistics and natural language. In D. Davidson & G. Harman (Eds.), *Semantics of natural language*. Dordrecht, Netherlands: D. Reidel Publishing, 1972, pp. 545–665. (b)

Lakoff, R. T. Some reasons why there can't be any *some-any* rule. *Language*, 1969, *45*, 608–616.

Lakoff, R. T. If's, and's, and but's about conjunctions. In C. J. Fillmore & D. T. Langendoen (Eds.), *Studies in linguistic semantics*. New York: Holt, Rinehart and Winston, 1971, pp. 115–149.

Lakoff, R. T. Questionable answers and answerable questions. In B. B. Kachru, R. B. Lees, Y. Malkiel, A. Pietrangeli, & S. Saporta (Eds.), *Papers in linguistics in honor of Henry and Renée Kahane*. Edmonton, Ill.: Linguistic Research, 1973, pp. 453–467.

Langacker, R. W. Pronominalization and the chain of command. In D. Reibel & S. Schane (Eds.), *Modern studies in English*. Englewood Cliffs, N.J.: Prentice-Hall, 1969, pp. 160–186.

Langacker, R. W. *Language and its structure* (2nd ed.). New York: Harcourt Brace Jovanovich, 1973.

Langacker, R. W. *Fundamentals of linguistic analysis*. New York: Harcourt Brace Jovanovich, 1974. (a)

Langacker, R. W. Movement rules in functional perspective. *Language*, 1974, *50*, 630–664. (b)

Langendoen, D. T. *Essentials of English grammar*. New York: Holt, Rinehart and Winston, 1970.

Lashley, K. S. The problem of serial order in behavior. In L. A. Jeffress (Ed.), *Cerebral mechanisms in behavior*. New York: John Wiley & Sons, 1951, pp. 112–136.

Leech, G. *Towards a semantic description of English*. London: Longman, 1969.

Leech, G. *Semantics*. Baltimore: Penguin Books, 1974.

Legum, S. The acquisition of adverbial noun complements. *Papers and Reports on Child Language Development* (Stanford University), 1975, *10*, 178–187.

Lehiste, I., & Peterson, G. Vowel amplitude and phonemic stress in American English. *Journal of the Acoustical Society of America*, 1959, *31*, 428–435.

Lehmann, W. P. On converging theories in linguistics. *Language*, 1972, *48*, 266–275.

Lehmann, W. P. A structural principle of language and its implications. *Language*, 1973, *49*, 47–66.

Lehrer, A. Semantic cuisine. *Journal of Linguistics*, 1969, *5*, 39–55.

Lehrer, A. Indeterminacy in semantic description. *Glossa*, 1970, *4*, 87–110.

Lehrer, A. *Semantic fields and lexical structure*. Amsterdam: North-Holland Publishing, 1974.

Lehrman, D. S. A critique of Konrad Lorenz's theory of instinctive behavior. *The Quarterly Review of Biology*, 1953, *28*, 337–363.

Lempers, J., Flavell, E. L., & Flavell, J. H. The development in very young children of tacit knowledge concerning visual perception. *Genetic Psychology Monographs*, 1977, *95*, 3–53.

Lenneberg, E. H. Understanding language without ability to speak: A case report. *Journal of Abnormal and Social Psychology*, 1962, *65*, 419–425.

Lenneberg, E. H. *Biological foundations of language*. New York: John Wiley & Sons, 1967.

Lenneberg, E. H., & Roberts, J. M. The language of experience: A study in methodology. *International Journal of American Linguistics*, 1956, Memoir *13*.

Leopold, W. F. *Speech development of a bilingual child* (4 vols.). Evanston, Ill.: Northwestern University Press, 1939–1949.

Levelt, W. J. M. Hierarchical clustering algorithm in the psychology of grammar. In G. B. Flores d'Arcais & W. J. M. Levelt (Eds.), *Advances in psycholinguistics*. Amsterdam: North-Holland Publishing, 1970, pp. 101–140. (a)

Levelt, W. J. M. Hierarchical chunking in sentence processing. *Perception and Psychophysics*, 1970, *8*, 99–102. (b)

Levelt, W. J. M. *Formal grammars in linguistics and psycholinguistics, Vol. 3: Psycholinguistic applications*. The Hague: Mouton Publishers, 1974.

Levelt, W. J. M. What became of LAD? From *Ut videam: Contributions to an understanding of linguistics, for Pieter Verburg on the occasion of his 70th birthday*. Lisse, Netherlands: Peter de Ridder Press, 1975, pp. 171–190.

Levelt, W. J. M., & Bonarius, M. Suffixes as deep structure clues. *Methodology and Science*, 1973, *6*, 7–37.

Levin, H., & Silverman, I. Hesitation phenomena in children's speech. *Language and Speech*, 1965, *8*, 67–85.

Levin, H., Silverman, I., & Ford, B. L. Hesitations in children's speech during explanation and description. *Journal of Verbal Learning and Verbal Behavior*, 1967, *6*, 560–564.

Lewis, M., & Freedle, R. O. Mother-infant dyad: The cradle of meaning. In P. Pliner, L. Krames, & T. Alloway (Eds.), *Communication and affect*. New York: Academic Press, 1973, pp. 127–155.

Lewis, M. M. *Infant speech: A study of the beginnings of language* (2nd ed.). London: Routledge & Kegan Paul, 1951.

Li, C. N., & Thompson, S. A. Historical change of word order: A case study in Chinese and its implications. In J. M. Anderson & C. Jones (Eds.), *Historical linguistics I: Syntax, morphology, internal and comparative reconstruction*. Amsterdam: North-Holland Publishing, 1974, pp. 199–217.

Li, C. N., & Thompson, S. A. The semantic function of word order: A case study in Mandarin. In C. N. Li (Ed.), *Word order and word order change*. Austin: University of Texas Press, 1975, pp. 163–195.

Liberman, A. M., Cooper, F., Shankweiler, D., & Studdert-Kennedy, M. Perception of the speech code. *Psychological Review*, 1967, *74*, 431–459.

Liberman, A. M., Harris, K. S., Hoffman, H. S., & Griffith, B. C. The discrimination of speech sounds within and across phoneme boundaries. *Journal of Experimental Psychology*, 1957, *54*, 358–368.

Lieberman, P. *Intonation, perception, and language*. Cambridge, Mass.: M.I.T. Press, 1967.

Lieberman, P., Klatt, D. H., & Wilson, W. H. Vocal tract limitations on the vowel repertoires of Rhesus monkey and other non-human primates. *Science*, 1969, *164*, 1185–1187.

Lieven, E. V. M. Conversations between mothers and young children: Individual differences and their possible implication for the study of language learning. Paper presented at the Third International Child Language Symposium, London, September 1975.

Lilly, R. S. The qualification of evaluative adjectives by frequency adverbs. *Journal of Verbal Learning and Verbal Behavior*, 1968, *7*, 333–336. (a)

Lilly, R. S. Multiplying values of intensive, probabilistic, and frequency adverbs when combined with potency adjectives. *Journal of Verbal Learning and Verbal Behavior*, 1968, *7*, 854–858. (b)

Lilly, R. S. Adverbial qualification of adjectives connoting activity. *Journal of Verbal Learning and Verbal Behavior*, 1969, *8*, 313–315.

Limber, J. The genesis of complex sentences. In T. E. Moore (Ed.), *Cognitive development and the acquisition of language*. New York: Academic Press, 1973, pp. 169–185.

Linde, C., & Labov, W. Spatial networks as a site for the study of language and thought. *Language*, 1975, *51*, 924–939.

Linden, E. *Apes, men, and language*. New York: E. P. Dutton, 1975.

Lisker, L., & Abramson, A. A cross-language study of voicing in initial stops: Acoustical measurements. *Word*, 1964, *20*, 384–422.

Lisker, L., & Abramson, A. The voicing dimension: Some experiments in comparative phonetics. *Proceedings of Sixth International Congress of Phonetic Sciences, Prague, 1967*. Prague: Academia, 1970, pp. 563–567.

Loftus, E. F. Leading questions and the eyewitness report. *Cognitive Psychology*, 1975, 7, 560–572.

Loftus, E. F., & Zanni, G. Eyewitness testimony: The influence of the wording of a question. *Bulletin of the Psychonomic Society*, 1975, *5*, 86–88.

Loftus, G. R., & Loftus, E. F. *Human memory: The processing of information*. Hillsdale, N.J.: Lawrence Erlbaum Associates, 1976.

Lord, C. Variations in the pattern of acquisition of negation. *Papers and Reports on Child Language Development* (Stanford University), 1974, *8*, 78–86.

Lorenz, K. Z. *King Solomon's ring*. London: Methuen, 1961.

Lounsbury, F. G. A semantic analysis of the Pawnee kinship usage. *Language*, 1956, *32*, 158–194.

Lumsden, E. A., & Poteat, B. W. S. The salience of the vertical dimension in the concept of "bigger" in five- and six-year-olds. *Journal of Verbal Learning and Verbal Behavior*, 1968, 7, 404–408.

Lyons, J. *Introduction to theoretical linguistics*. Cambridge: Cambridge University Press, 1968.

Lyons, J. (Ed.). *New horizons in linguistics*. Baltimore: Penguin Books, 1970.

Lyons, J. *Semantics* (2 vols.). Cambridge: Cambridge University Press, 1977.

Maccoby, E. E., & Bee, H. L. Some speculations concerning the lag between perceiving and performing. *Child Development*, 1965, *36*, 367–377.

MacKay, D. G. To end ambiguous sentences. *Perception and Psychophysics*, 1966, *1*, 426–436.

MacKay, D. G. Mental diplopia: Towards a model of speech perception. In G. B. Flores d'Arcais & W. J. M. Levelt (Eds.), *Advances in psycholinguistics*. Amsterdam: North-Holland Publishing, 1970, pp. 76–98. (a)

MacKay, D. G. Spoonerisms: The structure of errors in the serial order of speech. *Neuropsychologia*, 1970, *8*, 323–350. (b)

MacKay, D. G. The structure of words and syllables: Evidence from errors in speech. *Cognitive Psychology*, 1972, *3*, 210–227.

MacKay, D. G. Aspects of the theory of comprehension, memory and attention. *Quarterly Journal of Experimental Psychology*, 1973, *25*, 22–40. (a)

MacKay, D. G. Complexity in output systems: Evidence from behavioral hybrids. *American Journal of Psychology*, 1973, *86*, 785–806. (b)

MacKay, D. G. On the retrieval and lexical structure of verbs. *Journal of Verbal Learning and Verbal Behavior*, 1976, *15*, 169–182.

Maclay, H., & Osgood, C. E. Hesitation phenomena in spontaneous English speech. *Word*, 1959, *15*, 19–44.

Macnamara, J. (Ed.). *Language learning and thought*. New York: Academic Press, 1977.

MacNeilage, P. F. Motor control of serial ordering of speech. *Psychological Review*, 1970, *77*, 182–196.

Macrae, A. J. *Meaning relations in language development: A study of some converse pairs and directional opposites*. Unpublished doctoral dissertation, University of Edinburgh, 1976.

MacWhinney, B. *How Hungarian children learn to speak*. Unpublished doctoral dissertation, University of California, Berkeley, 1974.

Mahl, G. F. Disturbances and silences in the patient's speech in psychotherapy. *Journal of Abnormal and Social Psychology*, 1956, *53*, 1–15.

Major, D. R. *First steps in mental growth*. New York: Macmillan, 1906.

Mandler, J. M., & Johnson, N. S. Remembrance of things parsed. Story structure and recall. *Cognitive Psychology*, 1977, *9*, 111–151.

Maratsos, M. P. Preschool children's use of definite and indefinite articles. *Child Development*, 1974, *45*, 446–455.

Maratsos, M. P. *The use of definite and indefinite reference in young children: An experimental study of semantic acquisition*. Cambridge: Cambridge University Press, 1976.

Marks, L. E., & Miller, G. A. The role of semantic and syntactic constraints in the memorization of English sentences. *Journal of Verbal Learning and Verbal Behavior*, 1964, *3*, 1–5.

Marshall, J. Psychological linguistics: Psychological aspects of semantic structure. In A. R. Meetham (Ed.), *Encyclopedia of linguistics, information and control*. London: Pergamon Press, 1969, pp. 442–444.

Marslen-Wilson, W. D. Linguistic structure and speech shadowing at very short latencies. *Nature*, 1973, *244*, 522–523.

Marslen-Wilson, W. D. Sentence perception as an interactive parallel process. *Science*, 1975, *189*, 226–228.

Martin, E. Toward an analysis of subjective phrase structure. *Psychological Bulletin*, 1970, *74*, 153–166.

Martin J. E. Some competence-process relationships in noun phrases with pre-nominal and post-nominal ordering. *Journal of Verbal Learning and Verbal Behavior*, 1969, *8*, 471–480. (a)

Martin, J. E. Semantic determinants of preferred adjective order. *Journal of Verbal Learning and Verbal Behavior*, 1969, *8*, 697–704. (b)

Martin, J. G. Some acoustic and grammatical features of spontaneous speech. In D. L. Horton & J. J. Jenkins (Eds.), *The perception of language.* Columbus, Ohio: Charles E. Merrill, 1971, pp. 47–68.

Martin, J. G. Rhythmic (hierarchical) versus serial structure in speech and other behavior. *Psychological Review*, 1972, *79*, 487–509.

Martin, J. G., & Strange, W. The perception of hesitation in spontaneous speech. *Perception and Psychophysics*, 1968, *3*, 427–432.

Massaro, D. Preperceptual images, processing time, and perceptual units in auditory perception. *Psychological Review*, 1972, *79*, 124–145.

Matthews, P. H. *Morphology: An introduction to the theory of word-structure.* Cambridge: Cambridge University Press, 1974.

Matthews, P. H. (Review of *A first language: The early stages* by R. Brown.) *Journal of Linguistics*, 1975, *11*, 322–343.

McCawley, J. D. Prelexical syntax. In R. J. O'Brien (Ed.), Linguistics: Developments of the sixties—Viewpoints of the seventies. *Monograph Series in Languages and Linguistics*, 1971, *24*, 19–33.

McCawley, J. D. The role of lexicographic information in dictionary definitions. Paper presented at the Annual Conference of the International Linguistic Association, New York, March 1975.

McDaniel, C. K. Basic color terms: Their neurophysiological bases. Paper presented at the Annual Meeting of the American Anthropological Association, Mexico City, November 1974.

McNeill, D. Developmental psycholinguistics. In F. Smith & G. A. Miller (Eds.), *The genesis of language: A psycholinguistic approach.* Cambridge, Mass.: M.I.T. Press, 1966, pp. 15–84. (a)

McNeill, D. A study of word association. *Journal of Verbal Learning and Verbal Behavior*, 1966, *5*, 548–557. (b)

McNeill, D. *The acquisition of language: The study of developmental psycholinguistics.* New York: Harper & Row, 1970.

McNeill, D., & Lindig, K. The perceptual reality of phonemes, syllables, words, and sentences, *Journal of Verbal Learning and Verbal Behavior.* 1973, *12*, 419–430.

McNeill, D., & McNeill, N. B. What does a child mean when he says "no"? In C. A. Ferguson & D. I. Slobin (Eds.), *Studies of child language development.* New York: Holt, Rinehart and Winston, 1973, pp. 619–627.

Mehler, J. Some effects of grammatical transformations on the recall of English sentences. *Journal of Verbal Learning and Verbal Behavior*, 1963, *2*, 250–262.

Menn, L. Phonotactic rules in beginning speech. *Lingua*, 1971, *26*, 225–251.

Menn, L. *Pattern, control, and contrast in beginning speech: A case study in the development of word form and word function.* Unpublished doctoral dissertation, University of Illinois, 1976.

Menyuk, P. Children's learning and reproduction of grammatical and nongrammatical phonological sequences. *Child Development*, 1968, *39*, 849–859.

Menyuk, P. *The acquisition and development of language.* Englewood Cliffs, N.J.: Prentice-Hall, 1971.

Meringer, R., & Mayer, K. *Versprechen und Verlesen.* Stuttgart, Germany: Göschensche Verlagsbuchhandlung, 1895.

Mervis, C. B., Catlin, J., & Rosch, E. Development of the structure of color categories. *Developmental Psychology*, 1975, *11*, 54–60.

Messer, S. Implicit phonology in children. *Journal of Verbal Learning and Verbal Behavior*, 1967, *6*, 609–613.

Meyer, B. J. F. *The organization of prose and its effects on memory.* Amsterdam: North-Holland Publishing, 1975.

Meyer, D. E. Verifying affirmative and negative propositions: Effects of negation on memory retrieval. In S. Kornblum (Ed.), *Attention and performance* (Vol. 4). New York: Academic Press, 1973, pp. 379–394.

Mikeš, M. Acquisition des catégories grammaticales dans le langage de l'enfant. *Enfance*, 1967, *20*, 289–298.

Miller, C., & Swift, K. *Words and woman: New language in new times.* New York: Doubleday, 1976.

Miller, G. A. The perception of speech. In M. Halle (Ed.), *For Roman Jakobson.* The Hague: Mouton Publishers, 1956, pp. 353–359.

Miller, G. A. Some psychological studies of grammar. *American Psychologist*, 1962, *17*, 748–762.

Miller, G. A. English verbs of motion: A case study in semantics and lexical memory. In A. W. Melton & E. Martin (Eds.), *Coding processes in human memory.* Washington, D.C.: V. H. Winston & Sons, 1972, pp. 335–372.

Miller, G. A., Heise, G., & Lichten, W. The intelligibility of speech as a function of the context of the test materials. *Journal of Experimental Psychology*, 1951, *41*, 329–335.

Miller, G. A., & Isard, S. Some perceptual consequences of linguistic rules. *Journal of Verbal Learning and Verbal Behavior*, 1963, *2*, 217–228.

Miller, G. A., & Johnson-Laird, P. N. *Language and perception.* Cambridge, Mass.: Harvard University Press, 1976.

Miller, G. A., & McKean, K. O. A chronometric study of some relations between sentences. *Quarterly Journal of Experimental Psychology*, 1964, *16*, 297–308.

Miller, G. A., & Nicely, P. An analysis of perceptual confusions among some English consonants. *Journal of the Acoustical Society of America*, 1955, *27*, 338–352.

Miller, M. H. Pragmatic constraints on the linguistic realization of "semantic intentions" in early child language. Paper presented at the

Third International Child Language Symposium, London, September 1975.

Miller, W., & Ervin, S. M. The development of grammar in child language. In U. Bellugi & R. Brown (Eds.), The acquisition of language. *Monographs of the Society for Research in Child Development*, 1964, *29* (Serial No. 92), 9–34.

Minsky, M. A framework for representing knowledge. In P. Winston (Ed.), *The psychology of computer vision*. New York: McGraw-Hill, 1975, pp. 211–277.

Mistler-Lachman, J. L. Depth of comprehension and sentence memory. *Journal of Verbal Learning and Verbal Behavior*, 1974, *13*, 98–106.

Miyawaki, K., Strange, W., Verbrugge, R., Liberman, A. M., Jenkins, J. J., and Fujimura, O. An effect of linguistic experience. The discrimination of [r] and [l] by native speakers of Japanese and English. *Perception and Psychophysics*, 1975, *18*, 331–340.

Moffitt, A. R. Consonant cue perception by twenty- to twenty-four week old infants. *Child Development*, 1971, *42*, 717–731.

Moore, T. E. (Ed.). *Cognitive development and the acquisition of language*. New York: Academic Press, 1973.

Moravcsik, E. A. Agreement. *Working Papers in Language Universals* (Stanford University), 1971, *5*, A1–A69.

Moray, N. Attention in dichotic listening: Affective cues and the influence of instructions. *Quarterly Journal of Experimental Psychology*, 1959, *11*, 56–60.

Moray, N. *Attention: Selective processes in vision and hearing*. London: Hutchinson, 1969.

Morse, P. A. The discrimination of speech and nonspeech stimuli in early infancy. *Journal of Experimental Child Psychology*, 1972, *14*, 477–492.

Morton, J., & Smith, N. V. Some ideas concerning the acquisition of phonology. In *Problèmes actuels en psycholinguistique / Current problems in psycholinguistics*. Paris: Editions du C.N.R.S., 1974, pp. 161–176.

Moskowitz, A. I. The two-year-old stage in the acquisition of English phonology. *Language*, 1970, *46*, 426–441.

Mowrer, O. H. *Learning theory and symbolic processes*. New York: John Wiley & Sons, 1960.

Moyer, R. S., & Bayer, R. H. Mental comparison and the symbolic distance effect. *Journal of Verbal Learning and Verbal Behavior*, 1976, *8*, 228–246.

Mueller, E. The maintenance of verbal exchanges between young children. *Child Development*, 1972, *43*, 930–938.

Müller, E., Hollien, H., & Murry, T. Perceptual responses to infant crying: Identification of cry types. *Journal of Child Language*, 1974, *1*, 89–95.

Mussen, P. H., Conger, J. J., & Kagan, J. *Child development and personality* (4th ed.). New York: Harper & Row, 1974.

Nash-Webber, B. The role of semantics in automatic speech understanding. In D. G. Bobrow and A. M. Collins (Eds.), *Representation and understanding: Studies in cognitive science*. New York: Academic Press, 1975, pp. 351–382.

Nelson, K. Structure and strategy in learning to talk. *Monographs of the Society for Research in Child Development*, 1973, *38* (Serial No. 149).

Nelson, K. Concept, word, and sentence: Interrelations in acquisition and development. *Psychological Review*, 1974, *81*, 267–285.

Nelson, K. The nominal shift in semantic-syntactic development. *Cognitive Psychology*, 1975, *7*, 461–479.

Nooteboom, S. G. The tongue slips into patterns. In *Nomen, Leyden studies in linguistics and phonetics*. The Hague: Mouton Publishers, 1969, pp. 114–132.

Norman, D. A. Memory while shadowing. *Quarterly Journal of Experimental Psychology*, 1969, *21*, 85–94.

Norman, D. A. *Memory and attention* (2nd ed.). New York: John Wiley & Sons, 1976.

Norman, D. A., Rumelhart, D. E., & the LNR Research Group. *Explorations in cognition*. San Francisco: W. H. Freeman, 1975.

Obusek, C. J., & Warren, R. M. Relation of the verbal transformation and the phonemic restoration effects. *Cognitive Psychology*, 1973, *5*, 97–107.

Oldfield, R. C., & Wingfield, A. Response latencies in naming objects. *Quarterly Journal of Experimental Psychology*, 1965, *17*, 273–281.

Oller, D. K., Wieman, L. A., Doyle, W. J., & Ross, C. Infant babbling and speech. *Journal of Child Language*, 1976, *3*, 1–11.

Olmsted, D. *Out of the mouth of babes*. The Hague: Mouton Publishers, 1971.

Olson, D. R. Language and thought: Aspects of a cognitive theory of semantics. *Psychological Review*, 1970, *77*, 257–273.

Olson, D. R. Language use for communicating, instructing and thinking. In J. B. Carroll & R. O. Freedle (Eds.), *Language comprehension and the acquisition of knowledge*. Washington, D.C.: V. H. Winston & Sons, 1972, pp. 139–167.

Olson, D. R., & Filby, N. On the comprehension of active and passive sentences. *Cognitive Psychology*, 1972, *3*, 361–381.

Olson, G. M. Developmental changes in memory and the acquisition of language. In T. E. Moore (Ed.), *Cognitive development and the acquisition of language*. New York: Academic Press, 1973, pp. 145–157.

Olson, G. M., & Clark, H. H. Research methods in psycholinguistics. In E. C. Carterette & M. P. Friedman (Eds.), *Handbook of perception* (*Vol. 7*). *Language and speech*. New York: Academic Press, 1976, pp. 25–74.

Olson, G. M., & Laxar, K. Asymmetries in processing the terms "right" and "left." *Journal of Experimental Psychology*, 1973, *100*, 284–290.

Olson, G. M., & Laxar, K. Processing the terms "right" and "left." *Journal of Experimental Psychology*, 1974, *102*, 1135–1137.

Omar, M. K. *The acquisition of Egyptian Arabic as a native language*. The Hague: Mouton Publishers, 1973.

Osgood, C. E. Interpersonal verbs and interpersonal behavior. In J. L. Cowan (Ed.), *Studies in thought and language*. Tucson: University of Arizona Press, 1970, pp. 133–228.

Osgood, C. E. Where do sentences come from? In D. A. Steinberg & L. A. Jakobovits (Eds.), *Semantics: An interdisciplinary reader in philosophy, linguistics, and psychology*. Cambridge: Cambridge University Press, 1971, pp. 497–529.

Osgood, C. E., & Richards, M. M. From yang and yin to *and* or *but*. *Language*, 1973, *49*, 380–412.

Osgood, C. E., Suci, G. J., & Tannenbaum, P. H. *The measurement of meaning*. Urbana: University of Illinois Press, 1957.

Paige, J. M., & Simon, H. A. Cognitive processes in solving algebra word problems. In B. Kleinmuntz (Ed.), *Problem solving*. New York: John Wiley & Sons, 1966, pp. 51–148.

Paivio, A. *Imagery and verbal processes*. New York: Holt, Rinehart and Winston, 1971.

Palermo, D. S. More about *less*: A study of language comprehension. *Journal of Verbal Learning and Verbal Behavior*, 1973, *12*, 211–221.

Palmer, F. R. *Semantics: A new outline*. Cambridge: Cambridge University Press, 1976.

Perez, B. *Les trois premières années de l'enfant*. Paris: Alcan, 1892.

Perfetti, C. A., & Goldman, S. R. Thematization and sentence retrieval. *Journal of Verbal Learning and Verbal Behavior*, 1974, *13*, 70–79.

Phillips, J. R. Syntax and vocabulary of mothers' speech to young children: Age and sex comparisons. *Child Development*, 1973, *44*, 182–185.

Piaget, J. [*Play, dreams, and imitation in childhood* (trans. of *La formation du symbole chez l'enfant*).] New York: W. W. Norton, 1951.

Piaget, J. *The origins of intelligence in the child*. London: Routledge & Kegan Paul, 1953.

Piaget, J. *The child's construction of reality*. London: Routledge & Kegan Paul, 1955.

Piaget, J., & Inhelder, B. *The psychology of the child*. London: Routledge & Kegan Paul, 1969.

Piaget, J., & Szeminska, A. *The child's conception of number*. New York: Humanities Press, 1952.

Pisoni, D. B. Auditory and phonetic memory codes in the discrimination of consonants and vowels. *Perception and Psychophysics*, 1973, *13*, 253–260.

Pisoni, D. B. Speech perception. In W. K. Estes (Ed.), *Handbook of learning and cognitive processes* (Vol. 5). Hillsdale, N.J.: Lawrence Erlbaum Associates, 1977.

Pisoni, D. B., & Sawusch, J. R. Some stages of processing in speech perception. In A. Cohen & S. G. Nooteboom (Eds.), *Structure and process in speech perception*. Heidelberg, W. Germany: Springer-Verlag, 1975, pp. 16–34.

Pisoni, D. B. & Tash, J. Reaction times to comparisons within and across phonetic categories. *Perception and Psychophysics*, 1974, *15*, 285–290.

Pollack, I., & Pickett, J. M. Intelligibility of excerpts from fluent speech: Auditory vs. structural context. *Journal of Verbal Learning and Verbal Behavior*, 1964, *3*, 79–84.

Pompi, R. F., & Lachman, R. Surrogate processes in short-term retention of connected discourse. *Journal of Experimental Psychology*, 1967, *75*, 143–150.

Postal, P. M. (Review of *Elements of general linguistics* by André Martinet.) *Foundations of Language*, 1966, *2*, 151–186.

Postman, L., & Keppel, G. *Norms of word associations*. New York: Academic Press, 1970.

Potts, G. R. Information processing strategies used in the encoding of linear orderings. *Journal of Verbal Learning and Verbal Behavior*, 1972, *11*, 727–740.

Potts, G. R. Memory for redundant information. *Memory and Cognition*, 1973, *1*, 467–470.

Potts, G. R. Storing and retrieving information about ordered relationships. *Journal of Experimental Psychology*, 1974, *103*, 431–439.

Premack, A. J., & Premack, D. Teaching language to an ape. *Scientific American*, 1972, *227*, 92–99.

Premack, D. Language in chimpanzee? *Science*, 1971, *172*, 808–822. (a)

Premack, D. On the assessment of language competence in the chimpanzee. In A. M. Schrier & F. Stollnitz (Eds.), *Behavior of nonhuman primates* (Vol. 4). New York: Academic Press, 1971, pp. 185–228. (b)

Propp, V. *Morphology of the folktale*. Austin: University of Texas Press, 1968.

Pullum, G. K. Word order universals and grammatical relations. In P. Cole & J. M. Sadock (Eds.), *Syntax and semantics, Vol. 8: Grammatical relations*. New York: Academic Press, 1977.

Putnam, H. The meaning of "meaning." *Mind, language and reality* (Philosophical Papers, Vol. 2). Cambridge: Cambridge University Press, 1975, pp. 215–271.

Pylyshyn, Z. W. What the mind's eye tells the mind's brain: A critique of mental imagery. *Psychological Bulletin*, 1973, *80*, 1–24.

Quirk, R., Greenbaum, S., Leech, G., & Svartvik, J. *A grammar of contemporary English*. London: Longman, 1972.

Quirk, R., & Svartvik, J. *Investigating linguistic acceptability*. The Hague: Mouton Publishers, 1966.

Radulović, L. *Acquisition of language: Studies of Dubrovnik children*. Unpublished doctoral dissertation, University of California, Berkeley, 1975.

Reber, A. S. What clicks may tell us about speech perception. *Journal of Psycholinguistic Research*, 1973, *2*, 287–288.

Reber, A. S., & Anderson, J. R. The perception of

clicks in linguistic and nonlinguistic messages. *Perception and Psychophysics*, 1970, *8*, 81–89.

Reddy, D. R. (Ed.). *Speech recognition*. New York: Academic Press, 1975.

Remick, H. W. *The maternal environment of language acquisition*. Unpublished doctoral dissertation, University of California, Davis, 1971.

Rheingold, H. L. Sharing at an early age. Presidential address, Division 7, Annual Meeting of the American Psychological Association, Montreal, 1973.

Ricks, D. M. Vocal communication in preverbal normal and autistic children. In N. O'Connor (Ed.), *Language, cognitive deficits, and retardation*. London: Butterworth, 1975, pp. 75–80.

Rips, L. J. Inductive judgments about natural categories. *Journal of Verbal Learning and Verbal Behavior*, 1975, *14*, 665–681.

Rips, L. J., Shoben, E. J., & Smith E. E. Semantic distance and the verification of semantic relations. *Journal of Verbal Learning and Verbal Behavior*, 1973, *12*, 1–20.

Rochester, S. R. The significance of pauses in spontaneous speech. *Journal of Psycholinguistic Research*, 1973, *2*, 51–81.

Rogers, S. (Ed.). *Children and language: Readings in early language and socialization*. Oxford: Oxford University Press, 1975.

Romney, A. K., & d'Andrade, R. G. Cognitive aspects of English kin terms. In A. K. Romney & R. G. d'Andrade (Eds.), Transcultural studies in cognition. *American Anthropologist*, 1964, *66* (3, Pt. 2), 146–170.

Romney, A. K., Shepard, R. N., & Nerlove, S. B. *Multidimensional scaling: Theory and applications in the behavioral sciences* (Vol. 2). New York: Seminar Press, 1972.

Rosch, E. On the internal structure of perceptual and semantic categories. In T. E. Moore (Ed.), *Cognitive development and the acquisition of language*. New York: Academic Press, 1973, pp. 111–144.

Rosch, E. Linguistic relativity. In A. Silverstein (Ed.), *Human communication: Theoretical perspectives*. New York: Halsted Press, 1974, pp. 95–121.

Rosch, E. Cognitive representations of semantic categories. *Journal of Experimental Psychology: General*, 1975, *104*, 192–233.

Rosch, E. Human categorization. In N. Warren (Ed.), *Advances in cross-cultural psychology* (Vol. 1). London: Academic Press, 1977.

Rosch, E., & Mervis, C. B. Family resemblances: Studies in the internal structure of categories. *Cognitive Psychology*, 1975, *7*, 573–605.

Rosch, E., Mervis, C. B., Gray, W., Johnson, D., & Boyes-Braem, P. Basic objects in natural categories. *Cognitive Psychology*, 1976, *8*, 382–439.

Rosch, E., Simpson, C., & Miller, R. S. Structural bases of typicality effects. *Journal of Experimental Psychology: Human Perception and Performance*, 1976, *2*, 491–502.

Rosen, C., & Rosen, H. *The language of primary school children*. Baltimore: Penguin Books, 1973.

Ross, J. R. On the cyclic nature of English pronominalization. In *To honor Roman Jakobson: Essays on the occasion of his 70th birthday*. The Hague: Mouton Publishers, 1967, pp. 1669–1682.

Rubin, D. C. Within word structure in the tip-of-the-tongue phenomenon. *Journal of Verbal Learning and Verbal Behavior*, 1975, *14*, 392–397.

Rudel, R. G., & Teuber, H. L. Discrimination of the direction of line by children. *Journal of Comparative and Physiological Psychology*, 1963, *56*, 892–898.

Rūke-Draviņa, V. On the emergence of inflection in child language: A contribution based on Latvian speech data. In C. A. Ferguson & D. I. Slobin (Eds.), *Studies of child language development*. New York: Holt, Rinehart and Winston, 1973, pp. 252–267.

Rumbaugh, D., Gill, T. V., & von Glaserfeld, E. C. Reading and sentence completion by a chimpanzee (Pan). *Science*, 1973, *183*, 731–733.

Rumelhart, D. E. Notes on a schema for stories. In D. G. Bobrow & A. M. Collins (Eds.), *Representations and understanding: Studies in cognitive science*. New York: Academic Press, 1975, pp. 211–236.

Rumelhart, D. E. Understanding and summarizing brief stories. In D. LaBerge & S. J. Samuels (Eds.), *Basic processes in reading: Perception and comprehension*. Hillsdale, N.J.: Lawrence Erlbaum Associates, 1977.

Rumelhart, D. E., Lindsay, P. H., & Norman, D. A. A process model for long-term memory. In E. Tulving & W. Donaldson (Eds.), *Organization of memory*. New York: Academic Press, 1972, pp. 197–246.

Rumelhart, D. E., & Ortony, A. The representation of knowledge in memory. In R. C. Anderson, R. J. Spiro, & W. E. Montague (Eds.), *Schooling and the acquisition of knowledge*. Hillsdale, N.J.: Lawrence Erlbaum Associates, 1977.

Ryle, G. Thinking and language. *Proceedings of the Aristotelian Society*. Supplementary Volume 25, 1951, 65–82.

Sachs, J. S. Recognition memory for syntactic and semantic aspects of connected discourse. *Perception and Psychophysics*, 1967, *2*, 437–442.

Sachs, J. S., Brown, R., & Salerno, R. A. Adults' speech to children. In W. van Raffler Engel & Y. LeBrun (Eds.), *Baby talk and infant speech* (*Neurolinguistics 5*). Amsterdam: Swets & Zeitlinger, 1976, pp. 240–245.

Sachs, J. S., & Johnson, M. Language development in a hearing child of deaf parents. In W. von Raffler Engel & Y. LeBrun (Eds.), *Baby talk and infant speech* (*Neurolinguistics 5*). Amsterdam: Swets & Zeitlinger, 1976, pp. 246–252.

Sacks, H., Schegloff, E. A., & Jefferson, G. A simplest systematics for the organization of turn-taking for conversation. *Language*, 1974, *50*, 696–735.

Sadock, J. M. *Towards a linguistic theory of speech acts.* New York: Academic Press, 1974.

Sampson, G. *The form of language.* London: George Weidenfeld & Nicolson, 1975.

Sanders, G. On the explanation of constituent order universals. In C. N. Li (Ed.), *Word order and word order change.* Austin: University of Texas Press, 1975, pp. 389–436.

Sankoff, G., & Brown, P. The origins of syntax in discourse: A case study of Tok Pisin relatives. *Language,* 1976, *52,* 631–666.

Santa, J. L., & Ranken, H. B. Effects of verbal coding on recognition memory. *Journal of Experimental Psychology,* 1972, *93,* 268–278.

Sapir, E. Grading: A study in semantics. *Philosophy of Science,* 1944, *11,* 93–116.

Savić, S. Aspects of adult-child communication: The problem of question acquisition. *Journal of Child Language,* 1975, *2,* 251–260.

Schaffer, H. R. *Studies in mother-infant interaction.* London: Academic Press, 1977.

Schane, S. A. *Generative phonology.* Englewood Cliffs, N.J.: Prentice-Hall, 1973.

Schank, R. C. Conceptual dependency: A theory of natural language understanding. *Cognitive Psychology,* 1972, *3,* 552–631.

Schank, R. C., & Abelson, R. P. Scripts, plans and knowledge. Paper presented at the Fourth International Conference on Artificial Intelligence, Tbilisi, USSR, August 1975.

Schegloff, E. A. Sequencing in conversational openings. *American Anthropologist,* 1968, *70,* 1075–1095.

Schegloff, E. A. Notes on a conversational practice: Formulating place. In D. N. Sudnow (Ed.), *Studies in social interaction.* New York: The Free Press, 1972, pp. 75–119.

Schegloff, E. A., & Sacks, H. Opening up closings. *Semiotica,* 1973, *8,* 289–327.

Schlesinger, I. M. A note on the relationship between psychological and linguistic theories. *Foundations of Language,* 1967, *3,* 397–402.

Schlesinger, I. M. *Sentence structure and the reading process.* The Hague: Mouton Publishers, 1968.

Schlesinger, I. M. Production of utterances and language acquisition. In D. I. Slobin (Ed.), *The ontogenesis of grammar: A theoretical symposium.* New York: Academic Press, 1971, pp. 63–101.

Schlesinger, I. M. Relational concepts underlying language. In R. L. Schiefelbusch & L. L. Lloyd (Eds.), *Language perspectives—Acquisition, retardation and intervention.* Baltimore: University Park Press, 1974, pp. 129–151.

Schmerling, S. F. Asymmetric conjunction and rules of conversation. In P. Cole & J. L. Morgan (Eds.), *Syntax and semantics, Vol. 3: Speech acts.* New York: Seminar Press, 1975, pp. 211–231.

Schöler, H. Verstehen und Imitation temporaler Satzformen. In H. Grimm, H. Schöler, & M. Wintermantel (Eds.), *Zur Entwicklung*

sprachlicher Strukturformen bei Kindern. Weinheim, W. Germany: J. Beltz Verlag, 1975, pp. 132–152.

Scholz, K., & Potts, G. R. Cognitive processing of linear orderings. *Journal of Experimental Psychology,* 1974, *102,* 323–326.

Schourup, L. Unique New York unique New York unique New York. In *Papers from the Ninth Regional Meeting, Chicago Linguistic Society,* 1973, pp. 587–596.

Scollon, R. T. *One child's language from one to two: The origins of construction.* Unpublished doctoral dissertation, University of Hawaii, 1974.

Searle, J. R. What is a speech act? In M. Black (Ed.), *Philosophy in America.* London: George Allen & Unwin, 1965, pp. 221–239.

Searle, J. R. *Speech acts.* Cambridge: Cambridge University Press, 1969.

Searle, J. R. A taxonomy of illocutionary acts. In K. Gunderson (Ed.), *Minnesota studies in the philosophy of language.* Minneapolis: University of Minnesota Press, 1975, pp. 344–369. (a)

Searle, J. R. Indirect speech acts. In P. Cole & J. L. Morgan (Eds.), *Syntax and semantics, Vol. 3: Speech acts.* New York: Seminar Press, 1975, pp. 59–82. (b)

Seymour, P. H. K. Response latencies in classification of word-shape pairs. *British Journal of Psychology,* 1969, *60,* 443–451.

Seymour, P. H. K. Generation of a pictorial code. *Memory and Cognition,* 1974, *2,* 224–232.

Shatz, M. The comprehension of indirect directives: Can two-year-olds shut the door? Paper presented at the Summer Meeting of the Linguistic Society of America, Amherst, Massachusetts, July 1974.

Shatz, M., & Gelman, R. The development of communication skills: Modifications in the speech of young children as a function of listener. *Monographs of the Society for Research in Child Development,* 1973, *38* (Serial No. 152).

Shepard, R. N. The analysis of proximities: Multidimensional scaling with an unknown distance function. I and II. *Psychometrika,* 1962, *27,* 125–140; 219–246.

Shepard, R. N. Psychological representation of speech sounds. In E. E. David & P. B. Denes (Eds.), *Human communication: A unified view.* New York: McGraw-Hill, 1972, pp. 67–113.

Shepard, R. N., & Chipman, S. Second-order isomorphism of internal representations: Shapes of states. *Cognitive Psychology,* 1971, *1,* 1–17.

Shepard, R. N., Kilpatric, D. W., & Cunningham, J. P. The internal representation of numbers. *Cognitive Psychology,* 1975, *7,* 82–138.

Shepard, R. N., & Metzler, J. Mental rotation of three-dimensional objects. *Science,* 1971, *171,* 701–703.

Sherman, M. A. Bound to be easier? The negative prefix and sentence comprehension. *Journal of Verbal Learning and Verbal Behavior,* 1973, *12,* 76–84.

Sherman, M. A. Adjectival negation and the comprehension of multiply negated sentences. *Journal of Verbal Learning and Verbal Behavior*, 1976, *15*, 143–157.

Shields, J. L., McHugh, A., & Martin, J. G. Reaction time to phoneme targets as a function of rhythmic cues in continuous speech. *Journal of Experimental Psychology*, 1974, *102*, 250–255.

Shoben, E. J. The verification of semantic relations in a same-different paradigm: An asymmetry in semantic memory. *Journal of Verbal Learning and Verbal Behavior*, 1976, *15*, 365–379.

Shulman, H. G. Encoding and retention of semantic and phonemic information in short-term memory. *Journal of Verbal Learning and Verbal Behavior*, 1970, *9*, 499–508.

Shulman, H. G. Semantic confusion errors in short-term memory. *Journal of Verbal Learning and Verbal Behavior*, 1972, *11*, 221–227.

Shvachkin, N. Kh. The development of phonemic speech perception in early childhood. In C. A. Ferguson & D. I. Slobin (Eds.), *Studies of child language development*. New York: Holt, Rinehart and Winston, 1973, pp. 91–127.

Siegman, A. W., & Pope, B. Effects of question specificity and anxiety producing messages on verbal fluency in the initial interview. *Journal of Personality and Social Psychology*, 1965, *2*, 522–530.

Sinclair-de Zwart, H. Language acquisition and cognitive development. In T. E. Moore (Ed.), *Cognitive development and the acquisition of language*. New York: Academic Press, 1973, pp. 9–25.

Sinclair, H., & Bronckart, J. P. SVO A linguistic universal? A study in developmental psycholinguistics. *Journal of Experimental Child Psychology*, 1972, *14*, 329–348.

Sinclair, J. McH., & Coulthard, R. M. *Towards an analysis of discourse: The English used by teachers and pupils*. Oxford: Oxford University Press, 1975.

Slobin, D. I. Grammatical transformations and sentence comprehension in childhood and adulthood. *Journal of Verbal Learning and Verbal Behavior*, 1966, *5*, 219–227. (a)

Slobin, D. I. The acquisition of Russian as a native language. In F. Smith & G. A. Miller (Eds.), *The genesis of language: A psycholinguistic approach*. Cambridge, Mass.: M.I.T. Press, 1966, pp. 129–148. (b)

Slobin, D. I. Universals of grammatical development in children. In G. B. Flores d'Arcais & W. J. M. Levelt (Eds.), *Advances in psycholinguistics*. Amsterdam: North-Holland Publishing, 1970, pp. 174–186.

Slobin, D. I. Cognitive pre-requisites for the acquisition of grammar. In C. A. Ferguson & D. I. Slobin (Eds.), *Studies of child language development*. New York: Holt, Rinehart and Winston, 1973, pp. 175–208.

Slobin, D. I. The more it changes . . . On understanding language by watching it move through time. *Papers and Reports on Child Language Development* (Stanford University), 1975, *10*, 1–30.

Slobin, D. I., & Welsh, C. A. Elicited imitation as a research tool in developmental psycholinguistics. In C. A. Ferguson & D. I. Slobin (Eds.), *Studies of child language development*. New York: Holt, Rinehart and Winston, 1973, pp. 485–497.

Smith, C. S. An experimental approach to children's linguistic competence. In J. R. Hayes (Ed.), *Cognition and the development of language*. New York: John Wiley & Sons, 1970, pp. 109–135.

Smith, E. E. Theories of semantic memory. In W. K. Estes (Ed.), *Handbook of learning and cognitive processes* (Vol. 5). Hillsdale, N.J.: Lawrence Erlbaum Associates, 1977.

Smith, E. E., Balzano, G. J., & Walker, J. Nominal, perceptual, and semantic codes in picture categorization. In J. Cotton & R. L. Klatzky (Eds.), *Semantic factors in cognition*. Hillsdale, N.J.: Lawrence Erlbaum Associates, 1977.

Smith, E. E., Rips, L. J., & Shoben, E. J. Semantic memory and psychological semantics. In G. H. Bower (Ed.), *The psychology of learning and motivation* (Vol. 8). New York: Academic Press, 1974, pp. 1–45.

Smith, E. E., Shoben, E. J., & Rips, L. J. Structure and process in semantic memory: A featural model for semantic decisions. *Psychological Review*, 1974, *81*, 214–241.

Smith, K. H., & McMahon, L. E. Understanding order information in sentences: some recent work at Bell Laboratories. In G. B. Flores d'Arcais & W. J. M. Levelt (Eds.), *Advances in psycholinguistics*. Amsterdam: North-Holland Publishing, 1970, pp. 253–274.

Smith, N. V. *The acquisition of phonology: A case study*. Cambridge: Cambridge University Press, 1973.

Smith, N. V. Universal tendencies in the child's acquisition of phonology. In N. O'Connor (Ed.), *Language, cognitive deficits, and retardation*. London: Butterworth, 1975, pp. 47–65.

Smith, P. T. Feature-testing models and their application to perception and memory for speech. *Quarterly Journal of Experimental Psychology*, 1973, *25*, 511–534.

Smith, P. T., & Jones, K. F. Some hierarchical scaling methods for confusion matrix analysis II. Applications to large matrices. *British Journal of Mathematical and Statistical Psychology*, 1975, *28*, 30–45.

Snow, C. E. Mothers' speech to children learning language. *Child Development*, 1972, *43*, 549–565.

Snow, C. E. The development of conversation between mothers and babies. *Journal of Child Language*, 1977, *4*.

Snow, C. E., Arlman-Rupp, A., Hassing, Y., Jobse, J., Joosten, J., & Vorster, J. Mothers' speech in three social classes. *Journal of Psycholinguistic Research*, 1976, *5*, 1–20.

Snow, C. E., & Ferguson, C. A. (Eds.). *Talking to children: Language input and acquisition.* Cambridge: Cambridge University Press, 1977.

Spooner, W. A. How to reek spite. *Psycholinguistix Illustrated,* 1891, *9,* 1–99.

Springston, F. J. *Some cognitive aspects of presupposed coreferential anaphora.* Unpublished doctoral dissertation, Stanford University, 1975.

Springston, F. J., & Clark, H. H. *And* and *or,* or the comprehension of pseudoimperatives. *Journal of Verbal Learning and Verbal Behavior,* 1973, *12,* 258–272.

Steinberg, D. D. Phonology, reading, and Chomsky and Halle's optimal orthography. *Journal of Psycholinguistic Research,* 1973, *2,* 239–258.

Stern, C., & Stern, W. *Die Kindersprache: Eine psychologische und sprachtheoretische Untersuchung* (4th revised ed.). Leipzig, Germany: Barth, 1928.

Stern, D. N. Mother and infant at play: The dyadic interaction involving facial, vocal, and gaze behaviors. In M. Lewis & L. Rosenblum (Eds.), *The effect of the infant on its caretaker.* New York: John Wiley & Sons, 1974, pp. 187–213.

Stern, W. *Psychology of early childhood.* New York: Holt, 1930.

Stevens, K. N. Toward a model for speech recognition. *Journal of the Acoustical Society of America,* 1960, *32,* 47–55.

Stevens, K. N., & House, A. S. Speech perception. In J. V. Tobias (Ed.), *Foundations of modern auditory theory* (Vol. 2). New York: Academic Press, 1972, pp. 3–62.

Stolz, W. A study of the ability to decode grammatically novel sentences. *Journal of Verbal Learning and Verbal Behavior,* 1967, *6,* 867–873.

Strohner, H., & Nelson, K. E. The young child's development of sentence comprehension: Influence of event probability, nonverbal context, syntactic form, and strategies. *Child Development,* 1974, *45,* 567–576.

Stross, B. Acquisition of botanical terminology by Tzeltal children. In M. S. Edmonson (Ed.), *Meaning in Mayan languages.* The Hague: Mouton Publishers, 1973, pp. 107–141.

Studdert-Kennedy, M. The perception of speech. In T. A. Sebeok (Ed.), *Current trends in linguistics, Vol. 12: Linguistics and adjacent arts and sciences.* The Hague: Mouton Publishers, 1974, pp. 2349–2385.

Studdert-Kennedy, M. Speech perception. In N. J. Lass (Ed.), *Contemporary issues in experimental phonetics.* Springfield, Ill.: Charles C. Thomas, 1975, pp. 243–293.

Suci, G. J., Ammon, P. R., & Gamlin, P. The validity of the probe-latency technique for assessing structure in language. *Language and Speech,* 1967, *10,* 69–80.

Sudnow, D. N. (Ed.). *Studies in social interaction.* New York: The Free Press, 1972.

Sulin, R. A., & Dooling, D. J. Intrusion of a thematic idea in retention of prose. *Journal of Experimental Psychology,* 1974, *103,* 255–262.

Sutherland, N. S. Visual discrimination of orientation and shape by *Octopus. Nature,* 1957, *179,* 505.

Sutherland, N. S. Visual discrimination of orientation by *Octopus:* Mirror images. *British Journal of Psychology,* 1960, *51,* 9–18.

Talmy, L. Semantic causative types. In M. Shibatani (Ed.), *Syntax and semantics, Vol. 6: The grammar of causative constructions.* New York: Academic Press, 1976, pp. 43–116.

Tannenbaum, P. H., & Williams, F. Generation of active and passive sentences as a function of subject or object focus. *Journal of Verbal Learning and Verbal Behavior,* 1968, *7,* 246–250.

Tannenbaum, P. H., Williams, F., & Hillier, C. S. Word predictability in the environment of hesitations. *Journal of Verbal Learning and Verbal Behavior,* 1965, *4,* 134–140.

Taylor, I. Content and structure in sentence production. *Journal of Verbal Learning and Verbal Behavior,* 1969, *8,* 170–175.

Teller, P. Some discussion and extension of Manfred Bierwisch's work on German adjectivals. *Foundations of Language,* 1969, *5,* 185–217.

Templin, M. Certain language skills in children: Their development and interrelationships. *Institute of Child Welfare Monograph 26.* Minneapolis: University of Minnesota Press, 1957.

Thomson, J. R., & Chapman, R. S. Who is "Daddy"? The status of two-year-olds' overextended words in use and comprehension. *Papers and Reports on Child Language Development* (Stanford University), 1975, *10,* 59–68.

Thorndyke, P. W. Cognitive structures in comprehension and memory of narrative discourse. *Cognitive Psychology,* 1977, *9,* 77–110.

Tieman, D. G. *Recognition memory for comparative sentences.* Unpublished doctoral dissertation, Stanford University, 1972.

Trabasso, T., & Riley, C. A. On the construction and use of representations involving linear order. In R. L. Solso (Ed.), *Contemporary issues in cognitive psychology.* Washington, D.C.: Lawrence Erlbaum Associates, 1975, pp. 381–410.

Trabasso, T., Rollins, H., & Shaughnessy, E. Storage and verification stages in processing concepts. *Cognitive Psychology,* 1971, *2,* 239–289.

Traugott, E. C. Explorations in linguistic elaboration: Language change, language acquisition, and the genesis of spatio-temporal terms. In J. M. Anderson & C. Jones (Eds.), *Historical linguistics I: Syntax, morphology, internal and comparative reconstruction.* Amsterdam: North-Holland Publishing, 1974, pp. 263–314.

Treisman, A. M. Verbal cues, language and meaning in selective attention. *American Journal of Psychology,* 1964, *77,* 206–219. (a)

Treisman, A. M. The effect of irrelevant material on the efficiency of selective listening. *American Journal of Psychology,* 1964, *77,* 533–546. (b)

Trudgill, P. *Sociolinguistics: An introduction.* Baltimore: Penguin Books, 1974.

Tulving, E. Episodic and semantic memory. In E. Tulving & W. Donaldson (Eds.), *Organization of memory.* New York: Academic Press, 1972, pp. 381–403.

Turner, E. A., & Rommetveit, R. The effects of focus of attention on storing and retrieving of active and passive voice sentences. *Journal of Verbal Learning and Verbal Behavior,* 1968, 7, 543–548.

Turner, J. *Cognitive development* (Essential Psychology Series, C-2). London: Methuen, 1975.

Ullmann, S. *Semantics: An introduction to the study of meaning.* Oxford: Basil Blackwell & Mott, 1962.

Ultan, R. Some general characteristics of interrogative systems. *Working Papers in Language Universals* (Stanford University), 1969, 1, 41–63a.

Umiker-Sebeok, D. J. *The conversational skills of preschool children.* Unpublished doctoral dissertation, Indiana University, 1976.

van Dijk, T., & Kintsch, W. Cognitive psychology and discourse: Recalling and summarizing stories. In W. U. Dressler (Ed.), *Trends in text-linguistics.* New York and Berlin, W. Germany: De Gruyter, 1977.

Velten, H. V. The growth of phonemic and lexical patterns in infant language. *Language,* 1943, 19, 281–292.

Vendler, Z. *Linguistics in philosophy.* Ithaca, N.Y.: Cornell University Press, 1967.

Vendler, Z. *Adjectives and nominalizations.* The Hague: Mouton Publishers, 1968.

Vennemann, T. Explanation in syntax. In J. Kimball (Ed.), *Syntax and semantics* (Vol. 2). New York: Seminar Press, 1973, pp. 1–50.

Vennemann, T. Topics, subjects, and word order: From SXV to SVX via TVX. In J. M. Anderson & C. Jones (Eds.), *Historical linguistics I: Syntax, morphology, internal and comparative reconstruction.* Amsterdam: North-Holland Publishing, 1974, pp. 339–376.

Vennemann, T. An explanation of drift. In C. N. Li (Ed.), *Word order and word order change.* Austin: University of Texas Press, 1975, pp. 269–305.

Vernon, S. M., & Gordon, J. What happens when negation fails to falsify? Paper presented at the Annual Convention of the American Psychological Association, Chicago, September 1975.

Volterra, V. Il "no": Prime fasi dello sviluppo della negazione nel linguaggio infantile. *Archivio de Psicologia, Neurologia e Psichiatria,* 1972, 33, 16–53.

Wales, R. J., & Campbell, R. On the development of comparison and the comparison of development. In G. B. Flores d'Arcais & W. J. M. Levelt (Eds.), *Advances in psycholinguistics.* Amsterdam: North-Holland, 1970, pp. 373–396.

Wallace, A. F. C., & Atkins, J. The meaning of kinship terms. *American Anthropologist,* 1960, 62, 58–79.

Wanner, E. *On remembering, forgetting, and understanding sentences.* The Hague: Mouton Publishers, 1974.

Warden, D. A. The influence of context on children's use of identifying expressions and references. *British Journal of Psychology,* 1976, 67, 101–112.

Warren, R. M. Perceptual restoration of missing speech sounds. *Science,* 1970, 167, 392–393.

Warren, R. M., & Obusek, C. J. Speech perception and phonemic restorations. *Perception and Psychophysics,* 1971, 9, 358–362.

Warren, R. M., Obusek, C. J., Farmer, R. M., & Warren, R. P. Auditory sequence: Confusion of patterns other than speech or music. *Science,* 1969, 164, 586–587.

Warren, R. M., & Warren, R. P. Auditory illusions and confusions. *Scientific American,* 1970, 223, 30–36.

Wason, P. C. The processing of positive and negative information. *Quarterly Journal of Experimental Psychology,* 1959, 11, 92–107.

Wason, P. C. Response to affirmative and negative binary statements. *British Journal of Psychology,* 1961, 52, 133–142.

Wason, P. C. The contexts of plausible denial. *Journal of Verbal Learning and Verbal Behavior,* 1965, 4, 7–11.

Wason, P. C. In real life negatives are false. *Logique et Analyse,* 1972, 57–58, 17–38.

Wason, P. C., & Johnson-Laird, P. N. *Psychology of reasoning: Structure and content.* London: B. T. Batsford, 1972.

Wason, P. C., & Jones, S. Negatives: Denotation and connotation. *British Journal of Psychology,* 1963, 54, 299–307.

Waterson, N. Child phonology: A prosodic view. *Journal of Linguistics,* 1971, 7, 179–211.

Watt, W. C. Comments on the Brown and Hanlon paper. In J. R. Hayes (Ed.), *Cognition and the development of language.* New York: John Wiley & Sons, 1970, pp. 55–78. (a)

Watt, W. C. On two hypotheses concerning psycholinguistics. In J. R. Hayes (Ed.), *Cognition and the development of language.* New York: John Wiley & Sons, 1970, pp. 137–220. (b)

Watt, W. C. Competing economy criteria. In *Problèmes actuels en psycholinguistique / Current problems in psycholinguistics.* Paris: Editions du C.N.R.S., 1974, pp. 361–389. (a)

Watt, W. C. Mentalism in linguistics, II. *Glossa,* 1974, 8, 3–40. (b)

Watt, W. C. (Review of *Behavior of nonhuman primates* [Vol. 4] edited by A. M. Shrier & F. Stollnitz.) *Behavioral Science,* 1974, 19, 70–75. (c)

Webb, R. A., Oliveri, M. E., & O'Keeffe, L. Investigations of the meaning of "different" in the language of young children. *Child Development,* 1974, 45, 984–991.

Weinreich, U. Travels through semantic space. *Word*, 1958, *14*, 346–366.

Weir, R. H. *Language in the crib*. The Hague: Mouton Publishers, 1962.

Weir, R. H. Questions on the learning of phonology. In F. Smith & G. A. Miller (Eds.), *The genesis of language: A psycholinguistic approach*. Cambridge, Mass.: M.I.T. Press, 1966, pp. 153–168.

Weisenburger, J. L. A choice of words: Two-year-old speech from a situational point of view. *Journal of Child Language*, 1976, *3*, 275–281.

Wetstone, H. S., & Friedlander, B. Z. The effect of word order on young children's responses to simple questions and commands. *Child Development*, 1973, *44*, 734–740.

Whorf, B. L. Science and linguistics. In J. B. Carroll (Ed.), *Language, thought and reality: Selected writings of Benjamin Lee Whorf*. Cambridge, Mass.: M.I.T. Press, 1956, pp. 207–219.

Whynant, R. Tokyo tongue twist. *The Guardian*, March 20, 1976.

Wickelgren, W. Distinctive features and errors in short-term memory for English vowels. *Journal of the Acoustical Society of America*, 1965, *38*, 583–588.

Wickelgren, W. Distinctive features and errors in short-term memory for English consonants. *Journal of the Acoustical Society of America*, 1966, *39*, 388–398.

Wieman, L. A. *The stress pattern of early child language*. Unpublished doctoral dissertation, University of Washington, Seattle, 1974.

Wieman, L. A. Stress patterns of early child language. *Journal of Child Language*, 1976, *3*, 283–286.

Wilson, D. *Presuppositions and non-truth-conditional semantics*. New York: Academic Press, 1975.

Wingfield, A. Perceptual and response hierarchies in object identification. *Acta Psychologica*, 1967, *26*, 216–226.

Wingfield, A. Effects of frequency on identification and naming of objects. *American Journal of Psychology*, 1968, *81*, 226–234.

Winitz, H., & Irwin, O. C. Syllabic and phonetic structure of infants' early words. *Journal of Speech and Hearing Research*, 1958, *1*, 250–256.

Winograd, T. *Understanding natural language*. New York: Academic Press, 1972.

Winograd, T. A procedural model of language understanding. In R. C. Schank & K. M. Colby (Eds.), *Computer models of thought and language*. San Francisco: W. H. Freeman, 1973, pp. 152–186.

Wittgenstein, L. *Philosophical investigations*. New York: Macmillan, 1953.

Wittgenstein, L. *The blue and brown books*. New York: Harper & Row, 1958.

Wolff, P. H. The natural history of crying and other vocalizations in early infancy. In B. M. Foss (Ed.), *Determinants of infant behavior* (Vol. 4). London: Methuen, 1966, pp. 81–109.

Wood, C. *Processing units in reading*. Unpublished doctoral dissertation, Stanford University, 1974.

Woods, W. A. Procedural semantics for a question-answer machine. *Proceedings of Fall Joint Computer Conference*. New York: Spartan Books, 1968, pp. 457–471.

Woods, W. A. Transition network grammars for natural language analysis. *Communications of the A. C. M.*, 1970, *13*, 591–606.

Woods, W. A. An experimental parsing system for transition network grammars. In R. Rustin (Ed.), *Natural language processing*. Englewood Cliffs, N.J.: Prentice-Hall, 1973, pp. 111–154.

Woods, W. A. Syntax, semantics, and speech. In D. R. Reddy (Ed.), *Speech recognition*. New York: Academic Press, 1975, pp. 345–400.

Woods, W. A., & Makhoul, J. Mechanical inference problems in continuous speech understanding. *Proceedings of the Third International Joint Conference on Artificial Intelligence*. Stanford, Calif.: Stanford Research Institute, 1973, pp. 200–207.

Wright, P. Transformations and the understanding of sentences. *Language and Speech*, 1969, *12*, 156–166.

Wright, P. Some observations on how people answer questions about sentences. *Journal of Verbal Learning and Verbal Behavior*, 1972, *11*, 188–195.

Yngve, V. H. A model and an hypothesis for language structure. *Proceedings of the American Philosophical Society*, 1960, *104*, 444–466.

Zajonc, R. B. Attitudinal effects of mere exposure. *Journal of Personality and Social Psychology, Monograph Supplement*, 1968, *9* (2, Pt. 2), 1–27.

Ziff, P. *Semantic analysis*. Ithaca, N.Y.: Cornell University Press, 1960.

Zimmer, K. E. Affixal negation in English and other languages: An investigation of restricted productivity. *Word*, 1964, *20* (2, Pt. 2).

Zipf, G. K. *The psycho-biology of language*. Boston: Houghton Mifflin, 1935.

Zipf, G. K. *Human behavior and the principle of least effort*. Cambridge, Mass.: Addison-Wesley Publishing, 1949.

Name Index

Subject Index

Basic level. *See* Categories; Category names

before-after

  in acquisition, 357–59, 507–08; in planning, 240

Behaghel's First Law, 545

Bias in reconstructing sentences from memory, 148–50

big-small, 498–99

Bilabial consonants, 24, 180

  in acquisition, 392–93, 402; in speech perception, 201

Biological specialization, and language, 518–23

black board-blackboard, 183–84

Blends, as speech errors, 274, 471

Brain lateralization, 519

Bridging assumptions. *See* Implicatures

but, 456

Case relations

  defined, 306–09; precursors to, in acquisition, 303–06, 501–02; in two-word utterances, 309–12

Categorical perception, and phonetic stage, 199–202

Categories

  basic level, 254, 528–30; cognitive, 536–41; perceptual, 523–36; social, 541–44; typicality of membership in, 464–65. *See also* Category names

Category names

  basic level, 254, 407, 500–01, 527–30; featural approach, 464–65; and features, 466–68; network approach to, 462–64; and verifying category statements, 465–66

Causation, and change, 423–25, 510–13, 539–40

Causatives, 510–13

Cause. *See* Causation, and change

Change, and causation, 423–25, 510–13, 539–40

Change-of-state, and state, 423, 510, 539–40

Channels, in perception of consonants, 193–94

Characteristic features, 466–67

Child-based representations of words, 384

Children. *See* Acquisition; Child's Language

Child's language, 295–96

  case relations in, 303–12; context and strategy in, 501–09; elaboration of function in, 363–72; elaboration of structure in, 342–63; operating principles in, 339–42; and perception of speech sounds, 376–87; precursors to first utterances, 300–02; and production of speech sounds, 387–403; semantic components, 509–13. *See also* Acquisition; Language; Meaning

Chimpanzee language, 520–23

Clang associations, 479

Classifiers, 531–33, 545

Clause, 10–11, 68–70

  adverbial, 11, 59, 357–59; phonemic, 267; relative, 11, 69–70, 355–57

Click displacements, 54–55

Closing section, conversation, 230

Cluster analysis, 432

Cognitive categories, 536–37

  cause and effect, 539–41; negation, 538–39; number, 537; time, 540–41

Cognitive complexity, 337–38

Cognitive difficulty in speech planning, 271–72

Color terms, basic, 524–27

Color vision, opponent theory of, 526

Combining propositions, 13–15, 347–48, 355–63

Commands, direct and indirect, 28–29, 124–28

Commissives, 88, 89

  and directives in child's language, 364–66

Common topic contract, 128–29

Communication, and language, 1, 25, 296–99

Comparative adjective, 23, 505–06

Comparisons, 240

Competence, linguistic, 6–7

Complement, 15, 62

  in acquisition, 360–63

Complementation, 15, 16, 355

Complex adjective, 428–29

Complexity

  cognitive, 337–38; of expression, 523–24; formal, 338–39; in language, 337–39; learning, processing, and, 334–42; of meaning, 487–88; principle, 523; sources, 30–31

Complex noun, 428

Component, semantic

  in acquisition, 509–13; as procedure, 439–41

Componential analysis, 416–19

  applications of, 423–32; formal advantages of, 419–22; limitations of, 429–32; semantic fields studied by, 430, 497–500

Componential view of lexical entry, 413

Comprehension, 4

  and adult speech to children, 320–30; and ambiguity, 80–84; answering WH- questions in, 113–17; answering yes/no questions in, 100–12; of category names, 462–68; children's strategies in, 501–09; construction process in, 45–49; defined, 43–45; following instructions in, 117–21; identification of isolated speech sounds in, 191–200; indirect utilization of utterances in, 121–31; of inherent negatives, 452–57; memorization in, 141–43; and memory, 133–36; memory for stories in, 166–72; memory for substance in, 153–66; memory for unrelated sentences in, 143–53; of modifiers, 457–62; overextensions in, 496–97; perception of continuous speech in, 210–19; and production in children, 298–99, 487; recording assertions in, 91–100; semantic approach to, 72–79; short-term memory in, 137–41; speech perception in, 175; syntactic approach to, 57–72; and surface constituents, 50–57; utilization process in, 90–91. *See also* Acquisition; Meaning; Memory; Sentence(s); Speech perception; Strategy

Conceptual knowledge, and semantic, 489–90

Conceptual salience, 238

Conceptual unity of constituents, 50–51

Condensing sentences, 16–19

Congruence principle, 90–91, 112

Conjunctive rule, 439

Consonant(s), 180–82

  bilabial, 24, 180, 201; clusters, in child's speech, 398–99; confusion, and signal-to-noise ratio, 191–93; contrasts, 392–93; distinctive features, 187; of four-year-olds, 396; fricatives, 181; perception of pieces, 193–95; stop, 24, 181

Constituent(s), 47–48, 144

  as aids in perception, 51–52; anticipating, 75–76; building up, 58–65; conceptual unity of, 50–51; discontinuous, 60; immediate, 48; and propositions, 53–54, 144–45; in speech execution, 262–65; in speech planning, 265–68; ultimate, 48; in working memory, 52. *See also* Surface constituents

Constituent boundaries, as hesitation points, 267–68

Constituent plans, 224, 248–57

Construction process
of interpretations, 47–49; semantic approaches to, 72–79; syntactic approaches to, 57–72; underlying representations, 45–47

Contact vernacular, 550

Content of description, 232

Content words, 21–22, 63–64
anticipating, 61; in building up constituents, 61–63; as hesitation points, 268; selection of, 278

Context
and strategy, in child's language, 501–09; tying sentences to, 76–78

Context-dependent cues, 197

Context-independent cues, 197

Contextual ellipsis, 17

Contextual neutralization, 524

Contextual pronominalization, 17–18

Continuity in infant babbling, 389–91

Continuous speech, perception of, 210–19

Contract
common topic, 128–29; given-new, 91–93, 123; order of mention, 129–30, 358, 506–08

Contradictories, 155, 422

Contraries, 155, 422

Contrasts
acquisition of sound, 392; consonant, 392–93; vowel, 393

Conventional pause, 261

Conversation
adjacency pairs, 228–29; closing, 230–32; opening, 229–30; turn taking, 227–28, 324–25

Conversational implicature, 124

Conversational lessons in adult speech, 327–28

Conversational turns, 324–25

Converses, 422, 438

Cooperative principle, 72–73, 122–24
in acquisition, 327–28; in speech planning, 225–26

Coordination, 14, 16, 355. *See also and; but*

Correction
in adult speech to children, 325–26; as speech error, 262

Correction phrase, 264, 270–71

Creativity, lexical, 444, 446–47

Creole vs. pidgin, 550–51

Critical periods for language acquisition, 520

Decision table for motion verbs, 440–41

Declarations, 88, 89
and expressives in child's language, 366–67

Declaratives, 27–28

Defining features, 466–67

Denials, 98–100
verifying, 107–11

Dental consonants, 180

Derivational complexity theory, 144

Description, 232–33
of apartments, 233–36; and arrays, 251–52

Dictionary and encyclopedia, mental, 410–12

Dimension(s)
dominance relations among, 536; natural, 534–35; in semantic space, 433–36

Dimensional relations, 505–06

Dimensional terms, 498–99

Direct command, 28–29

Directives, 88, 89
and commissives, in child's language, 364–66

Direct speech acts, 28–29, 244–45

Discontinuity in infant babbling, 389–91

Discontinuous constituent, 60

Discourse, 35, 224
conversations, 227–32; descriptions, 232–36; memory for stories, 166–72; referents in, 159–60; structure of, 236–37; structuring, hesitation in, 272

Discreteness of sounds, 176

Disjunctive rule, 439

Distinguishability among categories, 529

Dominance relations, dimensions, 536

Effect, and cause, 539–41

electric-electricity, 178, 188

Ellipsis, 16–17, 18

Encyclopedia and dictionary, mental, 410–12

Encyclopedic knowledge, and features, 467–68

Encyclopedic view of lexical entry, 413

Entailment, 409

Episode of story, 168

Essential rule, for speech acts, 242

Event in story, 169

Exclamations, as attention getters, 321

Execution, speech. *See* Production

Experiencer case, 305

Experiential chunking, 238–39

Experiment, 37, 38

Expertise, and category names, 529–30, 552–55

Expression, complexity of, 523–24

Expressives, 88, 89
and declarations, in child's language, 366–67

Extension and intension, 410

External evidence in sentence verification, 112

Factor analysis, 432

Fallibility of short-term memory, 137–38

False starts, 262

Family resemblances and features, 467

Featural approach to category names, 464–65

Features
in articulatory program, 276–77; defining and characteristic, 466–67; distinctive, 186–90, 194–95; and encyclopedic knowledge, 467–68; and family resemblances, 467; semantic, 415

Felicity conditions, 125–26, 242–43

Figure, good, 531

Filled pause, 262

Final segments, omission in child's speech, 397–98

"Fis" phenomenon, 384–85, 387

Fixed structure, principle of, 66–67

Focal colors, 525–26

Focal stress, 32
in child's language, 318–19; and sentence structure, 370–72

Folk tales and schemata, memory for, 167–68

334–37; model, 320; objective content, 548–49; perceptual categories in, 523–36; physiological factors in, 518–20; processes in use of, 7–10, 35–39; processing constraints in, 545–51; psychology of, 3–4; social categories, 541–44; stress timed vs. syllable timed, 215; study of, 4–7, 37–39; and thought, 554–57; universals and relativity of, 515–18; variation in, 551–57. *See also* Acquisition; Child's language; Language function; Language structure; Meaning; Word(s)

Language function, 24–35, 333
 children's elaboration of, 363–72; process, structure, and, 7–10

Language structure, 10–24, 333
 children's elaboration of, 342–63; process, function, and, 7–10. *See also* Language; Structure

Latency components, 110

Lateralization, brain, 519

Laterals, 181, 182

Learning
 complexity, processing, and, 334–42; hypothesis testing in, 336–37; by imitation, 334–35; and reinforcement, 336; theories of, 334–37

Level
 of abstraction, in categories, 254, 407, 500–01, 527–30; of description, 232

Lexical creativity, 444, 446–47

Lexical entry, 411–14

Lexicon vs. encyclopedia, mental, 411–12

Linear arrays, 161–63

Linguistic competence, 6

Linguistic performance, 6

Linguistic relativity
 Sapir-Whorf hypothesis, 554–57; and universals, 515–18

Linguistics, as empirical science, 38–39

Linguistic universals, 515–18

Listener
 acknowledgement, and child's language, 319–20; capacity for processing speech, 55–57; knowledge, in problem solving, 225

Listening, 87–88
 to propositional and thematic content, 89; selective, 216–19; and speaking, 3–4; and speech acts, 88–89; for stress, 215–16; and utilization, 90–91. *See also* Comprehension

Locative case, 306

Logic of semantic components, 420–21

long-short, 426–28, 534

Long-term memory, 135–36
 vs. short-term, 138–41. *See also* Memory

Main clause, 11, 68–70, 358

Malapropisms, 287–88, 472

Mammals, semantic space for, 435

man, 417, 440, 451–52, 478–80

Manipulation, experimental, 37

Manner, maxim of, 123

Many meanings theory of ambiguity, 81–82

Mapping
 acoustic-phonetic, 205; and communication, 296

Mapping lessons in adult speech, 328

Marked adjectives, and unmarked, 426–28,

455–56, 498–99, 513, 533–36, 538–39

Markedness, 427, 523–24

Maxim of manner, 123

Maxim of quality, 123

Maxim of quantity, 123

Maxim of relation, 123

Meaning
 and children, 485–90; complexity of, 487–88; complications in representation of, 444–47; comprehension of, 450–68; early, 490–501; functional approach to, 439–43; image theory of, 409–10; indirect, 126–30, 160–61; issues in acquisition of, 486–90; and memorization, 142; nature of, 408–14; with no overlap, 491–92; over-extensions, 492–97; and process, 450; production, 468–82; quantificational representations of, 432–38; referential and picture theories of, 409–10; relations, in componential analysis, 421–22; selection of, 278; semantic components, 414–23, 431–32; semantic fields, 429–30, 497–501; study of, 408–10; under-extensions, 491. *See also* Acquisition; Child's language; Language; Speech; Word(s)

Means-oriented instruction, 117

Memorization, 141–43

Memory
 auditory, 198–99, 202; bias in reconstructing sentences from, 148–53; capacity, 65–68, 137; factors affecting, 133–34; and input, 134–35; and instructions, 150–53; integrating information into, 95–98; long-term, 135–36; modality-specific, 165; for other message, in selective listening, 216–17; and output, 135, 136; phonetic, 202–04; prompts, 145–46; propositional and non-propositional, 164–65; propositions in, 143–48; savings, 459–60; search and recall, propositions in, 146–48; short-term, 137–41; span, and simplification, 401; and storage, 135–36; for stories, 166–72; and structure in paragraphs, 165–66; for substance, 153–66; and thought, 556; for unrelated sentences, 143–53; working, 52–53, 135

Mental operations
 in building sentences, 8; procedures as, 441–42; in sentence verification, 111

Message, other, in selective listening, 216–18

Minimal distance principle, 360

Misderivation, as speech error, 274

Misfits in global representations, 163

Misperceptions, speech, 214–15

Mixed theory of ambiguity, 82–84

Modality-specific memory, 165

Modification in the noun phrase, 251

Modifiers
 and comprehension, 457–62; intensive adverbs, 458–59; and memory savings, 459–60; order of, 475; planning, and nouns, 250–51

Modulation, as attention getter, 321

more-less, 505–06

Morphemes
 added, and universals, 523–24; grammatical, acquisition of, 342–46; and inflections, 22–23

Motor theory of speech perception, 207–10

Mouth, positions of articulation in, 181

Movables, child's knowledge of, 301–02

Movement, over-extensions based on, 493, 494

Planning stage, in following simple instructions, 118

Plural vs. singular, 23
in acquisition, 344, 345; as category, 537; in word formation, 189–90

Pointing, as precursor to speech acts, 313

Politeness, and indirect speech acts, 128, 244–45

Pollyanna hypothesis, 538–39

Polysemy, 444–46

Positive, good, and normal, 538–39

Possession verbs, 499–500

Possessive nouns, 23, 190, 344, 345

Power semantic and solidarity semantic, 256–57

Practice and sound play in child's speech, 402–03

Pre-closing statement, 230

Predicate negatives, vs. denials, 111

Predicate vs. subject, 33–34
in planning speech, 246–48; in two-word utterances, 310–12

Predication, 45–47, 415–16

Prediction, in experiments, 37

Preparatory rule, for speech acts, 242

present-absent, 453–55, 457

Principle of fixed structure, 66–67

Principle of natural serialization, 547

Principle of two sentences, 67

Probe-latency technique, 52

Problem solving
in answering questions, 116; in following instructions, 121; and labeling, 556–57; speech planning as, 225–26

Procedural semantics, 439–42
limitations, 442–43

Procedures
components as, 439–41; flexibility of, 443; for inherent negatives, 453–54; as mental operations, 441–42

Process
and meaning, 450; structure, function, and, 7–10; in use of language, 35–39

Processing
depth and focus of, 151–53; learning, complexity, and, 334–42; real-time, 55–57. *See also* Process; Processing constraints

Processing constraints
invented language, 550–51; paradigms, 549–50; word groups, 545–46; word order, 546–49

Production, 4
of adjective order, 472–77; articulatory program in, 273–92; child's elaboration of function in, 364–72; child's elaboration of structure in, 342–63; constituent plans in, 248–57; discourse plans in, 227–37; execution of speech plans in, 259–60; of names, 469–72; of one- and two-word utterances, 300–20; planning and execution in, 260–73; planning vs. execution, 223–26; sentence plans in, 237–48; of speech sounds by children, 387–403; of word associations, 477–82. *See also* Acquisition; Slips of the tongue; Speech; Speech planning

Progressive verb, 23, 345

promise, 361–62, 365–66

Prompts, memory, 145

Pronomenalization, 16, 17–18

Pronouns, 17–18

in cluster analysis, 436, 437; nominative vs. objective, 29; personal, and terms of address, 255–57; in planning, 254–55; in two-word utterances, 388–89

Proposition(s), 11, 165
combining, 13–16; and constituents, 53–55, 144–45; defined, 46–47; functions of, 29–30; in memory, 143–48, 164–65; in recall and memory search, 146–48; in units of meaning, 11–12, 408. *See also* Component, semantic

Propositional content, 29–31
complexity sources, 30–31; and listening, 89; rule, for speech acts, 242; of sentence, 29–31, 237–41; and thematic, 89

Propositional functions, 46

Propositional memory, and non-propositional, 164–65

Prototype, 464–65

Psychology of Everyday Life (Freud), 282

Psychology of language, 3–10

Quality, maxim of, 123

Quantificational representations of meaning, 432–38

Quantity, maxim of, 123

Questions
in child's language, 351–54; complicated, 116–17; simple, 114–15; WH-, 113–17; yes/no, 100–13

Reaching, as precursor to speech acts, 313

Reactions, in story, 169

Reality principle, 72–73, 226

Real-time processing, 55–57

Recall
and memory search, propositions in, 146–48; of stories, 170–72. *See also* Memory

Recipients, child's knowledge of, 302

Recording assertions, 91–95
denials in, 98–100; integrating information into memory, 95–98

Recursion, 16, 169

Redundancy rules in componential analysis, 419

Reduplication in child's speech, 400–01

Reference and sense, 410

Referent
in constructing interpretations, 47, 76–78; and memory for substance, 156–60; in representation of meaning, 409–10; and semantic procedures, 439–40

Referential theory of meaning, 409–10

Regularity and rhythm in articulatory program, 289–90

Reinforcement and learning, 336

Relation
of description elements, 232; grammatical, 19–20; maxim of, 123

Relative clause, 11
in child's language, 355–57; in comprehension, 69–70

Relativity and universals, 515–18

Relativization, 14–15, 16, 355

Repeats, as speech errors, 262

Representation(s)
adult-based, 385–87; complications in, for

Representation(s) *(continued)*
  meaning, 444–47; quantificational, for meaning, 432–38; underlying, and construction process, 45–47; underlying vs. surface structure, 12–13
Representational ability, and simplification, 401
Representatives, 88, 89, 313–16, 364
Requests, 88
  in acquisition, 314–16, 364–65; felicity conditions for, 125; indirect, 124–28, 367–68; as instructions, 117–21
Response latencies, 36–37
Response time, 36–37
Retention interval, 133
Retraced false starts, as speech errors, 262
Reversal, as speech error, 274
Rhythm
  in speech perception, 215–16; and timing in articulatory program, 288–91
Rich interpretation of child's language, 299
Rule(s)
  in child's language, 344, 382, 397–99; in describing apartments, 234; felicity conditions, 242; of grammar, 5–6; phonological, 188–91; in verification model, 103, 105, 109–10, 453–54; in word associations, 479–82; in word formation, 283–86

Sapir-Whorf hypothesis of linguistic relativity, 554–57
Savings, memory, 459–60
Scaling, multidimensional, 432, 434–36
Schema, 168
Schwa, 183
Search and recall, memory, 146–48
Segmentation lessons in adult speech, 328
Segments. *See* Phonetic segments
Selection of content words, 278
Selective adaptation, 201–02
Selective listening, 216–19
Self-contradiction, 409, 420
Self-embedded sentence, 61
Semantic, power vs. solidarity, 256–57
Semantic approach to construction, 72–79
Semantic clusters, 436
Semantic coherence in child's language, 340–41
Semantic complexity
  and acquisition of grammatical morphemes, 345–46; in acquisition of meaning, 498–501
Semantic components
  in child's language, 509–13; logic of, 420–21; nature of, 430–31; negation, 513. *See also* Semantic field; Semantics
Semantic differential, 432–33
Semantic factors, 432
Semantic field, 418, 429–30
  of basic-level terms, 500–01; of dimensional terms, 498–99; of possession verbs, 499–500
Semantic knowledge, and conceptual, 489–90
Semantic planning, 266–67
Semantic power vs. solidarity, 256–57
Semantic procedures, as mini-strategies, 451–52
Semantics, 5, 408
  componential approach to, 414–32; functional approach to, 439–43; procedural, 439–43; quantificational approach to, 432–38

Semantic space, 433–36
  adequacy of, 438
Semivowels, 180, 181, 182
Sense
  and reference, 410; of words, 444–46
Sensori-motor stage of child's development, 300–01
Sentence(s)
  active and passive, 93–95, 105–06; ambiguous, 18–19; analysis into propositions, 11–12; bias in reconstructing from memory, 143–53; combining propositions in, 13–16; complex, 355–63; complexity sources, 30–31; condensing, 16–19; frames, 326–27; grammatical relations in, 19–20; ideal delivery, 261–62; illocutionary content, 241–45; making sense of, 73–76; negative and interrogative, 347–54; passive, 93–95, 105–06; plans, 224, 237–48; propositional content, 29–31, 237–41; representing, 429; right-branching, 56; self-embedded, 56, 61; and structure, 10–11; surface structure, 12–13; thematic structure, 31–35, 245–48, 316–20, 368–72; tying to context, 76–78; underlying representation, 12–13; unrelated, memory for, 143–53; verification, 101, 105–06, 111–12. *See also* Acquisition; Child's language; Language; Sentence structure; Speech perception; Word(s)
Sentence structure
  and focal stress in child's language, 370–72; surface, and underlying representation, 12–13; thematic, 31–35, 245–48. *See also* Sentence(s); Structure
Sentential ellipsis, 17
Sequences
  perception of, 380–82; and phonetic segments, 379–80
Setting of story, 168
Shadowing, 217, 218
Shape
  names, 530–33; over-extensions based on, 492–93
Shortcuts in articulatory program, 290–91
Shorthand expressions, 252–53
Short-term memory, 135
  fallibility of, 137–38; vs. long-term, 138–41. *See also* Memory
Signal-to-noise ratio, and confusion of consonants, 191–93
Sign language, 521–23
Silent pause, 262, 263, 265, 267–68, 270, 271–73
Simplicity criterion, 239–41
Simplification, in child's speech sounds, 397–401
Sincerity rule, for speech acts, 242
Situational anxiety, and speech error, 272
Size, over-extensions based on, 493, 494
Skeleton + constituent model, of planning, 248–49, 262–64, 279
Slips of the tongue, 273–75
  and availability, 283. *See also* Articulation; Articulatory program
Social categories
  kinship terms, 541–43; pronouns, 543–44
Social factors in speech planning difficulty, 272–73
Solidarity semantic, 256–57
Sound, over-extensions based on, 493, 494

606